The Celebrity Address

Directory & Autograph

Collector's Guide

3nd Edition - 2008

By: Lee Ellis

Americana Group Publishing

The Celebrity Address Directory & Autograph Collector's Guide
3nd Edition 2007

Copyright 2007 by Lee Ellis

Americana Group Publishing
54 Woodridge Drive West
River Falls, WI 54022
E-mail at: american@pressenter.com
Telephone: 715-425-9653
Fax: 715-425-5347
Website: www.americanagrouppublishing.com

ISBN: 0-9759569-2-2

10 9 8 7 6 5 4 3 2 1

Printed May 2007

Printed and bound in the United States of America

p.258 cm.

$39.95

Notice of Liability

The information is distributed on an "As Is" basis, without warranty. While every precaution has been taken in the preparation of this book, neither the author nor Americana Group Publishing shall have any liability to any person or entity with any respect to any liability, loss, or damage caused or alleged to be caused directly or indirectly by the information and instructions contained in this book.

About the Book

This book is a collaborative effort between David R. Moore and myself. Mr. Moore is a retired school teacher and a well respected autograph collector.

I chose to do the research on the celebrity names and references while Mr. Moore edited my material. Many parts of the book have changed since the first edition of this title in 2000. The changes are in the form of about 2500 additional celebrity names as well as new areas of research. It is my goal to provide you, the reader with useful information. The research is information that readers have requested over time and include celebrity hobbies and charities, celebrity hangouts and sightings and a complete birthday list of celebrities. It is my hope that this additional information gives you something to share or show you have in common with the celebrity you are writing to.

My wish is that you have as much fun and enjoyment sending letters and receiving celebrity autographs as I have had. May you have many good autograph times.

Acknowledgements

Many individuals contributed in some way or another to the completion of this book. The people at Digital Dynamics gave their technical advice and expertise that was invaluable in the production of this book. The crew at Americana Group Publishing guided the path of this book and made it a reality. Most importantly, I wish to thank my family, who gave me the support and encouragement to seek the rewards of this project.

Colophon

This book was created using Adobe PageMaker 7.0 on a Dell Dimension 4600 computer. Adobe Book Antiqua 36 point was used for the headings and Adobe Garamond 18 point was used for the sub-headings. Lucida Sans 12 point and Arial 10 & 8 point was used for the body copy. The content of this book was printed using a Hewlett-Packard 8100DN printer.

Author: Lee Ellis
Editor: David R. Moore
Assistant Editor: Mollie Cleary
Cover Design: Scott A. Ellis
Index: Multiplex Inc.

Table of Contents

Table of Contents

Table of Contents

The Basics:

Getting Started in

Collecting Autographs

Through the Mail

Tips for the collector
Questions with answers about autograph collecting
Sample letters that have gotten results
Celebrities who have received the Eagle Scout Award
Hobbies of Celebrities
Charities of Celebrities

Be courteous- in collecting autographed material through the mail, the rules of common courtesy suggest that you always use a stamped, self-addressed envelope with your request.

Be legible- a letter that has good handwriting or is typed is a must. A neat, well-written letter always gets attention.

Get to the point- requests for autographs should be concise and clear. There is no need to be lengthy or over complimentary. Requests that are sincere and show interest in that persons career or hobby receive attention. Letters that relate to the celebrity's interest are more likely to receive a reponse.

Be informed- knowing the celebrity's interests can come from many sources. Newspaper and magazine articles appear daily about a variety of topics celebrities are involved in. Celebrities promote their work by TV appearances and by books they have written.

Make a request- do not procrastinate- many times a simple request can be in the form of: My hobby is collecting autographs of (business) leaders. Naturally, I would like to add your signature to my collection. I would be most grateful if you would send it to me in the enclosed self-addressed envelope.

Best regards,

Do not be greedy- once you have made a request don't ask for more than what would be polite. Remember that a celebrity knows what his or her autograph is worth. Please don't ruin the chances of other people receiving signatures.

Be patient- receiving a signature from a celebrity can take a long time. Waiting 4 to 6 weeks for a return is not unusual in autograph collecting. If you believe it has been too long in waiting for your request, rewrite your letter explaining what has happened.

Keep good records- keep a log or chart containing the names, dates and descriptions of all requests. It might be a good idea to code the envelope with a small number in a corner. Celebrity autograph requests can take a long time to be sent and celebrities do not always have a recognizable signature.

Do not send valuable items that have monetary or sentimental value to be signed without first securing permission from the celebrity. It is also important to have the item insured with the post office or agent delivering the item.

After I have mailed a request for an autograph, how long does it take to get a response?

Answer: It can vary from a few days to a few months. Some celebrities are quick to respond to a request while others lag in their accommodation of a request. Celebrities can view the signing of autograph requests as appreciation of the fan's interest or it can be viewed as a task. A normal wait is four to twelve weeks. If you have not heard from the celebrity by that time, you may want to contact the celebrity again.

How do I know if the autograph I receive in the mail from a celebrity is real?

Answer: Sometimes it is very hard to know if an autograph is authentic. It could be genuine or it could be an autopen (mechanical reproduction) or a secretarial signature. An autopen signature has telltale signs that it is a reproduction. In all cases, the line of ink has a regular width (from even pressure) and in some cases has squiggles (curves or twists) from too much pressure. Also, there is definite start and stop points that may show as a ball of ink at the end of a line. A secretarial signature is a signature that is usually authorized by the celebrity to sign autographs on his /her behalf. The best examples of this are presidential signatures in which a secretary or staff member is given permission by the president to sign certain autograph requests. Other non-authentic autographs are photocopies and rubber stamps, which most people have an easy time to tell if it is real.

If I'm not sure if the autograph is real, can I have it authenticated?

Answer: The way to have an autograph authenticated is to have the autograph seen by a professional. Some autograph dealers will authenticate autograph material. In some instances, the dealer will request that a copy or a fax be sent to him. In some cases, the dealer may have to see the original autograph. Therefore, it is important to get to know an autograph dealer whom you can trust. Bringing your autographs to a dealer for authenication can save you sad moments in time and money.

I have sent out 100 autograph requests, how many reponses should I expect to receive?

Answer: After a survey was conducted on the success autograph collectors had receiving autographs through the mail, an autograph magazine article stated that the success rate was about 50 percent. So, if you receive more than 50 responses, consider yourself one of the lucky ones.

Why do some celebrities have the same address or more than one address?

Answer: Most addresses for celebrities are not their home address. For privacy reasons, celebrities have their mail sent to their agent and/or other mailing address. Celebrities receive hundreds or thousands of autograph requests and delivery to a home would be impractical. So, celebrities who have the same agent or mailing service may have the same address or more than one address.

If I write to a celebrity, will they answer my request?

Answer: Most celebrities are agreeable and willing to sign for fans to keep a good public relationship (PR). However, some celebrities by their nature want to protect their privacy (they may fear for their safety) and not sign autograph requests. Celebrities may also dislike the idea of someone making money from their autograph. But, for the most part, celebrities enjoy hearing from and seeing their fans and accommodate most autograph requests.

How much is an autograph worth?

Answer: It depends on a few factors. One factor is popularity. Like other collectibles, demand is key. Celebrities who are well liked, top in their field of profession, or receive awards or positive recognition will have signatures in demand. Another factor is what the celebrity has signed. A common signed article is an 8 x 10-color photograph. Generally, values are based on the time a celebrity uses to personalize an article. So, a more valuable item would be a personal letter showing a facet of the celebrity's life. Another factor affecting value or price is condition. Predictably, an autograph that is faded or worn will receive a lower value. To be aware of prices paid for autographs, one should research autograph prices in an autograph price book such as "Sander's Price Guide to Autographs" which is available at most bookstores.

How does the 911 attack on America or the anthrax scare affect autograph collecting through the mail?

Answer: Besides an increase in the suspicion of articles going through the mail, I have seen some terrible things happen to paper that has been irradiated by the U. S. Postal Service. The machine that destroys any anthrax spores in the letter uses a high heat source. The heat from these machines turns the paper brittle and yellow. Luckily, the locations of these machines are government offices such as congress or the senate. If I was sending a request through the mail to a senator or congressman I would note on the envelope, "Autograph Request, Please Do Not Irradiate."

W. Edwards Deming
123 Anywhere St.
Washington, DC 20011

Joseph Avery
456 Ridge Rd.
Black Falls, MN 55413

Mr. Deming;
    I would like to take this time to thank you for contribution to manufacturing quality. You have led the world in your innovative approach in solving the basic problems of business, industry, education, how we teach our children and how we deal with others.

    Although I am not a professional engineer, the articles I have read make sense to what you have labeled " A New World Order."

    I am however, an autograph collector and would enjoy receiving your signature on the card I have provided. I will continue to read and discuss your books and articles, and I hope your capitalist revolution becomes universally accepted very soon.

                                              Thank You,

Neil Armstrong
123 Pine Ave.
Anywhere, USA 12345

Thomas Hammond
1849 Rock Rd.
Rock Creek, VA 34234

Mr. Armstrong;

    I am a sixth grade science teacher in Rock Creek, VA. My class is presently studying the manned space flights to the moon. I am trying to make the subject as exciting for my students as it was for me in July of 1969 watching your historic walk on the moon. I am also an autograph collector and thought it would be interesting to show my students your signature. It is my hope that your autograph will stimulate my students to think more seriously about careers in engineering and science. I have enclosed a card for you to sign with a return envelope.

                                              Thank You,

Bo Jackson
Box 2000
Anaheim, CA 92801

Curt Major
1514 Sunset
Pine City, MN 54128

Dear Mr. Jackson;

I want to congratulate you on your return to professional sports after your hip surgery. I heard that this is the first time anyone has returned to professional sports after a double hip replacement. Although you may not want to think about it too much, I believe it took a lot of courage and determination.

I recently saw your picture on a GQ magazine and thought it would be a good picture to have an autograph on. I would be grateful if you would sign it and return it to me. I have enclosed a stamped self-addressed envelope.

Thank You,

George Foreman
6 West Rivercrest Dr.
Houston, TX 77042

Simon Walter
18 Willow Creek
River Falls, WI 54022

Dear George;

Congratulations on your regaining the World's Heavyweight Championship. I was thrilled to hear that a man my age was able to compete and win against men much younger. I am also an autograph collector and would like to have your signature on the enclosed card. I would like to wish you continued good fortune in your career.

Thank You,

Greetings from The President of The United States

Presidential greetings are given to newborns, couples celebrating their 50th wedding anniversary and individuals celebrating their 80th birthday.

The card is official white house stationary and contains an autopen (machine copy) of the president's signature. It is an impressive gift to anyone celebrating an event mentioned above.

Anyone can request a greeting from the president for someone they know who is celebrating an event mentioned.

Make sure you include the name and address of the person celebrating the event and the date that the event occurs. The address of the greeting office is:

> The Greeting Office
> The White House
> Washington, DC 20500

The Greeting Office
The White House
Washington, DC 20500

Samuel Most
9003 Harbor Drive
Boston, MA. 08902

Dear Greeting Office:

I would like to request a Presidential Greeting for my mother who will be 80 years old on August 29, 2000. Please address the greeting to :

> Rachel Most
> 230 North 2nd Street
> International Falls, MN. 55673

Thank You,

Senator Harry Reid   B. Johnston
528 Hart Senate Office Building   4312 5th Street
Washington, DC 20510   Niles, MI 49120

Dear Senator Reid:

I was at your office on Friday the 11ᵗʰ and I'm sorry I missed you. I was looking forward to visiting with you and discussing the book you wrote about Searchlight, Nevada.

First I must say that I was delighted to read your book. I thought searchlight was portrayed in a positive and realistic way. I am a geographer by training and was impressed by the organization, research and documentation in your book.

Searchlight has become interesting to me for several reasons. I have been a coin collector for many years and I am aware of the precious metal gold in coins. On my first vacation to Nevada, I passed through Searchlight on my way to Laughlin from Las Vegas. I noticed the mineshafts in Searchlight. I was surprises to see old mineshafts and wanted to know more about Searchlight's mines. Your description of the mines and mining life in your book was informative and enjoyable to read. My wife and I have passed through Searchlight many times in our travels from Las Vegas to Laughlin. Each time we pass through Searchlight, new points of interest appear. We always stop and eat at the local diner. We also do some gambling there. Searchlight has kind of grown on us; we are staying longer and seeing more things. I am finding old mines, gambling, and the small town atmosphere of Searchlight to be unique and enjoyable.

The people you describe in your book "Searchlight" seem to fit my personality. I admire the individualism and self-reliance that the miners demonstrate in your book. Besides the movie star you describe in your book, another celebrity resided in Searchlight. Up to his death in 1996, the first three time Indy 500 winner Louie Meyer lived in Searchlight. On one of my last visits to Searchlight, I tried to find out where he lived. I stopped at the post office and asked the clerk if she knew. She responded that he had lived nearby but had passed away in the fall of the previous year. I was curious as to why he lived there and not closer to racing centers such as Indianapolis or Charlottesville. If you know why he chose to live in Searchlight, I would like to hear from you.

Growing up in Searchlight was harder than I realized. Besides the hard economic times, you had to endure the harsh climate conditions. After reading your book I think we all can appreciate your first hand comments on the life and times of the residents in Searchlight.

 I hope on my next visit to Washington DC we are able to meet and discuss Searchlight. I left my copy of "Searchlight" at your office with your scheduler. If possible, please sign the book I left there and mail it to the address I gave your scheduler.
　　　　Thank you very much.　　　Best Regards,

Sample Letters Requesting An Autograph

Tom Arnold
Brillstein Entertainment
9150 Wilshire Blvd
Beverly Hills, CA 90211

Marge Cummings
National MD Association
124 Seminole Avenue
Tempe, AZ 89247

January 4, 2003

Hello Mr. Arnold,

The National MD Association is holding its 3rd annual "Ride for the Stars" gala on April 14th at the Marriot Hotel in Bakersfield, CA. We are thankful for your donation last year and now ask for your continued support. We are asking all the celebrities we know who are motorcycle enthusiasts to donate an item or autographed photo for the celebrity auction we are having the night of the gala.

You are also invited to attend the gala banquet dinner to be held at 7:00PM at the ballroom of the Marriot Hotel in Bakersfield. In keeping with the theme of the gala, celebrities will be dressed in motorcycle fashion. If you want, please come to the gala on your motorcycle and dazzle our guests.

Please feel free to contact me if you have any questions. Please send all donations to the above address.

Thanks again, Marge Cummings

Michael Bloomberg
Office of the Mayor
New York, New York 10211

Ed Rizwall
7693 Lake Ridge Road
Rosemount, NY 10958

Mayor Michael Bloomberg,

In the ceremonies at the Boy Scout of America Post 187 in Rosemount, New York on the 20th of May, 2004 my son, John P. Rizwall will receive the Eagle Scout Award from Scoutmaster Paul Lucas.

It is my understanding you are a recipient of the Eagle Scout Award and I would like to request your presence at this ceremony. If you are not able to attend, I would like you to send a congratulatory letter to my son John on his well earned Eagle Scout Award.

John's project to receive his Eagle Scout badge was to clean a one mile riverbank along the Hudson River near Rosemount and make the signs and rest areas more clean, safe and beautiful for the residents and visitors to enjoy. His project lasted over 6 months and logged about 1000 hours. The project called "Beautify the Hudson" was highlighted in the local newspaper and received an honorable mention in the Boy Scout Press.

Ant correspondence can be sent to John's address above. Thanks for your time, John Rizwall

Celebrities Who Have Received The Eagle Scout Award

Here is a ready reference for those who wish to contact a celebrity requesting an appearance or a congratulatory autograph from a celebrity who has received the Eagle Scout Award from the Boy Scouts of America.

Note: You can find the addresses of these celebrities under Government and Astronauts

Bill Alexander - U.S. Representative from Arkansas

Neil Armstrong - astronaut, first man on moon, from Wapakoneta, OH

Henry Aaron - Baseball player, home run king - the Mobile Press Register quoted Henry as saying that the greatest positive influence in his life was his involvement in scouting

Charles E. Bennett - U.S. Representative from Florida

William Bennett - Former Secretary of Education

Michael Bloomberg - Mayor of New York City, founder of Bloomberg News

Bill Bradley - Pro basketball star and U.S. Senator from NJ

James Brady - Former Press Secretary to President Reagan

Milton A. Caniff - Comic strip artist "Steve Canyon"

William E. Dannemeyer - U.S. Representative from California

William Devries - M.D., transplanted first artificial heart

David Farabee - Texas State Representative

Gerald Ford - U.S. President (1st Eagle to be President)

Steven Fossett - Tried several times to fly solo around the world in a hot air balloon and finally did it in 2002, won the Chicago to Mackinaw boat races, competed in the Iditarod dog race, and competed in several iron man triathelons, and among other things lives the Scouting mottos both Cub and Boy Scout by doing his best and being prepared

Steven W. Lindsey - Astronaut - He was the pilot for STS-95 when John Glen returned to space as a Senator. He made eagle in troop 161 in Temple City, California.

Gary Locke, Governor of the State of Washington, the first Chinese-American Governor in the contiguous United States, and selected as a Distinguished Eagle Scout by NESA

James Lovell - Navy pilot and astronaut, President of National Eagle Scout Association. Flew on Gemini 7, 12 & Apollo 8, 13 At one time had seen more sunrises than any other human being

Richard Lugar - Senator from Indiana (presidential canidate 1996)

Sam Nunn - U.S. Senator from Georgia

H. Ross Perot - Self-made billionaire and presidential canidate

Rick Perry - Governor, State of Texas

J. J. Pickle - U.S. Representative from Texas, proudly displays his Eagle plaque inside his office

Samuel R. Pierce - Former Sec. Housing & Urban Development

Donald Rumsfeld - Secretary of Defense

Jeff Sessions - Junior Senator from Alabama is an Eagle Scout from the troop in Camden, AL.

William Sessions - Former FBI director

Steven Spielberg - Movie producer, from Scottsdale, AZ, made a movie of his troop while getting Photography MB. Helped to design requirements for the cinematography MB.

Percy Sutton - Attorney, Chairman of the Board of City Broadcasting Corp.

John Tesh - TV celebrity and pianist

Hobbies of Celebrities

Abdul, Paula	Enjoys pets	Dungy, Tony	Fishing
Affleck, Ben	Baseball as a spectator, gambling	Eastwood, Alison	Enjoys pets
Anderson, Pamela	Enjoys pets	Elliott, Chris	Monster trucks
Applegate, Christina	Enjoys pets	Ellison, Larry	Yacht racing
Arnold, Tom	Riding motorcycles	Everhart, Angie	Enjoys pets
Arquette, Courtney Cox	Enjoys pets	Fisher, Joely	Enjoys pets
Arquette, David	Enjoys pets	Fonda, Peter	Riding motorcycles
Arquette, Rosanna	Enjoys pets	Ford, Faith	Enjoys pets
Asner, Ed	Playing poker	Ford, William C. Jr.	Fly Fishing
Aykroyd, Dan	Riding motorcycles	Fraser, Brendan	Enjoys pets
Bacharach, Burt	Horse racing & breeding	Garner, James	Golf
Baio, Scott	Enjoys pets	Garofalo, Janeane	Enjoys pets
Baldwin, Daniel	Playing poker	Gates, Bill	Golf, Stave Jigsaw Puzzles
Barberie, Jillian	Enjoys pets	Gershon, Gina	Enjoys pets
Bateman, Jason	Playing poker	Gillette, Penn (of Penn & Teller)	Playing poker
Bochco, Steven	Watching horse racing	Glover, Danny	Baseball as a spectator
Bottualuci, Michael	Watching horse racing	Goldberg, Whoopi	Watching horse racing
Bruckheimer, Jerry	Plays hockey	Gooding, Cuba Jr.	Plays hockey
Buffet, Warren	Golf, Stave Jigsaw Puzzles	Gordon, Jeff	Playing poker
Burton, Tim	Enjoys pets	Graham, Lauren	Playing poker
Busey, Gary	Playing poker	Grier, David Alan	Enjoys pets
Bush, George	Fishing, Baseball	Hanks, Tom	Collects 1940s typewriters
Buss, Jerry	Playing poker	Harris, Steve	Watching horse racing
Caan, James	Enjoys pets	Hart, Mary	Riding motorcycles
Cain, Dean	Enjoys pets	Hedren, Tipi	Enjoys pets
Campbell, Billy	Enjoys Recreational Vehicle	Hennessy, Jill	Riding motorcycles
Cheney, Dick	Fly Fishing	Henstridge, Natasha	Enjoys pets
Cher	Riding motorcycles	Hopper, Dennis	Riding motorcycles
Coppola, Francis Ford	Enjoys Recreational Vehicle	Hudson, Kate	Enjoys pets
Crystal, Billy	Baseball - New York Yankees	Hunter, Rachel	Enjoys pets
Day, Doris	Enjoys pets	Hutton, Lauren	Riding motorcycles
Deluise, Dom	Playing poker	Ice-T	Enjoys pets
Derek, Bo	Enjoys pets	Iglesias, Enrique	Windsurfing
Dickinson, Angie	Playing poker	Immelt, Jeffrey	Golf
Doherty, Shannen	Enjoys pets	Jameson, Jenna	Golf
		Johnson, Don	Raising race horses
		Johnston, Kristen	Enjoys pets

Hobbies of Celebrities

Johnston, Kristen	Enjoys pets	O'Boyle, Maureen	Enjoys pets
Jones, Tommy Lee	Polo player	O'Neal, Shaquil	Electronic devices
Kaplan, Gabe	Playing poker	Osborne, Ozzy	Collects Victorian art
Kellerman, Sally	Enjoys pets	Osmond, Donnie	Watching horse racing
Kennedy, Robert Jr.	Raising hawks	Osmond, Donny	Coin collector
Kudrow, Lisa	Billiards or pool player	Oteri, Cheri	Enjoys pets
Lagasse, Emeril	Playing the drums	Perry, Matthew	Playing poker
Larroquette, John	Antique collector	Pesci, Joe	Watching horse racing
Lee, Spike	Basketball as a spectator	Pfeiffer, DeDee	Enjoys pets
Leno, Jay	Collects antique autos	Pfeiffer, Michelle	Watching horse racing
Lopez, George	Golf	Phillips, Lou Diamond	Playing poker
Lowe, Rob	Enjoys pets	Puck, Wolfgang	Enjoys pets
Mac, Bernie	Collects pistols and rifles	Quinlan, Kathleen	Surfer
MacDonald, Norm	Playing poker	Rogers, Mimi	Playing poker
Macy, William H.	Enjoys pets	Rooney, Mickey	Playing poker
Malick, Wendie	Watching horse racing	Rue, Sarah	Playing poker
Malone, Carl	Monster trucks	Schwarzenegger, A.	Riding motorcycles
Manheim, Camryn	Riding motorcycles	Shatner, William	Horse breeding
Martin, Steve	Art collector	Shepard, Cybill	Watching horse racing
Mazar, Deborah	Enjoys pets	Sheridan, Nicolette	Enjoys pets
McGuire, Tobey	Playing poker	Shore, Paulie	Enjoys pets
McGwire, Mark	Golf	Stevens, Connie	Enjoys pets
Metcalf, Laurie	Watching horse racing	Stiller, Ben	Enjoys pets
Milano, Alyssa	Collects religious art objects	Struthers, Sally	Enjoys pets
Ming-Na	Playing poker	Sutherland, Keifer	Plays hockey
Montana, Joe	Golf	Tambor, Jeffrey	Enjoys pets
Moore, Julianne	Loves to read & Enjoys pets	Thornton, Billy Bob	Spectator sport of baseball
Mortensen, Viggo	Mets baseball fan	Tilly, Jennifer	Playing poker
Murray, Bill	Owns minor league team	Travolta, John	Flying airplanes
Myers, Mike	War history enthusiast	Trebek, Alex	Horse breeding
Na, Ming	Playing poker	Van Dyke, Jerry	Playing poker
Neeson, Liam	Riding motorcycles	Van Patten, Dick	Horse racing, Playing poker
Neill, Sam	Making wine	Van Patten, Vince	Tennis, Playing poker
Newman, Paul	Auto racing	Whitman, Meg	Fly Fishing
Nicholson, Jack	Golf & watching Lakers games	Williams, Robbie	Enjoys pets
Nicholson, Jack	Watching horse racing	Woods, James	Playing poker
Norman, Greg	Fishing, Scuba Diving, Yachting	Wuhrer, Kari	Enjoys pets

Charities of Celebrities

Abdul, Paula	Animal Rights - pet owner	Burton, Lavar	Children's education
Aerosmith	AIDS	Burton, Tim	Animal Rights - pet owner
Affleck, Ben	Alcoholism & cancer	Busey, Gary	Autism & Scleroderma
Agassi, Andre	College Preparatory School	Busfield, Tim	Planned Parenthood
Ali, Mohammed	Parkinson's Disease & UN Peace	Bush, Barbara	1000 Points of Light Foundation
Alley, Kirstie	Supports Church of Scientology	Bush, George W.	Thyroid cancer
Alpert, Herb	Painted Turtle Camp	Buttons, Red	Starkey Hearing Foundation, giving
Anderson, Pamela	Animal Rights - pet owner	free hearing devices to poor children around the world	
Annie Glenn	Stuttering disorders	Caan, James	Animal Rights - pet owner
Anniston, Jennifer	AIDS, Unicef & St. Judes Hospital	Cain, Dean	Animal Rights - pet owner
Applegate, Christina	Animal Rights - pet owner	Calloway, Wayne	Prostrate cancer
Archer, Ann	Supports Church of Scientology	Cannell, Stephen J.	Dyslexia
Armstrong, Lance	Cancer	Carew, Rod	Bone Marrow Donor Registration
Arness, James	The United Cerebral Palsy Foundation	Carey, Mariah	Drug addiction
Arquette, Courtney Cox	Animal Rights - pet owner	Carson, Johnny	Faith Regional Health Services Fond.
Arquette, David	Breast cancer	Carter, Jimmy & Rosalynn	Habitat for Humanity
Arquette, Rosanna	Animal Rights - pet owner	Cattrall, Kim	Avocate for senior citizens
Arthur, Bea	AIDS	Cher	Dyslexia
Aspen, Jennifer	Supports Church of Scientology	Clemens, Roger	The Roger Clemens Foundation is an
Asner, Ed	Defenders of Wildlife		entity dedicated to helping children.
Baio, Scott	Animal Rights - pet owner	Clinton, William Jefferson	AIDS
Baldwin, Alec	Breast Cancer Foundation	Combs, Sean	Daddy's House Social Programs
Baldwin, Stephen	Breast Cancer Foundation	Connery, Sean	Prostrate cancer
Baldwin, William	Breast Cancer Foundation	Coolio	Heritage Begins Within
Barberie, Jillian	Animal Rights - pet owner	Copperfield, David	Project Magic Fund
Barker, Bob	Animal Rights Activist	Cosby, Bill	Higher education
Beatty, Ned	Ned Beatty Hope for Children Classic,	Crawford, Cindy	St. Judes Hospital
	Louisville Easter Seals	Cronkite, Walter	Starkey Hearing Foundation
Begley, Ed Jr.	Environmental issues	Crosby, Norm	Starkey Hearing Foundation
Belafonte, Harry	Dyslexia	Cruise, Tom	Dyslexia
Belafonte, Harry	Prostrate cancer	Cruise, Tom	Supports Church of Scientology
Bell, Catherine	Supports Church of Scientology	Cruz, Penelope	Sabera Foundation- helps impover-
Belushi, John	Education	ished Indian Women & Children	
Bolton, Michael	Safe Space of New Haven	Culp, Robert	Starkey Hearing Foundation
Boone, Pat	Church on the Way	Cuomo, Kerry Kennedy	Save the Children
Boone, Pat	Prostrate cancer	Curtis, Tony	Starkey Hearing Foundation
Borman, Frank	Prostrate cancer	Danson, Ted	American Oceans Campaign, Marine
Bostwick, Barry	Prostrate cancer		Fish Conservation Network
Brady, James & Sarah	Gun control	Day, Doris	Doris Day Pet Foundation
Bridges, Jeff	End Hunger Network,	Degeneres, Ellen	Supports non-violent programs
Broderick, Matthew	United Way	DeNiro, Robert	Prostrate cancer
Brokaw, Tom	Conservation International; American	Derek, Bo	Animal Rights - pet owner
	Museum of Natural History	DeVito, Danny	Education
Brooks, Garth	The Touch 'Em All Foundation, College	Dion, Celine	Cancer
	Prospects of America	Doherty, Shannen	Animal Rights - pet owner
Buffett, Jimmy	Save the Manatee Club	Dole, Bob	Prostate cancer
		Douglas, Kirk	Stroke

Charities of Celebrities

Duke, Patty	Bipolar condition
Dungy, Tony	Mentors for Life
Eastwood, Alison	Animal Rights - pet owner
Elfman, Bodhi	Supports Church of Scientology
Elfman, Jenna	Supports Church of Scientology
Elway, John	Supports Cancer Research
Erving, Julius	Ahtletes Against Drugs Foundation
Esiason, Boomer	Cystic Fibrosis (esiason.org)
Everhart, Angie	Animal Rights - pet owner
Farr, Jamie	Kroger Classic Golf Tournament
Farrakahn, Louis	Prostrate cancer
Fisher, Eddie	Prostrate cancer
Fisher, Joely	Animal Rights - pet owner
Fleming, Peggy	Breast cancer
Flockhart, Calista	St. Judes Hospital
Flutie, Doug	Doug Flutie Foundation - Autism
Fonda, Jane	Campaign for Adolescent Pregnancy Prevention
Ford, Faith	Animal Rights - pet owner
Ford, Whitey	Prostrate cancer
Fox, Michael J.	Foundation for Parkinson's Research
Fraser, Brendan	Animal Rights - pet owner
Frazier, Walt	Walt Frazier Youth Foundation
Funicello, Annette	Multiple Sclerosis
Garofalo, Janeane	Animal Rights - pet owner
Garr, Terri	Multiple Sclerosis
Garth, Jennie	Animal Rights Activist
Gere, Richard	International Campaign For Tibet
Gershon, Gina	Animal Rights - pet owner
Gertz, Jamie	Painted Turtle- homes for sick kids
Getty, Estelle	Parkinson's Disease
Gibons, Leeza	Alzheimer's
Gifford, Kathie Lee	The Association to Benefit Children
Giuliani, Rudolph	Prostrate cancer
Glover, Danny	Dyslexia
Goldberg, Whoopi	Dyslexia
Goldblum, Jeff	End Hunger Network
Goulet, Robert	Prostrate cancer
Graham, Billy	Parkinson's Disease
Grammer, Kelsey	Save The Children Care Skills
Grier, David Alan	Animal Rights - pet owner
Griffin, Merv	Prostrate cancer
Grove, Andy	Prostrate cancer
Guthrie, Arlo	Guthrie Foundation, Musical outreach and educational programs for children

Hagman, Larry	Organ donation
Hamill, Dorothy	Arthritis
Hammond, Daryl	KaBoom, which builds playgrounds for kids
Harman, Katie	Breast cancer
Harper, Valerie	End Hunger Network
Hasselhoff, David	Alcoholism & United Way
Hayes, Isaac	Supports Church of Scientology
Hedren, Tippi	Shambala Preserve for exotic animals
Hefner, Hugh	Playboy Fndt. for social and political causes
Henstridge, Natasha	St. Judes Hospital & Animal Rights
Heston, Charlton	Alzheimer's
Heston, Charlton	Prostrate cancer
Hilfiger, Tommy	The Fresh Air Fund
Houston, Allan	Foundation for Disadvantaged Youth
Houston, Whitney	Foundation for Children
Howard, Ron	Education
Hudson, Kate	Animal Rights - pet owner
Hunter, Rachel	Animal Rights - pet owner
Huston, Angelica	Brain related disorders
Ice-T	Animal Rights - pet owner
Imus, Don	Imus Ranch for children with illnesses
Jackson, Bo	Joint replacement
Jackson, Michael	Skin Disease
Jackson, Samuel L.	Drug addiction
Jackson, Zina	Tennis program in Houston, TX
Janney, Allison	National Breast Cancer Foundation
Jansen, Dan	Cancer- Leukemia
Jenner, Bruce	Dyslexia
Jeter, Derek	Turn 2 Foundation which promotes a healthy and drug free lifestyle to youths in New York, Tampa, Forida and western Michigan.
Jewel	Ground for Humanity, Diversity Works
Joel, Billy	Drug addiction & Depression
John, Elton	Elton John AIDS Foundation
Johnson, Magic	AIDS
Johnson, Tom	Depression
Johnston, Kristen	Animal Rights - pet owner
Jolie, Angelina	UN Ambassador for refuges
Jordon, Michael	Under underprivileged kids
Judd, Naomi	Liver disorders
Kaczmarek, Jane	St. Judes Hospital
Katzenberg, Jeffrey	Cedars-Sinai Medical Center and The UCLA Foundation
Kellerman, Sally	Animal Rights - pet owner
Kennedy, Jayne	Endometriosis
Kennedy, Robert Jr.	Environmental causes & Asthma

Charities of Celebrities

Kennedy,George	Starkey Hearing Foundation		McMahon, Ed	Neighborhood watch -
Kerr, Deborah	Parkinson's Disease		McNabb, Donovan	Foundation contributes to fighting diabetes
Kerry, John	Prostate cancer			
Kidder, Margot	Mental disorders		Mellancamp, John	Farm Aid
Killebrew, Harmon	Harmon Killebrew Foundation		Meskimen, Jim	Supports Church of Scientology
King, B.B.	Diabetes		Michaels, Lorne	City Parks Foundation; International

Kennedy,George — Starkey Hearing Foundation
Kerr, Deborah — Parkinson's Disease
Kerry, John — Prostate cancer
Kidder, Margot — Mental disorders
Killebrew, Harmon — Harmon Killebrew Foundation
King, B.B. — Diabetes
King, Larry — The Larry King Cardiac Foundation
and Starkey Hearing Foundation, giving free hearing devices
King, Stephen — Education
Klugman, Jack — Throat cancer
Koontz, Dean — Canine Companions for Independence
Kwan, Michelle — Children's Miracle Network
Lander, David "Squiggy" — Multiple Sclerosis
Lawrence, Sharon — Alzheimer's
Lear, Norman — National Hispanic Media Institute
Leary, Denis — Firefighters Association
Lee, Brenda — Musical Cares Foundation
Leno, Jay — Dyslexia
Leno, Jay — Medicine & Screen Actors Guild
Leno, Mavis — Afghanistan's women & girls
Letterman, David — Indiana Special Olympics
Levy, Marv — Prostrate cancer
Lewis, Jerry — Muscular Dystrophy
Lewis, Jerry — Prostrate cancer
Lewis, Juliette — Supports Church of Scientology
Limbaugh, Rush — Hearing Disorders
Logins, Greg — AIDS & Animal Rights
Lopez, George — Men's food bank of Simi Valley
Lougainis, Greg — Dyslexia
Lowe, Rob — Cancer
Lucas, George — Education
Macy, William H. — Animal Rights - pet owner
Manning, Peyton — Sports equipment for underprivileged youths
Marino, Dan — Foundation - Autism - Miami Hospital
Marshall, Penny — Californian commemorative quarters
Martin, Steve — Starkey Hearing Foundation
Masterson, Danny — Supports Church of Scientology
Mays, Willie — Sey Hey Foundation for underprivileged kids
Mazar, Deborah — Animal Rights - pet owner
McCartney, Heather Mills — Land mine removal & Animal rights
McClanahan, Rue — Breast Cancer
McCormick, Eric — Meals to people with AIDS
McGwire, Mark — Foundation to help abused children
McIntrye, Reba — Supports Habitat for Humanity

McMahon, Ed — Neighborhood watch -
McNabb, Donovan — Foundation contributes to fighting diabetes
Mellancamp, John — Farm Aid
Meskimen, Jim — Supports Church of Scientology
Michaels, Lorne — City Parks Foundation; International Rescue Committee; The Children's Health
Midler, Bette — New York Restoration Project
Miller, Reggie — Foundation - Burn Victims
Milos, Sofia — Supports Church of Scientology
Ming-Na — Breast cancer
Minnelli, Liza — Drug and alcohol addiction
Minnesota Wild — 10,000 Rinks Foundation supports kid's hockey programs and goodwill ambassadors for childhood illnesses
Montana, Joe — High Blood Pressure - Hypertension
Moore, Julianne — Animal Rights - pet owner
Moore, Mary Tyler — Diabetes
Moore, Roger — UNICEF goodwill ambassador
Murdoch, Rupert — Prostrate cancer
Mutombo, Dikembe — Health Centers in his home Congo
Nelly — Bone marrow donation
Nelson, Willie — Farm Aid
Newrnan, Paul — The Nature Conservancy & The Hole in the Wall Camp
Newton, Wayne — The Children's Cancer Research Fund
NFL — United Way
Nicklaus, Jack — Heart Disease & Hip replacement
Nixon, Cynthia — Better Public Schools
Nolte, Nick — Alcoholism
Norville, Deborah — Depression
Nuegent, Ted — Gun Rights
O'Boyle, Maureen — Animal Rights - pet owner
O'Connor, Sandra Day — Breast cancer
O'Donnell, Rosie — The For All Kids Foundation
Ono, Yoko — Casita Maria Settlement House
Osborne, Sharon — Cancer- Colon
Osmond, Donny — One Heart Organization
Osmond, Marie — Children's Miracle Network
Oteri, Cheri — Animal Rights - pet owner
Palmer, Arnold — Quit smoking campaign
Paltrow, Gwyneth — Cancer
Parker, Fess — Prostrate cancer
Parton, Dolly — Imagination Library program
Pauley, Jane — United Way - Bipolar conditions
Perry, Matthew — Drug addiction
Pfeiffer, DeDee — Animal Rights - pet owner
PGA (The) — Goodwill Industries

Charities of Celebrities

Pierce, David Hyde	Alzheimer's
Pitt, Brad	Children's Discovery Center
Poitier, Sidney	Prostrate cancer
Powell, Colin	Youth organizations
Powers, Stephanie	William Holden Wildlife Foundation
Presley, Priscilla	Supports Church of Scientology
Preston, Kelly	New York Police Widows Charities
Prior, Richard	Multiple Sclerosis
Puck, Wolfgang	Meals on Wheels of St. Vincent
Quayle, Dan	Thyroid cancer
Reagan, Nancy	Alzheimer's
Redford, Robert	Sundance Institute, Sundance Film Festival, Global Green USA
Remini, Leah	Supports Church of Scientology
Reno, Janet	Parkinson's Disease
Rice, Ann	Diabetes
Rice, Jerry	Children's Causes
Rivera, Geraldo	Foundation organizes aid to students
Roberts, Julia	Dignity-Haitian Literacy Fund
Rodriguez, Chi Chi	Modesta-Robbins School Partnership offers after school tutoring
Ross, Diana	Drug addiction
Roundtree, Richard	Breast cancer
Rowlings, J.K.	Multiple Sclerosis
Rue, Sarah	Breast cancer
Russert, Tim	Education
Sarbanes, Paul	Prostrate cancer
Schwab, Charles	Dyslexia
Schwarzenegger, Arnold	Inner-City Games Foundation, Scholastic and athletic events for children
Schwarzkopff, H. Norman	Prostrate cancer
Shepard, Cybill	St. Judes Hospital
Sheridan, Nicolette	Animal Rights - pet owner
Shore, Paulie	Animal Rights - pet owner
Shriver, Maria	Inner-City Games Foundation
Simmons, Jeff	Better Public Schools
Simmons, Richard	Weight Loss
Simon, Paul	The Children's Health Fund
Sinbad	Inner-City Games Foundation
Smith, Will	Youth organizations
Somers, Suzanne	Breast cancer
Spelling, Aaron	Los Angeles Police Historical Society
Spielberg, Steven	Starbright Foundation, Media-based programs for children with a prolonged injury or illness. Survivors of the Shoah Visual History Foundation, Cataloging eyewitness accounts of the Holocaust . The Righteous Persons Foundation, Israel Experience
Springsteen, Bruce	The Southern Poverty Law Center
Steinem, Gloria	Women's Rights & Breast cancer
Stevens, Connie	Animal Rights - pet owner
Stewart, Jackie	Dyslexia
Stiller, Ben	Animal Rights - pet owner
Sting	Rainforest Foundation Fund, Assistance to indian tribes in Peru, Latin America
Streisand, Barbra	The Salk Institute; John Wayne Cancer Institute
Struthers, Sally	Animal Rights - pet owner
Tambor, Jeffrey	Animal Rights - pet owner
Tarentino, Quentin	Dyslexia
Taylor, Elizabeth	AIDS
Theron, Charlize	Best Friends Animal Sanctuary
Thomas, Marlo	St. Judes Hospital
Thornton, Billy Bob	Drug addiction
Tillis, Mel	Stuttering disorders
Torre, Joe	Prostrate cancer
Torres, Joe	Safe at Home Foundation
Travolta, John	Supports Church of Scientology
Turner, Kathleen	Arthritis
Turner, Ted	Depression
Tutu, Bishop Desmond	Prostrate cancer
Twain, Shania	Food programs for kids
Vitale, Dick	Cancer & Boys & Girls Club
Walker, Clay	Band Against MS
Walton, Bill	NBA Former Players Charity
Ward, Sela	KFC's Colonel's Kids shelter for abused and neglected children
Warwick, Dionne	Health care & AIDS
Washington, Denzel	Boys Club of America
White, Betty	Animal Rights Activist
Wilder, Gene	Gilda's Club, Support for people with cancer
Williams, Montel	Multiple Sclerosis
Williams, Robbie	Animal Rights - pet owner
Williams, Vanessa	Missing and exploited children
Willis, Bruce	Adoption Advocate
Wilson, Brian	Drug addiction
Winfrey, Oprah	Oprah's Angel Network, Boys and Girls Clubs of America
Woodruff, Judy	Spina Bifida
Woods, James	American Stroke Association
Woods, Tiger	Start Something Program for Target
Wuhrer, Kari	Animal Rights - pet owner
Young, Neil	Farm Aid, Cerebral Palsy

The Basics:

Getting Started in

Collecting In-Person

Autographs

Tips for getting in-person autographs

Celebrity sightings & hangouts

Questions & answers to pro football training camps

Addresses of pro football training camps

MLB Cactus & Grapefruit League spring training camps

Getting autographs at a TV show production

Be prepared- you may see a celebrity on the street, in a restaurant or other public place. Always carry a small book of paper in case a celebrity appears, I like to carry a spiral bound book of 3x5 plain index cards. Also, carry proper inks, such as a sharpie or other pen.

Have your material ready- if you are seeing a celebrity at a signing, bring photos or other material with you to be signed. Don't assume that the celebrity will have photos or other material on hand. (Some celebrities do, some do not)

Be courteous- crowds and lines must be expected. Pushing only creates bad feelings toward others.

Know the lay of the land- know the entrances and exits the celebrity will be using. Most times the celebrity signs material after the function, so position yourself as close to the exit as possible.

Don't be greedy- unless it is a fee based signing; don't overload the celebrity with requests. This may make the celebrity feel you are a professional collector and decreases the chance that he (she) will oblige other requests.

Plan in advance- know where the celebrities will be. Ask for the itinerary from the celebrities agent or publicist. Confirm all dates, places and times as much as possible.

Be informed- be aware of autograph shows in your area and subscribe to all the major clubs and publications to be on top of all celebrity appearances.

Search for leads- always ask organizations that the celebrity may be a member if they plan any appearances.

Get on mailing lists- bookstores have many authors and other celebrities present at book signings.

Celebrity Sightings & Hangouts

Los Angeles Area Celebrities

The Viceroy Hotel
1819 Ocean Avenue
Santa Monica, California
Telephone 310-451-8711
viceroysatamonica.com
Since opening in July of 2002, the Viceroy Hotel has attracted many celebrities. Fran Dresher, Ben Kinsley, Matthew Perry, Dennis Hopper, Christina Ricci, Jennifer Love Hewitt, Jules Asner, Beck, Keri Russell, Belinda Carlisle have glided through the oversized glass doors which Thursday through Sunday are guarded by a doorman with the list. Your name must be on the list to enter. Reservations must be made at least three weeks in advance to receive any consideration. What attracts these celebrities to the Viceroy? It is its renovated decor, ambiance and food that draws the celebs. The owners of the Viceroy, the Kor Hotel Group, wanted the right feel and amount of people, not just to pack them in and fade away in a year or so. They created a long term goal, to be sophisticated, high end, service oriented establishment.

Sushi Roku
1401 Ocean Ave
Santa Monica, CA
(310) 458-4771
When Will Smith wants sushi he eats here.

Crustacean
9646 Santa Monica Blvd
Beverly Hills, CA
(310) 205-8990
Will Smith has also been seen eating here

El Cholo Restaurant
1121 S Western Avenue
Los Angeles, CA
(323) 734-2773
This restaurant as well as Teri Sushi is one of Tom Hanks favorite restaurants.

Teru Sushi
11940 Ventura Blvd
Studio City, CA
(818) 763-6201

Caffe Roma
350 N. Canon Drive
Beverly Hills, CA
(310)274-7834
If you ever have relatives that come out and want to see movie stars, they should go to lunch at Caffe Roma. They're all there everyday.

Eclipse Restaurant
West Hollywood
Co-owned by Whoopi Goldberg, Steven Segal and Joe Pesci

BaCar Hotel in California
Miro Restaurant
Celebrities seen are Debra Messing and Drew Barrymore

Cinegrill
Most famous cabaret on the west coast
Tony Danza and Sybil Shepard have performed here. Star gazing can be done in the lobby of this popular jazz club

Dolce
8284 Melrose Avenue
West Hollwood, CA
Although it promotes itself as a bastion of Italian peasant cuisine, Dolce is not a dining spot for the common folk. With over a dozen celebrity investors, (including about half the cast of "That '70s Show" including Ashton Kutcher), Dolce is so celeb-packed that you will have a hard time not going crazy with curiosity over who's in the private dining room.

Madre's Restaurant
897 Granite Drive
Pasadena, CA
Madre's, which is Spanish for Mothers, was created by Jennifer Lopez to celebrate her cultural heritage, and her family. Jennifer eats at her latin and Caribbean style restaurant four to five times a week and her father, David is the manager.

Atlanta Georgia Area Celebrities

Ted's Montana Grill
Atlanta, GA
Owned by Ted Turner
Turn of the century décor and Ted Turner lives upstairs so spotting him on occasion is common. The menu includes bison burgers which come from one of his many bison herds located throughout the west.

New York City Area Celebrities

Michael Jordan's The Steak House
Grand Central Terminal
23 Vanderbilt Avenue at 42rd Street
New York City
This restaurant owned by superstar Michael Jordan (in partnership with some experienced New York restaurateurs) is a masculine, mahogany steakhouse located inside the newly renovated Grand Central Terminal. Michael visits his eatery and on occasion you may see him enter his private dining room.

Tribeca Grill
New York City
Owned by Robert DeNiro
A place where a person can rub elbows with celebrities including Robert DeNiro. Upstairs is a screen room where many movie premieres and has become a New York City Landmark.

Philadelphia Pennsylvania Area Celebrities

Morimoto
723 Chestnut Street
Philadelphia, PA
Owned by Masahura Morimoto
It's a Japanese restaurant. It's totally impressive. Just beyond neon chartreuse glass doors, chef Morimoto's elongated culinary theater welcomes diners to a daring here and now. There are undulating bamboo ceilings, booths that change color, and, best of all, the "Iron Chef" himself presiding over a bustling sushi bar in back.

Illinois Area Celebrities

Lovell, Jim
Lovell's of Lake Forest Restaurant
915 South Waukegan
Lake Forest, IL
The flight of Apollo 13 is to be remembered as the space flight that was a failure and success. A failure that the crew did not land and walk on the moon, but a success in the sense that all crewmen and flight controllers in Houston had to work together in what seemed to be an impossible task of returning a damaged and crippled space craft to earth. The space flight that coined the phrase, "failure is not an option" is Jim Lovell's legacy of turning failure into success. He has also turned in another success. After being in the corporate world, he set his sights on the restaurant business. His son James Jr, is a world class chef and the two of them share running the restaurant. The restaurant is upscale and sometimes you will see astronaut colleagues of Jim Lovell's dining at this restaurant.

Arizona Area Celebrities

Alice Cooperstown
101 East Jackson
Phoenix, AZ
Rock-and-roll memorabilia, occasional live music and a staff made up like Alice. Located up the street from Bank One Ballpark and America West Arena, this former furniture warehouse is well placed to take advantage of Phoenix sports mania. Live music on the outdoor stage ties in with game nights, and larger-than-life video screens electrify the bar. The Alice connection comes in the form of memorabilia displays and the Cooperesque eye makeup worn by the staff, male and female alike. Alice himself visits the bar & grill about three to four times a week.

Utah, Wyoming, Montana Celebrities

Tree Room
Provo, Utah
Befitting its Sundance Resort home, Tree Room is the height of rustic elegance: Candlelight and white-linen tablecloths enrich the rough-hewn, lodgey look of the wood-heavy dining room. Floor-to-ceiling windows overlooking a forest-scape and a tree growing through the restaurant's roof bring patrons comfortably close to nature. Western bric-a-brac and Native American art from celebrity-owner Robert Redford's private collection cap the cozy feel and you may see the famous actor dining here during the Sundance Film Festival.

Question: What is the purpose of a football training camp?

Answer: The purpose is twofold. First, all the players, rookie and veteran alike, compete for the available positions on the team. Second, the coaching staff decides which player is best suited for the available position and the team.

Question: What goals do the players and coaches have?

Answer: The players are there to get physically conditioned and learn the playbook. The coaches are there to evaluate the ability of each player and set a game plan into action.

Question: What takes place at training camp?

Answer: The players perform a series of drills to get conditioned and understand the plays of the team. A lot of study time is necessary to become familiar with the complex plays of the team. The coaching staff determines which player(s) are the best choice(s) for the team and makes the cuts as necessary.

Question: When do training camps take place?

Answer: The camp usually starts in July and runs to the week before regular season.

Question: Where are the training camps held?

Answer: Training camps take place all across the U.S. A list of the training camps appear after these Q&A's.

Question: What are the training camps like for the spectator?

Answer: Most of the training camps are held in college towns to accommodate the classroom, dormitory and field requirements of the team. A spectator can expect a relaxed and casual time.

Question: How often do the players practice?

Answer: For most teams there two practices a day. There is one two hour practice in the morning and one two hour practice in the afternoon.

Question: How accessible are the players to sign autographs?

Answer: Usually the players are available after each practice session. Also, players have been known to sign autographs off-campus at golf courses, restaurauts and other local attractions.

Question: Will I get a famous player to sign an autograph?

Answer: Sometimes, sometimes not. A famous player like Joe Montana is known to slip out the back door of the locker room to avoid the crowds. However, I have also seen him come out to sign autographs and greet fans waiting to see him.

Question: Are there any other events where I can get a player's or coache's autograph?

Answer: There can be special events such as fan appreciation days where the autograph collector can go on to the field and obtain the signature of a favorite player or coach.

Question: Are there any photos of players at the training camps?

Answer: Usually not, I suggest that you bring with you all the material you want signed.

Question: What are the most popular items signed?

Answer: The players will sign almost anything within reason, including footballs, helmets and team posters.

Question: Besides training camp, are there other places that a player may be seen signing an autograph?

Answer: Many times a player or coach who is seen at a local golf course or restaurant will accommodate an autograph request.

Question: Can visiting training camps be a good vacation for the family?

Answer: Yes, I believe visiting training camps combined with autograph collecting can be fun for the whole family. Usually the training camps are located at a college or university town that provide amenities for the whole family. Lodging and meals are usually reasonable near training camps. Many times a football team selects a college for its training camp because of its pleasant surroundings. A good example is the training camp at the University of Wisconsin at River Falls. It is in a rural to suburban setting with cultural and natural attractions nearby.

Question: How do I plan a trip to a training camp?

Answer: The key is to know the schedule of the training camp. I would get brochures from the management of the university describing events and practice times at the training camp. I would also call the local area chamber of commerce to find out lodging, restaurants and other attractions in the area.

Addresses of Pro Football Training Camps

Arizona Cardinals
Training Camp
Northern Arizona University
Flagstaff, Arizona

Atlanta Falcons
Training Camp
Furman University
Greenville, South Carolina

Baltimore Ravens
Training Camp
Western Maryland College
Westminster, Maryland

Buffalo Bills
Training Camp
St. John Fisher College
Pittsford, New York

Carolina Panthers
Training Camp
Wofford College
Spartanburg, South Carolina

Chicago Bears
Training Camp
Olivet Nazarene University
Bourbonnais, Illinois

Cincinnati Bengals
Training Camp
Georgetown College
Georgetown, Kentucky

Cleveland Browns
Training Camp
Cleveland Browns Training Facility
Berea, Ohio

Dallas Cowboys
Training Camp
Alamodome
San Antonio, Texas

Denver Broncos
Training Camp
University of Northern Colorado
Greeley, Colorado

Detroit Lions
Training Camp
Lions Training Facility
Allen Park, Michigan

Green Bay Packers
Training Camp
St. Norbert College
De Pere, Wisconsin

Houston Texans
Training Camp
Reliant Park
Houston, Texas

Indianapolis Colts
Training Camp
Rose-Hulman Institute Of Technology
Terre Haute, Indiana

Jacksonville Jaguars
Training Camp
ALLTEL Stadium
Jacksonville, Florida

Kansas City Chiefs
Training Camp
University of Wisconsin - River Falls
River Falls, Wisconsin

Addresses of Pro Football Training Camps

Miami Dolphins
Training Camp
Nova University
Davie, Florida

Minnesota Vikings
Training Camp
University of Minnesota - Mankato
Mankato, Minnesota

New England Patriots
Training Camp
Bryant College
Smithfield, Rhode Island

New Orleans Saints
Training Camp
Nicholls State University
Thibodaux, Louisiana

New York Giants
Training Camp
University at Albany
Albany, New York

New York Jets
Training Camp
Hofstra University
Hempstead, New York

Oakland Raiders
Training Camp
Napa Valley Marriott Hotel
Napa, California

Philadelphia Eagles
Training Camp
Lehigh University
Bethlehem, Pennsylvania

Pittsburgh Steelers
Training Camp
St. Vincent College
Latrobe, Pennsylvania

St. Louis Rams
Training Camp
Western Illinois University
Macomb, illinois

San Diego Chargers
Training Camp
University of California - San Diego
La Jolla, California

San Francisco 49ers
Training Camp
University of the Pacific
Stockton, California

Seattle Seahawks
Training Camp
Eastern Washington University
Cheney, Washington

Tampa Bay Buccaneers
Training Camp
Disney Wide World of Sports
Lake Buena Vista, Florida

Tennessee Titans
Training Camp
Baptist Sports Park
Nashville, Tennessee

Washington Redskins
Training Camp
Dickinson College
Carlisle, Pennsylvania

MLB Cactus & Grapefruit League Spring Training Camps

Besides the possibility of getting autographs from individual MLB players, spring training offers the best of baseball on a budget. A relaxed atmosphere, being able to bring a bagged lunch, inexpensive seats and easy access to the players make the Cactus and Grapefruit Leagues an autograph collectors' paradise.

Listed are the addresses of MLB spring training locations.

Team	Stadium	Address	City	State	Zip
Anaheim Angeles	Diablo Stadium	2200 W. Alameda Drive	Tempe	Arizona	
Arizona Diamondbacks	Electric Park	2500 E. Ajo Way	Tucson	Arizona	
Atlanta Braves	Disney's Sports Complex	700 South Victory Way	Kissimmee	Florida	34747
Baltimore Orioles	Fort Lauderdale Stadium	5301 NW 12th Ave.	Fort Lauderdale	Florida	33309
Boston Red Sox	City of Palms Park	2201 Edison Ave.	Ft. Myers	Florida	33901
Chicago Cubs	Hohokam Park	1235 N. Center	Mesa	Arizona	
Chicago White Soxs	Electric Park	2500 E. Ajo Way	Tucson	Arizona	
Cincinnati Reds	Ed Smith Stadium	2700 12th Street	Sarasota	Florida	34237
Colorado Rockies	Hi Corbett Field	3400 E. Camino Campestre	Tucson	Arizona	
Detroit Tigers	Joker Marchant Stadium	2301 Lakeland Hills Blvd.	Lakeland	Florida	33805
Florida Marlins	Space Coast Stadium	5800 Stadium Parkway	Viera	Florida	32940
Houston Astros	Osceola County Stadium	1000 Bill Beck Blvd.	Kissimmee	Florida	34744
Kansas City Royals	Baseball City Stadium	300 Stadium Way	Davenport	Florida	33837
Los Angeles Dodgers	Holman Stadium/Dodgertown	4101 26th Street	Vero Beach	Florida	32960
Milwaukee Brewers	Maryvale Sports Park	3600 N. 51st Avenue	Phoenix	Arizona	
Minnesota Twins	Hammond Stadium	14100 Six Mile Cypress Pkwy	Ft. Myers	Florida	33912
Montreal Expos	Roger Dean Stadium	4751 Main Street	Jupiter	Florida	33458
New York Mets	Thomas J. White Stadium	525 NW Peacock Blvd.	Port St. Lucie	Florida	34986
New York Yankees	Legends Field	1 Steinbrenner Drive	Tampa	Florida	33614
Oakland A's	Municipal Stadium	5999 E. Van Buren	Phoenix	Arizona	
Philadelphia Phillies	Jack Russell Memorial Stadium	800 Phillies Drive	Clearwater	Florida	33755
Pittsburgh Pirates	McKechnie Field	1611 9th Street	West Bradenton	Florida	34208
San Diego Pardes	Peoria Sports Complex	16101 N. 83rd Avenue	Phoenix	Arizona	
San Francisco Giants	Scottsdale Stadium	7408 E. Osborn Road	Scottsdale	Arizona	
Seattle Mariners	Peoria Sports Complex	16101 N. 83rd Avenue	Phoenix	Arizona	
St. Louis Cardinals	Roger Dean Stadium	4751 Main Street	Jupiter	Florida	33458
Tampa Bay Devil Rays	Florida Power Park	180 2nd Avenue SE	St. Petersburg	Florida	33701
Texas Rangers	Charlotte County Stadium	2300 El Jobean Road	Port Charlotte	Florida	33948
Toronto Blue Jays	Dunedin Stadium at Grant Field	373 Douglas Avenue	Dunedin	Florida	34697

If you are planning to visit Los Angeles or live in the southern California area, then getting tickets to be in the audience of a TV show production could be the passport to receiving autographs from the cast of one of your favorite TV Shows. It is not guaranteed, but many cast members take time to greet members of the studio audience and grant autograph requests before the taping of TV shows. Listed below are the addresses of the studios for the 2002-2003 season. If you would like complete information on how to be a member of a studio audience, apply to be a contestant of a game show or appear on a reality or court TV please read Lee Ellis' book; Appearing on TV Shows for Fun, Fame & Fortune: A Guide for Audiences, Contestants & Guests. Available from the publisher for $19.95 plus shipping, call 1-800-206-7730 access code 35

SUNSET GOWER STUDIOS
1438 N. Gower, Hollywood, CA

Greetings From Tucson
Pablo Santos, Julio Oscar Mechoso

CBS STUDIO CENTER
4024 Radford Ave., Studio City, CA

According To Jim
Jim Belushi, Courtney Thorne-Smith

Charlie Lawrence
Nathan Lane, Laurie Metcalf

Good Morning Miami
Mark Feuerstein, Ashley Williams, Suzanne Pleshette

Grounded For Life
Donal Logue, Megyn Price

Half And Half
Rachel True, Essence Atkins, Telma Hopkins

Just Shoot Me
George Segal, Laura SanGiacomo, David Spade

Less Than Perfect
Sara Rue, Andy Dick, Eric Roberts

Still Standing
Mark Addy, Jami Gertz

That '70s Show
Ensemble cast comedy

Will & Grace
Eric McCormack, Debra Messing

Yes, Dear
Anthony Clark, Jean Louisa Kelly

CBS TELEVISION CITY
7800 Beverly Blvd., Los Angeles, CA

Abby
Sydney Tamiia Poitier, Sean O'Bryan

SONY PICTURES STUDIOS
3970 Overland Ave., Culver City, CA

The King of Queens
Kevin James, Leah Remini, Jerry Stiller

WALT DISNEY STUDIOS
500 S. Buena Vista, Burbank, CA

8 Simple Rules
John Ritter, Katey Sagal

Lost At Home
Mitch Rouse, Connie Britton, Gregory Hines

WARNER BROS. STUDIOS
4210 W. Olive Ave., Burbank, CA

Everybody Loves Raymond
Ray Romano, Patricia Heaton

George Lopez
George Lopez, Constance Marie

Off Centre
Sean Maguire, Eddie Kaye Thomas

The Drew Carey Show
Drew Carey, Kathy Kinney

What I Like About You
Amanda Bynes, Jennie Garth

20th CENTURY FOX STUDIOS
10201 W. Pico Blvd., Los Angeles, CA

Reba
Reba McEntire, Christopher Rich, Melissa Peterman

The Pitts
Dylan Baker, Kellie Waymire

UNIVERSAL STUDIOS
Barham & Lakeside Plaza Dr., Universal City, CA

Coupling
New NBC comedy based on the hit British series

Reference Sources For

The Autograph Collector

Autograph Associations & Clubs

Autograph Magazines & Periodicals

Autograph Dealer Listings

Autograph Collector Magazine
510-A South Corona Mall
Corona, CA 91719-1420
www.autographcollector.com

Eyes, Ears And Voice Of The Hobby Magazine
Publication Of IACC/DA

International Autograph Collectors Club
4575 Sheridan Street
Hollywood, FL 33021
www.ewol.com./Autos

The Manuscript Society
Dept. UA 350 N. Niagara Street
Burbank, CA 915505-3648

The Professional Autograph Dealers Assoc.
PO Box 1729-A Murray Hill Station
New York, NY 10156
www.padaweb.org

Free Autograph Collectors & Enthusiast
47 Webb Crescent, Dawley, Telford
Shropshire TF4 3D3, Eng.

International Autograph Dealers Alliance
4575 Sheridan Street
Hollywood, FL 33021

The Pen & Quill Magazine
Publication Of UACC

Universal Autograph Collectors Club
PO Box 6181
Washington, DC 20044-618

Autograph Dealers in the U.S.

The author or the publisher does not endorse or recommend any dealer listed. These listings are a possible source for buying or selling autographs. It is strongly urged that the reader contact the dealer before making any plans for visiting, some dealers may have unusual hours or may not have a showroom.

Name	Address	City, State, Zip	Phone
A. Lovell Elliott	93 Harris Meadows Ln.	Barnstable, MA 02630	508-362-2334
A. Lovell Elliott	940 Crescent Beach Rd.	Vero Beach, FL 32963	561-234-1034
Abraham Lincoln Book	357 West Chicago Ave.	Chicago, IL 60610	312-944-3085
Ad's Autographs	PO Box 8006	Webster, NY 14580	716-671-2651
Alexander Autographs	100 Melrose Ave.	Greenwich, CT 06830	203-622-8444
Amer. Historical Auction	24 Farnsworth Street	Boston, MA 02210	617-443-0791
American Memories	16901 N. Dallas Parkway	Addison, TX 75001	972-380-2657
Antique Paper Emporium	PO Box 85652	Cortaro, AZ 85652	520-744-0005
Archives Historical Auto	119 Chestnut Hill Road	Wilton, CT 06897	203-226-3920
Auction House	PO Box 969	Freeport, FL 32439	850-835-1249
Autograph Avenue	34545 Chope Place	Clinton Twsp, MI 48035	810-791-5867
Autos & Autos	PO Box 280	Elizabeth City, NC 27909	252-335-1117
A-Z Autograph Gallery	4201 Mass.Ave. NW.	Washington, DC 20016	
Barb Pengelly Autographs	13917 No. Meadows Road	Hagerstown, MD 21742	301-733-9070
Barry A. Smith	PO Box 38306	Greensboro, NC 27438	336-288-4375
Batchelder, Robert F.	1 West Butler Avenue	Ambler, PA 19002	215-643-1430
Beetz, Tom & Kimberly	PO Box 5838	Spring Hills, FL 34611	352-683-3337
Beverly Hills Autographs	9663 Santa Monica Blvd	Beverly Hills, CA 90210	310-826-3595
Bill Corcoran	9228 Sunflower Drive	Tampa, FL 33647	813-973-4727
Blumenthal, John	2853 Rikkard Drive	Thousand Oaks, CA 91362	805-493-5070
Bob Buckley's Red Door	176 Kenton Drive	Langhorne, PA 19047	215-752-2236
Bomsey, Edward N.	7317 Farr Street	Annandale, VA 22003-2516	703-642-2040
Books & Autographs	287 Goodwin Road	Eliot, ME 03903	207-439-4739
Brian & Maria Green	PO Box 1816	Kernersville, NC	336-993-5100
Celebrity Autographs	4161 S. Howell Avenue	Milwaukee, WI 53207	800-522-6037
Christophe Stickel Autog.	PO Box 569	Pacific Grove, CA 93950	831-656-0111
Cindi Thompson Autographs	PO Box 151824	Cape Coral, FL 33915	941-656-5502
Classic Rarities	PO Box 29109	Lincoln, NE 68529	402-467-2948
Cohasco Inc.	Postal 821	Yonkers, NY 10702	914-476-8500
Cohen, Daniel	869 Nashville Road	Kleinburg, Ont. Canada	905-893-2328
Coins Of The Realm	1331f Rockville Pike	Rockville, MD 20852	301-340-1640
Collectibles Of The Stars	4575 Sheridan Street	Hollywood, FL 33021	954-963-5238
Collectibles Unlimited	245 Somerset Way	Weston, FL 33024	954-963-5238
Collector's Mart Inc.	1629 W. Whitmore Ave.	Modesto, CA 95358	209-537-5221
David W. Foudy Collectibles	106 Pleasant Street	Dumont, NJ 07628	201-387-8761
Deco Memorabilia, Inc.	PO Box 5358	Scottsdale, AZ 85261	602-657-7448
Dennis Holzman Antiques	241 Washington Ave.	Albany, Ny 12210	518-449-5414
E.A.C. Gallery	99 Powerhouse Road	Roslyn Heights, NY 11577	516-484-6280
EDM Galleries	497 Allwood Road	Clifton, NJ 07012	973-472-1521
Elmer's Nostalgia, Inc.	3 Putnam Street	Sanford, ME 04073	207-324-2166
Empire Autograph Auction	1213 Station Place	Hewlett, NY 11557	516-562-2130
F. Don Nidiffer	PO Box 8148	Charlottesville,VA 22906	804-296-2027
Famous Autographs	10645 N. Tatum Blvd	Phoenix, AZ 85028	602-996-0187
Federal Hill Antiquities	PO Box 600	Phoenix, MD 21131-0600	410-584-8329
Fred Senese Autographs	Box 440	Goffstown, NH 03045	800-231-9758
Gallery Of History	3601 Sahara Avenue	Las Vegas, NV 89102	800-425-5379
Gerard Stodoloski	555 Canal Street	Manchester, NH 03101	603-647-0716
Golder State Autographs	PO Box 14776	Albuquerque, NM 87191	505-293-7407
Great Lakes Autographs	8903 Soutmoor Ave.	Highland, IN 46322	219-923-8884
Greg Tucker Autographs	PO Box 909	Broken Arrow, OK 74013	918-455-3689
H & L Collectibles	4908 Poplar Drive	Alexandria, VA 22310	
Harris Schaller Autographs	PO Box 746	Dubuque, IA 52004-0746	319-583-2757
Historical Collectibles	PO Box 975	Burlington, NC 27215	336-570-2803
Historical Collections	13190 Memorial Drive	Houston, TX 77231	713-723-0296
Historical Documents	13321 Sw 124th Street	Miami, FL 33186	305-233-7999
Historical Rarities	PO Box 200	Garryowen, MT 59031	

Houle Rare Books & Autos	7260 Beverly Blvd	Los Angeles, CA 90036	213-937-5858
J.B. Mums Art & Autographs	1162 Shattack Ave.	Berkeley, CA 94707	510-525-2420
Jack Bacon & Co.	3550 Southhampton Dr.	Reno, NV 89509	775-852-2215
Jack W. Heir Autographs	PO Box 88	Manalapan, NJ 07726	732-446-4758
Jan Schray Autographs	6721 Troost Avenue	No. Hollywood, CA 91606	
Jerry N. Showalter	PO Box 84	Ivy, VA 22945	804-295-6413
Jim Hayes Antiquarian	Drawer 12560	James Island, SC 29422	843-795-0732
Kenneth W. Rendell, Inc.	PO Box 9001	Wellsley, MA 02481	781-431-1776
Keya Gallery	110 West 25th Street	New York, NY 10001	800-906-5392
La Scala Autographs	PO Box 715	Pennington, NJ 08534	800-622-2702
Left Field Collectibles	7855 Blvd East # 25c	North Bergen, NJ 07047	201-869-1882
Legends Of History	PO Box 700918	Plymouth, MI 48170	734-451-1553
Les Perline & Co.	Two Gannett Drive #200	White Plains, NY 10604	800-567-2014
Lone Star Autographs	PO Box 10	Kaufman, TX 75142	972-932-6050
Lowe, James Autographs	30 East 60th Street	New York, NY 10022-1008	212-759-0775
Main Street Fine Books	206 North Main	Galena, IL 61036	815-777-3749
Matted Memories	134 Bengeyfield Dr.	East Williston, NY 11596	516-742-7266
Michael J. Amenta Autog.	28 Helene Avenue	Merrick, NY 11566	516-868-9208
Michael Wehrmann Autog.	70-40 Juno Street	Forest Hills, NY 11375	718-261-4183
Mike Hirsch Autographs	11 Phillips Mill Drive	Middleton, NJ 07748	732-787-1202
Mike Tipper Enterprises	2023 Madison Avenue	Redwood City, CA 94061	650-365-5390
Miller's Nostalgia	623 Ivy Court	Wheeling, IL 60090	847-398-1613
North Shore Manuscript	PO Box 458	Rosly Heights, NY 11577	516-484-6826
Novagraphics	PO Box 37197-t5	Tucson, AZ 85740	800-727-6682
Olla Podrida	4348 North 40th Street	Phoenix, AZ 85018	602-954-0972
P & P Autographs	92-c Main Street	Hampton, CT 06247	860-455-0784
Personalities Plus	PO Box 323	Arnolds Park, IA 51331	712-332-7251
Polk, Robert L.	4129 Leamington Avenue	Chicago, IL 60641	773-286-4543
Prime Collectibles	7267 West Kentucky Dr.	Lakewood, CO 80226	
Profiles In History	345 North Maple Drive	Beverly Hills, CA 90210	310-859-7701
Queen Esther Judaica	927 51st Street	Brooklyn, NY 11219	718-437-9305
R & R Enterprises	3 Chestnut Drive	Bedford, NH 03110	800-937-3880
R.M. Smythe	26 Broadway Suite 271	New York, NY 10004	800-622-1880
Raab, Steven S.	Box 471	Ardmore, PA 19003	610-446-6193
Rambod, Max	16161 Ventura Blvd	Encino, CA 91436	818-784-1776
Remains To Be Seen	3520 South Ocean Blvd	Palm Beach, FL 33480	561-547-3786
Remember When Auctions	Po Box 1829	Wells, ME 04090	207-646-2740
Rich Aitman Collectibles	3942 North 46th Ave.	Hollywood, FL 33021	954-986-0707
Rocky Mountain Rarities	PO Box 303	Bountiful, UT 84011	801-296-6276
Roger Gross Ltd.	225 East 57th Street	New Yory, NY 10022	212-759-2892
Rubinfine, Joseph	505 South Flag Drive	West Palm Beach, FL 33401	561-659-7077
Safka & Bareis Autog.	PO Box 886	Forest Hills, NY 11375	718-263-2276
Scott J. Winslow Assoc.	PO Box 10240	Bedford, NH 03110	800-225-6233
Seaport Autographs	6 Brandon Lane	Mystic, CT 06355	860-572-8441
Searle's Autographs	PO Box 9369	Ashville, TN 28815	704-299-0512
Second Story Books	12160 Parklawn Drive	Rockville, MD 20852	301-770-0477
Signature House	407 Liberty Ave.	Bridgeport, WY 26330	304-842-3386
Signatures In Time	PO Box 180	Scandinavia, WI 54977	715-445-2214
Signed Sealed Delivered	7320 Ashcroft # 204	Houston, TX 77081	713-664-1299
Sport Shop	2295 Needham St. # 15	El Cajon, CA 92020	619-447-0217
Stampede Investments	PO Box 843	Lagrange, IL 60525	708-788-9022
Star Shots	5389 Bearup Street	Port Charlotte, FL 33981	941-697-6935
Starbrite Autographs	PO Box 722020	San Diego, CA 92172	800-380-1777
Stephen Koschal Autog.	PO Box 1581	Boyton Beach, FL 33425	561-736-8409
Swann Galleries	104 East 25th Street	New York, NY 10010	212-254-4710
The History Buff	32 Via Mizner	Palm Beach, FL 33480	561-366-8255
The Written Word Autog.	PO Box 490	Tamworth, NH 03886	603-323-7563
Time Again Collectibles	Po Box 8042	Hilton Head, SC 29938	843-842-6616
Tollett & Harman	175 W. 76th Street	New York, NY 10023	212-877-1566
University Archives	49 Richmondville Ave.	Westport, CT 06880	800-237-5692
Vardakis, Mark	PO Box 1430	Coventry, RI 02816	800-342-0301
W.J. Burger Americana	PO Box 832	Pine Grove, CA 95665	209-296-7970
Walls Of Fame Autographs	PO Box 1053	Neptune, NJ 07753	732-988-0315
Walter Burks Autographs	PO Box 23097	Stanley, KS 66223	913-897-4674
Walter R. Benjamin	Scribner Hollow Road	Hunter, NY 12442	518-263-4133

The Address Directory: Entertainers

Academy Award Winners

Actors & Actresses Having Leading and Character Roles on TV and Film

James Bond Movie Personalities

Aussie Posse - Australian Actors

Supermodels

Comedians, Cartoonists

Authors, Directors, Producers, Writers,
Radio & TV Personalities, Architects, Artists, Chefs,
Fashion Designers, Magicians

Announcers, Composers, Dancers, Instrumentalists,
Groups & Bands, Vocalists, Music Halls of Fame

Celebrity Biographies on Web Sites & TV
Wed Sites of Celebrities

Academy Award Winners 1988 to 2008

Catagories	1988 (61st annual award)	1989 (62nd annual award)
Best Picture	Rain Man	Driving Miss Daisy
Best Actor	Dustin Hoffman	Daniel Day Lewis
Best Actress	Jodie Foster	Jessica Tandy
Best Supporting Actor	Kevine Kline	Denzel Washington
Best Supporting Actress	Geena Davis	Brenda Fricker
Best Director	Barry Levinson	Oliver Stone

Catagories	1990 (63rd annual award)	1991 (64th annual award)
Best Picture	Dances with Wolves	The Silence of the Lamb
Best Actor	Jeremy Irons	Anthony Hopkins
Best Actress	Kathy Bates	Jodie Foster
Best Supporting Actor	Joe Pesci	Jack Palance
Best Supporting Actress	Whoopi Goldberg	Mercedes Ruhl
Best Director	Kevin Costner	Jonathan Demme

Catagories	1992 (65th annual award)	1993 (66th annual award)
Best Picture	Unforgiven	Schindler's List
Best Actor	Al Pacino	Tom Hanks
Best Actress	Emma Thompson	Holly Hunter
Best Supporting Actor	Gene Hackman	Tommy Lee Jones
Best Supporting Actress	Marisa Tomei	Anna Pacquin
Best Director	Clint Eastwood	Steven Spielberg

Catagories	1994 (67th annual award)	1995 (68th annual award)
Best Picture	Forrest Gump	Braveheart
Best Actor	Tom Hanks	Nicolas Cage
Best Actress	Jessica Lange	Susan Sarandon
Best Supporting Actor	Martin Landau	Kevin Spacey
Best Supporting Actress	Dianne Wiest	Miro Sorvino
Best Director	Robert Zemeckis	Mel Gibson

Catagories	1996 (69th annual award)	1997 (70th annual award)
Best Picture	The English Patient	Titanic
Best Actor	Geoffrey Rush	Jack Nicholson
Best Actress	Frances McDormand	Helen Hunt
Best Supporting Actor	Cuba Gooding Jr.	Robin Williams
Best Supporting Actress	Juliet Binoche	Kim Basinger
Best Director	Anthony Minghella	James Cameron

Academy Award Winners 1988 to 2008

Categories	1998 (71st annual award)	1999 (72nd annual award)
Best Picture	Shakespeare in Love	American Beauty
Best Actor	Robert Benigni	Kevin Spacey
Best Actress	Gwyneth Paltrow	Hilary Swank
Best Supporting Actor	James Coburn	Michael Caine
Best Supporting Actress	Judi Dench	Angelina Jolie
Best Director	Steven Spielberg	Sam Mendes

Categories	2000 (73rd annual award)	2001 (74th annual award)
Best Picture	Gadiator	A Beautiful Mind
Best Actor	Russell Crowe	Denzel Washington
Best Actress	Julia Roberts	Halle Berry
Best Supporting Actor	Benicio Del Toro	Jim Broadbent
Best Supporting Actress	Marcia Gay Harden	Jennifer Connelly
Best Director	Steven Soderbergh	Ron Howard

Categories	2002 (75th annual award)	2003 (76th annual award)
Best Picture	Chicago	Lord of the Rings
Best Actor	Adrien Brody	Sean Penn
Best Actress	Nicole Kidman	Charlize Theron
Best Supporting Actor	Chris Cooper	Tim Robbins
Best Supporting Actress	Catherine Zeta-Jones	Renee Zellweger
Best Director	Roman Polansky	Peter Jackson

Categories	2004 (77th annual award)	2005 (78th Annual Award)
Best Picture	Million Dollar Baby	Crash
Best Actor	Jamie Foxx	Philip Seymour Hoffman
Best Actress	Hillary Swank	Reese Witherspoon
Best Supporting Actor	Morgan Freeman	George Clooney
Best Supporting Actress	Cate Blancett	Rachel Weisz
Best Director	Clint Eastwood	Ang Lee

Categories	2006 (79th annual award)	2007 (80th annual award)
Best Picture	The Departed	No Country for Old Men
Best Actor	Forest Whitaker	Daniel Day-Lewis
Best Actress	Helen Mirren	Marion Cotilland
Best Supporting Actor	Alan Arkin	Javier Bardem
Best Supporting Actress	Jennifer Hudson	Tilda Swinton
Best Director	Martin Scorsese	Joel & Ethan Coen

Abraham, F. Murray	Paradigm Talent Agency	360 N. Crescent Drive	Beverly Hills, CA 90210
Acker, Amy	Lesher Entertainment	1134 S Cloverdale Avenue	Los Angeles, CA 90019
Adams, Amy	Endeavor Talent Agency	9601 Wilshire Blvd. 3rd Floor	Beverly Hills, CA 90212
Adams, Joey Lauren	Intl. Creative Mgmt.	8942 Wilshire Blvd	Beverly Hills, CA 90211
Affleck, Ben	Endeavor Talent Agency	9601 Wilshire Blvd. 3rd Floor	Beverly Hills, CA 90212
Affleck, Casey	ID Public Relations	8409 Santa Monica Blvd	West Hollywood, CA 90069
Aghdashloo, Shohreh	Creative Artists Agency	2000 Avenue of The Stars	Beverly Hills, CA 90067
Aiello, Danny	Parseghian/Planco	23 East 22nd Street	New York, NY 10010
Aiken, Liam	Abrams Artists Agency	275 7th Avenue 26th Floor	New York, NY 10001
Alba, Jessica	Bragman/Nyman/Cafarelli	8687 Melrose Ave. 8th floor	Los Angeles, CA 90069
Alberghetti, Anna Marie	10333 Chrysanthemum Ln.	Los Angeles, CA 90077	
Alda, Alan	ICM-Toni Howard	8942 Wilshire Blvd	Beverly Hills, CA 90211
Aldridge, Kelly	Irene Marie Mgmt. Group	728 Ocean Drive	Miami Beach, FL 33139
Aldridge, Sabrina	Irene Marie Mgmt. Group	728 Ocean Drive	Miami Beach, FL 33139
Alexander, Erika	Innovative Artists	235 Park Ave. S.	New York, NY 10003
Alexander, Jane	William Morris Agency	One William Morris Place	Beverly Hills, CA 90212
Alexander, Jason	William Morris Agency	One William Morris Place	Beverly Hills, CA 90212
Allen, Joan	Intl. Creative Mgmt.	40 West 57th Street	New York, NY 10019
Allen, Karen	Paradigm Talent Agency	360 N. Crescent Drive	Beverly Hills, CA 90210
Allen, Krista	ROAR	9701 Wilshire Blvd	Beverly Hills, CA 90212
Allen, Woody	42 West	220 West 42nd Street	New York, NY 10036
Alonso, Daniella	The Gersh Agency	232 North Canon Dr.	Beverly Hills, CA 90210
Altice, Summer	Platform Public Relations	2666 North Beachwood Dr.	Los Angeles, CA 90068
Ambrose, Lauren	United Talent Agency	9560 Wilshire Blvd 5th Floor	Beverly Hills, CA 90212
Amerie	Feenix Entertainment	1360 Clifton Avenue	Clifton, NJ 07012
Amick, Madchen	The Gersh Agency	232 North Canon Drive	Beverly Hills, CA 90210
Amos, John	Diverse Talent Group	1875 Century Park East	Los Angeles, CA 90067
Anderson, Anthony	Principato Young Mgmt.	9465 Wilshire Blvd. Suite 880	Beverly Hills, CA 90212
Anderson, Gillian	Creative Artists Agency	2000 Avenue of The Stars	Beverly Hills, CA 90067
Anderson, Loni	Innovative Artists	1505 Tenth Street	Santa Monica, CA 90401
Anderson, Pamela	United Talent Agency	9560 Wilshire Blvd 5th Floor	Beverly Hills, CA 90212
Anderson, Paul Thomas	Endeavor Talent Agency	9601 Wilshire Blvd. 3rd Floor	Beverly Hills, CA 90212
Anderson, Richard Dean	Intl. Creative Mgmt.	10250 Constellation Blvd.	Los Angeles, CA 90067
Anderson, Wes	United Talent Agency	9560 Wilshire Blvd #500	Beverly Hills, CA 90212
Andrews, Julie	Hanson & Schwam PR	9350 Wilshire Blvd., Ste 315	Beverly Hills, CA 90212
Andrews, Naveen	Renee Jennett Management	10028 Farragut Drive	Culver City, CA 90232
Angarano, Michael	Coast to Coast Talent	3350 Barham Blvd.	Los Angeles, CA 90068
Aniston, Jennifer	Creative Artists Agency	2000 Avenue of The Stars	Beverly Hills, CA 90067
Anthony, Marc	Creative Artists Agency	2000 Avenue of The Stars	Beverly Hills, CA 90067
Anton, Susan	4625 S. Polaris Ste. 102	Las Vegas, NV 89103	
Appleby, Shiri	The Gersh Agency	232 North Canon Drive	Beverly Hills, CA 90210
Applegate, Christina	Wolf Kasteler PR	355 North Maple Dr.	Beverly Hills, CA 90210
Aquino, Amy	TalentWorks	3500 W. Olive Ave	Burbank, CA 91505
Archer, Ann	A.P.A.	405 S. Beverly Dr.	Los Angeles, CA 90212
Arcieri, Leila	Catch 23 Enter. c/o Darryl Taja	310 North Camden	Los Angeles, CA 90210
Arias, Yancey	Penner PR	8225 Santa Monica Blvd	Los Angeles, CA 90048
Arkin, Alan	Endeavor Talent Agency	9601 Wilshire Blvd. 3rd Floor	Beverly Hills, CA 90212
Armstrong, Bess	William Morris Agency	One William Morris Place	Beverly Hills, CA 90212
Armstrong, Samaire	Aquarius PR c/o Mia Hansen	5320 Slymar Ave.	Sherman Oaks, CA 91401
Arnaz, Desi Jr.	The Artists Agency	1180 So. Beverly Drive	Los Angeles, CA 90035
Arness, James	Ms. Janet Arness	PO Box 492163	Los Angeles, CA 90049
Arnett, Will	United Talent Agency	9560 Wilshire Blvd	Beverly Hills, CA 90212
Arnold, Tichina	APA Talent Agency	9200 Sunset Blvd.	Los Angeles, CA 90069
Arquette, Courteney Cox	Coquette Productions	8105 W. 3rd St.	West Hollywood, CA 90048

Arquette, David	Coquette Productions	8105 W. 3rd St.	West Hollywood, CA 90048
Arquette, Patricia	The Gersh Agency	232 North Canon Drive	Beverly Hills, CA 90210
Arquette, Rosanna	Creative Artists Agency	2000 Avenue of The Stars	Beverly Hills, CA 90067
Arroyave, Karina	Peter Strain & Associates	5455 Wilshire Blvd.	Los Angeles, CA 90036
Ashanti	TalentWorks	3500 West Olive Ave.	Burbank, CA 91505
Ashley, Elizabeth	Duva-Flack Associates	200 West 57th Street	New York, NY 10019
Ashmore, Shawn	Nancy Seltzer & Associates	6220 Del Valle Dr.	Los Angeles, CA 90048
Asner, Ed	Innovative Artists	1505 Tenth Street	Santa Monica, CA 90401
Aspen, Jennifer	Innovative Artists	1505 10th Street	Santa Monica, CA 90401
Astin, Sean	Patricola Lust PR	8383 Wilshire Blvd.	Beverly Hills, CA 90211
Atkins, Sharif	Stone Manners Agency	6500 Wilshire Blvd. Ste #550	Los Angeles, CA 90048
Atkins, Tom	Paradigm Talent Agency	360 N. Crescent Drive	Beverly Hills, CA 90210
Atkinson, Rowan	PBJ Management	7 Soho Street	London W1D 3DQ UK
Auberjonois, Rene	Peter Strain & Assoc.	5455 Wilshire Blvd.	Los Angeles, CA 90036
Avery, James	Cynthia Snyder PR	5739 Colfax Ave.	North Hollywood, CA 91601
Azaria, Hank	Endeavor Talent Agency	9601 Wilshire Blvd. 3rd Floor	Beverly Hills, CA 90212
Bacall, Lauren	Dakota Hotel	1 West 72nd Street No. 43	New York, NY 10023
Bach, Catherine	Rohr Talent PR	1901 Ave of the Stars Ste. 365	Los Angeles, CA 90067
Bacon, Kevin	PMK Public Relations	700 San Vicente Blvd.	West Hollywood, CA 90069
Bader, Diedrich	Paradigm Talent Agency	360 N. Crescent Drive	Beverly Hills, CA 90210
Bahr, Iris	Agency for the Performing Arts	9200 Sunset Blvd.	Beverly Hills, CA 90069
Bain, Barbara	Mark Bass Agency	9171 Wilshire Blvd.	Beverly Hills, CA 90210
Baio, Scott	TalentWorks	3500 W. Olive Ave.	Burbank, CA 91505
Bairstow, Scott	Endeavor Talent Agency	9601 Wilshire Blvd. 3rd Floor	Beverly Hills, CA 90212
Baker, Carroll	Abrams Artists Agency	9200 Sunset Blvd 11th Floor	Los Angeles CA 90067
Baker, Diane	The Gage Group	9255 Sunset Blvd	Los Angeles, CA 90069
Baker, Joe Don	The Artists Agency	1180 So. Beverly Drive	Los Angeles, CA 90035
Baker, Simon	ID Public Relations	8409 Santa Monica Blvd.	West Hollywood, CA 90069
Bakula, Scott	JDS - Jay D. Schwartz	3151 Cahuenga Blvd Suite	Los Angeles, CA 90068
Baldwin, Adam	Innovative Artists	1505 10th Street	Santa Monica, CA 90401
Baldwin, Alec	El Dorado Pictures	725 Arizona Ave.	Santa Monica, CA 90401
Baldwin, Daniel	Innovative Artists	1505 10th Street	Santa Monica, CA 90401
Baldwin, Stephen	TalentWorks	3500 W. Olive Ave.	Burbank, CA 91505
Bale, Christian	Endeavor Talent Agency	9601 Wilshire Blvd. 3rd Floor	Beverly Hills, CA 90212
Ball, Taylor	William Morris Agency	One William Morris Place	Beverly Hills, CA 90212
Bamber, Jamie	Pinnacle Public Relations	8265 Sunset Blvd	Los Angeles, CA 90046
Bana, Eric	William Morris Agency	One William Morris Place	Beverly Hills, CA 90212
Banderas, Antonio	Creative Artists Agency	2000 Avenue of The Stars	Beverly Hills, CA 90067
Banks, Elizabeth	I/D Public Relations	8409 Santa Monica Blvd.	West Hollywood, CA 90069
Baranski, Christine	United Talent Agency	9560 Wilshire Blvd #500	Beverly Hills, CA 90212
Barbeau, Adrienne	William Morris Agency	One William Morris Place	Beverly Hills, CA 90212
Barberie, Jillian	42 West	1801 Century Park E.	Los Angeles, CA 90067
Bardem, Javier	Endeavor Talent Agency	9601 Wilshire Blvd. 3rd Floor	Beverly Hills, CA 90212
Bardot, Brigitte	La Madrague	83990 St. Tropez	France
Barnes, Priscilla	AKA Talent Agency	6310 San Vicente Blvd.	Los Angeles, CA 90048
Barrett, Majel	PO Box 691370	W. Hollywood, CA 90211	
Barrymore, Drew	Flower Films	4000 Warner Blvd.	Burbank, CA 91522
Barton, Mischa	Baker Winokur Ryder	9100 Wilshire Blvd.	Beverly Hills, CA 90212
Basinger, Kim	Creative Artists Agency	2000 Avenue of The Stars	Beverly Hills, CA 90067
Bassett, Angela	Creative Artists Agency	2000 Avenue of The Stars	Beverly Hills, CA 90067
Bateman, Jason	United Talent Agency	9560 Wilshire Blvd.	Beverly Hills, CA 90212
Bates, Alan	Intl. Creative Mgmt.	10250 Constellation Blvd.	Los Angeles, CA 90067
Bates, Kathy	Susan Smith & Associates	121 N. San Vicente Blvd	Beverly Hills, CA 90211
Baxter, Meredith	Agency for the Performing Arts	888 Seventh Ave.	New York, NY 10106

Beach, Adam	Artistry Management	525 Westbourne Drive	Los Angeles, CA 90048
Beals, Jennifer	APA Talent Agency	888 Seventh Ave.	New York, NY 10106
Bean, Orson	Stone Manners Agency	6500 Wilshire Blvd. Ste #550	Los Angeles, CA 90048
Bean, Sean	Creative Artists Agency	2000 Avenue of The Stars	Beverly Hills, CA 90067
Beatty, Warren	Creative Artists Agency	2000 Avenue of The Stars	Beverly Hills, CA 90067
Beauvais, Garcelle	The Gersh Agency	232 North Canon Drive	Beverly Hills, CA 90210
Beckham, Victoria	Rogers & Cowan PR	8687 Melrose Ave., 7th Floor	Los Angeles, CA 90069
Beckinsale, Kate	Baker Winokur Ryder	9100 Wilshire Blvd.	Beverly Hills, CA 90212
Begley, Ed Jr.	Innovative Artists	1505 10th St	Santa Monica, CA 90401
Belafonte, Harry	William Morris Agency	One William Morris Place	Beverly Hills, CA 90212
Belafonte, Shari	William Morris Agency	One William Morris Place	Beverly Hills, CA 90212
Bell, Camilla	Creative Artists Agency	2000 Avenue of The Stars	Beverly Hills, CA 90067
Bell, Catherine	PMK Public Relations	700 San Vicente Blvd	West Hollywood, CA 90069
Bell, Kristen	Bragman & Nyman PR	8687 Melrose Ave	Los Angeles, CA 90069
Bell, Lake	United Talent Agency	9560 Wilshire Blvd	Beverly Hills, CA 90212
Bell, Zoe	James/Levy/Jacobson	3500 W. Olive Ave.	Burbank, CA 91505
Belle, Camilla	Creative Artists Agency	2000 Avenue of The Stars	Beverly Hills, CA 90067
Bello, Maria	Creative Artists Agency	2000 Avenue of The Stars	Beverly Hills, CA 90067
Bellucci, Monica	Creative Artists Agency	2000 Avenue of The Stars	Beverly Hills, CA 90067
Bellwood, Pamela	The Sanders Agency	8831 Sunset Blvd	Los Angeles, CA 90069
Belushi, Jim	Intl. Creative Mgmt.	10250 Constellation Blvd.	Los Angeles, CA 90067
Belzer, Richard	Don Buchwald & Associates	6500 Wilshire Blvd	Los Angeles, CA 90048
Benigni, Roberto	Nancy Seltzer & Associates	6220 Del Valle Dr.	Los Angeles, CA 90048
Bening, Annette	Creative Artists Agency	2000 Avenue of The Stars	Beverly Hills, CA 90067
Benjamin, Andre	William Morris Agency	One William Morris Place	Beverly Hills, CA 90212
Benjamin, Richard	The Gersh Agency	232 North Canon Drive	Beverly Hills, CA 90210
Bennett, Jimmy	Endeavor Talent Agency	9601 Wilshire Blvd. 3rd Floor	Beverly Hills, CA 90212
Bennett, Jonathan	Pinnacle PR	1424 Second Street	Santa Monica, CA 90401
Benrubi, Abraham	Stone Manners Agency	6500 Wilshire Blvd	Los Angeles, CA 90048
Benson, Amber	Innovative Artists	1505 10th St	Santa Monica, CA 90401
Benson, Robbie	Creative Artists Agency	2000 Avenue of The Stars	Beverly Hills, CA 90067
Bentley, Wes	William Morris Agency	1325 Ave of the Americas	New York NY 10019
Benzali, Daniel	Suite 555	9300 Wilshire Blvd	Beverly Hills, CA 90212
Bergen, Candice	Celebrity Consultants	3340 Ocean Park Blvd	Santa Monica, CA 90405
Bergen, Polly	TalentWorks	3500 W. Olive Ave	Burbank, CA 91505
Berkley, Elizabeth	Innovative Artists	1505 Tenth Street	Santa Monica, CA 90401
Bernal, Gael García	Endeavor Talent Agency	9601 Wilshire Blvd. 3rd Floor	Beverly Hills, CA 90212
Bernard, Carlos	Paul Kohner Agency	9300 Wilshire Blvd. Suite 555	Beverly Hills, CA 90212
Bernard, Crystal	IFA Talent Agency	8730 Sunset Blvd #490	Los Angeles, CA 90069
Bernsen, Corbin	Special Artists Agency	9465 Wilshire Blvd	Beverly Hills, CA 90212
Berry, Halle	Intl. Creative Mgmt.	10250 Constellation Blvd.	Los Angeles, CA 90067
Bertinelli, Valerie	PMK Public Relations	700 San Vicente Blvd.	West Hollywood, CA 90069
Bettany, Paul	Intl. Creative Mgmt.	10250 Constellation Blvd.	Los Angeles, CA 90067
Bibb, Leslie	Intl. Creative Mgmt.	10250 Constellation Blvd.	Los Angeles, CA 90067
Biel, Jessica	BWR	9100 Wilshire Blvd.	Beverly Hills, CA 90212
Bikel, Theodore	The Artists Group	3345 Wilshire Blvd	Los Angeles, CA 90010
Billingsley, Barbara	Michael Einfeld Mgmt.	10630 Moorpark 101	Toluca Park, CA 91602
Bilson, Rachel	Creative Artists Agency	2000 Avenue of The Stars	Beverly Hills, CA 90067
Bingham, Tracy	Acme Talent Agency	4727 Wilshire Blvd	Los Angeles, CA 90010
Binoche, Juliette	Endeavor Talent Agency	9601 Wilshire Blvd. 3rd Floor	Beverly Hills, CA 90212
Birney, David	Bret Adams Agency	448 W. 44th St.	New York, NY 10036
Bisset, Jacqueline	Guttman Associates	118 S. Beverly Dr.	Beverly Hills, CA 90212
Black, Jack	United Talent Agency	9560 Wilshire Blvd - 5th Floor	Beverly Hills, CA 90212
Black, Shirley Temple	115 Lakeview Drive	Woodside, CA 94062	

Blair, Selma	Creative Artists Agency	2000 Avenue of The Stars	Beverly Hills, CA 90067
Blake, Robert	11604 Dilling Street	Studio City, CA 91604	
Blakely, Susan	Defining Artists Agency	10 Universal City Plaza	Universal City, CA 91608
Blanc, Jennifer	TZ PR	15015 Sherman Way	Van Nuys, CA 91405
Blanchard, Rachel	Endeavor Talent Agency	9601 Wilshire Blvd. 3rd Floor	Beverly Hills, CA 90212
Blanchett, Cate	Creative Artists Agency	2000 Avenue of The Stars	Beverly Hills, CA 90067
Bledel, Alexis	Endeavor Talent Agency	9601 Wilshire Blvd. 3rd Floor	Beverly Hills, CA 90212
Bleeth, Yasmine	The Gersh Agency	232 North Canon Drive	Beverly Hills, CA 90210
Blethyn, Brenda	Nancy Seltzer & Associates	6220 Del Valle Dr	Los Angeles, CA 90048
Bloodgood, Moon	Paradigm Talent Agency	360 N. Crescent Drive	Beverly Hills, CA 90210
Bloom, Orlando	PMK/HBH	161 6th Ave. Ste. 10R	New York, NY 10013
Bochner, Lloyd	David Shapira & Assoc.	15821 Ventura Blvd # 235	Encino, CA 91436
Bonner, Frank	Guardian Angel Management	11271 Ventura Blvd	Studio City, CA 91604
Boreanaz, David	Visionary Entertainment	1558 North Stanley Ave.	West Hollywood, CA 90046
Borgnine, Ernest	3055 Lake Glen Drive	Beverly Hills, CA 90210	
Borstein, Alex	Endeavor Talent Agency	9601 Wilshire Blvd	Beverly Hills, CA 90210
Bostwick, Barry	Paradigm Talent Agency	360 N. Crescent Drive	Beverly Hills, CA 90210
Bosworth, Kate	United Talent Agency	9560 Wilshire Blvd 5th Floor	Beverly Hills, CA 90212
Bova, Raoul	Paradigm Talent Agency	360 N. Crescent Drive	Beverly Hills, CA 90210
Bowen, Andrea	McClure and Associates PR	5225 Wilshire Blvd.	Los Angeles, CA 90036
Bowen, Julie	United Talent Agency	9560 Wilshire Blvd #500	Beverly Hills, CA 90212
Boxleitner, Bruce	Domain Talent	9229 Sunset Blvd	Los Angeles, CA 90069
Boyd, Billy	Brunskill Management	169 Queensgate Suite 8a	London, SW7 5HE, UK
Bozilovic, Ivana	Guttman Associates	118 South Beverly Drive	Beverly Hills, CA 90212
Bracco, Lorraine	Innovative Artists	235 Park Avenue South	New York, NY 10003
Bradford, Jesse	Alchemy Entertainment	9229 Sunset Blvd.	Los Angeles, CA 90069
Braff, Zach	Creative Artists Agency	2000 Avenue of The Stars	Beverly Hills, CA 90067
Branagh, Kenneth	Special Artists Agency	9465 Wilshire Blvd	Beverly Hills, CA 90212
Bratt, Benjamin	ID Public Relations	8409 Santa Monica Blvd	West Hollywood, CA 90069
Bree "Brianne Siddall"	The Tisherman Agency	6767 Forest Lawn Dr	Los Angeles, CA 90068
Brenneman, Amy	Creative Artists Agency	2000 Avenue of The Stars	Beverly Hills, CA 90067
Brennen, Eileen	Peter Strain & Associates	5455 Wilshire Blvd	Los Angeles, CA 90036
Breslin, Spencer	Coast to Coast Talent Group	3350 Barham Blvd	Los Angeles, CA 90068
Brewster, Jordana	Management 360	9111 Wilshire Blvd.	Beverly Hills, CA 90210
Bridges, Angelica	Defining Artists Agency	10 Universal City Plaza	Universal City, CA 91608
Bridges, Beau	Creative Artists Agency	2000 Avenue of The Stars	Beverly Hills, CA 90067
Bridges, Chris "Ludacris"	William Morris Agency	One William Morris Place	Beverly Hills, CA 90212
Bridges, Jeff	Asis Films	316 N. Rossmore Avenue	Los Angeles, CA 90004
Briscoe, Brent	Red Baron Management	1600 Rosecrans Ave.	Manhattan Beach, CA 90266
Broderick, Matthew	Creative Artists Agency	2000 Avenue of The Stars	Beverly Hills, CA 90067
Brody, Adam	Endeavor Talent Agency	9601 Wilshire Blvd. 3rd Floor	Beverly Hills, CA 90212
Brody, Adrien	Creative Artists Agency	2000 Avenue of The Stars	Beverly Hills, CA 90067
Brolin, James	Intl. Creative Mgmt.	10250 Constellation Blvd.	Los Angeles, CA 90067
Brolin, Josh	William Morris Agency	One William Morris Place	Beverly Hills, CA 90212
Brook, Kelly	Paradigm Talent Agency	360 N. Crescent Drive	Beverly Hills, CA 90210
Brooks, Avery	Innovative Artists	1505 Tenth Street	Santa Monica, CA 90401
Brosnan, Pierce	Irish Dream Time	3110 Main St., Ste 200	Santa Monica, CA 90405
Brown, Melanie	William Morris Agency	One William Morris Place	Beverly Hills, CA 90212
Bryant, Joy	I/D Public Relations	8409 Santa Monica Blvd	West Hollywood, CA 90069
Bullock, Sandra	Fortis Films	8581 Santa Monica Blvd.	West Hollywood, CA 90069
Burghoff, Gary	Ruth Webb Enterprises	13834 Magnolia Blvd	Sherman Oaks, CA 91423
Burke, Delta	William Morris Agency	One William Morris Place	Beverly Hills, CA 90212
Burns, Brooke	Paradigm Talent Agency	360 N. Crescent Drive	Beverly Hills, CA 90210
Burns, Edward	ID Public Relations	155 Spring St.	New York, NY 10012

Burns, Jere II	Framework Entertainment	9057 Nemo St	West Hollywood, CA 90069
Burns, Regan	Omnipop Talent	4605 Lankershim Blvd	Toluca Lake, CA 91602
Burrows, Saffron	ID Public Relations	155 Spring St.	New York, NY 10012
Burstyn, Ellen	Creative Artists Agency	2000 Avenue of The Stars	Beverly Hills, CA 90067
Burton, LeVar	Jonas Public Relations	240 26th Street, Suite 3	Santa Monica, CA 90402
Buscemi, Steve	Polaris Public Relations	8135 W. 4th St	Los Angeles, CA 90048
Busey, Gary	Alinemedia PR	1460 4th St.	Santa Monica, CA 90401
Bush, Sophia	PYR Public Relations	139 South Beverly Dr.	Beverly Hills, CA 90212
Butler, Gerald	Creative Artists Agency	2000 Avenue of The Stars	Beverly Hills, CA 90067
Butler, Yancy	Writers & Artists Agency	19 W. 44th St.	New York, NY 10036
Butz, Norbert Leo	Creative Artists Agency	2000 Avenue of The Stars	Beverly Hills, CA 90067
Bynes, Amanda	Paula Heap Productions	331 Pleasant Ave.	New York, NY 10035
Byrne, Gabriel	Paradigm Talent Agency	360 N. Crescent Drive	Beverly Hills, CA 90210
Byrnes, Edd	The Agency	1800 Avenue of the Stars	Los Angeles, CA 90067
Caan, James	Rogers & Cowan PR	8687 Melrose Ave	Los Angeles , CA 90069
Caan, Scott	United Talent Agency	9560 Wilshire Blvd	Beverly Hills, CA 90212
Cage, Nicholas	Saturn Films	9000 Sunset Blvd., Ste 911	West Hollywood, CA 90069
Caine, Michael	Intl. Creative Mgmt.	10250 Constellation Blvd.	Los Angeles, CA 90067
Call, Brandon	5918 Van Nuys Blvd	Van Nuys, CA 91401	
Cameron, Kirk	Mark Craig Productions	1383 Callens	Ventura, CA 93003
Camp, Colleen	Colleen Camp Productions	6310 San Vicente Blvd.	Los Angeles, CA 90048
Campanella, Joseph	William Carroll Agency	139 N. San Bernadino Rd.	Burbank, CA 91502
Campbell, Bruce	Agency For Performing Art	9200 Sunset Blvd Suite 900	Los Angeles, CA 90069
Campbell, Neve	Intl. Creative Mgmt.	10250 Constellation Blvd.	Los Angeles, CA 90067
Cannon, Dyan	TalentWorks	3500 W. Olive Ave.	Burbank, CA 91505
Cannon, Nick	William Morris Agency	One William Morris Place	Beverly Hills, CA 90212
Cantone, Mario	Innovative Artists	1505 Tenth Street	Santa Monica, CA 90401
Caplan, Lizzy	The Gersh Agency	232 North Canon Drive	Beverly Hills, CA 90210
Capshaw, Jessica	William Morris Agency	One William Morris Place	Beverly Hills, CA 90212
Capshaw, Kate	Creative Artists Agency	2000 Avenue of The Stars	Beverly Hills, CA 90067
Cardellini, Linda	The Gersh Agency	232 North Canon Drive	Beverly Hills, CA 90210
Carell, Steve	Endeavor Talent Agency	9601 Wilshire Blvd. 3rd Floor	Beverly Hills, CA 90212
Carlson, Kelly	Anthem Entertainment	6100 Wilshire Blvd.	Los Angeles, CA 90048
Caron, Leslie	Artmedia	20 avenue Rapp	Paris 75008 France
Carpenter, Charisma	The Gersh Agency	232 North Canon Drive	Beverly Hills, CA 90210
Carradine, David	Rogers & Cowan PR	8687 Melrose Ave.	Los Angeles, CA 90069
Carradine, Keith	Innovative Artists	1505 Tenth Street	Santa Monica, CA 90401
Carrere, Tia	Innovative Artists	1505 Tenth Street	Santa Monica, CA 90401
Carrey, Jim	Marleah Leslie & Associates	8370 Wilshire Blvd.	Beverly Hills, CA 90211
Carter, Dixie	Innovative Artists	1505 Tenth Street	Santa Monica, CA 90401
Carter, Helena Bonham	Endeavor Talent Agency	9601 Wilshire Blvd.	Beverly Hills, CA 90210
Carter, Lynda	The Blake Industry	1333 Ocean Ave.	Santa Monica, CA 90401
Caruso, David	Intl. Creative Mgmt.	10250 Constellation Blvd.	Los Angeles, CA 90067
Carvey, Dana	Baker Winokur Ryder	9100 Wilshire Blvd	Beverly Hills, CA 90212
Cassel, Vincent	Creative Artists Agency	2000 Avenue of The Stars	Beverly Hills, CA 90067
Cassidy, Joanna	Bette Smith Management	499 North Canon Dr.	Beverly Hills, CA 90210
Cattrall, Kim	ICM C/O Carol Bodie	8942 Wilshire Blvd	Beverly Hills, CA 90211
Cauffiel, Jessica	Michael Greene & Associates	190 N. Canon Drive	Beverly Hills, CA 90210
Cavallari, Kristin	PMK/HBH	700 San Vicente Blvd	West Hollywood, CA 90069
Caviezel, James	Special Artists Agency	9465 Wilshire Blvd	Beverly Hills, CA 90212
Cedric The Entertainer	Creative Artists Agency	2000 Avenue of The Stars	Beverly Hills, CA 90067
Chabert, Lacey	Platform Public Relations	2666 North Beachwood Dr.	Los Angeles, CA 90068
Chalke, Sarah	United Talent Agency	9560 Wilshire Blvd #500	Beverly Hills, CA 90212
Chamberlain, Richard	Panacea Entertainment	10635 Santa Monica Blvd.	Los Angeles, CA 90025

Chambers, Justin	Industry Entertainment	955 South Carrillo Drive	Los Angeles, CA 90048
Chambers, Nanci	United Talent Agency	9560 Wilshire Blvd #500	Beverly Hills, CA 90212
Chan, Jackie	Creative Artists Agency	2000 Avenue of The Stars	Beverly Hills, CA 90067
Chandler, Kyle	Brillstein-Grey Enter.	9150 Wilshire Blvd, Ste. 350	Beverly Hills, CA 90212-3427
Channing, Stockard	Intl. Creative Mgmt.	10250 Constellation Blvd.	Los Angeles, CA 90067
Chappelle, Dave	The Gersh Agency	232 N. Canon Drive	Beverly Hills, Ca 90210
Chatwin, Justin	PMK/HBH-Stephen Huvane	700 San Vincente Blvd.	West Hollywood, CA 90069
Cheadle, Don	PMK/HBH-Stephen Huvane	700 San Vincente Blvd.	West Hollywood, CA 90069
Chen, Joan	Rigberg Entertainment Group	1180 South Beverly Dr.	Los Angeles, CA 90035
Chenoweth, Kristin	Creative Artists Agency	2000 Avenue of The Stars	Beverly Hills, CA 90067
Cher	Intl. Creative Mgmt.	10250 Constellation Blvd.	Los Angeles, CA 90067
Cherry, Jake	Leverage Management	3030 Pennsylvania Ave	Santa Monica, CA 90404
Chiklis, Michael	Endeavor Talent Agency	9601 Wilshire Blvd. 3rd Floor	Beverly Hills, CA 90212
Chiles, Lois	Abrams Artists Agency	9200 Sunset Blvd 11th Floor	Los Angeles CA 90067
Cho, Margaret	William Morris Agency	One William Morris Place	Beverly Hills, CA 90212
Choudhury, Sarita	Washington Square Arts	310 Bowery 2nd Floor	New York, NY 90046
Chow, China	Paul Kohner Agency	9300 Wilshire Blvd	Beverly Hills, CA 90212
Chriqui, Emmanuelle	Endeavor Talent Agency	9601 Wilshire Blvd. 3rd Floor	Beverly Hills, CA 90212
Christensen, Erika	United Talent Agency	9560 Wilshire Blvd #500	Beverly Hills, CA 90212
Christensen, Hayden	Forest Park Pictures	8228 Sunset Blvd., Ste. 209	West Hollywood, CA 90046
Christie, Julie	Endeavor Talent Agency	9601 Wilshire Blvd. 3rd Floor	Beverly Hills, CA 90212
Christopher, Tyler	Paradigm Talent Agency	360 N. Crescent Drive	Beverly Hills, CA 90210
Church, Thomas Hayden	Brillstein-Grey Entertainment	9150 Wilshire Boulevard	Beverly Hills, CA 90210
Clark, Anthony	The Gersh Agency	232 North Canon Drive	Beverly Hills, CA 90210
Clark, Susan	The Gersh Agency	232 North Canon Drive	Beverly Hills, CA 90210
Clarkson, Kelly	Creative Artists Agency	2000 Avenue of The Stars	Beverly Hills, CA 90067
Clarkson, Patricia	Creative Artists Agency	2000 Avenue of The Stars	Beverly Hills, CA 90067
Clary, Robert	10001 Sun Dial Lane	Beverly Hills, CA 90210	
Clayburgh, Jill	Innovative Artists	1505 10th St.	Santa Monica, CA 90401
Cleese, John	Creative Artists Agency	2000 Avenue of The Stars	Beverly Hills, CA 90067
Clooney, George	Smoke House	4000 Warner Blvd., Bldg. 15	Burbank, CA 91522
Close, Glenn	Trillium Productions	P.O. Box 1560	New Canaan, CT 06840
Coen, Ethan	United Talent Agency	9560 Wilshire Blvd #500	Beverly Hills, CA 90212
Coen, Joel	United Talent Agency	9560 Wilshire Blvd #500	Beverly Hills, CA 90212
Cohen, Sacha Baron	Endeavor Talent Agency	9601 Wilshire Blvd. 3rd Floor	Beverly Hills, CA 90212
Cohen, Scott	William Morris Agency	One William Morris Place	Beverly Hills, CA 90212
Cole, Dennis	Hartig, Hilepo Agency	54 West 21st Street	New York, NY 10010
Cole, Gary	Intl. Creative Mgmt.	10250 Constellation Blvd.	Los Angeles, CA 90067
Coleman, Dabney	The Gersh Agency	232 North Canon Drive	Beverly Hills, CA 90210
Coleman, Gary	The Tisherman Agency	6767 Forest Lawn Drive	Los Angeles, CA 90068
Coleman, Monique	Ellis Talent Agency	4705 Laurel Canyon Blvd	Valley Village, CA 91607
Collette, Toni	Endeavor Talent Agency	9601 Wilshire Blvd. 3rd Floor	Beverly Hills, CA 90212
Collins, Clifton Jr.	ROAR	9701 Wilshire Blvd	Beverly Hills, CA 90212
Collins, Gary	William Morris Agency	One William Morris Place	Beverly Hills, CA 90212
Coilins, Joan	TalentWorks	3500 W. Olive Ave	Burbank, CA 91505
Collins, Mo	Diverse Talent Group	1875 Century Park East	Los Angeles, CA 90067
Collins, Stephen	# 300 Envision Entertainment	10390 Santa Monica Blvd	Los Angeles, CA 90025
Coltrane, Robbie	William Morris Agency	One William Morris Place	Beverly Hills, CA 90212
Combs, Holly Marie	The Gersh Agency	232 North Canon Drive	Beverly Hills, CA 90210
Connelly, Jennifer	Intl. Creative Mgmt.	10250 Constellation Blvd.	Los Angeles, CA 90067
Connery, Sean	Creative Artists Agency	2000 Avenue of The Stars	Beverly Hills, CA 90067
Conrad, Robert	David Shapira & Assoc.	15821 Ventura Blvd # 235	Encino, CA 91436
Conroy, Frances	Intl. Creative Mgmt.	10250 Constellation Blvd.	Los Angeles, CA 90067
Considine, John	The Artists Mgmt. Group	9465 Wilshire Blvd	Beverly Hills, CA 90212

Coogan, Steve	United Talent Agency	9560 Wilshire Blvd	Beverly Hills, CA 90212
Cook, Dane	New Wave Entertainment	2660 West Olive Ave.	Burbank, CA 91505
Cook, Rachael Leigh	Nicole Nassar PR	1111 10th Street Ste. 104	Santa Monica, CA 90403
Coolidge, Jennifer	ID Public Relations	8409 Santa Monica Blvd	West Hollywood, CA 90069
Cooper, Chris	Paradigm Talent Agency	360 N. Crescent Drive	Beverly Hills, CA 90210
Cooper, Jackie	Contemporary Artists	610 Santa Monica Blvd.	Santa Monica, CA 90401
Coppola, Sofia	42West	220 W. 42nd St.	New York, NY 10036
Corduner, Allan	Hamilton Hodell Ltd	66 - 68 Margaret Street	LondonW1W 8SR UK
Cornell, Lydia	JKA Talent	12725 Ventura Blvd., Ste.H	Studio City, CA 91604
Coster, Ritchie	The Gersh Agency	232 North Canon Drive	Beverly Hills, CA 90210
Costner, Kevin	Rogers & Cowan PR	8687 Melrose Avenue	Los Angeles, CA 90069
Cox, Brian	IFA Talent Agency	8730 Sunset Blvd Ste. 490	Los Angeles, CA 90069
Cox, Nikki	United Talent Agengy	9560 Wilshire Blvd Ste. 500	Beverly Hills, CA 90212
Cox, Ronny	Levine Management	9028 West Sunset Blvd	Los Angeles, CA 90069
Coyote, Peter	TalentWorks	3500 W. Olive Ave	Burbank, CA 91505
Craig, Daniel	Creative Artists Agency	2000 Avenue of The Stars	Beverly Hills, CA 90067
Craine, Jeanne	1029 Arbolado	Santa Barbara, CA 93103	
Cranston, Bryan	United Talent Agency	9560 Wilshire Blvd #500	Beverly Hills, CA 90212
Crawford, Cindy	Creative Artists Agency	2000 Avenue of The Stars	Beverly Hills, CA 90067
Crawford, Johnny	Ruth Webb Enterprises	13834 Magnolia Blvd	Sherman Oaks, CA 91423
Crewson, Wendy	Wallman Public Relations	10323 Santa Monica Blvd	Los Angeles, CA 90025
Cromwell, James	SDB Partner Inc.	1801 Avenue of the Stars	Los Angeles, CA 90067
Crosby, Mary	Gold Marshak & Assoc.	3500 West Olive Avenue	Burbank, CA 91505
Cross, David	Creative Artists Agency	2000 Avenue of The Stars	Beverly Hills, CA 90067
Cross, Joseph	Innovative Artists	235 Park Ave. S.	New York, NY 10003
Cross, Marcia	Framework Entertainment	9057 Nemo St.	West Hollywood, CA 90069
Crowe, Russell	PMK/HBH C/O Robert Baum	161 6th Ave.Ste. 10R	New York, NY 10013
Cruise, Tom	Cruise Wagner Productions	10250 Constellation Blvd	Los Angeles, CA 90067
Cruz, Penelope	Creative Artists Agency	2000 Avenue of The Stars	Beverly Hills, CA 90067
Crystal, Billy	MBST Entertainment	345 North Maple Drive	Beverly Hills, CA 90210
Culkin, Kieran	Brookside Artist Mgmt	250 West 57th Street	New York, NY 10107
Culkin, Macaulay	Brookside Artist Mgmt	250 West 57th Street	New York, NY 10107
Culkin, Rory	Brookside Artist Mgmt	250 West 57th Street	New York, NY 10107
Culp, Robert	Elkins Entertainment	8306 Wilshre Blvd.	Beverly Hills, CA 90211
Culp, Steven	Paradigm Talent Agency	360 N. Crescent Drive	Beverly Hills, CA 90210
Culver, Molly	Jonas Public Relations	240 26th Street, Suite 3	Santa Monica, CA 90402
Cuoco, Kaley	SDB Partner Inc.	1801 Avenue of the Stars	Los Angeles, CA 90067
Curry, Mark	William Morris Agency	One William Morris Place	Beverly Hills, CA 90212
Curtis, Jamie Lee	Creative Artists Agency	2000 Avenue of The Stars	Beverly Hills, CA 90067
Curtis, Tony	William Morris Agency	One William Morris Place	Beverly Hills, CA 90212
Cusack, Joan	United Talent Agency	9560 Wilshire Blvd #500	Beverly Hills, CA 90212
Cusack, John	Wolf/Kasteler PR	355 North Maple Dr., Ste. 351	Beverly Hills, CA 90210
Cuthbert, Elisha	The Gersh Agency	232 North Canon Drive	Beverly Hills, CA 90210
Cyrus, Billy Ray	APA Talent and Literary	405 South Beverly Drive	Beverly Hills, CA 90212
Cyrus, Miley	PMK/HBH	700 San Vicente Blvd	West Hollywood, CA 90069
Dafoe, Willem	ID Public Relations	8409 Santa Monica Blvd	West Hollywood, CA 90069
Dalton, Kristen	Domain	9229 Sunset Blvd. Ste 415	Los Angeles, CA 90069
Daly, Timothy	United Talent Agency	9560 Wilshire Blvd 5th Floor	Beverly Hills, CA 90212
Daly, Tyne	Hartig, Hilepo Agency	54 West 21st Street Ste. 610	New York, NY 10010
Damon, Matt	PMK/HBH Public Relations	700 San Vicente Blvd	West Hollywood, CA 90069
Dane, Eric	Innovative Artists	1505 10th Street	Santa Monica, CA 90401
Danes, Claire	ID Public Relations	8409 Santa Monica Blvd	West Hollywood, CA 90069
D'Angelo, Beverly	Intl. Creative Mgmt.	10250 Constellation Blvd.	Los Angeles, CA 90067
Daniel, Brittany	PMK/HBH Public Relations	101 E. Erie Street Ste. 1100	Chicago, IL 60611

Daniels, Jeff	Wendy Morris Public Relations	332 East 84th Street	New York, NY 10028
Danner, Blythe	Creative Artists Agency	2000 Avenue of The Stars	Beverly Hills, CA 90067
Dano, Paul	The Gersh Agency	232 North Canon Drive	Beverly Hills, CA 90210
Danson, Ted	Wolf/Kasteler PR	355 North Maple Drive	Beverly Hills, CA 90210
Danza, Tony	Katie Face Productions	13351 Riverside Dr.	Sherman Oaks, CA 91423
D'Arcy, James	Markham & Froggatt Ltd.	4 Windmill Street	London, W1T 2HZ, UK
Davenport, Jack	Intl. Creative Mgmt.	10250 Constellation Blvd.	Los Angeles, CA 90067
David, Larry	Endeavor Talent Agency	9601 Wilshire Blvd. 3rd Floor	Beverly Hills, CA 90212
Davidson, Amy	John Carrabino Management	100 North Crescent Drive	Beverly Hills, CA 90210
Davidson, Tommy	John Lewis Entertainment	3071 S. Valley View	Las Vegas, NV 89102
Davies, Jeremy	PMK Public Relations	8500 Wilshire Blvd Ste. 700	Beverly Hills, CA 90211
Davis, Ann B.	23315 Eagle Gap	San Antonio, TX 78255	
Davis, Geena	Creative Artists Agency	2000 Avenue of The Stars	Beverly Hills, CA 90067
Davis, Hope	United Talent Agency	9560 Wilshire Blvd #500	Beverly Hills, CA 90212
Davis, Kristin	Endeavor Talent Agency	9601 Wilshire Blvd. 3rd Floor	Beverly Hills, CA 90212
Davoli, Andrew	Don Buchwald & Associates	6500 Wilshire Blvd	Los Angeles, CA 90048
Dawber, Pam	Gold Marshak & Assoc.	3500 West Olive Avenue	Burbank, CA 91505
Dawson, Rosario	Intl. Creative Mgmt.	10250 Constellation Blvd.	Los Angeles, CA 90067
Day, Doris	PO Box 223163	Carmel, CA 93922	
de Lancie, John	SDB Partner Inc.	1801 Avenue of the Stars	Los Angeles, CA 90067
de Matteo, Drea	42West	1801 Century Park East	Los Angeles, CA 90067
de Pablo, Cote	Paradigm Talent Agency	360 N. Crescent Drive	Beverly Hills, CA 90210
de Ravin, Emilie	Nancy Iannios PR	8271 Melrose Ave	Los Angeles, CA 90046
de Rossi, Portia	Intl. Creative Mgmt.	10250 Constellation Blvd.	Los Angeles, CA 90067
DeFer, Kaylee	Intl. Creative Mgmt.	10250 Constellation Blvd.	Los Angeles, CA 90067
DeGeneres, Ellen	ID Public Relations	8409 Santa Monica Blvd	West Hollywood, CA 90069
Del Toro, Benicio	The Firm c/o Rick Yorn	9465 Wilshire Blvd	Beverly Hills, CA 90212
Delaney, Kim	The Gersh Agency	232 North Canon Drive	Beverly Hills, CA 90210
Delpy, Julie	Rigberg Entertainment Group	1180 South Beverly Dr.	Los Angeles, CA 90035
DeMornay, Rebecca	The Gersh Agency	232 North Canon Drive	Beverly Hills, CA 90210
Dempsey, Patrick	Baker Winokur Ryder	9100 Wilshire Blvd	Beverly Hills, CA 90210
Dench, Judi	Julian Belfrage Associates	46 Albemarle Street	London, 1X 4PP UK
Deneuve, Catherine	United Talent Agency	9560 Wilshire Blvd #500	Beverly Hills, CA 90212
DeNiro, Robert	Creative Artists Agency	2000 Avenue of The Stars	Beverly Hills, CA 90067
Denisof, Alexis	United Talent Agency	9560 Wilshire Blvd #500	Beverly Hills, CA 90212
Dennehy, Brian	Susan Smith & Associates	121 N. San Vicente Blvd	Beverly Hills, CA 90211
Dent, Catherine	Guttman Associates	118 S. Beverly Dr.	Beverly Hills, CA 90212
Depardieu, Gerard	4 Place De La Chappelle	F-78380 Bougival	France
Depp, Johnny	Infinitum Nihil Productions	9100 Wilshire Blvd. Ste. 400W	Beverly Hills, CA 90212
Derek, Bo	Chasin Agency	8899 Beverly Blvd - 7th Floor	Los Angeles, CA 90048
Dern, Bruce	Creative Artists Agency	2000 Avenue of The Stars	Beverly Hills, CA 90067
Dern, Laura	Creative Artists Agency	2000 Avenue of The Stars	Beverly Hills, CA 90067
Deschanel, Zooey	Seven Summits	8906 West Olympic Blvd	Beverly Hills, CA 90211
DeVito, Danny	Jersey Films	10351 Santa Monica Blvd	Los Angeles, CA 90025
Dewan, Jenna	William Morris Agency	One William Morris Place	Beverly Hills, CA 90212
DeWitt, Joyce	# 403	1250 6th Street	Santa Monica, CA 90401
Dey, Susan	JDS - Jay D. Schwartz	3151 Cahuenga Blvd	Los Angeles, CA 90068
Diaz, Cameron	Bragman/Nyman/Cafarelli	8687 Melrose Avenue	Los Angeles, CA 90069
DiCaprio, Leonardo	The Firm c/o Rick Yorn	9465 Wilshire Blvd.	Beverly Hills, CA 90212
Dick, Andy	Intl. Creative Mgmt.	10250 Constellation Blvd.	Los Angeles, CA 90067
Dickinson, Angie	The Blake Industry	1327 Ocean Avenue	Santa Monica, CA 90401
Diesel, Vin	BWR	9100 Wilshire Blvd - 6th Floor	Los Angeles, CA 90067
Diggs, Taye	Endeavor Talent Agency	9601 Wilshire Blvd. 3rd Floor	Beverly Hills, CA 90212
Dillon, Kevin	Intl. Creative Mgmt.	10250 Constellation Blvd.	Los Angeles, CA 90067

Dillon, Matt	Banyon Tree	1 Worth St., 2nd Floor	New York, NY 10013
Discala, Jamie-Lynn	United Talent Agency	9560 Wilshire Blvd #500	Beverly Hills, CA 90212
Dixon, Donna	8955 Norman Place	Los Angeles, CA 90069	
Dixon, Ivan	# 103	8431 Compatible Way	Charlotte, NC 28263
Djimon Hounsou	The Gersh Agency	232 North Canon Drive	Beverly Hills, CA 90210
D'Lyn, Shea	Cunningham Escott Dipene	10635 Santa Monica Blvd	Los Angeles, CA 90025
Dogg, Snoop	William Morris Agency	One William Morris Place	Beverly Hills, CA 90212
Doherty, Shannen	Endeavor Talent Agency	9601 Wilshire Blvd. 3rd Floor	Beverly Hills, CA 90212
Dominic Chianese	Corner Stone Talent Agency	37 W. 20th Street-Ste. 1108	New York, NY 10011
Donahue, Elinor	APP	11333 Moorpark Street	Studio City, CA 91602
D'Onofrio, Vincent	United Talent Agency	9560 Wilshire Blvd #500	Beverly Hills, CA 90212
Dorff, Stephen	Intl. Creative Mgmt.	10250 Constellation Blvd.	Los Angeles, CA 90067
Dorfman, David	Abrams Artists Agency	9200 Sunset Blvd 11th Floor	Los Angeles CA 90067
Douglas, Donna	Ruth Webb Enterprises	13834 Magnolia Blvd	Sherman Oaks, CA 91423
Douglas, Illeana	Innovative Artists	1505 Tenth Street	Santa Monica, CA 90401
Douglas, Kirk	Warran Cowan & Associates	8899 Beverly Blvd.	Los Angeles, CA 90048
Douglas, Michael	Furthur Films	825 Eight Ave. 30th Floor	New York, NY 10019
Down, Lesley-Anne	PO Box 57593	Sherman Oaks, CA 91403	
Downey, Robert Jr.	Rogers & Cowan PR	8687 Melrose Avenue	Los Angeles, CA 90069
Downey, Roma	The Gersh Agency	41 Madison Ave., 33rd Floor	New York, NY 10010
Dratch, Rachel	Paradigm Talent Agency	360 N. Crescent Drive	Beverly Hills, CA 90210
Drescher, Fran	Intl. Creative Mgmt.	10250 Constellation Blvd.	Los Angeles, CA 90067
Dreyfus, Julia Louise	ID Public Relations	8409 Santa Monica Blvd	West Hollywood, CA 90069
Dreyfuss, Richard	Dreyfuss James Productions	1041 North Formosa Avenue	West Hollywood, CA 90046
Duchovney, David	Intl. Creative Mgmt.	10250 Constellation Blvd.	Los Angeles, CA 90067
Duff, Hillary	Rogers & Cowan PR	8687 Melrose Avenue	Los Angeles, CA 90069
Duffy, Julia	Peter Strain & Associates	5455 Wilshire Blvd., Ste. 1812	Los Angeles, CA 90036
Duffy, Patrick	Blueprint Management	5670 Wilshire Blvd	Los Angeles, CA 90036
Duhamel, Josh	Gersh Agency	41 Madison Avenue	New York, NY 10010
Dukakis, Olympia	William Morris Agency	One William Morris Place	Beverly Hills, CA 90212
Duke, Patty	Innovative Artists	1505 Tenth Street	Santa Monica, CA 90401
Dunaway, Faye	Innovative Artists	1505 Tenth Street	Santa Monica, CA 90401
Duncan, Michael Clarke	William Morris Agency	One William Morris Place	Beverly Hills, CA 90212
Dunst, Kirsten	PMK/HBH c/o Stephen Huvane	700 San Vicente Blvd	West Hollywood, CA 90069
Durning, Charles	Paradigm Talent Agency	360 N. Crescent Drive	Beverly Hills, CA 90210
Dushku, Eliza	The Gersh Agency	232 North Canon Drive	Beverly Hills, CA 90210
Duval, James	Artistry Management	525 Westbourne Dr	Los Angeles, CA 90048
Duvall, Clea	Endeavor Talent Agency	9601 Wilshire Blvd. 3rd Floor	Beverly Hills, CA 90212
Duvall, Robert	PO Box 520	The Plain, VA 22171	
Duvall, Shelley	The Gersh Agency	232 North Canon Drive	Beverly Hills, CA 90210
Dye, John	William Morris Agency	One William Morris Place	Beverly Hills, CA 90212
Eastwood, Clint	The Malpaso Company	4000 Warner Blvd. Bldg. 81	Burbank, CA 91522-0811
Eckhart, Aaron	Creative Artists Agency	2000 Avenue of The Stars	Beverly Hills, CA 90067
Edelstein, Lisa	IFA Talent Agency	8730 Sunset Blvd.	Los Angeles, CA 90069
Eden, Barbara	P.O. Box 5556	Sherman Oaks , CA 91403	
Edie Falco	Innovative Artists	235 Park Avenue South	New York, NY 10003
Edwards, Anthony	ID Public Relations	8409 Santa Monica Blvd	West Hollywood, CA 90069
Edwards, Stacy	TalentWorks	3500 W. Olive Ave	Burbank, CA 91505
Egan, Susan	ML Management	125 West 55th St, 8th Floor	New York, NY 10019
Eggar, Samantha	Halpern & Associates	10524 West Pico	Los Angeles, CA 90064
Eggert, Nicole	Roklin Management	8530 Wilshire Blvd	Beverly Hills, CA 90211
Ehle, Jennifer	Endeavor Talent Agency	152 W. 57th St.	New York, NY 10019
Ehlers, Beth	Stone Manners Agency	900 Broadway, Ste. 803	New York, NY 10003
Eikenberry, Jill	197 Oakdale	Mill Valley, CA 94941-5301	

Ekberg, Anita	Via Astro #1	00045 Genzano Di	Rome, Italy
Eldard, Ron	Management 360	9111 Wilshire Blvd	Beverly Hills, CA 90210
Electra, Carmen	United Talent Agency	9560 Wilshire Blvd #500	Beverly Hills, CA 90212
Elfman, Jenna	Creative Artists Agency	2000 Avenue of The Stars	Beverly Hills, CA 90067
Elizondo, Hector	The Gersh Agency	232 North Canon Drive	Beverly Hills, CA 90210
Elliot, Chris	United Talent Agency	9560 Wilshire Blvd #500	Beverly Hills, CA 90212
Elliott, David James	Creative Artists Agency	2000 Avenue of The Stars	Beverly Hills, CA 90067
Elliott, Sam	Intl. Creative Mgmt.	10250 Constellation Blvd.	Los Angeles, CA 90067
Ellis, Aunjanue	Creative Artists Agency	2000 Avenue of The Stars	Beverly Hills, CA 90067
Elson, Andrea	Flick East & West Talent	9057 Nemo	West Hollywood, CA 90068
Elwes, Cary	Innovative Artists	1505 Tenth Street	Santa Monica, CA 90401
Embry, Ethan	Paradigm Talent Agency	360 N. Crescent Drive	Beverly Hills, CA 90210
Eminem	Intl. Creative Mgmt.	10250 Constellation Blvd.	Los Angeles, CA 90067
Emmerich, Noah	William Morris Agency	One William Morris Place	Beverly Hills, CA 90212
Englund, Robert	Abrams Artists Agency	9200 Sunset Blvd 11th Floor	Los Angeles CA 90067
Epps, Omar	The Gersh Agency	232 North Canon Drive	Beverly Hills, CA 90210
Epps, Mike	Creative Artists Agency	2000 Avenue of The Stars	Beverly Hills, CA 90067
Erbe, Kathryn	The Gersh Agency	232 North Canon Drive	Beverly Hills, CA 90210
Ermy, R. Lee	4348 West Avenue N3	Palmdale, CA 93551	
Esposito, Jennifer	The Gersh Agency	232 North Canon Drive	Beverly Hills, CA 90210
Estes, Will	Paradigm Talent Agency	360 N. Crescent Drive	Beverly Hills, CA 90210
Estevez, Emilio	Endeavor Talent Agency	9601 Wilshire Blvd.	Beverly Hills, CA 90210
Estrada, Erik	William Morris Agency	One William Morris Place	Beverly Hills, CA 90212
Evans, Chris	Kass & Stokes Management	9229 Sunset Blvd.	Los Angeles, CA 90069
Evans, Linda	TalentWorks	3500 W. Olive Avenue	Burbank, CA 91505
Eve	Endeavor Talent Agency	9601 Wilshire Blvd.	Beverly Hills, CA 90210
Everett, Chad	The Artists Mgmt. Group	9465 Wilshire Blvd	Beverly Hills, CA 90212
Fabray, Nanette	J. Cast Productions	2550 Greenvalley Rd	Los Angeles, CA 90046
Fairchild, Morgan	Bauman Redanty & Shaul	5757 Wilshire Blvd.	Los Angeles, CA 90036
Falco, Edie	Innovative Artists	235 Park Avenue South	New York, NY 10003
Falk, Peter	Writers & Artists Agency	19 W. 44th St.	New York, NY 10036
Fallon, Jimmy	Ken Sunshine Consultants	75 Ninth Avenue	New York, NY 10011
Fanning, Dakota	Osbrink Talent Agency	4343 Lankershim Blvd.	Universal City, CA 91602
Fanning, Elle	Osbrink Talent Agency	4343 Lankershim Blvd	Universal City, CA 91602
Farentino, James	Marc Bass Agency	9171 Wilshire Boulevard	Beverly Hills, CA 90210
Farina, Dennis	Lori DeWaal & Associates	7080 Hollywood Blvd.	Los Angeles, CA 90028
Faris, Anna	The Gersh Agency	232 North Canon Drive	Beverly Hills, CA 90210
Farr, Diane	United Talent Agency	9560 Wilshire Blvd	Beverly Hills, CA 90212
Farr, Jamie	53 Ranchero Rd	Bell Canyon, CA 91307	
Farrell, Colin	Creative Artists Agency	2000 Avenue of The Stars	Beverly Hills, CA 90067
Farrell, Mike	Farrell Minoff Productions	14011 Ventura Blvd.	Sherman Oaks, CA 91423
Farrell, Sharon	H. David Moss & Assoc.	733 N. Seward Street	Los Angeles, CA 90038
Farreli, Terry	Buchwald & Associates	6500 Wilshire Blvd	Los Angeles, CA 90048
Farrow, Mia	Hofflund/Polone	9465 Wilshire Blvd., Ste. 820	Beverly Hills, CA 90212
Fauser, Mark	United Talent Agency	9560 Wilshire Blvd #500	Beverly Hills, CA 90212
Favreau, Jon	Creative Artists Agency	2000 Avenue of The Stars	Beverly Hills, CA 90067
Fawcett, Farrah	Jay Bernstein Productions	PO Box 1148	Beverly Hills, CA 90213
Fehr, Brendan	PMK/HBH - Gina Hoffman	700 San Vicente Blvd.	West Hollywood, CA 90069
Feldon, Barbara	Creative Artists Agency	2000 Avenue of The Stars	Beverly Hills, CA 90067
Fenn, Sherilyn	Agency For Performing Art	888 Seventh Ave.	New York, NY 10106
Ferguson, Colin	Wallman Public Relations	10323 Santa Monica Blvd	Los Angeles, CA 90025
Ferguson, Stacy	CESD Talent Agency	10635 Santa Monica Blvd.	Los Angeles, CA 90025
Ferland, Jodelle	Play Management Inc.	Suite 220 - 825 Powell Street	Vancouver, BC V6A 1H7
Ferlito, Vanessa	Innovative Artists	1505 Tenth Street	Santa Monica, CA 90401

Ferrell, Will	Baker Winokur Ryder	9100 Wilshire Blvd	Beverly Hills, CA 90212
Ferrer, Miguel	Leslie Allan Rice Management	1007 Maybrook Dr.	Beverly Hills, CA 90210
Ferrera, America	Endeavor Talent Agency	9601 Wilshire Blvd. 3rd Floor	Beverly Hills, CA 90212
Fey, Tina	Endeavor Talent Agency	9601 Wilshire Blvd. 3rd Floor	Beverly Hills, CA 90212
Fichtner, William	William Morris Agency	One William Morris Place	Beverly Hills, CA 90212
Field, Sally	Creative Artists Agency	2000 Avenue of The Stars	Beverly Hills, CA 90067
Fiennes, Joseph	I/D Public Relations	155 Spring Street	New York, NY 10012
Fiennes, Ralph	Creative Artists Agency	2000 Avenue of The Stars	Beverly Hills, CA 90067
Finney, Albert	Simkins Management	45-51 Whitfield Street	London W1T 4HB UK
Firth, Colin	Creative Artists Agency	2000 Avenue of The Stars	Beverly Hills, CA 90067
Fischer, Jenna	Endeavor Talent Agency	9601 Wilshire Blvd. 3rd Floor	Beverly Hills, CA 90212
Fisher, Frances	Melanie Green Management	425 N. Robertson Blvd.	Los Angeles, CA 90048
Fisher, Isla	Mosaic Media Group	9200 West Sunset Blvd.	Los Angeles, CA 90069
Fisher, Joely	The Gersh Agency	232 North Canon Drive	Beverly Hills, CA 90210
Flanery, Sean Patrick	The Gersh Agency	232 North Canon Drive	Beverly Hills, CA 90210
Fletcher, Louise	Don Buchwald & Associates	6500 Wilshire Blvd., Ste. 2200	Los Angeles, CA 90048
Flockhart, Calista	Intl. Creative Mgmt.	10250 Constellation Blvd.	Los Angeles, CA 90067
Foley, Dave	JDS - Jay D. Schwartz	3151 Cahuenga Blvd	Los Angeles, CA 90068
Foley, Scott	Baker Winokur Ryder	9100 Wilshire Blvd	Beverly Hills, CA 90212
Fonda, Bridget	IFA Talent Agency	8730 Sunset Blvd #490	Los Angeles, CA 90069
Fonda, Jane	Creative Artists Agency	2000 Avenue of The Stars	Beverly Hills, CA 90067
Fonda, Peter	5625 Foothills Drive	Bozeman, MT 59718	
Ford, Faith	Intl. Creative Mgmt.	10250 Constellation Blvd.	Los Angeles, CA 90067
Ford, Harrison	UTA- c/o Jim Berkus	9560 Wilshire Blvd #500	Beverly Hills, CA 90212
Ford, Willa	Agency For Performing Art	405 S. Beverly Drive	Beverly Hills, CA 90212
Forlani, Claire	WMA- C/O John Fogelmam	One William Morris Place	Beverly Hills, CA 90212
Forster, Robert	Paradigm Talent Agency	360 N. Crescent Drive	Beverly Hills, CA 90210
Forsythe, John	Talent Group	6300 Wilshire Blvd	Los Angeles, CA 90048
Forsythe, William	Innovative Artists	235 Park Avenue South	New York, NY 10003
Foster, Ben	Endeavor Talent Agency	9601 Wilshire Blvd. 3rd Floor	Beverly Hills, CA 90212
Foster, Jodie	PMK Public Relations	700 San Vicente Blvd	West Hollywood, CA 90069
Foster, Sara	Innovative Artists	235 Park Avenue South	New York, NY 10003
Fox, Jorja	Intl. Creative Mgmt.	10250 Constellation Blvd.	Los Angeles, CA 90067
Fox, Matthew	Intl. Creative Mgmt.	10250 Constellation Blvd.	Los Angeles, CA 90067
Fox, Michael J.	Baker Winokur Ryder	9100 Wilshire Blvd.	Beverly Hills, CA 90212
Fox, Vivica A.	Paradigm Talent Agency	360 N. Crescent Drive	Beverly Hills, CA 90210
Foxx, Jamie	Rogers & Cowan PR	8687 Melrose Avenue	Los Angeles, CA 90069
Franciosa, Anthony	Trademark Talent	338 1/2 North Ogden Drive	Los Angeles, CA 90036
Franco, James	PMK/HBH	161 6th Ave.	New York, NY 10013
Franken, Al	William Morris Agency	One William Morris Place	Beverly Hills, CA 90212
Frankes, Jonathan	c/o JLL Management, Inc.	1601 Cloverfield Blvd.	Santa Monica, CA 90404
Franz, Dennis	Paradigm Talent Agency	360 N. Crescent Drive	Beverly Hills, CA 90210
Fraser, Brenden	ID Public Relations	8409 Santa Monica Blvd	West Hollywood, CA 90069
Freeman, Morgan	Revelations Entertainment	1221 Second St.	Santa Monica, CA 90401
Fricker, Brenda	IFA Talent Agency	8730 Sunset Blvd Ste. 490	Los Angeles, CA 90069
Fugit, Patrick	The Gersh Agency	232 North Canon Drive	Beverly Hills, CA 90210
Fuller, Kurt	Agency For Performing Art	888 Seventh Ave.	New York, NY 10106
Fuller, Robert	Halpern & Associates	12304 Santa Monica Blvd	Los Angeles, CA 90025
Funicello, Annette	Intl. Creative Mgmt.	10250 Constellation Blvd.	Los Angeles, CA 90067
Furlong, Edward	Innovative Artists	1505 10th Street	Santa Monica, CA 90401
Gallagher, David	Aquarius Public Relations	5320 Slymar Ave.	Sherman Oaks, CA 91401
Gallagher, Patrick	Play Management Inc.	825 Powell Street	Vancouver, BC V6A 1H7 Canada
Gallagher, Peter	Creative Artists Agency	2000 Avenue of The Stars	Beverly Hills, CA 90067
Gandolfini, James	United Talent Agency	9560 Wilshire Blvd Ste.500	Beverly Hills, CA 90212

Garcia, Andy	Paradigm Talent Agency	500 5th Ave 37th Floor	New York, NY 10110
Garcia, Joanna	PMK PR c/o Jennifer Shoucair	8500 Wilshire Blvd.	Beverly Hills, CA 90211
Garlin, Jeff	3 Arts Entertainment	9460 Wilshire Blvd. 7th Floor	Beverly Hills, CA 90212
Garner, James	Cherokee Productions	8491 Sunset Blvd.	West Hollywood, CA 90069
Garner, Jennifer	Management 360 Nicole King	9111 Wilshire Blvd.	Beverly Hills, CA 90210
Garner, Kelli	United Talent Agency	9560 Wilshire Blvd.	Beverly Hills, CA 90212
Garofalo, Janeane	Creative Artists Agency	2000 Avenue of The Stars	Beverly Hills, CA 90067
Garr, Terri	Brillstein-Grey Enter.	9150 Wilshire Blvd, Ste. 350	Beverly Hills, CA 90212-3427
Garrett, Brad	William Morris Agency	One William Morris Place	Beverly Hills, CA 90212
Garrison, Lane	Endeavor Talent Agency	9601 Wilshire Blvd. 3rd Floor	Beverly Hills, CA 90212
Garth, Jennie	Nicole Nassar PR	1111 10th St.	Santa Monica, CA 90403
Gasteyer, Ana	ID Public Relations	155 Spring St.	New York, NY 10012
Gavankar, Janina	TalentWorks	3500 W. Olive Ave.	Burbank, CA 91505
Gayheart, Rebecca	The Gersh Agency	232 North Canon Drive	Beverly Hills, CA 90210
Gellar, Sarah Michelle	United Talent Agency	9560 Wilshire Blvd #500	Beverly Hills, CA 90212
George, Melissa	Paradigm Talent Agency	360 N. Crescent Drive	Beverly Hills, CA 90210
Geraghty, Brian	Osbrink Talent	4343 Lankershim Blvd	Universal City, CA 91602
Gere, Richard	Intl. Creative Mgmt.	10250 Constellation Blvd.	Los Angeles, CA 90067
Gershon, Gina	ID Public Relations	155 Spring St.	New York, NY 10012
Gertz, Jami	Intl. Creative Mgmt.	10250 Constellation Blvd.	Los Angeles, CA 90067
Gervais, Ricky	PDF C/O Duncan Hayes	Drury House, 34-43 Russell St.	London, WC2B 5HA, UK
Giamatti, Marcus	Don Buchwald & Associates	6500 Wilshire Blvd.	Los Angeles, CA 90048
Giamatti, Paul	ID Public Relations	8409 Santa Monica Blvd.	West Hollywood, CA 90069
Gibson, Henry	TalentWorks	3500 W. Olive Ave.	Burbank, CA 91505
Gibson, Mel	Rogers & Cowan PR	8687 Melrose Avenue	Los Angeles, CA 90069
Gilbert, Melissa	William Morris Agency	One William Morris Place	Beverly Hills, CA 90212
Gilbert, Sarah	16254 High Valley Drive	Encino, CA 91436	
Gilliam, Terry	Casarotto Ramsat Associates	7-12 Noel St.Waverley House	London, W1F 8GQ UK
Gilsig, Jessalyn	SDB Partners	1801 Avenue of the Stars	Los Angeles, CA 90067
Gish, Annabeth	Hyler Management	3000 W. Olympic Blvd.	Santa Monica, CA 90404
Givens, Robin	Marshak Zachary	8840 Wilshire Blvd.	Beverly Hills, CA 90211
Glaser, Paul Michael	SDB Partners	1801 Avenue of the Stars	Los Angeles, CA 90067
Gleason, Joanna	Innovative Artists	1505 Tenth Street	Santa Monica, CA 90401
Gless, Sharon	Don Buchwald & Associates	6500 Wilshire Blvd	Los Angeles, CA 90048
Glover, Danny	Rogers & Cowan PR	8687 Melrose Avenue	Los Angeles, CA 90069
Gold, Tracy	TalentWorks	3500 W. Olive Ave.	Burbank, CA 91505
Goldberg, Adam	Nancy Iannios PR	8271 Melrose Avenue	Los Angeles, CA 90046
Goldberg, Whoopi	William Morris Agency	One William Morris Place	Beverly Hills, CA 90212
Goldblum, Jeff	The Gersh Agency	232 N. Canon Dr.	Beverly Hills, CA 90210
Gong, Li	42West	220 W. 42nd St.	New York, NY 10036
Goode, Matthew	Dalzell and Beresford Ltd.	26 Astwood Mews	London, SW7 4DE UK
Gooding, Cuba Jr.	Creative Artists Agency	2000 Avenue of The Stars	Beverly Hills, CA 90067
Gooding, Omar	Innovative Artists	1505 Tenth Street	Santa Monica, CA 90401
Goodman, John	The Gersh Agency	232 N. Canon Dr.	Beverly Hills, CA 90210
Gordon-Levitt, Joseph	The Gersh Agency	232 North Canon Drive	Beverly Hills, CA 90210
Gorham, Christopher	Creative Artists Agency	2000 Avenue of The Stars	Beverly Hills, CA 90067
Gosling, Ryan	IFA Talent Agency	8730 Sunset Blvd.	Los Angeles, CA 90069
Gossett, Louis Jr.	Logo Entertainment	P.O. Box 6187	Malibu, CA 90265
Gould, Alexander	Intl. Creative Mgmt.	10250 Constellation Blvd.	Los Angeles, CA 90067
Gould, Elliott	Agency For Performing Art	888 Seventh Ave.	New York, NY 10106
Grace, Maggie	Aquarius Public Relations	5320 Slymar Ave.	Sherman Oaks, CA 91401
Grace, Topher	William Morris Agency	One William Morris Place	Beverly Hills, CA 90212
Graham, Heather	United Talent Agency	9560 Wilshire Blvd #500	Beverly Hills, CA 90212
Graham, Lauren	Good Game Entertainment	4000 Warner Blvd	Burbank, CA 91522

Grammer, Kelsey	Grammnet Inc	5555 Melrose Ave	Los Angeles, CA 90038
Grant, Hugh	42West	220 W. 42nd St.	New York, NY 10036
Grant, Lee	No. 7-B 610 West End Ave	New York, NY 10024	
Grassle, Karen	PO Box 913	Pacific Palisades, CA 90272	
Graves, Peter	William Morris Agency	One William Morris Place	Beverly Hills, CA 90212
Gray, Linda	Anonymous Content	3532 Hayden Ave	Culver City, CA 90232
Green, Eva	Endeavor Talent Agency	9601 Wilshire Blvd. 3rd Floor	Beverly Hills, CA 90212
Green, Seth	Endeavor Talent Agency	9601 Wilshire Blvd. 3rd Floor	Beverly Hills, CA 90212
Green, Tom	William Morris Agency	One William Morris Place	Beverly Hills, CA 90212
Greene, Graham	Susan Smith & Associates	121 N. San Vicente Blvd	Beverly Hills, CA 90211
Greenwood, Bruce	Binder & Associates	1465 Lindacrest Dr	Beverly Hills CA 90210
Greer, Judy	Creative Artists Agency	2000 Avenue of The Stars	Beverly Hills, CA 90067
Grenier, Adrian	Leverage Management	3030 Pennsylvania Ave.	Santa Monica, CA 90404
Grey, Jennifer	Envision Entertainment	9255 Sunset Blvd., Ste. 300	Los Angeles, CA 90069
Grey, Joel	Innovative Artists	1505 Tenth Street	Santa Monica, CA 90401
Grieco, Richard	Creative Artists Agency	2000 Avenue of The Stars	Beverly Hills, CA 90067
Grier, David Alan	Endeavor Talent Agency	9601 Wilshire Blvd. 3rd Floor	Beverly Hills, CA 90212
Grier, Pam	Innovative Artists	235 Park Ave. S.	New York, NY 10003
Griffin, Eddie	Intl. Creative Mgmt.	10250 Constellation Blvd.	Los Angeles, CA 90067
Griffin, Nikki	Pinnacle Entertainment	8265 Sunset Blvd	Los Angeles, CA 90046
Griffith, Andy	William Morris Agency	One William Morris Place	Beverly Hills, CA 90212
Griffith, Melanie	William Morris Agency	One William Morris Place	Beverly Hills, CA 90212
Griffiths, Rachel	Markham & Froggatt Ltd	4 Windmill Street	London, W1T 2HZ UK
Griffiths, Richard	Paradigm Talent Agency	360 N. Crescent Drive	Beverly Hills, CA 90210
Grint, Rupert	Actual Management	7 Great Russell Street	LondonWC1B 3NH UK
Groh, David	Henderson-Hogan Agency	247 S. Beverly Drive	Beverly Hills, CA 90210
Gugino, Carla	Creative Artists Agency	2000 Avenue of The Stars	Beverly Hills, CA 90067
Guillaume, Robert	Alan Davis Management	8840 Wilshire Blvd	Beverly Hills, CA 90211
Guillory, Sienna	William Morris Agency	One William Morris Place	Beverly Hills, CA 90212
Guiry, Tom	The Gersh Agency	232 N. Canon Dr	Beverly Hills, CA 90210
Gummer, Mamie	The Gersh Agency	232 N. Canon Dr	Beverly Hills, CA 90210
Guy, Jasmine	Stone Manners Agency	6500 Wilshire Blvd. Ste #550	Los Angeles, CA 90048
Guzman, Luis	The Gersh Agency	232 N. Canon Dr	Beverly Hills, CA 90210
Gyllenhaal, Jake	Creative Artists Agency	2000 Avenue of The Stars	Beverly Hills, CA 90067
Gyllenhaal, Maggie	Creative Artists Agency	2000 Avenue of The Stars	Beverly Hills, CA 90067
Haas, Lukas	United Talent Agency	9560 Wilshire Blvd #500	Beverly Hills, CA 90212
Hackman, Gene	Creative Artists Agency	2000 Avenue of The Stars	Beverly Hills, CA 90067
Hagman, Larry	Majlar Productions	9950 Sulphur Mt. Road	Ojai, CA 93023
Hale, Barbara	David Shapira & Assoc.	15821 Ventura Blvd # 235	Encino, CA 91436
Hall, Deidre	David Shapira & Assoc.	15821 Ventura Blvd # 235	Encino, CA 91436
Hamill, Mark	Marc Bass Agency	9171 Wilshire Blvd	Beverly Hills, CA 90210
Hamilton, George	Talent Works	3500 W. Olive Ave.	Burbank, CA 91505
Hamilton, Linda	Writers & Artists Agency	19 W. 44th St.	New York, NY 90036
Hamlin, Harry	Pinnacle Entertainment	8265 Sunset Blvd	Los Angeles, CA 90046
Hammer, Armie	Endeavor Talent Agency	9601 Wilshire Blvd. 3rd Floor	Beverly Hills, CA 90212
Handler, Evan	Agency For Performing Art	888 Seventh Ave	New York, NY 10106
Hanks, Tom	42West	1801 Century Park East	Los Angeles, CA 90067
Hannah, Daryl	Writers & Artists Agency	19 W. 44th St.	New York, NY 10036
Hannigan, Alyson	United Talent Agency	9560 Wilshire Blvd #500	Beverly Hills, CA 90212
Hanson, Curtis	United Talent Agency	9560 Wilshire Blvd #500	Beverly Hills, CA 90212
Harden, Marcia Gay	Creative Artists Agency	2000 Avenue of The Stars	Beverly Hills, CA 90067
Hargitay, Mariska	William Morris Agency	One William Morris Place	Beverly Hills, CA 90212
Harmon, Angie	Special Artists Agency	9465 Wilshire Blvd	Beverly Hills, CA 90212
Harmon, Mark	Paradigm Talent Agency	360 N. Crescent Drive	Beverly Hills, CA 90210

Harper, Valerie	616 N. Maple Drive	Beverly Hills, CA 90210-3410	
Harrelson, Woody	Creative Artists Agency	2000 Avenue of The Stars	Beverly Hills, CA 90067
Harrington, Desmond	PMK/HBH	700 San Vicente Blvd	West Hollywood, CA 90069
Harris, Danielle	United Talent Agency	9560 Wilshire Blvd #500	Beverly Hills, CA 90212
Harris, Ed	PMK/HBH	700 San Vicente Blvd	West Hollywood, CA 90069
Harris, Jared	Workhouse Publicity	133 West 25th Street	New York, NY 10013
Harris, Naomi	Yakety Yak	8A Bloomsbury Square	LondonWC1A 2NE, UK
Hart, Melissa Joan	Nine Yards Entertainmnet	8530 Wilshire	Beverly Hills, CA 90211
Hartley, Mariette	Cunningham Escott Dipene	10635 Santa Monica Blvd	Los Angeles, CA 90025
Hartnett, Josh	Creative Artists Agency	2000 Avenue of The Stars	Beverly Hills, CA 90067
Harvey, Steve	Creative Artists Agency	2000 Avenue of The Stars	Beverly Hills, CA 90067
Hasselhoff, David	Talent Works	3500 W. Olive	Burbank, CA 91505
Hatcher, Teri	Paradigm Talent Agency	360 N. Crescent Drive	Beverly Hills, CA 90210
Hathaway, Anne	Creative Artists Agency	2000 Avenue of The Stars	Beverly Hills, CA 90067
Hauer, Rutger	Hyler Management	3000 W. Olympic Blvd.	Santa Monica, CA 90404
Hawke, Ethan	Creative Artists Agency	2000 Avenue of The Stars	Beverly Hills, CA 90067
Hawn, Goldie	Endeavor Talent Agency	9601 Wilshire Blvd. 3rd Floor	Beverly Hills, CA 90212
Hayek, Selma	Baker Winoker PR	9100 Wilshire Blvd.	Beverly Hills, CA 90212
Hayes, Robert	Paradigm Talent Agency	360 N. Crescent Drive	Beverly Hills, CA 90210
Hayes, Sean	William Morris Agency	One William Morris Place	Beverly Hills, CA 90212
Haysbert, Dennis	Gersh Agency	41 Madison Avenue	New York, NY 10010
Headey, Lena	Creative Artists Agency	2000 Avenue of The Stars	Beverly Hills, CA 90067
Heald, Anthony	Endeavor Talent Agency	9601 Wilshire Blvd. 3rd Floor	Beverly Hills, CA 90212
Hearst, Patty	The Gersh Agency	41 Madison Ave., 33rd Floor	New York, NY 10010
Heath Ledger	Creative Artists Agency	2000 Avenue of The Stars	Beverly Hills, CA 90067
Heaton, Patricia	Fourboys Films	500 S. Buena Vista St.	Burbank, CA 91521
Heche, Ann	Creative Artists Agency	2000 Avenue of The Stars	Beverly Hills, CA 90067
Heder, John	BWR	9100 Wilshire Blvd 6th Floor	Beverly Hills, CA 90212
Hedron, Tippi	Media Artists Group	6404 Wilshire Blvd	Los Angeles, CA 90048
Heigl , Katherine	Paradigm Talent Agency	360 N. Crescent Drive	Beverly Hills, CA 90210
Helfer, Tricia	Innovative Artists	1505 10th Street	Santa Monica, CA 90401
Helmond, Katherine	William Morris Agency	One William Morris Place	Beverly Hills, CA 90212
Helms, Ed	Creative Artists Agency	2000 Avenue of The Stars	Beverly Hills, CA 90067
Henderson, Florence	Celebrity Consultants	3340 Ocean Park Blvd.	Santa Monica, CA 90405
Henderson, Martin	Management 360	9111 Wilshire Blvd	Beverly Hills, CA 90210
Henderson, Shirley	Endeavor Talent Agency	9601 Wilshire Blvd. 3rd Floor	Beverly Hills, CA 90212
Hennessy, Jill	William Morris Agency	One William Morris Place	Beverly Hills, CA 90212
Henson, Elden	The Kohner Agency	9300 Wilshire Blvd	Beverly Hills, CA 90212
Henson, Taraji	United Talent Agency	9560 Wilshire Blvd.	Los Angeles, CA 90046
Hernandez, Jay	Creative Artists Agency	2000 Avenue of The Stars	Beverly Hills, CA 90067
Herrmann, Edward	Agency For Performing Art	888 Seventh Ave.	New York, NY 10106
Hershey, Barbara	Intl. Creative Mgmt.	10250 Constellation Blvd.	Los Angeles, CA 90067
Hessmam, Howard	Stone Manners Agency	6500 Wilshire Blvd. Ste #550	Los Angeles, CA 90048
Heston, Charlton	Agamemnon Films	650 North Bronson Blvd	Los Angeles, CA 90004
Hewitt, Jennifer Love	Endeavor Talent Agency	9601 Wilshire Blvd. 3rd Floor	Beverly Hills, CA 90212
Hightower, Freddie	Artists Rights Group	4 Great Portland Street	London, W1W 8PA, England
Hilgenbrink, Tad	Innovative Artists	1505 10th Street	Santa Monica, CA 90401
Hilton, Nicky	Venture IAB	3122 Santa Monica Blvd	Santa Monica, CA 90404
Hilton, Paris	Paris Hilton Entertainment	250 North Canon Dr.	Beverly Hills, CA 90210
Hines, Cheryl	Intl. Creative Mgmt.	10250 Constellation Blvd.	Los Angeles, CA 90067
Hirch, Judd	Paradigm Talent Agency	360 N. Crescent Drive	Beverly Hills, CA 90210
Hirsch, Emile	The Collective -Sam Maydew	9100 Wilshire Boulevard	Beverly Hills, CA 90210
Hoffman, Dustin	ID Public Relations	8409 Santa Monica Blvd	West Hollywood, CA 90069
Hoffman, Philip Seymour	Cooper's Town Productions	302A W. 12th St.	New York, NY 10014

Hogan, Paul	55 Lavandar Place	Milson's Point	Sydney, 2060 Australia
Holbrook, Hal	Abrams Artists Agency	9200 Sunset Blvd 11th Floor	Los Angeles CA 90067
Holden, Alexandra	Artistry Management	525 Westbourne Dr.	Los Angeles, CA 90048
Holliman, Earl	Dayton Milrad cho	8899 Beverly BLV	Los Angeles, CA 90046
Holly, Lauren	Paradigm Talent Agency	360 N. Crescent Drive	Beverly Hills, CA 90210
Holm, Celeste	SMS Film Entertainment	8730 Sunset-Suite 440	Los Angeles, CA 90069
Holm, Ian	Intl. Creative Mgmt.	10250 Constellation Blvd.	Los Angeles, CA 90067
Holmes, Katie	Creative Artists Agency	2000 Avenue of The Stars	Beverly Hills, CA 90067
Hooks, Robert	House of Representatives	400 South Beverly Drive	Beverly Hills, CA 90212
Hope, Leslie	Wallman Public Relations	10323 Santa Monica	Los Angeles, CA 90025
Hopkins, Anthony	Rogers & Cowan PR	8687 Melrose Blvd	Los Angeles, CA 90069
Hopkins, Bo	Marion Rosenberg	8428 Melrose Place	Los Angeles, CA 90069
Hopper, Dennis	Intl. Creative Mgmt.	10250 Constellation Blvd.	Los Angeles, CA 90067
Horsley, Lee	Central Artists	3310 Burbank Blvd	Burbank, CA 91505
Hounsou, Djimon	The Gersh Agency	232 North Canon Drive	Beverly Hills, CA 90210
Howard, Bryce Dallas	Intl. Creative Mgmt.	10250 Constellation Blvd.	Los Angeles, CA 90067
Howard, Ron	Imagine Entertainment	9465 Wilshire Blvd	Beverly Hills, CA 90212
Howard, Terrence	William Morris Agency	One William Morris Place	Beverly Hills, CA 90212
Howard, Traylor	United Talent Agency	9560 Wilshire Blvd #500	Beverly Hills, CA 90212
Hudgens, Vanessa Anne	William Morris Agency	One William Morris Place	Beverly Hills, CA 90212
Hudson, Ernie	Innovative Artists	1505 Tenth Street	Santa Monica, CA 90401
Hudson, Jennifer	J B P Entertainment Group	6626 Kingspointe Pkwy	Orlando, FL 32819
Hudson, Kate	Bragman & Nyman PR	8687 Melrose Avenue	Los Angeles, CA 90069
Huffman, Felicity	Creative Artists Agency	2000 Avenue of The Stars	Beverly Hills, CA 90067
Hunnam, Charlie	Brillstein-Grey Enter.	9150 Wilshire Blvd, Ste. 350	Beverly Hills, CA 90212-3427
Hunt, Bonnie	Endeavor Talent Agency	9601 Wilshire Blvd. 3rd Floor	Beverly Hills, CA 90212
Hunt, Helen	PMK/HBH	700 San Vicente Blvd.	West Hollywood, CA 90069
Hunt, Linda	William Morris Agency	One William Morris Place	Beverly Hills, CA 90212
Hunter, Holly	Intl. Creative Mgmt.	10250 Constellation Blvd.	Los Angeles, CA 90067
Hunter, Rachel	Celebrity Consultants	3340 Ocean Park Blvd.	Santa Monica, CA 90405
Hurd-Wood, Rachel	Troika	74 Clerkenwell Road	LondonEC1M 5QA UK
Hurley, Elizabeth	Intl. Creative Mgmt.	10250 Constellation Blvd.	Los Angeles, CA 90067
Hurt, William	Creative Artists Agency	2000 Avenue of The Stars	Beverly Hills, CA 90067
Huston, Anjelica	Intl. Creative Mgmt.	10250 Constellation Blvd.	Los Angeles, CA 90067
Hutcherson, Josh	Intl. Creative Mgmt.	10250 Constellation Blvd.	Los Angeles, CA 90067
Hutton, Lauren	William Morris Agency	One William Morris Place	Beverly Hills, CA 90212
Hutton, Timothy	ID Public Relations	155 Spring St.	New York, NY 10012
Ice Cube "O'Shea Jackson"	Baker Winokur PR	9100 Wilshire Blvd.	Beverly Hills, CA 90212
Ifans, Rhys	Endeavor Talent Agency	9601 Wilshire Blvd. 3rd Floor	Beverly Hills, CA 90212
Iler, Robert	Innovative Artists	235 Park Avenue South	New York, NY 10003
Imperioli, Michael	United Talent Agency	9560 Wilshire Blvd #500	Beverly Hills, CA 90212
Innes, Laura	Creative Artists Agency	2000 Avenue of The Stars	Beverly Hills, CA 90067
Ireland, Kathy	William Morris Agency	One William Morris Place	Beverly Hills, CA 90212
Irons, Jeremy	Creative Artists Agency	2000 Avenue of The Stars	Beverly Hills, CA 90067
Irving, Amy	The Gersh Agency	232 North Canon Drive	Beverly Hills, CA 90210
Isaacs, Jason	The Gersh Agency	232 North Canon Drive	Beverly Hills, CA 90210
Ito, Robert	Chateau/Billings Agency	5657 Wilshire Blvd	Los Angeles, CA 90036
Izzard, Eddie	Creative Artists Agency	2000 Avenue of The Stars	Beverly Hills, CA 90067
Jackman, Hugh	Seed Productions	10201 W. Pico Blvd.	Los Angeles, CA 90035
Jackson, Jonathan	BWR	9100 Wilshire Blvd	Beverly Hills, CA 90212
Jackson, Joshua	William Morris Agency	One William Morris Place	Beverly Hills, CA 90212
Jackson, Kate	David Shapira & Assoc.	193 N. Robertson Blvd	Beverly Hills, CA 90211
Jackson, Samuel L.	Wolf/Kasteler PR	355 North Maple Dr., Ste. 351	Beverly Hills, CA 90210
James, Kevin	Endeavor Talent Agency	9601 Wilshire Blvd. 3rd Floor	Beverly Hills, CA 90212

Jameson, Jenna	Alley Katz Enterprises	9899 Santa Monica Blvd.	Beverly Hills, CA 90212
Jane, Tom	ID Public Relations	8409 Santa Monica Blvd.	West Hollywood, CA 90069
Janney, Allison	Paradigm Talent Agency	360 N. Crescent Drive	Beverly Hills, CA 90210
Janssen, Famke	I/D Public Relations	8409 Santa Monica Blvd	West Hollywood, CA 90069
Jillian, Ann	William Morris Agency	One William Morris Place	Beverly Hills, CA 90212
Johansson, Scarlet	William Morris Agency	One William Morris Place	Beverly Hills, CA 90212
Johns, Glynis	Marshak/Zachary	8840 Wilshire Blvd.	Beverly Hills, CA 90211
Johnson, Arte	Barbara J. Silver Mgt.	8099 Pinnacle	Las Vegas, NV 89113
Johnson, Don	Don Johnson Productions	9633 Santa Monica Blvd	Beverly Hills, CA 90210
Johnson, Dwayne	United Talent Agency	9560 Wilshire Blvd #500	Beverly Hills, CA 90212
Johnson, Russell	PO Box 11198	Bainbridge, WA 98110	
Jolie, Angelina	Media Talent Group	9200 Sunset Blvd.	West Hollywood, CA 90069
Jones, Cherry	William Morris Agency	One William Morris Place	Beverly Hills, CA 90212
Jones, Dean	Michael Einfeld Mgmt.	10630 Moorpark Ave	Toluca Lake, CA 91602
Jones, James Earl	Paradigm Talent Agency	500 5th Ave.	New York, NY 10110
Jones, January	United Talent Agency	9560 Wilshire Blvd #500	Beverly Hills, CA 90212
Jones, Shirley	The Gage Group	450 Seventh Ave	New York, NY 10123
Jones, Tommy Lee	PMK/HBH	700 San Vicente Blvd	West Hollywood, CA 90069
Judd, Ashley	William Morris Agency	One William Morris Place	Beverly Hills, CA 90212
Kaczmarek, Jane	Endeavor Talent Agency	9601 Wilshire Blvd. 3rd Floor	Beverly Hills, CA 90212
Kanakaredes, Melina	The Gersh Agency	41 Madison Ave.	New York, NY 10010
Kane, Carol	Creative Artists Agency	2000 Avenue of The Stars	Beverly Hills, CA 90067
Kash, Linda	OAZ c/o	438 Queen Street East	Toronto, ON M5A 1T4, Canada
Katt, Nicky	Endeavor Talent Agency	9601 Wilshire Blvd. 3rd Floor	Beverly Hills, CA 90212
Kattan, Chris	Endeavor Talent Agency	9601 Wilshire Blvd. 3rd Floor	Beverly Hills, CA 90212
Kaufman, Charlie	United Talent Agency	9560 Wilshire Blvd #500	Beverly Hills, CA 90212
Keach, Stacy	Guttman Associates PR	118 S. Beverly Dr.	Beverly Hills, CA 90212
Keaton, Diane	Endeavor Talent Agency	9601 Wilshire Blvd. 3rd Floor	Beverly Hills, CA 90212
Keaton, Michael	United Talent Agency	9560 Wilshire Blvd #500	Beverly Hills, CA 90212
Kebbel, Arielle	Aquarius Public Relations	5320 Slymar Ave.	Sherman Oaks, CA 91401
Keegan, Andrew	Liebman Entertainment	25 E. 21st St.	New York, NY 10010
Keener, Catherine	The Gersh Agency	232 North Canon Drive	Beverly Hills, CA 90210
Keitel, Harvey	Intl. Creative Mgmt.	10250 Constellation Blvd.	Los Angeles, CA 90067
Kellermen, Sally	Innovative Artists	1505 Tenth Street	Santa Monica, CA 90401
Kelly, Moira	The Gersh Agency	232 North Canon Drive	Beverly Hills, CA 90210
Kemp, Will	Creative Artists Agency	2000 Avenue of The Stars	Beverly Hills, CA 90067
Kennedy, George	Bauman, Redanty, Shaul	5757 Wilshire Blvd. Ste. 473	Los Angeles, CA 90036
Kennedy, Jamie	Creative Artists Agency	2000 Avenue of The Stars	Beverly Hills, CA 90067
Kerns, Joanna	Intl. Creative Mgmt.	10250 Constellation Blvd.	Los Angeles, CA 90067
Kerr, Deborah	Klosters	7250 Grisons	Switzerland
Kidder, Margot	Muse Management	1541 Ocean Ave.	Santa Monica, CA 90401
Kidman, Nicole	Creative Artists Agency	2000 Avenue of The Stars	Beverly Hills, CA 90067
Kikuchi, Rinko	Creative Artists Agency	2000 Avenue of The Stars	Beverly Hills, CA 90067
Kilcher, Q'orianka	Dramatic Artists Agency	250 South San Fernando Blvd.	Burbank, CA 91501
Kilmar, Val	Rogers & Cowan PR	8687 Melrose Avenue	Los Angeles, CA 90069
Kim, Yunjin	William Morris Agency	One William Morris Place	Beverly Hills, CA 90212
Kingsley, Ben	Creative Artists Agency	2000 Avenue of The Stars	Beverly Hills, CA 90067
Kingston, Alex	The Gersh Agency	232 North Canon Drive	Beverly Hills, CA 90210
Kinnear, Greg	Baker Winokur Ryder	9100 Wilshire Blvd	Beverly Hills, CA 90212
Kinski, Nastassja	Innovative Artists	1505 10th Street	Santa Monica, CA 90401
Kirk, Justin	Creative Artists Agency	2000 Avenue of The Stars	Beverly Hills, CA 90067
Kirshner, Mia	Paradigm Talent Agency	360 N. Crescent Drive	Beverly Hills, CA 90210
Kline, Kevin	Creative Artists Agency	2000 Avenue of The Stars	Beverly Hills, CA 90067
Klugman, Jack	22548 Pacific Coast Hwy.	Malibu, CA 90265-5053	

Knight, Shirley	Gage Group -Suite 505	14724 Ventura Blvd.	Sherman Oaks, CA 91403
Knightley, Keira	Endeavor Talent Agency	9601 Wilshire Blvd. 3rd Floor	Beverly Hills, CA 90212
Knowles, Beyonce	Rogers & Cowan	8687 Melrose Avenue	Los Angeles, CA 90069
Knoxville, Johnny	Creative Artists Agency	2000 Avenue of The Stars	Beverly Hills, CA 90067
Kodjoe, Boris	The Gersh Agency	232 North Canon Drive	Beverly Hills, CA 90210
Koenig, Walter	H. David Moss & Assoc.	733 N. Seward Street	Los Angeles, CA 90038
Kopell, Bernie	Jonas Public Relations	240 26th Street, Suite 3	Santa Monica, CA 90402
Korine, Harmony	Endeavor Talent Agency	9601 Wilshire Blvd. 3rd Floor	Beverly Hills, CA 90212
Krakowski, Jane	The Gersh Agency	232 North Canon Drive	Beverly Hills, CA 90210
Kramer, Stepfanie	Patricola Lust PR	8383 Wilshire Blvd	Beverly Hills, CA 90211
Krause, Peter	Creative Artists Agency	2000 Avenue of The Stars	Beverly Hills, CA 90067
Krauss, Alison	Shore Fire Media	32 Court St.	New York, NY 11201
Kreuk, Kristin	Pacific Artists Mgmt.	1285 West Broadway	Vancouver, BC V6H 3X8 Canada
Kruger, Diane	Creative Artists Agency	2000 Avenue of The Stars	Beverly Hills, CA 90067
Krumholtz, David	The Gersh Agency	232 North Canon Drive	Beverly Hills, CA 90210
Krupa, Joanna	Diverse Talent Group	1875 Century Park E.	Los Angeles, CA 90067
Kudrow, Lisa	Endeavor Talent Agency	9601 Wilshire Blvd. 3rd Floor	Beverly Hills, CA 90212
Kunis, Mila	Creative Artists Agency	2000 Avenue of The Stars	Beverly Hills, CA 90067
Kurtz, Swoosie	William Morris Agency	One William Morris Place	Beverly Hills, CA 90212
Kutcher, Ashton	Baker Winokur Ryder	9100 Wilshire Blvd	Beverly Hills, CA 90212
La Placa, Alison	Marshak/Zachary	8840 Wilshire Blvd	Beverly Hills, CA 90211
LaBeouf, Shia	PMK/HBH	700 San Vicente Blvd.	West Hollywood, CA 90069
Lachey, Nick	Brillstein-Grey Enter.	9150 Wilshire Blvd, Ste. 350	Beverly Hills, CA 90212-3427
Ladd, Cheryl	JDS - Jay D. Schwartz	3151 Cahuenga Blvd	Los Angeles, CA 90068
Ladd, Diane	The Chasin Agency	8899 Beverly Blvd., Suite 716	Los Angeles, CA 90048
Ladd, Jordan	3 Arts Entertainment	9460 Wilshire Blvd. 7th Floor	Beverly Hills, CA 90212
Laflin, Bonnie-Jill	Guttman Associates PR	118 S. Beverly Dr.	Beverly Hills, CA 90212
Lahti, Christine	Intl. Creative Mgmt.	10250 Constellation Blvd.	Los Angeles, CA 90067
Lamas, Lorenzo	David Shapira & Assoc.	193 N. Robertson Blvd	Beverly Hills, CA 90211
Lambert, Christopher	Special Artists Agency	9465 Wilshire Blvd	Beverly Hills, CA 90212
Landau, Martin	Guttman Associates PR	118 South Beverly Dr.	Beverly Hills, CA, 90212
Landers, Audrey	Media Artists Group	6404 Wilshire Blvd	Los Angeles, CA 90048
Lane, Diane	Endeavor Talent Agency	9601 Wilshire Blvd. 3rd Floor	Beverly Hills, CA 90212
Lane, Nathan	United Talent Agency	9560 Wilshire Blvd #500	Beverly Hills, CA 90212
Lange, Artie	Creative Artists Agency	2000 Avenue of The Stars	Beverly Hills, CA 90067
Lange, Hope	SDB Partner Inc.	1801 Avenue of the Stars	Los Angeles, CA 90067
Lange, Jessica	Creative Artists Agency	2000 Avenue of The Stars	Beverly Hills, CA 90067
Langton, Brooke	United Talent Agency	9560 Wilshire Blvd #500	Beverly Hills, CA 90212
Lansbury, Angela	Intl. Creative Mgmt.	10250 Constellation Blvd.	Los Angeles, CA 90067
Larroquette, John	Wolf/Kasteler PR	355 North Maple Dr., Ste. 351	Beverly Hills, CA 90210
Larson, Jack	(Jimmy Olsen of Superman)	449 North Skyeway Road	Los Angeles, CA 90049
Larter, Ali	Intl. Creative Mgmt.	10250 Constellation Blvd.	Los Angeles, CA 90067
Lathan, Sanaa	William Morris Agency	One William Morris Place	Beverly Hills, CA 90212
Latifah, Queen	William Morris Agency	One William Morris Place	Beverly Hills, CA 90212
Laurie, Hugh	Creative Artists Agency	2000 Avenue of The Stars	Beverly Hills, CA 90067
Law, Jude	PMK/HBH	700 San Vicente	West Hollywood, CA 90069
Lawless, Lucy	Endeavor Talent Agency	9601 Wilshire Blvd. 3rd Floor	Beverly Hills, CA 90212
Lawrence, Joey	Stone Manners Agency	6500 Wilshire Blvd	Los Angeles, CA 90048
Lawrence, Martin	United Talent Agency	9560 Wilshire Blvd #500	Beverly Hills, CA 90212
Lawson, Maggie	The Gersh Agency	232 N. Canon Dr.	Beverly Hills, CA 90210
Leachman, Cloris	Rohr Talent Public Relations	1901 Avenue of the Stars	Los Angeles, CA 90067
Learned, Michael	Innovative Artists	1505 Tenth Street	Santa Monica, CA 90401
Leary, Denis	Apostle	568 Broadway, Ste 301	New York, NY 10012
LeBlanc, Matt	ID Public Relations	8409 Santa Monica Blvd	West Hollywood, CA 90069
LeBrock, Kelly	MCO Financial Mgmt.	2445 Alamo Pintado Ave.	Los Olivos, CA 93441

Ledger, Heath	Creative Artists Agency	2000 Avenue of The Stars	Beverly Hills, CA 90067
Lee, Jason	Nancy Iannios PR	8271 Melrose Ave.	Los Angeles, CA 90046
Lee, Jason Scott	Sweet Mud Group	280 South Beverly Drive	Beverly Hills, CA 90212
Leeves, Jane	The Gersdh Agency	232 N. Canon Dr.	Beverly Hills, CA 90210
LeGros, James	IFA Talent Agency	8730 Sunset Blvd #490	Los Angeles, CA 90069
Leguizamo, John	William Morris Agency	One William Morris Place	Beverly Hills, CA 90212
Leigh, Janet	Amsel, Eisenstadt & Assoc.	5055 Wilshire Blvd.	Los Angeles, CA 90036
Leigh, Jennifer Jason	United Talent Agency	9560 Wilshire Blvd #500	Beverly Hills, CA 90212
Leo, Melissa	Don Buchwald & Assoc.	10 E. 44th St.	New York, NY 10017
Leonard, Robert Sean	William Morris Agency	One William Morris Place	Beverly Hills, CA 90212
Leslie, Mann	Endeavor Talent Agency	9601 Wilshire Blvd. 3rd Floor	Beverly Hills, CA 90212
Leto, Jared	Baker Winokur Ryder	9100 Wilshire Blvd	Beverly Hills, CA 90212
Leung, Katie	Hamilton College	Bothwell Road	Hamilton ML3 0AY UK
Levy, Eugene	United Talent Agency	9560 Wilshire Blvd #500	Beverly Hills, CA 90212
Lewis, Damian	Endeavor Talent Agency	9601 Wilshire Blvd. 3rd Floor	Beverly Hills, CA 90212
Lewis, Daniel Day	Julian Belfrage Associates	14 New Burlington St.	London W1S 3BQ UK
Lewis, Jason	United Talent Agency	9560 Wilshire Blvd.	Beverly Hills, CA 90212
Lewis, Juliette	Nancy Iannios PR	8271 Melrose Ave., Ste. 102	Los Angeles, CA 90046
Li, Jet	Wolf/Kasteler PR	355 North Maple Dr	Beverly Hills, CA 90210
Light, Judith	The Gersh Agency	232 N. Canon Dr.	Beverly Hills, CA 90210
Lil' Kim	Intl. Creative Mgmt.	10250 Constellation Blvd.	Los Angeles, CA 90067
Lillard, Matthew	Creative Artists Agency	2000 Avenue of The Stars	Beverly Hills, CA 90067
Lilly, Evangeline	Rogers & Cowan PR	8687 Melrose Avenue	Los Angeles, CA 90069
Linden, Hal	Stone Manners Agency	6500 Wilshire Blvd. Ste #550	Los Angeles, CA 90048
Lindsey, George-Goober	PO Box 121089	Nashville, TN 37212	
Ling, Lisa	William Morris Agency	One William Morris Place	Beverly Hills, CA 90212
Linney, Laura	Intl. Creative Mgmt.	10250 Constellation Blvd.	Los Angeles, CA 90067
Liotta, Ray	Endeavor Talent Agency	9601 Wilshire Blvd. 3rd Floor	Beverly Hills, CA 90212
Lithgow, John	Creative Artists Agency	2000 Avenue of The Stars	Beverly Hills, CA 90067
Liu, Lucy	PMK/HBH	700 San Vicente Blvd	West Hollywood, CA 90069
Livingston, Ron	Endeavor Talent Agency	9601 Wilshire Blvd. 3rd Floor	Beverly Hills, CA 90212
Llewelyn, Doug	Durkin Artists Agency	127 Broadway	Santa Monica, CA 90401
Lloyd, Christopher	The Gersh Agency	232 North Canon Drive	Beverly Hills, CA 90210
Lockhart, Anne	Henderson-Hogan Agency	247 S. Beverly Drive	Beverly Hills, CA 90210
Locklear, Heather	Intl. Creative Mgmt.	10250 Constellation Blvd.	Los Angeles, CA 90067
Locklin, Loryn	Abrams Artists Agency	9200 Sunset Blvd 11th Floor	Los Angeles CA 90067
Lohan, Lindsay	Creative Artists Agency	2000 Avenue of The Stars	Beverly Hills, CA 90067
Lohman, Alison	Endeavor Talent Agency	9601 Wilshire Blvd. 3rd Floor	Beverly Hills, CA 90212
Lohr, Aaron	Beth Rosner Management	15 Stuyvesant Oval	New York, NY 10009
Lohr, Chris	MKS & Associates	8675 West Washington	Culver City, CA 90232
Loken, Kristanna	James/Levy/Jacobson	3500 West Olive Ave	Burbank, CA 91505
London, Jeremy	Metropolitan Talent	4500 Wilshire Blvd	Los Angeles, CA 90010
Long, Justin	United Talent Agency	9560 Wilshire Blvd #500	Beverly Hills, CA 90212
Long, Matt	Creative Artists Agency	2000 Avenue of The Stars	Beverly Hills, CA 90067
Long, Nia	Paradigm Talent Agency	360 N. Crescent Drive	Beverly Hills, CA 90210
Long, Shelly	Intl. Creative Mgmt.	10250 Constellation Blvd.	Los Angeles, CA 90067
Longoria, Eva	Thruline Entertainment	9250 Wilshire Blvd.	Beverly Hills, CA 90212
Lopez, George	Marleah Leslie Associates	8370 Wilshire Blvd	Beverly Hills, CA 90211
Lopez, Jennifer	Nuyorican Productions	1100 Glendon Ave	Los Angeles, CA 90024
Lopez, Mario	Talent Works	3500 W. Olive Ave.	Burbank, CA 91505
Loren, Sophia	Laconcordia Ranch	1151 Hiden Valley Road	Thousand Oaks, CA 91361

Loughlin, Lori	Much & House PR	8075 W. Third Street	Los Angeles, CA 90048
Louis-Dreyfus, Julia	ID Public Relations	8409 Santa Monica Blvd.	West Hollywood, CA 90069
Louise, Tina	Michael Einfeld Mgmt.	10630 Moorpark Ave., Ste. 101	Toluca Lake, CA 91602
Love Hewitt, Jennifer	Love Spell Entertainment	4063 Radford Ave. #213	Studio City, CA 91604
Love, Courtney	Untitled Entertainment	331 N. Maple Dr.	Beverly Hills, CA 90210
Lover, Ed	Central Entertainment Group	485 Madison Ave., 21st Flr	New York, NY 10022
Lowe, Rob	Rogers & Cowan PR	8687 Melrose Ave.	Los Angeles, CA 90069
Lowell, Carey	Barking Dog Entertainment	9 Desbrosses St.	New York, NY 10013
Lucas, Josh	Creative Artists Agency	2000 Avenue of The Stars	Beverly Hills, CA 90067
Lucci, Susan	Brownstein and Associates	630 Ninth Avenue Suite 217	New York, NY 10036
Luft, Lorna	Stiletto Entertainmnet	PO Box 45348	Los Angeles, CA 90045
Luke, Derek	Intl. Creative Mgmt.	10250 Constellation Blvd.	Los Angeles, CA 90067
Lush, Billy	Barry, Haft, Brown Artists Agcy	249 East 48th Street	New York, NY 10017
Lyman, Dorothy	Stone Manners Agency	6500 Wilshire Blvd	Los Angeles, CA 90048
Lynch, Jane	Domain Talent	9229 Sunset Blvd.	Los Angeles, CA 90069
Lynley, Carol	The Agency	1800 Avenue of the Stars	Los Angeles, CA 90067
Lynskey, Melanie	I/D Public Relations	8409 Santa Monica Blvd.	West Hollywood, CA 90069
Lyonne, Natasha	Melanie Greene Management	425 N. Robertson	Los Angeles, CA 90048
Mac, Bernie	Baker Winokur PR	9100 Wilshire Blvd.	Beverly Hills, CA 90212
MacArthur, James	Henderson-Hogan Agency	247 S. Beverly Drive	Beverly Hills, CA 90210
MacDonald, Norm	Brillstein-Grey Enter.	9150 Wilshire Blvd, Ste. 350	Beverly Hills, CA 90212-3427
MacDowell, Andie	Intl. Creative Mgmt.	10250 Constellation Blvd.	Los Angeles, CA 90067
MacGraw, Ali	Rogers & Cowan PR	8687 Melrose Avenue	Los Angeles, CA 90069
Macht, Gabriel	Intl. Creative Mgmt.	10250 Constellation Blvd.	Los Angeles, CA 90067
MacLachlan, Kyle	The Gersh Agency	232 N. Canon Dr.	Beverly Hills, CA 90210
MacLaine, Shirley	Intl. Creative Mgmt.	10250 Constellation Blvd.	Los Angeles, CA 90067
Macnee, Patrick	39 Guilford Park Road	Guilford, Surrey	GUZ JNA England
Macy, William H.	Creative Artists Agency	2000 Avenue of The Stars	Beverly Hills, CA 90067
Mader, Rebecca	Innovative Artists	1505 10th Street	Santa Monica, CA 90401
Madigan, Amy	William Morris Agency	One William Morris Place	Beverly Hills, CA 90212
Madonna	Creative Artists Agency	2000 Avenue of The Stars	Beverly Hills, CA 90067
Madsen, Michael	Anderson Group	8060 Melrose Ave	Los Angeles, CA 90046
Madsen, Virginia	Creative Artists Agency	2000 Avenue of The Stars	Beverly Hills, CA 90067
Maestro, Mia	Special Artists Agency	9465 Wilshire Blvd	Beverly Hills, CA 90212
Maguire, Tobey	ID Public Rel. C/O Kelly Bush	8409 Santa Monica Blvd	West Hollywood, CA 90069
Majorino, Tina	Innovative Artists	1505 10th Street	Santa Monica, CA 90401
Majors, Lee	Diverse Talent Group	1875 Century Park E.	Los Angeles, CA 90067
Malave, Tina	Abrams Artists Agency	9200 Sunset Blvd.	Los Angeles, CA 90069
Malek, Rami	Defining Artists Agency	10 Universal City Plaza	Universal City, CA 91608
Malick, Wendie	Innovative Artists	1505 Tenth Street	Santa Monica, CA 90401
Malkovich, John	Mr. Mudd	5225 Wilshire Blvd.	Los Angeles, CA 90036
Malone, Jena	United Talent Agency	9560 Wilshire Blvd #500	Beverly Hills, CA 90212
Malthe, Natassia	Nancy Ionis PR	8271 Melrose Ave.	Los Angeles, CA 90046
Manheim, Camryn	Cunningham Escott Dipene	10635 Santa Monica Blvd	Los Angeles, CA 90025
March, Stephanie	ID Public Relations	8409 Santa Monica Blvd	West Hollywood, CA 90069
Marcil, Vanessa	Much & House PR	8075 W. Third Street	Los Angeles, CA 90048
Margret, Ann	AM Productions	8899 Beverly Blvd	Los Angeles, CA 90048
Margulies, Julianna	ID Public Relations	8409 Santa Monica Blvd	West Hollywood, CA 90069
Marin, Cheech	Jonas Public Relations	240 26th Street, Suite 3	Santa Monica, CA 90402
Markham, Monte	PMF - David D'Eugenio	11801 Mississippi Ave	Los Angles, CA 90025
Marrow, Tracy "Ice-T"	Jorge Hinojosa	1212 S Crescent Heights Blvd	Los Angeles, CA 90035

Marsters, James	The Kohner Agency	9300 Wilshire Blvd.	Beverly Hills, CA 90212
Martin, Kellie	The Gersh Agency	232 North Canon Drive	Beverly Hills, CA 90210
Mason, Marsha	Suite 402-B	320 Galisteo Street	Sante Fe, NM 87501
Masterson, Christopher	United Talent Agency	9560 Wilshire Blvd #500	Beverly Hills, CA 90212
Masterson, Danny	United Talent Agency	9560 Wilshire Blvd #500	Beverly Hills, CA 90212
Masterson, Mary Stuart	Creative Artists Agency	2000 Avenue of The Stars	Beverly Hills, CA 90067
Mastrantonia, Mary	PFD - Lindy King	Drury House, 34-43 Russell St.	London, WC2B 5HA UK
Matchett, Kari	Anderson Group	8060 Melrose Avenue	Los Angeles, CA 90046
Mathers, Jerry	23965 Via Aranda	Valencia, CA 91355	
Matheson, Hans	Lou Coulson Agency	37 Berwick Street	London, W1F 8RS UK
Matlin, Marlee	Innovative Artists	1505 Tenth Street	Santa Monica, CA 90401
Mazar, Debi	William Morris Agency	One William Morris Place	Beverly Hills, CA 90212
McAdams, Rachel	Special Artists Agency	9465 Wilshire Blvd	Beverly Hills, CA 90212
McBride, Chi	United Talent Agency	9560 Wilshire Blvd	Beverly Hills, CA 90212
McCallum, David	Marmont Management	Langham Hse, 308 Regent St.	London, W1B 3AT, UK
McCarthy, Andrew	Innovative Artists	1505 Tenth Street	Santa Monica, CA 90401
McCarthy, Jenny	William Morris Agency	One William Morris Place	Beverly Hills, CA 90212
McConaughey, Matthew	Rogers & Cowan PR	8687 Melrose Ave.	Los Angeles, CA 90069
McCord, Kent	David Shapira & Assoc.	15821 Ventura Blvd # 235	Encino, CA 91436
McCormack, Catherine	PFD	Drury House, 34-43 Russell St.	London, WC2B 5HA UK
McCormack, Eric	Endeavor Talent Agency	9601 Wilshire Blvd. 3rd Floor	Beverly Hills, CA 90212
McCormack, Mary	PMK Public Relations	700 San Vicente Blvd.	West Hollywood, CA 90069
McCormack, Will	The Gersh Agency	232 North Canon Drive	Beverly Hills, CA 90210
McCormick, Maureen	William Morris Agency	One William Morris Place	Beverly Hills, CA 90212
McCutcheon, Martine	Artists Rights Group	4 Great Portland St.	London W1W 8PA
McDaniel, James	Innovative Artists	1505 Tenth Street	Santa Monica, CA 90401
McDermott, Dylan	ID Public Relations	155 Spring Street	New York, NY 10012
McDonnell, Mary	The Gersh Agency	232 North Canon Drive	Beverly Hills, CA 90210
McDormand, Frances	Endeavor Talent Agency	9601 Wilshire Blvd. 3rd Floor	Beverly Hills, CA 90212
McDowell, Malcolm	Intl. Creative Mgmt.	10250 Constellation Blvd.	Los Angeles, CA 90067
McFadden, Gates	Innovative Artists	1505 Tenth Street	Santa Monica, CA 90401
McGill, Bruce	Stone Manners Agency	6500 Wilshire Blvd. Ste #550	Los Angeles, CA 90048
McGillis, Kelly	David Shapira & Assoc.	193 N. Robertson Blvd.	Beverly Hills, CA 90211
McGinley, John C.	William Morris Agency	One William Morris Place	Beverly Hills, CA 90212
McGinley, Ted	Innovative Artists	1505 Tenth Street	Santa Monica, CA 90401
McGoohan, Patrick	Innovative Artists	1505 Tenth Street	Santa Monica, CA 90401
McGowan, Rose	The Gersh Agency	232 North Canon Drive	Beverly Hills, CA 90210
McGregor, Ewan	PDF	Drury House, 34-43 Russell St.	London, WC2B 5HA, UK
McKenzie, Benjamin	William Morris Agency	One William Morris Place	Beverly Hills, CA 90212
McKeon, Nancy	The Gersh Agency	232 North Canon Drive	Beverly Hills, CA 90210
McLanahan, Rue	Barbara Lawrence	19264 Pacific Coast Hwy.	Malibu, CA 90265
McMahon, Julian	Creative Artists Agency	2000 Avenue of The Stars	Beverly Hills, CA 90067
Meadows, Jane	The Artists Mgmt. Group	9465 Wilshire Blvd	Beverly Hills, CA 90212
Meloni, Christopher	The Gersh Agency	232 North Canon Drive	Beverly Hills, CA 90210
Mendes, Eva	Creative Artists Agency	2000 Avenue of The Stars	Beverly Hills, CA 90067
Meriwether, Lee	Scott Sander & Assoc.	13701 Riverside Drive	Sherman Oaks, CA 91423
Merkerson, S. Epatha	ID Public Relations	8409 Santa Monica Blvd.	West Hollywood, CA 90069
Merrill, Dina	The Gersh Agency	232 North Canon Drive	Beverly Hills, CA 90210
Meskimen, Jim	Sutton, Barth & Vennari	145 South Fairfax	Los Angeles, CA 90036
Messing, Debra	The Gersh Agency	232 North Canon Drive	Beverly Hills, CA 90210
Metcalf, Laurie	Intl. Creative Mgmt.	10250 Constellation Blvd.	Los Angeles, CA 90067

Metcalfe, Jesse	Endeavor Talent Agency	9601 Wilshire Blvd. 3rd Floor	Beverly Hills, CA 90212
Meyer, Breckin	The Gersh Agency	232 North Canon Drive	Beverly Hills, CA 90210
Meyers, Jonathan Rhys	United Talent Agency	9560 Wilshire Blvd	Beverly Hills, CA 90212
Michalka, Alyson	Intl. Creative Mgmt.	10250 Constellation Blvd.	Los Angeles, CA 90067
Midler, Bette	Intl. Creative Mgmt.	10250 Constellation Blvd.	Los Angeles, CA 90067
Mikkelsen, Mads	Industry Entertainment	955 South Carrillo Drive	Los Angeles, CA 90048
Milano, Alyssa	Pariseau, Yorke, Raymond PR	139 S. Beverly Dr.	Beverly Hills, CA 90212
Milian, Christina	Endeavor Talent Agency	9601 Wilshire Blvd. 3rd Floor	Beverly Hills, CA 90212
Miller, Christa	United Talent Agency	9560 Wilshire Blvd #500	Beverly Hills, CA 90212
Miller, Penelope Ann	APA Talent Agency	405 S. Beverly Dr.	Beverly Hills, CA 90212
Miller, Sienna	Endeavor Talent Agency	9601 Wilshire Blvd. 3rd Floor	Beverly Hills, CA 90212
Miller, Wentworth	PMK/HBH Jennifer Allen	700 San Vicente Blvd.	West Hollywood, CA 90069
Mills, Alley	Stone Manners Agency	6500 Wilshire Blvd. Ste #550	Los Angeles, CA 90048
Milner, Martin	# 2409	10100 Santa Monica	Los Angeles, CA 90067
Minnillo, Vanessa	Rebel Entertainment	5700 Wilshire Blvd.	Los Angeles, CA 90036
Mirren, Helen	PMK/HBH	700 San Vicente Blvd.	West Hollywood, CA 90069
Mitchell, Beverly	Agency For Performing Art	888 Seventh Ave.	New York, NY 10106
Mitchell, Elizabeth	IFA Talent Agency	8730 Sunset Blvd	Los Angeles, CA 90069
Mitra, Rhona	Creative Artists Agency	2000 Avenue of The Stars	Beverly Hills, CA 90067
Moakler, Shanna	Don Buchwald & Assoc.	6500 Wilshire Blvd.	Los Angeles, CA 90048
Modine, Matthew	Innovative Artists	1505 10th St	Santa Monica, CA 90401
Mohr, Jay	Barry Katz Entertainment	1776 Broadway, Ste. 2001	New York, NY 10019
Mol, Gretchen	Intl. Creative Mgmt.	10250 Constellation Blvd.	Los Angeles, CA 90067
Molina, Alfred	William Morris Agency	One William Morris Place	Beverly Hills, CA 90212
Molinaro, Al	PO Box 9218	Glendale, CA 91226	
Moloney, Janel	The Gersh Agency	232 North Canon Drive	Beverly Hills, CA 90210
Monaco, Kelly	William Morris Agency	One William Morris Place	Beverly Hills, CA 90212
Moore, Christina	The Gersh Agency	232 North Canon Dr.	Beverly Hills, CA 90210
Moore, Demi	Creative Artists Agency	2000 Avenue of The Stars	Beverly Hills, CA 90067
Moore, Julianne	Creative Artists Agency	2000 Avenue of The Stars	Beverly Hills, CA 90067
Moore, Mandy	I/D Public Relations	8409 Santa Monica Blvd.	West Hollywood, CA 90069
Moore, Mary Tyler	United Talent Agency	9560 Wilshire Blvd #500	Beverly Hills, CA 90212
Moore, Roger	Chasin Agency	8899 Beverly Blvd - 7th Floor	Los Angeles, CA 90048
Moran, Erin	Feldman Management	10642 Santa Monica Blvd	Los Angeles, CA 90025
Moreno, Rita	Agency For Performing Art	888 Seventh Ave.	New York, NY 10106
Morgan, Harry	The Artists Mgmt. Group	9465 Wilshire Blvd	Beverly Hills, CA 90212
Morgenstern, Maia	Institute for Cultural Memory	Piata Presei Libere1-CP33-90	71341 Bucharest, Romania
Morris, Kathryn	Mosaic Media Group	9200 West Sunset Blvd.	Los Angeles, CA 90069
Morrison, Jennifer	Abrams Artists Agency	9200 Sunset Blvd.	Los Angeles, CA 90069
Morse, David	Endeavor Talent Agency	9601 Wilshire Blvd. 3rd Floor	Beverly Hills, CA 90212
Mortensen, Viggo	Endeavor Talent Agency	9601 Wilshire Blvd. 3rd Floor	Beverly Hills, CA 90212
Mortimer, Emily	Endeavor Talent Agency	9601 Wilshire Blvd. 3rd Floor	Beverly Hills, CA 90212
Morton, Samantha	Endeavor Talent Agency	9601 Wilshire Blvd. 3rd Floor	Beverly Hills, CA 90212
Moss, Carrie-Ann	William Morris Agency	One William Morris Place	Beverly Hills, CA 90212
Moura, Cinthia	The Gersh Agency	232 North Canon Drive	Beverly Hills, CA 90210
Moynahan, Bridget	Endeavor Talent Agency	9601 Wilshire Blvd. 3rd Floor	Beverly Hills, CA 90212
Mullally, Megan	The Gersh Agency	232 North Canon Drive	Beverly Hills, CA 90210
Mulroney, Dermot	Intl. Creative Mgmt.	10250 Constellation Blvd.	Los Angeles, CA 90067
Muniz, Frankie	Intl. Creative Mgmt.	10250 Constellation Blvd.	Los Angeles, CA 90067
Munn, Allison	Nancy Iannios PR	8271 Melrose Ave.	Los Angeles, CA 90046

Actors and Actresses Having Roles on TV and Film

Name	Agency	Address	City
Murphy, Brittany	Intl. Creative Mgmt.	10250 Constellation Blvd.	Los Angeles, CA 90067
Murphy, Eddie	William Morris Agency	One William Morris Place	Beverly Hills, CA 90212
Myers, Mike	Creative Artists Agency	2000 Avenue of The Stars	Beverly Hills, CA 90067
Najimy, Kathy	Intl. Creative Mgmt.	10250 Constellation Blvd.	Los Angeles, CA 90067
Nash, Niecy	LSPR	12198 Ventura Blvd.	Studio City, CA 91604
Neal, Elise	Anonymous Content	3532 Hayden Ave	Culver City, CA 90232
Neal, Patricia	PO Box 1043	Edgerton, MA 02539	
Neeson, Liam	Rogers & Cowan PR	8687 Melrose Avenue	Los Angeles, CA 90069
Neill, Noel	(Early Superman Lois Lane)	331 Sage Lane	Santa Monica, CA 90402
Neill, Sam	Intl. Creative Mgmt.	10250 Constellation Blvd.	Los Angeles, CA 90067
Nelson, Craig T.	Endeavor Talent Agency	9601 Wilshire Blvd. 3rd Floor	Beverly Hills, CA 90212
Nelson, Tim Blake	United Talent Agency	9560 Wilshire Blvd #500	Beverly Hills, CA 90212
Nettleson, Lois	The Artists Mgmt. Group	3345 Wilshire Blvd	Los Angeles, CA 90010
Neuwirth, Bebe	Intl. Creative Mgmt.	10250 Constellation Blvd.	Los Angeles, CA 90067
Newhart, Bob	Endeavor Talent Agency	9601 Wilshire Blvd. 3rd Floor	Beverly Hills, CA 90212
Newman, Paul	ICM- C/O Toni Howard	8942 Wilshire Blvd	Beverly Hills, CA 90211
Newmar, Julie	Richard Sindell & Assoc.	8271 Melrose Avenue	Los Angeles, CA 90046
Newton, Thandie	I/D Public Relations	155 Spring St.	New York, NY 10012
Nguyen, Dustin	JDS - Jay D. Schwartz	3151 Cahuenga Blvd	Los Angeles, CA 90068
Nichols, Rachel	Innovative Artists	1505 10th Street	Santa Monica, CA 90401
Nicholson, Jack	Bresler Kelly & Assoc.	11500 Olympic Blvd # 510	Los Angeles, CA 90064
Nielsen, Connie	Creative Artists Agency	2000 Avenue of The Stars	Beverly Hills, CA 90067
Nielson, Brigitte	Bohemia Group	8170 Beverly Blvd.	Los Angeles, CA 90048
Nielson, Leslie	Bresler Kelly & Assoc.	11500 Olympic Blvd # 510	Los Angeles, CA 90064
Nighy, Bill	Markham & Froggatt	4 Windmill Street	LondonW1T 2HZ UK
Nimoy, Leonard	The Gersh Agency	232 North Canon Drive	Beverly Hills, CA 90210
Nixon, Cynthia	William Morris Agency	One William Morris Place	Beverly Hills, CA 90212
Noble, James	Paradigm Talent Agency	360 N. Crescent Drive	Beverly Hills, CA 90210
Nolan, Christopher	Creative Artists Agency	2000 Avenue of The Stars	Beverly Hills, CA 90067
Nolin, Gena Lee	Shandrew Public Relations	1050 South Stanley Ave.	Los Angeles, CA 90019-6634
Nolte, Nick	Creative Artists Agency	2000 Avenue of The Stars	Beverly Hills, CA 90067
Norris, Chuck	Fenton Kritzer Entertainmnet	8840 Wilshire Blvd.	Beverly Hills, CA 90211
Norton, Edward	Endeavor Talent Agency	9601 Wilshire Blvd. 3rd Floor	Beverly Hills, CA 90212
Norwood, Brandy	William Morris Agency	One William Morris Place	Beverly Hills, CA 90212
Noth, Chris	United Talent Agency	9560 Wilshire Blvd #500	Beverly Hills, CA 90212
Nouri, Michael	Bauman, Redanty, Shaul	5757 Wilshire Blvd. Ste. 473	Los Angeles, CA 90036
O'Hurley, John	Anderson Group PR	8060 Melrose Avenue	Los Angeles, CA 90046
O'Bryan, Sean	Domain	9229 Sunset Blvd	Los Angeles, CA 90069
O'Connell, Jerry	Endeavor Talent Agency	9601 Wilshire Blvd. 3rd Floor	Beverly Hills, CA 90212
O'Connor, Frances	The Bauer Company	9720 Wilshire Blvd	Beverly Hills, CA 90212
O'Day, Aubrey	50855 Washington Street	LaQuinta, CA 92253-2891	
O'Donnell, Chris	William Morris Agency	One William Morris Place	Beverly Hills, CA 90212
O'Grady, Gail	Shelter Entertainment	9255 Sunset Blvd.	Los Angeles, CA 90069
Oh, Sandra	Baker Winokur Ryder	9100 Wilshire Blvd.	Beverly Hills, CA 90212
O'Hara, Catherine	Brillstein-Grey Entertainment	9150 Wilshire Blvd	Beverly Hills, CA 90212
O'Hara, Maureen	PO Box 1400	Christainhead, VI 00820	
Oka, Masi	Greater Vision Artists	9229 Sunset Blvd	Los Angeles, CA 90069
Oldman, Gary	SE8 Group	505 North Robertson Blvd.	Los Angeles, CA 90048
Olin, Ken	Creative Artists Agency	2000 Avenue of The Stars	Beverly Hills, CA 90067
Oliu, Ingrid	Suites 900 & 950	257 Park Avenue South	New York NY 10010

Olsen, Ashley	Dualstar Productions	1801 Century Park East	Los Angeles, CA 90067
Olsen, Mary-Kate	Dualstar Productions	1801 Century Park East	Los Angeles, CA 90067
Olyphant, Timothy	William Morris Agency	One William Morris Place	Beverly Hills, CA 90212
O'Neal, Ryan	Patricola Lust PR	8383 Wilshire Blvd.	Beverly Hills, CA 90211
O'Neill, Ed	Brillstein-Grey Entertainment	9150 Wilshire Blvd, Ste. 350	Beverly Hills, CA 90212-3427
O'Neill, Jennifer	The Blake Agency	1327 Ocean Avenue	Santa Monica, CA 90401
Ontiveros, Lupe	Latin Hollywood Films	2934 ½ Beverly Glen Circle	Bel Air, CA 90077
Ormond, Julia	Endeavor Talent Agency	9601 Wilshire Blvd. 3rd Floor	Beverly Hills, CA 90212
Osbourne, Jack	Endeavor Talent Agency	9601 Wilshire Blvd. 3rd Floor	Beverly Hills, CA 90212
Osbourne, Kelly	Endeavor Talent Agency	9601 Wilshire Blvd. 3rd Floor	Beverly Hills, CA 90212
Osbourne, Sharon	Endeavor Talent Agency	9601 Wilshire Blvd. 3rd Floor	Beverly Hills, CA 90212
Osment, Haley Joel	Coast to Coast Talent	3350 Barham Blvd	Los Angeles, CA 90068
O'Toole, Peter	Steve Kenis & Company	Royalty House-72-74 Dean St.	London, WID 3SG UK
Otto, Miranda	The Gersh Agency	232 North Canon Drive	Beverly Hills, CA 90210
Owen, Clive	42 West	220 W. 42nd St.	New York, NY 10036
Pacino, Al	Creative Artists Agency	2000 Avenue of The Stars	Beverly Hills, CA 90067
Padalecki, Jared	Jonas Public Relations	240 26th Street, Suite 3	Santa Monica, CA 90402
Page, Ellen	Gary Goddard Agency	#305-10 St. Mary Street	Toronto, ON M4Y 1P9 Canada
Paige, Elaine	Associated Intl. Mgmt.	1 Blythe Road	London W14 OHG UK
Palminteri, Chazz	William Morris Agency	One William Morris Place	Beverly Hills, CA 90212
Paltrow, Gwyneth	Creative Artists Agency	2000 Avenue of The Stars	Beverly Hills, CA 90067
Panettiere, Hayden	Rogers & Cowan PR	8687 Melrose Avenue	Los Angeles, CA 90069
Pankow, John	The Gersh Agency	232 North Canon Drive	Beverly Hills, CA 90210
Pantoliano, Joe	United Talent Agency	9560 Wilshire Blvd #500	Beverly Hills, CA 90212
Paolo, Connor	Abrams Artists Agency	275 Seventh Ave.	New York, NY 10001
Paquin, Anna	ID Public Relations	8409 Santa Monica Blvd	West Hollywood, CA 90069
Park, Grace	Characters Talent Agency	200-1505 West 2nd Avenue	Vancouver, BC V6H 3Y4 Canada
Park, Ray	Entertainment Legends Mgmt.	1100 Irvine Blvd. #661	Tustin, CA 92780
Parker, Fess	PO Box 908	Los Olivos, CA 93441	
Parker, Mary-Louise	William Morris Agency	One William Morris Place	Beverly Hills, CA 90212
Parker, Sarah Jessica	Pretty Matches Productions	1100 Avenue of Americas	New York, NY 10036
Pasdar, Adrian	Intl. Creative Mgmt.	10250 Constellation Blvd.	Los Angeles, CA 90067
Pastore, Vincent	Abrams Artists Agency	275 Seventh Ave.	New York, NY 10001
Pastorelli, Robert	Abrams Artists Agency	9200 Sunset Blvd 11th Floor	Los Angeles CA 90067
Patric, Jason	Rogers & Cowan PR	8687 Melrose Avenue	Los Angeles, CA 90069
Patrick, Robert	Endeavor Talent Agency	9601 Wilshire Blvd. 3rd Floor	Beverly Hills, CA 90212
Patton, Paula	William Morris Agency	One William Morris Place	Beverly Hills, CA 90212
Paul, Adrian	Mosaic Media Group	9200 West Sunset Blvd	Los Angeles, CA 90069
Paula Abdul	Jeff Ballard Public Relations	4814 North Lemona Ave.	Sherman Oaks, CA 91403
Paulson, Sarah	Intl. Creative Mgmt.	10250 Constellation Blvd.	Los Angeles, CA 90067
Paxton, Bill	Endeavor Talent Agency	9601 Wilshire Blvd. 3rd Floor	Beverly Hills, CA 90212
Paxton, Sara	Coast to Coast Talent Group	3350 Barham Blvd.	Los Angeles, CA 90068
Peck, Mizuo	The Artists Group	3345 Wilshire Blvd	Los Angeles, CA 90010
Peeples, Nia	Stone Manners Agency	6500 Wilshire Blvd	Los Angeles, CA 90048
Peet, Amanda	Management 360	9111 Wilshire Blvd	Beverly Hills, CA 90210
Peete, Holly Robinson	Dolores Robinson Enter.	3815 Hughes Ave.	Culver City, CA 90232
Peña, Elizabeth	Paradigm Talent Agency	360 N. Crescent Drive	Beverly Hills, CA 90210
Pena, Michael	Innovative Artists	1505 10th Street	Santa Monica, CA 90401
Penn, Kal	Jonas Public Relations	240 26th Street	Santa Monica, CA 90402
Penn, Robin Wright	ID Public Relations	8409 Santa Monica Blvd	West Hollywood, CA 90069

Actors and Actresses Having Roles on TV and Film

Penn, Sean	ID Public Relations	8409 Santa Monica Blvd	West Hollywood, CA 90069
Perabo, Piper	UTA c/o Allison Band	9560 Wilshire Blvd.	Beverly Hills, CA 90212
Perez, Vincent	PFD - Lindy King	Drury House, 34-43 Russell St.	London, WC2B 5HA UK
Perkins, Elizabeth	The Gersh Agency	232 North Canon Dr.	Beverly Hills, CA 90210
Perlman, Rhea	Intl. Creative Mgmt.	10250 Constellation Blvd.	Los Angeles, CA 90067
Perlman, Ron	Kritzer Entertainment	8840 Wilshire Blvd.	Beverly Hills, CA 90211
Perry, Luke	Rogers & Cowan PR	8687 Melrose Avenue	Los Angeles, CA 90069
Perry, Matthew	Wolf Kasteler PR	355 North Maple Dr.	Beverly Hills, CA 90210
Perry, Rachel	Abrams Artists Agency	9200 Sunset Blvd	Los Angeles, CA 90069
Pesci, Joe	Jay Julien Management	1501 Broadway, Ste. 2600	New York, NY 10036
Peters, Bernadette	William Morris Agency	One William Morris Place	Beverly Hills, CA 90212
Petersen, William L.	United Talent Agency	9560 Wilshire Blvd #500	Beverly Hills, CA 90212
Pettiford, Valerie	TalentWorks c/o Joel Dean	3500 West Olive Ave.	Burbank, CA 91505
Pfeiffer, Michelle	Creative Artists Agency	2000 Avenue of The Stars	Beverly Hills, CA 90067
Phifer, Mekhi	William Morris Agency	One William Morris Place	Beverly Hills, CA 90212
Phillippe, Ryan	United Talent Agency	9560 Wilshire Blvd #500	Beverly Hills, CA 90212
Phillips, Lou Diamond	Eddie Michaels & Associates	9025 Wilshire Blvd., Ste. 450	Beverly Hills, CA 90211
Phillips, Mackenzie	SDB Partner Inc.	1801 Avenue of the Stars	Los Angeles, CA 90067
Phoenix, Rain	Endeavor Talent Agency	9601 Wilshire Blvd. 3rd Floor	Beverly Hills, CA 90212
Phoenix, Summer	Iris Burton Agency	8916 Ashcroft Ave.	Los Angeles, CA 90048
Phoenix, Joaquin	Patricola Lust PR	8383 Wilshire Blvd	Beverly Hills, CA 90211
Pierce, David Hyde	Brillstein-Grey Enter.	9150 Wilshire Blvd, Ste. 350	Beverly Hills, CA 90212-3427
Pietz, Amy	Innovative Artists	1505 10th St	Santa Monica, CA 90401
Pine, Chris	SDB Partners Inc.	1801 Avenue of the Stars	Los Angeles, CA 90067
Pitt, Brad	Creative Artists Agency	2000 Avenue of The Stars	Beverly Hills, CA 90067
Piven, Jeremy	Platform Public Relations	2666 North Beachwood Dr.	Los Angeles, CA 90068
Place, Mary Kay	The Gersh Agency	232 North Canon Drive	Beverly Hills, CA 90210
Pleshette, Susan	TalentWorks c/o Joel Dean	3500 West Olive Ave.	Burbank, CA 91505
Poehler, Amy	United Talent Agency	9560 Wilshire Blvd.	Beverly Hills, CA 90212
Poitier, Sidney	Verdon Cedric Productions	P.O. Box 2639	Beverly Hills, CA 90213
Poitier, Sydney Tamiia	Innovative Artists	1505 10th St	Santa Monica, CA 90401
Pollack, Sydney	42West	220 W. 42nd St.	New York, NY 10036
Pollak, Kevin	Intl. Creative Mgmt.	10250 Constellation Blvd.	Los Angeles, CA 90067
Pollan, Tracy	Writers & Artists Agency	19 W. 44th St.	New York, NY 10036
Polley, Sarah	William Morris Agency	One William Morris Place	Beverly Hills, CA 90212
Polo, Teri	United Talent Agency	9560 Wilshire Blvd.	Beverly Hills, CA 90212
Pompeo, Ellen	Hofflund/Polone	9465 Wilshire Blvd.	Beverly Hills, CA 90212
Posey, Parker	Creative Artists Agency	2000 Avenue of The Stars	Beverly Hills, CA 90067
Poston, Tom	2930 Deep Canyon	Beverly Hills, CA 90210	
Potente, Franka	William Morris Agency	One William Morris Place	Beverly Hills, CA 90212
Potter, Monica	United Talent Agency	9560 Wilshire Blvd #500	Beverly Hills, CA 90212
Potts, Annie	Intl. Creative Mgmt.	10250 Constellation Blvd.	Los Angeles, CA 90067
Powell, Jane	# 26C	150 W. End Avenue	New York, NY 10023
Powers, Stefanie	The Gage Group	450 Seventh Ave	New York, NY 10123
Pratt, Victoria	Don Buchwald & Assoc.	6500 Wilshire Blvd	Los Angeles, CA 90048
Prentiss, Paula	The Gersh Agency	232 North Canon Drive	Beverly Hills, CA 90210
Prepon, Laura	United Talent Agency	9560 Wilshire Blvd #500	Beverly Hills, CA 90212
Presley, Priscilla	William Morris Agency	One William Morris Place	Beverly Hills, CA 90212
Pressly, Jaime	Roklin Management	8530 Wilshire Blvd.	Beverly Hills, CA 90211
Preston, Kelly	Wolf Kasteler PR	355 North Maple Dr.	Beverly Hills, CA 90210

Priestley, Jason	United Talent Agency	9560 Wilshire Blvd #500	Beverly Hills, CA 90212
Principal, Victoria	Victoria Principal Productions	23852 Pacific Coast Hwy	Malibu, CA 90265
Prinze, Freddie Jr	Intl. Creative Mgmt.	10250 Constellation Blvd.	Los Angeles, CA 90067
Procter, Emily	William Morris Agency	One William Morris Place	Beverly Hills, CA 90212
Provine, Dorothy	8832 Ferncliff NE	Bainbridge Island,	WA 98110
Pryce, Jonathan	Endeavor Talent Agency	9601 Wilshire Blvd. 3rd Floor	Beverly Hills, CA 90212
Pullman, Bill	One Entertainment	9220 Sunset Blvd.	Los Angeles, CA 90069
Quaid, Dennis	William Morris Agency	One William Morris Place	Beverly Hills, CA 90212
Quaid, Randy	Guttman Associates PR	118 S. Beverly Drive, Suite 201	Beverly Hills, CA 90212
Quigley, Maggie	Creative Artists Agency	2000 Avenue of The Stars	Beverly Hills, CA 90067
Quinn, Colin	The Agency Group	9348 Civic Center Drive	Beverly Hills, CA 90210
Radcliffe, Daniel	Special Artists Agency	9465 Wilshire Blvd	Beverly Hills, CA 90212
Raffin, Deborah	The Artists Agency	1180 So. Beverly Drive	Los Angeles, CA 90035
Rai, Aishwarya	Canyon Entertainment	POB # 256	Palm Springs, CA 92263
Rajskub, Mary Lynn	Endeavor Talent Agency	9601 Wilshire Blvd. 3rd Floor	Beverly Hills, CA 90212
Ramirez, Sara	Mitchell K. Stubbs & Assoc.	8675 West Washington Blvd.	Culver City, CA 90232
Rampling, Charlotte	Artmedia	20 Ave Rapp	75007 Paris, France
Ratzenberger, John	PO Box 515	Vashon, WA 98070	
Raver, Kim	Mosaic Media Group	9200 W. Sunset Blvd	Los Angeles, CA 90069
Redford, Robert	Creative Artists Agency	2000 Avenue of The Stars	Beverly Hills, CA 90067
Redgrave, Lynn	Paradigm Talent Agency	360 N. Crescent Drive	Beverly Hills, CA 90210
Redgrave, Vanessa	Creative Artists Agency	2000 Avenue of The Stars	Beverly Hills, CA 90067
Reed, Pamela	Innovative Artists	1505 Tenth Street	Santa Monica, CA 90401
Rees, Roger	Innovative Artists	1505 Tenth Street	Santa Monica, CA 90401
Reese, Della	UP Church	7985 Santa Monica Blvd	West Hollywood, CA 90046
Reeves, Keanu	PMK/HBH - Steve Huvane	700 San Vicente Blvd.	Beverly Hills, CA 90211
Reeves, Scott	United Talent Agency	9560 Wilshire Blvd.	Beverly Hills, CA 90212
Reid, Tara	PMK/HBH	700 San Vicente Blvd.	Beverly Hills, CA 90211
Reilly, John C.	United Talent Agency	9560 Wilshire Blvd #500	Beverly Hills, CA 90212
Reiner, Carl	Creative Artists Agency	2000 Avenue of The Stars	Beverly Hills, CA 90067
Reiner, Rob	Castle Rock Entertainmnet	335 N. Maple Drive	Beverly Hills, CA 90210
Reiser, Paul	Nuance Productions	4049 Radford Ave.	Studio City, CA 91604
Remini, Leah	Rogers & Cowan PR	8687 Melrose Avenue	Los Angeles, CA 90069
Renfro, Brad	William Morris Agency	One William Morris Place	Beverly Hills, CA 90212
Resser , Autumn	Agency For Performing Art	888 Seventh Ave.	New York, NY 10106
Reubens, Paul	ID Public Relations	8409 Santa Monica Blvd	West Hollywood, CA 90069
Reynolds, Burt	Intl. Creative Mgmt.	10250 Constellation Blvd.	Los Angeles, CA 90067
Reynolds, Debbie	Metropolitan Talent	4500 Wilshire Blvd	Los Angeles, CA 90010
Reynolds, Ryan	United Talent Agency	9560 Wilshire Blvd #500	Beverly Hills, CA 90212
Rhames, Ving	Oxbow Productions	1945 West Race Ave	Chicago, IL 60622
Rhys, Paul	The Gersh Agency	232 North Canon Drive	Beverly Hills, CA 90210
Rhys-Davies, John	APA Literary Talent	405 S. Beverly Dr.	Beverly Hills, CA 90212
Rhys-Meyers, Jonathan	United Talent Agency	9560 Wilshire Blvd #500	Beverly Hills, CA 90212
Ribisi, Giovanni	William Morris Agency	One William Morris Place	Beverly Hills, CA 90212
Ricci, Christina	Intl. Creative Mgmt.	10250 Constellation Blvd.	Los Angeles, CA 90067
Richards, Denise	Rogers & Cowan PR	8687 Melrose Avenue	Los Angeles, CA 90069
Richards, Michael	William Morris Agency	One William Morris Place	Beverly Hills, CA 90212
Richardson, Cameron	Leverage Management	3030 Pennsylvania Ave.	Santa Monica, CA 90404
Richardson, Miranda	Parseghian, Planco	23 E. 22nd St.	New York, NY 10010
Richardson, Natasha	Creative Artists Agency	2000 Avenue of The Stars	Beverly Hills, CA 90067

Actors and Actresses Having Roles on TV and Film

Richardson, Patricia	Innovative Artists	1505 Tenth Street	Santa Monica, CA 90401
Richie, Nicole	United Talent Agency	9560 Wilshire Blvd.	Beverly Hills, CA 90212
Richter, Andy	Special Artists Agency	9465 Wilshire Blvd	Beverly Hills, CA 90212
Rickman, Alan	Endeavor Talent Agency	9601 Wilshire Blvd. 3rd Floor	Beverly Hills, CA 90212
Ringwald, Molly	Untitled Entertainment	331 N. Maple Dr.	Beverly Hills, CA 90210
Ripa, Kelly	William Morris Agency	One William Morris Place	Beverly Hills, CA 90212
Ritter, Jason	Burstein Company	15304 Sunset Blvd. Suite 208	Pacific Palisades, CA 90272
Robb, AnnaSophia	CESD	10635 Santa Monica Blvd.	Los Angeles, CA 90025
Robbins, Tim	Creative Artists Agency	2000 Avenue of The Stars	Beverly Hills, CA 90067
Roberts, Emma	Sweeney Management	8033 Sunset Blvd. #1048	Los Angeles, CA 90046
Roberts, Julia	Engelman&Co.	156 5th Ave., Ste. 711	New York, NY 10010
Roberts, Tanya	JDS - Jay D. Schwartz	3151 Cahuenga Blvd	Los Angeles, CA 90068
Roberts, Tony	Innovative Artists	1505 Tenth Street	Santa Monica, CA 90401
Robertson, Kathleen	Innovative Artists	1505 Tenth Street	Santa Monica, CA 90401
Robinson, Zuleikha	The Gersh Agency	232 North Canon Drive	Beverly Hills, CA 90210
Rock, Chris	Endeavor Talent Agency	9601 Wilshire Blvd. 3rd Floor	Beverly Hills, CA 90212
Rockwell, Sam	The Gersh Agency	232 North Canon Drive	Beverly Hills, CA 90210
Rodríguez, Adam	Global Artists Agency	1648 N. Wilcox Ave.	Los Angeles, CA 90028
Rodríguez, Freddy	Wolf Kasteler PR	355 North Maple Dr.	Beverly Hills, CA 90210
Roemer, Sarah	Intl. Creative Mgmt.	10250 Constellation Blvd.	Los Angeles, CA 90067
Rogers, Mimi	ID Public Relations	8409 Santa Monica Blvd	West Hollywood, CA 90069
Rogers, Wayne	Stargazer Entertainmnet	11828 La Grange Ave.	Los Angeles, CA 90025
Rohm, Elisabeth	Special Artists Agency	9465 Wilshire Blvd	Beverly Hills, CA 90212
Romano, Ray	ID Public Relations	8409 Santa Monica Blvd	West Hollywood, CA 90069
Romijn, Rebecca	William Morris Agency	One William Morris Place	Beverly Hills, CA 90212
Rooney, Mickey	The Artists Group	10100 Santa Monica Blvd	Los Angeles, CA 90067
Roseanne	United Talent Agency	9560 Wilshire Blvd #500	Beverly Hills, CA 90212
Ross, Marion	The Artists Agency	1180 S. Beverly Dr.	Los Angeles, CA 90035
Ross, Tracee Ellis	Intl. Creative Mgmt.	10250 Constellation Blvd.	Los Angeles, CA 90067
Rossellini, Isabella	ID Public Relations	8409 Santa Monica Blvd	West Hollywood, CA 90069
Rossum, Emmy	BenderSpink C/O C. Donatelli	110 South Fairfax Ave.	Los Angeles, CA 90036
Roth, Eli	Creative Artists Agency	2000 Avenue of The Stars	Beverly Hills, CA 90067
Roth, Tim	Special Artists Agency	9465 Wilshire Blvd	Beverly Hills, CA 90212
Roundtree, Richard	Stone Manners Agency	6500 Wilshire Blvd. Ste #550	Los Angeles, CA 90048
Rourke, Mickey	Intl. Creative Mgmt.	10250 Constellation Blvd.	Los Angeles, CA 90067
Routh, Brandon	United Talent Agency	9560 Wilshire Blvd #500	Beverly Hills, CA 90212
Rowell, Victoria	Abrams Artists Agency	9200 Sunset Blvd 11th Floor	Los Angeles CA 90067
Rowlands, Gena	Intl. Creative Mgmt.	40 West 57th Street	New York, NY 10019
Roxburgh, Richard	Intl. Creative Mgmt.	10250 Constellation Blvd.	Los Angeles, CA 90067
Rubén Blades	United Talent Agency	9560 Wilshire Blvd #500	Beverly Hills, CA 90212
Ruehl, Mercedes	Innovative Artists	1505 Tenth Street	Santa Monica, CA 90401
Ruffalo, Mark	William Morris Agency	One William Morris Place	Beverly Hills, CA 90212
Rush, Geoffrey	Creative Artists Agency	2000 Avenue of The Stars	Beverly Hills, CA 90067
Russell, Keri	William Morris Agency	One William Morris Place	Beverly Hills, CA 90212
Russell, Kurt	Creative Artists Agency	2000 Avenue of The Stars	Beverly Hills, CA 90067
Russo, Rene	John Crosby Management	1310 N. Spaulding Ave.	Los Angeles, CA 90046
Ryan, Blanchard	The Gage Group	450 Seventh Ave	New York, NY 10123
Ryan, Jeri	Original Management	2045 South Barrington Ave	Los Angeles, CA 90025
Ryan, Meg	PMK/HBH	700 San Vicente Blvd	West Hollywood, CA 90069
Ryder, Winona	ID Public Relations	8409 Santa Monica Blvd	West Hollywood, CA 90069
Sabato, Antonio Jr.	Main Title Entertainmnet	5225 Wilshire Blvd.	Los Angeles, CA 90036

Sagal, Katey	7095 Hollywood Blvd # 792	Los Angeles, CA 90028	
Saget, Bob	William Morris Agency	One William Morris Place	Beverly Hills, CA 90212
Saint, Eve Maria	Warren Cowan & Associates	8899 Beverly Blvd.	Los Angeles, CA 90048
San Giacomo, Laura	ID Public Relations	8409 Santa Monica Blvd	West Hollywood, CA 90069
Sanchez, Kiele	The Gersh Agency	232 North Canon Drive	Beverly Hills, CA 90210
Sanchez, Roselyn	United Talent Agency	9560 Wilshire Blvd #500	Beverly Hills, CA 90212
Sandler, Adam	Happy Madison Productions	10202 W. Washington Blvd	Culver City, CA 90232
Santoro, Rodrigo	The Gersh Agency	232 North Canon Drive	Beverly Hills, CA 90210
Sara, Mia	The Gersh Agency	232 North Canon Drive	Beverly Hills, CA 90210
Sarandon, Susan	Intl. Creative Mgmt.	10250 Constellation Blvd.	Los Angeles, CA 90067
Sasso, Will	Nancy Iannios PR	8271 Melrose Ave.	Los Angeles, CA 90046
Savage, Fred	Creative Artists Agency	2000 Avenue of The Stars	Beverly Hills, CA 90067
Saxon, John	GVA Talent Agency	9025 Wilshire Blvd	Beverly Hills, CA 90211
Scacchi, Greta	Innovative Artists	1505 Tenth Street	Santa Monica, CA 90401
Scalia, Jack	Jonas Public Relations	240 26th Street, Suite 3	Santa Monica, CA 90402
Schell, Maximilian	The Blake Agency	1327 Ocean Avenue	Santa Monica, CA 90401
Schneider, Bonnie	N.S. Bienstock, Inc.	1740 Broadway	New York, NY 10019
Schneider, John	Johnenelly Productions	4000 Warner Blvd-Bldg.139	Burbank, CA 91522
Schneider, Rob	Stan Rosenfield PR	2029 Century Park E.	Los Angeles, CA 90067
Schram, Bitty	Innovative Artists	1505 10th Street	Santa Monica, CA 90401
Schreiber, Liev	Creative Artists Agency	2000 Avenue of The Stars	Beverly Hills, CA 90067
Schroder, Rick	Innovative Artists	1505 10th Street	Santa Monica, CA 90401
Schwartzman, Jason	United Talent Agency	9560 Wilshire Blvd #500	Beverly Hills, CA 90212
Schwarzenegger, Arnold	Creative Artists Agency	2000 Avenue of The Stars	Beverly Hills, CA 90067
Schwimmer, David	The Gersh Agency	232 North Canon Drive	Beverly Hills, CA 90210
Scoggins, Tracy	Amsel, Eisenstadt & Assoc.	5055 Wilshire Blvd.	Los Angeles, CA 90036
Scott, April	APA Literary Talent	405 S. Beverly Dr.	Los Angeles, CA 90212
Scott, Ashley	United Talent Agency	9560 Wilshire Blvd #500	Beverly Hills, CA 90212
Scott, Donna W.	TRC Entertainment	8424A Santa Monica Blvd	West Hollywood, CA 90069
Scott, Seann William	ID Public Relations	8409 Santa Monica Blvd	West Hollywood, CA 90069
Scott, Tom Everett	The Gersh Agency	232 North Canon Drive	Beverly Hills, CA 90210
Sedaris, Amy	Paradigm Talent Agency	360 N. Crescent Drive	Beverly Hills, CA 90210
Sedgwick, Kyra	ID Public Relations	155 Spring St.	New York, NY 10012
Selleca, Connie	Binder & Associates	1465 Lindcrest Drive	Beverly Hills, CA 90212
Selleck, Tom	Wolf Kasteler PR	355 North Maple Dr	Beverly Hills, CA 90210
Sellers, Victoria	Fries	1927 Vista Del Mar	Hollywood, CA 90068
Serkis, Andy	Lou Colson Associates	37 Berwick Street	LondonW1V 3RF UK
Sevigny, Chloe	Brillstein-Grey Enter.	9150 Wilshire Blvd, Ste. 350	Beverly Hills, CA 90212-3427
Sewell, Rufus	Endeavor Talent Agency	9601 Wilshire Blvd. 3rd Floor	Beverly Hills, CA 90212
Seyfried, Amanda	THJ Management	405 East 54th St. #3H	New York, NY 10022
Seymour, Jane	Anthem Entertainment	6100 Wilshire Blvd, Suite 1170	Los Angeles, CA 90048
Shadyac, Tom	Creative Artists Agency	2000 Avenue of The Stars	Beverly Hills, CA 90067
Shahi, Sarah	McKeon-Valeo Management	9150 Wilshire Blvd.	Beverly Hills, CA 90210
Shalhoub, Tony	Creative Artists Agency	2000 Avenue of The Stars	Beverly Hills, CA 90067
Shannon, Molly	Framework Entertainment	9057 Nemo St., Ste. C	West Hollywood, CA 90069
Sharif, Omar	Steve Kenis & Company	72-74 Dean Street	LondonWID 3SG
Shatner, William	TalentWorks	3500 W. Olive Ave.	Burbank, CA 91505
Shaw, Fiona	Intl. Creative Mgmt.	10250 Constellation Blvd.	Los Angeles, CA 90067
Shawkat, Alia	Innovative Artists	1505 Tenth Street	Santa Monica, CA 90401
Shear, Rhonda	J. Cast Productions	2550 Greenvalley Rd	Los Angeles, CA 90046
Sheedy, Ally	Buchwald & Associates	6500 Wilshire Blvd	Los Angeles, CA 90048

Sheen, Charlie	Endeavor Talent Agency	9601 Wilshire Blvd. 3rd Floor	Beverly Hills, CA 90212
Shelton, Marley	The Firm - Stacy Boniello	9465 Wilshire Blvd	Beverly Hills, CA 90212
Shepard, Cybill	Hofflund & Polone	9465 Wilshire Blvd #820	Beverly Hills, CA 90212
Shepard, Dax	Endeavor Talent Agency	9601 Wilshire Blvd	Beverly Hills, CA 90210
Shepard, Sam	Intl. Creative Mgmt.	10250 Constellation Blvd.	Los Angeles, CA 90067
Sheridan, Nicolette	Innovative Artists	1505 Tenth Street	Santa Monica, CA 90401
Shields, Brook	Intl. Creative Mgmt.	10250 Constellation Blvd.	Los Angeles, CA 90067
Shire, Talia	Elkins Entertainment	8306 Wilshre Blvd., #438	Beverly Hills, CA, 90211
Short, Martin	William Morris Agency	One William Morris Place	Beverly Hills, CA 90212
Shue, Elisabeth	Creative Artists Agency	2000 Avenue of The Stars	Beverly Hills, CA 90067
Sigler, Jamie Lynn	Evolution Talent Agency	1776 Broadway	New York, NY 10019
Silva, Henry	5226 Beckford Avenue	Tarzana, CA 91356-3102	
Silverstone, Alicia	First Kiss Productions	468 North Camden Dr	Beverly Hills, CA 90210
Simmons, Jean	Michael K. Stubbs	8695 W. Washington Blvd.	Culver City, CA 90232
Simpson, Ashlee	Creative Artists Agency	2000 Avenue of The Stars	Beverly Hills, CA 90067
Simpson, Jessica	Creative Artists Agency	2000 Avenue of The Stars	Beverly Hills, CA 90067
Sims, Molly	William Morris Agency	One William Morris Place	Beverly Hills, CA 90212
Singleton, John	United Talent Agency	9560 Wilshire Blvd #500	Beverly Hills, CA 90212
Sinise, Gary	Brillstein-Grey Enter.	9150 Wilshire Blvd, Ste. 350	Beverly Hills, CA 90212-3427
Sirico, Tony	Writers & Artists Agency	19 W. 44th St.	New York, NY 10036
Sirtis, Marina	Rohr Talent Public Relations	1901 Avenue of the Stars	Los Angeles, CA 90067
Sisto, Jeremy	Intl. Creative Mgmt.	10250 Constellation Blvd.	Los Angeles, CA 90067
Sites, Brian	Innovative Artists	1505 Tenth Street	Santa Monica, CA 90401
Sizemore, Tom	Innovative Artists	1505 Tenth Street	Santa Monica, CA 90401
Skerritt, Tom	Intl. Creative Mgmt.	10250 Constellation Blvd.	Los Angeles, CA 90067
Slater, Christan	ID Public Relations	8409 Santa Monica Blvd	West Hollywood, CA 90069
Smart, Amy	Endeavor Talent Agency	9601 Wilshire Blvd. 3rd Floor	Beverly Hills, CA 90212
Smith, Dylan	TalentWorks	3500 W. Olive Ave.	Burbank, CA 91505
Smith, Gregory	Endeavor Talent Agency	9601 Wilshire Blvd. 3rd Floor	Beverly Hills, CA 90212
Smith, Jaclyn	Intl. Creative Mgmt.	10250 Constellation Blvd.	Los Angeles, CA 90067
Smith, Jada Pinkett	Overbrook Entertainment	450 North Roxbury Dr., 4th Fl.	Beverly Hills, CA 90210
Smith, Kevin	Endeavor Talent Agency	9601 Wilshire Blvd. 3rd Floor	Beverly Hills, CA 90212
Smith, Maggie	Intl. Creative Mgmt.	10250 Constellation Blvd.	Los Angeles, CA 90067
Smith, Riley	Innovative Artists	1505 Tenth Street	Santa Monica, CA 90401
Smith, Shawnee	Agency for the Performing Arts	888 Seventh Ave	New York, NY 10106
Smith, Will	Creative Artists Agency	2000 Avenue of The Stars	Beverly Hills, CA 90067
Smits, Jimmy	Creative Artists Agency	2000 Avenue of The Stars	Beverly Hills, CA 90067
Snipes, Wesley	United Talent Agency	9560 Wilshire Blvd #500	Beverly Hills, CA 90212
Snow, Brittany	Intl. Creative Mgmt.	10250 Constellation Blvd.	Los Angeles, CA 90067
Sobieski, Leelee	Pinnacle PR	8265 Sunset Blvd	Los Angeles, CA 90046
Sokoloff, Marla	William Morris Agency	One William Morris Place	Beverly Hills, CA 90212
Somerhalder, Ian	Innovative Artists	1505 Tenth Street	Santa Monica, CA 90401
Somers, Suzanne	David Shapira & Assoc.	193 N. Robertson Blvd.	Beverly Hills, CA 90211
Song, Brenda	Intl. Creative Mgmt.	10250 Constellation Blvd.	Los Angeles, CA 90067
Sorbo, Kevin	Intl. Creative Mgmt.	10250 Constellation Blvd.	Los Angeles, CA 90067
Sorvino, Mira	I/D Public Relations	8409 Santa Monica Blvd.	West Hollywood, CA 90069
Sorvino, Paul	TalentWorks	3500 W. Olive Ave.	Burbank, CA 91505
Sossamon, Shannyn	Nancy Iannios PR	8271 Melrose Avenue	Los Angeles, CA 90046
Soul, David	Lip Service Casting Ltd.	60-66 Wardour Street	London W1F 0TA UK
Spacek, Sissy	Creative Artists Agency	2000 Avenue of The Stars	Beverly Hills, CA 90067
Spacey, Kevin	William Morris Agency	One William Morris Place	Beverly Hills, CA 90212

Spade, David	Baker Winokur Ryder	9100 Wilshire Blvd.	Beverly Hills, CA 90212
Spader, James	Intl. Creative Mgmt.	10250 Constellation Blvd.	Los Angeles, CA 90067
Sparks, Hal	Marsh Entertainment	12444 Ventura Blvd	Studio City, CA 91604
Speedman, Scott	Endeavor Talent Agency	9601 Wilshire Blvd. 3rd Floor	Beverly Hills, CA 90212
Spelling, Tori	United Talent Agency	9560 Wilshire Blvd #500	Beverly Hills, CA 90212
Spencer, John	Abrams Artists Agency	9200 Sunset Blvd 11th Floor	Los Angeles CA 90067
Spiner, Brent	Innovative Artists	1505 Tenth Street	Santa Monica, CA 90401
Stafford, Michelle	TalentWorks	3500 West Olive Ave.	Burbank, CA 91505
Stahl-David, Michael	The Gersh Agency	232 North Canon Drive	Beverly Hills, CA 90210
Stahl, Nick	PMK Public Relations	8500 Wilshire Blvd	Beverly Hills, CA 90211
Stallone, Sylvester	Rogers & Cowan PR	8687 Melrose	Los Angeles, CA 90069
Stamos, John	Bragman, Nyman, Caferelli	8687 Melrose Ave	Los Angeles, CA 90069
Stanford, Aaron	Endeavor Talent Agency	9601 Wilshire Blvd. 3rd Floor	Beverly Hills, CA 90212
Stapleton, Jean	Bauman, Redanty, Shaul	5757 Wilshire Blvd.	Los Angeles, CA 90036
Staunton, Imelda	Artist Rights Group (A.R.G)	4 Great Portland Street	LondonW1W 8PA, UK
Steenburgen, Mary	The Gersh Agency	232 North Canon Drive	Beverly Hills, CA 90210
Stevens, Fisher	Dan Clores PR	386 Park Avenue South	New York, NY 10016
Stevens, Gary	Intl. Creative Mgmt.	10250 Constellation Blvd.	Los Angeles, CA 90067
Stevens, Stella	MC Squared Entertainment	14724 Ventura Blvd	Sherman Oaks, CA 91403
Stevenson, Parker	Metropolitan Talent	4500 Wilshire Blvd.	Los Angeles, CA 90010
Stewart, French	A.P.A.	405 S. Beverly Dr.	Los Angeles, CA 90212
Stewart, Kristen	The Gersh Agency	232 North Canon Drive	Beverly Hills, CA 90210
Stewart, Patrick	ID Public Relations	8409 Santa Monica Blvd	West Hollywood, CA 90069
Stiers, David Ogden	Mitchell K. Stubbs & Assoc	8695 West Washington Blvd	Culver City, CA 90232
Stiles, Julia	Creative Artists Agency	2000 Avenue of The Stars	Beverly Hills, CA 90067
Stiles, Ryan	Liberman & Zerman	252 No. Larchmont Blvd	Los Angeles, CA 90004
Stiller, Ben	United Talent Agency	9560 Wilshire Blvd #500	Beverly Hills, CA 90212
Stock, Barbara	The Artists Mgmt. Group	9465 Wilshire Blvd	Beverly Hills, CA 90212
Stoltz, Eric	Creative Artists Agency	2000 Avenue of The Stars	Beverly Hills, CA 90067
Stone, Sharon	PMK Public Relations	161 6th Ave.	New York, NY 10013
Storch, Larry	330 West End Avenue	New York, NY 10023	
Storm, Gale	23831 Bluehill Bay	Dana Point, CA 92629	
Stormare, Peter	Endeavor Talent Agency	9601 Wilshire Blvd. 3rd Floor	Beverly Hills, CA 90212
Stowe, Madeleine	Brillstein-Grey Entertainment	9150 Wilshire Blvd.	Beverly Hills, CA 90212
Strait, Steven	Creative Artists Agency	2000 Avenue of The Stars	Beverly Hills, CA 90067
Strathairn, David	Intl. Creative Mgmt.	10250 Constellation Blvd.	Los Angeles, CA 90067
Strauss, Peter	TalentWorks	3500 West Olive Ave.	Burbank, CA 91505
Streep, Meryl	Creative Artists Agency	2000 Avenue of The Stars	Beverly Hills, CA 90067
Streisand, Barbra	Intl. Creative Mgmt.	10250 Constellation Blvd.	Los Angeles, CA 90067
Stringfield, Sherry	United Talent Agency	9560 Wilshire Blvd #500	Beverly Hills, CA 90212
Struthers, Sally	Sharp & Associates	8721 Sunset Blvd., Ste. 208	Los Angeles, CA 90069
Suchet, David	Ken McReddie Ltd	36 - 40 Glasshouse Street	LondonW1B 5DL UK
Sullivan, Nicole	William Morris Agency	One William Morris Place	Beverly Hills, CA 90212
Sullivan, Susan	Paradigm Talent Agency	360 N. Crescent Drive	Beverly Hills, CA 90210
Sumpter, Jeremy	United Talent Agency	9560 Wilshire Blvd #500	Beverly Hills, CA 90212
Sutherland, Donald	Creative Artists Agency	2000 Avenue of The Stars	Beverly Hills, CA 90067
Sutherland, Kiefer	Wolf/Kasteler PR	355 North Maple Dr., Ste. 351	Beverly Hills, CA 90210
Suvari, Mena	The Gersh Agency	232 North Canon Drive	Beverly Hills, CA 90210
Swain, Dominique	APA Literary Talent	405 S. Beverly Dr.	Beverly Hills, CA 90212
Swank, Hilary	Creative Artists Agency	2000 Avenue of The Stars	Beverly Hills, CA 90067
Swardson, Nick	The Gersh Agency	232 North Canon Drive	Beverly Hills, CA 90210

Swayze, Patrick	William Morris Agency	One William Morris Place	Beverly Hills, CA 90212
Sweeney, Alison	Reel Talent Management	980 Bundy Drive	Los Angeles, CA 90049
Swinton, Tilda	Endeavor Talent Agency	9601 Wilshire Blvd. 3rd Floor	Beverly Hills, CA 90212
Sykes, Wanda	William Morris Agency	One William Morris Place	Beverly Hills, CA 90212
Symone, Raven	Endeavor Talent Agency	9601 Wilshire Blvd. 3rd Floor	Beverly Hills, CA 90212
Szmanda, Eric	The Gersh Agency	232 North Canon Drive	Beverly Hills, CA 90210
Takei, George	Don Buchwald & Assoc.	6500 Wilshire Blvd	Los Angeles, CA 90048
Tamblyn, Amber	Endeavor Talent Agency	9601 Wilshire Blvd. 3rd Floor	Beverly Hills, CA 90212
Tambor, Jeffrey	The Gersh Agency	232 North Canon Drive	Beverly Hills, CA 90210
Tarantino, Quentin	William Morris Agency	One William Morris Place	Beverly Hills, CA 90212
Tarver, Antonio	GEM Public Relations	1101 S Robertson Blvd	Los Angeles, CA 90035
Tatum, Channing	Innovative Artists	1505 Tenth Street	Santa Monica, CA 90401
Tautou, Audrey	Creative Artists Agency	2000 Avenue of The Stars	Beverly Hills, CA 90067
Taylor, Christine	United Talent Agency	9560 Wilshire Blvd #500	Beverly Hills, CA 90212
Taylor, Elizabeth	PO Box 55995	Sherman Oaks, CA 91413	
Taylor, Holland	The Gersh Agency	232 North Canon Drive	Beverly Hills, CA 90210
Taylor, Noah	Intl. Creative Mgmt.	10250 Constellation Blvd.	Los Angeles, CA 90067
Taylor, Rod	2375 Bowmont	Beverly Hills, CA 90210	
Terra, Scott	Abrams Artists Agency	9200 Sunset Blvd 11th Floor	Los Angeles CA 90067
Theissen, Tiffani-Amber	Wolf/Kasteler PR	355 North Maple Dr.	Beverly Hills, CA 90210
Theron, Charlize	Denver & Delilah Productions	1041 N. Formosa Ave	Los Angeles, CA 90046
Theroux, Justin	3 Arts Entertainment	9460 Wilshire Blvd. 7th Floor	Beverly Hills, CA 90212
Thewlis, David	William Morris Agency	One William Morris Place	Beverly Hills, CA 90212
Thicke, Alan	1568 Blue Jay Way	Los Angeles, CA 90069	
Thinnes, Roy	Phoenix Artists	311 West 43rd St.	New York, NY 10036
Thomas, Eddie Kaye	The Gersh Agency	232 North Canon Drive	Beverly Hills, CA 90210
Thomas, Kristin Scott	Creative Artists Agency	2000 Avenue of The Stars	Beverly Hills, CA 90067
Thomas, Marlo	Creative Artists Agency	2000 Avenue of The Stars	Beverly Hills, CA 90067
Thomas, Richard	Creative Artists Agency	2000 Avenue of The Stars	Beverly Hills, CA 90067
Thomas, Robin	TalentWorks	3500 West Olive Ave.	Burbank, CA 91505
Thomas, Rozonda 'Chilli'	William Morris Agency	One William Morris Place	Beverly Hills, CA 90212
Thomas, Sean Patrick	Paradigm Talent Agency	360 N. Crescent Drive	Beverly Hills, CA 90210
Thompson, Emma	William Morris Agency	One William Morris Place	Beverly Hills, CA 90212
Thompson, Lea	7966 Woodrow Wilson Dr.	Los Angeles, CA 90046	
Thompson, Sada	Bauman, Hiller & Assoc.	5757 Wilshire Blvd. Ste. 473	Los Angeles, CA 90036
Thompson, Sarah	Brillstein-Grey Enter.	9150 Wilshire Blvd, Ste. 350	Beverly Hills, CA 90212-3427
Thoms, Tracie	The Gersh Agency	41 Madison Avenue	New York, NY 10010
Thornton, Billy Bob	Rogers & Cowan PR	8687 Melrose Avenue	Los Angeles, CA 90069
Thurman, Uma	Creative Artists Agency	2000 Avenue of The Stars	Beverly Hills, CA 90067
Tierney, Maura	Anonymous Content	3532 Hayden Ave	Culver City, CA 90232
Tilly, Jennifer	Innovative Artists	1505 10th St	Santa Monica, CA 90401
Tilly, Meg	The Gersh Agency	232 North Canon Drive	Beverly Hills, CA 90210
Tisdale, Ashley	Scott Appel PR	13547 Ventura Blvd.	Sherman Oaks, CA 91423
Titus, Christopher	Omnipop Talent Agency	4605 Lankershim Blvd.	Toluca Lake, CA 91602
Tom, Nicole	TalentWorks	3500 West Olive Ave.	Burbank, CA 91505
Tomei, Marisa	ID Public Relations	8409 Santa Monica Blvd	West Hollywood, CA 90069
Torn, Rip	Guttman Associates PR	118 South Beverly Drive	Beverly Hills, CA 90212
Torres, Gina	PMK Public Relations	700 San Vicente Blvd.	West Hollywood, CA 90069
Townsend, Stuart	Artists Independent Network	825 Nowita Place	Venice, CA 90291
Trachtenberg, Michelle	Intl. Creative Mgmt.	10250 Constellation Blvd.	Los Angeles, CA 90067
Travanti, Daniel J.	The Tisherman Agency	6767 Forest Lawn Drive	Los Angeles, CA 90068

Travis, Nancy	Endeavor Talent Agency	9601 Wilshire Blvd. 3rd Floor	Beverly Hills, CA 90212
Travolta, John	WMA-C/O Jim Wyatt	One William Morris Place	Beverly Hills, CA 90212
Tripplehorn, Jeanne	I/D Public Relations	8409 Santa Monica Blvd.	West Hollywood, CA 90069
Troyer, Vern	Fonolli Management	11218 Osborne St	Lakeview Terrace, CA 91342
Tucker, Jonathan	Endeavor Talent Agency	9601 Wilshire Blvd. 3rd Floor	Beverly Hills, CA 90212
Turner, Kathleen	Intl. Creative Mgmt.	10250 Constellation Blvd.	Los Angeles, CA 90067
Turturro, Aida	Framework Entertainment	9057 Nemo St. Suite C	West Hollywood, CA 90069
Turturro, John	Creative Artists Agency	2000 Avenue of The Stars	Beverly Hills, CA 90067
Twiggy, Lawson	PFD	Drury House, 34-43 Russell St.	London, WC2B 5HA UK
Tyler, Aisha	Endeavor Talent Agency	9601 Wilshire Blvd. 3rd Floor	Beverly Hills, CA 90212
Tyler, Liv	PMK Public Relations	700 San Vicente Blvd.	West Hollywood, CA 90069
Ubach, Alanna	The Gersh Agency	232 North Canon Drive	Beverly Hills, CA 90210
Ullman, Ricky	Nani/Saperstein Management	16 Penn Plaza	New York, NY 10001
Underwood, Blair	Thruline Entertainment	9250 Wilshire Blvd	Beverly Hills, CA 90212
Union, Gabrielle	United Talent Agency	9560 Wilshire Blvd.	Beverly Hills, CA 90212
Urban, Karl	Auckland Actors	Box 56 -460 Dominion Rd.	Aukland, New Zealand
Vaccara, Brenda	Waters & Nicolosi	4311 Wilshire Blvd.	Los Angeles, CA 90010-3717
Valderrama, Wilmer	United Talent Agency	9560 Wilshire Blvd #500	Beverly Hills, CA 90212
Valley, Mark	Paradigm Talent Agency	360 N. Crescent Drive	Beverly Hills, CA 90210
Van Ark, Joan	William Morris Agency	One William Morris Place	Beverly Hills, CA 90212
Van Damme, Jean Claude	Intl. Creative Mgmt.	10250 Constellation Blvd.	Los Angeles, CA 90067
Van Der Beek, James	The Gersh Agency	232 North Canon Drive	Beverly Hills, CA 90210
Van Dyke, Barry	William Morris Agency	One William Morris Place	Beverly Hills, CA 90212
Van Dyke, Dick	William Morris Agency	One William Morris Place	Beverly Hills, CA 90212
Van Dyke, Jerry	J. Cast Productions	2550 Greenvalley Rd	Los Angeles, CA 90046
Van Zandt, Steve	Shore Fire Media	32 Court Street	New York, NY 11201
Vardalos, Nia	Creative Artists Agency	2000 Avenue of The Stars	Beverly Hills, CA 90067
Vartan, Michael	Stephen Hanks Management	252 N Larchmont Blvd # 201	Los Angeles, CA 90008
Vaughn, Vince	United Talent Agency	9560 Wilshire Blvd #500	Beverly Hills, CA 90212
Vaugier, Emmanuelle	Innovative Artists	1505 10th Street	Santa Monica, CA 90401
Vega, Paz	William Morris Agency	One William Morris Place	Beverly Hills, CA 90212
Vel Johnson, Reginald	8637 Allenwood Drive	Los Angeles, CA 90046	
Velasquez, Patricia	DePaz Management	2011 North Vermont Ave.	Los Angeles, CA 90027
Velazquesz, Nadine	The Gersh Agency	232 North Canon Drive	Beverly Hills, CA 90210
Venora, Diane	Davila	9255 Sunset Blvd	Los Angeles, CA 90069
Ventimiglia, Milo	Divide Pictures	1545 Amherst Ave	Los Angeles, CA 90025
Vergara, Sofia	Endeavor Talent Agency	9601 Wilshire Blvd. 3rd Floor	Beverly Hills, CA 90212
Vidal, Christina	Writers & Artists Agency	19 W. 44th St.	New York, NY 10036
Vincent, Cerina	Bohemia Enter. Group	8170 Beverly Blvd. #102	Los Angeles, CA, 90048
Visnjic, Goran	Endeavor Talent Agency	9601 Wilshire Blvd. 3rd Floor	Beverly Hills, CA 90212
von Detten, Erik	Nancy Iannios PR	8271 Melrose Ave	Los Angeles, CA 90046
von Sydow, Max	United Talent Agency	9560 Wilshire Blvd #500	Beverly Hills, CA 90212
Waggoner, Lyle	The Artists Mgmt. Group	9465 Wilshire Blvd	Beverly Hills, CA 90212
Wagner, Lindsay	Intl. Creative Mgmt.	10250 Constellation Blvd.	Los Angeles, CA 90067
Wagner, Robert	Binder & Associates	1465 Lindacrest Drive	Beverly Hills, CA 90210
Wahlberg, Donnie	Wolf/Kasteler PR	355 North Maple Dr.	Beverly Hills, CA 90210
Wahlberg, Mark	Endeavor Talent Agency	9601 Wilshire Blvd. 3rd Floor	Beverly Hills, CA 90212
Walken, Christopher	ICM C/O Toni Howard	8942 Wilshire Blvd	Beverly Hills, CA 90211
Walker, Clint	10175 Joerschke # 1	Grass Valley, CA 95945	
Walker, Paul	Intl. Creative Mgmt.	10250 Constellation Blvd.	Los Angeles, CA 90067
Wallach, Eli	90 Riverside Drive	New York, NY 10024	

Walsh, Dylan	Creative Artists Agency	2000 Avenue of The Stars	Beverly Hills, CA 90067
Walsh, Kate	Innovative Artists	1505 Tenth Street	Santa Monica, CA 90401
Walter, Lisa Ann	United Talent Agency	9560 Wilshire Blvd #500	Beverly Hills, CA 90212
Walters, Julie	Intl. Creative Mgmt.	10250 Constellation Blvd.	Los Angeles, CA 90067
Wantanabe, Ken	Roar Entertainment	9701 Wilshire Blvd.	Beverly Hills, CA 90212
Ward, Fred	Innovative Artists	1505 Tenth Street	Santa Monica, CA 90401
Ward, Sela	Intl. Creative Mgmt.	10250 Constellation Blvd.	Los Angeles, CA 90067
Warner, Malcolm-Jamal	William Morris Agency	One William Morris Place	Beverly Hills, CA 90212
Warren, Estella	Paradigm Talent Agency	360 N. Crescent Drive	Beverly Hills, CA 90210
Warren, Lesley Ann	Innovative Artists	1505 Tenth Street	Santa Monica, CA 90401
Washington, Denzel	Intl. Creative Mgmt.	10250 Constellation Blvd.	Los Angeles, CA 90067
Washington, Isaiah	Jaymes/Nelson Entertainment	12444 Ventura Blvd.	Studio City, CA 91604
Washington, Kerry	Creative Artists Agency	2000 Avenue of The Stars	Beverly Hills, CA 90067
Waterston, Sam	Intl. Creative Mgmt.	10250 Constellation Blvd.	Los Angeles, CA 90067
Watson, Emma	Special Artists Agency	9465 Wilshire Blvd	Beverly Hills, CA 90212
Watts, Naomi	Creative Artists Agency	2000 Avenue of The Stars	Beverly Hills, CA 90067
Wayans, Damon	Tencer & Associates	9777 Wilshire Blvd	Beverly Hills, CA 90212
Wayans, Keenen Ivory	William Morris Agency	One William Morris Place	Beverly Hills, CA 90212
Wayans, Marlon	William Morris Agency	One William Morris Place	Beverly Hills, CA 90212
Wayans, Shawn	William Morris Agency	One William Morris Place	Beverly Hills, CA 90212
Wayne, Patrick	David Shapira & Assoc.	15821 Ventura Blvd # 235	Encino, CA 91436
Weatherly, Michael	Colden, McKuin & Frankel	141 El Camino Dr	Beverly Hills, CA 90212
Weathers, Carl	Abrams Artists Agency	9200 Sunset Blvd.	Los Angeles, CA 90069
Weaver, Sigourney	42West	220 W. 42nd St.	New York, NY 10036
Weaving, Hugo	ICM C/O Chris Andrews	8942 Wilshire Blvd	Beverly Hills, CA 90211
Wedgeworth, Ann	The Blake Agency	1327 Ocean Avenue	Santa Monica, CA 90401
Weigert, Robin	Bauman, Redanty & Shaul	5757 Wilshire Blvd.	Los Angeles, CA 90036
Weisz, Rachel	ID Public Relations	8409 Santa Monica Blvd	West Hollywood, CA 90069
Welch, Raquel	Innovative Artists	1505 Tenth Street	Santa Monica, CA 90401
Wells, Dawn	11684 Ventura Blvd # 985	Studio City, CA 91604	
Wen, Ming-Na	Intl. Creative Mgmt.	10250 Constellation Blvd.	Los Angeles, CA 90067
Wendt, George	Paradigm Talent Agency	360 N. Crescent Drive	Beverly Hills, CA 90210
Wenham, David	Endeavor Talent Agency	9601 Wilshire Blvd. 3rd Floor	Beverly Hills, CA 90212
West, Adam	Chasin Agency	8899 Beverly Blvd - 7th Floor	Los Angeles, CA 90048
West, Dominic	Creative Artists Agency	2000 Avenue of The Stars	Beverly Hills, CA 90067
West, Shane	William Morris Agency	One William Morris Place	Beverly Hills, CA 90212
Whitaker, Forest	William Morris Agency	One William Morris Place	Beverly Hills, CA 90212
White, Betty	PO Box 491965	Los Angeles, CA 90049	
White, Jaleel (Urkel)	William Morris Agency	One William Morris Place	Beverly Hills, CA 90212
White, Mike	William Morris Agency	One William Morris Place	Beverly Hills, CA 90212
White, Vanna	Wheel of Fortune	Sony Pictures Plaza	Culver City, CA 90232
Whitford, Bradley	Endeavor Talent Agency	9601 Wilshire Blvd. 3rd Floor	Beverly Hills, CA 90212
Whitman, Stuart	House of Representatives	400 South Beverly Drive	Beverly Hills, CA 90212
Whitmore, James	J. Michael Bloom & Assoc	9255 Sunset Blvd	Los Angeles, CA 90069
Whitworth, Johnny	TalentWorks	3500 W. Olive Ave	Burbank, CA 91505
Wiest, Diane	Intl. Creative Mgmt.	10250 Constellation Blvd.	Los Angeles, CA 90067
Wilde, Olivia	Creative Artists Agency	2000 Avenue of The Stars	Beverly Hills, CA 90067
Wilder, Gene	David Shapira & Assoc.	193 N. Robertson Blvd	Beverly Hills, CA 90211
Willard, Fred	Amsel, Eisenstadt & Assoc.	5055 Wilshire Blvd.	Los Angeles, CA 90036
Williams, Billy Dee	The Artists Agency	1180 So. Beverly Drive	Los Angeles, CA 90035
Williams, Cindy	William Morris Agency	One William Morris Place	Beverly Hills, CA 90212

Williams, Clarence III	Abrams Artists Agency	9200 Sunset Blvd 11th Floor	Los Angeles CA 90067
Williams, Kimberly	Creative Artists Agency	2000 Avenue of The Stars	Beverly Hills, CA 90067
Williams, Michelle	Creative Artists Agency	2000 Avenue of The Stars	Beverly Hills, CA 90067
Williams, Olivia	Intl. Creative Mgmt.	10250 Constellation Blvd.	Los Angeles, CA 90067
Williams, Robin	Creative Artists Agency	2000 Avenue of The Stars	Beverly Hills, CA 90067
Williams, Treat	One Entertainment	9220 Sunset Blvd.	Los Angeles, CA 90069
Williams, Vanessa L.	Intl. Creative Mgmt.	10250 Constellation Blvd.	Los Angeles, CA 90067
Willis, Bruce	Rogers & Cowan PR	8687 Melrose	Los Angeles, CA 90069
Willis, Katherine	Collier Talent Agency	2313 Lake Austin Blvd	Austin, TX 78703
Wilson, Bridgette	The Gersh Agency	232 North Canon Drive	Beverly Hills, CA 90210
Wilson, Debra	Rosenberg & Associates	145 B Allen Blvd.	Farmingdale, NY 11735
Wilson, Luke	Creative Artists Agency	2000 Avenue of The Stars	Beverly Hills, CA 90067
Wilson, Owen	United Talent Agency	9560 Wilshire Blvd #500	Beverly Hills, CA 90212
Wilson, Patrick	Creative Artists Agency	2000 Avenue of The Stars	Beverly Hills, CA 90067
Wilson, Peta	Wolf/Kasteler PR	355 North Maple Drive	Beverly Hills, CA 90210
Wilson, Rita	Creative Artists Agency	2000 Avenue of The Stars	Beverly Hills, CA 90067
Windom, William	Herb Tannen & Assoc.	8370 Wilshire Blvd	Beverly Hills, CA 90211
Winger, Debra	William Morris Agency	One William Morris Place	Beverly Hills, CA 90212
Winkler, Henry	Intl. Creative Mgmt.	10250 Constellation Blvd.	Los Angeles, CA 90067
Winnick, Katheryn	United Talent Agency	9560 Wilshire Blvd	Beverly Hills, CA 90212
Winningham, Mare	IFA Talent Agency	8730 Sunset Blvd #490	Los Angeles, CA 90069
Winslet, Kate	Creative Artists Agency	2000 Avenue of The Stars	Beverly Hills, CA 90067
Winstead, Mary Elizabeth	Paradigm Talent Agency	360 N. Crescent Drive	Beverly Hills, CA 90210
Witherspoon, Reese	Management 360	9111 Wilshire Blvd.	Beverly Hills, CA 90210
Wolf, Scott	Innovative Artists	1505 Tenth Street	Santa Monica, CA 90401
Wong, B.D.	Innovative Artists	1505 Tenth Street	Santa Monica, CA 90401
Wood, Elijah	William Morris Agency	One William Morris Place	Beverly Hills, CA 90212
Wood, Evan Rachel	I/D Public Relations	8409 Santa Monica Blvd.	West Hollywood, CA 90069
Woodard, Alfre	Intl. Creative Mgmt.	10250 Constellation Blvd.	Los Angeles, CA 90067
Woods, James	Intl. Creative Mgmt.	10250 Constellation Blvd.	Los Angeles, CA 90067
Woodward, Joanne	Westport Country Playhouse	P.O. Box 629	Westport, CT 06881
Wopat, Tom	The Agency Group	9348 Civic Center Drive	Beverly Hills, CA 90210
Wright, Bonnie	PDF C/O Ruth Young	Drury House, 34-43 Russell St.	London, WC2B 5HA, UK
Wright, Jeffrey	Creative Artists Agency	2000 Avenue of The Stars	Beverly Hills, CA 90067
Wright-Penn, Robin	Creative Artists Agency	2000 Avenue of The Stars	Beverly Hills, CA 90067
Wyle, Noah	Intl. Creative Mgmt.	10250 Constellation Blvd.	Los Angeles, CA 90067
Wynter, Sarah	Endeavor Talent Agency	9601 Wilshire Blvd. 3rd Floor	Beverly Hills, CA 90212
Yasbeck, Amy	William Morris Agency	One William Morris Place	Beverly Hills, CA 90212
Yeoh, Michelle	Endeavor Talent Agency	9601 Wilshire Blvd. 3rd Floor	Beverly Hills, CA 90212
York, Michael	Innovative Artists	1505 Tenth Street	Santa Monica, CA 90401
Young, Alan	The Tisherman Agency	6767 Forest Lawn Drive	Los Angeles, CA 90068
Young, Dey	Trademark Talent	338½ North Ogden Drive	Los Angeles, CA 90036
Zahn, Steve	Endeavor Talent Agency	9601 Wilshire Blvd. 3rd Floor	Beverly Hills, CA 90212
Zellwegger, Renee	Creative Artists Agency	2000 Avenue of The Stars	Beverly Hills, CA 90067
Zegers, Kevin	Intl. Creative Mgmt.	10250 Constellation Blvd.	Los Angeles, CA 90067
Zerbe, Anthony	Michael K. Stubbs	8695 W. Washington Blvd	Culver City, CA 90232
Zeta-Jones, Catherine	William Morris Agency	One William Morris Place	Beverly Hills, CA 90212
Zhang, Ziyi	William Morris Agency	One William Morris Place	Beverly Hills, CA 90212
Zimbalist, Efrem Jr.	1448 Holsted Drive	Solvang, CA 93463	
Zimbalist, Stephanie	Peter Strain & Associates	5455 Wilshire Blvd	Los Angeles, CA 90036

Title	James Bond	Leading Actress	Character	Director	Year
Dr. No	Sean Connery	Ursula Andress	Honey Ryder	Terence Young	1962
From Russia With Love	Sean Connery	Daniela Bianchi	Tatiana	Terence Young	1963
Goldfinger	Sean Connery	Honor Blackman	Pussy Galore	Guy Hamilton	1964
Thunderball	Sean Connery	Luciana Paluzzi	Fiona Volpe	Terence Young	1965
Casino Royale	David Niven	Ursula Andress	Vesper Lynd	Val Guest	1967
You Only Live Twice	Sean Connery	Mia Hama	Kissy Suzuski	Lewis Gilbert	1967
On Her Majesty's Secret Service	George Lazenby	Diana Rigg	Tracy Draco	Peter R. Hunt	1969
Diamonds Are Forever	Sean Connery	Jill St. John	Tiffany Case	Guy Hamilton	1971
Live And Let Die	Roger Moore	Jane Seymour	Solitaire	Guy Hamilton	1973
The Man With The Golden Gun	Roger Moore	Britt Eklund	MaryGoodnight	Guy Hamilton	1974
The Spy Who Loved Me	Roger Moore	Barbara Bach	Anya Amasova	Lewis Gilbert	1977
Moonraker	Roger Moore	Lois Chiles	Dr Goodhead	Lewis Gilbert	1979
For Your Eyes Only	Roger Moore	Carol Bouquet	Melina Havelock	John Glen	1981
Octopussy	Roger Moore	Maud Adams	Octopussy	John Glen	1983
Never Say Never Again	Sean Connery	Barbara Carrera	Fatima Blush	Irvin Kershner	1984
A View To Kill	Roger Moore	Grace Jones		John Glen	1985
The Living Daylights	Timothy Dalton	Maryam D'abo	Kara Milovy	John Glen	1987
License To Kill	Timothy Dalton	Talisa Sota	Lupe	John Glen	1989
Golden Eye	Pierce Brosnan	Izabella Scorupco	Natalya	Martin Campell	1996
Tomorrow Never Dies	Pierce Brosnan	Michelle Yeoh	Wai Lin	R.Spottiswoode	1997
World Is Not Enough	Pierce Brosnan	Sophie Marceau	Elektra King	Micheal Apted	1999
Die Another Day	Pierce Brosnan	Halle Berry	Jinx Johnson	Lee Tamahori	2002
Casino Royale	Daniel Craig	Eva Green	Vesper Lynd	Martin Campbell	2006

Adams, Maud	Bondstars.com	Pinewood Studios	Iver Heath, BUCKS SL0 0NH UK
Andress, Ursula	C/O IPO	Via F. Siacco 38	1-009197 Rome, Italy
Atkinson, Rowan	PBJ Mgmt Ltd.	7 Soho Square	LondonW1D 3DQ UK
Auger, Claudine	Artmedia	20 avenue Rapp	75008 Paris, France
Bach, Barbara	La Rocca Bella	14 Ave Princess Grace	Monte Carlo, Monoca
Baker, George	Intl. Creative Mgmt.	76 Oxford Street	London W1N 0AX UK
Baker, Joe Don	The Artists Agency	1180 S. Beverly Dr.	Los Angeles, CA 90035
Barnes, Priscilla	AKA Talent Agency	6310 San Vicente Blvd.	Los Angeles, CA 90048
Basinger, Kim	Wolf Kasteler PR	355 North Maple Dr.	Beverly Hills, CA 90210
Bassey, Shirley	24 Ave. Princess Grace	Monte Carlo, Monaco	
Bean, Sean	Rogers & Cowan PR	8687 Melrose Avenue	Los Angeles, CA 90069
Berkoff, Steven	Qvoice Talent Agency	8 King Street-Covent Garden	LondonWC2E 8HN UK
Beswicke, Martine	131 S. Sycamore Ave	Los Angeles, CA 90036	
Blackman, Honor	Qvoice Talent Agency	8 King Street-Covent Garden	LondonWC2E 8HN UK
Blake, Teresa	Stonne Manners Agcy.	8091 Selma Ave	Los Angeles, CA 90046
Bliss, Caroline	PFD Drury House	34-43 Russell St	London, WC2B 5HA UK
Bond, Samantha	Innovative Artists	1505 10th Street	Santa Monica, CA 90401
Bouquet, Carole	Intl. Creative Mgmt.	10250 Constellation Blvd.	Los Angeles, CA 90067
Brosnan, Pierce	Irish Dream Time	3110 Main St., Ste 200	Santa Monica, CA 90405
Carrera, Barbara	Alan David Management	8840 Wilshire Blvd., Ste. 200	Beverly Hills, CA 90211
Castalda, Jean-Pierre	Cineart	36 Rue De Ponthieu	75008 Paris France
Chiles, Lois	Abrams Artists Agency	9200 Sunset Blvd 11th Floor	Los Angeles CA 90067
Chin, Tsai	PFD 503/4 The Chambers	Chelsea Harbor, Lots Rd.	London SW10 0XF UK
Cleese, John	Creative Artists Agency	2000 Avenue Of The Stars	Los Angeles, CA 90067
Coltrane, Robbie	William Morris Agency	One William Morris Place	Beverly Hills, CA 90212
Connery, Sean	Nancy Seltzer & Associates	6220 Del Valle Drive	Los Angeles, CA 90048
Craig, Daniel	Creative Artists Agency	2000 Avenue Of The Stars	Los Angeles, CA 90067
Cumming, Alan	Creative Artists Agency	2000 Avenue Of The Stars	Los Angeles, CA 90067
D'Abo, Maryam	The Gage Group	450 Seventh Ave	New York, NY 10123
Dalton, Timothy	Intl. Creative Mgmt.	10250 Constellation Blvd.	Los Angeles, CA 90067
Dance, Charles	Intl. Creative Mgmt.	10250 Constellation Blvd.	Los Angeles, CA 90067
Davi, Robert	Stonne Manners Agcy.	6500 Wilshire Blvd	Los Angeles, CA 90048
Davies, John Rhys	Emptage Hallett	24 Poland Street	London, W1F 8QL UK
De Souza, Edward	8 Berkeley Road	London SW13 9LZ	England
Dean, Jimmy	# 210A	28035 Dorothy Drive	Agoura, CA 91301
Del Toro, Benicio	PMK/HBH	161 6th Ave.	New York, NY 10013

Dench, Judi	Julian Belfrage Assoc.	14 New Burlington St.	London W1S 3BQ UK
Doody, Alison	Julian Belfrage Assoc.	14 New Burlington St.	London W1S 3BQ UK
Driver, Minnie	Special Artists Agency	9465 Wilshire Blvd	Beverly Hills, CA 90212
Eaton, Shirley	Guild House	Upper St. Martin's Ln.	London WC2H 9EG UK
Ekland, Britt	Cohen/Thomas Mgmt.	1888 N. Crescent Hghts Blvd	Los Angeles, CA 90069
Fullerton, Fiona	London Mgmt.	2/4 Noel Street	London W1V 3RN UK
Gayson, Eunice	Spotlight	7 Leicester Pl.	London WC2H 7BP, UK
Gee, Prunella	MLPM	11 Southwick Mews	London W2 1JG, UK
Glover, Bruce	11449 Woodbine Street	Los Angeles, CA 90066	
Glover, Julian	Conway van Gelder	18-21 Jermyn Street	London SW1Y 6HP UK
Gordon, Serena	Cassie Mayer & Associates	5 Old Garden House	London SW11 3AD UK
Gray, Charles	2-4 Noel Street	London W1V 3RB	England
Hanley, Jenny	MBA Theatrical Agency	62 Grafton Way	London W1P 5LB UK
Hatcher, Terri	Special Artists Agency	9465 Wilshire Blvd	Beverly Hills, CA 90212
Hedison, David	PO Box 1470	Beverly Hills, CA 90213	
Hendry, Gloria	c/o Moss	733 N. Seward St. #PH	Los Angeles, CA 90038
Holder, Geoffrey	565 Broadway	New York, NY 10012	
Hollis, John	1a Shepperton House	Shepperton Road	London N1 30F, UK
James, Clifton	95 Buttonwood Drive	Dix Hills, NY 11746	
Janssen, Famke	ID Public Relations	8409 Santa Monica Blvd	West Hollywood, CA 90069
John, Gottfried	Conway van Gelder	18-21 Jermyn Street	London SW1Y 6HP
Johnson, Lynn-Holly	c/o Cavaleri	178 S. Victory Blvd. #205	Burbank, CA 91502
Jones, Grace	Central Entertainment	485 Madison Ave 21st floor	New York, NY 10022
Jourdan, Louis	1139 Maybrook	Beverly Hills, CA 90210	
Karyo, Tcheky	c/o Artmedia	20 avenue Rapp	75008 Paris, France
Keen, Geoffrey	50 Lock Road Ham.	Richmond	Surrey TW10 7LN, UK
Kiel, Richard	The Stevens Group	14011 Ventura Blvd	Sherman Oaks, CA 91423
Kotto, Yaphet	Diverse Talent Group	1875 Century Park E.	Los Angeles, CA 90067
Krabbe, Jeroen	Conway van Gelder	18-21 Jermyn Street	London SW1Y 6HP
Kwouk, Burt	Berlin Associates	14 Floral St	London WC2E 9DH UK
Lazenby, George	Hervey/Grimes Talent Agcy	10561 Missouri Ave	Los Angeles, CA 90025
Lee, Chris	c/o London Mgmt.	Noel House 2-4 Noel Street	London W1V 3RB, UK
Lee, Christopher	Intl. Creative Mgmt.	76 Oxford St.	London W1D 1BS UK
Leon, Valerie	Barry Burnett Grafton House	2-3 Golden Square #42-43	London W1R 3AD, UK
Locke, Philip	Conway, Robinson	18/21 Jermyn Street	London SW1Y 6HP UK
Lonsdale, Michael	Agence I. Kloucowski	16 Ru De Breteuil	75007 Paris France
Lowell, Carey	Barking Dog Entertainment	9 Desbrosses St.	New York, NY 10013

Lumley, Joanna	Intl. Creative Mgmt.	10250 Constellation Blvd.	Los Angeles, CA 90067
Lundgren, Dolph	Intl. Creative Mgmt.	10250 Constellation Blvd.	Los Angeles, CA 90067
MacNee, Patrick	PO Box 1685	Palm Springs, CA 90263	
Malik, Art	PFD	Drury House, 34-43 Russell St	London, WC2B 5HA UK
Marceau, Sophie	Intl. Creative Mgmt.	10250 Constellation Blvd.	Los Angeles, CA 90067
Maxwell, Lois	# 200	150 Carlton Street	Toronto, Ontario M5K 2E1
Moore, Roger	Diamond Management	31 Percy Street	London, W1T 2DD UK
Munro, Caroline	123B Hollydale Road	London SE15 2TF	England
Newton, Wayne	William Morris Agency	One William Morris Place	Beverly Hills, CA 90212
Palmer, Geoffrey	Conway van Gelder	18-21 Jermyn Street	LondonSW1Y 6HP
Price, Jonathan	Endeavor Talent Agency	9601 Wilshire Blvd.	Beverly Hills, CA 90210
Ravalec, Blanche	c/o Babette Pouget	6 Sq. Villaret de Joyeuse	75017 Paris, France
Richards, Denise Lee	The Gersh Agency	232 N. Canon Drive	Beverly Hills, CA 90210
Rigby, Terence	Emptage Hallett	24 Poland St.	LondonW1F 8QL
Rigg, Dame Dianna	Yakety Yak	8 Bloomsbury Square	LondonWC1A 2NE UK
Roberts, Tanya	Jay D. Schwartz	3151 Cahuenga Blvd W	Los Angeles, CA 90068
Schell, Catherine	Postfach 800504	Koln D-51005, Germany	
Scorupco, Izabella	Station 3	8522 National Blvd.	Culver City, CA 90232
Scoular, Angela	Hobson's International	62 Chiswick High Road	LondonW4 1SY UK
Seymour, Jane	Guttman Associates	118 S. Beverly Dr.	Beverly Hills, CA 90212
Smith, Madeline	Sunbury Island	Sunbury on Thames	Middlesex, England
Soto, Talisa	Agency For The Arts	9200 Sunset Blvd	Los Angeles, CA 90069
St. John, Jill	C/O Borinstein/Oreck	8271 Melrose Ave	Los Angeles, CA 90046
Stroud, John	1347 Gates Ave.	Manhattan Beach, CA 90266-6907	
Terry, John	25 W. 5200 North	Park City, UT 84098-6003	
Thomsen, Cecilie	Special Artists Agency	9465 Wilshire Blvd	Beverly Hills, CA 90212
Tiek Oh, Soon	Conan Carroll Associates	11350 Ventura Blvd.	Studio City, CA 91640
Vanner, Sue	Malone & Knight	26 Wellesley Rd.Cheswick	London W4 4BN, UK
Von Sydow, Max	Paradigm Talent Agency	500 5th Ave.	New York, NY 10110
Walken, Christopher	ID Public Relations	155 Spring St.	New York, NY 10012
Wallace, Julie	Annette Stone & Assoc	9 Newburgh Street	London W1V 1LH UK
Wilmer, Douglas	Belfrage	46 Albermarle Street	London W1X 4PP, UK
Wiseman, Joseph	c/o ICM	40 W. 57th St.	New York, NY 10019
Wisniewski, Andreas	c/o The Gage Group	9255 Sunset Blvd. #515	Los Angeles, CA 90069
Wood, Lana	TRC Entertainment	8424 A Santa Monica Blvd	West Hollywood, CA 90069
Yeoh, Michelle	Endeavor Talent Agency	9601 Wilshire Blvd	Beverly Hills, CA 90212
Zerbe, Anthony	1175 High Road	Santa Barbara, CA 93150	

Baker, Simon	Intl. Creative Mgmt.	10250 Constellation Blvd.	Beverly Hills, CA 90067
Bana, Eric	William Morris Agency	One William Morris Place	Beverly Hills, CA 90212
Blanchett, Cate	Creative Artists Agency	2000 Avenue Of The Stars	Los Angeles, CA 90067
Castle-Hughes, Keisha	Endeavor Talent Agency	9601 Wilshire Blvd.	Beverly Hills, CA 90210
Collette, Toni	Endeavor Talent Agency	9601 Wilshire Blvd.	Beverly Hills, CA 90210
Crowe, Russell	William Morris Agency	One William Morris Place	Beverly Hills, CA 90212
de Rossi, Portia	Intl. Creative Mgmt.	10250 Constellation Blvd.	Beverly Hills, CA 90067
Fisher, Isla	Creative Artists Agency	2000 Avenue Of The Stars	Los Angeles, CA 90067
Furness, Deborah-Lee	Endeavor Talent Agency	9601 Wilshire Blvd.	Beverly Hills, CA 90210
Gibson, Mel	Rogers & Cowan PR	8687 Melrose Avenue	Los Angeles, CA 90069
Griffiths, Rachel	ID Public Relations	8409 Santa Monica Blvd.	West Hollywood, CA 90069
Hogan, Paul	Creative Artists Agency	2000 Avenue Of The Stars	Los Angeles, CA 90067
Hunter, Rachel	Ford Model Agency	8826 Burton Way	Beverly Hills, CA 90211
Jackman, Hugh	Rogers & Cowan PR	8687 Melrose Avenue	Los Angeles, CA 90069
Kwanten, Ryan	Creative Artists Agency	2000 Avenue Of The Stars	Los Angeles, CA 90067
Lawless, Lucy	Endeavor Talent Agency	9601 Wilshire Blvd.	Beverly Hills, CA 90210
McMahon, Julian	Creative Artists Agency	2000 Avenue Of The Stars	Los Angeles, CA 90067
Minoque, Kylie	Primary Talent Intertnational	2-12 Pentonville Rd.	London N1 9PL UK
Monk, Sophie	Agency for Performing Arts	405 S. Beverly Dr.	Beverly Hills, CA 90212
Pearce, Guy	Creative Artists Agency	2000 Avenue Of The Stars	Los Angeles, CA 90067
Rigg, Rebecca	Endeavor Talent Agency	9601 Wilshire Blvd.	Beverly Hills, CA 90210
Roxburgh, Richard	Intl. Creative Mgmt.	10250 Constellation Blvd.	Beverly Hills, CA 90067
Rush, Geoffrey	Creative Artists Agency	2000 Avenue Of The Stars	Los Angeles, CA 90067
Urban, Karl	Auckland Actors	PO Box 56-460 Dominion Rd	Auckland, New Zealand
Watts, Naomi	Creative Artists Agency	2000 Avenue Of The Stars	Los Angeles, CA 90067
Weaving, Hugo	Intl. Creative Mgmt.	10250 Constellation Blvd.	Beverly Hills, CA 90067
Wenhem, David	Endeavor Talent Agency	9601 Wilshire Blvd.	Beverly Hills, CA 90210
Wilson, Peta	Wolf Kasteler Public Relations	355 North Maple Dr.	Beverly Hills, CA 90210

Alexis, Kim	PMK	2219 West Olive	Burbank, CA 91506
Alt, Carol	Metropolitan Talent	4526 Wilshire Blvd	Los Angeles, CA 90010
Alves, Michele	Marilyns	601 Norwalk St	Greensboro, NC 27407
Ambrosio, Alessandra	Elite Modeling	111 East 22nd Street	New York, NY 10010
Banks, Tyra	Paradigm Talent Agency	10100 Santa Monica Blvd	Los Angeles, CA 90067
Barros, Ana Beatriz	Women	199 Lafayette	New York, NY 10012
Benitez, Elsa	Elite Modeling	111 East 22nd Street	New York, NY 10010
Brinkley, Christie	William Morris Agency	One William Morris Place	Beverly Hills, CA 90212
Bundchen, Gisele	IMG Models	304 Park Avenue South	New York, NY 10010
Campbell, Naomi	Intl. Creative Mgmt.	8942 Wilshire Blvd	Beverly Hills, CA 90211
Casta, Laetitia	Artmédia	10 avenue George-V	75008 Paris, France
Crawford, Cindy	William Morris Agency	One William Morris Place	Beverly Hills, CA 90212
Diaz, Yamila	Next Models	23 Watts St., 6th floor	New York, NY 10013
Driegen, Dewi	Elite Modeling	111 East 22nd Street	New York, NY 10010
Dvoncova, Denisa	Elite Modeling	111 East 22nd Street	New York, NY 10010
Fontana, Isabeli	Women	199 Lafayette	New York, NY 10012
Hall, Bridget	IMG Models	304 Park Avenue South	New York, NY 10010
Herzigova, Eva	1 Management	424 W. Broadway	New York, NY
Hunter, Rachel	Ford Model Agency	344 E 59th St.	New York, NY 10022
Ireland, Kathy	William Morris Agency	One William Morris Place	Beverly Hills, CA 90212
Jeinsen, Elke	311 N. Robertson Blvd	Beverly Hills, CA 90211	
Kass, Carmen	Women	199 Lafayette	New York, NY 10012
Kebebe, Liya	IMG Models	304 Park Avenue South	New York, NY 10010
Kirseborn, Vendela	William Morris Agency	One William Morris Place	Beverly Hills, CA 90212
Klum, Heidi	IMG Models	304 Park Avenue South	New York, NY 10010
Kurkova, Karolina	DNA Model Mgmt	520 Broadway	New York, NY 10012
Lindner, Pernilla	Elite Modeling	111 East 22nd Street	New York, NY 10010
Lindvall, Angela	IMG Models	304 Park Avenue South	New York, NY 10010
MacPherson, Elle	Click Modeling Agency	129 W. 27th Penthouse	Manhattan, NY 10001
Mazza, Valerie	Elite Modeling	111 East 22nd Street	New York, NY 10010
Montana, Ashley	Ford Model Agency	344 E 59th St.	New York, NY 10022
Moss, Kate	IMG Models	304 Park Avenue South	New York, NY 10010
Mulder, Karen	Elite Modeling	111 East 22nd Street	New York, NY 10010
Nemcova, Petra	Next Models	23 Watts St., 6th floor	New York, NY 10013
Pestova, Daniela	Next Models	23 Watts St., 6th floor	New York, NY 10013
Peterson, Cristel Winther	Elite Modeling	111 East 22nd Street	New York, NY 10010
Porizkova, Paulina	Creative Artists Agency	9830 Wilshire Blvd	Beverly Hills, CA 90212
Rayder, Frankie	Women	199 Lafayette	New York, NY 10012
Romijn-Stamos, Rebecca	William Morris Agency	One William Morris Place	Beverly Hills, CA 90212
Ryan, Chanel	7095 Hollywood Blvd	Hollywood, CA 90028	
Schiffer, Claudia	United Talent Agency	9560 Wilshire Blvd	Beverly Hills, CA 90212
Seymore, Stephanie	Ford Model Agency	344 E 59th St.	New York, NY 10022
Sims, Molly	Next Models	23 Watts St., 6th floor	New York, NY 10013
Tavares, Fernada	Marilyns	601 Norwalk St	Greensboro, NC 27407
Thom, Ashley	STX Productions E-303	24881 Alicia Pkwy	Laguna Hills, CA 92653
Turlington, Christy	United Talent Agency	9560 Wilshire Blvd	Beverly Hills, CA 90212
Velasquez, Patricia	Ford Model Agency	344 E 59th St.	New York, NY 10022
Wheeler, Jacquetta	IMG Models	304 Park Avenue South	New York, NY 10010
Williams, Roshumba	N.S. Bienstock, Inc.	1740 Broadway	New York, NY 10019

Comedians

Allen, Marty	PO Box 929	Beverly Hills, CA 90213	
Allen, Tim	William Morris Agency	One William Morris Place	Beverly Hills, CA 90212
Altman, Jeff	Richard De La Font Agency	4845 South Sheridan Rd	Tulsa, OK 74145
Anderson, Louie	Richard De La Font Agency	4845 South Sheridan Rd	Tulsa, OK 74145
Arnold, Tom	Brillstein-Grey Entertainment	9150 Wilshire Blvd	Beverly Hills, CA 90212
Aykroyd, Dan	Creative Artists Agency	2000 Avenue of the Stars	Beverly Hills, CA 90212
Balan, Michele	Roberson Public Relations	8899 Beverly Blvd.. Ste. 616	West Hollywood, CA 90048
Ballantine, Carl	Stage 9 Management	1249 North Lodi Place	Hollywood, CA 90038
Belushi, James	Intl. Creative Mgmt.	10250 Constellation Blvd.	Los Angeles, CA 90067
Berman, Shelly	APA Talent Agency	405 S. Beverly Dr.	Beverly Hills, CA 90212
Bernhard, Sandra	William Morris Agency	One William Morris Place	Beverly Hills, CA 90212
Black, Lewis	APA Talent Agency	405 S. Beverly Dr.	Beverly Hills, CA 90212
Boosler, Elayne	The Gersh Agency	232 North Canon Drive	Beverly Hills, CA 90210
Brenner, David	Jonas Public Relations	240 26th Street, Suite 3	Santa Monica, CA 90402
Brooks, Albert	William Morris Agency	One William Morris Place	Beverly Hills, CA 90212
Brooks, Mel	Brooksfilms	9336 W. Washington Blvd	Culver City, CA 90232
Burnett, Carol	Intl. Creative Mgmt.	10250 Constellation Blvd.	Los Angeles, CA 90067
Butler, Brett	William Morris Agency	One William Morris Place	Beverly Hills, CA 90212
Buzzi, Ruth	Amsel, Eisenstadt & Frazier	5055 Wilshire Blvd.	Los Angeles, CA 90036
Byner, John	Richard De La Font Agency	4845 S. Sheridan Rd.	Tulsa, OK 74145
Caesar, Sid	1910 Loma Vista Drive	Beverly Hills, CA 90210	
Carey, Drew	Baker Winokur PR	9100 Wilshire Blvd.	Beverly Hills, CA 90212
Carlin, George	Jonas Public Relations	240 26th Street, Suite 3	Santa Monica, CA 90402
Carrey, Jim	Marleah Leslie & Associates	8370 Wilshire Blvd.	Beverly Hills, CA 90211
Carrot Top	Intl. Creative Mgmt.	10250 Constellation Blvd.	Los Angeles, CA 90067
Carter, Jack	The Cosden Agency	3518 Cahuengo Blvd	Los Angeles, CA 90068
Carvey, Dana	Creative Artists Agency	2000 Avenue of the Stars	Beverly Hills, CA 90212
Chapelle, Dave	The Gersh Agency	232 N. Canon Dr.	Beverly Hills, CA 90210
Chase, Chevy	Innovative Artists	1505 10th Street	Santa Monica, CA 90401
Cho, Margaret	William Morris Agency	One William Morris Place	Beverly Hills, CA 90212
Clay, Andrew Dice	8667 Metz Place	Los Angeles, CA 90069	
Cleese, John	Creative Artists Agency	2000 Avenue of the Stars	Beverly Hills, CA 90212
Conway, Tim	CESD	10635 Santa Monica Blvd.	Los Angeles, CA 90025
Correy, Rebecca	Rebel Entertainment Partners	5700 Wilshire Blvd.	Los Angeles, CA 90036
Cosby, Bill	William Morris Agency	One William Morris Place	Beverly Hills, CA 90212
Crosby, Norm	William Morris Agency	One William Morris Place	Beverly Hills, CA 90212
Crystal, Billy	Intl. Creative Mgmt.	10250 Constellation Blvd.	Los Angeles, CA 90067
Curtain, Jane	Intl. Creative Mgmt.	10250 Constellation Blvd.	Los Angeles, CA 90067
David, Larry	Endeavor Talent Agency	9601 Wilshire Blvd	Beverly Hills, CA 90210
Dana, Bill	PO Box 1792	Santa Monica, CA 90406	
Degeneres, Ellen	Intl. Creative Mgmt.	10250 Constellation Blvd.	Los Angeles, CA 90067
Deluise, Dom	Artists Group, Ltd	3345 Wilshire Blvd	Los Angeles, CA 90010
Diller, Phyllis	CESD	10635 Santa Monica Blvd.	Los Angeles, CA 90025
Einstein, Bob	"Crazy Dave Osborne"	8383 Wilshire Boulevard #500	Beverly Hills, CA 90211

Engvall, Bill	William Morris Agency	One William Morris Place	Beverly Hills, CA 90212
Fey, Tina	Endeavor Talent Agency	9601 Wilshire Blvd	Beverly Hills, CA 90210
Foxworthy, Jeff	Parallel Entertainment	9255 West Sunset Blvd	Los Angeles, CA 90069
Franken, Al	William Morris Agency	One William Morris Place	Beverly Hills, CA 90212
Gallagher, Leo	14984 Roan Court	West Palm Beach, FL	33414
Garofalo, Janeane	Creative Artists Agency	2000 Avenue of the Stars	Los Angeles, CA 90067
Garrett, Brad	William Morris Agency	One William Morris Place	Beverly Hills, CA 90212
Goldberg, Whoopi	Whoop One Ho Productions	375 Greenwich St.	New York, NY 10013
Goldthwait, Bobcat	The Gersh Agency	232 North Canon Drive	Beverly Hills, CA 90210
Gottfried, Gilbert	William Morris Agency	One William Morris Place	Beverly Hills, CA 90212
Hammond, Darrell	Jonas Public Relations	240 26th St.	Santa Monica, CA 90402
Hughley, D.L.	Intl. Creative Mgmt.	10250 Constellation Blvd.	Los Angeles, CA 90067
Idle, Eric	William Morris Agency	One William Morris Place	Beverly Hills, CA 90212
Kaplan, Gabe	9551 Hidden Valley Road	Beverly Hills, CA 90210	
Keaton, Michael	Rogers & Cowan PR	8687 Melrose Avenue	Los Angeles, CA 90069
Kline, Robert	William Morris Agency	One William Morris Place	Beverly Hills, CA 90212
Korman, Harvey	1136 Stradella	Los Angeles, CA 90077	
Larry the Cable Guy	Parallel Entertainment	9255 West Sunset Blvd	Los Angeles, CA 90069
Lawrence, Martin	United Talent Agency	9560 Wilshire Blvd	Beverly Hills, CA 90212
Leno, Jay	The Tonight Show	3000 West Almeda	Burbank, CA 91523
Letterman, David	The Late Show	1697 Broadway 111th Fl.	New York, NY 10019
Lewis, Jerry	Jerry Lewis Films # 816	3160 W. Sahara Avenue	Las Vegas, NV 84102
Lil' JJ	LSPR	12198 Ventura Blvd.	Studio City, CA 91604
Little, Rich	CESD	10635 Santa Monica Blvd.	Los Angeles, CA 90025
Lopez, George	Marleah Leslie & Associates	8370 Wilshire Blvd.	Beverly Hills, CA 90211
Lovitz, Jon	Jonas Public Relations	240 26th Street, Suite 3	Santa Monica, CA 90402
Macdonald, Norm	Brillstein-Grey Entertainment	9150 Wilshire Blvd	Beverly Hills, CA 90212
Martin, Steve	Intl. Creative Mgmt.	10250 Constellation Blvd.	Los Angeles, CA 90067
Mason, Jackie	William Morris Agency	One William Morris Place	Beverly Hills, CA 90212
Meara, Ann	Innovative Artists	1505 10th St	Santa Monica, CA 90401
Mencia, Carlos	Anderson Group PR	8060 Melrose Ave	Los Angeles, CA 90046
Miller, Dennis	Jonas Public Relations	240 26th Street, Suite 3	Santa Monica, CA 90402
Mochrie, Colin	Jonas Public Relations	240 26th Street, Suite 3	Santa Monica, CA 90402
Morris, Garrett	The Agency Group	361-373 City Rd.	LondonEC1V 1PQ UK
Murphy, Eddie	William Morris Agency	One William Morris Place	Beverly Hills, CA 90212
Murray, Bill	Yohalem & Gilman Company	477 Madison Ave	New York, NY 10022
Myers, Mike	CAA- David O'Connor	9830 Wilshire Blvd	Beverly Hills, CA 90212
Nealon, Kevin	Jonas Public Relations	240 26th St.	Santa Monica, CA 90402
Newhart, Bob	Endeavor Talent Agency	9601 Wilshire Blvd	Beverly Hills, CA 90210
Oswalt, Patton	Creative Artists Agency	2000 Avenue of the Stars	Los Angeles, CA 90067
Palin, Michael	Mayday Management	34 Tavistock Street	London, WC2E 7PB, UK
Paulsen, Pat	1551 So. Robertson Blvd	Los Angeles, CA 90035	
Penn (Jillette)	William Morris Agency	One William Morris Place	Beverly Hills, CA 90212
Poundstone, Paula	William Morris Agency	One William Morris Place	Beverly Hills, CA 90212
Proops, Greg	International Artistes Limited	Holborn Hall	LondonWC1V 7BD UK
Reiner, Carl	Creative Artists Agency	2000 Avenue of the Stars	Beverly Hills, CA 90212

Comedians

Reiser, Paul	Nuance Productions	4049 Radford Ave.	Studio City, CA 91604
Reubens, Paul	ID Public Relations	8409 Santa Monica Blvd.	West Hollywood, CA 90069
Rivers, Joan	William Morris Agency	One William Morris Place	Beverly Hills, CA 90212
Rock, Chris	BWR	9100 Wilshire Blvd.	Beverly Hills, CA 90212
Rodriguez, Paul	Intl. Creative Mgmt.	10250 Constellation Blvd.	Los Angeles, CA 90067
Romano, Ray	William Morris Agency	One William Morris Place	Beverly Hills, CA 90212
Roseanne	United Talent Agency	9560 Wilshire Blvd	Beverly Hills, CA 90212
Rudner, Rita	Jonas Public Relations	240 26th St.	Santa Monica, CA 90402
Russell, Mark	Richard De La Font Agency	4845 S. Sheridan Rd.	Tulsa, OK 74145
Saget, Bob	William Morris Agency	One William Morris Place	Beverly Hills, CA 90212
Sahl, Mort	2325 San Ysidro Drive	Beverly Hills, CA 90210	
Sandler, Adam	Happy Madison Productions	10202 W. Washington Blvd	Culver City, CA 90232
Seinfeld, Jerry	Shapiro West Associates	141 El Camino Drive	Beverly Hills, CA 90212
Shandling, Garry	Endeavor Talent Agency	9601 Wilshire Blvd	Beverly Hills, CA 90210
Shore, Pauly	Rogers & Cowan PR	8687 Melrose Avenue	Los Angeles, CA 90069
Short, Martin	William Morris Agency	One William Morris Place	Beverly Hills, CA 90212
Silverman, Sarah	BNC Public Relations	8687 Melrose Ave	Los Angeles, CA 90069
Sinbad	Creative Artists Agency	2000 Avenue of the Stars	Beverly Hills, CA 90212
Smirnoff, Yakov	Richard De La Font Agency	4845 S. Sheridan Rd.	Tulsa, OK 74145
Smith, Will	Creative Artists Agency	2000 Avenue of the Stars	Beverly Hills, CA 90212
Smothers, Dick	William Morris Agency	One William Morris Place	Beverly Hills, CA 90212
Smothers, Tom	William Morris Agency	One William Morris Place	Beverly Hills, CA 90212
Soupy Sales	J. Cast Productions	2550 Greenvalley Rd	Los Angeles, CA 90046
Spade, David	Endeavor Talent Agency	9601 Wilshire Blvd	Beverly Hills, CA 90210
Stiller, Ben	United Talent Agency	9560 Wilshire Blvd	Beverly Hills, CA 90212
Stiller, Jerry	Paul Kohner, Inc.	9300 Wilshire Blvd	Beverly Hills, CA 90212
Stone, Pam	The Gersh Agency	232 North Canon Drive	Beverly Hills, CA 90210
Taylor, Rip	Schiowitz, Clay & Assoc.	1680 North Vine St	Hollywood, CA 90028
Teller (Raymond)	William Morris Agency	One William Morris Place	Beverly Hills, CA 90212
Tenuta, Judy	warren Cowan & Associates	8899 Beverly Blvd.	Los Angeles, CA 90048
Tomlin, Lilly	William Morris Agency	One William Morris Place	Beverly Hills, CA 90212
Torn, Rip	Guttman Associates	118 S. Beverly Dr.	Beverly Hills, CA 90212
Travalena, Fred	J. Cast Productions	2550 Greenvalley Rd.	Los Angeles, CA 90046
Ullman, Tracey	Endeavor Talent Agency	9601 Wilshire Blvd.	Beverly Hills, CA 90210
Walker, Jimmy	#306	7767 Hollywood Blvd	Los Angeles, CA 90046
Wallace, George	The Gersh Agency	232 North Canon Dr.	Beverly Hills, CA 90210
Wayans, Damon	Cunningham, Escott, Dipene	10635 Santa Monica Blvd	Los Angeles, CA 90025
Wayans, Keenan	William Morris Agency	One William Morris Place	Beverly Hills, CA 90212
Wayans, Marlon	William Morris Agency	One William Morris Place	Beverly Hills, CA 90212
Wayans, Shawn	William Morris Agency	One William Morris Place	Beverly Hills, CA 90212
White, Ron	International Creative Mgmt.	10250 Constellation Blvd.	Los Angeles, CA 90067
Williams, Robin	Creative Artists Agency	2000 Avenue of the Stars	Beverly Hills, CA 90212
Winters, Jonathan	Rebel Entertainment Partners	5700 Wilshire Blvd.	Los Angeles, CA 90036

Adams, Scott	Harper Business	10 East 53rd Street	New York, NY 10022
Aldrich, Lance	Universal Press Syn.	4520 Main Street	Kansas City, MO 64111
Amend, Bill	Universal Press Syndicate	4520 Main Street	Kansas City, MO 64111
Anderson, Brad	United Feature Syn.	200 Madison Ave.	New York, NY 10016
Arriola, Gus	PO Box 3275	Carmel, CA 93521	
Auth, Tony	Philadelphia Inquirer	PO Box 8263	Philadelphia, PA 19101
Basset, Brian	Universal Press Syn.	4520 Main Street	Kansas City, MO 64111
Blake, Bud	PO Box 146	Damariscotta,	ME 04543
Brookins, Gary	Tribune Media Serv.	435 N. Michigan Ave.	Chicago, IL 60611
Browne, Dik	King Features Syn.	235 East 45th Street	New York, NY 10017
Busiek, Kurt	About Comics	217 Red Lane	Thousand Oaks, CA 91320
Chast, Roz	New Yorker Magazine	20 West 43rd Street	New York, NY 10036
Clowes, Daniel	Fantagraphics	7563 Lake City Way	Seattle, WA 98115
Cochran, Tony	Creators Syndicate	5777 W. Century Blvd	Los Angeles, CA 90045
Crumb, R.	Fantagraphics	7563 Lake City Way	Seattle, WA 98115
Davis, Jim	3300 Chadham Lane	Munice, IN 47302	
DeCarlo, Dan	Bongo Comic Group	1440 S. Sepulveda	Los Angeles, CA 90025
Drucker, Mort	C/O Mad Magazine	485 Madison Ave	New York NY 10022
Eisner, Will	Museum of Cartoon Art	201 Plaza Real	Boca Raton, FL 33432
Gary Trudeau	Suite 113	459 Columbus Ave.	New York, NY 10019
Gary, Wise	Universal Press Syn.	4520 Main Street	Kansas City, MO 64111
Gilchrist, Brad	Gilchrist Publishing	PO Box 1194	Canton, CT 06019
Goldberg, Stan	C/O Archie Comics	325 Fayette Ave.	Mamaroneck, NY 10543
Grace, Bud	King Features Syn.	235 East 45th Street	New York, NY 10017
Graham, Alex	Tribune Media Services	435 N. Michigan Ave.	Chicago, IL 60611
Griffith, Bill	King Features Syn.	235 East 45th Street	New York, NY 10017
Groening, Matt	10201 West Pico Blvd.	Los Angeles, CA 90035	
Guisewite, Cathy	Universal Press Syn.	4520 Main Street	Kansas City, MO 64111
Hillenburg, Stephen	Nickelodeon	231 West Olive Avenue	Burbank, CA 91502
Johnston, Lynn	United Feature Syn.	200 Madison Ave.	New York, NY 10016
Katchor, Ben	PO Box 2024	Cathedral Station	New York, NY 10025
Ketchum, Hank	512 Pierce St.	Monterey, CA 93940	
Kimball, Ward	Cartoon Art Museum	814 Mission Street	San Francisco, CA
Lasswell, Fred	1111 N. Westshore Blvd.	Tampa, FL 33607	
Lee, Stan	POW! Entertainment	9440 Santa Monica Blvd	Beverly Hills, CA 90210

Cartoonists

Lee, Vic	King Features Syn.	235 East 45th Street	New York, NY 10017
Locher, Dick	C/O Chicago Tribune	435 No. Michigan Ave	Chicago, IL 60611
Luckovich, Mike	Atlanta Journal	72 Marietta Street NW	Atlanta, GA 30303
Mankoff, Robert	New Yorker Magazine	4 Times Square	New York, NY 10036-6592
Marlette, Doug	Newsday	2 Park Avenue # 601	New York, NY 10016-5679
Matera & Saunders	King Features Syn.	235 East 45th Street	New York, NY 10017
McCoy, Glenn	Universal Press Syn.	4520 Main Street	Kansas City, MO 64111
McCracken, Craig	Cartoon Network	PO Box 7555	Atlanta, GA 30357
McDonnell, Patrick	King Features Syn.	235 East 45th Street	New York, NY 10017
McFarlane, Seth	20th Century TV	PO Box 900	Beverly Hills, CA 90213
McGruder, Aaron	Universal Press Syn.	919 Michigan Ave.	Chicago, IL 60611-1681
Meddick, Jim	United Feature Syn.	200 Madison Ave.	New York, NY 10016
Murphy, John C.	King Features Syn.	235 East 45th Street	New York, NY 10017
O'Hare, Mark	Universal Press Syn.	4520 Main Street	Kansas City, MO 64111
Parker & Hart	Creators Syndicate	5777 W. Century Blvd	Los Angeles, CA 90045
Parker, Trey	William Morris Agcy.	151 El Camino	Beverly Hills, CA 90212
Pekar, Harvey	3061 E. Overlook Road	Cleveland, OH 44118	
Pett, Mark	Creators Syndicate	5777 W. Century Blvd	Los Angeles, CA 90045
Piraro, Dan	Universal Press Syn.	4520 Main Street	Kansas City, MO 64111
Price, Hilary B.	King Features Syn.	235 East 45th Street	New York, NY 10017
Rosa, Don	Cartoon Art Museum	814 Mission Street	San Francisco, CA
Stantis, Scott	United Feature Syn.	200 Madison Ave.	New York, NY 10016
Stanton, Andrew	Pixar Studios	1200 Park Avenue	Emeryville, CA 94608
Stone, Matt	William Morris Agcy.	151 El Camino	Beverly Hills, CA 90212
Thaves, Bob	United Feature Syn.	200 Madison Ave.	New York, NY 10016
Toles, Tom	United Media	200 Madison Avenue	New York, NY 10016-5679
Tomorrow, Tom	Village Voice	36 Copper Square	New York, NY 10003
Toomey, Jim	King Features Syn.	235 East 45th Street	New York, NY 10017
Trudeau, Gary	Suite 200	459 Columbus Avenue	New York, NY 10024
Turner, Morrie	Cartoon Art Museum	814 Mission Street	San Francisco, CA
Wagner, Fred	No. American Synd.	235 45th Street	New York, NY 10017
Wagner, John	Universal Press Synd.	4520 Main Street	Kansas City, MO 64111
Walker, Mort	King Features 2nd Floor	888 7th Avenue	New York, NY 10019
Watterson, Bill	Andrews & Mcmeel	4520 Main Street	Kansas City, MO 64111
Wright, Will	Electronic Arts	209 Redwood Shores	Redwood, CA 94065

Albee, Edward	William Morris Agency	One William Morris Place	Beverly Hills, CA 90212
Albom, Mitch	Detroit Free Press	321 Lafayette	Detroit, MI 48226
Angelou, Maya	C/O Random House	201 East 50th Street	New York, NY 10022
Archer, Jeffrey	The Old Vicarage	Grantchester	Cambridge, England
Babbitt, Natalie	Childrens Marketing	Farrar, Straus & Giroux	19 Union Street
Benchley, Peter	35 Boudinot Street	Princeton, NJ 08540	
Benson, Milred	Blade	541 Superior Street	Toledo, OH 43660
Berendt, John	William Morris Agency	One William Morris Place	Beverly Hills, CA 90212
Berg, A. Scott	Creative Artists Agency	9830 Wilshire Blvd.	Beverly Hills, CA 90212
Blume, Judy	Harold Ober Assoc.	425 Madison Avenue	New York, NY 10017
Bly, Robert	308 First Street	Moose Lake, MN 55767	
Bradbury, Brad	Harold Matson Co.	276 5th Avenue	New York, NY 10010
Bradbury, Ray	10265 Cheviot Drive	Los Angeles, CA 90064	
Bradlee, Ben	C/O The Washington Post	Washington, DC 20071	
Bradshaw, John	1776 Yorktown	Houston, TX 77056	
Brooks, David	New York Times	229 West 43rd Street	New York, NY 10036
Brown, Dan	Doubleday Broadway Pub.	1745 Broadway	New York, NY 10019
Brown, Sandra	1000 North Bowden	Arlington, TX 76012	
Buckley, William F. Jr.	150 East 35th Street	New York, NY 10016	
Cambell, Bebe Moore	WMA- C/O Beth Swofford	151 El Camino	Beverly Hills, CA 90212
Cameron, Julie	Charter Books	200 Madison Avenue	New York, NY 10016
Chehak, Susan T.	Carol Abel	160 West 87th Street	New York, NY 10024
Clancy, Tom	PO Box 800	Huntington, MD 20639	
Clark, Mary H.	Mcintosh & Otis Inc.	475 5th Avenue	New York, NY 10017
Clarke, Richard	c/o Bruce Nichols	Simon & Schuster	1230 Avenue of the Americas
Collins, Jackie	Block-Korenbrot PR	110 S. Fairfax, Ste. 310	Los Angeles, CA 90036
Cometbus, Aaron	PO Box 4726	Berkeley, CA 94704	
Cornwell, Patricia	P. Cornwell Enterprise	PO Box 35686	Richmond, VA 23235
Coulter, Ann	Crown Publishing	280 Park Avenue	New York, NY 10017
Covey, Stephen	3507 N. University Ave.	Provo, UT 84606	
Crichton, Michael	Janklow and Nesbit Assoc	598 Madison Ave	New York, NY 10022
D'Souza, Dinesh	Hoover Institution	Stanford University	Stanford, CA 94305-6010
Desai, Kiran	Grove/Atlantic	841 Broadway	New York, NY 10003
Deutsch, Linda	Associated Press	221 South Figueroa Street	Los Angeles, CA 90012
Dickinson, Amy	Chicago Tribune "Ask Amy"	435 N. Michigan Avenue	Chicago, IL 60611
Dobson, James C.	James Dobson Inc.	1755 Telstar Drive	Colrado Springs, CO 80920
Drudge, Matt	Fox Channel News	1211 Ave of America	New York, NY 10036
Dyer, Wayne	50 Nohea Kai Drive	Lahaina, HI 96761-1943	
Ethan Coen	United Talent Agency	9560 Wilshire Blvd	Beverly Hills, CA 90212
Flynn, Vince	Atria Books - David Brown	1230 Avenue of the Americas	New York, NY 10022
Flynt, Larry	Larry Flynt Publishing	8484 Wilshire Blvd	Beverly Hills, CA 90211
Follett, Ken	PO Box 4, Knebworth	Hertfordshire SG3 6PT UK	
Foote, Horton	95 Horatio Street	New York, NY 10014	
Frazier, Charles	International Creative Mgmt.	8942 Wilshire Blvd.	Beverly Hills, CA 90211-1934
Friedman, Thomas	The New York Times	1627 I St. NW	Washington, DC 20006

Authors

George, Elizabeth	C/O Random House	1540 Broadway	New York, NY 10036
Gladwell, Malcolm	The New Yorker Magazine	4 Times Square	New York, NY 10036-6592
Godwin, Gail	C/O Ballintine Books	201 East 50th Street	New York, NY 10022
Goldman, William	William Morris Agency	One William Morris Place	Beverly Hills, CA 90212
Goodwin, Doris	Simon & Schuster	1230 Ave. of America	New York, NY 10020
Grisham, John	Writers Artists Agency	924 Westwood Blvd	Los Angeles, CA 90024
Hancock, Graham	Penguin Books	80 Strand	London WC2 ORL, England
Harris, Thomas	C/O Doubleday Publicity	1540 Broadway	New York, NY 10036
Hooks, Bell	291 West 12th Street	New York, NY 10014	
Irving, John	The Turnbull Agency	PO Box 757	Dorset, VT 05251
Kadohata, Cynthia	Simon&Schuster	1230 Avenue of the Americas	New York, NY 10020
Karon, Jan	Viking Publicity	375 Hudson Street	New York, NY 10014
Keillor, Garrison	45 East 7th Street	St. Paul, MN 55443	
Kellerman, Faye	Barney Karpfinger	500 5th Avenue	New York, NY 10110
Kelly, Tim	8730 Lookout Mountain	West Hollywood, CA 90046	
King, Stephen	49 Florida Ave	Bangor, MA 04401-3005	
Koontz, Dean	PO Box 9529	Newport Beach,	CA 92658
Krantz, Judith	Bantam Books	666 5th Avenue	New York, NY 10103
Lamb, Wally	63 Lewiston Avenue	Willimantic, CT 06226	
Least Heat-Moon, William	William Trogdon	8401 S Old Plank Road	Columbia, MO 65203-8720
Lecarre, John	Alfred A. Knopf Inc.	201 E. 50th Street	New York, NY 10022
Leonard, Elmore	2192 Yarmouth Road	Bloomfield Village, MI 48301	
Mailer, Norman	142 Columbia Rd	Brooklyn, NY 11201	
Mamet, David	Pantheon Books	201 East 50th Street	New York, NY 10022
Martin, George	Bantam Books	1745 Broadway	New York, NY 10019
McMurtry, Larry	PO Box 552	Archer City, TX 76351	
Morrison, Toni	ICM c/o Amanda Urban	40 West 57th Street	New York, NY 10019
Naifeh, Steven	Woodward, White Inc.	129 1st Ave S.W.	Aiken, SC 29801
Piers, Anthony	PO Box 2289	Inverness, FL 33451-2289	
Rice, Anne	1239 First Street	New Orleans, LA 70130	
Rowling, J.K.	C/O Scholastic	555 Broadway	New York, NY 10012
Salinger, J.D.	RR 3 Box 176	Cornishflat, NH 03746	
Schapiro, Miriam	Steinbaum Kraus	3550 N. Miami Avenue	Miami, FL 33127
Seddons, Ann Richards	Harper Collins Author Mail	10 East 53rd Street	New York, NY 10022-5244
Shashi Tharoor	Arcade Publishing	141 Fifth Avenue	New York, NY 10010
Shriver, Lionel	Scovil, Chicak & Galen	12 West 19th Street	New York, NY 10013
Shyamalan, M. Night	United Talent Agency	9560 Wilshire Blvd #500	Beverly Hills, CA 90212
Simon, Neal	10745 Chalon Rd.	Los Angeles, CA 90077	
Smith, Gregory	Woodward, White Inc.	129 1st Ave SW	Aiken, SC 29801
Steel, Danielle	Dell Publishing Co.	1540 Broadway	New York, NY 10036
Styron, William	R.F.D.	Roxbury, CT 06783	
Updike, John	675 Hale Street	Beverly Farms, MA 01915	
Von Furstenberg, Diane	Simon & Schuster	1230 Ave. of the Americas	New York, NY 10020
Walker, Alice	Harcourt, Brace	1250 6th Avenue	San Diego, CA 92101

Directors & Producers

Apted, Michael	Creative Artists Agency	2000 Avenue Of The Stars	Los Angeles, CA 90067
Arad, Avi	Marvel Studios	9242 Beverly Boulevard	Beverly Hills, CA 90210
Barris, Chuck	Carroll Graf Publishers	245 W. 17th Street	New York, NY 10011-5300
Bochco, Steven	Steven Bochco Productions	3000 Olympic Blvd.	Santa Monica, CA 90404
Bogdonovich, Peter	N2N Talent Agency	1230 Montana Ave.	Santa Monica, CA 90403
Bruckheimer, Jerry	Jerry Bruckheimer Films	1631 Tenth Street	Santa Monica, CA 90404
Burnett, Mark	Mark Burnett Productions	640 N Sepulveda Blvd	Los Angeles, CA 90049
Burrows, James	International Creative Mgmt.	10250 Constellation Blvd.	Los Angeles, CA 90067
Burton, Tim	William Morris Agency	One William Morris Place	Beverly Hills, CA 90212
Cannel, Steven J.	Creative Artists Agency	2000 Avenue Of The Stars	Los Angeles, CA 90067
Carpenter, John	William Morris Agency	One William Morris Place	Beverly Hills, CA 90212
Chase, David	United Talent Agency	9560 Wilshire Blvd.	Beverly Hills, CA 90212
Cimino, Michael	WWBCG&E	9665 Wilshire Blvd.	Beverly Hills, CA 90210
Coen, Joel	United Talent Agency	9560 Wilshire Blvd	Beverly Hills, CA 90212
Columbus, Chris	Creative Artists Agency	2000 Avenue Of The Stars	Los Angeles, CA 90067
Coppola, Francis Ford	American Zeotrope	6747 Milner Rd.	Los Angeles, CA 90068
Coppola, Sofia	Creative Artists Agency	2000 Avenue Of The Stars	Los Angeles, CA 90067
David, Larry	Endeavor Talent Agency	9601 Wilshire Blvd.	Beverly Hills, CA 90210
Doden, Stanley	Creative Artists Agency	2000 Avenue Of The Stars	Los Angeles, CA 90067
Gaghan, Stephen	William Morris Agency	One William Morris Place	Beverly Hills, CA 90212
Griffin, Merv	Merv Griffin Entertainment	130 S. El Camino Drive	Beverly Hills, CA 90212
Haggis, Paul	Paul Haggis Productions	9200 Sunset Blvd., Ste. 820	Los Angeles, CA 90069
Hallstrom, Lasse	Creative Artists Agency	2000 Avenue Of The Stars	Los Angeles, CA 90067
Heckerling, Amy	Creative Artists Agency	2000 Avenue Of The Stars	Los Angeles, CA 90067
Jonze, Spike	Creative Artists Agency	2000 Avenue Of The Stars	Los Angeles, CA 90067
Ladd, Alan Jr.	The Ladd Company	9465 Wilshire Blvd.	Beverly Hills, CA 90210
Lee, Spike	40 Arces & A Mule Film	124 Dekalb Avenue	Brooklyn, NY 11217
Levinson, Barry	International Creative Mgmt.	10250 Constellation Blvd.	Los Angeles, CA 90067
Linklater, Richard	Creative Artists Agency	2000 Avenue Of The Stars	Los Angeles, CA 90067
Lucas, George	Industrial Light & Magic	PO Box 29909	San Francisco, CA 94129
Lument, Sydney	International Creative Mgmt.	10250 Constellation Blvd.	Los Angeles, CA 90067
Mann, Michael	Creative Artists Agency	2000 Avenue Of The Stars	Los Angeles, CA 90067
Marshall, Penny	International Creative Mgmt.	10250 Constellation Blvd.	Los Angeles, CA 90067
Mendes, Sam	Creative Artists Agency	2000 Avenue Of The Stars	Los Angeles, CA 90067
Moore, Michael	Endeavor Talent Agency	9601 Wilshire Blvd.	Beverly Hills, CA 90210
Needham, Hal	PO Box 46609	Los Angeles, CA 90046	
Nichols, Mike	Creative Artists Agency	2000 Avenue Of The Stars	Los Angeles, CA 90067
Nichols, Paul	N.S. Bienstock, Inc.	1740 Broadway	New York, NY 10019
Osborne, Barrie M.	Emerald City Productions	9777 Wilshire Blvd., Ste 550	Beverly Hills, CA 90212
Payne, Alexander	William Morris Agency	One William Morris Place	Beverly Hills, CA 90212
Petersen, Wolfgang	Creative Artists Agency	2000 Avenue Of The Stars	Los Angeles, CA 90067
Polansky, Roman	International Creative Mgmt.	10250 Constellation Blvd.	Los Angeles, CA 90067
Rodriguez, Robert	Endeavor Talent Agency	9601 Wilshire Blvd.	Beverly Hills, CA 90210
Ross, Gary	Creative Artists Agency	2000 Avenue Of The Stars	Los Angeles, CA 90067
Sarsgaard, Peter	ID Public Relations	8409 Santa Monica Blvd.	West Hollywood, CA 90069
Scorsese, Martin	Endeavor Talent Agency	9601 Wilshire Blvd.	Beverly Hills, CA 90210
Scott, Ridley	William Morris Agency	One William Morris Place	Beverly Hills, CA 90212
Shyamalan, M. Night	Blinding Edge Pictures	100 Four Falls Corporate Center	Conshohocken, PA 19428
Silberling, Brad	William Morris Agency	One William Morris Place	Beverly Hills, CA 90212
Sorkin, Aaron	42 West	220 W. 42nd St.	New York, NY 10036
Spielberg, Steven	Creative Artists Agency	2000 Avenue Of The Stars	Los Angeles, CA 90067
Spurlock, Morgan	The Gersh Agency	232 N. Canon Dr.	Beverly Hills, CA 90210
Steen, Peter	N.S. Bienstock, Inc.	1740 Broadway	New York, NY 10019
Stone, Oliver	Creative Artists Agency	2000 Avenue Of The Stars	Los Angeles, CA 90067
Woo, John	Creative Artists Agency	2000 Avenue Of The Stars	Los Angeles, CA 90067
Zwick, Edward	Creative Artists Agency	2000 Avenue Of The Stars	Los Angeles, CA 90067

Asner, Jules	William Morris Agency	One William Morris Place	Beverly Hills, CA 90211
Banfield, Ashley	MSNBC TV	One MSNBC Plaza	Secaucus, NJ 07094
Banks, Tyra	Bankable Productions	6310 San Vicente Blvd.	Los Angeles, CA 90048
Barberie, Jillian	William Morris Agency	One William Morris Place	Beverly Hills, CA 90211
Barker, Bob	The Price is Right	5757 Wilshire Blvd	Los Angeles, CA 90036
Barris, Chuck	Hyperion Publishing	77 West 66th Street	New York, NY 10023
Barsamian, David	Alternative Radio	PO Box 551	Boulder, CO 80306
Behar, Joy	The View - ABC Television	320 West 66th St.	New York, NY 10023
Behrendt, Greg	BWR	9100 Wilshire Blvd.	Beverly Hills, CA 90212
Bonaduce, Danny	William Morris Agency	One William Morris Pl.	Beverly Hills, CA 90212
Brokaw, Tom	NBC News	30 Rockefeller Plaza	New York, NY 10012
Brothers, Dr. Joyce	William Morris Agency	One William Morris Place	Beverly Hills, CA 90212
Brown, Aaron	CNN New York Bureau	5 Penn Plaza	New York, NY 10112
Brown, Campbell	NBC Weekend Today	30 Rockefeller Plaza	New York, NY 10012
Buchanan, Pat	MSNBC TV	One MSNBC Plaza	Seacusus, NJ 07094
Burbano, Mindy	Carolyn Aguayo - KTLA-TV	5800 Sunset Blvd.	Los Angeles, CA 90028
Burke , Brooke	William Morris Agency	One William Morris Pl.	Beverly Hills, CA 90212
Champion, Sam	Good Morning America	147 Columbus Avenue	New York, NY 10023
Chung, Connie	Cable News Network	One CNN Center	Atlanta, GA 30303
Cohn, Linda	ESPN TV	ESPN Plaza	Bristol, CT 06010
Colbert, Steve	The Colbert Report	513 West 54th Street	New York, NY
Colmes, Alan	Fox News Channel	1211 Avenue of the Americas	New York, NY 10036
Cooper, Anderson	Cable News Network	One CNN Center	Atlanta, GA 30303
Couric, Katie	NBC News - Today	30 Rockefeller Plaza	New York, NY 10012
Cowell, Simon	Creative Artists Agency	9830 Wilshire Blvd.	Beverly Hills, CA 90212
Crier, Catherine	Catherine Crier Live	600 Third Avenue	New York, NY 10016
Cronkite, Walter	Cronkite Unit CBS	51 West 52nd Street	New York, NY 10036
Cumia, Anthony	Robert Eatman Enterprises	P.O. Box 853	Pacific Palisades, CA 90272
Cuomo, Chris	Good Morning America	147 Columbus Avenue	New York, NY 10023
Curry, Ann	Dateline-NBC News	30 Rockefeller Plaza	New York, NY 10112
D'Amato, Alfonse	Fox News Channel	1211 Avenue of the Americas	New York, NY 10036
Daly, Carson	Carson Daly Productions	3500 W. Olive Avenue	Burbank, CA 91505
DeGeneres, Ellen	ICM	10250 Constellation Blvd	Los Angeles, CA 90067
Deutsch, Donny	Open City Films	122 Hudson Street	New York, NY 10013
Devlin, Ryan	Innovative Artists	235 Park Ave. S.	New York, NY 10003
Dhue, Laurie	Fox News Channel	1211 Avenue of the Americas	New York, NY 10036
Dobbs, Lou	Cable News Network	One CNN Center	Atlanta, GA 30303
Donahue, Phil	N.S. Bienstock, Inc.	1740 Broadway	New York, NY 10019
Donovan, Carrie	New York Times	228 W. 43rd Street	New York, NY 10036
Downs, Hugh	Arizona State University	Communications Dept.	Tempe, AZ 85287
Dunne, Dominick	Catherine Crier Live	600 Third Avenue	New York, NY 10016
Ebert, Roger	Chicago Sun Times	401 North Wabash Avenue	Chicago, IL 60611
Ellerbee, Linda	Lucky Duck	96 Morton Street	New York, NY 10014
Estrich, Susan	Fox News Channel	1211 Avenue of the Americas	New York, NY 10036
Ferraro, Geraldine	Fox News Channel	1211 Avenue of the Americas	New York, NY 10036
Fiducia, Donna	Fox News Channel	1211 Avenue of the Americas	New York, NY 10036
Francisco, Don	9405 N.W. 41st St.	Miami, FL 33178	
Franken, Al	William Morris Agency	One William Morris Place	Beverly Hills, CA 90212
Frost, David	William Morris Agency	One William Morris Place	Beverly Hills, CA 90212
Fuentas, Daisy	William Morris Agency	One William Morris Place	Beverly Hills, CA 90212
Geist, Bill	N.S. Bienstock, Inc.	1740 Broadway	New York, NY 10019
Gibbons, Leeza	Celebrity Consultants	3340 Ocean Park Blvd	Santa Monica, CA 90405
Gibson, Charles	Good Morning America	147 Columbus Avenue	New York, NY 10023
Gifford, Kathie Lee	William Morris Agency	One William Morris Place	Beverly Hills, CA 90212
Gotti, Victoria	N.S. Bienstock, Inc.	1740 Broadway	New York, NY 10019
Grace, Nancy	Cable News Network	One CNN Center	Atlanta, GA 30303
Hall, Monty	Hatos-Hall Productions	519 North Arden Drive	Beverly Hills, CA 90210
Hannity, Sean	Fox News Channel	1211 Avenue of the Americas	New York, NY 10036

Hansen, Chris	Dateline-NBC	30 Rockefeller Plaza	New York, NY 10112
Harris, Samantha	Ken Lindner & Associates	2049 Century Park East	Los Angeles, CA 90067
Hart, Mary	Entertainment Tonight	5555 Melrose Ave.	Hollywood, CA 90038
Harvey, Paul	1035 Park Avenue	River Forest, IL 60305	
Hasselbeck, Elisabeth	The View - ABC Television	320 West 66th St.	New York, NY 10023
Hewitt, Don	CBS News	524 West 57th Street	New York, NY 10019
Holt, Lester	NBC - Weekend Today	30 Rockefeller Plaza	New York, NY 10012
Huffington, Arianna	Los Angeles Times	218 South Spring St.	Los Angeles, CA 90012
Hughes, "Opie" Gregg	Robert Eatman Enterprises	P.O. Box 853	Pacific Palisades, CA 90272
Hume, Brit	Fox News Channel	1211 Avenue of the Americas	New York, NY 10036
Ifill, Gwen	WETA-TV	2275 South Quincy Street	Arlington, VA 22206
Imus, Dick	MSNBC TV	One MSNBC Plaza	Seacusus, NJ 07094
Imus, Don	ICM	10250 Constellation Blvd.	Los Angeles, CA 90067
Iovanna, Carol	Fox News Channel	1211 Avenue of the Americas	New York, NY 10036
Jones, Jenny	454 N. Columbus Dr.	Chicago, IL 60611	
Kalter, Alan	The Late Show	1679 Broadway	New York, NY 10019
Kasem, Casey	138 N. Mapleton Drive	Los Angeles, CA 90077	
Kilborn, Craig	Creative Artists Agency	2000 Avenue Of The Stars	Los Angeles, CA 90067
Kimmel, Jimmy	El Capitan Entert. Center	6840 Hollywood Blvd.	Los Angeles, CA 90028
King, Larry	CNN America	6430 Sunset Blvd	Los Angeles, CA 90028
Koppel, Ted	ABC News Nightline	500 S. Buena Vista St	Burbank, CA 91521
Lake, Ricki	The Gersh Agency	232 North Canon Drive	Beverly Hills, CA 90210
Lamb, Brian	C-Span	Washington, DC 20016?	
Lauer, Matt	NBC	30 Rockefeller Plaza # 701	New York, NY 10112
Leach, Robin	Diverse Talent Group	1875 Century Park E.	Los Angeles CA 90067
Lehrer, Jim	WETA-TV	3620 South 27th St.	Arlington, VA 22206
Leno, Jay	The Tonight Show	3000 W. Alameda Avenue	Burbank, CA 91523
Letterman, David	The Late Show	1697 Broadway	NY, NY 10019
Levin, Harvey	N.S. Bienstock, Inc.	1740 Broadway	New York, NY 10019
Lewis, Ananda	The Insider- Paramount TV	5555 Melrose Avenue	Hollywood, CA 90038
Limbaugh, Rush	The Rush Limbaugh Show	1270 Avenue of the Americas	New York, NY 10020
Linkletter, Art	1100 Bel Air Road	Los Angeles, CA 90077	
Logan, Lara	60 Minutes	524 West 57th Street	New York, NY 10019
Magliozzi, Ray	PO Box 3500	Car Talk - Harvard Square	Cambridge, MA 02238
Magliozzi, Tom	PO Box 3500	Car Talk - Harvard Square	Cambridge, MA 02238
Maher, Bill	Creative Artists Agency	2000 Avenue Of The Stars	Los Angeles, CA 90067
Mandell, Howie	Creative Artists Agency	2000 Avenue Of The Stars	Los Angeles, CA 90067
Marshall, Peter	16714 Oakview Drive	Encino, CA 91316	
Matalin, Mary	PO Box 15129	Washington, DC 20037	
Matthews, Chris	Hardball	ONE MSNBC Plaza	Secaucus, NJ 07094
McGraw, Phillip	PO Box 140143	Irving, TX 75014-0143	
McMahon, Ed	CED	10635 Santa Monica Blvd	Los Angeles, CA 90025
Merrill, Carrol	Hatos-Hall Productions	519 North Arden Drive	Beverly Hills, CA 90210
Michaels, Lorne	Creative Artists Agency	2000 Avenue Of The Stars	Los Angeles, CA 90067
Miller, Dennis	Jonas Public Relations	240 26th Street, Ste. 3	Santa Monica, CA 90402
Mitchell, Andrea	2710 Chain Bridge Rd NW	Washington, DC 20016	
Molinari, Susan	141 New Drop Lane	Staten Island, NY 10306	
Morales, Natalie	MSNBC Today Show	30 Rockefeller Plaza	New York, NY 10112
Moyers, Bill	76 Fourth Street	Garden City	Long Island, NY 11530
North, Oliver	Fox News Channel	1211 Avenue of the Americas	New York, NY 10036
Norville, Deborah	Inside Edition	555 West 57th Street	New York, NY 10019
O'Brian, Conan	NBC Productions	30 Rockefeller Plaza	NY, NY 10011
O'Donnell, Rosie	The View - ABC Television	320 West 66th St.	New York, NY 10023
O'Reilly, Bill	N.S. Bienstock, Inc.	1740 Broadway	New York, NY 10019
O'Brien, Pat	Access Hollwood	3000 Wesy Alameda Avenue	Burbank, CA 91523
O'Brien, Soledad	Cable News Network	One CNN Center	Atlanta, GA 30303
Pauley, Jane	William Morris Agency	One William Morris Place	Beverly Hills, CA 90211
Pennington, Ty	Lock & Key Productions	1149 S. Gower Street	Los Angeles, CA 90038
Philbin, Regis	William Morris Agency	One William Morris Place	Beverly Hills, CA 90211
Phillips, Stone	Dateline NBC	30 Rockefeller Plaza	New York, NY 10012

Pinsky, Drew (Dr.)	William Morris Agency	One William Morris Place	Beverly Hills, CA 90211
Povich, Maury	Studios USA	15 Penn Plaza/Ballroom	New York, NY 10001
Probst, Jeff	William Morris Agency	One William Morris Place	Beverly Hills, CA 90211
Raphael, S. Jessy	Creative Artists Agency	2000 Avenue Of The Stars	Los Angeles, CA 90067
Rather, Dan	CBS News	524 West 57th Street	New York, NY 10019
Recana, Victoria	The Insider- Paramount TV	5555 Melrose Avenue	Hollywood, CA 90038
Rhodes, Randi	Tim Allan Walker	3 Park Avenue	New York, NY 10016
Rivera, Geraldo	William Morris Agency	One William Morris Place	Beverly Hills, CA 90211
Roberts, Cokie	1717 Desales St NW	Washington, DC 20036	
Roberts, Robin	Good Morning America	Broadway & 44th St.	New York, NY
Robinson, Anne	Penrose Media	19 Victoria Grove	LondonW8 5RW
Roeper, Richard	Chicago Sun Times	401 North Wabash Avenue	Chicago, IL 60611
Roker, Al	NBC News - Today	30 Rockefeller Plaza	New York, NY 10012
Rooney, Andy	CBS News	524 West 57th Street	New York, NY 10019
Rose, Charlie	Charlie Rose Inc.	731 Lexington Avenue	New York, NY 10022
Rowe, Mike	Katz, Golden and Sullivan	2001 Wilshire Blvd	Santa Monica, CA 90403
Russert, Tim	Meet the Press	4001 Nebraska Ave. NW	Washington, DC 20016
Safer, Morley	CBS News	524 West 57th Street	New York, NY 10019
Sajak, Pat	Wheel of Fortune	10202 W. Washington Blvd	Culver City, CA 90232
Sawyer, Diane	Good Morning America	147 Columbus Avenue	New York, NY 10023
Scarborough, Joe	MSNBC TV	One MSNBC Plaza	Seacusus, NJ 07094
Scelsa, Vin	WFUV Radio	Fordham Univ. Rosehill	Bronx, NY 10458
Schieffer, Bob	CBS Face the Nation	2020 M Street NW	Washington, DC 20036
Schlessinger, Laura	GCI Group	6100 Wilshire Blvd	LA, CA 90048
Scott, Willard	NBC News - Today	30 Rockefeller Plaza	New York, NY 10012
Seacrest, Ryan	William Morris Agency	One William Morris Pl.	Beverly Hills, CA 90212
Shaw, Bernard	Cable Network News	820 1st Street NE	Washington, DC 20002
Shields, Mark	Creator Syndicate	577 W. Century Blvd	Los Angeles, CA 90045
Smiley, Tavis	The Smiley Group	3870 Crenshaw Blvd.	Los Angeles, CA 90008
Smith, Shepard	Fox News Channel	1211 Avenue of the Americas	New York, NY 10036
Snyder, Tom	CBS-TV City	7800 Beverly Blvd	LA, CA 90036
Spencer, Lara	The Insider- Paramount TV	5555 Melrose Avenue	Hollywood, CA 90038
Springer, Jerry	Linda Shafran	454 North Columbus Dr.	Chicago, IL 60611
Stahl, Lesley	William Morris Agency	One William Morris Pl.	Beverly Hills, CA 90212
Stein, Ben	Endeavor Talent Agency	10th Fl. 9701 Wilshire Blvd.	Beverly Hills, CA 90212
Stern, Howard	K-Rock Radio	40 West 57th Street	New York, NY, 10019
Stewart, Jon	Comedy Central Viewer	1775 Broadway - 10th Floor	New York, NY 10019
Stewart, Martha	Chelsea Studios	221 W 26th St	New York, NY
Stossel, John	N.S. Bienstock, Inc.	1740 Broadway	New York, NY 10019
Trebek, Alex	Jeopary	10202 W. Wash. Blvd	Culver City, CA 90232
Van Susteren, Greta	Fox News Channel	1211 Avenue of the Americas	New York, NY 10036
Vargas, Elizabeth	NBC News	30 Rockefeller Plaza	New York, NY 10112
Vieira, Meredith	ABC Television Studios	30 West 67th Street	New York, NY 10023
Vila, Bob	BobVila.com	115 Kingston Street	Boston, MA 02111
Wallace, Chris	Fox News Channel	1211 Avenue of the Americas	New York, NY 10036
Wallace, Mike	CBS News	524 West 57th Street	New York, NY 10019
Walters, Barbara	The View - ABC Television	320 West 66th St.	New York, NY 10023
Westheimer, Ruth	900 West 190th Street	New York, NY 10040	
Williams, Armstrong	201 Massachusetts Ave. NE	Washington, DC 20002	
Williams, Brian	NBC News	30 Rockefeller Plaza	New York, NY 10112
Williams, Montel	433 West 53rd Street	New York, NY 10019	
Winfrey, Oprah	Harpo Productions	110 No. Carpenter St.	Chicago, IL 60607
Woodruff, Bob	ABC News	147 Columbus Ave	New York, NY 10023
Woodruff, Judy	PO Box 2626	Washington, DC 20013	
Zahn, Paula	N.S. Bienstock, Inc.	1740 Broadway	New York, NY 10019

Architects

Calatrava, Santiago	Parkring 11	8002 Zürich	Switzerland
Gehry, Frank O.	Gehry Partners	12541 Beatrice Street	Los Angeles, CA 90066
Holl, Steven	Steven Holl Architects	450 West 31st Street	New York, NY 10001
Libeskind, Daniel	Studio Daniel Libeskind	Windscheidstr 18	D-10627 Berlin, Germany
Lin, T.Y	T.Y. Lin International	Two Harrison Street, Suite 500	San Francisco, CA 94105
Mayne, Thom	Morphiss Architecture	2041 Colorado Avenue	Santa Monica, CA 90404
McDonough, William	William McDonough Prtns	200 East Jefferson St.	Charlottsville, VA 22903
Nixon, Norman	Freedom Ship Intl.	P.O. Box 5020	Sarasota, Florida 34239
Pei, Ieoh Ming	Pei, Cobb, Freed	88 Pine Street	New York, NY 10005
Pelli, Cesar	Cesar Pelli Associates	322 8th Avenue	New York NY 10001
Piano, Renzo	Renzo Piano Workshop	Via Rubens, 29	16158 Genova, Italy
St. Florian, Friedrich	112 Union Street	Providence, RI 02903	

Artists & Art Critics

Aikten, Doug	303 Gallery	525 22nd Street	New York, NY 10011
Beckett, Wendy	BBC TV Centre	Wood Lane	London W12 7RJ, UK
Bontecou, Lee	Michael Rosenfeld Gallery	24 West 57th Street	New York, NY 10019
Britto, Romero	Britto Central	818 Lincoln Road	Miami Beach, FL 33139
Carone, Nicolas	Apt. B937	463 West Street	New York, NY 10014
Celmins, Vija	McKee Galleries	745 Fifth Avenue	New York, NY 10151
Chihuly, Dale	Chihuly Studios	509 NE Northlake Way	Seattle, WA 98105
Cristo	C/O Harry N. Abrams	110 East 59th Street	New York, NY 10022
Gorman, R.C.	Navajo Gallery	PO Box 1756	Taos, NM 87571
Hammons, David	c/o Jack Tilton Galleries	49 Greene Street	New York, NY 10013
Kappos, Marina	I-20 Gallery	557 West 53rd Street	New York, NY 10011
Kinkade, Thomas	Media Arts Group	521 Charcot Avenue	San Jose, CA 95131
Lin, Maya	Maya Lin Studio	112 Prince Street, 4th Fl.	New York, NY 10012
Max, Peter	118 Riverside Drive	New York, NY 10024	
Morris, Burton	Atelier House	64 Pratt Street	London NW1 0LF UK
Nechita, Alexandra	Nechita Enterprises	PO Box 9129	Whittier, CA 90608
Neiman, Leroy	Hammer Galleries	33 West 57th Street	New York, NY 10019
Redlin, Terry	Redlin Art Center	Interstate 29 & Hwy 212	Watertown, SD 57201
Richter, Gerhard	Distributed Art Publishers	155 Sixth Avenue	New York, NY 10013
Rodrigue, George	Rodrigue Studio Lafayette	2021 Pinhook Rd	Lafayette, LA 70508
Sarkisian, Peter	I-20 Gallery	557 West 53rd Street	New York, NY 10011
Sherman, Cindy	c/o Metro Pictures	519 W. 24th Street	New York, NY 10011
Sleigh, Sylvia	I-20 Gallery	557 West 53rd Street	New York, NY 10011
Taintor, Anne	PO Box 9	Youngsville, NM 87064	
Thiebaud, Wayne	1617 7th Avenue	Sacramento, CA 95818	
Warner, Debora	I-20 Gallery	557 West 53rd Street	New York, NY 10011
Wasserman, Martabel	I-20 Gallery	557 West 53rd Street	New York, NY 10011
Wolfe, Art	1944 First Avenue	Seattle, WA 98134	
Wong, Sherry	I-20 Gallery	557 West 53rd Street	New York, NY 10011
Zittel, Andrea	Andrea Rosen Gallery	525 West 24th Street	New York, NY 10011

Magicians

Blaine, David	Jason Weinberg & Assoc.	122-124 E. 25th Street	New York, NY 10010
Burton, Lance	The Monte Carlo Hotel	3770 Las Vegas Blvd	Las Vegas, NV 89109
Copperfield, David	Alberta Rettig	11777 San Vicente Blvd	Los Angeles, CA 90048
The Amazing Jonathan	Weirdstuff	PO Box 10462	Marina Del Ray, CA 90265
The Amazing Kreskin	Rubenstein Public Relation	1345 Ave. of the Americas	New York, NY 10105-0109
The Amazing Randi	J. Randi Education Found.	201 SE 12th Street	Fort Lauderdale, FL 33316
Penn & Teller	Rio Hotel & Casino	3700 W. Flamingo Road	Las Vegas, NV 89103
Siegfried (Fischbacher) & Roy (Horn)	Mirage Hotel & Casino	3400 S. Las Vegas Blvd	Las Vegas, NV 89109

Designers - Fashion - Fragrance - Video - Autos

Armani, Giorgio	Palazzo Durini 242012	Milano, Italy	
Duke, Randolph	Special Artists Agency	9465 Wilshire Blvd	Beverly Hills, CA 90212
Giannulli, Mossimo	Mossimo Inc.	2016 Broadway Blvd	Santa Monica, CA 90404
Hillfiger, Tommy	485 Fifth Ave. 6th Floor	New York, NY 10017	
Karan, Donna	Donna Karan Co.	550 7th Avenue	New York, NY 10018
Klein, Calvin	Calvin Klein Ldt.	205 W. 39th Street	New York, NY 10018
Mackie, Bob	FAO Schwarz	767 Fifth Ave.	New York, NY 10153
Mead, Syd	The Gnomon Workshop	1015 N.Cahuenga Blvd.	Hollywood, CA 90038
Sassoon, Vidal	General Motors Plaza	757 Fifth Avenue	New York, NY 10023
Versace, Donatella	Keeble Cavaco & Duka	Suite 604 450 W. 15th St.	New York, NY 10011
Wang, Vera	Vera Wang Corp. Hdqtrs.	225 West 39th Street	New York, NY 10018
Wintaur, Anna	Editor, Vogue Magazine	350 Madison Ave.	New York, NY 10017
Edelbrock, Vic Jr.	Edelbrock Corp.	2700 California Street	Torrance, CA 90503
Barris, George	Edward Lozzi & Associates	9454 Wilshire Boulevard	Beverly Hills, California 90212
Farr, Bruce	613 Third Streeet Suite 20	P.O. Box 4964	Annapolis MD 21403
Bravo, Rose Marie	Burberry Ltd.	18-22 Haymarket	London SW 1Y 4DQ England
Cole, Kenneth	610 Fifth Avenue	New York, NY	212-373-5800
Posen, Zac	1317 Laight Street	New York, NY 10013	
Prada, Miuccia	2 Via Andres Maffei	Milano, 20135 Italy	
Rodriguez, Narciso	Narciso Rodriguez Perfumes	28/32 Victor Hugo Avenue	75116 Paris, France
Silva, Daniel	M. Ducksworth at Putnam	375 Hudson Street	New York, NY 10014
Spade, Kate	Kate Spade LLC	48 West 25th Street	New York, NY 10010
Vuitton, Louis	2 rue du Pont-Neuf	75034 Paris Cedex 01	France
Beck, Kent	Three Rivers Institute	PO Box 128	Merlin, OR 97532
Glaser, Milton	Milton Glaser Inc.	207 East 32nd Street	New York, NY 10016
Wright, Will	Electronic Arts / Maxis	2121 North California Blvd	Walnut Creek, CA 94596

Photographers

Ballen, Roger	Hamburg Kennedy	75 West Street 17C	New York, New York 10006
Blackmon, Julie	Hamburg Kennedy	75 West Street 17C	New York, New York 10006
Colbert, Gregory	Bianimale Foundation	210 East 5th Street	New York, NY 10003
diCorcia, Philip-Lorca	Hamburg Kennedy	75 West Street 17C	New York, New York 10006
Dijkstra, Rineke	Hamburg Kennedy	75 West Street 17C	New York, New York 10006
Doubilet, David	National Geographic	P.O. Box 98199	Washington, D.C. 20090-8199
Eastman, Michael	Hamburg Kennedy	75 West Street 17C	New York, New York 10006
Eggleston, William	Hamburg Kennedy	75 West Street 17C	New York, New York 10006
Erwitt, Elliott	Hamburg Kennedy	75 West Street 17C	New York, New York 10006
Fen, Weng	Hamburg Kennedy	75 West Street 17C	New York, New York 10006
Friedlander, Lee	c/o Janet Borden Inc.	560 Broadway	New York, NY 10012
Fuss, Adam	Hamburg Kennedy	75 West Street 17C	New York, New York 10006
Galella, Ron	Hamburg Kennedy	75 West Street 17C	New York, New York 10006
Höfer, Candida	Hamburg Kennedy	75 West Street 17C	New York, New York 10006
Hondros, Chris	Getty Images	601 North 34th Street	Seattle, WA 98103
Klein, William	Hamburg Kennedy	75 West Street 17C	New York, New York 10006
Klum, Mattias	Svanliden, Hammarskog	SE-755 91 Uppsala	Sweden
Kusama, Yayoi	Hamburg Kennedy	75 West Street 17C	New York, New York 10006
La Chapelle, David	CXA c/o Steven Pranica	416 West 13th Street	New York NY 10014
Leibovitz, Annie	Houk Galleries	745 Fifth Avenue	New York, NY 10151
Mann, Sally	Hamburg Kennedy	75 West Street 17C	New York, New York 10006
McCurry, Steve	2 Fifth Avenue	New York, NY 10011	
Tunick, Spencer	I-20 Gallery	557 West 53rd Street	New York, NY 10011
van Empel, Ruud	Hamburg Kennedy	75 West Street 17C	New York, New York 10006
Vitali, Massimo	Hamburg Kennedy	75 West Street 17C	New York, New York 10006

Announcers

Crook, Lorianne	Great American Country	PO Box 50970	Knoxville, TN 37950
Alexander, Suzanne	Great American Country	PO Box 50970	Knoxville, TN 37950
Clark, Dick	William Morris Agency	One William Morris Place	Beverly Hills, CA 90212
Cody, Bill	Great American Country	PO Box 50970	Knoxville, TN 37950
Kasem, Casey	138 N. Mapleton Drive	Los Angeles, CA 90077	

Composers

Adams, John	Boosey & Hawkes	24 East 21 St Street	New York, NY 10010
Arden, Jann	Shore Fire Media	32 Court Street, Suite 1600	New York, NY 11201
Bacharach, Burt	Linda Dozoretz Comm.	8033 W. Sunset Blvd	Los Angeles, CA 90046
Blades, Rubén	Shore Fire Media	32 Court Street, Suite 1600	New York, NY 11201
Browne, Jackson	Shore Fire Media	32 Court Street, Suite 1600	New York, NY 11201
Carpenter, Richard	PO Box 3787	Thousand Oaks, CA 91359	
Claypool, Les	Shore Fire Media	32 Court St.	Brooklyn, NY 11201
Conti, Bill	117 Freemont Place	Los Angeles, CA 90068	
Dr. John	The Agency Group	361-373 City Road	London EC1V 1PQ UK
Edelman, Randy	Gorfaine/Schwartz Agcy	4111 West Alameda Ave	Burbank, CA 91505
Elling, Kurt	Shore Fire Media	32 Court St.	Brooklyn, NY 11201
Enya	Shore Fire Media	32 Court St.	Brooklyn, NY 11201
Gabriel, Peter	Primary Talent Intl.	2-12 Pentonville Road	London N1 9PL UK
Hamlisch, Marvin	970 Park Ave #501	New York, NY 10028	
Harper, Ben	Virgin Records	150 Fifth Street	New York, NY 10011-4311
Jones, Quincy	William Morris Agency	One William Morris Place	Beverly Hills, CA 90212
Kander, John	Intl. Creative Mgmt.	8942 Wilshire Blvd	Beverly Hills, CA 90211
Kelly, Paul	Shore Fire Media	32 Court St.	Brooklyn, NY 11201
Lloyd Webber, Andrew	725 Fifth Avenue	New York, NY 10022	
Martin, George	Air Edel Associates	18 Rodmarton Street	London, W1U 8BJ UK
Maxwell	William Morris Agency	One William Morris Place	Beverly Hills, CA 90212
McGuinn, Roger	Shore Fire Media	32 Court St.	Brooklyn, NY 11201
Miller, Marcus	Shore Fire Media	32 Court St.	Brooklyn, NY 11201
Neptune	Star Trak Entertainment	PO Box 1938	Radio City Station
Newman, Randy	Gorfaine Schwartz Agcy	4111 West Alameda Ave.	Burbank, CA 91505
Previn, Andre	180 West 80th Street	New York, NY 10024	
Rosey	Creative Artists Agency	2000 Avenue of the Stars	Los Angeles, CA 90067
Schaffer, Paul	The Late Show	1697 Broadway 11th Floor	New York, NY 10019
Slatkin, Leonard	Washington Synphony	Kennedy Center	Washington, DC 20011
Sondheim, Steven	246 East 49th Street	New York, NY 10017	
Stigers, Curtis	Shore Fire Media	32 Court St.	Brooklyn, NY 11201
Stuart, Marty	William Morris Agency	One William Morris Place	Beverly Hills, CA 90212-1825
Tesh, John	PO Box 6010-72	Sherman Oaks, CA 91413	
Thompson, Linda	Shore Fire Media	32 Court St.	Brooklyn, NY 11201
Van Zandt, Steve	Shore Fire Media	32 Court Street, Suite 1600	New York, NY 11201
Weller, Paul	Shore Fire Media	32 Court Street, Suite 1600	New York, NY 11201
Wilhorn, Frank	Plymouth Theatre	23 West 45th Street	New York, NY 10036
Williams, John	Boston Orchestra	301 Massachuchetts	Boston. MA 02115
Wyclef, Jean	Richard DeLaFont Agcy	4845 S. Sheridan Rd.	Tulsa, OK 74145

Dancers

Abdul, Paula	William Morris Agency	One William Morris Place	Beverly Hills, CA 90212-1825
Allen, Debbie	607 Marguerita Ave.	Santa Monica, CA 90402	
Baryshnikov, Mikhail	Creative Artists Agency	2000 Avenue of the Stars	Los Angeles, CA 90067
Burke, Cheryl	Guttman Associates	118 S. Beverly Dr. Ste. 201	Beverly Hills, CA 90212
Flatley, Michael	Creative Artists Agency	2000 Avenue of the Stars	Los Angeles, CA 90067
Glover, Savion	1501 Broadway # 404	New York, NY 10036	
Jamison, Judith	Alvin Ailey Dance Studio	211 West 61st Street	New York, NY 10023
Marshall, Susan	Dance Continuum Inc.	Box 707 Cooper Stat.	New York, NY 10276
Miller, Bebe	Bebe Miller Dance Co.	54 W. 21st Street	New York, NY 10010
Neuwirth, Bebe	Shubert Theatre	225 West 44th Street	New York, NY 10036
Rhodes, Cynthia	# 900	15250 Ventura Blvd	Sherman Oaks, CA 91403
Rivera, Chita	William Morris Agency	One William Morris Place	Beverly Hills, CA 90212-1825
Tune, Tommy	50 East 89th Street	New York, NY 10128	

Instrumentalists-Musicians

Alpert, Herb	Almo/Irving Music	360 N. LaCienga Blvd	Los Angeles, CA 90048
Ben-Ari, Miri	Univeral Music Group	2220 Colorado Avenue	Santa Monica, CA 90404
Brown, Jr.	Thompson Brown Co.	PO Box 690715	Tulsa, OK 74169-0715
Cherry, Eagle Eye	Beth Rosner Mgmt.	15 Stuyvesant Oval	New York, NY 10009
Claypool, Les	Shore Fire Media	32 Court Street, Suite 1600	Brooklyn, New York, NY 11201
Coleman, Steve	M-Base Concepts	PO Box 114	Allentown, PA 18105-0114
Didley, Bo	PO Box 474	Archer, FL 32618	
Douglas, Dale	Sooya Arts	PO Box 87	Tappan, NY 10983-0087
Elfman, Danny	Kraft-Engel Mngt.	15233 Ventura Blvd	Sherman Oaks, CA 91403
Gorlick, Kenny	Creative Artists Agency	2000 Avenue of the Stars	Los Angeles, CA 90067
Hammond, John	Shore Fire Media	32 Court St.	Brooklyn, NY 11201
Harper, Ben	Virgin Records	150 Fifth Avenue	New York, NY 10011-4311
Hill, Andrew	167 Wayne Street	Jersey City, NJ 07302-3401	
Joel, Billy	Sony Music Enter.	550 Madison Ave, 24th Fl	New York, NY 10022-3211
Lee, Tommy	Creative Artists Agency	2000 Avenue of the Stars	Los Angeles, CA 90067
Lewis, Ramsey	Shore Fire Media	32 Court Street, Suite 1600	New York, NY 11201
Ma, Yo-Yo	Intl. Creative Mgmt.	8942 Wilshire Blvd	Beverly Hills, CA 90211
Mangione, Chuck	Richard De La Font Agcy	4845 South Sheridan Rd	Tulsa, OK 74145
Marsalis, Wynton	Creative Artists Agency	2000 Avenue of the Stars	Los Angeles, CA 90067
Moby	William Morris Agency	One William Morris Place	Beverly Hills, CA 90212
Ramsey Lewis	APA Talent & Literary	9200 Sunset Blvd.	Los Angeles, CA 90069
Santana, Carlos	Creative Artists Agency	2000 Avenue of the Stars	Los Angeles, CA 90067
Severinsen, Doc	De La Font Agency	4845 South Sheridan Rd	Tulsa, OK 74145
Steve Van Zandt	Writers & Artists Agency	19 West 44th St.	New York, NY 10036
Van Zandt, Steve	Endeavor Talent Agency	9601 Wilshire Blvd	Beverly Hills, CA 90210
Wilson, Cassandra	Shore Fire Media	32 Court Street, Suite 1600	Brooklyn, New York, NY 11201
Wylde, Zakk	Spitfire Records	22 West 38th Street	New York, NY 10018

Producers

Brown, Anastasia	Creative Artists Agency	2000 Avenue of the Stars	Los Angeles, CA 90067
Fuller, Simon	33 Ransomes Dock-35-37	Parkgate Road	LondonSW11 4NP UK
Neptunes	Star Trak Entertainment	PO Box 1938	New York, NY 10101-1938

Bands- Groups

50 Cent	William Morris Agency	One William Morris Place	Beverly Hills, CA 90212
Aerosmith	Mitch Schneider Org.	14724 Ventura Blvd	Sherman Oaks, CA 91403
Alabama	William Morris Agency	1600 Division Street	Nashville, TN 37203
Beastie Boys	Endeavor Talent Agency	9601 Wilshire Blvd.	Beverly Hills, CA 90210
Beck	Creative Artists Agency	2000 Avenue of the Stars	Los Angeles, CA 90067
Black Eyed Peas	A&M Records	2220 Colorado Avenue	Santa Monica, CA 90404
Brooks & Dunn	De La Font Agcy	4845 Sheridan Road	Tulsa, OK 74145
Bush	# 1230	10900 Wilshire Blvd	Los Angeles, CA 9024
Byrds (The)	# 458	9850 Sandalfoot Road	Boca Raton, FL 33428
C & C Music Factory	# 500	1700 Broadway	New York, NY 10019
Chantels (The)	Veta Gardner	1789 S.W. McAllister Ln	Hendersonville, TN 34953
Charlie Daniels Band	17060 Central Pike	Lebanon, TN 37090	
Chicago	# 200 HK Mgmt.	8900 Wilshire Blvd	Beverly Hills, CA 90211
Chieftans	BMG	1540 Broadway	New York, NY 10036
Coasters (The)	4905 S. Atlantic Avenue	Daytona Beach, FL 32114	
Coldplay	Capital Records	1750 North Vine Street	Hollywood, CA 90028
Commodores (The)	Mang Associates	1920 Benson Ave.	St. Paul, MN 55116
Creed	PO Box 20346	Tallahassee, FL 32316	
Crickets (The)	Gould Mountain	2 Music Circle # 212	Nashville, TN 37203-5708
Crystals (The)	Gardner	1789 SW McAllister LN.	Hendersonville, TN 34953
Def Leppard	Island Records	825 Eighth Street	New York, NY 10019
Destiny's Child	Worldwide Management	PO Box 710450	Houston, TX 77271
Dixie Chicks	Creative Artists Agency	2000 Avenue of the Stars	Los Angeles, CA 90067
DMX	William Morris Agency	One William Morris Place	Beverly Hills, CA 90212-1825
Doobie Brothers (The)	15140 Sanoma Hwy.	Glen Ellen, CA 95442	
Doodlebops	Cookie Jar Entertainment	4500 Wilshire Blvd.	Los Angeles, CA 90010
Doors (The)	3011 Ledgewood Drive	Los Angeles, CA 90068	
Drifters, (The)	10 Chelsea Court	Neptune, NJ 07753	
Duran Duran	Shore Fire Media	32 Court Street, Suite 1600	New York, NY 11201
Eagles (The)	Suite 1000	9200 Sunset Blvd.	Los Angeles, CA 90069
Everly Brothers (The)	William Morris Agency	One William Morris Place	Beverly Hills, CA 90212-1825
Fleetwood Mac	# 582 2899 Agoura Rd.	Westlake Village, CA	91361
Foreigner	Creative Artists Agency	2000 Avenue of the Stars	Los Angeles, CA 90067
Four Tops (The)	ABC Associates	1995 Broadway # 501	New York, NY 10023
Gatlin Brothers (The)	# 202	207 Westport Road	Kansas City, MO 64111
Goo Goo Dolls	3300 Warner Blvd	Burbank, CA 91510	
Grass Roots (Rob Grill)	Paradise Artists	108 East Matilija Street	Ojai, CA 93023
Green Day	Reprise Records	3300 Warner Blvd	Burbank, CA 91505
Guns N' Roses	CAA- Mitch Rose	9830 Wilshire Blvd	Beverly Hills, CA 90212
Immature	Pyramid -7th Floor	89 Fifth Avenue	New York, NY 10003
Indigo Girls	# 755	315 Ponce De Leon Avenue	Decatur, GA 30030
Iron Butterfly	8803 Mayne Street	Bellflower, CA 90706	
Jan & Dean	C/O Bill Hollingshead	1720 N. Ross Street	Santa Clara, CA 92706
Judas Priest	The Agency Group	1775 Broadway # 430	New York, NY 10019
KC&The Sunshine Band	# 458	9850 Sandalfoot Road	Boca Raton, FL 33428
Kingston Trio (The)	PO Box 34397	San Diego, CA 92103	
Kiss (Gene Simmons)	Kleinberg ,Lopez, Lange	2049 Century Park East	Los Angeles, CA 90067
Lennon Sisters	1984 State Highway 165	Branson, MO 65616	
Little Anthony	& The Imperials	3567 Fair Bluff Street	Las Vegas, NV 89135
Los Lobos	Hollywood Records	500 S. Buena Vista Street	Burbank, CA 91521

Music Bands & Groups Continued

Marvelettes (The)	9936 Majorca Place	Boca Raton, FL 33434	
Mike & The Mechanics	Hit & Run Music	25 Ives Street	GB-London SW3 2ND Eng.
Monkees (The)	8369A Sausalito Ave.	West Hills, CA 91304	
N Sync	Po Box 692109	Orlando, Fl 32869-2109	
Nasty Boys (The)	PO Box 105366	Atlanta, GA 30348	
Nine Inch Nails	Island Records	22 St. Peter's Square	London W6 9NW Eng.
Nitty Gritty Dirt Band	Robertson Agency	1227 17th Avenue So.	Nashville, TN 37212
Oak Ridge Boys (The)	88 New Schackle Isd. Rd.	Hendersonville, TN 37075	
Outcast	Laface Records	3350 Peachtree Road NE	Atlanta GA 30326
Pearl Jam	PO Box 4570	Seattle, WA 98104	
Peter, Paul & Mary	Shelly Belusar	121 Mount Hermon Way	Ocean Grove, NJ 07756
Red Hot Chili Peppers	Creative Artists Agency	2000 Avenue of the Stars	Los Angeles, CA 90067
Reo Speedwagon	15003 Greenleaf Street	Sherman Oaks, CA 91403	
Riders In The Sky	Suite 300	38 Music Sq. East	Nashville, TN 37203
Salt N' Pepa	Famous Artists # 1803	555 8th Avenue	New York, NY 10018
Sam & Mark	Ambush Artist Mgmt	32 Ransomes Dock	London SW11 4NP UK
Sawyer Brown	PO Box 150637	Nashville, TN 37215	
Sha-Na-Na	15760 Ventura Blvd	#2011	Encino, CA 91436
Smashing Pumpkins	Annie Ohayon Media	525 Broadway- 6th Floor	New York, NY 10012
Spice Girls (The)	Virgin Records	533-579 Harrow Road	GB-London W10 4RH Eng.
Statler Brothers	PO Box 2703	Staunton, VA 24402	
Temptations(Otis Williams)	Hal Ray c/o ICM	8942 Wilshire Blvd	Beverly Hills, CA 90211
Ten Thousand Maniacs	# 1A	2525 Michigan Avenue	Santa Monica, CA 90404
Three Dog Night	Business Office	PO Box 96597	Las Vegas, NV 89193
Turtles (The)	Paradise Talent Agency	108 East Matilija Street	Ojai, CA 93023
Wallflowers (The)	# 300	8900 Wilshire Blvd	Beverly Hills, CA 90211

Vocalists

Adams, Bryan	Bruce Allen Talent Agency	500-425 Carrall Street	Vancouver, BC V6B 6E3 Canada
Adkins, Trace	William Morris Agency	1600 Division Street	Nashville, TN 37203
Adu, Sade	Creative Artists Agency	2000 Avenue of the Stars	Los Angeles, CA 90067
Aguilera, Christina	Creative Artists Agency	2000 Avenue of the Stars	Los Angeles, CA 90067
Aiken, Clay	Ambush Artist Mgmt	32 Ransomes Dock	London SW11 4NP UK
Alexakis, Art	Pinnacle	83 Riverside Drive	New York, NY 10024
Amerie	Feenix Entertainment	1360 Clifton Avenue Ste 318	Clifton, NJ 07012
Amos, Tori	Creative Artists Agency	2000 Avenue of the Stars	Los Angeles, CA 90067
Anderson, John	Sony BMG Music	1400 18th Ave S	Nashville, TN 37212
Anderson, Lynn	De La Font Agency	4845 South Sheridan Rd	Tulsa, OK 74145
Andrews, Jessica	Creative Artists Agency	3310 West End Avenue	Nashville, TN 37203
Andrews, Julie	William Morris Agency	One William Morris Place	Beverly Hills, CA 90212
Anka, Paul	William Morris Agency	One William Morris Place	Beverly Hills, CA 90212
Antonthy, Marc	Creative Artists Agency	2000 Avenue of the Stars	Los Angeles, CA 90067
Apple, Fiona	Sony BMG Music	550 Madison Avenue	New York, NY 10022
Arden, Jann	Shore Fire Media	32 Court Street, Suite 1600	New York, NY 11201
Ashanti	De La Font Agency	4845 South Sheridan Rd	Tulsa, OK 74145
Austin, Patti	De La Font Agency	4845 South Sheridan Rd	Tulsa, OK 74145
Austin, Sherrie	William Morris Agency	1600 Division Street	Nashville, TN 37203
Avalon, Frankie	# 1	6311 Desoto Street	Woodland Hills, CA 91367
Babyface	Edmonds Entertainment	1635 North Cahuenga Blvd.	Los Angeles, CA 90028

Baez, Joan	Vanguard Records	2700 Pennsylvania Ave	Santa Monica, CA 90404
Baker, Anita	All Baker's Music	804 Crescent Drive	Beverly Hills, CA 90210
Barrino, Fantasia	Ambush Artist Mgmt	32 Ransomes Dock a	London SW11 4NP UK
Bass, Lance	William Morris Agency	One William Morris Place	Beverly Hills, CA 90212
Battle, Kathleen	Columbia Artist Mgmt.	165 West 57th Street	New York, NY 10019
Belafonte, Harry	William Morris Agency	One William Morris Place	Beverly Hills, CA 90212
Benatar, Pat	William Morris Agency	One William Morris Place	Beverly Hills, CA 90212
Bennett, Tony	RPM Music Suite 90	130 West 57th Street	New York, NY 10019
Benson, George	De La Font Agency	4845 South Sheridan Rd	Tulsa, OK 74145
Bent, Amel	Ambush Artist Mgmt	32 Ransomes Dock	London SW11 4NP UK
Bentley, Dierks	Erv Woolsey Company	1000- 18th Avenue South	Nashville, TN 37212
Berry, Chuck	William Morris Agency	One William Morris Place	Beverly Hills, CA 90212
Beyonce	Rogers & Cowan PR	Pacific Design Center 8687	Los Angeles, CA 90067
Bice, Bo	Ambush Artist Mgmt	32 Ransomes Dock	London SW11 4NP UK
Big Boi	William Morris Agency	One William Morris Place	Beverly Hills, CA 90212
Binns, Henry	Evolution Talent Agency	1776 Broadway - 15th Floor	New York, NY 10019
Bjork	William Morris Agency	One William Morris Place	Beverly Hills, CA 90212
Black, Clint	William Morris Agency	1600 Division Street	Nashville, TN 37203
Blythe, Stephanie	ICM	40 West 57th Street	New York, NY 10019
Bocelli, Andrea	Galleria Del Corso 4	Milan I-20122	ITALY
Bolton, Michael	Creative Artists Agency	2000 Avenue of the Stars	Los Angeles, CA 90067
Boltz, Ray	# 209	4205 Hillsboro Rd.	Nashville, TN 37215
Bon Jovi, Jon	Creative Artists Agency	2000 Avenue of the Stars	Los Angeles, CA 90067
Bono "Paul Hewson"	Principle Management	250 West 57th Street	New York, NY 10107
Boone, Pat	William Morris Agency	One William Morris Place	Beverly Hills, CA 90212
Branch, Michelle	Maverick Records	9348 Civic Center Drive	Beverly Hills, CA 90210
Branigan, Laura	Intl. Creative Mgmt.	10250 Constellation Blvd.	Los Angeles, CA 90067
Braxton, Toni	William Morris Agency	One William Morris Place	Beverly Hills, CA 90212
Brewer, Teresa	384 Pinebrook Blvd	New Rochelle, NY 10803	
Brightman, Sarah	Evolution Talent Agency	1776 Broadway - 15th Floor	New York, NY 10019
Brooks, Garth	William Morris Agency	One William Morris Place	Beverly Hills, CA 90212
Brown, Bobby	William Morris Agency	One William Morris Place	Beverly Hills, CA 90212
Brown, Junior	Thompson Brown Co.	PO Box 690715	Tulsa, OK 74169-0715
Browne, Jackson	Creative Artists Agency	2000 Avenue of the Stars	Los Angeles, CA 90067
Bryson, Peabo	De La Font Agency	4845 South Sheridan Rd	Tulsa, OK 74145
Buble, Michael	Bruce Allen Talent	500 - 425 Carrall Street	Vancouver, BC V6B 6E3 Canada
Buffett, Jimmy	HK Management	9200 Sunset Blvd	Los Angeles, CA 90069
Bunton, Emma	Ambush Artist Mgmt	32 Ransomes Dock	London SW11 4NP UK
Cagle, Chris	P.O. Box 121901	Nashville, TN 37212	
Campbell, Glen	William Morris Agency	One William Morris Place	Beverly Hills, CA 90212
Cannon, Freddie	"Boom Boom"	18641 Cassandra	Tarzana, CA 91356
Cara, Irene	Lloyd Talent Management	3675 W. Teco Avenue	Las Vegas, NV 89118
Carey, Mariah	Creative Artists Agency	2000 Avenue of the Stars	Los Angeles, CA 90067
Carnes, Kim	De La Font Agency	4845 South Sheridan Rd	Tulsa, OK 74145
Carpenter, Mary C.	William Morris Agency	One William Morris Place	Beverly Hills, CA 90212
Carr, Vikki	PO Box 780968	San Antonio, TX 78278	
Carreras, Jose	William Morris Agency	One William Morris Place	Beverly Hills, CA 90212
Carter, Aaron	William Morris Agency	One William Morris Place	Beverly Hills, CA 90212
Carter, Benny	JMK Concerts	2523 Crowder Lane	Tampa, FL 33629
Carter, Deana	Creative Artists Agency	2000 Avenue of the Stars	Los Angeles, CA 90067
Carter, Nick	It Girl Public Relations	5301 Beethoven Street	Los Angeles, CA 90066
Cassidy, David	MGM Grand Hotel	3799 Las Vegas Blvd So.	Las Vegas, NV 89109

Music Vocalists

Channing, Carol	William Morris Agency	One William Morris Place	Beverly Hills, CA 90212
Chapman, Beth Neilsen	De La Font Agency	4845 South Sheridan Rd	Tulsa, OK 74145
Chapman, Steven Curtis	PO Box 150156	Nashville, TN 37215	
Chapman, Tracy	William Morris Agency	One William Morris Place	Beverly Hills, CA 90212
Checker, Chubby	Twisted Enterprise	320 Fayette Street	Conshohocken, PA 17428
Cher	Intl. Creative Mgmt.	10250 Constellation Blvd.	Los Angeles, CA 90067
Chesney, Kenny	RCA Label Group	1400 18th Avenue South	Nashville, TN 37212
Chingy	William Morris Agency	One William Morris Place	Beverly Hills, CA 90212
Christie, Lou	Dick Fox Enter.	1650 Broadway	New York, NY 10019
Church, Charlotte	William Morris Agency	One William Morris Place	Beverly Hills, CA 90212
Ciara	William Morris Agency	One William Morris Place	Beverly Hills, CA 90212
Clapton, Eric	Creative Artists Agency	2000 Avenue of the Stars	Los Angeles, CA 90067
Clark, Roy	1800 Forrest Blvd	Tulsa, OK 74114	
Clarkson, Kelly	Creative Artists Agency	2000 Avenue of the Stars	Los Angeles, CA 90067
Cocker, Joe	Creative Artists Agency	2000 Avenue of the Stars	Los Angeles, CA 90067
Cole, Natalie	William Morris Agency	One William Morris Place	Beverly Hills, CA 90212
Cole, Paula	509 Hartnell	Monterey, CA 93940	
Collins, Judy	Entertainment Unlimited	64 Division Ave. #216	Levittown, NY 11856
Collins, Phil	30 Ives Street	London, 3W3 2ND UK	
Connick, Harry Jr.	Creative Artists Agency	2000 Avenue of the Stars	Los Angeles, CA 90067
Coolidge, Rita	Intl. Creative Mgmt.	10250 Constellation Blvd.	Los Angeles, CA 90067
Coolio	Esterman Entertainment	1360 Clifton Avenue	Clifton, NJ 07013
Cooper, Alice	4135 East Kelm Drive	Paradise Valley, AZ 85253	
Costello, Elvis	William Morris Agency	One William Morris Place	Beverly Hills, CA 90212
Crawford, Michael	Intl. Creative Mgmt.	10250 Constellation Blvd.	Los Angeles, CA 90067
Criss, Peter	Mercury Records	825 8th Avenue	New York, NY 10019
Crosby, David	Creative Artists Agency	2000 Avenue of the Stars	Los Angeles, CA 90067
Crow, Sheryl	De La Font Agency	4845 South Sheridan Rd	Tulsa, OK 74145
Cyrus, Billy Ray	Cyrus Spirit	PO Box 1206	Franklin, TN 37065-1206
Daltrey, Roger	TalentWorks	3500 West Olive Ave	Burbank, CA 91505
Damone, Vic	International Ventures Inc.	25864 Tournament Rd	Valencia, CA 91355
Daniels, Charlie	14410 Central Pike	Mount Joliet, TN 37122	
Daughtry, Chris	Ambush Artist Mgmt	32 Ransomes Dock	London SW11 4NP UK
Day, Doris	PO Box 223163	Carmel, CA 93922	
Des'ree	William Morris Agency	One William Morris Place	Beverly Hills, CA 90212
Diamond, Neil	Friends of Neil Diamond	PO Box 3357	Hollywood, CA 90028
Difranco, Ani	Righteous Babe Records	PO Box 95 Elliott Sta.	Buffalo, NY 14205
DiGarmo, Diane	Ambush Artist Mgmt	32 Ransomes Dock	London SW11 4NP UK
Dion, Celine	Feeling Productions	2540 Daniel Johnson Blvd.	Laval, Quebec H7T2S3
Dogg, Snoop	William Morris Agency	One William Morris Place	Beverly Hills, CA 90212
Doherty, Denny	1262 Contour Drive	Mississauga, ON L5H 1B2	CANADA
Dolenz, Micky	Grant Management	1158 26th Street	Santa Monica, CA 90403
Donovan	William Morris Agency	One William Morris Place	Beverly Hills, CA 90212
Dylan, Bob	Creative Artists Agency	2000 Avenue of the Stars	Los Angeles, CA 90067
Easton, Sheena	De La Font Agency	4845 South Sheridan Rd	Tulsa, OK 74145
Elliott, Missy	De La Font Agency	4845 South Sheridan Rd	Tulsa, OK 74145
Eminem	United Talent Agency	9560 Wilshire Blvd	Beverly Hills, CA 90212
Enya	Shore Fire Media	32 Court Street, Suite 1600	New York, NY 11201
Estatof, Steeve	Ambush Artist Mgmt	32 Ransomes Dock a	London SW11 4NP UK
Estefan, Gloria	Creative Artists Agency	2000 Avenue of the Stars	Los Angeles, CA 90067
Etheridge, Melissa	True Public Relations	6725 Sunset Blvd., #570	Los Angeles, CA 90028

Evans, Dustin	Giantslayer Records	1103 17th Avenue South	Nashville, TN 37212
Evans, Faith	De La Font Agency	4845 South Sheridan Rd	Tulsa, OK 74145
Evans, Sara	William Morris Agency	1600 Division Street	Nashville, TN 37203
Eve "Jihan Jeffers"	42West	1801 Century Park E.	Los Angeles, CA 90067
Faithfull, Marianne	Susan Dewsap	235 Footscray Road	New Eltham, London, UK
Federline, Kevin	Dmand Entertainment	1777 Westwood Blvd.	Los Angeles, CA 90024
Ferguson, Stacy "Fergie"	CESD Agency	10635 Santa Monica Blvd.	Los Angeles, CA 90025
Fogerty, John	Creative Artists Agency	2000 Avenue of the Stars	Los Angeles, CA 90067
Ford, Willa	Media Talent Group	9200 Sunset Blvd	West Hollywood, CA 90069
Frampton, Peter	CESD Agency	10635 Santa Monica Blvd.	Los Angeles, CA 90025
Francis, Connie	6413 West 102nd Terrace	Parkland, FL 33076-2357	
Franklin, Aretha	William Morris Agency	One William Morris Place	Beverly Hills, CA 90212
Frehley, Ace	Creative Artists Agency	2000 Avenue of the Stars	Los Angeles, CA 90067
Furtado, Nelly	Creative Artists Agency	2000 Avenue of the Stars	Los Angeles, CA 90067
Gabriel, Peter	William Morris Agency	One William Morris Place	Beverly Hills, CA 90212
Garfunkel, Art	William Morris Agency	One William Morris Place	Beverly Hills, CA 90212
Gates, Gareth	Ambush Artist Mgmt	32 Ransomes Dock	London SW11 4NP UK
Gaynor, Gloria	De La Font Agency	4845 South Sheridan Rd	Tulsa, OK 74145
George, Boy	William Morris Agency	One William Morris Place	Beverly Hills, CA 90212
Ghostface Killah	Evolution Talent Agency	1776 Broadway - 15th Floor	New York, NY 10019
Gibb, Barry	Middle Ear Studio	1801 Bay Road	Miami Beach, FL 33139
Gibson, Deborah	J. Cast Productions	2550 Greenvalley Rd	Los Angeles, CA 90046
Goldsboro, Bobby	De La Font Agency	4845 South Sheridan Rd	Tulsa, OK 74145
Gore, Lesley	De La Font Agency	4845 South Sheridan Rd	Tulsa, OK 74145
Grant, Amy	Creative Artists Agency	2000 Avenue of the Stars	Los Angeles, CA 90067
Gray, Macy	Creative Artists Agency	2000 Avenue of the Stars	Los Angeles, CA 90067
Green, Al	William Morris Agency	One William Morris Place	Beverly Hills, CA 90212
Green, Danny	Giantslayer Records	1103 17th Avenue South	Nashville, TN 37212
Greenwood, Lee	William Morris Agency	One William Morris Place	Beverly Hills, CA 90212
Grill, Rob (Grass Roots)	Paradise Artists	108 East Matilija Street	Ojai, CA 93023
Groban, Josh	Special Artists Agency	9465 Wilshire Blvd	Beverly Hills, CA 90212
Haggard, Merle	P.O. Box 536	Palo Cedro, CA 96073	
Hammer, M.C.	De La Font Agency	4845 South Sheridan Rd	Tulsa, OK 74145
Hanson, Zac	William Morris Agency	One William Morris Place	Beverly Hills, CA 90212
Hayes, Isaac	Intl. Creative Mgmt.	10250 Constellation Blvd.	Los Angeles, CA 90067
Hetfield, James	Electra Entertainment	75 Rockefeller Plaza	New York, NY 10019
Hill, Faith	Faith's Friends	PO Box 24266	Nashville, TN 37202
Hill, Lauryn	William Morris Agency	One William Morris Place	Beverly Hills, CA 90212
Ho, Don	Century Records	PO Box 90039	Honolulu, HI 96835
Hooker, John Lee	De La Font Agency	4845 South Sheridan Rd	Tulsa, OK 74145
Hopkins, Telma	JDS - Jay D. Schwartz	3151 Cahuenga Blvd	Los Angeles, CA 90068
Horne, Lena	203 East 74th Street	New York, NY 10021	
Houston, Whitney	William Morris Agency	One William Morris Place	Beverly Hills, CA 90212
Humperdinck, Engelbert	Intl. Creative Mgmt.	10250 Constellation Blvd.	Los Angeles, CA 90067
Hunt-Lieberman, Lorraine	Nonesuch Records	1290 Avenue of Americas	New York, NY 10104
Iglesias, Enrique	The Firm	9465 Wilshire Blvd.	Beverly Hills, CA 90212
Iglesias, Julio	5 Indian Creek Drive	Miami, FL 33154	
India.Arie	Creative Artists Agency	2000 Avenue of the Stars	Los Angeles, CA 90067
Ingram, James	867 Muirfield Road	Los Angeles, CA 90005	
Jackson, Alan	Creative Artists Agency	2000 Avenue of the Stars	Los Angeles, CA 90067
Jackson, Curtis "50-Cent"	William Morris Agency	One William Morris Place	Beverly Hills, CA 90212
Jackson, Janet	Special Artists Agency	9465 Wilshire Blvd	Beverly Hills, CA 90212

Jackson, Latoya	# 1970	301 Park Avenue	New York, NY 10022
Jackson, Michael	Cunningham, Escott, Dipene	10635 Santa Monica Blvd	Los Angeles, CA 90025
Jadakiss	De La Font Agency	4845 South Sheridan Rd	Tulsa, OK 74145
Jagger, Mick	Virgin Records America	338 NorthFoothill Rd	Beverly Hills, CA 90210
Jarreau, Al	Creative Artists Agency	2000 Avenue of the Stars	Los Angeles, CA 90067
Jay-Z	Roc-A-Fella Records	825 Eigth Street	New York, NY 10019-7416
Jett, Joan	Paradise Artists-R. Birk	108 East Matilija Street	Ojai, CA 93023
Jewel	Creative Artists Agency	2000 Avenue of the Stars	Los Angeles, CA 90067
Joe, Fat	Creative Artists Agency	2000 Avenue of the Stars	Los Angeles, CA 90067
Joel, Billy	Writers & Artists Agency	8383 Wilshire Blvd	Beverly Hills, CA 90211
John, Elton	Rogers & Cowan	8687 Melrose Avenue	Los Angeles, CA 90069
Jones, Davy	Fire Inside Productions	PO Box 400	Beavertown, PA 17813
Jones, George	48 Music Square	Nashville, TN 37203	
Jones, Jack	J. Cast Productions	2550 Greenvalley Rd	Los Angeles, CA 90046
Jones, Kimerly "Lil' Kim"	De La Font Agency	4845 South Sheridan Rd	Tulsa, OK 74145
Jones, Norah	S.L. Feldman & Assoc.	#200-1505 West 2nd Avenue	Vancouver, BC V6H 3Y4 Canada
Jones, Shirley	Don Buchwald & Assoc.	6500 Wilshire Blvd	Los Angeles, CA 90048
Jones, Tom	Creative Artists Agency	2000 Avenue of the Stars	Los Angeles, CA 90067
Jordan, Montell	De La Font Agency	4845 South Sheridan Rd	Tulsa, OK 74145
Jordan, Oscar	Atkins & Associates	303 S. Crescent Hieghts	Los Angeles, CA 90048
Judd, Naomi	William Morris Agency	One William Morris Place	Beverly Hills, CA 90212
Judd, Wynonna	William Morris Agency	One William Morris Place	Beverly Hills, CA 90212
Juvenile	De La Font Agency	4845 South Sheridan Rd	Tulsa, OK 74145
Kazan, Lainie	Warren Cowan & Assoc	8899 Beverly Blvd.	Los Angeles, CA 90048
Keith, Toby	Greenlight Management	315 S. Beverly Drive	Beverly Hills, CA 90212
Kelly, R	William Morris Agency	One William Morris Place	Beverly Hills, CA 90212
Kershaw, Doug	De La Font Agency	4845 South Sheridan Rd	Tulsa, OK 74145
Kershaw, Sammy	De La Font Agency	4845 South Sheridan Rd	Tulsa, OK 74145
Keyes, Alicia	William Morris Agency	One William Morris Place	Beverly Hills, CA 90212
Khan, Chaka	Evolution Talent Agency	1776 Broadway - 15th Floor	New York, NY 10019
Kid Rock "Robert Richie"	Creative Artists Agency	2000 Avenue of the Stars	Los Angeles, CA 90067
Kilcher, Jewel	Creative Artists Agency	2000 Avenue of the Stars	Los Angeles, CA 90067
King, BB	1414 Sixth Ave	New York, NY 10019	
King, Carole	Bully Music	12300 Wilshire Blvd	Los Angeles, CA, 90025
Kitt, Eartha	CESD Agency	10635 Santa Monica Blvd	Los Angeles, CA 90025
Knight, Gladys	William Morris Agency	One William Morris Place	Beverly Hills, CA 90212
Krauss, Alison	Shore Fire Media	32 Court Street, Suite 1600	New York, NY 11201
Kravitz, Lenny	Creative Artists Agency	2000 Avenue of the Stars	Los Angeles, CA 90067
Labelle, Patti	Creative Artists Agency	2000 Avenue of the Stars	Los Angeles, CA 90067
Lachey, Nick	ICM	10250 Constellation Blvd.	Los Angeles, CA 90067
Lang, K.D.	William Morris Agency	One William Morris Place	Beverly Hills, CA 90212
Larsen, Blaine	Giantslayer Records	1103 17th Avenue South	Nashville, TN 37212
Latifa, Queen	Flavor Unit Entertainment	155 Morgan St.	Jersey City, NJ 07302
Lauper, Cyndi	De La Font Agency	4845 South Sheridan Rd	Tulsa, OK 74145
Lavigne, Avril	Nettwerk Management	8730 Wilshire Blvd., Ste. 304	Beverly Hills, CA 90211
Led Zeppelin	WEA Records	28 Kennsington Church St.	London, W8 4EP Eng.
Lee, Brenda	2175 Carson Street	Nashville, TN 37210	
Lee, Peggy	Stanley Weinstein Mgmt.	408 Charleston Road	Hampton, NJ 08827
Legend, John	Esterman Entertainment	1360 Clifton Ave	Clifton, NJ 07013
Lennox, Annie	Creative Artists Agency	2000 Avenue of the Stars	Los Angeles, CA 90067
Lenon, Sean	William Morris Agency	One William Morris Place	Beverly Hills, CA 90212
Levesque, Joanna 'JoJo'	Barnes, Morris, Klein	1424 Second Street	Santa Monica, CA 90401

Lewis, Gary	PO Box 53664	Indianapolis, IN 46253	
Lewis, Huey	Bob Brown Management	P.O. Box 779	Mill Valley, CA 94942
Lewis, Jerry Lee	Brasstack Alliance	P.O. Box 143	Morris Plains, NJ 07950
Lil' Kim	Intl. Creative Mgmt.	10250 Constellation Blvd.	Los Angeles, CA 90067
Lil' Romeo	Nickelodeon Studios	231 West Olive Avenue	Burbank, CA 91502
Limp Bizkit	Interscope Records	2220 Colorado Ave	Santa Monica, CA 90404
Lindsay, Mark	Steppin' Out	PO Box 754	Sandy, OR 97055
Little Richard	De La Font Agency	4845 South Sheridan Rd	Tulsa, OK 74145
LL Cool J	PMK Public Relations	8500 Wilshire Blvd	Beverly Hills, CA 90211
Loggins, Kenny	De La Font Agency	4845 South Sheridan Rd	Tulsa, OK 74145
Lopez, Jennifer	William Morris Agency	One William Morris Place	Beverly Hills, CA 90212
Loring, Gloria	J. Cast Productions	2550 Greenvalley Rd	Los Angeles, CA 90046
Lovano, Joe	Blue Note Capital	304 Park Avenue	New York, NY 10010
Love, Courtney	United Talent Agency	9560 Wilshire Blvd	Beverly Hills, CA 90212
Loveless, Patty	William Morris Agency	One William Morris Place	Beverly Hills, CA 90212
Lovett, Lyle	De La Font Agency	4845 South Sheridan Rd	Tulsa, OK 74145
Ludacris "Chris Bridges"	William Morris Agency	One William Morris Place	Beverly Hills, CA 90212
Lulu	PO Box 22	Sunbury-on-Thames	Middlesex TW165RT UK
Macy, Gary	Epic Records	550 Madison Avenue	New York, NY 10022
Madonna	Creative Artists Agency	2000 Avenue of the Stars	Los Angeles, CA 90067
Manchester, Mellissa	Columbia Artists Mgmt.	165 West 57th Street	New York, NY 10019
Mandrell, Barbara	Creative Artists Agency	2000 Avenue of the Stars	Los Angeles, CA 90067
Mandrell, Louise	Artists Management Inc.	555 West Madison Street	Chicago, IL 60661
Manilow, Barry	William Morris Agency	One William Morris Place	Beverly Hills, CA 90212
Manson, Marilyn	Creative Artists Agency	2000 Avenue of the Stars	Los Angeles, CA 90067
Martin, Joey	Giantslayer Records	1103 17th Avenue South	Nashville, TN 37212
Martin, Ricky	Creative Artists Agency	2000 Avenue of the Stars	Los Angeles, CA 90067
Mathis, Johnny	William Morris Agency	One William Morris Place	Beverly Hills, CA 90212
Mattea, Kathy	William Morris Agency	One William Morris Place	Beverly Hills, CA 90212
Matthews, Dave	Dave Matthews Band	509 Hartnell Street	Monterey, CA 93940
Mayer, John	Ken Sunshine Consultant	149 5th Avenue	New York, NY 10010
McBride, Martina	Creative Artists Agency	2000 Avenue of the Stars	Los Angeles, CA 90067
McCartney, Paul	Waterfall Estates	Near Peamarsh	St. Leonard-on-Sea UK
McCoo, Marilyn	William Morris Agency	One William Morris Place	Beverly Hills, CA 90212
McCready, Mindy	1209 16th Avenue South	Nashville, TN 37212	
McDonald, Michael	William Morris Agency	One William Morris Place	Beverly Hills, CA 90212
McEntire, Reba	Creative Artists Agency	2000 Avenue of the Stars	Los Angeles, CA 90067
McGraw, Tim	Creative Artists Agency	2000 Avenue of the Stars	Los Angeles, CA 90067
McKnight, Brian	William Morris Agency	One William Morris Place	Beverly Hills, CA 90212
McLachlan, Sarah	Nettwerk Management	8730 Wilshire Blvd	Beverly Hills, CA 90211
McNight, Brian	Richard	4845 South Sheridan Rd	Tulsa, OK 74145
McPhee, Katharine	Untitled Entertainment	331 N. Maple Drive	Beverly Hills, CA 90210
Medley, Bill	William Morris Agency	One William Morris Place	Beverly Hills, CA 90212
Mellencamp, John	Route 1 Box 361	Nashville, IN 47448	
Messina, Jo Dee	De La Font Agency	4845 South Sheridan Rd	Tulsa, OK 74145
Michael, George	Creative Artists Agency	2000 Avenue of the Stars	Los Angeles, CA 90067
Midler, Bette	Creative Artists Agency	2000 Avenue of the Stars	Los Angeles, CA 90067
Milian, Christina	Evolution Talent Agency	1776 Broadway - 15th Floor	New York, NY 10019
Milsap, Ronnie	Ronnie Milsap Theatre	3015 Theatre Drive	Myrtle Beach, SC 29577
Minnelli, Liza	Innovative Artists	1505 10th St	Santa Monica, CA 90401
Money, Eddie	De La Font Agency	4845 South Sheridan Rd	Tulsa, OK 74145
Monica	Handprint Entertainment	1100 Glendon Ave	Los Angeles, CA 90024

Moore, Chante	Creative Artists Agency	2000 Avenue of the Stars	Los Angeles, CA 90067
Moreno, Rita	APA Talent and Literary	9200 Sunset Blvd	Los Angeles, CA 90069
Morgan, Lorrie	# 300	38 Music Square	Nashville, TN 37203
Morissette, Alanis	Creative Artists Agency	2000 Avenue of the Stars	Los Angeles, CA 90067
Morrison, Van	De La Font Agency	4845 South Sheridan Rd	Tulsa, OK 74145
Murphy, Mark	High Note Records	106 West 71st Street	New York, NY 10023
Murray, Anne	Bruce Allen Talent	500 - 425 Carrall Street	Vancouver, BC V6B 6E3 Canada
Musiq	William Morris Agency	One William Morris Place	Beverly Hills, CA 90212
Mya "Marie Harrison"	Idea Public Relations	3940 Laurel Canyon Blvd.	Studio City, CA 91604
Nabors, Jim	PO Box 10364	Honolulu, HI 96816	
Nash, Graham	Creative Artists Agency	2000 Avenue of the Stars	Los Angeles, CA 90067
Nelly "Cornell Haynes Jr."	Upton / Universal Records	1755 Broadway	New York, NY 10019
Nelson, Willie	William Morris Agency	One William Morris Place	Beverly Hills, CA 90212
Nesmith, Michael	The Agency Group	9348 Civic Center Drive	Beverly Hills, CA 90210
Neville, Aaron	Shore Fire Media	32 Court Street, Suite 1600	New York, NY 11201
Newkirk, Anastacia	Evolution Talent Agency	1776 Broadway - 15th Floor	New York, NY 10019
Newton, Wayne	Flying Eagle Inc.	3422 Happy Lane	Las Vegas, NV 89101
Newton-John, Olivia	Creative Artists Agency	2000 Avenue of the Stars	Los Angeles, CA 90067
Noone, Peter	9265 Robin Lane	Los Angeles, CA 90069	
Norwood, Brandy	William Morris Agency	One William Morris Place	Beverly Hills, CA 90212
Nugent, Ted	800 Eckert	Concord, MI 49239	
O'Connor Sinead	Vanguard Records	2700 Pennsylvania Ave	Santa Monica, CA 90404
Ocean, Billy	Ascot	Berkshire, England	
O'Neil, Melissa	Ambush Artist Mgmt	32 Ransomes Dock	London SW11 4NP UK
Ono, Yoko	Studio One	1 West 72nd Street	New York, NY 10023
Orlando, Tony	3220 Falls Parkway	Branson, MO 65616	
Osborne, Ozzy	Creative Artists Agency	2000 Avenue of the Stars	Los Angeles, CA 90067
Osmond, Donny	Suite 424	51 West Center	Orem, UT 84057
Osmond, Marie	William Morris Agency	One William Morris Place	Beverly Hills, CA 90212
Page, Patti	Gurtman & Murtha	450 Seventh Avenue	New York, NY 10123
Paisley, Brad	William Morris Agency	One William Morris Place	Beverly Hills, CA 90212
Parton, Dolly	Dollywood	1020 Dollywood Lane	Pigeon Forge, TN 37683
Patty, Sandi	De La Font Agency	4845 South Sheridan Rd	Tulsa, OK 74145
Paycheck, Johnny	PO Box 121377	Nashville, TN 37212	
Peck, Danielle	Orbison Myers Mgmt	1625 Broadway	Nashville, TN 37203
Petty, Tom	PO Box 260159	Encino, CA 91426	
Pink "Alecia Moore"	William Morris Agency	One William Morris Place	Beverly Hills, CA 90212
Piondexter, Buster	APA Talent and Literary	9200 Sunset Blvd	Los Angeles, CA 90069
Pop, Iggy	533-579 Harrow Road	London, England W104RH	
Porter, Kalan	Ambush Artist Mgmt	32 Ransomes Dock	London SW11 4NP UK
Presley, Lisa Maria	William Morris Agency	One William Morris Place	Beverly Hills, CA 90212
Preston, Billy	De La Font Agency	4845 South Sheridan Rd	Tulsa, OK 74145
Pride, Charlie	PO Box 670507	Dallas, TX 75367	
Prince "Roger Nelson"	The Lippin Group	369 Lexington Avenue	New York, NY 10017-6506
Puckett, Gary	GP Music, Inc.	36181 East Lake Rd, #107	Palm Harbor, Fl 34685
Q-Tip	Creative Artists Agency	2000 Avenue of the Stars	Los Angeles, CA 90067
Raitt, Bonnie	De La Font Agency	4845 South Sheridan Rd	Tulsa, OK 74145
Ray, Amy	High Road Touring	751 Ridgeway- 3rd Floor	Sausalito, CA 94965
Redbone, Leon	179 Aquestong Road	New Hope, PA 18938	
Reddy, Helen	De La Font Agency	4845 South Sheridan Rd	Tulsa, OK 74145

Redman, Joshua	Shore Fire Media	32 Court Street, Suite 1600	New York, NY 11201
Reed, Jerry	153 Rue De Grande	Brentwood, TN 37027	
Reese, Dela	William Morris Agency	One William Morris Place	Beverly Hills, CA 90212
Reeves, Martha	1300 Lafayette	Detriot, MI 48207	
Richie, Lionel	Creative Artists Agency	2000 Avenue of the Stars	Los Angeles, CA 90067
Rihanna	Def Jam Recordings	825 Eighth Avenue	New York, NY 10019
Rimes, LeAnn	Special Artists Agency	9465 Wilshire Blvd	Beverly Hills, CA 90212
Rivers, Johnny	De La Font Agency	4845 South Sheridan Rd	Tulsa, OK 74145
Robinson, Smokey	William Morris Agency	One William Morris Place	Beverly Hills, CA 90212
Rogers, Kenny	William Morris Agency	One William Morris Place	Beverly Hills, CA 90212
Ronstadt, Linda	De La Font Agency	4845 South Sheridan Rd	Tulsa, OK 74145
Ross, Diana	Rogers & Cowan PR	1888 Century Park East	Los Angeles, CA 90067
Royal, Billie Joe	Bobby Roberts Company	PO Box 1547	Goodlettesville, TN 37070
Ryder, Mitch	ESI	6400 Pleasant Park Drive	Chanhassen, MN 55317
Sade	Creative Artists Agency	2000 Avenue of the Stars	Los Angeles, CA 90067
Saint-Marie, Buffy	RR1 Box 368	Kapaa , Kauai, HI 96746	
Saliers, Emily	Sony MusicEntertainment	550 Madison Avenue	New York, NY 10022
Scaggs, Boz	De La Font Agency	4845 South Sheridan Rd	Tulsa, OK 74145
Scott, Jill	Hidden Beach Records	3030 Nebraska Ave.	Santa Monica, CA 90404
Scruggs, Randy	Creative Artists Agency	2000 Avenue of the Stars	Los Angeles, CA 90067
Seal	Creative Artists Agency	2000 Avenue of the Stars	Los Angeles, CA 90067
Seals, Dan	PO Box 1770	Hendersonville, Tn 37077	
Sean 'P. Diddy' Combs	Bad Boy Films	1710 Broadway	New York, NY 10019
Sebastian, John	Dave Bendett	2431 Briarcrest Rd	Beverly Hills, CA 90210
Secada, John	William Morris Agency	One William Morris Place	Beverly Hills, CA 90212
Sedaka, Neil	De La Font Agency	4845 South Sheridan Rd	Tulsa, OK 74145
Seger, Bob	Creative Artists Agency	2000 Avenue of the Stars	Los Angeles, CA 90067
Shakira "Isabel Ripoll"	William Morris Agency	One William Morris Place	Beverly Hills, CA 90212
Sherman, Bobby	Paradise Talent-R. Birk	108 East Matilija Street	Ojai, CA 93023
Short, Bobby	De La Font Agency	4845 South Sheridan Rd	Tulsa, OK 74145
Sierra, Jessica	Talent Master Agency	PO Box 218014	Nashville, TN 37221
Simmons, Gene	Kleinberg Lopez Lange	2049 Century Park East	Los Angeles, CA 90067 USA
Simon, Paul	Creative Artists Agency	2000 Avenue of the Stars	Los Angeles, CA 90067
Simpson, Ashlee	Creative Artists Agency	2000 Avenue of the Stars	Los Angeles, CA 90067
Simpson, Jessica	Creative Artists Agency	2000 Avenue of the Stars	Los Angeles, CA 90067
Skaggs, Ricky	54 Music Square East	Nashville, TN 37203	
Slick, Grace	5956 Kanan Dume Road	Malibu, CA 90265	
Smothers, Dick	William Morris Agency	One William Morris Place	Beverly Hills, CA 90212
Smothers, Tom	William Morris Agency	One William Morris Place	Beverly Hills, CA 90212
Spears, Britney	Evolution Talent Agency	1776 Broadway - 15th Floor	New York, NY 10019
Springfield, Rick	APA Talent and Literary	9200 W, Sunset Blvd	Los Angeles, CA 90069
Springsteen, Bruce	Creative Artists Agency	2000 Avenue of the Stars	Los Angeles, CA 90067
Stanley, Paul	Mercury Records	825 8th Avenue	New York, NY 10019
Starr, Ringo	Primary Talent Intl.	5th Floor, 2-12 Pentonville Rd	London, N1 9PL UK
Stefani, Gwen	Interscope Records	2220 Colorado Avenue	Santa Monica, CA 90404
Stevens, Rachel	Ambush Artist Mgmt	32 Ransomes Dock	London SW11 4NP UK
Stevens, Ray	William Morris Agency	1600 Division Street	Nashville, TN 37203
Stewart, Rod	Stiefel Entertainment	421 North Robertson Blvd.	West Hollywood, CA 90048
Sting	Markham & Froggatt Ltd	4 Windmill Street	London, W1T 2HZ UK
Stone, Joss	EMI USA	6255 West Sunset Blvd	Hollywood, CA 90028
Strait, George	C/O Woolsey	1000 18th Avenue So.	Nashville, TN 37212

Streisand, Barbra	Solters & Digney	8383 Wilshire Blvd.	Beverly Hills, CA 90211
Studdard, Ruben	Creative Artists Agency	2000 Avenue of the Stars	Los Angeles, CA 90067
Studt, Amy	Ambush Artist Mgmt	32 RansomesParkgate Road	London SW11 4NP UK
Summer, Donna	Enter Talking PR	PO Box 18834	Beverly Hills, CA 90209
Taylor, James	Gorfaine/Schwartz Agency	4111 West Alameda Ave.	Burbank, CA 91505
Tenacious D	Creative Artists Agency	2000 Avenue of the Stars	Los Angeles, CA 90067
Tennille, Tony	De La Font Agency	4845 South Sheridan Rd	Tulsa, OK 74145
Thomas, B.J.	Gloria Thomas	1424 Crownhill Drive	Arlington, TX 76012
Tillis, Pam	De La Font Agency	4845 South Sheridan Rd	Tulsa, OK 74145
Tork, Peter	Fantasma Productions	2000 S. Dixie Highway	West Palm Beach, FL. 33401
Travis, Randy	Intl. Creative Mgmt.	10250 Constellation Blvd.	Los Angeles, CA 90067
Tritt, Travis	William Morris Agency	One William Morris Place	Beverly Hills, CA 90212
Tucker, Tanya	William Morris Agency	One William Morris Place	Beverly Hills, CA 90212
Turner, Ike	Shore Fire Media	32 Court Street, Suite 1600	New York, NY 11201
Turner, Tina	Creative Artists Agency	2000 Avenue of the Stars	Los Angeles, CA 90067
Twain, Shania	Creative Artists Agency	3310 West End Avenue	Nashville, TN 37203
Tyrell, Steve	Soundtrack Music	2229 Cloverfield Blvd.	Santa Monica, CA 90405
Underwood, Carrie	RCA Music Group	1540 Broadway	New York, NY 10036
Urban, Keith	Creative Artists Agency	2000 Avenue of the Stars	Los Angeles, CA 90067
Usher	Jonas Public Relations	240 26th Street, Ste. 3	Santa Monica, CA 90402
Vallie, Frankie	5603 No. Winton Ct.	Calbassas, CA 91302	
Van Halen, Eddie	31736 Broad Beach	Malibu, CA 90265	
Van Shelton, Ricky	De La Font Agency	4845 South Sheridan Rd	Tulsa, OK 74145
Vaughn, Jimmie	De La Font Agency	4845 South Sheridan Rd	Tulsa, OK 74145
Vee, Bobby	PO Box 41	Sauk Rapids, MN 56378	
Vinton, Bobby	PO Box 6010	Branson, MO 65615	
Wagoner, Porter	PO Box 290785	Nashville, TN 37229	
Waits, Tom	Endeavor Talent Agency	9601 Wilshire Blvd. Floor 3	Beverly Hills, CA 90210
Warwick, Dionne	Intl. Creative Mgmt.	10250 Constellation Blvd	Los Angeles, CA 90067
West, Kanye	William Morris Agency	One William Morris Place	Beverly Hills, CA 90212
Whatmore, Sarah	Ambush Artist Mgmt	32 RansomesParkgate Road	London SW11 4NP UK
Williams, Andy	2540 W. Hwy. 76	Branson, MO 65616	
Williams, Deniece	De La Font Agency	4845 South Sheridan Rd	Tulsa, OK 74145
Williams, Hank Jr.	William Morris Agency	One William Morris Place	Beverly Hills, CA 90212
Williams, Lucinda	De La Font Agency	4845 South Sheridan Rd	Tulsa, OK 74145
Williams, Vanesa L.	Intl. Creative Mgmt.	8942 Wilshire Blvd	Beverly Hills, CA 90211
Wilson, Brian	William Morris Agency	One William Morris Place	Beverly Hills, CA 90212
Wilson, Carnie	William Morris Agency	One William Morris Place	Beverly Hills, CA 90212
Wilson, Cassandra	Shore Fire Media	32 Court Street, Suite 1600	New York, NY 11201
Wilson, Gretchen	Sony Music Nashville	1400 18th Avenue South	Nashville, TN 37212
Wilson, Mary	JDS - Jay D. Schwartz	3151 Cahuenga Blvd	Los Angeles, CA 90068
Wilson, Nancy	Peters Management	1212 Old Topanga CanyonRd	Topanga, CA 90290
Winans, CeCe	William Morris Agency	One William Morris Place	Beverly Hills, CA 90212
Womack, Lee Ann	DeLaFont Agency	4845 S. Sheridan Rd.	Tulsa, OK 74145
Wonder, Stevie	Creative Artists Agency	2000 Avenue of the Stars	Los Angeles, CA 90067
Wynette, Tammy	MCA Records	60 Music Square East	Nashville, TN 37203
Yearwood, Trisha	William Morris Agency	One William Morris Place	Beverly Hills, CA 90212
Yoakam, Dwight	William Morris Agency	One William Morris Place	Beverly Hills, CA 90212
Young, Will	Ambush Artist Mgmt	32 RansomesParkgate Road	London SW11 4NP UK
Yunus, Monica	Mirshak Artists Mgmt	15 West 28th Street	New York, NY 10001

Music Halls of Fame

The Rock & Roll Hall of Fame is in Cleveland, Ohio.

Unfortunately, the Hall of Fame does not forward autograph requests to inductees, however, the list is impressive and is a good starting place to build a collection of music related autographs.

1986
Chuck Berry
James Brown
Ray Charles
Sam Cooke
Fats Domino
The Everly Brothers
Buddy Holly
Jerry Lee Lewis
Elvis Presley
Little Richard
Non-Performers
Alan Freed
Sam Phillips
Early-Influences
Robert Johnson
Jimmie Rodgers
Jimmy Yancey
Lifetime Achievement
Morton, Jelly Roll
John Hammond
1987
The Coasters
Eddie Cochran
Bo Diddley
Aretha Franklin
Marvin Gaye
Bill Haley
B. B. King
Clyde McPhatter
Ricky Nelson
Roy Orbison
Carl Perkins
Smokey Robinson
Big Joe Turner
Muddy Waters
Jackie Wilson
Non-Performers
Leonard Chess
Ahmet Ertegun
J. Leiber and M. Stoller
Jerry Wexler
Early Influences
Louis Jordan
T-Bone Walker

Early Influ. 1987 Contined
Hank Williams
1988
The Beach Boys
The Beatles
The Drifters
Bob Dylan
The Supremes
Non-Performers
Berry Gordy, Jr.
Early Influences
Woody Guthrie
Lead Belly
Les Paul
1989
Dion
Otis Redding
The Temptations
Stevie Wonder
Non-Performer
Phil Spector
Early Influences
The Ink Spots
Bessie Smith
The Soul Stirrers
1990
Hank Ballard
Bobby Darin
The Four Seasons
The Four Tops
The Kinks
The Platters
Simon and Garfunkel
The Who
Non-Performers
Gerry Goffin
and Carole King
Holland & Dozier
Early Influences
Louis Armstrong
Charlie Christian
Ma Rainey

1991
La Vern Baker
The Byrds
John Lee Hooker
The Impressions
Wilson Pickett
Jimmy Reed
Ike and Tina Turner
Non-Performers
Dave Bartholomew
Ralph Bass
Early Influence
Howlin' Wolf
Lifetime Achievement
Nesuhi Ertegun
1992
Bobby "Blue" Bland
Booker T. and the M.G.'s
The Rolling Stones

Jimi Hendrix
Isley Brothers
Sam and Dave
The Yardbirds
Non-Performers
Leo Fender
Bill Graham
Doc Pomus
Early Influences
Elmore James
Professor Longhair
1993
Ruth Brown
Cream
Creedence Clearwater
Revival
The Doors
Etta James
Frankie Lymon
and The Teenagers
Van Morrison
Sly and the Family Stone
Non-Performers
Dick Clark
Milt Gabler

Early Influence 1993
Dinah Washington
1994
The Animals
The Band
Duane Eddy
Grateful Dead
Elton John
John Lennon
Bob Marley
Rod Stewart
Non-Performer
Johnny Otis
Early Influence
Willie Dixon
1995
The Allman Brothers Band
Al Green
Johnny Cash

Led Zeppelin
Martha and the Vandellas
Neil Young
Frank Zappa
Non-Performer
Paul Ackerman
Early Influence
The Orioles
David Bowie
Jefferson Airplane
Little Willie John
Gladys Knight and the Pips
Pink Floyd
The Shirelles
The Velvet Underground
Non-Performer
Tom Donahue
Early Influence
Pete Seeger
1997
Bee Gees, The
Buffalo Springfield
Crosby, Stills and Nash
Jackson Five, The
Mitchell, Joni

1997-continued
Parliament-Funkadelic
(Young) Rascals, The
Non-Performer
Nathan, Syd
Early Influences
Jackson, Mahalia
Monroe, Bill
1998
Eagles, The
Fleetwood Mac
Mamas and the Papas
Price, Lloyd
Santana
Vincent, Gene
Non-Performer
Toussaint, Allen
Early Influence
Janis Joplin
1999
Joel, Billy
Mayfield, Curtis
McCartney, Paul
Shannon, Del
Springfield, Dusty
Springsteen, Bruce
Staple Singers, The
Non-Performer
Martin, George
Early Influences
Charles Brown
Bob Wills
and Texas Playboys
2000
Eric Clapton
Earth, Wind & Fire
Lovin' Spoonful
The Moonglows
Bonnie Raitt
Early Influences
Nat King Cole
Billie Holiday

Music Halls of Fame

Rock and Roll Hall of Fame - continued

2001

Performers

Aerosmith

Burke, Solomon

The Flamingos

Jackson, Michael

Queen

Simon, Paul

Steely Dan

Valens, Ritchie

Sidemen

Burton, James

Johnson, Johnnie

Non-performers

Chris Blackwell

2002

Performers

Hayes, Isaac

Lee, Brenda

Tom Petty and the Heartbreakers

Pitney, Gene

Ramones

Talking Heads

Sidemen

Chet Atkins

Non-Performers

Jim Stewart

2003

Performers

AC/DC

The Clash

Elvis Costello & the Attractions

The Police

Righteous Brothers

Sidemen

Benny Benjamin

Floyd Cramer

Steve Douglas

Non-performers

Mo Ostin

2004

Performers

Jackson Browne

The Dells

Harrison, George

Prince

Seger, Bob

Traffic

ZZ Top

Lifetime Achievement

Wenner, Jann S.

Music Halls of Fame

Election to the Country Music Hall of Fame is the highest honor in country music. The Hall of Fame award was created in 1961 by the Country Music Association (CMA), the country music industry's leading trade organization. The award recognizes persons who have made outstanding contributions to country music over the lengths of their careers. Addresses of Country Music Hall of Fame inductees can be found in the list of musicians.

*Deceased

1961 Jimmie Rodgers*
1961 Fred Rose*
1961 Hank Williams*
1962 Roy Acuff*
1964 Tex Ritter*
1965 Ernest Tubb*
1966 Eddy Arnold
1966 James R. Denny*
1966 George D. Hay*
1966 Uncle Dave Macon*
1967 Red Foley*
1967 J. L. Frank*
1967 Jim Reeves*
1967 Stephen H. Sholes*
1968 Bob Wills*
1969 Gene Autry*
1970 Bill Monroe*
1970 Original Carter Family
1971 Arthur Satherley*
1972 Jimmie H. Davis*
1973 Chet Atkins*
1973 Patsy Cline*
1974 Owen Bradley*
1974 Frank "Pee Wee" King
1975 Minnie Pearl*
1976 Kitty Wells
1976 Paul Cohen*
1977 Merle Travis*
1978 Grandpa Jones*
1979 Hubert Long*
1979 Hank Snow*
1980 Connie B. Gay*
1980 Sons of the Pioneers
1980 Johnny Cash*
1981 Vernon Dalhart*
1981 Grant Turner*

1982 Lefty Frizzell*
1982 Marty Robbins*
1982 Roy Horton*
1983 Little Jimmy Dickens
1984 Ralph S. Peer*
1984 Floyd Tillman*
1985 Lester Flatt* & Earl Scruggs
1986 Wesley H. Rose*
1986 Whitey Ford*
1987 Rod Brasfield*
1988 Roy Rogers*
1988 Loretta Lynn
1989 Cliffie Stone*
1989 Hank Thompson
1989 Jack Stapp*
1990 Tennessee Ernie Ford*
1991 Felice and Boudleaux Bryant*
1992 George Jones
1992 Frances William Preston*
1993 Willie Nelson
1994 Merle Haggard
1995 Jo Walker-Meador
1995 Roger Miller*
1996 Patsy Montana*
1996 Buck Owens
1996 Ray Price
1997 Harlan Howard*
1997 Brenda Lee
1997 Cindy Walker
1998 George Morgan*
1998 Elvis Presley*
1998 E.W. "Bud" Wendell
1998 Tammy Wynette
1999 Johnny Bond*
1999 Dolly Parton
1999 Conway Twitty*

2000 Charley Pride
2000 Faron Young *
2001 Bill Anderson
2001 The Delmore Brothers *
2001 The Everly Brothers
2001 Don Gibson
2001 Homer & Jethro *
2001 Waylon Jennings *
2001 The Jordanaires
2001 Don Law *
2001 The Louvin Brothers Ira Loudermilk*
2001 Ken Nelson
2001 Webb Pierce *
2001 Sam Phillips
2002 Bill Carlisle *
2002 Porter Wagoner
2003 Floyd Cramer*
2003 Carl Smith

Websites of Celebrity Biographies

I recommend **www.imdb.com** "The IMDB Internet Movie Database." It is an excellent source of information about actors, movies, directors and cast members of movies over the past 100 years.

Here are some of the stats held in the "IMDB Internet Movie Database":
1. Over 203,000 entries of movie and tv series titles since 1895.
2. 45,000 award title entries
3. Listings of titles in current production and future productions.
4. The IMDB has over 20 occupation categories with 240,000 actor entries, 145,000 actress entries and 35,000 director entires.
5. The IMDB also has cast lists, crew lists, plot summaries and biographies.

www.who2.com
A good general purpose celebrity biographic site. The biographies are about one page in length.

www.astronautix.com
One of the few astronaut biography web sites. However, some of the biographies are short compared to others.

Biography.com
This web site holds the information on over 25,000 celebrities.

TV Shows That Feature Celebrity Biographies

The Biography Channel
The Biography Channel takes the viewer into a world of exceptional people. Biography shows the many facets of the celebrity; offering a fascinating view of celebrities and the forces that shape them.

Revealed with Jules Asner
A good, in depth look at todays celebrities

Actors Studio by Bravo TV Networks
Interview style of actors and their biographies

VH-1 Behind the Music
A good job of documenting the lives of music celebrities

ESPN Sports Century
One of the best if not the best program telling the story of sport figure lives. Program is one hour and covers the celebrities entire life, the good side as well as the not so good side.

Beyond the Glory
A good sports figure reference source. It is presented by Fox Sports and does an in depth report on the life of a sports figure.

Headliners & Legends with Matt Laurer

Web Sites of Celebrities

Affleck, Ben	http://www.affleck.com/	Cleese, John	http://thejohncleese.com/
Aguilera, Christina	http://www.christina-A.com/	Cohen, Sacha Baron	http://www.alig.com/
Allen, Tim	http://www.timallen.com/	Collette, Toni	http://www.pfd.co.uk/
Amos, Tori	http://toriamos.com/	Collins, Clifton Jr.	http://www.FilmKitchen.com/mysweetkiller
Anderson, Gillian	http://www.gilliananderson.ws/	Connery, Sean	http://www.seanconnery.com/
Anderson, Louie	http://www.louieanderson.com/	Connick, Harry Jr.	http://www.harryconnickjr.com/
Anderson, Pamela	http://www.clubpam.com/	Cook, Rachael Leigh	http://rachaelleighcook.com/
Angarano, Michael	http://www.kidactors.com/angarano	Coolidge, Rita	http://www.RitaCoolidge.com/
Anka, Paul	http://www.paulanka.com/	Cooper, Alice	http://www.alicecooper.com/
Anniston, Jennifer	http://www.jenniferaniston.com/	Cornell, Lydia	http://www.lydiacornell.com/
Antonthy, Marc	http://www.marcanthonyonline.com/	Costner, Kevin	www.kevincostner.com
Arness, James	www.jamesarness.com	Cox, Courteney	http://www.courteney-fan.net/
Astin, Sean	http://www.seanastin.com/	Coyote, Peter	http://www.petercoyote.com/
Aykroyd, Dan	http://hob.com/	Crawford, Cindy	http://www.cindy.com/
Bacon, Kevin	http://www.baconbros.com/	Crawford, Michael	http://www.mcifa.com/
Baez, Joan	http://baez.woz.org/	Criss, Peter	http://www.petercriss.net/
Baio, Scott	www.sitcomsonline.com/baiobiog.html	Cross, David	http://www.bobanddavid.com/
Barbeau, Adrienne	http://www.abarbeau.com/	Crow, Sheryl	http://www.sherylcrow.com/
Barberie, Jillian	http://www.jilliansworld.com/	Crowe, Russell	http://www.russellcrowe.com/
Bell, Catherine	http://www.catherinebellonline.com/	Culver, Molly	http://www.mollyculver.com/
Benson, Amber	http://www.efanguide.com/~amber/	Curry, Mark	http://www.markcurry.com/
Berman, Shelly	http://www.shelleyberman.com	Curtis, Tony	http://www.tonycurtis.com/
Bernhard, Sandra	http://www.sandrabernhard.com	Daly, Tyne	http://www.tynedaly.com/
Berry, Halle	http://www.hallewood.com/	Dangerfield, Rodney	http://www.rodney.com/
Bolton, Michael	http://www.michaelbolton.com/	Danza, Tony	http://www.tonydanza.com/
Borstein, Alex	http://www.alexborstein.com/	Day, Doris	http://www.ddal.org/
Bova, Raoul	http://www.raoulbova.it/	de Rossi, Portia	http://www.portia-derossi.com/
Boyd, Billy	http://www.billyboyd.net/	Degeneres, Ellen	http://ellen.warnerbros.com/
Branigan, Laura	http://www.laurabraniganonline.com	Del Toro, Benicio	http://www.beniciodeltoro.com/
Buffett, Jimmy	http://margaritaville.com/	Delany, Dana	http://www.danadelany.com/
Burke, Delta	http://www.delta-burke.com/	Deluise, Dom	http://www.domdeluise.com/
Butler, Brett	http://www.brettbutler.com/	Dempsey, Patrick	http://www.patrickdempsey.net/
Buzzi, Ruth	http://www.ruthbuzzi.com/	Deneuve, Catherine	http://www.cdeneuve.com/
Caesar, Sid	http://www.sidcaesar.com/	Denver, Bob	http://www.bobdenver.com/
Callas, Charlie	http://www.charliecallas.com/	Derek, Bo	http://www.boderek.com/
Campbell, Neve	http://www.nevecampbell.org/	DeVito, Danny	http://www.jerseyfilms.com/
Cannon, Dyan	http://www.dyancannon.com/	Dicaprio, Leonardo	http://www.leonardodicaprio.com/
Cara, Irene	http://www.irenecara.com/	Difranco, Ani	http://www.righteousbabe.com/index.asp
Carlin, George	http://www.georgecarlin.com/	Dion, Celine	http://www.celineonline.com/
Carr, Vikki	http://www.VikkiCarr.net/	Doherty, Denny	http://www.dennydoherty.com/
Carradine, David	http://www.davidcarradine.org/	Douglas, Michael	http://www.michaeldouglas.com/
Carrot Top	http://www.carrottop.com/	Down, Lesley-Anne	http://www.lesleyannedown.com/
Carter, Deana	http://www.deana.com/	Downey, Roma	http://www.roma-downey.com/roma.htm
Carvey, Dana	http://www.danacarvey.net/	Duke, Patty	http://www.officialpattyduke.com/
Cher	http://www.cher.com/	Eden, Barbara	http://www.fansource.com/eden.htm
Chiklis, Michael	http://www.michaelchiklis.com/	Egan, Susan	http://www.susanegan.net/
Cho, Margaret	http://www.margaretcho.net/	Elfman, Jenna	http://www.jennaelfman.com/
Christensen, Hayden	http://www.erikachristensen.com/	Eminem	http://www.eminem.com/
Christie, Lou	http://www.lou-christie.com/	Englund, Robert	http://www.robertenglund.com/
Clarkson, Kelly	http://www.kellyclarksonweb.com/	Ermy, R. Lee	http://www.rleeermey.com/

Web Sites of Celebrities

Estes, Will	http://www.willestes.com/		Ho, Don	http://www.donho.com/
Fairchild, Morgan	http://www.morganfairchild.com/		Hooks, Robert	http://www.necinc.org/
Faithfull, Marianne	http://www.marianne-faithfull.net/		Hope, Leslie	http://www.lesliehope.com/
Falk, Peter	http://www.peterfalk.com/		Hopper, Dennis	http://www.dennis-hopper.com/
Faris, Anna	http://www.annafaris.de/		Humperdinck, Engelbert	http://www.engelbert.com/
Farrell, Colin	http://www.colinfarrell.ie/		Hutton, Lauren	http://www.laurenhutton.com/
Favreau, Jon	http://www.gettingitmade.com/		Ice Cube	http://www.icecubemusic.com/
Fehr, Brendan	http://www.brendanfehr.com/		Idle, Eric	http://www.pythononline.com/
Fox, Michael J.	http://www.michaeljfox.org/		Iglesias, Enrique	http://www.enriqueiglesias.com/
Fox, Vivica A.	http://www.vivicafox.com/		India.Arie	http://www.indiaarie.com/
Francis, Connie	http://www.conniefrancis.com/		Ireland, Kathy	http://www.kathyireland.com/
Franken, Al	http://www.al-franken.com/		Jackson, Alan	http://www.alanjackson.com/index2.html
Franken, Al	http://www.al-franken.com/		Jackson, Janet	http://www.janet-jackson.com/
Fraser, Brenden	http://www.brendanfraser.com/		Jackson, Michael	http://www.michaeljackson.com/
Freeman, Morgan	http://www.revelationsent.com/		Jett, Joan	http://www.joanjett.com/
Fuentas, Daisy	http://www.daisyfuentes.com/		Jewel	http://www.jeweljk.com/
Fuller, Robert	http://www.robertfuller.tv		Joel, Billy	http://www.billyjoel.com/
Furlong, Edward	http://www.edward-furlong.com/		Johnson, Don	http://www.donjohnson.com/
Gallagher, Leo	http://gallaghersmash.com/		Johnson, Dwayne	http://www.therock.com/
Gallagher, Peter	http://www.petergallagher.com/		Johnson, Russell	http://www.russell-johnson.com/
Garth, Jennie	http://www.jenniegarth.com/		Jones, Davy	http://www.davyjones.net/
Gere, Richard	http://www.gerefoundation.org/		Jones, Jenny	http://www.jennyjones.com/
Gifford, Kathie Lee	http://www.kathieleegifford.com/		Jones, Shirley	http://www.castproductions.com/shirleyjones.html
Gilbert, Melissa	http://www.gilbert-boxleitner.com/		Jones, Tom	http://www.tomjones.com/
Gilliam, Terry	http://www.pythononline.com/plugs/gilliam/		Kazan, Lainie	http://www.lainiekazan.com/
Gish, Annabeth	http://www.allthingsannabeth.com/		Keach, Stacy	http://www.stacykeach.com/
Glaser, Paul Michael	http://www.paulmichaelglaser.org		Kennedy, Jamie	http://www.jamiekennedyworld.com/
Gorshin, Frank	http://www.frankgorshin.com/		Kid Rock	http://www.kidrock.com/
Gossett, Louis Jr.	http://www.louisgossettjr.info/		Kilmar, Val	http://www.valkilmer.com/
Grammer, Kelsey	http://www.kelseylive.com/		King, BB	http://bbking.mca.com/
Gray, Linda	http://www.lindagray.com/		King, Carole	http://www.caroleking.com/
Green, Seth	http://www.sethgreenonline.com/		Kingsley, Ben	http://www.benkingsley.com/
Green, Tom	http://www.tomgreen.com/		Kitt, Eartha	http://www.earthakitt.com/
Griffith, Andy	http://www.andygriffithmusic.com/		Knotts, Don	http://donknotts.tv/
Griffith, Melanie	http://www.melaniegriffith.com/		Knowles, Beyonce	http://www.destinyschild.com/
Grint, Rupert	http://rupertgrint.co.uk/		Kodjoe, Boris	http://www.borisonline.com/
Guzman, Luis	http://www.luisguzman.com/		Koenig, Walter	http://www.walterkoenig.com/
Gyllenhaal, Jake	http://www.jakegyllenhaal.com/		Kopell, Bernie	http://www.berniekopell.com/
Hall, Deidre	http://www.marlena.com/		Kramer, Stepfanie	http://www.stepfaniekramer.com/
Hargitay, Mariska	http://www.mariska.com/		Kravitz, Lenny	http://www.lennykravitz.com/
Harper, Valerie	http://www.valerieharper.com/		Kunis, Mila	http://www.milakunis.com/
Hasselhoff, David	http://www.davidhasselhoff.com/		La Beouf, Shia	http://www.celebritykidz.com/ShiaLaBeouf/default.htm
Hauer, Rutger	http://www.rutgerhauer.com/		Labelle, Patti	http://www.pattilabelle.com/
Hayek, Selma	http://www.hayekheaven.net/		Lachey, Nick	http://www.nicklachey.com
Heaton, Patricia	http://www.patriciaheaton.com/		Ladd, Cheryl	http://www.cherylladd.com/
Hedron, Tippi	http://www.shambala.org/		Ladd, Diane	http://www.dianeladd.com/
Hetfield, James	http://www.intersandman.com		Lamas, Lorenzo	http://www.lorenzo-lamas.com/
Hewitt, Jennifer Love	http://www.jenniferlovehewitt.com/		Lambert, Christopher	http://www.christopherlambert.org/
Hill, Faith	http://faithhill.com/		Lane, Diane	http://www.dianelane.com/
Hill, Lauryn	http://www.lauryn-hill.com/		Lauper, Cyndi	http://www.cyndilauper.com/

Web Sites of Celebrities

Lavigne, Avril	http://www.avril-lavigne.com/
Leary, Denis	http://www.learyfirefightersfoundation.org/
LeBlanc, Matt	http://www.nbc.com/Friends/bios/Matt_LeBlanc.html
Lee, Jason	http://www.jasonleefoundation.org/
Lee, Peggy	http://www.peggylee.com/
Leto, Jared	http://www.thirtysecondstomars.com/
Lewis, Huey	http://www.hln.org/
Lewis, Jerry	http://www.jerrylewiscomedy.com/
Lewis, Jerry Lee	http://www.jerryleelewis.com/
Li, Jet	http://www.jetli.com/
Light, Judith	http://www.judithlight.com/
Lil' Kim	http://lilkim.com/
Lillard, Matthew	http://www.matthewlillard.com/
Limbaugh, Rush	http://www.rushlimbaugh.com/
Limp Bizkit	http://www.LimpBizkit.com/
Lindsay, Mark	http://www.marklindsay.com/
Lockhart, Anne	http://www.annelockhart.com/
Lohan, Lindsay	http://llrocks.com/
Loken, Kristanna	http://www.kristannaloken.net/
Lopez, George	http://www.georgelopez.com/
Lopez, Jennifer	http://www.jenniferlopez.com
Loren, Sophia	http://www.sophialoren.com/
Loring, Gloria	http://www.glorialoring.com/
Love Hewitt, Jennifer	http://www.jenniferlovehewitt.com/
Love, Courtney	http://www.courtneylove.com/
Love, Courtney	http://www.courtneylove.com/
Lucci, Susan	http://www.susanlucci.com/
Ludacris	http://www.ludacris.net/
Luft, Lorna	http://www.lornaluftonline.com/
Lulu	http://www.lulu.co.uk/
Lynley, Carol	http://www.pscelebrities.com/cl.html
Lynskey, Melanie	http://www.melanie-lynskey.com/
MacArthur, James	http://www.jmdigitalscrapbook.com/
MacDowell, Andie	http://web.pinknet.cz/AndieMacDowell/
MacLachlan, Kyle	http://www.kylemaclachlan.com
MacLaine, Shirley	http://www.shirleymaclaine.com/
Madonna	http://www.maverickent.com/
Madsen, Michael	http://www.michaelmadsen.com/
Maher, Bill	http://www.billmaher.tv/
Manheim, Camryn	http://www.camryn.com/
Manilow, Barry	http://www.manilow.com/
Margret, Ann	http://www.ann-margret.com/
Martin, Ricky	http://www.rickymartin.com/
Martin, Steve	http://www.stevemartin.com/
Martino, Al	http://www.almartino.com/
Mathis, Johnny	http://www.johnnymathis.com/
Matlin, Marlee	http://www.marleeonline.com/
Mayo, Virginia	http://www.virginiamayo.com/
McBride, Martina	http://www.martina-mcbride.com/
McCarthy, Andrew	http://www.andrewmccarthy.com/
McCartney, Paul	http://www.paulmccartney.com
McCord, Kent	http://www.kentmccord.com/
McCormack, Eric	http://www.ericmccormack.com/
McCormick, Maureen	http://www.ttinet.com/mccormick/
McCutcheon, Martine	http://www.martinemccutcheon.com/
McEntire, Reba	http://www.reba.com/
McLachlan, Sarah	http://www.sarahmclachlan.com/
Mcnee, Patrick	http://www.patrickmacnee.com/
Mellencamp, John	http://www.mellencamp.com/
Meloni, Christopher	http://www.christopher-meloni.com/
Mendes, Eva	http://www.evamendes.com/
Meskimen, Jim	http://www.appliedsilliness.com/
Michael, George	http://www.georgemichael.com
Milner, Martin	http://www.hookup690.com/
Modine, Matthew	http://www.matthewmodine.com/
Mohr, Jay	http://www.JayMohrLive.com/
Molina, Alfred	http://www.alfred-molina.com/
Monica	http://www.monica.com/
Moore, Demi	http://members.aol.com/inzax580/demi.html
Moore, Mary Tyler	http://www.jdf.org/
Morissette, Alanis	http://www.alanismorissette.com/
Mullally, Megan	http://meganmullally.net/
Muniz, Frankie	http://www.celebritykidz.com/FrankieMuniz/
Najimy, Kathy	http://www.kathynajimy.com/
Nash, Graham	http://www.grahamnash.com/
Neill, Sam	http://www.twopaddocks.co.nz/
Nesmith, Michael	http://www.videoranch.com/
Newhart, Bob	http://www.bob-newhart.com/
Newhart, Bob	http://www.bob-newhart.com/
Newman, Paul	http://www.newmansown.com/
Nimoy, Leonard	http://www.leonardnimoyphotography.com/
Noone, Peter	http://www.peternoone.com/
Norris, Chuck	http://www.chucknorris.com/
Norwood, Brandy	http://www.foreverbrandy.com/
Olsen, Mary Kate&Ashley	http://www.mary-kateandashley.com/
O'Neill, Jennifer	http://www.jenniferoneill.com/
Osborne, Ozzy	http://www.ozzy.com/
Osbourne, Jack	http://www.jackosbourne.com/
Osbourne, Kelly	http://www.kellyosbourne.com/
Osment, Haley Joel	http://www.haleyjoelosment.net/
Osmond, Donny	http://www.donny.com/
Owens, Buck	http://www.buckowens.com/
Page, Patti	www.misspattipage.com
Palin, Michael	http://www.palinstravels.co.uk/
Paltrow, Gwyneth	http://www.gwynethpaltrow.com/
Panettiere, Hayden	http://www.haydenpanettiere.com/
Pantoliano, Joe	http://www.joeypants.com/
Paul, Adrian	http://www.adrianpaul.net/
Paxton, Bill	http://www.billpaxton.com/
Peete, Holly Robinson	http://www.hollyrobinsonpeete.com/

Perry, Luke	http://www77.pair.com/timem/perry/	Shatner, William	http://www.williamshatner.com/
Peters, Bernadette	http://www.bernadettepeters.com/	Shear, Rhonda	http://www.rhondashear.com/
Petty, Tom	http://www.tompetty.com/	Shepard, Cybill	http://www.cybill.com/
Pollak, Kevin	http://www.kevinpollak.net/	Shields, Brook	http://www.brookeshields.com/
Potente, Franka	http://www.franka-potente.de/	Shore, Pauly	http://www.paulyshore.com/
Powers, Stefanie	http://www.whwf.org/welcome.htm	Simmons, Gene	http://www.genesimmons.com
Pride, Charlie	http://www.charleypride.com/	Simon, Paul	http://www.paulsimon.com/
Principal, Victoria	http://www.victoriaprincipal.com/	Simpson, Ashlee	http://www.ashleesimpsonmusic.com/
Proops, Greg	http://www.gregproops.com/	Simpson, Jessica	http://www.jessicasimpson.com/
Pryor, Richard	http://www.richardpryor.com	Singleton, John	http://www.johnsingletonfilms.com/
Randolph, Boots	http://www.bootsrandolph.com/	Sirtis, Marina	http://www.marinasirtis.tv/
Rawls, Lou	http://www.lourawls.com/	Smirnoff, Yakov	http://www.yakov.com/
Redbone, Leon	http://www.leonredbone.com/	Smith, Jaclyn	http://www.jaclynsmith.com/
Reddy, Helen	http://www.helenreddy.com/	Smith, Kevin	http://www.viewaskew.com/
Redford, Robert	http://www.sundance.org/	Smith, Riley	http://www.rileysmith.tv/
Redgrave, Lynn	http://www.redgrave.com/	Smith, Will	http://www.willsmith.com/
Reiner, Rob	http://www.castle-rock.com/	Smothers, Dick	http://www.smothersbrothers.com/
Remini, Leah	http://www.leahremini.net/	Smothers, Tom	http://www.smothersbrothers.com/
Reynolds, Burt	http://www.burtreynolds.com/	Sobieski, Leelee	http://www.leeleesobieski.com/
Reynolds, Debbie	http://www.debbiereynolds.com/	Somers, Suzanne	http://www.suzannesomers.com/
Richards, Denise	http://www.deniserichards.com/	Sorbo, Kevin	http://www.kevinsorbo.net/
Rimes, LeAnn	http://www.rimestimes.com/	Sparks, Hal	http://www.halsparks.com/
Rivera, Geraldo	http://www.geraldo.com/	Spears, Britney	http://www.britneyspears.com/
Robinson, Smokey	http://www.sangsistasang.com/smokey.html	Spelling, Tori	http://www.tori-spelling.com/
Rodriguez, Paul	http://www.paulrodriguez.com/	Springer, Jerry	http://www.jerryspringer.com/
Romano, Ray	http://www.rayromano.com/	Springfield, Rick	http://www.rickspringfield.com/
Rooney, Mickey	http://www.mickeyrooney.com/	Stallone, Sylvester	http://www.sylvesterstallone.com/
Roseanne	http://www.roseanneworld.com/	Stanford, Aaron	http://www.aaronstanford.com/
Roseanne	http://www.roseanneworld.com/	Stein, Ben	http://www.benstein.com/
Rossum, Emmy	http://www.angelfire.com/tx3/emmyrossum/	Stevens, Gary	http://www.garystevens.com/
Roundtree, Richard	http://www.theoriginalshaft.com/	Stevens, Ray	http://www.raystevens.com/
Rowell, Victoria	http://www.faithfoxent.com/VRowell.htm	Stevens, Stella	http://www.stellavisions.com/
Rudner, Rita	www.ritafunny.com	Stiles, Julia	http://www.juliastiles.net/
Russell, Keri	http://www.kerirussell.com/	Sting	http://www.sting.com/
Russell, Mark	http://www.markrussell.net/	Strait, George	http://www.georgestrait.com/
Ryan, Jeri	http://www.jerilynn.com/	Streisand, Barbra	http://www.barbrastreisand.com/
Rydell, Bobby	http://www.bobbyrydell.com/	Summer, Donna	http://www.donna-summer.com/
Sade	http://www.sade.com/sade/	Swayze, Patrick	http://www.patrickswayze.net/
Sagal, Katey	http://www.kateysagal.net	Sykes, Wanda	http://www.wandasykes.com/
Saint-Marie, Buffy	http://www.creative-native.com/	Takei, George	http://www.georgetakei.com/
Sandler, Adam	http://www.adamsandler.com/	Tamblyn, Amber	http://www.amtam.com/
Sandler, Adam	http://www.adamsandler.com/	Tarantino, Quentin	http://www.abandapart.com/
Santana, Carlos	http://www.santana.com/	Taylor, Rip	http://www.riptaylor.com/
Scalia, Jack	http://www.jackscalia.com/	Tennille, Tony	http://captainandtennille.net/
Scoggins, Tracy	http://www.tracyscoggins.com/	Tenuta, Judy	http://www.judytenuta.com/
Scott, Jill	http://www.jillscott.com/	Theissen, Tiffani-Amber	http://www.tiffanithiessen.com
Seal	http://www.seal.com/homeNew.html	Theron, Charlize	http://www.charlizetheron.com/
Sedaka, Neil	http://www.neilsedaka.com/	Theroux, Justin	http://www.justintheroux.net/
Serkis, Andy	http://www.serkis.com/	Thicke, Alan	http://alanthicke.tripod.com/
Seymour, Jane	http://www.janeseymour.com/	Thinnes, Roy	http://miraclefilms.com/thinnes.htm

Web Sites of Celebrities

Thornton, Billy Bob	http://www.billybobthornton.net/
Tillis, Pam	http://www.pamtillis.com/
Tomlin, Lilly	http://www.lilytomlin.com/
Tork, Peter	http://www.petertork.com/
Travis, Randy	http://www.randy-travis.com/
Tritt, Travis	http://www.travis-tritt.com/
Tucker, Tanya	http://www.tanyatucker.com/
Turner, Tina	http://www.tina-turner.com/
Twain, Shania	http://www.shania-twain.com/
Twiggy, Lawson	http://www.twiggylawson.co.uk/
Ubach, Alanna	http://www.alannaubach.net/
Usher	http://www.usherworld.com/
Van Damme, Jean Claude	

http://www.jeanclaudevandamme.net/

Van Halen, Eddie	http://www.van-halen.com/
Vaughn, Vince	http://www.blue-visions.org/~vince/
Vidal, Christina	http://www.christina-vidal.com/
Waggoner, Lyle	http://www.starwaggons.com/
Wagner, Robert	http://www.robert-wagner.com/
Wahlberg, Mark	http://www.markwahlberg.com/
Ward, Sela	http://www.selawardtv.com/
Watson, Emma	http://www.EWofficial.tk
Wells, Dawn	http://www.dawn-wells.com/
Wen, Ming-Na	http://www.ming-na.com/
West, Adam	http://www.adamwest.com/
Whitaker, Forest	http://www.forestwhitaker.com/
Willard, Fred	http://www.fredwillard.com/
Williams, Cindy	http://www.cindywilliams.com/
Williams, Kimberly	http://www.kimberlywilliams-paisley.com/
Williams, Vanessa L.	http://www.vanessawilliams.de/
Willis, Bruce	http://www.brucewillis.com/
Willis, Katherine	http://www.kwillis.com/
Wilson, Peta	http://www.petawilson-online.com/
Windom, William	http://www77.pair.com/timem/windom/
Woods, James	http://www.jameswoods.com/
Wyle, Noah	http://www.theblank.com/
Wynette, Tammy	http://tammywynette.com/
Yearwood, Trisha	http://www.trishayearwood.com/
Yoakam, Dwight	http://www.dwightyoakam.net/
York, Michael	http://www.michaelyork.net/
Young, Alan	http://www.mister-ed.tv/
Zeta-Jones, Catherine	http://www.catherinezetajones.com/
Zhang, Ziyi	http://www.helloziyi.com/

The Address Directory: Sports

Baseball Hall of Fame

Major League Baseball Team Rosters

Basketball Hall of Fame Members

Harlem Globetrotters

National Basketball Association Team Rosters

International Boxing Hall of Fame Members

Pro Football Hall of Fame Members

National Football League Team Rosters

National Hockey League Team Rosters

All Professional Golf Association Members

International Tennis Hall of Fame Members

Indy 500 Winners & Auto Racers

Olympians

The National Baseball Hall of Fame will forward requests for autographs of a member. Please leave room on the envelope for the inductee's address. Please note on envelope to forward to inductee.

Address requests for Baseball Hall of Fame members to:

Name of Inductee
National Baseball Hall of Fame
25 Main Street
Cooperstown, NY 13326

Photos of inductees may be ordered from the Baseball Hall of Fame Photo Department. Please call
1-607-547-0370 (Photo Collection Manager) for price and availability of a member's photo. Below is a list of the living members of The Baseball Hall of Fame.

Name	Inducted	Name	Inducted
Aaron, Hank	1982	MacPhail, Lee	1998
Anderson, Sparky	2000	Marichal, Juan	1983
Aparicio, Luis	1984	Mays, Willie	1979
Banks, Ernie	1977	Mazeroski, Bill	2001
Bench, Johnny	1989	McCovey, Willie	1986
Berra, Yogi	1972	Molitor, Paul	2004
Brett, George	1999	Morgan, Joe	1990
Brock, Lou	1985	Murray, Eddie	2003
Bunning, Jim	1996	Musial, Stan	1969
Carew, Rod	1991	Niekro, Phil	1997
Carter, Gene	2003	Palmer, Jim	1990
Carlton, Steve	1994	Perez, Tony	2000
Cepeda, Orlando	1999	Perry, Gaylord	1991
Doerr, Bobby	1986	Puckett, Kirby	2001
Eckersley, Dennis	2004	Rizzuto, Phil	1994
Feller, Bob	1962	Roberts, Robin	1976
Fingers, Rollie	1992	Robinson, Brooks	1983
Fisk, Carlton	2000	Robinson, Frank	1982
Ford, Whitey	1974	Ryan, Nolan	1999
Gibson, Bob	1981	Schmidt, Mike	1995
Irvin, Monte	1973	Schoendienst, Red	1989
Jackson, Reggie	1993	Seaver, Tom	1992
Jenkins, Fergie	1991	Smith, Ozzie	2002
Kaline, Al	1980	Snider, Duke	1980
Kell, George	1983	Sutton, Don	1998
Killebrew, Harmon	1984	Weaver, Earl	1996
Kiner, Ralph	1975	Williams, Billy	1987
Koufax, Sandy	1972	Winfield, Dave	2001
Lasorda, Tommy	1997	Yastrzemski, Carl	1989
Lopez, Al	1977	Yount, Robin	1999

The major league player roster remains at 25 players throughout the regular season until the 1st of September, when it is increased to 40 players. If the team makes it into post-season play, the roster returns to 25 players. If a player is placed on the disabled list, he can be replaced with an additional player.

All major league baseball team rosters are listed on the following pages. Match the player you select with the team address listed below.

(Name Of Player)
Colorado Rockies
Coors Field
2001 Blake Street
Denver, Co 80209

Anaheim Angels	Angel Stadium	2000 Gene Autry Way	Anaheim, CA 92806
Arizona Diamondbacks	Bankone Ballpark	401 Jefferson	Phoenix, AZ 85004
Atlanta Braves	Turner Field	755 Hank Aaron Drive	Atlanta, GA 30315
Baltimore Orioles	Oriole Park	333 Camden Street	Baltimore, MD 212002
Boston Red Soxs	Fenway Park	4 Yawkee Way	Boston, MA 02215
Chicago Cubs	Wrigley Field	1060 Addison Street	Chicago, IL 60613
Chicago White Soxs	Comisky Park	333 W. 35th Street	Chicago. IL 60616
Cincinnati Reds	Great American Ballpark	100 Main Street	Cincinnati, OH 45202
Cleveland Indians	Jacobs Field	2401 Ontario Street	Cleveland, OH 44115
Colorado Rockies	Coors Field	2001 Blake Street	Denver, CO 80205
Detroit Tigers	Comerica Park	2100 Woodland Avenue	Detroit, MI 48201
Florida Marlins	Pro Player Stadium	2267 Dan Marino Blvd.	Miami, FL 33056
Houston Astros	Minute Maid Park	PO Box 288	Houston, TX 77001
Kansas City Royals	Kaufman Stadium	1 Royal Way	Kansas City, MO 64141
Los Angeles Dodgers	Dodger Stadium	1000 Elysian Way	Los Angeles, CA 90012
Milwaukee Brewers	Miller Park	One Brewers Way	Milwaukee, WI 53214
Minnesota Twins	HHH Metrodome	34 Kirby Puckett Way	Minneapolis, MN 55415
Montreal Expos	Olympic Stadium	4549 Pierre-de-Coubertin Ave	Montreal, Quebec H1V3N7
New York Mets	Shea Stadium	123-01 Roosevelt Avenue	Flushing, NY 11368
New York Yankees	Yankee Stadium	Bronx, NY 10451	
Oakland Athletics	Network Coliseum	7000 Coliseum Way	Oakland, CA 94621
Philadelphia Phillies	Citizens Bank Ballpark	One Citizens Bank Way	Philadelphia, PA 19148
Pittsburgh Pirates	PNC Park	115 Federal Street	Pittsburgh, PA 15212
San Diego Padres	PETCO Park	PO Box 122000	San Diego, CA 92112
San Francisco Giants	SBC Park	24 Willie Mays Plaza	San Francisco, CA 94107
Seattle Mariners	Safeco Field	First & Atlantic	Seattle, WA 98104
St Louis Cardinals	Busch Stadium	250 Stadium Plaza	St Louis, MO 63102
Tampa Bay Devils	Tropicana Field	One Tropicana Drive	St Petersburg, FL 33705
Texas Rangers	Ameriquest Field	1000 Ballpark Way	Arlington, TX 76011
Toronto Blue Jays	Skydome Stadium	1 Blue Jay Way	Toronto, Ontario M5V 1J1

Anaheim Angels	Arizona D-backs Cont.	Atlanta Braves - cont.	Balt Orioles - Cont.	Boston Red Sox - Cont.
Amezaga, Alfredo	DeVore, Doug	Franco, Julio	Majewski, Val	Reese, Pokey
Anderson, Garret	Durbin, Chad	Furcal, Rafael	McDonald, Darnell	Roberts, Dave
Colon, Bartolo	Fassero, Jeff	Giles, Marcus	Mora, Melvin	Schilling, Curt
DaVanon, Jeff	Fetters, Mike	Green, Nick	Newhan, David	Shiell, Jason
Donnelly, Brendan	Fossum, Casey	Gryboski, Kevin	Palmeiro, Rafael	Timlin, Mike
Dunn, Scott	Gil, Jerry	Hampton, Mike	Parrish, John	Varitek, Jason
Eckstein, David	Gonzalez, Edgar	Jones, Andruw	Ponson, Sidney	Wakefield, Tim
Erstad, Darin	Gonzalez, Luis	Jones, Chipper	Raines, Tim Jr.	Williamson, Scott
Escobar, Kelvim	Good, Andrew	LaRoche, Adam	Rakers, Aaron	Youkilis, Kevin
Figgins, Chone	Gosling, Mike	Marrero, Eli	Riley, Matt	**Chicago Cubs**
Glaus, Troy	Green, Andy	Martin, Tom	Roberts, Brian	Alou, Moises
Gregg, Kevin	Hairston, Scott	Meyer, Dan	Rodriguez, Eddy	Bako, Paul
Guerrero, Vladimir	Hammock, Robby	Ortiz, Russ	Ryan, B.J.	Barrett, Michael
Halter, Shane	Hill, Koyie	Perez, Eddie	Segui, David	Borowski, Joe
Hensley, Matt	Hillenbrand, Shea	Ramirez, Horacio	Surhoff, B.J.	Clement, Matt
Kennedy, Adam	Johnson, Randy	Reitsma, Chris	Tejada, Miguel	Dempster, Ryan
Kotchman, Casey	Kata, Matt	Smith, Travis	Williams, Todd	DiFelice, Mike
Lackey, John	Koplove, Mike	Smoltz, John	**Boston Red Sox**	Dubois, Jason
McPherson, Dallas	Kroeger, Josh	Thomas, Charles	Adams, Terry	Farnsworth, Kyle
Molina, Bengie	Lyon, Brandon	Thomson, John	Arroyo, Bronson	Garciaparra, Nomar
Molina, Jose	Mantei, Matt	Wise, Dewayne	Bellhorn, Mark	Goodwin, Tom
Ortiz, Ramon	McCracken, Quinton	Wright, Jaret	Burks, Ellis	Grieve, Ben
Paul, Josh	Nance, Shane	**Baltimore Orioles**	Cabrera, Orlando	Grudzielanek, Mark
Percival, Troy	Randolph, Stephen	Bauer, Rick	Damon, Johnny	Hawkins, LaTroy
Pride, Curtis	Reynolds, Shane	Bedard, Erik	DiNardo, Lenny	Hollandsworth, Todd
Quinlan, Robb	Service, Scott	Bigbie, Larry	Embree, Alan	Lee, Derrek
Riggs, Adam	Sexson, Richie	Borkowski, Dave	Foulke, Keith	Leicester, Jon
Rodriguez, Francisco	Snyder, Chris	Cabrera, Daniel	Gutierrez, Ricky	Macias, Jose
Salmon, Tim	Sparks, Steve	Chen, Bruce	Hyzdu, Adam	Maddux, Greg
Sele, Aaron	Terrero, Luis	Cordova, Marty	Kapler, Gabe	Martinez, Ramon
Shields, Scot	Tracy, Chad	DuBose, Eric	Leskanic, Curtis	Mercker, Kent
Washburn, Jarrod	Webb, Brandon	Gibbons, Jay	Lowe, Derek	Mitre, Sergio
Arizona D-backs	Zinter, Alan	Gil, Geronimo	Martinez, Pedro	Murray, Calvin
Aquino, Greg	**Atlanta Braves**	Grimsley, Jason	McCarty, Dave	Patterson, Corey
Baerga, Carlos	Alfonseca, Antonio	Groom, Buddy	Mientkiewicz, Doug	Perez, Neifi
Bautista, Danny	Betemit, Wilson	Hairston, Jerry Jr.	Millar, Kevin	Prior, Mark
Brito, Juan	Byrd, Paul	Julio, Jorge	Mirabelli, Doug	Ramirez, Aramis
Bruney, Brian	Cruz, Juan	Leon, Jose	Mueller, Bill	Remlinger, Mike
Choate, Randy	DeRosa, Mark	Lopez, Javy	Myers, Mike	Rusch, Glendon
Cintron, Alex	Drew, J.D.	Lopez, Luis	Nixon, Trot	Sosa, Sammy
Colbrunn, Greg	Drew, Tim	Lopez, Rodrigo	Ortiz, David	Walker, Todd
Cormier, Lance	Estrada, Johnny	Machado, Robert	Ramirez, Manny	Wellemeyer, Todd

Chicago Cubs - Cont.
Wood, Kerry
Wuertz, Michael
Zambrano, Carlos

Chicago White Sox
Adkins, Jon
Alomar, Roberto
Alomar, Sandy
Bajenaru, Jeff
Borchard, Joe
Buehrle, Mark
Burke, Jamie
Contreras, Jose
Cotts, Neal
Crede, Joe
Davis, Ben
Diaz, Felix
Everett, Carl
Garcia, Freddy
Garland, Jon
Gload, Ross
Grilli, Jason
Harris, Willie
Konerko, Paul
Lee, Carlos
Marte, Damaso
Munoz, Arnie
Perez, Timo
Politte, Cliff
Rowand, Aaron
Schoeneweis, Scott
Takatsu, Shingo
Thomas, Frank
Uribe, Juan
Valdez, Wilson
Valentin, Jose

Cincinnati Reds
Acevedo, Jose
Bragg, Darren
Casey, Sean
Castro, Juan
Claussen, Brandon
Cruz, Jacob

Cinci Reds -Cont.
Dunn, Adam
Freel, Ryan
Graves, Danny
Griffey Jr., Ken
Hall, Josh
Hancock, Josh
Harang, Aaron
Hudson, Luke
Jimenez, D'Angelo
Kearns, Austin
Larkin, Barry
LaRue, Jason
LaRue, Jason
Lopez, Felipe
Machado, Anderson
Mattox, D.J.
Norton, Phil
Pena, Wily Mo
Riedling, John
Romano, Jason
Valentine, Joe
Valentin, Javier
Van Poppel, Todd
Vander Wal, John
Wagner, Ryan
White, Gabe
Wilson, Paul

Cleveland Indians
Bard, Josh
Bartosh, Cliff
Belliard, Ronnie
Betancourt, Rafael
Blake, Casey
Boone, Aaron
Broussard, Ben
Cabrera, Fernando
Crisp, Coco
Cruceta, Francisco
Davis, Jason
Dawley, Joe
Denney, Kyle
Elarton, Scott

Cleve. Indians -Cont.
Gerut, Jody
Guthrie, Jeremy
Hafner, Travis
Howry, Bob
Laker, Tim
Lawton, Matt
Lee, Cliff
Ludwick, Ryan
Martinez, Victor
McDonald, John
Merloni, Lou
Miller, Matt
Peralta, Jhonny
Phelps, Josh
Phillips, Brandon
Riske, David
Robbins, Jake
Sabathia, C.C.
Sizemore, Grady
Stanford, Jason
Traber, Billy
Vizquel, Omar
Westbrook, Jake
White, Rick
Wickman, Bob
Young, Ernie

Colorado Rockies
Atkins, Garrett
Barmes, Clint
Bernero, Adam
Burnitz, Jeromy
Castilla, Vinny
Chacon, Shawn
Clayton, Royce
Closser, J.D.
Cook, Aaron
Dohmann, Scott
Estes, Shawn
Francis, Jeff
Freeman, Choo
Fuentes, Brian
Gissell, Chris

Colo. Rockies - Cont.
Gonzalez, Luis
Greene, Todd
Harikkala, Tim
Hawpe, Brad
Helton, Todd
Holliday, Matt
Jennings, Jason
Johnson, Charles
Kennedy, Joe
Lopez, Javier
Miles, Aaron
Neagle, Denny
Piedra, Jorge
Reed, Steve
Simpson, Allan
Stark, Denny
Sullivan, Cory
Sweeney, Mark
Tracy, Andy
Tsao, Chin-hui
Wilson, Preston
Wright, Jamey
Young, Jason

Detroit Tigers
Bonderman, Jeremy
Colyer, Steve
Cornejo, Nate
German, Franklyn
Granderson, Curtis
Guillen, Carlos
Higginson, Bobby
Infante, Omar
Inge, Brandon
Johnson, Jason
Knotts, Gary
Ledezma, Wilfredo
Levine, Al
Logan, Nook
Maroth, Mike
Monroe, Craig
Munson, Eric
Novoa, Roberto

Detroit Tigers - Cont.
Pena, Carlos
Raburn, Ryan
Robertson, Nate
Rodriguez, Ivan
Shelton, Chris
Smith, Jason
Spurling, Chris
Thames, Marcus
Urbina, Ugueth
Vina, Fernando
Walker, Jamie
White, Rondell
Yan, Esteban
Young, Dmitri

Florida Marlins
Aguila, Chris
Beckett, Josh
Benitez, Armando
Bump, Nate
Burnett, A.J.
Cabrera, Miguel
Castillo, Luis
Conine, Jeff
Cordero, Wil
Easley, Damion
Encarnacion, Juan
Fox, Chad
Gonzalez, Alex
Harris, Lenny
Howard, Ben
Kensing, Logan
Koch, Billy
Lo Duca, Paul
Lowell, Mike
Manzanillo, Josias
Mordecai, Mike
Mota, Guillermo
Pavano, Carl
Perisho, Matt
Pierre, Juan
Redmond, Mike
Seanez, Rudy

Florida Marlins - Cont.
Small, Aaron
Spooneybarger, Tim
Treanor, Matt
Valdez, Ismael
Weathers, David
Willis, Dontrelle

Houston Astros
Alfaro, Jason
Ausmus, Brad
Backe, Brandon
Bagwell, Jeff
Beltran, Carlos
Berkman, Lance
Biggio, Craig
Bruntlett, Eric
Burke, Chris
Chavez, Raul
Clemens, Roger
Duckworth, Brandon
Ensberg, Morgan
Everett, Adam
Gallo, Mike
Harville, Chad
Kent, Jeff
Lamb, Mike
Lane, Jason
Lidge, Brad
Miceli, Dan
Miller, Wade
Munro, Pete
Oliver, Darren
Oswalt, Roy
Palmeiro, Orlando
Pettitte, Andy
Qualls, Chad
Redding, Tim
Springer, Russ
Tremie, Chris
Vizcaino, Jose
Wheeler, Dan

Kansas City Royals
Affeldt, Jeremy
Anderson, Brian
Bautista, Denny
Berroa, Angel
Buck, John
Camp, Shawn
Carrasco, D.J.
Cerda, Jaime
DeJesus, David
Field, Nate
George, Chris
Gobble, Jimmy
Gotay, Ruben
Graffanino, Tony
Greinke, Zack
Harvey, Ken
MacDougal, Mike
May, Darrell
Murphy, Donnie
Nunez, Abraham
Phillips, Paul
Pickering, Calvin
Randa, Joe
Relaford, Desi
Reyes, Dennys
Serrano, Jimmy
Snyder, Kyle
Stairs, Matt
Stinnett, Kelly
Sullivan, Scott
Sweeney, Mike
Wood, Mike

LA Dodgers
Alvarez, Wilson
Beltre, Adrian
Bradley, Milton
Brazoban, Yhency
Carrara, Giovanni
Choi, Hee-Seop
Cora, Alex
Dessens, Elmer
Dreifort, Darren

LA Dodgers - Cont.
Finley, Steve
Flores, Jose
Gagne, Eric
Grabowski, Jason
Green, Shawn
Hernandez, Jose
Hundley, Todd
Izturis, Cesar
Lima, Jose
Mayne, Brent
Penny, Brad
Perez, Odalis
Ross, David
Saenz, Olmedo
Sanchez, Duaner
Shuey, Paul
Stewart, Scott
Thurston, Joe
Venafro, Mike
Ventura, Robin
Weaver, Jeff
Werth, Jayson
Wilson, Tom

Milwaukee Brewers
Adams, Mike
Bennett, Gary
Bennett, Jeff
Branyan, Russell
Capuano, Chris
Clark, Brady
Counsell, Craig
Davis, Doug
De La Rosa, Jorge
Ford, Ben
Ginter, Keith
Glover, Gary
Hall, Bill
Helms, Wes
Hendrickson, Ben
Jenkins, Geoff
Johnson, Mark
Kieschnick, Brooks

Mil. Brewers Cont.
Kolb, Dan
Krynzel, Dave
Liriano, Pedro
Magruder, Chris
Moeller, Chad
Obermueller, Wes
Overbay, Lyle
Phelps, Travis
Podsednik, Scott
Santos, Victor
Sheets, Ben
Spivey, Junior
Vizcaino, Luis
Wise, Matt

Minnesota Twins
Balfour, Grant
Bartlett, Jason
Beimel, Joe
Blanco, Henry
Borders, Pat
Crain, Jesse
Cuddyer, Michael
Durbin, J.D.
Ford, Lew
Fultz, Aaron
Guerrier, Matt
Guzman, Cristian
Hunter, Torii
Jones, Jacque
Koskie, Corey
Kubel, Jason
LeCroy, Matthew
Lohse, Kyle
Mauer, Joe
Mays, Joe
Miller, Corky
Morneau, Justin
Mulholland, Terry
Nathan, Joe
Offerman, Jose
Ojeda, Augie
Punto, Nick

Minnesota Twins - Cont.
Radke, Brad
Restovich, Michael
Rincon, Juan
Rivas, Luis
Roa, Joe
Romero, J.C.
Santana, Johan
Silva, Carlos
Stewart, Shannon
Tiffee, Terry

Montreal Expos
Biddle, Rocky
Carroll, Jamey
Church, Ryan
Cordero, Chad
Day, Zach
Downs, Scott
Eischen, Joey
Harris, Brendan
Horgan, Joe
Johnson, Nick
Labandeira, Josh
Majewski, Gary
Pascucci, Val
Patterson, John
Rauch, Jon
Schneider, Brian
Sledge, Terrmel
Smith, Dan
Tucker, T.J.
Wilkerson, Brad

New York Mets
Bell, Heath
Benson, Kris
Bottalico, Ricky
Brazell, Craig
Cameron, Mike
Darensbourg, Vic
DeJean, Mike
Delgado, Wilson
Diaz, Victor
Feliciano, Pedro

New York Mets - Cont.

Floyd, Cliff
Fortunato, Bartolome
Franco, John
Garcia, Danny
Ginter, Matt
Glavine, Tom
Heilman, Aaron
Hidalgo, Richard
Hietpas, Joe
Keppinger, Jeff
Leiter, Al
Looper, Braden
Matsui, Kazuo
McEwing, Joe
Phillips, Jason
Piazza, Mike
Reyes, Jose
Roberts, Grant
Seo, Jae Weong
Stanton, Mike
Strickland, Scott
Trachsel, Steve
Valent, Eric
Vaughn, Mo
Williams, Gerald
Wilson, Vance
Wright, David
Yates, Tyler
Yates, Tyler
Zeile, Todd

New York Yankees

Brown, Kevin
Cairo, Miguel
Clark, Tony
Crosby, Bubba
Flaherty, John
Giambi, Jason
Gordon, Tom
Halsey, Brad
Heredia, Felix
Hernandez, Orlando
Jeter, Derek

NY Yankees - Cont.

Karsay, Steve
Lee, Travis
Lieber, Jon
Loaiza, Esteban
Lofton, Kenny
Marsonek, Sam
Matsui, Hideki
Mussina, Mike
Nitkowski, C.J.
Olerud, John
Phillips, Andy
Posada, Jorge
Prinz, Bret
Proctor, Scott
Quantrill, Paul
Rivera, Mariano
Rodriguez, Alex
Sheffield, Gary
Sierra, Ruben
Sturtze, Tanyon
Vazquez, Javier
Williams, Bernie
Wilson, Enrique

Oakland Athletics

Blanton, Joe
Bradford, Chad
Byrnes, Eric
Chavez, Eric
Crosby, Bobby
Dotel, Octavio
Duchscherer, Justin
Durazo, Erubiel
Dye, Jermaine
Ellis, Mark
Garcia, Jairo
German, Esteban
Hammond, Chris
Harden, Rich
Hatteberg, Scott
Hudson, Tim
Johnson, Dan
Kielty, Bobby

Oakland A's - Cont.

Kotsay, Mark
Lehr, Justin
McLemore, Mark
McMillon, Billy
Mecir, Jim
Melhuse, Adam
Miller, Damian
Mulder, Mark
Redman, Mark
Rhodes, Arthur
Rincon, Ricardo
Rose, Mike
Saarloos, Kirk
Scutaro, Marco
Swisher, Nick
Zito, Barry

Phil. Phillies

Abreu, Bobby
Bell, David
Burrell, Pat
Byrd, Marlon
Collier, Lou
Cormier, Rheal
Floyd, Gavin
Geary, Geoff
Glanville, Doug
Hernandez, Roberto
Hinch, A.J.
Howard, Ryan
Jones, Todd
Lidle, Cory
Lieberthal, Mike
Madson, Ryan
Michaels, Jason
Millwood, Kevin
Milton, Eric
Myers, Brett
Padilla, Vicente
Perez, Tomas
Polanco, Placido
Powell, Brian
Pratt, Todd

Phil. Phillies - Cont.

Rodriguez, Felix
Rollins, Jimmy
Telemaco, Amaury
Thome, Jim
Utley, Chase
Wagner, Billy
Wolf, Randy
Wooten, Shawn
Worrell, Tim

Pittsburgh Pirates

Alvarez, Tony
Bautista, Jose
Bay, Jason
Boehringer, Brian
Brooks, Frank
Burnett, Sean
Castillo, Jose
Corey, Mark
Cota, Humberto
Davis, J.J.
Figueroa, Nelson
Fogg, Josh
Gonzalez, Mike
Grabow, John
Hill, Bobby
House, J.R.
Kendall, Jason
Mackowiak, Rob
Meadows, Brian
Mesa, Jose
Nunez, Abraham
Perez, Oliver
Redman, Tike
Sanchez, Freddy
Snell, Ian
Torres, Salomon
Van Benschoten, John
Vogelsong, Ryan
Ward, Daryle
Wells, Kip
Wigginton, Ty
Williams, Dave
Wilson, Craig
Wilson, Jack

San Diego Padres

Ashby, Andy
Aurilia, Rich
Burroughs, Sean
Bynum, Mike
Eaton, Adam
Fick, Robert
Germano, Justin
Giles, Brian
Gonzalez, Alex S.
Greene, Khalil
Guzman, Freddy
Hansen, Dave
Hernandez, Ramon
Hoffman, Trevor
Klesko, Ryan
Lawrence, Brian
Linebrink, Scott
Long, Terrence
Loretta, Mark
Nady, Xavier
Neal, Blaine
Nevin, Phil
Ojeda, Miguel
Osuna, Antonio
Otsuka, Akinori
Payton, Jay
Peavy, Jake
Quintero, Humberto
Robinson, Kerry
Stone, Ricky
Sweeney, Brian
Vazquez, Ramon
Watkins, Steve
Wells, David
Witasick, Jay

San Francisco Giants

Aardsma, David
Alfonzo, Edgardo
Bonds, Barry
Brower, Jim
Burba, Dave
Christiansen, Jason

San Fran Giants - Cont.	S. Mariners - Cont.	St. Louis Cards - Cont.	Tampa D-Rays - Cont.	Texas Rangers - Cont.
Correia, Kevin	Jacobsen, Bucky	Luna, Hector	Ritchie, Todd	Shouse, Brian
Cruz, Deivi	Kida, Masao	Mabry, John	Rolls, Damian	Soriano, Alfonso
Dallimore, Brian	Leone, Justin	Marquis, Jason	Sanchez, Rey	Teixeira, Mark
Durham, Ray	Lopez, Jose	Matheny, Mike	Seay, Bobby	Wasdin, John
Ellison, Jason	Lopez, Mickey	Molina, Yadier	Sosa, Jorge	Young, Chris
Eyre, Scott	Madritsch, Bobby	Morris, Matt	Upton, B.J.	Young, Eric
Feliz, Pedro	Martinez, Edgar	Pujols, Albert	Waechter, Doug	Young, Michael
Foppert, Jesse	Mateo, Julio	Renteria, Edgar	Webb, John	**Toronto Blue Jays**
Franklin, Wayne	Meche, Gil	Rolen, Scott	**Texas Rangers**	Adams, Russ
Grissom, Marquis	Moyer, Jamie	Sanders, Reggie	Alexander, Manny	Batista, Miguel
Hennessey, Brad	Nageotte, Clint	Simontacchi, Jason	Allen, Chad	Berg, Dave
Herges, Matt	Olivo, Miguel	Suppan, Jeff	Almanzar, Carlos	Bush, David
Hermanson, Dustin	Putz, J.J.	Taguchi, So	Barajas, Rod	Cash, Kevin
Knoedler, Justin	Reed, Jeremy	Tavarez, Julian	Benoit, Joaquin	Catalanotto, Frank
Ledee, Ricky	Rivera, Rene	Walker, Larry	Blalock, Hank	Chacin, Gustavo
Linden, Todd	Santiago, Ramon	Williams, Woody	Brocail, Doug	Chulk, Vinnie
Lowry, Noah	Sherrill, George	Womack, Tony	Callaway, Mickey	Crozier, Eric
Mohr, Dustan	Snelling, Chris	**Tampa Bay Devil Rays**	Cordero, Francisco	Delgado, Carlos
Nen, Robb	Spiezio, Scott	Baez, Danys	Dellucci, David	Douglass, Sean
Pierzynski, A.J.	Suzuki, Ichiro	Baldelli, Rocco	Dickey, R.A.	Estalella, Bobby
Ransom, Cody	Taylor, Aaron	Bell, Rob	Drese, Ryan	File, Bob
Rueter, Kirk	Thornton, Matt	Blum, Geoff	Fox, Andy	Frasor, Jason
Schmidt, Jason	Villone, Ron	Brazelton, Dewon	Francisco, Frank	Frederick, Kevin
Snow, J.T.	Williams, Randy	Cantu, Jorge	Fullmer, Brad	Glynn, Ryan
Tomko, Brett	Wilson, Dan	Carter, Lance	Gonzalez, Adrian	Gomez, Chris
Torcato, Tony	Winn, Randy	Crawford, Carl	Greer, Rusty	Gross, Gabe
Torrealba, Yorvit	**St. Louis Cardinals**	Cruz, Jose	Huckaby, Ken	Halladay, Roy
Tucker, Michael	Anderson, Marlon	Cummings, Midre	Hughes, Travis	Hinske, Eric
Walker, Tyler	Ankiel, Rick	Diaz, Matt	Jordan, Brian	Hudson, Orlando
Williams, Jerome	Calero, Kiko	Fordyce, Brook	Laird, Gerald	Johnson, Reed
Seattle Mariners	Cali, Carmen	Gaudin, Chad	Lewis, Colby	League, Brandon
Atchison, Scott	Carpenter, Chris	Halama, John	Loe, Kameron	Ligtenberg, Kerry
Baek, Cha Seung	Cedeno, Roger	Hall, Toby	Mahay, Ron	Lilly, Ted
Bloomquist, Willie	Edmonds, Jim	Harper, Travis	Matthews, Gary Jr.	Menechino, Frank
Bocachica, Hiram	Eldred, Cal	Hendrickson, Mark	Mench, Kevin	Miller, Justin
Boone, Bret	Flores, Randy	Huff, Aubrey	Nelson, Jeff	Myers, Greg
Cabrera, Jolbert	Haren, Danny	Kazmir, Scott	Nix, Laynce	Quiroz, Guillermo
Dobbs, Greg	Isringhausen, Jason	Lugo, Julio	Park, Chan Ho	Rios, Alexis
Franklin, Ryan	King, Ray	Martinez, Tino	Perry, Herbert	Speier, Justin
Guardado, Eddie	Kline, Steve	Miller, Trever	Powell, Jay	Towers, Josh
Hasegawa, Shigetoshi	Lankford, Ray	Nunez, Franklin	Ramirez, Erasmo	Wells, Vernon
Ibanez, Raul	Lincoln, Mike	Perez, Eduardo	Rogers, Kenny	Woodward, Chris
				Zaun, Gregg

Selected Additional Baseball Names & Addresses

Aaron, Hank	1611 Adams Dr. SW.	Atlanta, GA 30311	
Alou, Felipe	San Francisco Giants	24 Willie Mays Plaza	San Francisco, CA 94107
Anderson, Sparky	C/O Detroit Tigers	Tiger Stadium	Detriot, MI 48126
Baker, Dusty	Chicago Cubs	1060 Addison Street	Chicago, IL 60613
Baylor, Don	New York Mets	123-01 Roosevelt Avenue	Flushing, NY 11368
Bench, Johnny	324 Bishopsbridge Drive	Cincinnati, OH 45255	
Berra, Lawrence "Yogi"	19 Highland Avenue	Montclair, NJ 07042	
Blue, Vida	PO Box 1449	Pleasonton, CA 94566	
Bochy, Bruce	San Diego Padres	PO Box 122000	San Diego, CA 92112
Boddicker, Mike	11324 West 121st Street	Overalnd Park, KS 66213	
Boggs, Wade	599 Marmora Ave.	Tampa, FL 33606	
Bouton, Jim	Jim Bouton Enterprises	P.O. Box 188	N. Egremont, MA 01252
Bowa, Larry	Philadelphia Phillies	One Citizens Bank Way	Philadelphia, PA 19148
Branca, Ralph	Westchester Country Club	Rye, NY 10580	
Brett, George	Kansas City Royals	1 Royal Way	Kansas City, MO 64141
Brock, Lou	St Louis Cardinals	250 Stadium Plaza	St Louis, MO 63102
Buck, Joe	William Morris Agency	One William Morris Place	Beverly Hills, CA 90212-1825
Buckner, Bill	4405 East Wild Horse Lane	Boise, ID 83712	
Canseco, Joe	3025 Meadow Lane	Ft. Lauderdale, Fl 33331	
Carew, Rod	Minnesota Twins	34 Kirby Puckett Way	Minneapolis, MN 55415
Carey, Chip	Chicago Cubs	1060 Addison Street	Chicago, IL 60613
Cashman, Brian	New York Yankees	Yankee Stadium	Bronx, NY 10451
Cey, Ron	22714 Creole Rd	Woodland Hills, CA 91364	
Clemens, Roger	10131 Beekman Dr.	Houston, TX 77043	
Cox, Bobby	Atlanta Braves	755 Hank Aaron Drive	Atlanta, GA 30315
Craig, Roger	26658 San Felipe Rd	Warner Springs, CA 92086	
Davis, Tommy	9767 Whirlaway	Alta Loma, CA 91701	
Dempsey, Rick	Indian Oak Lane #101	Oak Park, CA 91301	
DeWitt, William O. Jr.	St Louis Cardinals	250 Stadium Plaza	St Louis, MO 63102
Dolan, Lawrence J.	Cleveland Indians	2401 Ontario Street	Cleveland, OH 44115
Elia, Lee	Tampa Bay Devils	One Tropicana Drive	St Petersburg, FL 33705
Erskine, Carl	6214 S. Madison Ave	Anderson, IN 46013	
Fidrych, Mark	260 West Street	Northboro, MA 01532-1223	
Foley, Tom	Tampa Bay Devils	One Tropicana Drive	St Petersburg, FL 33705
Francona, Terry	Boston Red Soxs	4 Yawkee Way	Boston, MA 02215
Gaetti, Gary	Houston Astros	PO Box 288	Houston, TX 77001
Gardenhire, Ron	Minnesota Twins	34 Kirby Puckett Way	Minneapolis, MN 55415
Garvey, Steve	11718 Barrington Court #6	Los Angeles, CA 90049	
Gibbons, John	Toronto Blue Jays	1 Blue Jay Way	Toronto, Ontario M5V 1J1
Gibson, Bob	St Louis Cardinals	250 Stadium Plaza	St Louis, MO 63102
Gibson, Kirk	17108 Mack Ave	Grosse Pointe, MI 48230	
Glass, David	Kansas City Royals	1 Royal Way	Kansas City, MO 64141
Godfrey, Paul V.	Toronto Blue Jays	1 Blue Jay Way	Toronto, Ontario M5V 1J1
Gossage, Goose	Colorado Rockies	2001 Blake Street	Denver, CO 80205
Guidry, Ron	Po Box 278	Scott, LA 70583-0278	
Guillen, Ozzie	Chicago White Soxs	333 W. 35th Street	Chicago. IL 60616
Hatcher, Billy	Tampa Bay Devils	One Tropicana Drive	St Petersburg, FL 33705
Hatcher, Mickey	4202 East Crescent Avenue	Mesa, AZ 85206	
Henderson, Ricky	10561 Englewood Drive	Oakland, CA 94621	
Hershiser, Orel	Texas Rangers	1000 Ballpark Way	Arlington, TX 76011
Hicks, Thomas O.	Texas Rangers	1000 Ballpark Way	Arlington, TX 76011
Hoffman, Glenn	201 Old Bridge Road	Anaheim Hills, CA 92807	
Hooton, Burt	3619 Granby Court	San Antonio, TX 78217	
Hough, Charlie	2266 Shade Tree Circle	Brea, CA, 92621	
Howard, Frank	6574 Palisades Ave	Centreville, VA 22020	
Howe, Art	New York Mets	123-01 Roosevelt Avenue	Flushing, NY 11368
Howe, Steve	P.O. Box 1355	Warsaw, IN 46581	
Hurdle, Clint	Colorado Rockies	2001 Blake Street	Denver, CO 80205
Ilitch, Michael	Detroit Tigers	2100 Woodland Avenue	Detroit, MI 48201
Jackson, Reggie	New York Yankees	Yankee Stadium	Bronx, NY 10451
Jansen, Larry	3207 NW Hwy 47	Forest Grove, OR 97116	

Selected Additional Baseball Names & Addresses

John, Tommy	Edmonton Trappers	10233 - 96th Avenue	Edmonton, Alberta, Canada
Kaline, Al	945 Timberlake Drive	Bloomfield, MI 48013	
Killebrew, Harmon	PO Box 14550	Scottsdale, AZ 85267	
Koufax, Sandy	P.O. Box 8306	Vero Beach, FL 32963	
Kubek, Tony	N8323 North Shore Drive	Menasha, WI 54942	
La Russa, Tony	St Louis Cardinals	250 Stadium Plaza	St Louis, MO 63102
Labine, Clem	311 N. Grove Isle Cir	Vero Beach, FL 32962	
Lacy, Lee	4424 Webster St	Oakland, CA 94609	
Lagrow, Lerrin	12271 East Turquoise	Scootsdale, AZ 85259	
Lahoud, Joe	Hut Hill Road Box 165	Bridgewater, CT 06752	
Lasorda, Tommy	Los Angeles Dodgers	1000 Elysian Way	Los Angeles, CA 90012
Lefebvre, Jim	9120 N. 106th Place	Scottsdale, AZ 85258	
Leyritz, Jim	7911 Eglington Ct.	Cicinnati, OH 45230	
Lillis, Bob	5107 Cherry Tree Lane	Orlando, FL 32819	
Lincoln, Howard	Seattle Mariners	First & Atlantic	Seattle, WA 98104
Lindner, Carl H.	Cincinnati Reds	100 Main Street	Cincinnati, OH 45202
Lonborg, Jim	498 First Parish Road	Sctuate, MA 02066-3201	
Lopes, Davey	17762 Vineyard Lane	Poway, CA 92064	
Lopes, Davey	San Diego Padres	PO Box 122000	San Diego, CA 92112
Loria, Jeffrey H.	Florida Marlins	2267 Dan Marino Blvd.	Miami, FL 33056
Macha, Ken	Oakland Athletics	7000 Coliseum Way	Oakland, CA 94621
MacPhail, Andrew B.	Chicago Cubs	1060 Addison Street	Chicago, IL 60613
Maddux, Mike	Milwaukee Brewers	One Brewers Way	Milwaukee, WI 53214
Magadan, Dave	San Diego Padres	PO Box 122000	San Diego, CA 92112
Malzone, Frank	16 Aletha Road	Needham, MA 02192	
Mattinging, Don	Route 5 Box 74	Evansville, IN 47711	
Mattingly, Don	New York Yankees	Yankee Stadium	Bronx, NY 10451
Mays, Willie	San Francisco Giants	24 Willie Mays Plaza	San Francisco, CA 94107
Mazzilli, Lee	Baltimore Orioles	333 Camden Street	Baltimore, MD 212002
McAuliffe, Dick	9 Crossroad Lane	Avon, CT 06001	
McClatchy, Kevin S.	Pittsburgh Pirates	115 Federal Street	Pittsburgh, PA 15212
McClendon, Lloyd	Pittsburgh Pirates	115 Federal Street	Pittsburgh, PA 15212
McCourt, Frank	Los Angeles Dodgers	1000 Elysian Way	Los Angeles, CA 90012
McCovey, Willie	San Francisco Giants	24 Willie Mays Plaza	San Francisco, CA 94107
McDaniel, Lindy	Route 2 Box 353A	Hollis, OK 73550	
McKeon, Jack	Florida Marlins	2267 Dan Marino Blvd.	Miami, FL 33056
Messersmith, Andy	200 Lagunita Drive	Soquel, CA 95073	
Miley, Dave	Cincinnati Reds	100 Main Street	Cincinnati, OH 45202
Molitor, Paul	Seattle Mariners	First & Atlantic	Seattle, WA 98104
Monday, Rick	10915 Portobelo Drive	San Diego, CA 92124	
Monfort, Charles K.	Colorado Rockies	2001 Blake Street	Denver, CO 80205
Montgomery, David	Philadelphia Phillies	One Citizens Bank Way	Philadelphia, PA 19148
Moon, Wally	1415 Angelina Circle	College Station, TX 77840	
Moores, John	San Diego Padres	PO Box 122000	San Diego, CA 92112
Mota, Manny	Los Angeles Dodgers	1000 Elysian Way	Los Angeles, CA 90012
Naimoli, Vincent J.	Tampa Bay Devils	One Tropicana Drive	St Petersburg, FL 33705
Necciai, Ron	201 Rosewood Drive	Monongahela, PA 15063	
Newcombe, Don	7077 Alvern Street #A206	Los Angeles, CA 90045	
Niedenfuer, Tom	3933 Losillias Drive	Sarasota, FL 34238	
Oliva, Tony	212 Spring Valley Drive	Bloomington, MN 55420	
Osteen, Claude	6419 Saddle Ridge Road	Arlington, TX 76016	
Owen, Mickey	604 West Division	Mount Vernon, MO 65712	
Pafko, Andy	1420 Blackhawk Dr	Mount Prospect, IL 60056	
Pedrique, Al	Arizona Diamondbacks	401 Jefferson	Phoenix, AZ 85004
Peña, Tony	Kansas City Royals	1 Royal Way	Kansas City, MO 64141
Perranoski, Ron	3805 Indian River Drive	Vero Beach, FL 32963	
Perry, Jim	2608 Ridgeview Way	Sioux Falls, SD 57105	
Phil Garner	Houston Astros	PO Box 288	Houston, TX 77001
Piazza, Mike	PO Box 864	Oakwood Lane	Valley Forge, PA 19481
Piniella, Lou	Tampa Bay Devils	One Tropicana Drive	St Petersburg, FL 33705
Podres, Johnny	1 Colonial Court	Glen Falls, NY 12801	

Selected Additional Baseball Names & Addresses

Pohlad, Carl R.	Minnesota Twins	34 Kirby Puckett Way	Minneapolis, MN 55415
Pujols, Luis	San Francisco Giants	24 Willie Mays Plaza	San Francisco, CA 94107
Randolph, Willie	New York Yankees	Yankee Stadium	Bronx, NY 10451
Regan, Phil	1375 108th St	Byron Center, MI 49315	
Reinsdorf, Jerry	Chicago White Soxs	333 W. 35th Street	Chicago. IL 60616
Richards, Gene	4360 Panorama Drive	La Mesa, CA 92041	
Rizzutto, Phil "Scooter"	912 Westminster Ave.	Hillside, NJ 07205	
Roberts, Robin	504 Terrace Hill Drive	Temple Terrace, FL 33617	
Robinson, Brooks	PO Box 1168	Baltimore, MD 21203	
Robinson, Frank	15557 Aqua Verde Drive	Los Angeles, CA 90024	
Roe, Elwin 'Preacher'	204 Wildwood Terrace	West Plains, MO 65775	
Roebuck, Ed	3434 Warwood Rd	Lakewood, Ca 90712	
Roenicke, Ron	2212 Avenida Las Ramblas	Chino Hills, CA 91709	
Rose, Pete	8570 Crescent Drive	Los Angeles, CA 90046	
Ryan, Nolan	Nolan Ryan Foundation	2925 S. Bypass Highway 35	Alvin, TX 77511
Santo, Ron	WGN Radio	435 N. Michigan Avenue	Chicago, IL 60611
Sauer, Hank	207 Vallejo Court	Millbrae, CA 94030	
Sax, Steve	201 Wesley Ct	Roseville, CA 95661	
Schmidt, Mike	PO Box 2575	Philadelphia, Pa 19101	
Schoendienst, Red	St Louis Cardinals	250 Stadium Plaza	St Louis, MO 63102
Schott, Steve	Oakland Athletics	7000 Coliseum Way	Oakland, CA 94621
Scioscia, Mike	Anaheim Angels	2000 Gene Autry Way	Anaheim, CA 92806
Score, Herb	C/O Wknr Radio	9446 Broadview Road	Cleveland, OH 44147
Scully, Vin	1555 Capri Dr	Pacific Palisades, CA 90272	
Selig, Bud	C/O Milwaukee Brewers	Po Box 3099	Miiwaukee, WI 53201
Selig-Prieb, Wendy A.	Milwaukee Brewers	One Brewers Way	Milwaukee, WI 53214
Sheffield, Gary	6731 30th St	South St. Petersburg, FL 33712	
Shelby, John	2232 Broadhead Lane	Lexington, KY 40515	
Sherry, Larry	27181 Arena Lane	Mission Viejo, CA 92675	
Showalter, Buck	Texas Rangers	1000 Ballpark Way	Arlington, TX 76011
Shuba, George	3421 Bent Willow Lane	Youngstown, OH 44511-2502	
Sinatro, Matt	Tampa Bay Devils	One Tropicana Drive	St Petersburg, FL 33705
Singer, Bill	4572 Arrowhead Drive SE	Decatur, AL 35603	
Smith, Reggie	6186 Coral Pink Circle	Woddland Hills, CA 91367	
Smith, Tal	Houston Astros	PO Box 288	Houston, TX 77001
Snider, Edwin 'Duke'	3037 Lakemount Dr	Fallbrook, CA 92028	
Steinbrenner, George	New York Yankees	Yankee Stadium	Bronx, NY 10451
Stottlemyre, Mel	New York Yankees	Yankee Stadium	Bronx, NY 10451
Sutcliff, Rick	25911 99th Street	Lees Summit, MO 64063	
Sutton, Don	1145 Mountain Ivy Drive	Roswell, GA 30075	
Torborg, Jeff	5208 Ciesta Cove Drive	Sarasota, FL 34242	
Torre, Joe	New York Yankees	Yankee Stadium	Bronx, NY 10451
Tracy, Jim	Los Angeles Dodgers	1000 Elysian Way	Los Angeles, CA 90012
Trammell, Alan	Detroit Tigers	2100 Woodland Avenue	Detroit, MI 48201
Ueberroth, Peter	184 Emerald Bay	Laguna Beach, FL 92651	
Uecker, Bob	201 South 46th Street	Milwaukee, WI 53214	
Valentine, Bobby	4102 Flower Garden Court	Arlington, TX 76016	
Valenzuela, Fernando	3004 North Beachwood Drive	Los Angeles, CA 90027	
Veryzer, Tom	41 Union Avenue	Islip, NY 11751	
Webster, Mitch	4935 Quail Creek Drive	Great Bend, KS 67530	
Wedge, Eric	Cleveland Indians	2401 Ontario Street	Cleveland, OH 44115
Welch, Bob	10800 E. Cactus Rd. #33	Scottsdale, AZ 85259	
Williams, Stan	4702 Hayter Ave	Lakewood, CA 90712	
Wilpon, Fred	New York Mets	123-01 Roosevelt Avenue	Flushing, NY 11368
Winfield, Dave	San Diego Padres	PO Box 122000	San Diego, CA 92112
Woods, Alvis	2518 60th Street	Oakland, CA 94605	
Yastrzemski, Carl	Eaton Vance Corp.	24 Federal Street	Boston, MA 02110
Yeager, Steve	P.O. Box 34184	Granada Hills, CA 91394	
Yost, Ned	Milwaukee Brewers	One Brewers Way	Milwaukee, WI 53214
Zimmer, Don	Tampa Bay Devils	One Tropicana Drive	St Petersburg, FL 33705

Basketball Hall of Fame

Contact: Basketball Hall of Fame
1150 W Columbus Ave.
PO Box 179
Springfield, MA 01101-0179

Autograph requests of members should be addressed to The Basketball Hall of Fame, with room on the front of the letter to forward to the member. Due to the September 11th tradegy, only the Inductees with an *asterisk will allow mail to be forwarded to them.

1999
Billie Moore, Player
Fred Zollner, Coach
John Thompson, Coach
Kevin McHale, Player
Wayne Embry, Player

1998
Larry Bird, Player
Marques Haynes, Coach
Jody Conradt, Player
*Arnie Risen, Coach
Alex Hannum, Player
Aleksandar Nikolic, Coach

1997
Alex English, Player
Pete Carril, Player
*Don Haskins, Coach
*Joan Crawford, Coach
*Bailey Howell, Player
Antonio Diaz - Miguel, Player

1996
George Gervin, Player
Gail Goodrich, Player
Nancy Lieberman, Player
David Thompson, Player
*George Yardley, Player

1995
Kareem Abdul Jabbar, Player
*Anne Donovan, Player
Aleksandr Gomelsky, Player
*John Kundla, Coach
Vern Mickkelsen, Coach
Cheryl Miller, Player
*John Wooden

1994
Carol Blazejowski, Player
*Denzel Crum, Player
Charles Daly, Coach
Harry Jeannette, Coach
Cesare Rubini- Trieste, Player

1993
*Walter Bellamy
Julius Erving, Player
Daniel Issel, Player
Ann E. Meyers, Player
*Dick Mcguire, Player
Calvin Murphy, Player
*Bill Walton, Player

1992
Lou Carnesecca, Player
Cornelius Hawkins, Coach
Bob Lanier, Player
Al Mcguire, Player
*John Ramsay, Coach
*Lusia Harris Stewart, Coach
Nera D. White, Player

1991
Nate Archibald, Player
*Dave Cowens, Player
Harry J. Gallitin, Player
Bob Knight Massillon, Player
Larry Fleisher, Coach

1990
Vernon Monroe, Player
*David Bing, Player
Elvin Hayes, Player
*Denise Curry
*Clarence Gaines

1989
William Gates
K. C. Jones, Player
Lenny Wilkens, Player

1988
Clyde E. Lovelette
Ralph Miller
Wes Unseld

1987
Rick Barry, Player
Walter Frazier, Player
Bob Houbregs, Player
Robert Wanzer, Player

1986
Billy Cunningham
Tom Heinsohn, Player
William Holzman, Player
Fred R. Taylor, Referee
Stanley Watts, Coach

1984
*Al Cervi, Player
Nate Thurmond, Player
*Marv Harshman, Coach
Margaret Wade, Coach
Senda Abbott, Coach

1983
John Havlecek, Player
Sam Jones, Player
Jack Gardner, Player

1982
Bill Bradley, Player
Dave Debusschere, Player
Lloyd Leith, Player
Dean Smith, Referee
*Jack Twyman, Coach
* Robert Kurland

1981
Hal Greer, Coach
*Slater Martin, Player
*Frank Ramsey, Player
*Willis Reed, Player

1979
Lester Harrison
Jerry Lucus, Contributor
Oscar Robertson, Player
Jerry A. West, Referee

1978
Wilt Chamberlain, Player
John B. McLendon, Coach
*Ray Meyer, Coach
*Pete Newell, Coach

1977
*Paul J. Arizin, Player
Clifforf Hagan, Player
John Nucatola, Player

1976
Elgin Baylor, Player

1975
*Tom Gola, Player
Harry Litwack, Player
*Bill Sharman, Coach

1970
*Bob Cousey, Player
Bob Pettit, Player

1969
Ben Carnevale, Coach

1968
Red Auerbach, Coach
*Morgan Wooten

2000
*Danny Biasone, Contributor
Robert McAdoo, Player
Charles Newton, Contributor
Pat Head Summitt, Coach
Isiah Thomas, Player
Morgan Wootten, Coach

2001
John Chaney, Coach
Mike Krzyzewski, Coach
Moses Malone, Player

2002
Harlem Globetrotters, Team
Larry Brown, Coach
Earvin" Magic" Johnson, Player
Lute Olson, Coach
Drazen Petrovic, Player
Kay Yow, Coach

2003
Leon Barmore, Coach
Chick Hearn, Contributor
Meadowlark Lemon, Contributor
Earl Lloyd, Contributor
Dino Meneghin, Player
Robert Parish, Player
James Worthy, Player

Known as the "good will ambassadors to the world", the Harlem Globetrotters have been entertaining audiences since 1927.

Here are some interesting facts about the harlem globetrotters.

1. Did you know that the globetrotters completed their 20,000[th] game on January 18, 1998?

2. The Harlem Globetrotters have played in over 114 countries and before 100 million fans.

3. The Globetrotters provide summer camps to hundreds of kids across the U.S. If you would like more information call 1-800-641-4667 or visit the Harlem Globetrotter's web site at www. globetrotters.com

4. The Harlem Globetrotters appreciate their fans and they set aside 15 minutes after each game for signing autographs.

Or, one can write to a current or retired player at:

(Name Of Player)
The Harlem Globetrotters
Suite 300
400 East Van Buren
Phoenix, Az 85004

No.	Name	Height	Weight	Pos.	College	Birthdate
15	Anthony Blakes	6-2	188	G	Wyoming '00	Dec. 6, 1976
26	Kris Bruton	6-7	218	F	Benedict College '94	Jan. 10, 1971
	Kevin Daley	6-5	220	F	Azusa Pacific '00	Oct. 7, 1976
31	Eugene Edgerson	6-7	245	F	Arizona '01	Feb. 10, 1978
32	Paul Gaffney	6-6	230	F	Tenn. Wesleyan '90	Jan. 26, 1968
23	Matt Jackson	6-4	230	G	Savannah State '83	Dec. 21, 1961
17	Curley Johnson	5-11	175	G	Loras '87	Feb. 10, 1966
12	Otis Key	6-10	240	F/C	Lincoln University '96	Oct. 10, 1974
22	Herbert Lang	6-3	170	G	Centenary '98	Aug. 1, 1976
	Gordon Malone	6-11	225	C	West Virginia '97	July 17, 1974
3	Michael Moncrief	6-7	200	F/F	Sterling College '04	May 19, 1982
10	Eathan O'Bryant	5-11	190	G	Nevada '95	Sept. 5, 1972
54	Ron Rollerson	6-10	320	C	Temple '02	Sept. 20, 1980
44	Antwan Scott	6-8	210	F	Wake Forest '02	Sept. 1, 1979
11	Keiron Shine	5-10	180	G	Memphis '00	June 13, 1977
8	Lazarus Sims	6-5	224	G	Syracuse '96	March 28, 1972
24	Mike St. Julien	6-5	215	F	McNeese State '92	Sept. 5, 1969
44	Wun Versher	6-5	193	G	Arizona State '93	Oct. 23, 1970
7	Charles Wells	6-6	235	F	Austin Peay '97	July 26, 1974
25	Michael Wilson	6-5	185	F	Memphis '96	July 22, 1972
	Damond Williams	6-5	210	F	McNeese St. '03	October 10, 1980

COACHES: Rod Baker, Charles "Tex" Harrison , "Sweet" Lou Dunbar, and Clyde Sinclair

All NBA team rosters are listed on the following pages. Match the player you select with the team address listed below.

Example: (Name of Player)
           Houston Rockets
           1510 Polk Street
           Houston, TX 77002

Atlanta Hawks	Centennial Tower	101 Marietta Street N.W.	Atlanta, GA 30303
Boston Celtics	151 Merrimac Street	Boston, MA 02114	
Charlotte Bobcats	129 West Trade Street	Suite 700	Charlotte, NC 28202
Chicago Bulls	United Center	1901 West Madison Street	Chicago, IL 60212-2459
Cleveland Cavaliers	Gund Arena	One Center Court	Cleveland, OH 44115
Dallas Mavericks	The Pavilion	2909 Taylor Street	Dallas, TX 75226
Denver Nuggets	Pepsi Center	1000 Chopper Circle	Denver, CO 80204
Detroit Pistons	The Palace of Auburn Hills	4 Championship Drive	Auburn Hills, Mi 48326
Golden State Warriors	1011 Broadway	Oakland, CA 94621	
Houston Rockets	1510 Polk Street	Houston, TX 77002	
Indiana Pacers	Conseco Fieldhouse	125 So. Pennsylvania St.	Indianapolis, IN 46204
L A Clippers	Staples Center	1111 South Figueroa St.	Los Angeles, CA 90017
Los Angeles Lakers	Staples Center	1111 S. Figueroa Street	Los Angeles, CA 90015
Memphis Grizzlies	Suite 150	175 Toyota Plaza	Memphis, TN 38103
Miami Heat	American Airlines Arena	601 Biscayne Boulevard	Miami, FL 33132
Milwaukee Bucks	The Bradley Center	1001 North Fourth Street	Milwaukee, WI 53203
Minnesota Timberwolves	Target Center	600 First Avenue North	Minneapolis, MN 55403
New Jersey Nets	390 Murray Hill Parkway	East Rutherford	New Jersey 07073
New Orleans Hornets	1501 Girod Street	New Orleans, LA 70113	
New York Knicks	Madison Square Garden	Two Pennsylvania Plaza	New York, NY 10121
Orlando Magic	8701 Maitland Summit Blvd.	Orlando, FL 32810	
Philadelphia 76ers	First Union Center	3601 South Broad St.	Philadelphia, PA 19148
Phoenix Suns	America West Arena	201 E. Jefferson St.	Phoenix, AZ 85001
Portland Trail Blazers	7325 SW Childs Road	Portland, OR 97224	
Sacramento Kings	Arco Arena	One Sports Parkway	Sacramento, CA 95834
San Antonio Spurs	SBC Center	One SBC Center	San Antonio, TX 78219
Seattle SuperSonics	Suite 500	351 Elliott Avenue West	Seattle, WA 98119
Toronto Raptors	Air Canada Centre	40 Bay Street	Toronto, Ontario M5J 2N8
Utah Jazz	Delta Center	301 West South Temple	Salt Lake City, UT 84101
Washington Wizards	MCI Center	601 F Street NW	Washington, DC 20004

National Basketball Association Team Rosters

Atlanta Hawks
Kenny Anderson
Jon Barry
Lonny Baxter
Reggie Butler
Josh Childress
Jason Collier
Chris Crawford
Tony Delk
Boris Diaw
Predrag Drobnjak
Al Harrington
Royal Ivey
Anthony Miller
Jeff Myers
Donta Smith
Josh Smith
Antoine Walker
Saddi Washington
Kevin Willis
Coach
Mike Woodson

Boston Celtics
Tony Allen
Marcus Banks
Dana Barros
Mark Blount
Ernest Brown
Ricky Davis
Tom Gugliotta
Al Jefferson
Raef LaFrentz
Walter McCarty
Gary Payton
Kendrick Perkins
Paul Pierce
Justin Reed
Michael Stewart
Jiri Welsch
Delonte West
Coaches
Doc Rivers
Tony Brown
Dave Wohl
Jim Brewer

Charlotte Bobcats
Corey Benjamin
Primoz Brezec
Omar Cook
Melvin Ely
Jason Hart
Eddie House
Brandon Hunter
Jason Kapono
Brevin Knight
Emeka Okafor
Bernard Robinson
Jamal Sampson
Tamar Slay
Steve Smith
Theron Smith
Gerald Wallace
Jahidi White
Coach
Bernie Bickerstaff

Chicago Bulls
Tyson Chandler
Eddy Curry
Antonio Davis
Luol Deng
Chris Duhon
Ben Gordon
Adrian Griffin
Othella Harrington
Kirk Hinrich
Andres Nocioni
Jannero Pargo
Eric Piatkowski
Jared Reiner
Eddie Robinson
Tommy Smith
Gary Trent
Cezary Trybanski
Mike Wilks
Frank Williams
Coach
Scott Skiles

Cleveland Cavaliers
DeSagana Diop
Drew Gooden
Lucious Harris
Jimmie Hunter
Zydrunas Ilgauskas
Luke Jackson
LeBron James
Art Long
Jeff McInnis
Ira Newble
Aleksandar Pavlovic
Eric Snow
Robert Traylor
Anderson Varejao
Dajuan Wagner
Scott Williams
Coach
Paul Silas

Dallas Mavericks
Tariq Abdul-Wahad
Calvin Booth
Shawn Bradley
Erick Dampier
Marquis Daniels
Dan Dickau
Evan Eschmeyer
Michael Finley
Devin Harris
Alan Henderson
Josh Howard
Avery Johnson
DJ Mbenga
Dirk Nowitzki
Pavel Podkolzin
Jerry Stackhouse
Jason Terry
Coach
Don Nelson

Denver Nuggets
Carmelo Anthony
Earl Boykins
Greg Buckner
Marcus Camby
Francisco Elson
Marcus Hatten
Arthur Johnson
Billy Keys
Voshon Lenard
Kenyon Martin
Andre Miller
Nenê
Desmond Penigar
Mark Pope
Soumaila Samake
Melvin Sanders
Nikoloz Tskitishvili
Rodney White
Coach
Jeff Bzdelik

Detroit Pistons
Chauncey Billups
Elden Campbell
Derrick Coleman
Carlos Delfino
Nigel Dixon
Ronald Dupree
Darvin Ham
Richard Hamilton
Lindsey Hunter
Horace Jenkins
Antonio McDyess
Darko Milicic
Smush Parker
Rickey Paulding
Tayshaun Prince
Terrence Shannon
Ben Wallace
Rasheed Wallace
Coach
Larry Brown

Golden State Warriors
Brandon Armstrong
Andris Biedrins
Matt Carroll
Calbert Cheaney
Speedy Claxton
Dale Davis
Mike Dunleavy
Derek Fisher
Luis Flores
Adonal Foyle
Troy Murphy
Eduardo Najera
Mickael Pietrus
Jason Richardson
Clifford Robinson
Ansu Sesay
Coach
Mike Montgomery

Houston Rockets
Ryan Bowen
Reece Gaines
David Hawkins
Juwan Howard
Jim Jackson
Mark Jackson
Tyronn Lue
Tracy McGrady
Dikembe Mutombo
Bostjan Nachbar
Scott Padgett
Brooks Sales
Vassilis Spanoulis
Bob Sura
Maurice Taylor
Charlie Ward
Clarence Weatherspoon
Yao Ming
Derrick Zimmerman
Coach
Jeff Van Gundy

Indiana Pacers
Ron Artest
Jonathan Bender
Austin Croshere
John Edwards
Desmon Farmer
Jeff Foster
Eddie Gill
David Harrison
Randy Holcomb
Stephen Jackson
Anthony Johnson
Fred Jones
James Jones
Reggie Miller
Jermaine O'Neal
Scot Pollard
Jamaal Tinsley
Rashad Wright
Coach
Rick Carlisle

LA Clippers
Elton Brand
Rick Brunson
Lionel Chalmers
Kaniel Dickens
Marcus Fleming
Jerry Holman
Marko Jaric
Chris Kaman
Kerry Kittles
Trajan Langdon
Shaun Livingston
Corey Maggette
Josh Moore
Mikki Moore
Terence Morris
Brandon Mouton
Mamadou N'diaye
Doug Overton
Zeljko Rebraca
Quinton Ross
Bobby Simmons
Chris Wilcox
Coach
Mike Dunleavy

LA Lakers
Chucky Atkins
Tony Bobbitt
Tierre Brown
Kobe Bryant
Caron Butler
Brian Cook
Vlade Divac
Marcus Douthit
Devean George
Brian Grant
Horace Grant
Nate Johnson
Jumaine Jones
Karl Malone
S. Medvedenko
Chris Mihm
Lamar Odom
Kareem Rush
Bryon Russell
Sasha Vujacic
Luke Walton
Coach
Rudy Tomjanovich

Memphis Grizzles
Shane Battier
Troy Bell
Antonio Burks
Brian Cardinal
Andre Emmett
Pau Gasol
Ryan Humphrey
Dahntay Jones
Sergei Lishouk
Mike Miller
Bo Outlaw
41 James Posey
Stromile Swift
Jake Tsakalidis
Earl Watson
Bonzi Wells
Jason Williams
Lorenzen Wright
Coach
Hubie Brown

Miami Heat
Malik Allen
Jerome Beasley
Rasual Butler
Bimbo Coles
Michael Doleac
Keyon Dooling
50 Matt Freije
Tang Hamilton
Udonis Haslem
Damon Jones
Eddie Jones
Christian Laettner
Albert Miralles
Shaquille O'Neal
Wesley Person
Dwyane Wade
John Wallace
Dorell Wright
Wang Zhizhi
Coach
Stan Van Gundy

Milwaukee Bucks
Tommy Adams
T.J. Ford
Dan Gadzuric
Marcus Haislip
Zendon Hamilton
Juaquin Hawkins
Mike James
Lonnie Jones
Toni Kukoc
Desmond Mason
Jelani McCoy
Zaza Pachulia
Michael Redd
Daniel Santiago
Joe Smith
Erick Strickland
Keith Van Horn
Brandon Williams
Maurice Williams
Coach
Terry Porter

Minnesota Twolves
Jackie Butler
Anthony Carter
Sam Cassell
Ndudi Ebi
Kevin Garnett
Anthony Goldwire
Eddie Griffin
Trenton Hassell
Fred Hoiberg
Troy Hudson
Ervin Johnson
Mark Madsen
Michael Olowokandi
Kasib Powell
Rick Rickert
Latrell Sprewell
Blake Stepp
Wally Szczerbiak
John Thomas
Coach
Flip Saunders

New Jersey Nets
Travis Best
Andre Brown
Rodney Buford
Jason Collins
Kyle Davis
Christian Drejer
Richard Jefferson
Jason Kidd
Nenad Krstic
Ron Mercer
Alonzo Mourning
Zoran Planinic
Darius Rice
Brian Scalabrine
Alex Scales
Jacque Vaughn
Aaron Williams
Eric Williams
Coach
Lawrence Frank

New Orleans Hornets
Chris Andersen
Darrell Armstrong
P.J. Brown
Baron Davis
Tremaine Fowlkes
Alex Garcia
Junior Harrington
Britton Johnsen
George Lynch
Jamaal Magloire
Jamal Mashburn
Lee Nailon
Tim Pickett
Rodney Rogers
J.R. Smith
David Wesley
David West
Nate Williams
Coach
Byron Scott

New York Knicks
Shandon Anderson
Trevor Ariza
Vin Baker
Andre Barrett
Mengke Bateer
Jamison Brewer
Jamal Crawford
Anfernee Hardaway
Allan Houston
Stephon Marbury
Nazr Mohammed
Tracy Murray
Moochie Norris
Bruno Sundov
Mike Sweetney
Kurt Thomas
Tim Thomas
Jerome Williams
Brent Wright
Coach
Lenny Wilkens

Orlando Magic
Stacey Augmon
Tony Battie
Keith Bogans
Michael Bradley
Kelvin Cato
Andrew DeClercq
Corsley Edwards
Steve Francis
Pat Garrity
Grant Hill
Dwight Howard
Mario Kasun
Cuttino Mobley
Jameer Nelson
DeShawn Stevenson
Hidayet Turkoglu
Coach
Johnny Davis

Philadelphia Sixers
Kedrick Brown
Samuel Dalembert
Josh Davis
Willie Green
Kirk Haston
Andre Iguodala
Allen Iverson
Marc Jackson
Nate James
Kyle Korver
Aaron McKie
Kevin Ollie
Glenn Robinson
John Salmons
Brian Skinner
Kenny Thomas
Corliss Williamson
Coach
Jim O'Brien

Phoenix Suns
Leandro Barbosa
Zarko Cabarkapa
Derrick Dial
Howard Eisley
Steven Hunter
Casey Jacobsen
Joe Johnson
Maciej Lampe
Shawn Marion
Steve Nash
Quentin Richardson
Paul Shirley
Amare Stoudemire
Yuta Tabuse
Jake Voskuhl
Jackson Vroman
Coach
Mike D'Antoni

Portland Trail Blazers
Shareef Abdur-Rahim
Derek Anderson
Geno Carlisle
Richie Frahm
Viktor Khryapa
Darius Miles
Sergei Monia
Travis Outlaw
Ruben Patterson
Joel Przybilla
Zach Randolph
Theo Ratliff
Ha Seung-Jin
Vladimir Stepania
Damon Stoudamire
Sebastian Telfair
Nick Van Exel
Qyntel Woods
Coach
Maurice Cheeks

Sacramento Kings
Courtney Alexander
Matt Barnes
Mike Bibby
David Bluthenthal
Doug Christie
Erik Daniels
Maurice Evans
Anwar Ferguson
Alton Ford
Bobby Jackson
Kevin Martin
Brad Miller
Ricky Minard
Greg Ostertag
Adam Parada
Darius Songaila
Predrag Stojakovic
Chris Webber
Liu Wei
Coach
Rick Adelman

San Antonio Spurs
Brent Barry
Ruben Boumtje
Bruce Bowen
Devin Brown
Tim Duncan
Emanuel Ginobili
Robert Horry
Linton Johnson
Sergei Karaulov
Sean Marks
Tony Massenburg
Vatler Monteiro
Radoslav Nesterovic
Tony Parker
Marque Perry
Malik Rose
Viktor Sanikidze
Romain Sato
James Thomas
Beno Udrih
Coach
Gregg Popovich

Seattle Supersonics
Ray Allen
Mateen Cleaves
Nick Collison
Antonio Daniels
Reggie Evans
Danny Fortson
Jerome James
Ibrahim Kutluay
Rashard Lewis
Ronald Murray
Vitaly Potapenko
Vladimir Radmanovic
Luke Ridnour
Leon Smith
Robert Swift
Damien Wilkins
Galen Young
Coach
Nate McMillan

Toronto Raptors
Rafer Alston
Rafael Araujo
Corie Blount
Matt Bonner
Chris Bosh
Vince Carter
Ousmane Cisse
Michael Curry
Dion Glover
Donyell Marshall
Roger Mason Jr.
Jerome Moiso
Lamond Murray
Milt Palacio
Morris Peterson
Norm Richardson
Jalen Rose
Pape Sow
Rod Strickland
Alvin Williams
Loren Woods
Coach
Sam Mitchell

Utah Jazz
Carlos Arroyo
Raja Bell
Carlos Boozer
Curtis Borchardt
Jarron Collins
Peter Cornell
Gordan Giricek
Matt Harpring
Cedric Henderson
Kris Humphries
Andrei Kirilenko
Raul Lopez
Keith McLeod
Jason Miskiri
Mehmet Okur
A. Radojevic
Kirk Snyder
Coach
Jerry Sloan

Washington Wizards
Gilbert Arenas
Steve Blake
Kwame Brown
Mitchell Butler
Juan Dixon
Gerald Fitch
Jarvis Hayes
Brendan Haywood
Larry Hughes
Antawn Jamison
Jared Jeffries
Anthony Peeler
Laron Profit
Peter Ramos
Michael Ruffin
Jon Smith
Billy Thomas
Etan Thomas
Samaki Walker
Chris Whitney
Coach
Eddie Jordan

Selected Additional Basketball Names & Addresses

Abdul-Jabbar, Kareem	Sports Placement Service	5458 Wilshire Blvd.	Los Angeles, CA 90036
Adams, Alvan	Phoenix Suns	201 E. Jefferson St.	Phoenix, AZ 85001
Allen, Paul G.	Portland Trail Blazers	7325 SW Childs Road	Portland, OR 97224
Arison, Micky	Miami Heat	601 Biscayne Boulevard	Miami, FL 33132
Atlanta Dance Team	Atlanta Hawks	101 Marietta Street N.W.	Atlanta, GA 30303
Auerbach, Arnold "Red"	Boston Celtics	151 Merrimac Street	Boston, MA 02114
Automotion Dance Team	Detroit Pistons	4 Championship Drive	Auburn Hills, MI 48326
Baylor, Elgin	Staples Center	1111 South Figueroa St.	Los Angeles, CA 90017
Bird, Larry	Indiana Pacers	125 So. Pennsylvania St.	Indianapolis, IN 46204
Blazer Dancers	Portland Trail Blazers	7325 SW Childs Road	Portland, OR 97224
Bobcats Dance Team	Charlotte Bobcats	129 West Trade Street	Charlotte, NC 28202
Bogues, Tyrone "Muggsy"	Always Believe Foundation	PO Box 1555	Greensboro, NC 27401
Cavalier Girls	Cleveland Cavaliers	One Center Court	Cleveland, OH 44115
Chambers, Tom	Phoenix Suns	201 E. Jefferson St.	Phoenix, AZ 85001
Chapman, Rex	Phoenix Suns	201 E. Jefferson St.	Phoenix, AZ 85001
Chicago Luvabulls	C.C. Company of Illinois	P.O. Box 4712	Wheaton, IL 60189
Colangelo, Jerry	Phoenix Suns	201 E. Jefferson St.	Phoenix, AZ 85001
Colson, Gary	Memphis Grizzlies	175 Toyota Plaza	Memphis, TN 38103
Cousy, Bob	Boston Celtics	151 Merrimac Street	Boston, MA 02114
Cuban, Mark	Dallas Mavericks	2909 Taylor Street	Dallas, TX 75226
Energee Dance Team	Milwaukee Bucks	1001 North Fourth Street	Milwaukee, WI 53203
Erving, Julius	Orlando Magic	8701 Maitland Summit Blvd.	Orlando, FL 32810
Grizzles Dance Team	Memphis Grizzlies	175 Toyota Plaza	Memphis, TN 38103
Grousbeck, Wyc	Boston Celtics	151 Merrimac Street	Boston, MA 02114
Hawkins, Connie	Phoenix Suns	201 E. Jefferson St.	Phoenix, AZ 85001
Heat Dancers	Miami Heat	601 Biscayne Boulevard	Miami, FL 33132
Indiana Pacemates	Indiana Pacers	125 So. Pennsylvania St.	Indianapolis, IN 46204
Isiah Thomas	New York Knicks	Two Pennsylvania Plaza	New York, NY 10121
Jazz Dancers	Delta Center	301 West South Temple	Salt Lake City, UT 84101
Johnson, Ervin "Magic"	United Talent Agency	9560 Wilshire Blvd.	Beverly Hills, CA 90212
Jordan, Michael	Estee Portney # 580	5335 Wisconsin Ave NW	Washington, DC 20015
Knicks City Dancers	New York Knicks	Two Pennsylvania Plaza	New York, NY 10121
Knight, Billy	Atlanta Hawks	101 Marietta Street N.W.	Atlanta, GA 30303
Knight, Bobby	Texas Tech Athletic Dept.	Lubbuck, TX 10523	
Kohl, Herb	Milwaukee Bucks	1001 North Fourth Street	Milwaukee, WI 53203
Kroenke, E. Stanley	Denver Nuggets	1000 Chopper Circle	Denver, CO 80204
Krzyzewski, Mike	Duke University	Durham, NC 27708	
Laker Girls	Staples Center	1111 S. Figueroa Street	Los Angeles, CA 90015
Lucas, Jerry	Lucas Education	P.O. Box 728	Templeton, CA 93465
Magic Dancers	Orlando Magic	8701 Maitland Summit Blvd.	Orlando, FL 32810
Mavs Dancers	Dallas Mavericks	2909 Taylor Street	Dallas, TX 75226
New Jersey Nets	390 Murray Hill Parkway	East Rutherford	New Jersey 07073
Nuggets Dancers	Denver Nuggets	1000 Chopper Circle	Denver, CO 80204
Pippen, Scottie	2320 Shady Lane	Highland Park, IL 60035	
Pitino, Rick	Boston Celtics	151 Merrimac Street	Boston, MA 02114
Raptors Dance Pak	Air Canada Centre	40 Bay Street	Toronto, Ontario M5J 2N8
Reed, Willis	New Orleans Hornets	1501 Girod Street	New Orleans, LA 70113
Riley, Pat	Miami Heat	601 Biscayne Boulevard	Miami, FL 33132
Rockets Power Dancers	Houston Rockets	1510 Polk Street	Houston, TX 77002
Rodman, Dennis	4809 Seashore Drive	Newport Beach, CA 92663	
Russell, Bill	Boston Celtics	151 Merrimac Street	Boston, MA 02114
Salley, John	Endeavor Talent Agency	10th Fl. 9701 Wilshire Blvd.	Beverly Hills, CA 90212
Shinn, George	New Orleans Hornets	1501 Girod Street	New Orleans, LA 70113
Silver Dancers	SBC Center	One SBC Center	San Antonio, TX 78219
Sixers Dancers	First Union Center	3601 South Broad St.	Philadelphia, PA 19148
Sonics Dance Team	Suite 500	351 Elliott Avenue West	Seattle, WA 98119
Spirit Dance Team	Staples Center	1111 South Figueroa St.	Los Angeles, CA 90017
Sterling, Donald T.	Staples Center	1111 South Figueroa St.	Los Angeles, CA 90017
T-wolves Dancers	Target Center	600 First Avenue North	Minneapolis, MN 55403
Valentine, Darnell	Portland Trail Blazers	7325 SW Childs Road	Portland, OR 97224
Van Arsdale, Dick	Phoenix Suns	201 E. Jefferson St.	Phoenix, AZ 85001
Versace, Dick	Memphis Grizzlies	175 Toyota Plaza	Memphis, TN 38103
Vitale, Bob	ESPN Plaza	935 Middle Street	Bristol, CT 06010
Warrior Girls	Golden State Warriors	1011 Broadway	Oakland, CA 94621
West, Jerry	Memphis Grizzlies	175 Toyota Plaza	Memphis, TN 38103
West, Mark	Phoenix Suns	201 E. Jefferson St.	Phoenix, AZ 85001
Wilkins, Dominique	Atlanta Hawks	101 Marietta Street N.W.	Atlanta, GA 30303
Wizards Dance Team	MCI Center	601 F Street NW	Washington, DC 20004

The International Boxing Hall of Fame will forward autograph requests to inductees if request is addressed:

Please Forward To:
(Name of Inductee)
C/O The International Boxing Hall of Fame
1 Hall of Fame Drive
Canastota, NY 13032

Deceased*

Ali, Muhammad	Arguello, Alexis	Armstrong, Henry *
Basilio, Carman	Benitez, Wilfred	Benvenuti, Nino
Berg, Jackie (Kid) *	Brown, Joe*	Burley, Charley *
Cerdan, Marcel *	Charles, Ezzard *	Conn, Billy *
Elorde, Gabriel (Flash)*	Foster, Bob	Frazier, Joe
Fullmer, Gene	Gavilan, Kid	Giardello, Joey
Gomez, Wilfred	Graham, Billy *	Graziano, Rocky *
Griffith, Emile	Hagler, Marvin	Harada, Masahiko
Jack, Beau*	Jofre, Eder	Johnson, Harold
Lamotta, Joe	Leonard, Sugar Ray	Liston, Sonny *
Marciano, Rocky *	Maxim, Joey	Montgomery, Bob *
Monzon, Carlos*	Moore, Archie*	Napoles, Jose
Norton, Ken	Olivares, Ruben	Ortiz, Carlos
Ortiz, Manuel*	Patterson, Floyd	Pep, Willie
Perez, Pasqual*	Pryor, Aaron	Robinson, Sugar Ray *
Rodriguez, Luis	Sadler, Sandy	Sanchez, Salvador*
Schmeling, Max	Spinks, Michael	Tiger, Dick *
Torres, Jose	Walcott, Jersey Joe *	Williams, Ike *
Wright, Chalky *	Zale, Tony *	Zarate, Carlos
Zivic, Fritzie *		

Selected Additional Boxing Names & Addresses

Ali, Muhammad	PO Box 187	Berrien Springs, MI 49103	
Austin, Tim	Don King Productions	501 Fairway Drive	Deerfield Beach, FL 33441
Bailey, Randall	Don King Productions	501 Fairway Drive	Deerfield Beach, FL 33441
Bowe, Riddick	C/O Spencer Promotions	1025 Vermont Ave NW	Washington, DC 20005
Bradley, Lonnie	Don King Productions	501 Fairway Drive	Deerfield Beach, FL 33441
Camacho, Hector	4751 Yardman Lane	Boyton Beach, FL 33436	
Chavez, Jesus	C/O Main Events	390 Murray Hill Parkway	East Rutherford, NJ 07073
De La Hoya, Oscar	2401 South Atlantic Blvd	Monterey Park, CA 91754	
Dundee, Angelo	1487 Camellia Circle	Weston, FL 33326	
Foreman, George	Po Box 14267	Humble, TX 77347	
Forrest, Vernon	C/O Main Events	390 Murray Hill Parkway	East Rutherford, NJ 07073
Frazier, Joe	2917 N. Broad Street	Philadelphia, PA 19132	
Gatti, Arturo	C/O Main Events	390 Murray Hill Parkway	East Rutherford, NJ 07073
Girgrah, Isra	Don King Productions	501 Fairway Drive	Deerfield Beach, FL 33441
Golotta, Andrew	C/O Main Events	390 Murray Hill Parkway	East Rutherford, NJ 07073
Guinn, Dominic	C/O Main Events	390 Murray Hill Parkway	East Rutherford, NJ 07073
Hall, Richard	Don King Productions	501 Fairway Drive	Deerfield Beach, FL 33441
Hanshaw, Anthony	C/O Main Events	390 Murray Hill Parkway	East Rutherford, NJ 07073
Harris, Vivian	C/O Main Events	390 Murray Hill Parkway	East Rutherford, NJ 07073
Hearns, Thomas	C/O Emmanual Steward	19600 West Mc Nichol	Detroit, MI 48219
Hollyfield, Evander	Don King Productions	501 Fairway Drive	Deerfield Beach, FL 33441
Holmes, Keith	Don King Productions	501 Fairway Drive	Deerfield Beach, FL 33441
Holmes, Larry	413 Northampton Street	Easton, PA 18042	
Jones, Roy Jr.	Endeavor Talent Agency	9601 Wilshire Blvd	Beverly Hills, CA 90212
Joppy, William	Don King Productions	501 Fairway Drive	Deerfield Beach, FL 33441
Judah, Zabdiel	C/O Main Events	390 Murray Hill Parkway	East Rutherford, NJ 07073
Julio, Jorge	Don King Productions	501 Fairway Drive	Deerfield Beach, FL 33441
King, Don	Don King Productions	501 Fairway Drive	Deerfield Beach, FL 33441
Lamotta, Jake	400 E. 57th Street	New York, NY 10022	
Laracuente, Belinda	Don King Productions	501 Fairway Drive	Deerfield Beach, FL 33441
Lazcano, Juan	C/O Main Events	390 Murray Hill Parkway	East Rutherford, NJ 07073
Leonard, Sugar Ray	# 303	4401 East-West Highway	Bethesda, MD 20814
Lewis, Lennox	C/O Main Events	390 Murray Hill Parkway	East Rutherford, NJ 07073
Lopez, Jose Luis	C/O Main Events	390 Murray Hill Parkway	East Rutherford, NJ 07073
Lopez, Ricardo	Don King Productions	501 Fairway Drive	Deerfield Beach, FL 33441
Lucero, Emmanuel	C/O Main Events	390 Murray Hill Parkway	East Rutherford, NJ 07073
Mancini, Ray	12524 Indianapolis St.	Los Angeles, CA 90066	
Martin, Christy	Don King Productions	501 Fairway Drive	Deerfield Beach, FL 33441
Mayweather, Floyd	Top Rank Inc.	3980 Howard Hughes Pkwy	Las Vegas, NV 89109
Mitchell, Shamba	Don King Productions	501 Fairway Drive	Deerfield Beach, FL 33441
Moorer, Michael	C/O Main Events	390 Murray Hill Parkway	East Rutherford, NJ 07073
Page, James	Don King Productions	501 Fairway Drive	Deerfield Beach, FL 33441
Quartey, Ike	C/O Main Events	390 Murray Hill Parkway	East Rutherford, NJ 07073
Robinson, Ivan	C/O Main Events	390 Murray Hill Parkway	East Rutherford, NJ 07073
Ruiz, John	Don King Productions	501 Fairway Drive	Deerfield Beach, FL 33441
Salamone, Melissa	Don King Productions	501 Fairway Drive	Deerfield Beach, FL 33441
Sencion, Luis	C/O Main Events	390 Murray Hill Parkway	East Rutherford, NJ 07073
Somers, Daniella	Don King Productions	501 Fairway Drive	Deerfield Beach, FL 33441
Tiozza, Fabrice	Don King Productions	501 Fairway Drive	Deerfield Beach, FL 33441
Trinadad, Felix	Don King Productions	501 Fairway Drive	Deerfield Beach, FL 33441
Tyson, Mike	NKS Management Suite 1300	10100 Santa Monica Blvd	Los Angeles, CA 90067
Vargas, Fernado	C/O Main Events	390 Murray Hill Parkway	East Rutherford, NJ 07073
Wright, Robert "Winky"	Intl. Boxing Federation	516 Main Street	East Orange, NJ 07018

If you have something you would like to send to an enshrinee,
   Please send it to:

> Please Forward To:
> (Name of Enshrinee)
> Pro Football Hall of Fame
> 2121 George Halas Drive NW
> Canton, Ohio 44708

And the Pro Football Hall of Fame will forward it to the Hall of Fame member. Please be sure that the enshrinee's name is on front of the envelope so that it will be forwarded correctly.

Name	Year	Position	Team	No. Of Years Played
Adderley, Herb	1980	Cornerback	Grenbay & Dallas	12 Playing Seasons
Allen, George	2002	Coach	LA Rams & Redskins	No Playing Season
Allen, Marcus	2003	Running Back	LA Raiders KC Chiefs	15 Playing Seasons
Alworth, Lance	1978	Wide Receiver-San Deigo	And Dallas Cowboys	11 Playing Seasons
Atkins, Doug	1982	Defensive End-Cleveland	Chicago - New Orleans	17 Playing Seasons
Badgro, Morris (Red)	1981	End	New York Giants	8 Playing Seasons
Barney, Lem	1992	Cornerback	Detroit	11 Playing Seasons
Baugh, Sammy	1963	Q-Back For Washington	Assist Coach Houston	16 Playing Seasons
Bednarik, Chuck	1967	Center And Linebacker	Philadelphia Eagles	14 Playing Seasons
Bell, Bobby	1983	Linebacker -Defense End	Kansas City Chiefs	12 Playing Seasons
Berry, Raymond	1973	End-Baltimore Colts	Head Coach-New Eng.	13 Playing Seasons
Bethea, Elvin	2003	Defensive End	Houston Oilers	16 Playing Seasons
Biletnikoff, Fred	1988	Wide Receiver	Oakland Raiders	14 Playing Seasons
Blanda, George	1981	Q-Back & Placekicker	Bears-Colts-Oilers	26 Playing Seasons
Blount, Mel	1989	Cornerback	Pittsburgh Steelers	14 Playing Seasons
Bradshaw, Terry	1989	Quarterback	Pittsburgh Steelers	14 Playing Seasons
Brown, Bob (Boomer)	2004	Tackle	Eagles & Raiders	10 Playing Seasons
Brown, Jim	1971	Fullback	Cleveland Browns	8 Playing Seasons
Brown, Roosevelt	1967	Offensive Tackle	New York Giants	13 Playing Seasons
Brown, Willie	1984	Cornerback	Denver & Oakland	16 Playing Seasons
Buoniconti, Nick	2001	Linebacker - Miami	Boston Patriots	14 Playing Seasons
Butkis, Dick	1979	Linebacker	Chicago Bears	9 Playing Seasons
Campell, Earl	1991	Running Back	Houston -New Orleans	8 Playing Seasons
Canadeo, Tony	1974	Halfback	Greenbay Packers	11 Playing Seasons
Casper, Dave	2002	Tight End	LA Raiders & Oilers	10 Playing Seasons
Connor, George	1975	Tackle & Linebacker	Chicago Bears	8 Playing Seasons
Creekmur, Lou	1996	Offensive Tackle, Guard	Detroit Lions	10 Playing Seasons
Csonka, Larry	1987	Fullback	Miami Dolphins	11 Playing Seasons
Davis, Al	1992	President And Former	Head Coach La Raiders	No Playing Season
Davis, Willie	1981	Defensive End	Cleveland & Greenbay	12 Playing Seasons
Dawson, Len	1987	Quartback For Steelers	Browns, Dallas, Chiefs	19 Playing Seasons
DeLamielleure, Joe	2003	Guard	Bills & Browns	13 Playing Seasons

Dickerson, Eric	1999	Running Back	La, Atlanta	12 Playing Seasons
Dierdorf, Dan	1996	Tackle, Center	St. Louis Cardinals	13 Playing Seasons
Ditka, Mike	1988	Tightend For Chicago	Head Coach Chicago	12 Playing Seasons
Donovan, Art	1968	Defensive Tackle For	Baltimore, N.Y., Dallas	12 Playing Seasons
Dorsett, Tony	1994	Running Back	Dallas Cowboys	12 Playing Seasons
Dudley, Bill	1966	Halfback	Pittsburgh, Detroit	9 Playing Seasons
Eller, Carl	2004	Defensive End	Minnesota Vikings	16 Playing Seasons
Elway, John	2004	Quarterback	Denver Broncos	16 Playing Seasons
Ewbank, Weeb	1978	Head Coach Baltimore	New York Jets	No Playing Season
Fears, Tom	1970	End- LA Rams	Head Ch. New Orleans	9 Playing Seasons
Fortmann, Daniel	1965	Guard	Chicago Bears	8 Playing Seasons
Fouts, Dan	1993	Quarterback	San Diego Chargers	15 Playing Seasons
Gatski, Frank	1985	Center-Cleveland And	Detroit Lions	12 Playing Seasons
Gibbs, Joe	1996	Coach	Washington Redskins	No Playing Season
Gifford, Frank	1977	Halfback	New York Giants	12 Playing Seasons
Gillman, Sid	1983	End- Cleveland Rams	Head Coach-San Diego	1 Playing Season
Grant, Bud	1994	End- Philadelphia	Head Coach- Minnesota	2 Playing Seasons
Greene, Joe	1987	Def. Tackle-Steeler	Assist. Coach- Miami	13 Playing Seasons
Gregg, Forest	1977	Tackle- Guard Greenbay	Coach-Browns, Gr.Bay	15 Playing Seasons
Griese, Bob	1990	Quarterback	Miami	14 Playing Seasons
Groza, Lou	1974	Tackle & Placekicker	Cleveland Browns	21 Playing Seasons
Ham, Jack	1988	Linebacker	Steelers	12 Playing Seasons
Hampton, Dan	2002	Defensive Tackle/End	Chicago Bears	12 Playing Seasons
Hannah, John	1991	Guard	New England	13 Playing Seasons
Harris, Franco	1990	Running Back	Pittsburgh Steelers	13 Playing Seasons
Haynes, Michael	1997	Cornerback	New Eng. & La Raiders	14 Playing Seasons
Hendricks, Ted	1990	Linebacker	Baltimore	15 Playing Seasons
Hirsch, Elroy (Crazylegs)	1968	Halfback & End	Chicago & La Rams	12 Playing Seasons
Horning, Paul	1986	Running Back- Green Bay	Packers	9 Playing Seasons
Houston, Ken	1986	Safety	Houston Oilers	14 Playing Seasons
Huff, Sam	1982	Linebacker- New York	Giants	13 Playing Seasons
Hunt, Lamar	1972	Founder-Afl Present	Owner Of Kc Chiefs	No Playing Season
Hutson, Don	1963	End & Assistant Coach	Green Bay Packers	11 Playing Seasons
Johnson, Jimmy	1994	Cornerback- 49er's	Head Coach- Dallas	16 Playing Seasons
Johnson, John Henry	1987	Fullback-49er's-Lions	& Steelers	13 Playing Seasons
Joiner, Charlie	1996	Receiver	Houston, Cinci, S.D.	18 Playing Seasons
Jones, David "Deacon"	1980	Defensive End- La Rams	San Diego & Washing.	14 Playing Seasons
Jones, Stan	1991	Guard-Bears & Redskins	Assist. Coach Denver	13 Playing Seasons
Jurgensen, Sonny	1983	Quarterback-Eagles &	Washington Redskins	18 Playing Seasons
Kelly, Jim	2002	Quarterback	Buffalo Bills	11 Playing Seasons
Kelly, Leroy	1994	Running Back-Cleveland	Browns	10 Playing Seasons
Krause, Paul	1998	Safety	Minnesota Vikings	15 Playing Seasons
Lambert, Jack	1990	Linebacker- Pittsburgh	Steelers	11 Playing Seasons
Landry, Tom	1990	Head Coach Dallas	Cowboys	No Playing Season
Lane, Richard	1974	Cornerback-La Rams	Detroit Lions	14 Playing Seasons
Langer, Jim	1987	Center- Vikings &	Miami Dolphins	12 Playing Seasons

Lanier, Willie	1986	Linebacker- Kansas City	Chiefs	11 Playing Seasons
Largent, Steve	1995	Wide Receiver	Seattle	14 Playing Seasons
Lary, Yale	1979	Safety	Detroit Lions	11 Playing Seasons
Lavelli, Dante	1975	End	Cleveland Browns	11 Playing Seasons
Levy, Marv	2001	Coach	Buffalo Bills	No Playing Season
Lilly, Bob	1980	Defensive Tackle	Dallas Cowboys	14 Playing Seasons
Little, Larry	1993	Guard	San Diego And Miami	14 Playing Seasons
Lofton, James	2003	Wide Receiver	Packers, Rams, Eagles	16 Playing Seasons
Long, Howie	2000	Defensive End	L.A. Raiders	12 Playing Seasons
Lott, Ronnie	2000	Safety	San Fracisco 49er's	13 Playing Seasons
Luckman, Sid	1965	Quarterback- Chicago	Bears	12 Playing Seasons
Mack, Tom	1999	Guard	La Rams	13 Playing Seasons
Mackey, John	1992	Tight End- Baltimore	& San Diego	10 Playing Seasons
Mara, Wellington	1997	President & Owner	New York Giants	Contributor
Marchetti, Gino	1972	Defensive End- Baltimore	Colts	14 Playing Seasons
Matson, Ollie	1972	Halfback- La Rams &	Philadelphia Eagles	14 Playing Seasons
Maynard, Don	1987	Wide Receiver	New York Jets	15 Playing Seasons
McAfee, George	1966	Halfback- Chicago Bears	Game Official 59-65 Nfl	8 Playing Seasons
McCormack, Mike	1984	Tackle-Cleveland	President-Carolina	10 Playing Seasons
McDonald, Tommy	1998	Wide Receiver	Phily, Dallas, La, Atl,	11 Playing Seasons
McElhennny, Hugh	1970	Halfback- 49er's	Vikings, Giants, Lions	13 Playing Seasons
Mitchell, Bobby	1983	Wide Receiver & Halfback	Browns, Redskins	11 Playing Seasons
Mix, Ron	1979	Offensive Tackle	Chargers, Raiders	11 Playing Seasons
Montana, Joe	2000	Quarterback	San Francisco 49er's	15 Playing Seasons
Moore, Leonard	1975	Flanker-Running Back	Colts	12 Playing Seasons
Motley, Marion	1968	Fullback	Browns	12 Playing Seasons
Munchak, Mike	2001	Guard	Houston Oilers	11 Playing Seasons
Munoz, Anthony	1998	Offensive Tackle	Cincinnati Bengals	12 Playing Seasons
Musso, George	1982	Guard-Tackle	Bears	12 Playing Seasons
Namath, Joe	1985	Quarterback	Jets	13 Playing Seasons
Newsome, Ozzie	1999	Tight End	Cleveland Browns	13 Playing Seasons
Nitschke, Ray	1978	Linebacker	Packers	13 Playing Seasons
Noll, Chuck	1993	Head Coach- Steelers,	Coach-Chargers	6 Playing Seasons
Nomellini, Leo	1969	Defensive Tackle	San Francisco 49er's	14 Playing Seasons
Olsen, Merlin	1982	Defensive Tackle	Los Angeles Rams	15 Playing Seasons
Otto, Jim	1980	Center	Los Angeles Raiders	15 Playing Seasons
Page, Alan	1988	Defensive Tackle	Minnesota Vikings	15 Playing Seasons
Parker, Jim	1973	Guard-Tackle	Baltimore Colts	11 Playing Seasons
Parker,Clarence (Ace)	1972	Quarterback- Brooklyn	Dodgers- Boston Yank	7 Playing Seasons
Payton, Walter	1993	Running Back	Chicago Bears	13 Playing Seasons
Perry, Fletcher (Shorty)	1969	Fullback	San Francisco 49er's	16 Playing Seasons
Pihos, Pete	1970	End	Philadelphia Eagles	9 Playing Seasons
Renfro, Mel	1996	Cornerback, Safety	Dallas Cowboys	14 Playing Seasons
Riggins, John	1992	Running Back	Ny Jets & Redskins	14 Playing Seasons
Ringo, Jim	1981	Center-Packers, Eagles	Assist Coach Bills	15 Playing Seasons

Robustelli, Andy	1971	Defensive End-Rams &	Giants	14 Playing Seasons
Rooney, Dan	2000	Contributor	Pittsburgh	No Playing Season
Rozelle, Pete	1985	Commissioner- NFL		No Playing Season
Sanders, Barry	2004	Running Back	Detroit Lions	10 Playing Seasons
Sayers, Gale	1977	Halfback	Chicago Bears	7 Playing Seasons
Schmidt, Joe	1973	Linebacker- Lions	Head Coach- Lions	13 Playing Seasons
Schramm, Tex	1991	G.M. Cowboys, President	World League	No Playing Season
Selmon, Lee Roy	1995	Defensive End	Tampa Bay Buccaneers	9 Playing Seasons
Shaw, Billy	1999	Guard	Buffalo Bills	9 Playing Seasons
Shell, Art	1989	Tackle-Raiders	Head Coach- Raiders	15 Playing Seasons
Shula, Don	1997	Coach	Miami Dolphins	No Playing Season
Simpson, O.J.	1985	Running Back	Buffalo Bills	11 Playing Seasons
Singletary, Michael	1998	Linebacker	Chicago Bears	12 Playing Seasons
Slater, Jackie	2001	Tackle	LA & St. Louis Rams	20 Playing Seasons
Smith, Jackie	1994	Tight End- St Louis	Cardinals	16 Playing Seasons
St. Clair, Bob	1990	Tackle	San Francisco 49er's	11 Playing Seasons
Stallworth, John	2002	Wide Receiver	Pittsburgh Steelers	13 Playing Seasons
Starr, Bart	1977	Quarterback-Packers	Head Coach-Packers	16 Playing Seasons
Staubach, Roger	1985	Quarteback	Dallas Cowboys	11 Playing Seasons
Stautner, Ernie	1969	Defensive Tackle	Steelers	14 Playing Seasons
Stenerud, Jan	1991	Placekicker-Chiefs	Packers- Vikings	19 Playing Seasons
Stephenson, Dwight	1998	Center	Miami Dolphins	8 Playing Seasons
Stram, Hank	2003	Coach	KC Chiefs & NO Saints	No Playing Season
Swann, Lynn	2001	Wide Receiver	Pittsburgh Steelers	9 Playing Seasons
Tarkenton, Fran	1986	Quaterback	Vikings & Giants	18 Playing Seasons
Taylor, Charlie	1984	Wide Receiver	Back-Redskins	13 Playing Seasons
Taylor, Jim	1976	Fullback	Greenbay Packers	10 Playing Seasons
Taylor, Lawrence	1999	Linebacker	New York Giants	13 Playing Seasons
Tittle, Y.A.	1971	Quarterback	Colts & 49er's	17 Playing Seasons
Trippi, Charley	1968	Halfback & Quarterback	Chicago Cardinals	9 Playing Seasons
Turner, Clyde (Bulldog)	1966	Center- Linbacker	Bears	13 Playing Seasons
Upshaw, Gene	1987	Guard	Steelers	15 Playing Seasons
Van Buren, Steve	1965	Halfback- Eagles	Assist Coach- Eagles	8 Playing Seasons
Walker, Doak	1986	Halfback	Detroit Lions	6 Playing Seasons
Walsh, Bill	1993	Head Coach	San Francisco 49er's	No Playing Season
Warfield, Paul	1983	Wide Receiver	Cleveland Browns	13 Playing Seasons
Webster, Michael	1997	Center	Pittsburgh & Kans. City	16 Playing Seasons
Weinmeister, Arnie	1984	Defensive Tackle	New York Yankees	6 Playing Seasons
White, Randy	1994	Defensive Tackle	Cowboys	14 Playing Seasons
Wilcox, Dave	2000	Linebacker	San Francisco 49er's	11 Playing Seasons
Willis, Bill	1977	Guard	Cleveland Browns	8 Playing Seasons
Wilson, Larry	1978	Safety-St Louis Cards	Coach Cardinals	13 Playing Seasons
Winslow, Kellen	1995	Tight End	Chargers	9 Playing Seasons
Wood, Willie	1989	Safety	Green Bay Packers	12 Playing Seasons
Yary, Ron	2001	Tackle	Minnesota Vikings	14 Playing Seasons
Youngblood, Jack	2001	Defensive End	LA Rams	14 Playing Seasons

All National Football League team rosters are listed on the following pages.
Match a selected player to the team address appearing below.

(Name of Player)
Denver Broncos
Training Facility
13655 Broncos Parkway
Englewood, CO 80112

Arizona Cardinals	PO Box 888	Phoenix	Arizona 85001-0888
Atlanta Falcons	4400 Falcon Parkway	Flowery Branch	Georgia 30542
Baltimore Ravens	Training Facility	1 Winning Drive	Owings Mills, MD 21117
Buffalo Bills	Ralph Wilson Stadium	One Bills Drive	Orchard Park, NY 14127
Carolina Pathers	Bank of America Stadium	800 South Mint Street	Charlotte, NC 28202-1502
Chicago Bears	Halas Hall	1000 Football Drive	Lake Forest, IL 60045
Cincinnati Bengals	Paul Brown Stadium	1 Paul Brown Stadium	Cincinnati, OH 45202
Cleveland Browns	Cleveland Browns Stad.	1085 West 3rd Street	Cleveland, OH 44114
Dallas Cowboys	Texas Stadium	2401 E. Airport Freeway	Irving, TX 75062
Denver Broncos	Training Facility	13655 Broncos Parkway	Englewood, CO 80112
Detroit Lions	222 Republic Drive	Allen Park	Michigan 48101
Green Bay Packers	PO Box 10628	Greenbay	Wisconsin 54307
Houston Texans	Two Reliant Park	Houston	Texas 77054
Indianapolis Colts	7001 West 56th Street	Indianaplois	Indiana 46254
Jacksonville Jaguars	ALLTEL Stadium	One Alltel Stadium Place	Jacksonville, FL 32202
Kansas City Chiefs	Arrowhead Stadium	One Arrowhead Drive	Kansas City, MO 64129
Miami Dolphins	7500 SW 30th Street	Davie	Florida 33314
Minnesota Vikings	HHH Metrodome	500 11th Avenue South	Minneapolis, MN 55415
New England Patriots	Gillette Stadium	One Patriot Place	Foxborough, MA 02035-1388
New Orleans Saints	5800 Airline Drive	Metairie	Louisiana 70003
New York Giants	Giants Stadium	50 Route 120	East Rutherford, NJ 07073
New York Jets	Giants Stadium	50 Route 120	East Rutherford, NJ 07073
Oakland Raiders	Network Asso.Coliseum	7000 Coliseum Way	Oakland, CA 94621
Philadelphia Eagles	Veterans Stadium	3501 South Broad Street	Philadelphia, PA 19148
Pittsburgh Steelers	Heinz Field	100 Art Rooney Avenue	Pittsburgh, PA 15212
San Diego Chargers	P.O. Box 609609	San Diego	California 92160-9609
San Francisco 49er's	Marie DeBartolo Centre	4949 Centennial Blvd	Santa Clara, CA 95054
Seattle Seahawks	11220 NE 53rd Street	Kirkland	Washington 98033
St. Louis Rams	One Rams Way	St. Louis	Missouri 63045
Tampa Bay Bucs	Raymond James Stad.	T. Bay Rd. & Dale Mabry	Tampa, FL 33607
Tennessee Titans	Adelphia Coliseum	1914 Church Street	Nashville, TN 37221
Washington Redskins	21300 Redskin Park Dr.	Ashburn	Virgina 20147

National Football League Team Rosters

Arizona Cardinals	Atlanta Falcons	Baltimore Ravens	Buffalo Bills	Carolina Panthers
Ayanbadejo, Obafemi	Beasley, Aaron	Abney, Derek	Adams, Sam	Allen, Brian
Berry, Bert	Beverly, Eric	Anderson, Bennie	Aiken, Sam	Armstead, Jessie
Blizzard, Bobby	Bibla, Martin	Baxter, Gary	Anderson, Tim	Branch, Colin
Boldin, Anquan	Blakley, Dwayne	Boller, Kyle	Baker, Rashad	Broussard, Jamall
Bridges, Jeremy	Brooking, Keith	Boulware, Peter	Bannan, Justin	Brzezinski, Doug
Bryant, Wendell	Carpenter, Keion	Brooks, Ethan	Bledsoe, Drew	Buckner, Brentson
Carter, Dyshod	Coleman, Roderick	Brown, Cornell	Burns, Joe	Burns, Antoine
Clement, Anthony	Crumpler, Alge	Brown, Orlando	Campbell, Mark	Carstens, Jordan
Croom, Larry	Detmer, Ty	Carlyle, Calvin	Clements, Nate	Carter, Drew
Dansby, Karlos	Draft, Chris	Carter, Dale	Crowell, Angelo	Ciurciu, Vinny
Darling, James	Duckett, T.J.	Cook, Damion	Denney, Ryan	Colbert, Keary
Davis, Leonard	Duncan, Jamie	Darling, Devard	Dorenbos, Jon	Cooper, Jarrod
Davis, Russell	Dunn, Warrick	Demps, Will	Edwards, Ron	Davis, Stephen
Diamond, Lorenzo	Echols, Mike	Dinkins, Darnell	Esposito, Jasen	Delhomme, Jake
Dockett, Darnell	Farris, Jimmy	Douglas, Marques	Euhus, Tim	Duckett, Damane
Edwards, Eric	Feely, Jay	Edwards, Dwan	Evans, Lee	Fields, Mark
Fitzgerald, Larry	Finneran, Brian	Flynn, Mike	Fletcher, London	Fordham, Todd
Hambrick, Troy	Forney, Kynan	Franklin, Aubrayo	Greer, Jabari	Foster, DeShaun
Hamilton, Lawrence	Garza, Roberto	Fuller, Corey	Haddad, Drew	Gaines, Michael
Harris, Quentin	Glymph, Junior	Green, Rod.	Haggan, Mario	Gamble, Chris
Hayes, Gerald	Griffith, Justin	Gregg, Kelly	Henry, Travis	Goings, Nick
Hill, Renaldo	Hall, Cory	Harris, Josh	Jennings, Jonas	Gross, Jordan
Hodel, Nathan	Hall, DeAngelo	Hartwell, Edgerton	Kelsay, Chris	Hampton, William
Hodgins, James	Hall, Travis	Heap, Todd	Lindell, Rian	Hankton, Karl
Joe, Leon	Herndon, Steve	Hymes, Randy	Losman, J.P.	Harris, Joey
Johnson, Bryant	Jasper, Edward	Johnson, Jarret	Matthews, Shane	Hawkins, Artrell
Jones, Freddie	Jenkins, Michael	Johnson, Kevin	McFarland, Dylan	Hoover, Brad
Keys, Isaac	Johnson, Eric	Johnson, Pat	McGahee, Willis	Houghton, Mike
King, Kenny	Kerney, Patrick	Jones, Terry	McGee, Terrence	Jackson, Eddie
King, Shaun	King, Austin	Kemoeatu, Ma'ake	Milloy, Lawyer	Jenkins, Kris
Kolodziej, Ross	Lake, Antwan	Lewis, Ray	Moorman, Brian	Johnson, Adam
Leckey, Nick	Lavalais, Chad	Maese, Joe	Moulds, Eric	Jordan, Omari
Lewis, Chris	Mathis, Kevin	McAlister, Chris	Neufeld, Ryan	Kadela, Dave
Macklin, David	McCadam, Kevin	Milons, Freddie	Peters, Jason	Kasay, John
Mayes, Adrian	McClure, Todd	Moore, Clarence	Posey, Jeff	Kyle, Jason
McCown, Josh	Melton, Terrence	Morrow, Harold	Price, Marcus	LaFavor, Tron
McKinnon, Ronald	Mohr, Chris	Mughelli, Ovie	Prioleau, Pierson	Maddox, Nick
Navarre, John	Moore, Michael	Mulitalo, Edwin	Pruce, David	Mangum, Kris
Newhouse, Reggie	Mosley, Kendrick	Norton, Zach	Pucillo, Mike	Manning, Ricky
Newton, Jim	Pearson, Dave	Ogden, Jonathan	Reed, Josh	Minter, Mike
Ohalete, Ifeanyi	Peck, Jared	Ogden, Marques	Reese, Izell	Mitchell, Jeff
Pace, Calvin	Pinkney, Cleveland	Pashos, Tony	Ritzmann, Constantin	Moorehead, Kindal
Player, Scott	Price, Peerless	Rabach, Casey	Sape, Lauvale	Morgan, Dan
Poole, Nate	Pritchett, Stanley	Reed, Ed	Schobel, Aaron	Muhammad, Muhsin
Rackers, Neil	Pruitt, Etric	Ricard, Alan	Shelton, Daimon	Nelson, Bruce
Reuber, Alan	Rackley, Derek	Richey, Wade	Smith, Jonathan	Peete, Rodney
Rue, Josh	Riley, Karon	Rimpf, Brian	Smith, Lawrence	Peppers, Julius
Scobey, Josh	Robinson, Travaris	Sams, B.J	Spikes, Takeo	Pittman
Shelton, L.J.	Rossum, Allen	Sanders, Deion	Stamer, Josh	Proehl, Ricky
Shipp, Marcel	Sanders, Darnell	Scott, Bart	Teague, Trey	Rasmussen, Kemp
Smith, Antonio	Schaub, Matt	Slaughter, T.J.	Thomas, Kevin	Reyes, Tutan
Smith, Emmitt	Scott, Bryan	Smith, Musa	Towns, Daryl	Richardson, Damien
Spikes, Cameron	Shabazz, Siddeeq	Smith, Trent	Tucker, Ross	Rucker, Mike
Starks, Duane	Shaffer, Kevin	Stewart, Kordell	Villarrial, Chris	Rutherford, Rod
Stepanovich, Alex	Smith, Brady	Stover, Matt	Vincent, Troy	Sauerbrun, Todd
Stone, Michael	Stewart, Matt	Suggs, Terrell	Williams, Mike	Seidman, Mike
Tate, Robert	Stewart, Steve	Taylor, Chester	Williams, Pat	Short, Brandon
Thompson, Raynoch	Ulmer, Artie	Taylor, Travis	Williams, Shaud	Smart, Rod
Vanden Bosch, Kyle	Vaughn, Khaleed	Thomas, Adalius	Wilson, George	Smith, Steve
Wakefield, Fred	Vick, Michael	Veal, Demetrin	Wire, Coy	Tillman, Travares
Wells, Reggie	Webster, Jason	Walls, Raymond	Zolman, Greg	Tufts, Sean
Williams, Karl	Weiner, Todd	Weaver, Anthony		Tylski, Rich
Wilson, Adrian	White, Dez	Wilcox, Daniel		Wallace, Al
Woods, LeVar	Williams, Demorrio	Williams, Chad		Weinke, Chris
Zellner, Peppi	Wilson, Quincy	Winborne, Jamaine		Wesley, Dante
		Wright, Anthony		Wharton, Travelle
		Zastudil, Dave		Willig, Matt
		Zielinski, Matt		Witherspoon, Will

Chicago Bears
Anderson, Bryan
Azumah, Jerry
Berrian, Bernard
Boone, Alfonso
Briggs, Lance
Brown, Alex
Brown, Mike
Brown, Ruben
Cain, Jeremy
Campbell, Darrell
Clark, Desmond
Colombo, Marc
Dorsey, Quinn
Droege, Rob
Edinger, Paul
Edwards, Steve
Ford, Carl
Gage, Justin
Gandy, Mike
Gibson, Aaron
Gilmore, John
Gray, Bobby
Green, Mike
Grossman, Rex
Harris, Tommie
Haynes, Michael
Hillenmeyer, Hunter
Hutchinson, Chad
Idonije, Israel
Jenkins, Corey
Johnson, Bryan
Johnson, Terry
Johnson, Todd
Jones, Thomas
Kashama, Alain
Krenzel, Craig
Kreutz, Olin
Lyman, Dustin
Mannelly, Patrick
Marshall, Alfonso
Maynard, Brad
McKie, Jason
McMillon, Todd
McQuarters, R.W.
Metcalf, Terrence
Miller, David
Mitchell, Qasim
Odom, Joe
Ogunleye, Adewale
Peterson, Adrian
Pierson, Shurron
Pinkard, Mike
Quinn, Jonathan
Reese, Marcus
Reid, Gabriel
Russell, Fred
Scott, Ian
Tait, John
Terrell, David
Thomas, Anthony
Tillman, Charles
Tucker, Rex
Urlacher, Brian
Vasher, Nathan
Wade, Bobby
Washburn, Cliff
Worrell, Cameron

Cincinnati Bengals
Abdullah, Khalid
Anderson, Willie
Andrews, Stacy
Askew, Matthias
Augustin, Allen
Bauman, Rashad
Beckett, Rogers
Braham, Rich
Bramlet, Casey
Brooks, Greg
Chamberlin, Frank
Clemons, Duane
Fontenot, Jerry
Geathers, Robert
Ghent, Ronnie
Graham, Shayne
Hardy, Kevin
Herring, Kim
Houshmandzadeh, T.J.
Jackson, LaDairis
James, Tory
Johnson, Belton
Johnson, Chad
Johnson, Jeremi
Johnson, Landon
Johnson, Rudi
Jones, Levi
Joseph, Ricot
Kaesviharn, Kevin
Kelly, Reggie
Kitna, Jon
Kooistra, Scott
Larson, Kyle
Lougheed, Pete
Lynch, James
Mabry, Mike
Mann, Maurice
Miller, Caleb
Mitchell, Anthony
Moore, Langston
Moore, Larry
Myles, Reggie
O'Neal, Deltha
Palmer, Carson
Perry, Chris
Powell, Carl
Ratliff, Keiwan
Richardson, Kyle
Roberts, Terrell
Russell, Cliff
Schobel, Matt
Scott, Greg
Smith, Justin
St. Louis, Brad
Steinbach, Eric
Stevens, Larry
Stewart, Tony
Sulfsted, Alex
Thornton, John
Walter, Kevin
Warrick, Pete
Washington, Kelley
Watson, Kenny
Weathersby, Dennis
Webster, Nate
Wilkins, Marcus
Williams, Bobbie
Williams, Madieu
Williams, Tony

Cleveland Browns
Alston, Richard
Beasley, Chad
Bentley, Kevin
Bodden, Leigh
Boyer, Brant
Brown, Courtney
Bryant, Antonio
Chambers, Kirk
Claybrooks, Felipe
Clemons, Chris
Collins, Javiar
Crocker, Chris
Davis, Andra
Davis, Andre
Dawson, Lew
Dawson, Phil
DeMar, Enoch
Eason, Nick
Echemandu, A.
Ekuban, Ebenezer
Faine, Jeff
Fowler, Melvin
Frost, Derrick
Garay, Antonio
Garcia, Jeff
Gardner, Barry
Garmon, Kelvin
Gonzalez, Joaquin
Gordon, Amon
Grant, Michael
Green, William
Griffith, Robert
Harris, Sterling
Heiden, Steve
Heinrich, Keith
Henry, Anthony
Holcomb, Kelly
Holdman, Warrick
Jackson, Corey
Jackson, Frisman
Jackson, James
Jameson, Michael
Jones, C.J.
Jones, Sean
King, Andre
Lang, Kenard
Lehan, Michael
Little, Earl
McCown, Luke
McCutcheon, Daylon
McIntyre, Corey
McKinley, Alvin
Miller, Ben
Morton, Christian
Mustard, Chad
Myers, Michael
Northcutt, Dennis
Pontbriand, Ryan
Rogers, Tyrone
Roye, Orpheus
Sanders, Lewis
Shea, Aaron
Smith, Terrelle
Suggs, Lee
Taylor, Ben
Thompson, Chaun
Tucker, Ryan
Unck, Mason
Verba, Ross
Warren, Gerard
Westmoreland, Eric

Dallas Cowboys
Adams, Flozell
Allen, Larry
Anderson, Richie
Barnes, Darian
Bickerstaff, Erik
Campbell, Dan
Cargile, Steve
Carson, Leonardo
Claybrooks, Devone
Coakley, Dexter
Coleman, Kenyon
Cooper, Chris
Copper, Terrance
Crayton, Patrick
Cundiff, Billy
Davis, Keith
DiNapoli, Gennaro
Dixon, Tony
Eaton, Chad
Ellis, Greg
Fowler, Ryan
Frazier, Lance
George, Eddie
Glenn, Terry
Glover, La'Roi
Gurode, Andre
Henson, Drew
Hunter, Pete
James, Bradie
Johnson, Al
Johnson, Keyshawn
Jones, Julius
Jones, Nathan
Lee, Reshard
Lehr, Matt
McBriar, Mat
Morgan, Quincy
Newman, Terence
Nguyen, Dat
Noll, Ben
O'Neil, Keith
Ogbogu, Eric
Peterman, Stephen
Pierce, Brett
Reeves, Jacques
Robinson, Jeff
Rogers, Jacob
Romo, Tony
Ryan, Sean
Scott, Lynn
Shanle, Scott
Singleton, Alshermond
Testaverde, Vinny
Thornton, Bruce
Thornton, Kalen
Trusty, Landon
Tucker, Torrin
Vollers, Kurt
Walter, Tyson
Ward, Dedric
Wiley, Marcellus
Williams, Lenny
Williams, Randal
Williams, Roy
Williams, Tyrone
Witten, Jason
Woodson, Darren

Denver Broncos
Alexander, P.J.
Alexander, Roc
Anderson, Mike
Bailey, Champ
Beard, Santonio
Bell, Tatum
Brandon, Sam
Carlisle, Cooper
Chukwurah, Patrick
Coleman, Marco
Crenshaw, Romar
Davis, Dorsett DT
Droughns, Reuben
Elam, Jason
Elliss, Luther
Fatafehi, Mario
Ferguson,
Foster, George
Green, Cornell
Green, Louis
Griffin, Quentin
Hamilton, Ben
Hape, Patrick
Hayward, Reggie
Hearst, Garrison
Herndon, Kelly
Holland, Darius
Jackson, Nate
Johnson, B.J.
Johnson, Ellis
Johnson, Kyle
Johnson, Raylee
Kanell, Danny
Kennedy, Kenoy
Knorr, Micah
LeSueur, Jeremy
Leach, Mike
Lelie, Ashley
Lepsis, Matt
Luke, Triandos
Lynch, John
Mauck, Matt
McNeal, Bryant
Middlebrooks, Willie
Miree, Brandon
Nalen, Tom
Neil, Dan
Palepoi, Anton
Pierce, Terry
Plummer, Jake
Pope, Monsanto
Pryce, Trevor
Putzier, Jeb
Sapp, Cecil
Sewell, Josh
Shoate, Jeff
Smith, Rod
Spragan, Donnie
Sykes, Jashon
Van Pelt, Bradlee
Walls, Lenny
Watts, Darius
Williams, D.J.
Wilson, Al
Young, Chris

National Football League Team Rosters

Detroit Lions	Green Bay Packers	Houston Texans	Indianapolis Colts	Jacksonville Jaguars
Alexander, Stephen	Barker, Bryan	Acholonu, D.D.	Allen, Brian	Adibi, Nathaniel
Babers, Roderick	Barnett, Nick	Anderson, Charlie	Bacon, Waine	Alexis, Rich
Backus, Jeff	Barry, Kevin	Anderson, Jason	Bashir, Idrees	Ayodele, Akin
Bailey, Boss	Bedell, Brad	Armstrong, Derick	Bird, Cory	Barnes, Lionel
Bell, Marcus	Carroll, Ahmad	Babin, Jason	Brackett, Gary	Bolden, Juran
Belton, Thump	Chatman, Antonio	Banks, Tony	Brock, Raheem	Brady, Kyle
Bethea, James	Clifton, Chad	Baxter, Jarrod	Brown, Travis	Bubin, Sean
Bly, Dre'	Cole, Colin	Bell, Jason	Carthon, Ran	Cherry, Matt
Bryant, Fernando	Curtin, Brennan	Bell, Marcus	Clark, Dallas	Compton, Mike
Bryson, Shawn	Davenport, Najeh	Bradford, Corey	David, Jason	Cooper, Deke
Butler, Kelly	Davis, Rob	Brown, Eric	DeMulling, Rick	Cordova, Jorge
Cash, Chris	Davis, Shockmain	Brown, Kris	Diem, Ryan	Darius, Donovin
Cobourne, Avon	Diggs, Na'il	Brown, Milford	Doss, Mike	Edwards, Marc
Curry, Donte'	Driver, Donald	Bruener, Mark	Eiland, Deandre	Edwards, Troy
Davis, James	Favre, Brett	Carr, David	Fletcher, Bryan	Favors, Greg
DeVries, Jared	Ferguson, Robert	Coleman, Marcus	Floyd, Anthony	Fletcher, Derrick
Drummond, Eddie	Fisher, Tony	Davis, Domanick	Freeney, Dwight	Fuamatu-Ma'afala, C.
Edwards, Kalimba	Flanagan, Mike	Davis, Jason	Freitas, Makoa	Garrard, David
Fitzsimmons, Casey	Franks, Bubba	DeLoach, Jerry	Gardner, Gilbert	Gilbert, Tony
Fox, Vernon	Gbaja-Biamila, Kabeer	Earl, Glenn	Glenn, Tarik	Grant, Deon
Goodman, Andre'	Green, Ahman	Evans, Brandon	Harper, Nicholas	Gray, Quinn
Hakim, Az-Zahir	Harris, Al	Evans, Troy	Harrison, Marvin	Green, Brandon
Hall, James	Hawthorne, Michael	Faggins, Demarcus	Hartsock, Ben	Hankton, Cortez
Hanson, Jason	Henderson, William	Foreman, Jay	Hill, Eric	Hanson, Chris
Harrington, Joey	Herrion, Atlas	Gaffney, Jabar	Houchin, Thomas	Henderson, John
Harris, Nick	Horton, Jason	Glenn, Aaron	Hutchins, Von	Hendricks, Tommy
Holmes, Earl	Hunt, Cletidus	Hollings, Tony	Hutton, Trevor	Jones, Brian
Holt, Terrence	Jackson, Grady	Ioane, Junior	James, Edgerrin	Jones, Greg
Hopson, Tyrone	Jenkins, Cullen	Johnson, Andre	Jefferson, Joseph	Leftwich, Byron
Jones, Kevin	Johnson, Chris	Jones, Garrick	June, Cato	Leonard, Matt
Joyce, Matt	Jue, Bhawoh	Joppru, Bennie	Lilja, Ryan	Lewis, Jermaine
Kircus, David	Kampman, Aaron	Lord, Jammal	Lopienski, Tom	Luzar, Chris
Lehman, Teddy	Kight, Kelvin	McCree, Marlon	Manning, Peyton	Maddox, Anthony
Lewis, Alex	Leach, Vonta	McKinney, Steve	Mathis, Robert	Manuwai, Vincent
Littleton, Jody	Lee, James	Miller, Billy	Moorehead, Aaron	Marler, Seth
Loverne, David	Lenon, Paris	Moses, J.J.	Morris, Rob	Mathis, Rashean
Marion, Brock	Longwell, Ryan	Murphy, Matt	Mungro, James	McCray, Bobby
McCoy, Matt	Luchey, Nicolas	Norris, Moran	Nelson, Jim	Meester, Brad
McDougle, Stockar	Marshall, Torrance	O'Sullivan, Dennis	Peko, Tupe	Meier, Rob
McMahon, Mike	Martin, David	Orr, Shantee	Pollard, Marcus	Naeole, Chris
Mirer, Rick	McHugh, Sean	Payne, Seth	Pope, Kendyll	Nyenhuis, Gabe
Owens, John	Morley, Steve	Peek, Antwan	Pyatt, Brad	Patterson, Elton
Pinner, Artose	Nall, Craig	Pittman, Bryan	Reagor, Montae	Pearson, Mike
Porcher, Robert	Navies, Hannibal	Pitts, Chester	Rhodes, Dominic	Peterson, Mike
Pritchett. Kelvin	O'Sullivan, J.T.	Polk, Dashon	Sanders, Bob	Ransom, Derrick
Rainer, Wali	Pederson, Doug	Ragone, Dave	Sapp, Gerome	Richardson, David
Raiola, Dominic	Peterson, Kenny	Robinson, Dunta	Saturday, Jeff	Romberg, Brett
Redding, Cory	Rivera, Marco	Sears, Corey	Scioli, Brad	Salaam, Ephraim
Rogers, Charles	Rogers, Nick	Sharper, Jamie	Scott, Jake	Scobee, Josh
Rogers, Shaun	Roman, Mark	Simmons, Jason	Smith, Hunter	Smith, Daryl
Rogers, Victor	Ruegamer, Grey	Smith, Robaire	Snow, Justin	Smith, Jimmy
Schlesinger, Cory	Sander, B.J.	Spears, Marcus	Sorgi, Jim	Sorensen, Nick
Shull, Andrew	Sharper, Darren	Stanley, Chad	Standeford, John	Spicer, Paul
Sidney, Dairion	Smith, Larry	Starling, Kendrick	Stewart, Jason	Stroud, Marcus
Smith, Keith	Steele, Ben	Symons, B.J.	Stokley, Brandon	Tate, Joe
Smith, Paul	Tauscher, Mark	Thomas, Sloan	Strickland, Donald	Taylor, Fred
Stephens, Leonard	Thomas, Joey	Wade, Todd	Thomas, Josh	Thomas, Kiwaukee
Streets, Tai	Thurman, Andrae	Walker, Gary	Thornton, David	Thompson, Chris
Swinton, Reginald	Truluck, R-Kal	Walker, Ramon	Tripplett, Larry	Toefield, LaBrandon
Trejo, Stephen	Wahle, Mike	Wand, Seth	Utecht, Ben	Washington, DeWayne
Vines, Scottie	Walker, Javon	Washington, Todd	Vanderjagt, Mike	Whitfield, Bob
Walker, Bracy	Washington, Donnell	Weary, Fred	Venzke, Patrick	Wilford, Ernest
Walker, Brian	Wells, Scott	Wells, Jonathan	Walters, Troy	Williams, Maurice
Wilkinson, Dan	Williams, Corey	Wiegert, Zach	Wayne, Reggie	Williams, Reggie
Williams, Roy	Williams, Walter	Wong, Kailee	Whiteside, Keyon	Wrighster, George
Woody, Damien G	Williams, Wendell	Works, Renaldo	Williams, Josh	Yoder, Todd
	Young, David	Wright, Kenny	Wright, Keith	Zelenka, Joe

Kansas City Chiefs	Miami Dolphins	Minnesota Vikings	New Eng. Patriots	New Orleans Saints
Allen, Jared	Akins, Chris	Andersen, Morten	Abdullah, Rabih	Allen, James
Baber, Billy	Ayanbadejo, Brendon	Angulo, Richard	Alexander, Eric	Ambrose, Ashley
Barber, Shawn	Bell, Yeremiah	Bennett, Darren	Andruzzi, Joe	Archibald, Ben
Bartee, William	Bellamy, Ronald	Bennett, Michael	Ashworth, Tom	Bellamy, Jay
Battle, Julian	Booker, Marty	Berton, Sean	Bailey, Rodney	Bentley, LeCharles
Beisel, Monty	Boston, David	Birk, Matt	Banta-Cain, Tully	Berger, Mitch
Black, Jordan	Bowens, David	Brown, Ralph	Brady, Tom	Bockwoldt, Colby
Blaylock, Derrick	Bowens, Tim	Burleson, Nate	Branch, Deion	Booker, Fred
Bober, Chris	Bryant, Matt	Campbell, Kelly	Brown, Troy	Bouman, Todd
Boerigter, Marc	Bua, Tony	Celestin, Oliver	Bruschi, Tedy	Brooks, Aaron
Browning, John	Carey, Vernon	Chavous, Corey	Chapman, Kory	Brown, Fakhir
Caver, Quinton	Chambers, Chris	Claiborne, Chris	Chatham, Matt	Bryant, Tony
Cheek, Steve	Chester, Larry	Clark, Kenny	Cherry, Je'Rod	Carney, John
Collins, Todd	Edwards, Antuan	Conaty, Billy	Cobbs, Cedric	Carter, Ki-Jana
Connot, Scott	Feeley, A.J.	Culpepper, Daunte	Colvin, Rosevelt	Conwell, Ernie
Dalton, Lional	Fiedler, Jay	Davis, Rod	Davey, Rohan	Craft, Jason
Dunn, Jason	Flemons, Ronald	Dixon, David	Davis, Don	Folau, Spencer
Easy, Omar	Forsey, Brock	Dorsey, Nat	Dillon, Corey	Gandy, Wayne
Fox, Keyaron	Freeman, Arturo	Dugan, Jeff	Faulk, Kevin	Gardner, Talman
Fujita, Scott	Gilmore, Bryan	Elling, Aaron	Fauria, Christian	Gleason, Steve
Gammon, Kendall	Gordon, Lamar	Elliott, Blake	Flemister, Zeron	Grant, Charles
Golliday, Aaron	Greenwood, Morlon	Frerotte, Gus	Gay, Randall	Grant, Cie
Gonzalez, Tony	Hadnot, Rex	Goldberg, Adam	Givens, David	Green, Howard
Green, Trent	Henry, Leonard	Haayer, Adam	Gorin, Brandon	Hall, Lamont
Hall, Dante	Howard, Reggie	Henderson, E.J.	Graham, Daniel	Henderson, Devery
Harts, Shaunard	James, Jeno	Herrera, Anthony	Green, Jarvis	Hilton, Zach
Hicks, Eric	Jerman, Greg	Hill, Shaun	Harrison, Rodney	Hodge, Sedrick
Holliday, Vonnie	King, Vick	Hoag, Ryan	Hill, Marquise	Holland, Montrae
Holmes, Priest	Knight, Sammy	Hosack, Aaron	Hochstein, Russ	Horn, Joe
Horn, Chris	Konrad, Rob	Hovan, Chris	Izzo, Larry	Houser, Kevin
Huard, Damon	Lee, Donald	Howry, Keenan	James, Cedric	Howard, Darren
Ingram, Johnathan	Madison, Sam	Irvin, Ken	Johnson, Bethel	Jacox, Kendyl
Johnson, Larry	Mare, Olindo	Johnson, Spencer	Johnson, Ted	Jones, Tebucky
Jones, Fred	Martin, Jamar	Johnstone, Lance	Kasper, Kevin	Karney, Mike
Kennison, Eddie	McIntosh, Damion	Kleinsasser, Jim	Kelley, Ethan	Kingsbury, Kliff
Maslowski, Mike	McKinney, Seth	Liwienski, Chris	Klecko, Dan	Knight, Roger
McCleon, Dexter	McMichael, Randy	Loeffler, Cullen	Klemm, Adrian	Leisle, Rodney
McIntyre, Jeris	Minor, Travis	Martin, Steve	Koppen, Dan	Lewis, Michael
Miller, Matt	Moore, Eddie	McKinnie, Bryant	Kurpeikis, Justin	McAfee, Fred
Mitchell, Kawika	Morris, Sammy	Mixon, Kenny	Law, Ty	McAllister, Deuce
Morton, Johnnie	Newson, Kendall	Moore, Mewelde	Light, Matt	McKenzie, Mike
Parker, Samie	Pape, Tony	Moss, Randy	McGinest, Willie	Mitchell, Mel
Pile, Willie	Perry, Ed	Nattiel, Mike	Miller, Jim	Montgomery, Delmonico
Richardson, Tony	Poole, Will	Ned, Larry	Miller, Josh	Morris, Carl
Roaf, Willie	Pope, Derrick	Nelson, Ben	Moreland, Earthwind	Nesbit, Jamar
Sampson, Kevin	Robinson, Bryan	Nelson, Rhett	Mruczkowski, Gene	Pathon, Jerome
Sapp, Benny	Romero, Dario	Newman, Keith	Neal, Steve	Poli-Dixon, Brian
Scanlon, Rich	Rosenfels, Sage	Newton, Brandon	Pass, Patrick	Riley, Victor
Sharpe, Montique	Roundtree, Alphonso	Offord, Willie	Patten, David	Rodgers, Derrick
Shields, Will	Seau, Junior	Owens, Richard	Paxton, Lonie	Ruff, Orlando
Siavii, Junior	Shaw, Josh	Robinson, Marcus	Phifer, Roman	Schurman, Nate
Sims, Ryan	Sippio, Bobby	Rosenthal, Mike	Poole, Tyrone	Setterstrom, Chad
Smith, Richard	Smith, Wade	Ross, Derek	Rasmussen, Buck	Smith, Kenny
Stills, Gary	St. Clair, John	Russell, Brian	Reid, Dexter	Smith, Shaun
Tynes, Lawrence	Stuber, Tim	Scott, Darrion	Sam, P.K.	Smith, Will
Warfield, Eric	Surtain, Patrick	Shaw, Terrance	Samuel, Asante	Stallworth, Donte
Waters, Brian	Taylor, Jason	Smith, Raonall	Scott, Guss	Stecker, Aaron
Welbourn, John	Thomas, Zach	Thomas, Dontarrious	Seymour, Richard	Stinchcomb, Jon
Wesley, Greg	Thompson, Derrius	Udeze, Kenechi	Traylor, Keith	Sullivan, Johnathan
Wiegmann, Casey	Tolver, J.R.	Wallace, Butchie	Vinatieri, Adam	Thomas, Fred
Wilkerson, Jimmy	Turk, Matt	Wiggins, Jermaine	Vrabel, Mike	Watson, Courtney
Williams, Brett	Welker, Wes	Wiley, Chuck	Warren, Ty	Whitehead, Willie
Willis, Donald	Whitley, Taylor	Wiley, Grant	Watson, Ben	Williams, Boo
Wilson, Kris	Williams, Jay	Williams, Brian	Weaver, Jed	Young, Brian
Woods, Jerome	Williams, Quintin	Williams, Kevin	Wilfork, Vince	
	Williams, Renauld	Williams, Moe	Wilson, Eugene	
	Wilson, Eric	Winfield, Antoine	Yates, Billy	
	Wooden, Shawn	Withrow, Cory		

New York Giants	New York Jets	Oakland Raiders	Philadelphia Eagles	Pittsburgh Steelers	St. Louis Rams
Alexander, Brent	Abraham, Donnie	Anderson, Courtney	Adams, Keith	Batch, Charlie	Alford, Darnell
Allen, Kenderick	Abraham, John	Anderson, Marques	Akers, David	Battles, Ainsley	Anderson, Dwight
Allen, Will	Askew, B.J.	Asomugha, Nnamdi	Allen, Ian	Bell, Kendrell	Archuleta, Adam
Anelli, Mark	Baker, Chris	Badger, Brad	Andrews, Shawn	Bettis, Jerome	Brake, Mike
Barber, Tiki	Barrett, David	Brayton, Tyler	Bartrum, Mike	Bowman, Grant	Bronson, Zack
Brewer, Jack	Barton, Eric	Buchanan, Ray	Blake, Jeff	Brooks, Barrett	Bruce, Isaac
Bromell, Lorenzo	Becht, Anthony	Buchanon, Phillip	Brown, Sheldon	Brown, Dante	Bulger, Marc
Burns, Curry	Bollinger, Brooks	Clark, Danny	Buckhalter, Correll	Burress, Plaxico	Burley, Nick
Carter, Tim	Brien, Doug	Collins, Kerry	Burgess, Derrick	Carter, Tyrone	Butler, Jerametris
Chase, Martin	Brown, Mark	Crockett, Zack	Clarke, Adrien	Clancy, Kendrick	Chandler, Chris
Christie, Steve	Bryant, Roderick	Curry, Ronald	Darilek, Trey	Cobb, Zamir	Chandler, Jeff
Cloud, Michael	Buckley, Terrell	Downs, Chris	Dawkins, Brian	Colclough, Ricardo	Chillar, Brandon
Cousin, Terry	Burnell, Keith	Engemann, Bret	Detmer, Koy	Cushing, Matt	Cleeland, C.
Davis, Chris	Carter, Jonathan	Fargas, Justin	Douglas, Hugh	Duff, Vontez	Coady, Richard
Dayne, Ron	Carter, Quincy	Francis, Carlos	Ephraim, Alonzo	Faneca, Alan	Coleman, Michael
Deloatch, Curtis	Cavka, Marko	Gabriel, Doug	Fraley, Hank	Farrior, James	Curtis, Kevin
Diehl, David	Caylor, Drew	Gallery, Robert	Grasmanis, Paul	Foote, Larry	Dishman, Chris
Douglas, Chris	Chrebet, Wayne	Gannon, Rich	Green, Jamaal	Gardocki, Chris	Faulk, Marshall
Ellis, Ed	Coleman, Erik	Gbaja-Biamila, Akbar	Hall, Andy	Haggans, Clark	Faulk, Trev
Emmons, Carlos	Cotchery, Jerricho	Gibson, Derrick	Hall, Branden	Hampton, Casey	Fisher, Bryce
Feagles, Jeff	Cowart, Sam	Grant, DeLawrence	Hicks, Artis G	Harrison, James	Fisher, Travis
Finn, Jim	Davis, Josh	Green, DeJuan	Hood, Roderick	Hartings, Jeff	Flowers, Erik
Geathers, Jason	Davison, Andrew	Grove, Jake	Jackson, Jamaal	Haynes, Verron	Furrey, Mike
Green, Barrett	Dearth, James	Hamilton, Bobby	Jenkins, Justin	Hoke, Chris	Garrett, Kevin
Greisen, Nick	Ellis, Shaun	Harris, Napoleon	Johnson, Dirk	Hope, Chris	Goodspeed, Joey
Hand, Norman	Evans, Josh	Irons, Grant	Jones, Dhani	Iwuoma, Chidi	Groce, Dejuan
Hilliard, Ike	Fabini, Jason	Janikowski, Sebastian	Kalu, Ndukwe	Jackson, Alonzo	Hargrove, Tony
Hollowell, T.J.	Ferguson, Jason	Jimenez, Jason	Kearse, Jevon	Jones, Jim	Harris, Arlen
Jones, Mark	Gessner, Chas	Johnson, Teyo	Labinjo, Mike	Keisel, Brett	Holt, Torry
Joseph, William	Glenn, Jason	Johnson, Tim	Levens, Dorsey	Kirschke, Travis	Howard, Brian
Kuehl, Ryan	Goodwin, Jonathan	Jolley, Doug	Lewis, Chad	Kranchick, Matt	Jackson, Steven
Lawton, Luke	Gowin, Toby	Kelly, Tommy	Lewis, Greg	Kreider, Dan	Jackson, Tyoka
Legree, Lance	Harper, Alan	Lechler, Shane	Lewis, Michael	Kriewaldt, Clint	Jensen, Erik
Lewis, Kevin	Henderson, Jamie	Lekkerkerker, Brad	Mahe, Reno	Lacy, Bo	Kennedy, Jimmy
Lucier, Wayne	Hobson, Victor	Middleton, Frank	Mayberry, Jermane	Logan, Mike	Landeta, Sean
Mallard, Wesly	Johnson, Trevor	Morant, Johnnie	McCoo, Eric	Maddox, Tommy	Lewis, Damione
Manning, Eli	Jones, Adrian	Nash, Keyon	McDougle, Jerome	Mays, Lee	Little, Leonard
Maxwell, Jim	Jordan, LaMont	Niklos, J.R.	McMullen, Billy	Morey, Sean	Looker, Dane
Monds, Mario	Kearney, Carl	Parrella, John	McNabb, Donovan	Okobi, Chukky	Loyd, Jeremy
O'Hara, Shaun	Kendall, Pete	Porter, Jerry	Mikell, Quintin	Parker, Willie	Lucas, Justin
Orr, Raheem	Martin, Curtis	Redmond, J.R.	Mitchell, Freddie	Polamalu, Troy	Manumaleuna, B.
Palmer, Jesse	Mawae, Kevin	Rivers, David	Owens, Terrell	Porter, Joey	Massey, Chris
Pears, Morgan	McCareins, Justin	Sands, Terdell	Parry, Josh	Quinn, Mike	McCollum, Andy
Peterson, William	McClover, Darrell	Sapp, Warren	Perry, Bruce	Randle El, Antwaan	McDonald, Shaun
Petitgout, Luke	McGraw, Jon	Schweigert, Stuart	Pinkston, Todd	Reed, Jeff	McGrorty, Dusty
Ponder, Willie	McKenzie, Kareem	Sims, Barry	Rayburn, Sam	Riemersma, Jay	Newson, Tony
Rivers, Marcellus	Mickens, Ray	Slaughter, Chad	Reed, J.R.	Roethlisberger, Ben	Nutten, Tom
Robbins, Fred	Moore, Brandon	Smith, Travian	Reese, Ike	Roper, Dedrick	Pace, Orlando
Seubert, Rich	Moss, Santana	Stone, John	Richmond, Greg	Ross, Oliver	Pickett, Ryan
Shiancoe, Visanthe	Pagel, Derek	Stone, Ron	Ritchie, Jon	Schneck, Mike	Polley, Tommy
Shockey, Jeremy	Pennington, Chad	Terrell, David	Runyan, Jon	Scott, Chad	Renteria, D.J.
Snee, Chris	Ray, Ricky	Treu, Adam	Sciullo, Steve	Simmons, Kendall	Saipaia, Blaine
Stokes, Barry	Reed, James	Tuiasosopo, Marques	Sheppard, Lito	Smith, Aaron	Shivers, Jason
Stoutmire, Omar	Robertson, Dewayne	Walker, Denard	Short, Jason	Smith, Marvel	Smoker, Jeff
Strahan, Michael	Smith, Brent	Walker, Langston	Simon, Corey	St. Pierre, Brian	Tercero, Scott
Sullivan, Marques	Sowell, Jerald	Washington, Ted	Simoneau, Mark	Staley, Duce	Thomas, Robert
Taylor, Jamaar	Strait, Derrick	Wheatley, Tyrone	Smith, L.J.	Starks, Max	Timmerman, Adam
Thomas, Art	Stubbs, Terrence	Whitted, Alvis	Strojny, Drew	Stuvaints, Russell	Tinoisamoa, Pisa
Toomer, Amani	Thomas, Bryan	Williams, Brock	Tapeh, Thomas	Taylor, Eric	Turley, Kyle
Torbor, Reggie	Tongue, Reggie	Williams, Roland	Thomas, Hollis	Taylor, Ivan	Turner, Larry
Tyree, David	Vilma, Jonathan	Williams, Sam	Thomas, Tra	Townsend, Deshea	Wahlroos, Drew
Umenyiora, Osi	Washington, Rashad	Wong, Joe	Trafford, Rod	Tuman, Jerame	Wilkins, Jeff
Walker, Frank	Wright, Kenyatta	Woodson, Charles	Trotter, Jeremiah	Vincent, Keydrick	Williams, Aeneas
Walker, Gregory	Yovanovits, Dave	Zereoue, Amos	Walker, Darwin	Von Oelhoffen, Kimo	Williams, Grant
Ward, Derrick			Ware, Matt	Ward, Hines	
Warner, Kurt			Wayne, Nate	Williams, Willie	
Washington, Keith			Westbrook, Brian	Young, Walter	
Whittle, Jason			Wynn, Dexter		
Williams, Shaun					
Wilson, Gibril					

San Diego Chargers	San Fran. 49ers	Seattle Seahawks	Tampa Bay Bucs	Tennessee Titans	Wash. Redskins
Ball, Dave	Adams, Anthony	Alexander, Shaun	Allen, Will	Amano, Eugene	Albright, Ethan
Ball, Jason	Adams, Mike	Babineaux, Jordan	Alston, Charles	Amato, Ken	Arrington, LaVar
Bingham, Ryon	Barlow, Kevan	Bannister, Alex	Alstott, Mike	Anderson, Gary	Barnes, Brandon
Binn, David	Battle, Arnaz	Bates, Solomon	Barber, Ronde	Beckham, Tony	Barrow, Mike
Brandt, David	Beasley, Fred	Bernard, Rocky	Bidwell, Josh	Bell, Jacob	Baxter, Fred
Brees, Drew	Brown, Tony	Bierria, Terreal	Bradley, Jon	Bennett, Drew	Betts, Ladell
Butler, Robb	Carpenter, Dwaine	Boulware, Michael	Brooks, Derrick	Berlin, Eddie	Boschetti, Ryan
Caldwell, Reche	Carter, Andre	Brown, Chad	Brown, Tim	Boiman, Rocky	Bowen, Matt
Cesaire, Jacques	Conway, Curtis	Brown, Josh	Burns, Keith	Brown, Chris	Brown, Ray
Chatman, Jesse	Cooper, Josh	Carter, Kerry	Clayton, Michael	Bulluck, Keith	Brown, Rufus
Cooper, Stephen	Davis, Jerome	Cochran, Antonio	Coleman, Cosey	Calico, Tyrone	Brunell, Mark
Davis, Sammy	Dorsey, Ken	Darche, J.P.	Comella, Greg	Calmus, Rocky	Campbell, Khary
Dielman, Kris	Engelberger, John	Davis, Chris	Cook, Jameel	Carter, Kevin	Cartwright, Rock
Dingle, Adrian	Fleck, P.J.	Dilfer, Trent	Cooper, Marquis	Clauss, Jared	Clark, Ryan
Downing, Eric	Gragg, Scott	Engram, Bobby	Cox, Torrie	Cramer, Casey	Clemons, Nic
Dwight, Tim	Gutierrez, Brock	Evans, Heath	Darby, Chartric	Danielsen, Lane	Coles, Laveranues
Edwards, Donnie	Hamilton, Derrick	Gray, Chris	Davis, Anthony	Devoe, Todd	Cooley, Chris
Fisk, Jason	Hanson, Joselio	Hackett, D.J.	Deese, Derrick	Dyson, Andre	Daniels, Phillip
Fletcher, Jamar	Harris, Kwame	Hamlin, Ken	Dilger, Ken	Ena, Justin	Dennis, Pat
Florence, Drayton	Heard, Ronnie	Hannam, Ryan	Dudley, Rickey	Fleming, Troy	Dockery, Derrick
Floyd, Malcom	Heitmann, Eric	Harden, Michael	Edwards, Mario	Gardner, Rich	Elisara, Pita
Flutie, Doug	Herrion, Thomas	Hasselbeck, Matt	Galloway, Joey	Hall, Carlos	Evans, Demetric
Foley, Steve	Hicks, Maurice	Hollenbeck, Joey	Garner, Charlie	Hartwig, Justin	Franz, Todd
Fonoti, Toniu	Isom, Jasen	Huard, Brock	Garrett, Jason	Haynesworth, Albert	Friedman, Lennie
Gates, Antonio	Jackson, Terry	Huff, Orlando	Gold, Ian	Hentrich, Craig	Gardner, Rod
Godfrey, Randall	Jennings, Brian	Hunter, Wayne	Gooch, Jeff	Hill, Darrell	Griffin, Cornelius
Goff, Mike	Johnson, Eric	Hutchinson, Steve	Graham, Earnest	Holcombe, Robert	Haley, Jermaine
Hardwick, Nick	Jordan, James	Jackson, Darrell	Gramatica, Martin	Hopkins, Brad	Hall, John
Hart, Clinton	Katnik, Norm	Jones, Donnie	Gregory, Damian	Johnson, Doug	Harris, Walt
Haw, Brandon	Kosier, Kyle	Jones, Walter	Griese, Brian	Johnson, Shawn	Hasselbeck, Tim
Hicks, Reese	Lee, Andy	Kacyvenski, Isaiah	Heller, Will	Kassell, Brad	Jacobs, Taylor
Jammer, Quentin	Leverette, Otis	Koutouvides, Niko	Howell, John	Kinney, Erron	Jansen, Jon
Johnson, Leon	Lewis, Keith	Lewis, D.D.	Ivy, Corey	Kramer, Jordan	Jimoh, Ade
Jordan, Leander	Lloyd, Brandon	Locklear, Sean	Jackson, Scott	LaBoy, Travis	Kimrin, Ola
Joseph, Carlos	Moore, Brandon	Lucas, Ken	Johnson, Brad	Long, Rien	Kozlowski, Brian
Kaeding, Nate	Murphy, Rob	Luke, R.J.	Jurevicius, Joe	Martin, Matt	Lott, Andre
Kiel, Terrence	Newberry, Jeremy	Manuel, Marquand	Kelly, Brian	Mason, Derrick	Marshall, Lemar
Krause, Ryan	Parrish, Tony	Mili, Itula	Knight, Marcus	Mathews, Jason	McCants, D.
Leber, Ben	Peterson, Julian	Mitchell, Brandon	Lawrie, Nate	McAddley, Jason	McCullough, S.
Lemon, Cleo	Peterson, Todd	Moore, Rashad	Lee, Charles	McGarrahan, Scott	Molinaro, Jim
Milligan, Hanik	Pickett, Cody	Morris, Maurice	Mahan, Sean	McNair, Steve	Morton, Chad
Moreno, Zeke	Plummer, Ahmed	Okeafor, Chike	McFarland, Anthony	Meier, Shad	Noble, Brandon
Neal, Lorenzo	Rasheed, Saleem	Parker, Arnold	Moore, Dave	Miller, Fred	Pierce, Antonio
Oben, Roman	Rattay, Tim	Rice, Jerry	Murphy, Frank	Nedney, Joe	Portis, Clinton
Olivea, Shane	Reed, Rayshun	Richard, Kris	Nece, Ryan	Nickey, Donnie	Ramsey, Patrick
Olshansky, Igor	Robertson, Jamal	Robinson, Damien	O'Dwyer, Matt	Odom, Antwan	Raymer, Cory
Osgood, Kassim	Rumph, Mike	Robinson, Koren	Phillips, Jermaine	Olson, Benji	Royal, Robert
Parker, Eric	Seigler, Richard	Rouen, Tom	Pittman, Michael	Payton, Jarrett	Salave'a, Joe
Peelle, Justin	Smiley, Justin	Simmons, Anthony	Quarles, Shelton	Piller, Zach	Samuels, Chris
Phillips, Shaun	Smith, Derek	Stevens, Jerramy	Rice, Simeon	Portis, Marico	Scott, Gari
Pinnock, Andrew	Sopoaga, Isaac	Strong, Mack	Rubin, DeAndrew	Reynolds, Robert	Sellers, Michael
Pippens, Jerrell	Spencer, Shawntae	Taylor, Bobby	Savage, Josh	Rolle, Samari	Simon, John
Polk, Carlos	Stewart, Daleroy	Terrill, Craig	Schroeder, Bill	Sandy, Justin	Smoot, Fred
Pollard, Robert	Ulbrich, Jeff	Terry, Chris	Shepherd, Edell	Schobel, Bo	Springs, Shawn
Quinnie, Willie	Walker, Aaron	Tobeck, Robbie	Simms, Chris	Schulters, Lance	Taylor, Sean
Rivers, Philip	Whiting, Brandon	Trufant, Marcus	Smart, Ian	Sirmon, Peter	Thomas, Randy
Ross, Micah	Williams, Andrew	Tubbs, Marcus	Smith, Corey	Smith, Antowain	Thrash, James
Scifres, Mike	Williams, Jimmy	Urban, Jerheme	Smith, Dwight	Spencer, Cody	Tupa, Tom
Scott, DeQuincy	Wilson, Cedrick	Wallace, Seneca	Spires, Greg	Starks, Randy	Warner, Ron
Shaw, Bobby	Winborn, Jamie	Wallace, Taco	Steussie, Todd	Thomas, Juqua	Washington, Marcus
Tomlinson, LaDainian	Woods, Rashaun	White, Tracy	Stinchcomb, Matt	Thompson, Lamont	Wilds, Garnell
Turner, Michael	Young, Bryant	Willis, Jason	Terry, Jeb	Troupe, Ben	Wilson, Dennard
VanBuren, Courtney		Wistrom, Grant	Wade, John	Volek, Billy	Wilson, Mark
Wilhelm, Matt		Womack, Floyd	Walker, Kenyatta	Waddell, Michael	Wynn, Renaldo
Williams, Jamal		Woodard, Cedric	Whitaker, Ronyell	Williams, Tank	
Wilson, Jerry		Wunsch, Jerry	White, Dewayne	Williams, Todd	
			White, Jamel	Woolfolk, Andre	
			Wyms, Ellis		

Aikman, Troy	PO Box 630227	Irving, TX 75063	
Alexander, Paul	Paul Brown Stadium	1 Paul Brown Stadium	Cincinnati, OH 45202
Allen, Marcus	332 Center St.	El Segundo, CA 90245	
Allen, Paul G.	Seattle Seahawks	11220 NE 53rd Street	Kirkland, WA 98033
Anderson, Dick	Anderson Insurance Group	7751 S.W. 62 Avenue	South Miami, FL 33143
Atkins, Gene	Atkins Sports	4729 N.W. 183 Street	Miami, FL 33055
Babb, Charlie	Raymond Building Supply	7751 Bayshore Road	North Fort Myers, FL 33917
Bailey, Robert	KCB Sports Marketing	4000 Island Blvd	Aventura, FL 33160
Barisich, Carl	Tayler Jordan & Associates	6030 Daybreak Circle	Clarksville, MD 21029
Belichick, Bill	New England Patriots	One Patriot Place	Foxborough, MA 02035
Bennett, Woody	New Destiny Intl. Christian Ctr.	8745 N.W. 57 Street	Tamarac, FL 33351
Bidwill, William V.	Arizona Cardinals	PO Box 888	Phoenix, AZ 85001-0888
Billick, Brian	Baltimore Ravens	1 Winning Drive	Owings Mills, MD 21117
Bisciotti, Stephen J.	Baltimore Ravens	1 Winning Drive	Owings Mills, MD 21117
Blanda, George	78001 Lago Drive	La Quinta, CA 92253	
Blank, Arthur	Atlanta Falcons	4400 Falcon Parkway	Flowery Branh, GA 30542
Bleir, Rocky	706 Ivy Street	Pittsburgh, PA 15232	
Bowlen, Pat	Denver Broncos	13655 Broncos Parkway	Englewood, CO 80112
Bowser, Charles	Sound Stage Audio	2605 Hawkshead Court	Silver Springs, MD 20904
Bradshaw, Terry	Steve Bradshaw	Highway 635	Zuni, VA 23898
Braggs, Stephen	Braggs Youth Fndt.	120 Powerhouse Road	Lawndale, NC 28090
Brown, Willie	Oakland Raiders	7000 Coliseum Way	Oakland, CA 94621
Capers, Dom	Houston Texans	Two Reliant Park	Houston, TX 77054
Cefalo, Jimmy	Cefalo's Wine Cellar	8867 S.W. 132 Street	Miami, FL 33176
Clancy, Sean	Advest, Inc.	672 E. Hallandale Beach Blvd.	Hallandale, FL 33009
Coughlin, Tom	New York Giants	Giants Stadium	East Rutherford, NJ 07073
Cowher, Bill	Pittsburgh Steelers	100 Art Rooney Avenue	Pittsburgh, PA 15212
Craig, Roger	271 Vista Verde Way	Portola Valley, CA 94028	
Crusan, Doug	P.O. Box 3686	Carmel, IN 46082	
Csonka, Larry	ZONK! Productions, Inc.	P.O. Box 39	Oak Hill, FL 32759
Curtis, Tom	Dolphin Digest	8033 N.W. 36 Street	Miami, FL 33166
Davis, Al	Oakland Raiders	7000 Coliseum Way	Oakland, CA 94621
Davis, Butch	Cleveland Browns	1085 W. 3rd Street	Cleveland, OH 44114
Del Rio, Jack	Jacksonville Jaguars	One Alltel Stadium Place	Jacksonville, FL 32202
Dellenbach, Jeff	Promotional Solutions	1351 Shotgun Road	Weston, FL 33326
Dennard, Mark	Wings N' More Restaurants	111 University Drive E.	College Station, TX 77840
Diana, Rich	CT Orthopaedic	2408 Whitney Avenue	Hamden, CT 06518
Donahoe, Tom	Ralph Wilson Stadium	One Bills Drive	Orchard Park, NY 14127
Dorsett, Tony	6116 No. Central Expwy.	Dallas, TX 75206	
Dungy, Tony	Indianapolis Colts	7001 West 56th Street	Indianaplois, IN 46254
Edwards, Herman	New York Jets	Giants Stadium	East Rutherford, NJ 07073
Eller, Carl	1035 Washburn Avenue N.	Minneapolis, MN 55441	

Elway, John	10030 E. Arapahoe Road	Englewood, CO 80112-3702	
Erickson, Dennis	Marie DeBartolo Centre	4949 Centennial Blvd	Santa Clara, CA 95054
Everett, Jim	31741 Contijo Way	Coto de Caza, CA 92679-3614	
Fisher, Jeff	Tennessee Titans	1914 Church Street	Nashville, TN 37221
Ford, William Clay	Detroit Lions	222 Republic Drive	Allen Park, MI 48101
Fox, John	Carolina Pathers	800 South Mint Street	Charlotte, NC 28202-1502
Gibbs, Alex	Atlanta Falcons	4400 Falcon Parkway	Flowery Branh, GA 30542
Gibbs, Joe	Washington Redskins	21300 Redskin Park Dr.	Ashburn, VA 20147
Graf, Rick	Fazoli's	11108 Bluestem Lane	Eden Prairie, MN 55347
Green, Dennis	Arizona Cardinals	PO Box 888	Phoenix, AZ 85001-0888
Green, Tim	C/O Fox Sports Net	1440 Sepulveda Blvd	Los Angeles, CA 90025
Greene, Joe	Pittsburgh Steelers	100 Art Rooney Avenue	Pittsburgh, PA 15212
Grimsley, John	World Class Expeditions	P.O. Box 16388	Sugar Land, TX 77496
Haden, Pat	8525 Wilson Avenue	San Marino, CA 91108	
Hampton, Lorenzo	LH Sports	1251 Nottoway Trail	Marietta, GA 30066
Haslett, Jim	New Orleans Saints	5800 Airline Drive	Metairie, Louisiana 70003
Higgs, Mark	M&T Transportation	2500 Kensington Blvd	Davie, FL 33325
Hill, Ike	Danley Lumber Co.	4019 St. Charles Road	Bellwood, IL 60104
Holmgren, Mike	Seattle Seahawks	11220 NE 53rd Street	Kirkland, WA 98033
Holtz, Lou	Athletic Department	Notre Dame University	South Bend, IN 46556
Hunt, Lamar	Kansas City Chiefs	One Arrowhead Drive	Kansas City, MO 64129
Hutton, Tom	Boyle Investment Co.	5900 Poplar Ave.	Memphis, TN 38119
Irsay, James	Indianapolis Colts	7001 West 56th Street	Indianaplois, IN 46254
Jackson, Bo	PO Box 2000	Anaheim, CA 92803	
Jackson, Frank	Law Offices of F. Johnson	2612 Boll Street	Dallas, TX 75204
Jensen, Jim	Henry & June, Inc.	1411 S. University Dr.	Plantation, FL 33324
Jones, Jerry	Dallas Cowboys	2401 E. Airport Freeway	Irving, TX 75062
Kelly, Jim	Jim Kelly Enterprise	355 Harlem Rd.	West Seneca, NY 14224
Kosar, Bernie	6969 Rin Park Place	Youngstown, OH 44512	
Lerner, Randolf D.	Cleveland Browns	1085 W. 3rd Street	Cleveland, OH 44114
Lofton, James	San Diego Chargers	P.O. Box 609609	San Diego, CA 92160-9609
Lott, Ronnie	11342 Canyon View Circle	Cupertino, CA 95014	
Madden, John	5304 Backhawk Drive	Danville, CA 94506	
Malone, Darrell	Heaven & Earth Salon	981 N. Nob Hill Road	Plantation, FL 33324
Manning, Archie	Special Olympics Louisiana	1615 Poydras Street	New Orleans, LA 70112
Mara, Wellington T.	New York Giants	Giants Stadium	East Rutherford, NJ 07073
Marino, Dan	Miami Dolphins	2269 N.W. 199th Street	Miami, FL 32056
Mariucci, Steve	Detroit Lions	222 Republic Drive	Allen Park, MI 48101
Martz, Mike	St. Louis Rams	One Rams Way	St. Louis, Missouri 63045
McNair, Robert C.	Houston Texans	Two Reliant Park	Houston, TX 77054
McNeal, Don	Dade Christian School	6601 N.W. 167 Street	Miami, FL 33015

Montana, Joe	# 1250	21515 Hawthorne Blvd	Torrence, CA 90503
Mora, Jim	Atlanta Falcons	4400 Falcon Parkway	Flowery Branh, GA 30542
Moreau, Doug	Attorney's Office	222 St. Louis Street	Baton Rouge, LA 70802
Mularkey, Mike	Ralph Wilson Stadium	One Bills Drive	Orchard Park, NY 14127
Noll, Chuck	201 Grant Street	Sewickley, PA 15143	
Nottingham, Don	AG Intl. Ins. Agency	8305 S.E. 58 Avenue	Ocala, FL 34480
Offerdahl, John	Offerdahls	929 Shotgun Road	Sunrise, FL 33326
Oliver, Louis	Home America, Inc.	18755 Biscayne Blvd.	Aventura, FL 33180
Olsen, Merlin	1080 Lorain Road	San Marino, CA 91108	
Otto, Jim	Oakland Raiders	7000 Coliseum Way	Oakland, CA 94621
Parcells, Bill	Dallas Cowboys	2401 E. Airport Freeway	Irving, TX 75062
Pearson, Drew	3721 Mount Vernon Way	Plano, TX 75025	
Pendergast, Clancy	Arizona Cardinals	PO Box 888	Phoenix, AZ 85001-0888
Phillips, Ted	Halas Hall	1000 Football Drive	Lake Forest, IL 6004
Phillips, Wade	San Diego Chargers	P.O. Box 609609	San Diego, CA 92160-9609
Porter, Daryl	Porter's Place	4535 N. Pine Island Rd	Sunrise, FL 33351
Pruitt, James	AFCG Consulting	500 S. Australian Ave.	West Palm Beach, FL 33409
Reid, Andy	Philadelphia Eagles	3501 South Broad Street	Philadelphia, PA 19148
Rice, Jerry	Sports Management Group	# 1008 - 222 S. Central	St. Louis, MO 63105
Rooney, Daniel M.	Pittsburgh Steelers	100 Art Rooney Avenue	Pittsburgh, PA 15212
Sanders, Barry	Detroit Loins	PO Box 4200	Pontiac, MI 48057
Sanders, Deion	Parker & Associates	1080 Stnd. Federal Hwy.	Fort Wayne, IN 46802
Schottenheimer, Marty	San Diego Chargers	P.O. Box 609609	San Diego, CA 92160-9609
Shanahan, Mike	Denver Broncos	13655 Broncos Parkway	Englewood, CO 80112
Sherman, Mike	Green Bay Packers	PO Box 10628	Greenbay, WI 54307
Shula, Dave & Don	Shula's Steakhouse	6843 Main Street	Miami Lakes, FL 33014
Smith, Lovie	Halas Hall	1000 Football Drive	Lake Forest, IL 6004
Smith, Tom	The Wine News	P.O. Box 142096	Coral Gables, FL 33114
Spanos, Alex G.	San Diego Chargers	P.O. Box 609609	San Diego, CA 92160-9609
Stabler, Ken	Crimson Tide Sports Mkt.	PO Box 11010	Northport, Al 35486
Starr, Bart	2065 Royal Fern Lane	Birmingham, Al 35244	
Staubach, Roger	Staubach Co.	6750 LBJ Freeway	Dallas, TX 75240-6512
Stenerud, Jan	1201 Walnut Street # 700	Kansas City, MO 64106-2136	
Stephenson, Dwight	D. Stephenson Constr, Inc.	1180 S. Powerline Road	Pompano Beach, FL 33069
Stofa, John	Medical Mutual of Ohio	9961 Brewster Lane	Columbus, OH 43065
Theismann, Joe	C/O ESPN	Espn Plaza	Bristol, Ct 06010
Thomas, Thurman	Thurman Thomas Corp.	9328 Westover Club Circle	Windermere, FL 34786
Tice, Mike	Minnesota Vikings	500 11th Avenue South	Minneapolis, MN 55415
Turner, Norv	Oakland Raiders	7000 Coliseum Way	Oakland, CA 94621
Vermeil, Dick	Kansas City Chiefs	One Arrowhead Drive	Kansas City, MO 64129
Vigorito, Tom	Roosevelt & Cross	20 Exchange Place	New York, NY 10005
Wannstedt, Dave	Miami Dolphins	7500 SW 30th Street	Davie, Florida 33314
Weaver, Wayne	Jacksonville Jaguars	One Alltel Stadium Place	Jacksonville, FL 32202
Wolford, Will	Louisville Fire Football	P.O. Box 21607	Louisville, KY 40221
Wyatt, Alvin	Bethune-Cookman Athletic Dept.	640 Dr. Mary McLeod Bethune Blvd	Daytona Beach, FL 32114-3099
Young, Steve	261 Broadway	Salt Lake City	Utah 84111
Youngblood, Jack	Orlando Predators	20 N. Orange Avenue	Orlando, FL 32801
Zorn, Jim	Seattle Seahawks	11220 NE 53rd Street	Kirkland, WA 98033

You can write to your favorite ESPN personality at:

ESPN

ESPN Plaza

Bristol, CT 06010

Among the ESPN personalities you will find Jim Kelly, Chris Berman and Joe Theismann.

David Aldridge	Rich Eisen	Mel Kiper Jr.	Sal Paolantonio	Pam Shriver
John Anderson	Len Elmore	Marlo Klain	Bob Papa	Dan Shulman
Teddy Atlas	Brian Engblom	Ray Knight	Benny Parsons	Dave Sims
Dave Barnett	Dave Feldman	Suzy Kolber	Dan Patrick	Shelley Smith
Tony Barnhardt	Phil Ferguson	Tony Kornheiser	Mike Patrick	Tommy Smyth
Jon Beekhuis	Mary Joe Fernandez	Andrea Kremer	Kyle Petty	Jayson Stark
Larry Beil	Roy Firestone	Tim Kurkjian	Richard "Digger" Phelps	Melissa Stark
Chris Berman	Julie Foudy	Steve Levy	Bob Picozzi	Charley Steiner
Al Bernstein	Chris Fowler	Bob Ley	Bill Pidto	Bob Stevens
Steve Berthiaume	Ron Franklin	David Lloyd	Andy Pollin	J.W. Stewart
Jay Bilas	Jim Frazier	Kevin Loughery	Dr. Jerry Punch	Fred Stolle
Rolando Blackman	Peter Gammons	Mike Macfarlane	Derek Rae	Rob Stone
Dan Bonner	Greg Garber	John Mackovic	Bill Raftery	Dave Strader
John Buccigross	Rod Gilmore	Paul Maguire	Dr. Jack Ramsay	Jon Sundvold
Ric Bucher	Hank Goldberg	Joe Magrane	Leo Rautins	Rick Sutcliffe
Quinn Buckner	Mike Golic	Seamus Malin	Karl Ravech	Joe Theismann
Dave Campbell	Mike Gottfried	Mark Malone	Larry Rawson	Gary Thorne
Bob Carpenter	Mike Greenberg	Chris Marlowe	Marty Reid	Mike Tirico
Fred Carter	Mimi Griffin	Buck Martinez	Dave Revsine	Roger Twibell
Todd Christensen	Bob Halloran	Kenny Mayne	Harold Reynolds	Bob Valvano
John Clayton	Kirk Herbstreit	Bill McDermott	Kenny Rice	Bob Varsha
Bill Clement	Mike Hill	Patrick McEnroe	Jimmy Roberts	Lesley Visser
Linda Cohn	Merril Hoge	Chris McKendry	Robin Roberts	Dick Vitale
Larry Conley	Jason Jackson	Brian McRae	Betsy Ross	Rich Waltz
Beano Cook	Tom Jackson	Barry Melrose	Holly Rowe	Pam Ward
Kevin Corke	Ron Jaworski	Ann Meyers	Dave Ryan	Malivai Washington
Lee Corso	Ned Jarrett	Gary Miller	Jim St. Andre	Whit Watson
Bill Curry	Bob Jenkins	Jon Miller	Sean Salisbury	Bill Weber
Steve Cyphers	Gary Jobson	Chris Moore	Lisa Salters	Ed Werder
Dan Davis	Adrian Karsten	Joe Morgan	Tommy Sanders	Ann Werner
Rece Davis	Andy Katz	Al Morganti	John Saunders	Solomon Wilcots
Joe D'ambrosio	Max Kellerman	Chris Mortensen	Dick Schaap	Chuck Wilson
John Paul Dellacamera	Jim Kelly, Play-by-Play	Beth Mowins	Jeremy Schaap	Keith Wilson
Rob Dibble	Jim Kelly, NFL Analyst	Anthony Muñoz	Phil Schoen	Trey Wingo
Cliff Drysdale	Brian Kenny	Brad Nesslerr	Gene Wojciechowski	Matt Yocum
Ray Dunlap	Ty Keough	Andy North	Mark Schwarz	
Jimmy Dykes	John Kernan	Iain Page	Stuart Scott	
Jack Edwards	Michael Kim	Darren Pang	Sterling Sharpe	

National Hockey League Team Addresses

All National Hockey League team rosters are listed on the following pages.
Match a selected player to the team address appearing below.

(Name of Player)
Pittsburgh Penguins
Civic Arena
66 Mario Lemieux Place
Pittsburgh, PA 15219

Anaheim Mighty Ducks	Disney Sports Enterprises Inc.	2695 East Katella Avenue	Anaheim, CA 92803
Atlanta Thrashers	Centennial Towers	101 Marietta Street NW	Atlanta, GA 30303
Boston Bruins	One FleetCenter	Suite 250	Boston, MA 02114-1303
Buffalo Sabres	HSBC Arena	One Seymour H. Knox III Plaza	Buffalo, NY 14203
Calgary Flames	P.O. Box 1540 Station M	Calgary, Alberta T2P 3B9	
Carolina Hurricanes	RBC Center	1400 Edwards Mill Road	Raleigh, NC 27607
Chicago Blackhawks	United Center	1901 W. Madison Street	Chicago, IL 60612
Colorado Avalanche	Pepsi Center	100 Chopper Place	Denver, CO 80204
Columbus Blue Jackets	Nationwide Arena	200 W. Nationwide Blvd	Columbus, OH 43215
Dallas Stars Hockey	Dr. Pepper StarCenter	211 Cowboys Parkway	Irving, TX 75063
Detroit Red Wings	Joe Louis Arena	600 Civic Center	Detroit, MI 48226
Edmonton Oilers Hockey	11230 - 110 Street	Edmonton, Alberta	Canada T5G 3H7
Florida Panthers	One Pather Parkway	Sunrise, FL 33323	
Los Angeles Kings	STAPLES Center	1111 S. Figueroa Street	Los Angeles, CA 90015
Minnesota Wild	Excel Arena	Kellogg Blvd	Saint Paul, MN 55105
Montreal Canadiens	1275 St. Antoine Street West	Montreal, QC, CANADA	H3C 5L2
Nashville Predators	501 Broadway	Nashville, TN 37203	
New Jersey Devils	Continental Airlines Arena	50 Route 120 North PO Box 504	East Rutherford, NJ 07073
New York Islanders	Nassau Vetrs. Mem. Coliseum	1255 Hempstead Turnpike	Uniondale, NY 11553
New York Rangers	Madison Square Garden	2 Penn Plaza	New York, NY 10121
Ottawa Senators	Corel Centre	1000 Palladium Drive	Kanata, ON K2V 1A4
Philadelphia Flyers	3601 South Broad Street	Philadelphia, PA 19148	
Phoenix Coyotes Hockey	Suite 350	5800 W. Glenn Drive	Glendale, AZ 85301
Pittsburgh Penguins	Mellon Arena	66 Mario Lemieux Place	Pittsburgh, PA 15219
San Jose Sharks	HP Pavilion	525 West Santa Clara Street	San Jose, CA 95113
St. Louis Blues	Savvis Center	1401 Clark Avenue	St. Louis, MO 63103-2709
Tampa Bay Lightning	St. Pete Times Forum	401 Channelside Drive	Tampa, FL 33602
Toronto Maple Leafs	Air Canada Centre	40 Bay Street, Suite 300	Toronto, ON M5J 2X2
Vancouver Canucks	General Motors Place	800 Griffiths Way	Vancouver, B.C. V6B 6G1
Washington Capitals	Market Square North	401 Nineht Street N.W.	Washington, D.C. 20004

National Hockey League Team Rosters

Anaheim Mighty Ducks
Bryzgalov, Ilya
Burnett, Garrett
Carney, Keith
Fedorov, Sergei
Giguere, Jean-Sebastien
Kunitz, Chris
Leclerc, Mike
Lupul, Joffrey
Malec, Tomas
Mcdonald, Andy
Niedermayer, Rob
Ozolinsh, Sandis
Pahlsson, Samuel
Rucchin, Steve
Salei, Ruslan
Skoula, Martin
Sykora, Petr
Vishnevski, Vitaly
Ward, Lance

Atlanta Thrashers
Serge Aubin
Kip Brennan
Garnet Exelby
Niclas Havelid
Dany Heatley
Jani Hurme
Tomas Kloucek
Ilya Kovalchuk
Vyacheslav Kozlov
Brad Larsen
Kari Lehtonen
Francis Lessard
Ivan Majesky
Shawn Mceachern
Scott Mellanby
Jaroslav Modry
Pasi Nurminen
Ronald Petrovicky
Marc Savard
Ben Simon
Patrik Stefan
Andy Sutton
Daniel Tjarnqvist
J.P. Vigier

Boston Bruins
P.J. Axelsson
Nick Boynton
Tom Fitzgerald
Hal Gill
Jonathan Girard
Sergei Gonchar
Ivan Huml
Zdenek Kutlak
Martin Lapointe
Robert Liscak
Ian Moran
Sergei Samsonov
P.J. Stock
Joe Thornton
Andrew Raycroft

Buffalo Sabres
Afinogenov, Maxim
Bartovic, Milan
Biron, Martin
Boulton, Eric
Briere, Daniel
Brown, Brad
Campbell, Brian
Connolly, Tim
Drury, Chris
Dumont, Jean-Pierre
Fitzpatrick, Rory
Grier, Mike
Hecht, Jochen
Janik, Doug
Jillson, Jeff
Kalinin, Dmitri
Kotalik, Ales
Mair, Adam
Mckee, Jay
Miller, Ryan
Milley, Norm
Noronen, Mika
Patrick, James
Peters, Andrew
Pominville, Jason

Calgary Flames
Roman Turek
Mike Commodore
Jordan Leopold
Steve Montador
Chuck Kobasew
Dave Lowry
Stephane Yelle
Jarome Iginla
Chris Simon
Shean Donovan
Chris Clark
Matthew Lombardi
Daymond Langkow
Lynn Loyns
Andrew Ference
Martin Gelinas
Ville Nieminen
Byron Ritchie
Marcus Nilson
Steven Reinprecht
Robyn Regehr
Jason Wiemer
Toni Lydman
Miikka Kiprusoff
Rhett Warrener

Carolina Hurricanes
Matt Cullen
Justin Williams
Kevyn Adams
Marty Murray
Rod Brind'amour
Radim Vrbata
Pavel Brendl
Erik Cole
Jesse Boulerice
Josef Vasicek
Jeff O'neill
Glen Wesley
Aaron Ward
Frantisek Kaberle
Bret Hedican
Niclas Wallin
Martin Gerber

Chicago Blackhawks
Arnason, Tyler
Barnaby, Matthew
Bell, Mark
Berard, Bryan
Brown, Curtis
Calder, Kyle
Cullimore, Jassen
Daze, Eric
Mccarthy, Steve
Nichol, Scott
Poapst, Steve
Robidas, Stephane
Ruutu, Tuomo
Thibault, Jocelyn

Colorado Avalanche
Joe Sakic
Alex Tanguay
Milan Hejduk
Peter Forsberg
Rob Blake
Vincent Damphousse
Steve Konowalchuk
John-Michael Liles
Chris Gratton
Brett Mclean
Adam Foote
Antti Laaksonen
Ian Laperriere
Karlis Skrastins
Dan Hinote
Kurt Sauer
Ossi Vaananen
Darby Hendrickson
Bob Boughner
Peter Worrell
Riku Hahl
Philippe Sauve
David Aebischer

Columbus Blue Jackets
Cassels, Andrew
Letowski, Trevor
Malhotra, Manny
Marchant, Todd
Wright, Tyler
Mcdonell, Kent
Vyborny, David
13 Zherdev, Nikolai
Nash, Rick
Sanderson, Geoff
Shelley, Jody
Klesla, Rostislav
Lachance, Scott
Richardson, Luke
Scoville, Darrel
Spacek, Jaroslav
Suchy, Radoslav
Westcott Duvie
Denis, Marc
Irbe, Arturs

Dallas Stars
Arnott, Jason
Barnes, Stu
Boucher, Philippe
Daley, Trevor
Dimaio, Rob
Downey, Aaron
Erskine, John
Guerin, Bill
Kapanen, Niko
Klemm, Jon
Lehtinen, Jere
Modano, Mike
Morrow, Brenden
Ott, Steve
Svoboda, Jaroslav
Sweeney, Don
Turco, Marty
Turgeon, Pierre
Zubov, Sergei

Detroit Red Wings	Edmonton Oilers	Florida Panthers	Los Angeles Kings	Minnesota Wild
Pavel Datsyuk	Shawn Horcoff	Jay Bouwmeester	Derek Armstrong	Brunette, Andrew
Steve Yzerman	Mike York	Branislav Mezei	Jeff Cowan	Burns, Brent
Robert Lang	Brad Isbister	Stephen Weiss	Esa Pirnes	Chouinard, Marc
Jason Williams	Ethan Moreau	Olli Jokinen	Sean Avery	Daigle, Alexandre
Kris Draper	Ryan Smyth	Juraj Kolnik	Luc Robitaille	Dupuis, Pascal
Mark Mowers	Raffi Torres	Niklas Hagman	Craig Conroy	Fernandez, Manny
Brendan Shanahan	Radek Dvorak	Ty Jones	Alexander Frolov	Gaborik, Marian
Henrik Zetterberg	Ales Hemsky	Nathan Horton	Eric Belanger	Henry, Alex
Ray Whitney	Georges Laraque	Kristian Huselius	Trent Klatt	Johnson, Matt
Tomas Holmstrom	Sean McAlsan	Darcy Hordichuk	Ryan Flinn	Kuba, Filip
Kirk Maltby	Fernando Pisani	Mike Van Ryn	Martin Straka	Mitchell, Willie
Darren Mccarty	Marc-Andre Bergeron	Christian Berglund	Mike Weaver	Park, Richard
Steve Thomas	Eric Brewer	Mathieu Biron	Aaron Miller	Roloson, Dwayne
Derian Hatcher	Cory Cross	Eric Beaudoin	Stephane Quintal	Rolston, Brian
Jamie Rivers	Alexei Semenov	Vaclav Nedorost	Nathan Dempsey	Schultz, Nick
Nicklas Lidstrom	Jason Smith	Eric Cairns	Mattias Norstrom	Veilleux, Stephane
Jiri Fischer	Steve Staios	Sean Hill	Lubomir Visnovsky	Walz, Wes
Mathieu Dandenault	Igor Ulanov	Serge Payer	Joe Corvo	Zyuzin, Andrei
Jason Woolley	Ty Conklin	Joel Kwiatkowski	Jason Holland	
Mathieu Schneider	Jussi Markkanen	Alexander Karpovtsev	Mathieu Garon	
Chris Chelios		Roberto Luongo	Roman Cechmanek	
Niklas Kronwall		Jamie McLennan		
Marc Lamothe				
Curtis Joseph				
Manny Legace				

Montreal Canadiens	Nashville Predators	New Jersey Devils	New York Islanders	New York Rangers
Mike Komisarek	Martin Erat	Bicek, Jiri	Rick DiPietro	Jason Marshall
Saku Koivu	Scott Hartnell	Brodeur, Martin	Arron Asham	Michael Nylander
Radek Bonk	Jim McKenzie	Brown, Sean	Shawn Bates	Jason Strudwick
Richard Zednik	David Legwand	Brylin, Sergei	Jason Blake	Tom Poti
Steve Bégin	Greg Johnson	Elias, Patrik	Eric Godard	Dale Purinton
Pierre Dagenais	Denis Arkhipov	Friesen, Jeff	Trent Hunter	Darius Kasparaitis
Alex Kovalev	Adam Hall	Gionta, Brian	Oleg Kvasha	Bobby Holik
Karl Dykhuis	Scott Walker	Gomez, Scott	Justin Papineau	Jamie Lundmark
Jim Dowd	Steve Sullivan	Hrdina, Jan	Mark Parrish	Karel Rachunek
Niklas Sundstrom	Jeremy Stevenson	Kozlov, Viktor	Michael Peca	Jaromir Jagr
Jan Bulis	Vladimir Orszagh	Langdon, Darren	Dave Scatchard	Kevin Weekes
Patrice Brisebois	Marek Zidlicky	Langenbrunner, Jamie	Mattias Weinhandl	Mike Dunham
Sheldon Souray	Mark Eaton	Madden, John	Alexei Yashin	Dan Blackburn
Francis Bouillon	Andreas Lilja	Marshall, Grant	Adrian Aucoin	
Craig Rivet	Jamie Allison	Martin, Paul	Sven Butenschon	
Mike Ribeiro	Shane Hnidy	Matvichuk, Richard	Roman Hamrlik	
Michael Ryder	Kimmo Timonen	Niedermayer, Scott	Kenny Jonsson	
Andrei Markov	Tomas Vokoun	Oliwa, Krzysztof	Radek Martinek	
Yanic Perreault	Chris Mason	Pandolfo, Jay	Janne Niinimaa	
Cristobal Huet		Rafalski, Brian		
Jose Theodore		Rasmussen, Erik		
		Stevens, Scott		
		White, Colin		

Ottawa Senators
Emery, Ray
Prusek, Martin
Hasek, Dominik
Pothier, Brian
Chara, Zdeno
Phillips, Chris
de Vries, Greg
Redden, Wade
Havlat, Martin
Alfredsson, Daniel
Fisher, Mike
Schaefer, Peter
Hossa, Marian
Spezza, Jason
Vermette, Antoine
Smolinski, Bryan
Volchenkov, Anton
Neil, Chris
Varada, Vaclav
White, Todd
Langfeld, Josh
Kelly, Chris

Philadelphia Flyers
Mattias Timander
Kim Johnsson
John LeClair
Tony Amonte
Simon Gagne
Branko Radivojevic
Radovan Somik
Mike Knuble
Sami Kapanen
Keith Primeau
Michal Handzus
Turner Stevenson
Marcus Ragnarsson
Todd Fedoruk
Eric Desjardins
Sean Burke
Robert Esche
Danny Markov
Donald Brashear
Jeremy Roenick

Phoenix Coyotes
Brent Johnson
Brian Boucher
Derek Morris
Denis Gauthier
David Tanabe
Matthew Spiller
Daniel Cleary
Brett Hull
Mike Johnson
Mike Rupp
Jeff Taffe
Boyd Devereaux
Ladislav Nagy
Tyson Nash
Shane Doan
Fredrik Sjostrom
Sean O'Donnell
Paul Mara
Jason Chimera
Cale Hulse
Krystofer Kolanos
Mike Ricci
Andrei Nazarov
Brad Ference
Brian Savage
Mike Comrie
Oleg Saprykin
Petr Nedved

Pittsburgh Penguins
Mike Eastwood
Milan Kraft
Mario Lemieux
Matt Bradley
Konstantin Koltsov
Ryan Malone
Lasse Pirjeta
Mark Recchi
Ryan VandenBussche
Ramzi Abid
Rico Fata
Ric Jackman
Josef Melichar
Brooks Orpik
Michal Rozsival
Martin Strbak
Dick Tarnstrom
Sebastien Caron

San Jose Sharks
Cheechoo, Jonathan
Davison, Rob
Dimitrakos, Niko
Ehrhoff, Christian
Ekman, Nils
Fahey, Jim
Goaltender
Goc, Marcel
Hannan, Scott
Korolyuk, Alex
Marleau, Patrick
McCauley, Alyn
McLaren, Kyle
Michalek, Milan
Nabokov, Evgeni
Preissing, Tom
Primeau, Wayne
Rathje, Mike
Smith, Mark
Stuart, Brad
Sturm, Marco
Thornton, Scott
Toskala, Vesa

St. Louis Blues
Eric Boguniecki
Petr Cajanek
Dallas Drake
Ryan Johnson
Reed Low
Doug Weight
Murray Baron
Barret Jackman
Alexander Khavanov
Christian Backman
Eric Weinrich
Reinhard Divis
Jamal Mayers
Mark Rycroft
Peter Sejna
Mike Sillinger
Keith Tkachuk
Al MacInnis
Chris Pronger
Bryce Salvador
Matt Walker
Patrick Lalime

Tampa Bay Lightning
Vincent Lecavalier
Ile Bizard
Martin Cibak
Eric Perrin
Brad Richards
Tim Taylor
Chris Dingman
Ruslan Fedotenko
Dave Andreychuk
Dmitry Afanasenkov
Fredrik Modin
Cory Stillman
Ben Clymer
Martin St. Louis
Andre Roy
Stan Neckar
Pavel Kubina
Cory Sarich
Dan Boyle
Brad Lukowich
Darren Rumble
Nolan Pratt
Darryl Sydor
Nikolai Khabibulin
John Grahame

Toronto Maple Leafs
Aki Berg
Alexander Mogilny
Alexei Ponikarovsky
Brian Leetch
Bryan McCabe
Chad Kilger
Darcy Tucker
Drake Berehowsky
Ed Belfour
Gary Roberts
Joe Nieuwendyk
Karel Pilar
Ken Klee
Mats Sundin
Nathan Perrott
Nik Antropov
Owen Nolan
Tie Domi
Tomas Kaberle
Wade Belak

Vancouver Canucks
Bryan Allen
Marc Bergevin
Todd Bertuzzi
Tyler Bouck
Artem Chubarov
Dan Cloutier
Matt Cooke
Ed Jovanovski
Mike Keane
Trevor Linden
Mats Lindgren
Marek Malik
Brad May
Brendan Morrison
Markus Naslund
Mattias Ohlund
Martin Rucinsky
Jarkko Ruutu
Sami Salo
Daniel Sedin
Henrik Sedin
Brent Sopel

Washington Capitals
Aulin, Jared
Boumedienne, Josef
Cutta, Jakub
Daigneault, Maxime
Doig, Jason
Eminger, Steve
Fleischmann, Tomas
Fussey, Owen
Gordon, Boyd
Halpern, Jeff
Johansson, Jonas
Klepis, Jakub
Kolzig, Olie
Laich, Brooks
Mink, Graham
Morrisonn, Shaone
Ouellet, Maxime
Paul, Jeff
Peat, Stephen
Pettinger, Matt
Semin, Alexander
Stana, Rastislav
Stroshein, Garret
Sutherby, Brian
Tvrdon, Roman
Verot, Darcy
Whitfield, Trent
Willsie, Brian
Witt, Brendan

Additional Hockey Names & Addresses

Anschutz, Philip F.	Los Angeles Kings	STAPLES Center	1111 S. Figueroa Street	Los Angeles, CA 90015
Armstrong, Doug	Dallas Stars Hockey	Dr. Pepper StarCenter	211 Cowboys Parkway	Irving, TX 75063
Babcock, Mike	Anaheim Mighty Ducks	Disney Sports Enterprises	2695 East Katella Avenue	Anaheim, CA 92803
Bowness, Rick	Phoenix Coyotes Hockey	Suite 350	5800 W. Glenn Drive	Glendale, AZ 85301
Burns, Pat	New Jersey Devils	Continental Airlines Arena	50 Route 120 North	East Rutherford, NJ 07073
Clarke, Bob	Philadelphia Flyers	3601 South Broad Street	Philadelphia, PA 19148	
Coates, Al	Anaheim Mighty Ducks	Disney Sports Enterprises	2695 East Katella Avenue	Anaheim, CA 92803
Crawford, Marc	Vancouver Canucks	General Motors Place	800 Griffiths Way	Vancouver, B.C. V6B 6G1
Ellman, Steve	Phoenix Coyotes Hockey	Suite 350	5800 W. Glenn Drive	Glendale, AZ 85301
Ferguson, John	Toronto Maple Leafs	Air Canada Centre	40 Bay Street, Suite 300	Toronto, ON M5J 2X2
Gallant, Gerard	Columbus Blue Jackets	Nationwide Arena	200 W. Nationwide Blvd	Columbus, OH 43215
Gillett, George N. Jr.	Montreal Canadiens	1275 St. Antoine Street W.	Montreal, QC, CANADA	H3C 5L2
Golisano, B. Thomas	Buffalo Sabres	HSBC Arena	1 Seymour H. Knox III Plaza	Buffalo, NY 14203
Gosselin, Mario	3225 NE 16th Street	Pompano Beach, FL 33062		
Goulet, MIchael	817 Fairchild Drive	Highlands Ranch, CO	80126	
Graham, Dirk	7238 East Tyndall Street	Mesa, AZ 85207		
Granato, Tony	11657 E. Basrry Drive	Englewood, CO 80111		
Gretzky, Wayne	Phoenix Coyotes Hockey	Suite 350	5800 W. Glenn Drive	Glendale, AZ 85301
Hanlon, Glen	Washington Capitals	Market Square North	401 Nineht Street N.W.	Washington, D.C. 20004
Hartley, Bob	Atlanta Thrashers	Centennial Towers	101 Marietta Street NW	Atlanta, GA 30303
Hitchcock, Ken	Philadelphia Flyers	3601 South Broad Street	Philadelphia, PA 19148	
Howe, Gordie	6645 Peninsula Drive	Traverse City, MI 49684		
Ilitch, Mike	Detroit Red Wings	Joe Louis Arena	600 Civic Center	Detroit, MI 48226
Jacobs, Jeremy M.	Boston Bruins	Suite 250	One FleetCenter	Boston, MA 02114-1303
Jamison, Greg	San Jose Sharks	HP Pavilion	525 West Santa Clara Street	San Jose, CA 95113
Julien, Claude	Montreal Canadiens	1275 St. Antoine Street W.	Montreal, QC, CANADA	H3C 5L2
Keenan, Mike	Florida Panthers	One Pather Parkway	Sunrise, FL 33323	
Kitchen, Mike	St. Louis Blues	Savvis Center	1401 Clark Avenue	St. Louis, MO 63103-2709
Lacroix, Pierre	Colorado Avalanche	Pepsi Center	100 Chopper Place	Denver, CO 80204
Lamoriello, Louis A.	New Jersey Devils	Continental Airlines Arena	50 Route 120 North	East Rutherford, NJ 07073
Laurie, Bill	St. Louis Blues	Savvis Center	1401 Clark Avenue	St. Louis, MO 63103-2709

Additional Hockey Names & Addresses

Laviolette, Peter	Carolina Hurricanes	RBC Center	1400 Edwards Mill Road	Raleigh, NC 27607
Leipold, Craig	Nashville Predators	501 Broadway	Nashville, TN 37203	
Lemaire, Jacques	Minnesota Wild	Excel Arena	Kellogg Blvd	Saint Paul, MN 55105
Lewis, Dave	Detroit Red Wings	Joe Louis Arena	600 Civic Center	Detroit, MI 48226
MacLean, Doug	Columbus Blue Jackets	Nationwide Arena	200 W. Nationwide Blvd	Columbus, OH 43215
MacTavish, Craig	Edmonton Oilers Hockey	11230 - 110 Street	Edmonton, Alberta	Canada T5G 3H7
Martin, Jacques	Florida Panthers	One Pather Parkway	Sunrise, FL 33323	
McPhee, George	Washington Capitals	Market Square North	401 Nineht Street N.W.	Washington, D.C. 20004
Milbury, Mike	New York Islanders	Nassau Vetrs.Coliseum	1255 Hempstead Turnpike	Uniondale, NY 11553
Muckler, John	Ottawa Senators	Corel Centre	1000 Palladium Drive	Kanata, ON K2V 1A4
Murray, Andy	Los Angeles Kings	STAPLES Center	1111 S. Figueroa Street	Los Angeles, CA 90015
Murray, Bryan	Ottawa Senators	Corel Centre	1000 Palladium Drive	Kanata, ON K2V 1A4
Quenneville, Joel	Colorado Avalanche	Pepsi Center	100 Chopper Place	Denver, CO 80204
Quinn, Pat	Toronto Maple Leafs	Air Canada Centre	40 Bay Street, Suite 300	Toronto, ON M5J 2X2
Renney, Tom	New York Rangers	Madison Square Garden	2 Penn Plaza	New York, NY 10121
Risebrough, Doug	Minnesota Wild	Excel Arena	Kellogg Blvd	Saint Paul, MN 55105
Ruff, Lindy	Buffalo Sabres	HSBC Arena	1 Seymour H. Knox III Plaza	Buffalo, NY 14203
Rutherford, Jim	Carolina Hurricanes	RBC Center	1400 Edwards Mill Road	Raleigh, NC 27607
Sather, Glen	New York Rangers	Madison Square Garden	2 Penn Plaza	New York, NY 10121
Stirling, Steve	New York Islanders	Nassau Vetrs.Coliseum	1255 Hempstead Turnpike	Uniondale, NY 11553
Sullivan, Mike	Boston Bruins	Suite 250	One FleetCenter	Boston, MA 02114-1303
Sullivan, Red	Pittsburgh Penguins	Mellon Arena	66 Mario Lemieux Place	Pittsburgh, PA 15219
Sutter, Brian	Chicago Blackhawks	United Center	1901 W. Madison Street	Chicago, IL 60612
Sutter, Darryl	Calgary Flames	P.O. Box 1540 Station M	Calgary, Alberta T2P 3B9	Canada T2P 3B9
Tippett, Dave	Dallas Stars Hockey	Dr. Pepper StarCenter	211 Cowboys Parkway	Irving, TX 75063
Trotz, Barry	Nashville Predators	501 Broadway	Nashville, TN 37203	
Waddell, Don	Atlanta Thrashers	Centennial Towers	101 Marietta Street NW	Atlanta, GA 30303
Wilson, Ron	San Jose Sharks	HP Pavilion	525 West Santa Clara Street	San Jose, CA 95113
Wirtz, William W.	Chicago Blackhawks	United Center	1901 W. Madison Street	Chicago, IL 60612

Aaron, Tommy	IMG	1360 East 9th Street	Cleveland, OH 44114
Abell, David	Nick Price Group	900 S. U.S. Highway 1	Jupiter, FL 33477
Allem, Fulton	Players Group, Inc.	1851 Alexander Bell Dr.	Reston, VA 20191-4345
Allen, Stephan	Gaylord Sports Mgmt.	14646 N. Kierland Blvd.	Scottsdale, AZ 85254
Allenby, Robert	IMG	1360 East 9th Street	Cleveland, OH 44114
Ames, Stephan	IMG 1 St. Clair Avenue E	Toronto, Ontario	Canada M4T 2V7
Andrade, Billy	Woolf Associates	101 Huntington St.	Boston, MA 02199
Aoki, Isao	IMG	1360 East 9th Street	Cleveland, OH 44114
Appleby, Stuart	IMG	1360 East 9th Street	Cleveland, OH 44114
Archambault, Mary	Signature Sports Group	801 Park Avenue	Minneapolis, MN 55404
Armour, Tommy	William H. Thibodeau	391 E. Las Colinas Blvd.	Irving, TX 75039
Armstrong, Ty	Signature Sports Group	801 Park Avenue	Minneapolis, MN 55404
Armstrong, Wally	Gator Golf	P.O. Box 941911	Maitland, FL 32794
Aubrey, Emlyn	Blue Chip Promotions	1314 Falcon Ledge	Ausitn, TX 78746
Austin, Woody	Benchmark SEG	2300 Computer Ave.	Willow Grove, PA 19090
Azinger, Paul	Leader Enterprises, Inc.	1101 N. Kentucky Ave.	Winter Park, FL 32789
Baiocchi, Hugh	Pro Assistants, Inc.	3656 Half Moon Drive	Orlando, FL 32812
Baiocchi, Lauren	Pro Assistants, Inc.	3656 Half Moon Drive	Orlando, FL 32812
Baird, Briny	Pros, Inc.	7100 Forest Ave.	Richmond, VA 23226
Baird, Butch	Pinnacle Enterprises, Inc.	8221 Old Courthouse Rd.	Vienna, VA 22182
Ballesteros, Seve	c/pasaje de Pena	n' 2 curata planta	Santander, Spain 39008
Barber, Miller	IMG	1360 East 9th Street	Cleveland, OH 44114
Barlow, Craig	Adam Lenkin, Esq.	4644 Reservoir Road, N.W.	Washington, DC 20007
Barnes, Brian	PrioritySport	1515 N. Federal Hwy.	Boca Raton, FL 33432
Barnhardt, Mac	Pros, Inc.	7100 Forest Ave.	Richmond, VA 23226
Barr, Dave	10620 Southdale Road	Richmond, BC	V7A 2W7 Canada
Bartie, Scott	Outside the Box Marketing	7590 East Gray Road	Scottsdale, AZ 85260
Bateman, Brian	Pros, Inc.	7100 Forest Ave.	Richmond, VA 23226
Bates, Ben	Timothy P. Flynn	3291 N. Buffalo Drive	Las Vegas, NV 89128
Bates, Pat	Links Mgmt. Group, Inc.	5068 W. Plano Parkway	Plano, TX 75093
Baumert, John	Gil Morgan, Ltd.	P.O. Box 806	Edmond, OK 73083
Bean, Andy	IMG	1360 East 9th Street	Cleveland, OH 44114
Beard, Frank	Tour Talent	843 N. Cleveland-Massillon	Akron, OH 44333
Beckman, Cameron	SFX Sports Group	5335 Wisconsin Ave. N.W.	Washington, D.C. 20015
Beem, Rich	Gaylord Sports Mgmt.	14646 N. Kierland Blvd.	Scottsdale, AZ 85254
Begay, Notah	Imani Sports, LLC	800 Washington Ave. N.	Minneapolis, MN 55401
Bentley, Bill	TwinHill Golf Company	1255 B Park Avenue	Emeryville, CA 94608
Berganio, David	IMG	1360 East 9th Street	Cleveland, OH 44114
Bertsch, Shane	Signature Sports Group	801 Park Avenue	Minneapolis, MN 55404
Black, Ronnie	Burt Kinert & Associates	5355 E. Williams Cr.	Tucson, AZ 85711
Blackburn, Woody	Frank W. Brown & Assoc.	P.O. Box 215	Orange Park, FL 32067
Blackmar, Phil	Integrated Sports Intl.	One Meadows Plaza	East Rutherford, NJ 07073
Bland, John	IMG	1360 East 9th Street	Cleveland, OH 44114
Blankenship, Bob	Pro Players Group	12900 Walden Rd.	Montgomery, TX 77356
Bolt, Tommy	Tour Talent	843 N. Cleveland-Massillon	Akron, OH 44333
Booker, Eric	Chi Chi Rodriguez Mgmt.	3916 Clock Point Circle	Stow, OH 44224
Boros, Guy	Integrated Sports Intl.	One Meadows Plaza	East Rutherford, NJ 07073
Bowden, Craig	Brian Symonds	47 Rutland Lane	Boynton Beach, FL 33436
Bradley, Michael	SFX Sports Group	5335 Wisconsin Ave. N.W.	Washington, D.C. 20015
Brame, Tom	T&J Ventures	P.O. Box 11375	Winston-Salem, NC 27116
Bratton, Alan	Links Mgmt. Group, Inc.	5068 W. Plano Parkway	Plano, TX 75093
Breed, Giff	Pros, Inc.	7100 Forest Ave.	Richmond, VA 23226
Brent Summers	Tarlow Jordan & Schrader	P.O. Box 230669	Portland, OR 97281
Brisky, Mike	SportsLink Consulting	545 Delaney Ave.	Orlando, FL 32801
Broeck, Lance Ten	IMG	1360 East 9th Street	Cleveland, OH 44114
Brooks, Mark	Hambric Sports Mgmt.	2515 McKinney Ave.	Dallas, TX 75201
Brown, Billy Ray	IMG	1360 East 9th Street	Cleveland, OH 44114
Browne, Olin	Signature Sports Group	801 Park Avenue	Minneapolis, MN 55404
Brue, Bob	Sports Marketing & Mgmt.	111 E. Kilbourn Ave.	Milwaukee, WI 53233
Bryant, Bart	Total Sports, Inc.	1133 Mission Ridge Ct.	Orlando, FL 32835
Bryant, Brad	Dyer Enterprises	5850 T.G. Lee Blvd.	Orlando, FL 32822
Buffoni, Brad	Signature Sports Group	801 Park Avenue	Minneapolis, MN 55404
Buha, Jason	Career Sports Mgmt.	200 Galleria Parkway	Atlana, GA 30339
Burke, Patrick	Benchmark SEG	2300 Computer Ave.	Willow Grove, PA 19090

Burns, Bob	Integrated Sports Intl.	One Meadows Plaza	East Rutherford, NJ 07073
Burns, George	IMG	1360 East 9th Street	Cleveland, OH 44114
Byrum, Curt	Pros, Inc.	7100 Forest Ave.	Richmond, VA 23226
Byrum, Tom	Signature Sports Group	801 Park Avenue	Minneapolis, MN 55404
Calcavecchia, Mark	IMG	1360 East 9th Street	Cleveland, OH 44114
Caldwell, Rex	Pro Players Group	12900 Walden Rd.	Montgomery, TX 77356
Callazzo, Kim	Pros, Inc.	7100 Forest Ave.	Richmond, VA 23226
Canizares, Jose M.	Armstrong Mgmt. Group	Two Soundview Drive	Greenwich, CT 06830
Carroll, Val	Turner Communications	1234 W. Cove Drive	Gilbert, AZ 85233
Carter, Jim	Gaylord Sports Mgmt.	14646 N. Kierland Blvd.	Scottsdale, AZ 85254
Casper, Billy	Pinnacle Enterprises, Inc.	8221 Old Courthouse Rd.	Vienna, VA 22182
Chalmers, Greg	IMG	1360 East 9th Street	Cleveland, OH 44114
Chamblee, Brandel	Intl. Golf Partners	3300 PGA Boulevard	Palm Beach Gardens, FL 33410
Charles, Bob	IMG	1360 East 9th Street	Cleveland, OH 44114
Chen, T.C.	Dr. Drew Winston	13436 Chalon Road	Los Angeles, CA 90049
Choi, K.J.	IMG	1360 East 9th Street	Cleveland, OH 44114
Cink, Stewart	IMG	1360 East 9th Street	Cleveland, OH 44114
Claar, Brian	Gaylord Sports Mgmt.	14646 N. Kierland Blvd.	Scottsdale, AZ 85254
Clarke, Darren	Intl. Sports Mgmt.	Stocks Lane, Over Peover	Cheshire, WA16 8TW England
Claxton, Paul	Pros, Inc.	7100 Forest Ave.	Richmond, VA 23226
Clearwater, Keith	Players Group, Inc.	1851 Alexander Bell Dr.	Reston, VA 20191-4345
Cochran, Bobby	Links Mgmt. Group, Inc.	5068 W. Plano Parkway	Plano, TX 75093
Cochran, Russ	Pay Pro Sports	2400 East Katella Ave.	Anaheim, CA 92806
Colbert, Jim	Jim Colbert, Inc.	222 South Rainbow	Las Vegas, NV 89128
Cole, Bobby	IMG	1360 East 9th Street	Cleveland, OH 44114
Conner, Frank	ProLink	The Harvard Bldg.	Pinehurst, NC 28374
Coody, Charles	IMG	1360 East 9th Street	Cleveland, OH 44114
Cook, John	Players Group, Inc.	1851 Alexander Bell Dr.	Reston, VA 20191-4345
Cooper, Hank	Jerry Hamilton	1705 S.E. 9th Street	Mineral Wells, TX 76067
Cosina, Dennis	Trudy Cosina	211 Main Street	East 'windsor, CT 06088
Couch, Chris	SFX Sports Group	5335 Wisconsin Ave. N.W.	Washington, D.C. 20015
Couples, Fred	Players Group, Inc.	1851 Alexander Bell Dr.	Reston, VA 20191-4345
Crampton, Bruce	Marlene Y. Crampton	80-47 Pebble Beach	La Quinta, CA 92253-4623
Crenshaw, Ben	Scott Sayers, Jr.	1800 Nueces Street	Austin, TX 78701
Cupit, Jacky	William Reppeto, Jr.	8214 Westchester Dr.	Dallas, TX 75225
Dalton, Skip	Sports Partners, Inc.	719 Vassar Street	Orlando, FL 32804
Daly, John	SFX Sports Group	5335 Wisconsin Ave. N.W.	Washington, D.C. 20015
Damron, Robert	IMG	1360 East 9th Street	Cleveland, OH 44114
Davis, Jay	Kevin Richardson	1551 Forum Pl.	West Palm Beach, FL 33401
Day, Glen	Intl. Golf Partners	3300 PGA Boulevard	Palm Beach Gardens, FL 33410
Decker, Adam	SFX Sports Group	5335 Wisconsin Ave. N.W.	Washington, D.C. 20015
Delsing, Jay	Vantage Sports Mgmt.	40 Wall Street	New York, NY 10005
Dennis, Clark	SFX Sports Group	5335 Wisconsin Ave. N.W.	Washington, D.C. 20015
Dent, Jim	Willye Dent, Esq.	P.O. Box 290656	Tampa, FL 33687-0656
Devlin, Bruce	Pinnacle Enterprises, Inc.	8221 Old Courthouse Rd.	Vienna, VA 22182
Dill, Terry	IMG	1360 East 9th Street	Cleveland, OH 44114
DiMarco, Chris	IMG	1360 East 9th Street	Cleveland, OH 44114
Dodds, Trevor	Links Mgmt. Group, Inc.	5068 W. Plano Parkway	Plano, TX 75093
Donovan, Kimberly	SFX Sports Group	5335 Wisconsin Ave. N.W.	Washington, D.C. 20015
Dooley, Adam	Signature Sports Group	801 Park Avenue	Minneapolis, MN 55404
Dougherty, Ed	John Reynolds	57 E. 64th Street	New York, NY 10021
Doyle, Allen	Pros, Inc.	7100 Forest Ave.	Richmond, VA 23226
Driscoll, Paul	Woolf Associates	101 Huntington St.	Boston, MA 02199
Duke, Ken	PrioritySport	1515 N. Federal Hwy.	Boca Raton, FL 33432
Dunakey, Doug	Chi Chi Rodriguez Mgmt.	3916 Clock Point Circle	Stow, OH 44224
Dunlap, Scott	Agliano, Hodges, P.A.	P.O. Box 190	Tampa, FL 33601
Durant, Joe	Pros, Inc.	7100 Forest Ave.	Richmond, VA 23226
Duval, David	IMG	1360 East 9th Street	Cleveland, OH 44114
Eaks, R.W.	Arbesman Golf Entpr.	P.O. Box 3140	Carefree, AZ 85377
Eastwood, Bob	First Intl. Financial, Inc.	8131 LBJ Freeway	Dallas, TX 75251
Ekington, Steve	Ekington Course Design	13131 Chapmions Dr.	Houston, TX 77069
Elder, Brad	Players Group, Inc.	1851 Alexander Bell Dr.	Reston, VA 20191-4345
Elder, Lee	The Elder Group, Inc.	129-A Powerline Rd.	Pompano Beach, FL 33069
Els, Ernie	P.O. Box 653278	Benmore 2010	Republic of South Africa

Estes, Bob	Hambric Sports Mgmt.	2515 McKinney Ave.	Dallas, TX 75201
Fair, Keith	Sports Properties, Ltd.	8708 Tantallon Circle	Tampa, FL 33647-2240
Faldo, Nick	CSS Stellar Golf	12 Great Newport Street	London, England WC2H 7JA
Faxon, Brad	Pros, Inc.	7100 Forest Ave.	Richmond, VA 23226
Feherty, David	Tour Talent	843 N. Cleveland-Massillon	Akron, OH 44333
Fehr, Rick	Signature Sports Group	801 Park Avenue	Minneapolis, MN 55404
Fernandez, Vincente	Armstrong Mgmt. Group	Two Soundview Drive	Greenwich, CT 06830
Fiori, Ed	SFX Sports Group	5335 Wisconsin Ave. N.W.	Washington, D.C. 20015
Fleisher, Bruce	Vantage Sports Mgmt.	40 Wall Street	New York, NY 10005
Flesch, Steve	Hambric Sports Mgmt.	2515 McKinney Ave.	Dallas, TX 75201
Floyd, Raymond	The Raymond Floyd Grp.	231 Roayl Palm Way	Palm Beach, FL 33480
Foisman, Gerald A.	Roisman Pro-Rep	31 Grand Street	Hartford, CT 06106-4692
Foltz, Gerald	Joesph Athletic Mgmt.	P.O. Box 2080	Greensboro, N.C. 27402
Forsbrand, Anders	Hurst Grove	Sanford Lane	Berkshire RG10 OSQ Eng.
Forsman, Dan	IMG	1360 East 9th Street	Cleveland, OH 44114
Franco, Carlos	IMG	1360 East 9th Street	Cleveland, OH 44114
Frazar, Harrison	Hambric Sports Mgmt.	2515 McKinney Ave.	Dallas, TX 75201
Freeman, Robin	Intl. Golf Partners	3300 PGA Boulevard	Palm Beach Gardens, FL 33410
Friend, Bob	SFX Sports Group	5335 Wisconsin Ave. N.W.	Washington, D.C. 20015
Frost, David	David Frost Wine Co.	13355 Noel Road	Dallas, TX 75240
Fryatt, Edward	Benchmark SEG	2321 A Devine Street	Columbia, SC 29205
Funk, Fred	Scott Sports Mgmt.	10334 Champions Way	Laurel, MD 20723
Furyk, Jim	Goal Marketing	226 East 81st Street	New York, NY 10028
Gallagher Jr., Jim	Gallagher-Meeks	104 West Park Avenue	Greenwood, MS 38930
Gallagher, Jeff	Chi Chi Rodriguez Mgmt.	3916 Clock Point Circle	Stow, OH 44224
Gamez, Rovert	Fuzzy Zoeller Prod.	12701 Covered Bridge Rd.	Shellersburg, IN 47172
Garcia, Sergio	Strategies & Solutions	2655 Lejeune Road	Coral Gables, FL 33134
Gay, Brian	SFX Sports Group	5335 Wisconsin Ave. N.W.	Washington, D.C. 20015
Geiberger, Al	Cross Consulting	5 Cathy Place	Melno Park, CA 94025
Geiberger, Brent	Cross Consulting	5 Cathy Place	Melno Park, CA 94025
Giannone, Alberto	Armstrong Mgmt. Group	Two Soundview Drive	Greenwich, CT 06830
Gibson, Fred	John Svenson	244 Mercury Cr.	Pomona, CA 91768
Gibson, Kelly	Robert E. Kennedy	2809 Prytania Street	New Orleans, LA 70115
Giffin, Doc	Arnold Palmer Enterprises	P.O. Box 52	Youngstown, PA 15696
Gilbert Jr., Gibby	Creative Sports Mgmt.	2835 Townsgate Rd.	Westlake Village, CA 91361
Gilbert Sr., Gibby	Creative Sports Mgmt.	2835 Townsgate Rd.	Westlake Village, CA 91361
Gilder, Bob	Jeff Sanders Promotions	5671 S.W. Artic Drive	Beaverton, OR 97005-4153
Giles, Vinny	Pros, Inc.	7100 Forest Ave.	Richmond, VA 23226
Gilford, David	19 Higher Lane	Lymm, Cheshire	WA13 OAR Eng.
Glasson, Bill	Links Mgmt. Group, Inc.	5068 W. Plano Parkway	Plano, TX 75093
Gleaton, Todd	SFX Sports Group	5335 Wisconsin Ave. N.W.	Washington, D.C. 20015
Goetz, Dick	Piper and Gray Enterprises	600 Kenrick, Suite #C-26	Houston, TX 77060
Gogel, Matt	Chi Chi Rodriguez Mgmt.	3916 Clock Point Circle	Stow, OH 44224
Goggin, Matt	Gaylord Sports Mgmt.	7373 N. Scottsdale Rd.	Scottsdale, AZ 85253
Gore, Jason	Cross Consulting	5 Cathy Place	Melno Park, CA 94025
Gotsche, Steve	Adam Lenkin, Esq.	4644 Reservoir Road, N.W.	Washington, DC 20007
Gove, Jeff	Pros, Inc.	7100 Forest Ave.	Richmond, VA 23226
Goydos, Paul	Integrated Sports Intl.	One Meadows Plaza	East Rutherford, NJ 07073
Graham, Lou	Intl. Licensing & Mgmt.	10880 Wilshire Blvd.	Los Angeles, CA 90024
Graham, Paul	PTG, Inc.	1219 Devine Street	Columbia, SC 29205
Gray, Gary	Piper and Gray Enterprises	600 Kenrick, Suite #C-26	Houston, TX 77060
Green, Hubert	IMG	1360 East 9th Street	Cleveland, OH 44114
Green, Jimmy	Benchmark SEG	2300 Computer Ave.	Willow Grove, PA 19090
Green, Ken	Kevin Richardson	1551 Forum Pl.	West Palm Beach, FL 33401
Groh, Gary	IMG	1360 East 9th Street	Cleveland, OH 44114
Gross, Drew	ProLink	The Harvard Bldg.	Pinehurst, NC 28374
Gullion, Joey	Signature Sports Group	801 Park Avenue	Minneapolis, MN 55404
Gump, Scott	Imani Sports, LLC	800 Washington Ave. N.	Minneapolis, MN 55401
Haas, Freddie	Ted Haas	147 E. Oakridge Park	Metairie, LA 70005
Haas, Jay	Players Group, Inc.	1851 Alexander Bell Dr.	Reston, VA 20191-4345
Hall, Walter	Pros, Inc.	7100 Forest Ave.	Richmond, VA 23226
Hallberg, Gary	K&E Golf Productions	9457 S. University	Highlands Ranch, CO 80126
Halldorson, Dan	Dick Lloyd	93339 East Paraiso Drive	Scottsdale, AZ 85255
Hammond, Donnie	Intl. Resource Group, Ltd.	P.O. Box 1326	Los Angeles, CA 90049

Hancock, Phil	Ed Curtis, III	915 Main Street	Evansville, IN 47708
Harrington, Dennis	Links Mgmt. Group, Inc.	5068 W. Plano Parkway	Plano, TX 75093
Hart, Dudley	IMG	1360 East 9th Street	Cleveland, OH 44114
Hart, Steve	Runnymede Sports Mgmt.	35 Park Avenue	Dayton, OH 45419
Hatalsky, Morris	Signature Sports Group	801 Park Avenue	Minneapolis, MN 55404
Hayes, J.P.	Integrated Sports Intl.	One Meadows Plaza	East Rutherford, NJ 07073
Hayes, Larry	Runnymede Sports Mgmt.	35 Park Avenue	Dayton, OH 45419
Heard, Jerry	Cross Consulting	5 Cathy Place	Melno Park, CA 94025
Heinen, Mike	TwinHill Golf Company	1255 B Park Avenue	Emeryville, CA 94608
Heintz, Bob	Pros, Inc.	7100 Forest Ave.	Richmond, VA 23226
Hendrickson, Dick	On the Tee, Inc	19 Huntly Drive	Palm Beach Gardens, FL 33418
Henke, Nolan	Players Group, Inc.	1851 Alexander Bell Dr.	Reston, VA 20191-4345
Henning, Harold	Pinnacle Enterprises, Inc.	8221 Old Courthouse Rd.	Vienna, VA 22182
Henninger, Brian	Pros, Inc.	7100 Forest Ave.	Richmond, VA 23226
Henry, J.J.	IMG	1360 East 9th Street	Cleveland, OH 44114
Herron, Alissa	Signature Sports Group	801 Park Avenue	Minneapolis, MN 55404
Herron, Tim	Signature Sports Group	801 Park Avenue	Minneapolis, MN 55404
Hietala, Ryan	Cross Consulting	5 Cathy Place	Melno Park, CA 94025
Higashi, Satoshi	Bridgestone Sports	15320 Ind. Park Blvd. N.E.	Covington, GA 30014
Hill, Guy	SFX Sports Group	5335 Wisconsin Ave. N.W.	Washington, D.C. 20015
Hill, Peter	Pinnacle Enterprises, Inc.	8221 Old Courthouse Rd.	Vienna, VA 22182
Hinkle, Lon	Gaylord Sports Mgmt.	14646 N. Kierland Blvd.	Scottsdale, AZ 85254
Hinson, Larry	Stephanie Diane Burton	879 Cherry Street; #1	Macon, GA 31201
Hjertstedt, Gabriel	IMG	1360 East 9th Street	Cleveland, OH 44114
Hoch, Scott	SFX Sports Group	5335 Wisconsin Ave. N.W.	Washington, D.C. 20015
Holtgrieve, Jim	Pros, Inc.	7100 Forest Ave.	Richmond, VA 23226
Howell, Jamie	Links Mgmt. Group, Inc.	5068 W. Plano Parkway	Plano, TX 75093
Howison, Ryan	Benchmark SEG	2300 Computer Ave.	Willow Grove, PA 19090
Hughes, Bradley	Gaylord Sports Mgmt.	14646 N. Kierland Blvd.	Scottsdale, AZ 85254
Hulbert, Mike	Pros, Inc.	7100 Forest Ave.	Richmond, VA 23226
Huston, John	Elliot Consulting	6481 Taeda Drive	Sarasota, FL 34241
Hyland, Scott	Tour Talent	843 N. Cleveland-Massillon	Akron, OH 44333
Irwin, Hale	Hale Irwin Golf Design	8800 Gainey Center Dr.	Scottsdale, AZ 85258
Jacklin, Tony	Astrid Jacklin	415 E. Washington St.	Lewisburg, WV 24901
Jacobs, John	Cross Consulting	5 Cathy Place	Melno Park, CA 94025
Jacobsen, Peter	Peter Jacobsen Prod.	8700 SW Nimbus Ave.	Beaverton, OR 97008
Janzen, Lee	SportsLink Consulting	545 Delaney Ave.	Orlando, FL 32801
Jim Thorpe	GolfServ, Inc.	632 Stonefield Loop	Heathrow, FL 32746
JobeBrant	IMG	1360 East 9th Street	Cleveland, OH 44114
Johansson, Per-Ulrik	Parallel Murray Mgmt. Ltd.	56 Ennismore Gardens	London England SW7 1AJ
John Wilson	Links Mgmt. Group, Inc.	5068 W. Plano Parkway	Plano, TX 75093
Johnson, George	T&J Ventures	P.O. Box 11375	Winston-Salem, NC 27116
Johnson, John	Kerri Kaiser	236 Hemlock Street	Oxnard, CA 93033
Johnston, Jimmy	Pros, Inc.	7100 Forest Ave.	Richmond, VA 23226
Johnston, Mark	Total Sports, Inc.	1133 Mission Ridge Ct.	Orlando, FL 32835
Jones, Kent	Signature Sports Group	801 Park Avenue	Minneapolis, MN 55404
Jones, Steve	Marlo Millikin	1627 W. Main Street	Bozeman, MT 59715
Jordan, Pete	Adam Lenkin, Esq.	4644 Reservoir Road, N.W.	Washington, DC 20007
Jurgensen, Steve	Eustis Benefits	Three Riverway	Houston, TX 77056
Kanada, Craig	Links Mgmt. Group, Inc.	5068 W. Plano Parkway	Plano, TX 75093
Katz, Richard	Pinnacle Enterprises, Inc.	8221 Old Courthouse Rd.	Vienna, VA 22182
Kaye, Johnathan	Integrated Sports Intl.	One Meadows Plaza	East Rutherford, NJ 07073
Kazami, Hiroshi	Vis A Vision	38 E. 64th Street, #6	New York, NY 10021
Kelly, Jan	Links Mgmt. Group, Inc.	5068 W. Plano Parkway	Plano, TX 75093
Kelly, Jerry	Cross Consulting	5 Cathy Place	Melno Park, CA 94025
Kendrick, Jill	Players Group, Inc.	1851 Alexander Bell Dr.	Reston, VA 20191-4345
Kite, Tom	Pros, Inc.	7100 Forest Ave.	Richmond, VA 23226
Kiyabu, Sachiko	Vis A Vision	38 E. 64th Street, #6	New York, NY 10021
Knox, Kenny	Sports Properties, Ltd.	8708 Tantallon Circle	Tampa, FL 33647-2240
Koch, Gary	Pros, Inc.	7100 Forest Ave.	Richmond, VA 23226
Kostis, Peter	Tour Talent	843 N. Cleveland-Massillon	Akron, OH 44333
Kraft, Greg	IMG	1360 East 9th Street	Cleveland, OH 44114
Kratzert, Billy	Tour Talent	843 N. Cleveland-Massillon	Akron, OH 44333
Kuehne, Hank	IMG	1360 East 9th Street	Cleveland, OH 44114

La Voie, Fran	Johnny Miller Enterprises	P.O. Box 2260	Napa, CA 94558
Lancaster, Neal	Image Marketing, Inc.	1428 Orchard Lake Dr.	Charlotte, N.C. 28270
Langer, Bernhard	IMG	Pier House Strand	Chiswick, London W4-3NN
Langham, Franklin	Career Sports Mgmt.	200 Galleria Parkway	Atlana, GA 30339
Laoretti, Larry	Vantage Sports Mgmt.	40 Wall Street	New York, NY 10005
Lee, Patrick	Links Mgmt. Group, Inc.	5068 W. Plano Parkway	Plano, TX 75093
Leen, Randy	Imani Sports, LLC	800 Washington Ave. N.	Minneapolis, MN 55401
Leggatt, Ian	PrioritySport	1515 N. Federal Hwy.	Boca Raton, FL 33432
Lehman, James M.	Signature Sports Group	801 Park Avenue	Minneapolis, MN 55404
Lehman, Tom	Signature Sports Group	801 Park Avenue	Minneapolis, MN 55404
Leonard, Justin	Pros, Inc.	7100 Forest Ave.	Richmond, VA 23226
Lickliter, Frank	SportsLink Consulting	545 Delaney Ave.	Orlando, FL 32801
Limbaugh, Tommy	SportsLink Consulting	545 Delaney Ave.	Orlando, FL 32801
Lohr, Bob	Bob Lohr	5156 City St. #125	Orlando, Fl 32839
Loustalot, Tim	Timothy P. Flynn	3291 N. Buffalo Drive	Las Vegas, NV 89128
Love, Davis	Pros, Inc.	7100 Forest Ave.	Richmond, VA 23226
Lovio, Tresa	Run Wild Sports, Inc.	100 Mulberry Lane	Pittsburgh, PA 15235
Lowery, Steve	Total Sports, Inc.	1133 Mission Ridge Ct.	Orlando, FL 32835
Lunstrom, David	ProLink	The Harvard Bldg.	Pinehurst, NC 28374
Lye, Mark	Adam Lenkin, Esq.	4644 Reservoir Road, N.W.	Washington, DC 20007
Magee, Andrew	IMG	1360 East 9th Street	Cleveland, OH 44114
Maggert, Jeff	IMG	1360 East 9th Street	Cleveland, OH 44114
Maginnes, John	Tour Talent	843 N. Cleveland-Massillon	Akron, OH 44333
Mahaffey, John	IMG	1360 East 9th Street	Cleveland, OH 44114
Maltbie, Rodger	SFX Sports Group	5335 Wisconsin Ave. N.W.	Washington, D.C. 20015
Maraghy, Dave	Sports Mgmt. Intl, Inc.	105 Doverland Road	Richmond, VA 23229
Marquina, Jose	Strategies & Solutions	2655 Lejeune Road	Coral Gables, FL 33134
Marsh, Graham	Mark Amundson	6829 Honeysuckle Ct.	Sioux Falls, SD 57106
Martin, Casey	Imani Sports, LLC	800 Washington Ave. N.	Minneapolis, MN 55401
Martin, Doug	IMG	1360 East 9th Street	Cleveland, OH 44114
Mascatello, John	SFX Sports Group	5335 Wisconsin Ave. N.W.	Washington, D.C. 20015
Mast, Dick	Imani Sports, LLC	800 Washington Ave. N.	Minneapolis, MN 55401
May, Bob	IMG	1360 East 9th Street	Cleveland, OH 44114
Mayfair, Billy	Gaylord Sports Mgmt.	14646 N. Kierland Blvd.	Scottsdale, AZ 85254
McCann, Ronnie	Marc J. Chamberland	112 Weston Road	Ft. Lauderdale, FL 33326
McCarron, Scott	Cross Consulting	5 Cathy Place	Melno Park, CA 94025
McClenaghan, Eric	Chi Chi Rodriguez Mgmt.	3916 Clock Point Circle	Stow, OH 44224
McCord, Gary	Tour Talent	843 N. Cleveland-Massillon	Akron, OH 44333
McCumber, Mark	McCumber Golf	P.O. Box 7879	Jacksonville, FL 32238-0879
McGovern, James	SportsLink Consulting	545 Delaney Ave.	Orlando, FL 32801
McRoy, Spike	Adam Lenkin, Esq.	4644 Reservoir Road, N.W.	Washington, DC 20007
Mediate, Rocco	Gaylord Sports Mgmt.	14646 N. Kierland Blvd.	Scottsdale, AZ 85254
Melnyk, Steve	Sports Partners, Inc.	719 Vassar Street	Orlando, FL 32804
Menyes, Tom	Tour Talent	843 N. Cleveland-Massillon	Akron, OH 44333
Micheel, Shaun	Creative Sports Mgmt.	2835 Townsgate Rd.	Westlake Village, CA 91361
Mickelson, Phil	Gaylord Sports Mgmt.	14646 N. Kierland Blvd.	Scottsdale, AZ 85254
Mikesell, Beverly	Larry Nelson Enterprises	P.O. Box 674646	Marietta, GA 30006-0002
Miller, Johnny	Johnny Miller Enterprises	P.O. Box 2260	Napa, CA 94558
Mitchell, Stiles	Signature Sports Group	801 Park Avenue	Minneapolis, MN 55404
Mize, Larry	Signature Sports Group	801 Park Avenue	Minneapolis, MN 55404
Montgomerie, Colin	IMG	Pier House Strand	Chiswick, London W4-3NN
Moody, Orville	IMG	1360 East 9th Street	Cleveland, OH 44114
Moorman, David	SportsLink Consulting	545 Delaney Ave.	Orlando, FL 32801
Morgan, Gil	Gil Morgan, Ltd.	P.O. Box 806	Edmond, OK 73083
Morgan, John	Armstrong Mgmt. Group	Two Soundview Drive	Greenwich, CT 06830
Morgan, Kelly	Gil Morgan, Ltd.	P.O. Box 806	Edmond, OK 73083
Morgan, Walter	Geraldine T. Morgan	136 Governors Road	Ponte Vedra Beach, FL 32082
Morris, Robert	Pinnacle Enterprises, Inc.	8221 Old Courthouse Rd.	Vienna, VA 22182
Moss, Perry	SFX Sports Group	5335 Wisconsin Ave. N.W.	Washington, D.C. 20015
Murphy, Bob	Tour Talent	843 N. Cleveland-Massillon	Akron, OH 44333
Murphy, Sean	Gene Murphy	1004 June Place	Lovington, N.M. 88260
Nelson, Larry	Larry Nelson Enterprises	P.O. Box 674646	Marietta, GA 30006-0002
Nemer, R.J.	Chi Chi Rodriguez Mgmt.	3916 Clock Point Circle	Stow, OH 44224
Nichols, Bobby	VIP Sports	15601 Triple Crown Ct.	Ft. Myers, FL 33912

Nichols, Rick	VIP Sports	15601 Triple Crown Ct.	Ft. Myers, FL 33912
Nicklaus, Gary	Golden Bear Intl, Inc.	11780 U.S. Hwy. 1	N. Palm Beach, FL 33408
Nicklaus, Jack	Golden Bear Intl, Inc.	11780 U.S. Hwy. 1	N. Palm Beach, FL 33408
Nimmer, Ann	Players Group, Inc.	1851 Alexander Bell Dr.	Reston, VA 20191-4345
Nobilo, Frank	IMG	1360 East 9th Street	Cleveland, OH 44114
Nolan, Keith	IMG	1360 East 9th Street	Cleveland, OH 44114
Norman, Greg	Great White Shark Entrpr.	501 North A1A	Jupiter, FL 33477
Norris, Tim	Edwards, Belk	6070 Gateway East	El Paso, TX 79905
North, Andy	IMG	1360 East 9th Street	Cleveland, OH 44114
O'Connor Jr., Christy	PrioritySport	1515 N. Federal Hwy.	Boca Raton, FL 33432
Ogilvie, Joe	Chi Chi Rodriguez Mgmt.	3916 Clock Point Circle	Stow, OH 44224
Ogrin, David	Signature Sports Group	801 Park Avenue	Minneapolis, MN 55404
Olazabal, Jose Maria	Sergio Gomez	Apartado 26	San Sebastian, Spain 20080
O'Meara, Mark	IMG	1360 East 9th Street	Cleveland, OH 44114
Oosterhuis, Peter	Tour Talent	843 N. Cleveland-Massillon	Akron, OH 44333
Ozaki, Joe	Turner Communications	1234 W. Cove Drive	Gilbert, AZ 85233
Ozaki, Joel	Imani Sports, LLC	800 Washington Ave. N.	Minneapolis, MN 55401
Palmer, Arnold	Arnold Palmer Enterprises	P.O. Box 52	Youngstown, PA 15696
Pappas, Deane	SFX Sports Group	5335 Wisconsin Ave. N.W.	Washington, D.C. 20015
Parker, David K.	Links Mgmt. Group, Inc.	5068 W. Plano Parkway	Plano, TX 75093
Parker, Thomas	Pros, Inc.	7100 Forest Ave.	Richmond, VA 23226
Parnevik, Jesper	IMG	1360 East 9th Street	Cleveland, OH 44114
Parry, Craig	IMG	1360 East 9th Street	Cleveland, OH 44114
Pate, Jerry	Jerry Pate Golf	100 E. Robert Road	Pensacola, FL 32534
Pate, Steve	Pros, Inc.	7100 Forest Ave.	Richmond, VA 23226
Paulson, Carl	Ned Paulson	216 B 72nd Street	Virginia Beach, VA 23451
Paulson, Dennis	Benchmark SEG	2300 Computer Ave.	Willow Grove, PA 19090
Pavin, Corey	Links Mgmt. Group, Inc.	5068 W. Plano Parkway	Plano, TX 75093
Peete, Calvin	Calvin Peete Enterprises	P.O. Box 2645	Ponte Vedra Beach, FL 32004
Peoples, David	Signature Sports Group	801 Park Avenue	Minneapolis, MN 55404
Perks, Craig	Guidry & Guidry	324 South Main Street	St. Martinville, LA 70582
Pernice, Tom	Greg Hood	5108 N. Maroa	Fresno, CA 93704
Perry, Chris	Signature Sports Group	801 Park Avenue	Minneapolis, MN 55404
Perry, Kenny	Links Mgmt. Group, Inc.	5068 W. Plano Parkway	Plano, TX 75093
Peterson, Tony	NB Asscociates	18034 Ventura Blvd.	Encino, CA 91316
Plate, Jerry	IMG	1360 East 9th Street	Cleveland, OH 44114
Player, Gary	Gary Player Group	3930 RCA Blvd.	Palm Beach Gardens, FL 33410
Pohl, Dan	Cross Consulting	5 Cathy Place	Melno Park, CA 94025
Pooley, Don	Signature Sports Group	801 Park Avenue	Minneapolis, MN 55404
Porter, Lee	Intl. Golf Partners	3300 PGA Boulevard	Palm Beach Gardens, FL 33410
Powell, Jimmy	Sports Marketing Group	930 Tahoe Blvd.	Incline Village, NV 89451
Price, Nick	Nick Price Group	900 S. U.S. Highway 1	Jupiter, FL 33477
Pride, Dickey	Intl. Golf Partners	3300 PGA Boulevard	Palm Beach Gardens, FL 33410
Purdy, Ted	Jim Purdy	10016 N. 55th Street	Scottsdale, AZ 85253
Purtzer, Tom	Players Group, Inc.	1851 Alexander Bell Dr.	Reston, VA 20191-4345
Quigley, Brett	PTG, Inc.	1219 Devine Street	Columbia, SC 29205
Quigley, Dana	IMG	1360 East 9th Street	Cleveland, OH 44114
Randolph, Sam	TwinHill Golf Company	1255 B Park Avenue	Emeryville, CA 94608
Raulerson, Charles	Signature Sports Group	801 Park Avenue	Minneapolis, MN 55404
Regaldo, Victor	Intl. Licensing & Mgmt.	10880 Wilshire Blvd.	Los Angeles, CA 90024
Reid, Mike	Pros, Inc.	7100 Forest Ave.	Richmond, VA 23226
Restino, John	The Legend Group	3290 RCA Blvd.	Palm Beach Gardens, FL 33410
Ricks, Charlie	PrioritySport	1515 N. Federal Hwy.	Boca Raton, FL 33432
Riley, Chirs	SFX Sports Group	5335 Wisconsin Ave. N.W.	Washington, D.C. 20015
Riley, Kevin	SFX Sports Group	5335 Wisconsin Ave. N.W.	Washington, D.C. 20015
Rilly, Terry	SFX Sports Group	5335 Wisconsin Ave. N.W.	Washington, D.C. 20015
Rinker, Larry	SFX Sports Group	5335 Wisconsin Ave. N.W.	Washington, D.C. 20015
Rinker, Lee	Intl. Golf Partners	3300 PGA Boulevard	Palm Beach Gardens, FL 33410
Roach, O. Lynn Jr.	Players Group, Inc.	1851 Alexander Bell Dr.	Reston, VA 20191-4345
Roberts, Loren	Links Mgmt. Group, Inc.	5068 W. Plano Parkway	Plano, TX 75093
Rocca, Costantino	Lake Lindero Country Club	5719 Lake Lindero Drive	Agoura Hills, CA 91301
Rodriguez, Anthony	Chi Chi Rodriguez Mgmt.	3916 Clock Point Circle	Stow, OH 44224
Rodriguez, Chi Chi	Chi Chi Rodriguez Mgmt.	3916 Clock Point Circle	Stow, OH 44224
Rollins, John	Pros, Inc.	7100 Forest Ave.	Richmond, VA 23226

Rosburg, Bob	IMG	1360 East 9th Street	Cleveland, OH 44114
Rose, Calarence	Keystone Marketing	101 S. Stratford Rd.	Winston-Salem, NC 27104
Royer, Hugh	Michael S. Seekings	177 Meeting Street	Charleston, SC 29401
Rummells, David	Creative Sports Mgmt.	2835 Townsgate Rd.	Westlake Village, CA 91361
Russell, Raymond	Parallel Murray Mgmt., Ltd.	56 Ennismore Gardens	London England SW7 1AJ
Rustand, Eric	Imani Sports, LLC	800 Washington Ave. N.	Minneapolis, MN 55401
Rymer, Charlie	Intl. Golf Partners	3300 PGA Boulevard	Palm Beach Gardens, FL 33410
Sabbatini, Rory	Burt Kinert & Associates	5355 E. Williams Cr.	Tucson, AZ 85711
Sanders, Doug	Doug Sanders Enterprises	8828 Sandringham	Houston, TX 77024
Sanders, Jeff	Jeff Sanders Promotions	5671 S.W. Artic Drive	Beaverton, OR 97005-4153
Scherrer, George	George Scherrer Mgmt.	3394 Eastlake Road	Skaneateles, N.Y. 13152
Scherrer, Tom	George Scherrer Mgmt.	3394 Eastlake Road	Skaneateles, N.Y. 13152
Schroeder, John	Cross Consulting	5 Cathy Place	Melno Park, CA 94025
Schulz, Ted	Signature Sports Group	801 Park Avenue	Minneapolis, MN 55404
Schwarzrock, Brent	SFX Sports Group	5335 Wisconsin Ave. N.W.	Washington, D.C. 20015
Seawell, David	Benchmark SEG	2300 Computer Ave.	Willow Grove, PA 19090
Senior, Peter	IMG	1360 East 9th Street	Cleveland, OH 44114
Shannon, Tim	Pay Pro Sports	2400 East Katella Ave.	Anaheim, CA 92806
Shearer, Bob	IMG- 281 Clarence Street	Sydney, NSW	2000 Australia
Shepherd, Rita	Nick Price Group	900 S. U.S. Highway 1	Jupiter, FL 33477
Siegel, Jeff	Vantage Sports Mgmt.	40 Wall Street	New York, NY 10005
Siegel, Scott	Vantage Sports Mgmt.	222 West Comstock Ave.	Winter Park, FL 32789
Sifford, Charles	Roisman Pro-Rep	31 Grand Street	Hartford, CT 06106-4692
Simpson, Scott	Signature Sports Group	801 Park Avenue	Minneapolis, MN 55404
Simpson, Tim	SFX Sports Group	5335 Wisconsin Ave. N.W.	Washington, D.C. 20015
Sindelar, Joey	IMG	1360 East 9th Street	Cleveland, OH 44114
Singh, Vijay	IMG	1360 East 9th Street	Cleveland, OH 44114
Skinner, Sonny	Creative Sports Mgmt.	2835 Townsgate Rd.	Westlake Village, CA 91361
Sluman, Jeff	Players Group, Inc.	1851 Alexander Bell Dr.	Reston, VA 20191-4345
Small, Mike	Signature Sports Group	801 Park Avenue	Minneapolis, MN 55404
Small, Shirley	Pros, Inc.	7100 Forest Ave.	Richmond, VA 23226
Smith, Chirs	Pros, Inc.	7100 Forest Ave.	Richmond, VA 23226
Smith, Eddie	PrioritySport	1515 N. Federal Hwy.	Boca Raton, FL 33432
Smith, Jerry	Outside the Box Marketing	7590 East Gray Road	Scottsdale, AZ 85260
Smith, Mike	Robert Martin	2713 Moffett Court	Plano, TX 75093
Snead, J. C.	Run Wild Sports, Inc.	100 Mulberry Lane	Pittsburgh, PA 15235
Snead, Sam Jr.	Sam Snead Enterprises	P.O. Box 741	Hot Springs, VA 24445
Sneed, Ed	IMG	1360 East 9th Street	Cleveland, OH 44114
Solomita, Andrea	Signature Sports Group	801 Park Avenue	Minneapolis, MN 55404
Spence, Craig	Gaylord Sports Mgmt.	14646 N. Kierland Blvd.	Scottsdale, AZ 85254
Sposa, Mike	Pros, Inc.	7100 Forest Ave.	Richmond, VA 23226
Spratley, Vernon	Pros, Inc.	7100 Forest Ave.	Richmond, VA 23226
Stadler, Graig	Players Group, Inc.	1851 Alexander Bell Dr.	Reston, VA 20191-4345
Standly, Mike	Signature Sports Group	801 Park Avenue	Minneapolis, MN 55404
Stankowski, Paul	Gaylord Sports Mgmt.	14646 N. Kierland Blvd.	Scottsdale, AZ 85254
Stiles, Darron	SFX Sports Group	5335 Wisconsin Ave. N.W.	Washington, D.C. 20015
Still, Ken	Linda Still	1210 Princeton	Fircrest, WA 98466
Stockton Jr., Dave	Cross Consulting	5 Cathy Place	Melno Park, CA 94025
Stockton, Dave	Cross Consulting	5 Cathy Place	Melno Park, CA 94025
Strange, Curtis	IMG	1360 East 9th Street	Cleveland, OH 44114
Stricker, Steve	IMG	1360 East 9th Street	Cleveland, OH 44114
Sullivan, Mike	Sports Mgmt. Intl., Inc.	105 Doverland Road	Richmond, VA 23229
Supple, Shane	Benchmark SEG	2300 Computer Ave.	Willow Grove, PA 19090
Sutherland, David	Pinnacle Enterprises, Inc.	8221 Old Courthouse Rd.	Vienna, VA 22182
Sutherland, Kevin	Integrated Sports Intl.	One Meadows Plaza	East Rutherford, NJ 07073
Sutton, Hal	Hal Sutton Management	212 Texas Street	Shreveport, LA 71101
Sweeney, Joel	Sports Marketing & Mgmt.	111 E. Kilbourn Ave.	Milwaukee, WI 53233
Tataurangi, Phil	IMG	1360 East 9th Street	Cleveland, OH 44114
Terjesen, Barry	Tour Talent	843 N. Cleveland-Massillon	Akron, OH 44333
Tesori, Paul	Benchmark SEG	2300 Computer Ave.	Willow Grove, PA 19090
Tewell, Doug	Links Mgmt. Group, Inc.	5068 W. Plano Parkway	Plano, TX 75093
Thompson, Leonard	Pinnacle Enterprises, Inc.	8221 Old Courthouse Rd.	Vienna, VA 22182
Thomson, Peter	Jack Cook, Jr.	P.O. Box 326	Austin, TX 78767

Thorsen, Jeff	SFX Sports Group	5335 Wisconsin Ave. N.W.	Washington, D.C. 20015
Tidland, Chris	IMG	1360 East 9th Street	Cleveland, OH 44114
Tolles, Tommy	Players Group, Inc.	1851 Alexander Bell Dr.	Reston, VA 20191-4345
Toms, David	Links Mgmt. Group, Inc.	5068 W. Plano Parkway	Plano, TX 75093
Toski, Bob	IMG	1360 East 9th Street	Cleveland, OH 44114
Trevino, Lee	Assured Mgmt. Co.	1901 West 47th Place	Westwood, KS 66205
Triplett, Kirk	Intl. Golf Partners	3300 PGA Boulevard	Palm Beach Gardens, FL 33410
Tryba, Ted	SFX Sports Group	5335 Wisconsin Ave. N.W.	Washington, D.C. 20015
Turner, Robert	Turner Communications	1234 W. Cove Drive	Gilbert, AZ 85233
Tway, Bob	Hambric Sports Mgmt.	2515 McKinney Ave.	Dallas, TX 75201
Twiggs, Greg	Signature Sports Group	801 Park Avenue	Minneapolis, MN 55404
Van Pelt, Bo	Players Group, Inc.	1851 Alexander Bell Dr.	Reston, VA 20191-4345
Vaughan, Bruce	Links Mgmt. Group, Inc.	5068 W. Plano Parkway	Plano, TX 75093
Venturi, Ken	Tour Talent	843 N. Cleveland-Massillon	Akron, OH 44333
Verplank, Scott	SFX Sports Group	5335 Wisconsin Ave. N.W.	Washington, D.C. 20015
Wadkins, Bobby	Pros, Inc.	7100 Forest Ave.	Richmond, VA 23226
Wadkins, Lanny	Pros, Inc.	7100 Forest Ave.	Richmond, VA 23226
Waite, Grant	IMG	1360 East 9th Street	Cleveland, OH 44114
Waldorf, Duffy	Intl. Golf Partners	3300 PGA Boulevard	Palm Beach Gardens, FL 33410
Wargo, Tom	SFX Sports Group	5335 Wisconsin Ave. N.W.	Washington, D.C. 20015
Warren, Charles	Pros, Inc.	7100 Forest Ave.	Richmond, VA 23226
Watson, Tom	Assured Mgmt. Co.	1901 West 47th Place	Westwood, KS 66205
Watts, Brian	Hambric Sports Mgmt.	2515 McKinney Ave.	Dallas, TX 75201
Weaver, DeWitt	Linksman Financial	7208 Sand Lake Rd.	Orlando, Fl 32819
Weilbring, D.A.	Golf Resources Group	1850 Crown Drive	Dallas, TX 75234
Weir, Mike	IMG 1 St. Clair Avenue E	Toronto, Ontario	Canada M4T 2V7
Weiskopf, Tom	IMG	1360 East 9th Street	Cleveland, OH 44114
Wentworth, Kevin	SFX Sports Group	5335 Wisconsin Ave. N.W.	Washington, D.C. 20015
Westwood, Lee	Intl. Sports Mgmt.	Stocks Lane, Over Peover	Cheshire, WA16 8TW England
Wi, Charlie	Creative Sports Mgmt.	2835 Townsgate Rd.	Westlake Village, CA 91361
Wiebe, Mark	SFX Sports Group	5335 Wisconsin Ave. N.W.	Washington, D.C. 20015
Wollmann, Chirs	Chi Chi Rodriguez Mgmt.	3916 Clock Point Circle	Stow, OH 44224
Wood, Willie	IMG	1360 East 9th Street	Cleveland, OH 44114
Woods, Tiger	IMG	1360 East 9th Street	Cleveland, OH 44114
Wrenn, Robert	Pros, Inc.	7100 Forest Ave.	Richmond, VA 23226
Zambri, Chris	Creative Sports Mgmt.	2835 Townsgate Rd.	Westlake Village, CA 91361
Zembriski, Walter	Lisa Zembriski Agamie	303 E. 7th Avenue	Windemere, FL 34786
Ziegler, Larry	Integrated Sports Intl.	One Meadows Plaza	East Rutherford, NJ 07073
Zinkon, Dennis	Adam Lenkin, Esq.	4644 Reservoir Road, N.W.	Washington, DC 20007
Zoeller, Fuzzy	Fuzzy Zoeller Prod.	12701 Covered Bridge Rd.	Shellersburg, IN 47172
Zokol, Richard	2605 Alma Street	Vancouver, BC	Canada V6R 3S1

The International Tennis Hall of Fame will forward autograph requests to inductees. Please use the following address:

Please Forward To:
(Name of Inductee)
International Tennis Hall of Fame
Newport Casino
Newport, RI 02840-3586

Alex Olmedo	John Newcombe
Angela Mortimer Barrett	Joseph F. Cullman
Ann Haydon Jones	Ken McGregor
Art Larsen	Ken Rosewall
Arthur W. "Bud" Collins	Lamar Hunt
Ashley Cooper	Lesley Turner Bowrey
Billie Jean King	Louise Brough Clapp
Bjorn Borg	Malcolm Anderson
Bob Falkenburg	Manuel Santana
Bob Hewitt	Margaret Osbourne du Pont
Chris Evert	Margaret Smith Court
Darlene Hard	Maria Bueno
Dennis Ralston	Martina Navratilova
Dick Savitt	Neale Fraser
Doris Hart	Nicola Pietrangeli
Evonne Goolagong Cawley	Pancho Segura
Frank Sedgman	Pauline Betz Addie
Fred Stolle	Robert Kelleher
Frew McMillan	Rod Laver
Gardnar Mulloy	Rosemary 'Rosie' Casals
Gene Mako	Roy Emerson
Gladys Heldman	Shirley Fry-Irvin
Guillermo Vilas	Sidney Wood
Hana Mandlikova	Stan Smith
Ilie Nastase	Ted Schroeder
Jack Kramer	Tony Roche
Jan Kodes	Tony Trabert
Jaroslav Drobny	Tracy Austin
Jimmy Connors	Vic Seixas
	Virginia Wade

These professional tennis players can be contacted at:

ATP Tours
201 ATP Tour Blvd.
Ponte Verda, FL 32082

Agassi, Andre (USA)
Bjorkman, Jonas (SWE)
Black, Byron (ZIM)
Bruguera, Sergi (ESP)
Chang, Michael (USA)
Chesnokov, Andrei (RUS)
Corretja, Alex (ESP)
Courier, Jim (USA)
Enqvist, Thomas (SWE)
Ferreira, Wayne (RSA)
Ferrero, Juan Carlos
Fromberg, Richard (AUS)
Furlan, Renzo (ITA)
Gambill, Jan-Michael (USA)
Golmard, Jerome (FRA)
Gustafsson, Magnus (SWE)
Haas, Tommy (GER)
Henman, Tim (GBR)
Hewitt, Lleyton (AUS)
Ivanisevic, Goran (CRO)
Johansson, Thomas (SWE)
Kafelnikov, Yevgeny (RUS)
Kiefer, Nicolas (GER)
Koubek, Stefan (AUT)
Krajicek, Richard (NED)
Kroslak, Jan (SVK)
Kucera, Karol (SVK)

Kuerten, Gustavo
Kulti, Nicklas (SWE)
Lapentti, Nicolas (ECU)
Larsson, Magnus (SWE)
Martin, Todd (USA)
Medvedev, Andrei (UKR)
Moya, Carlos (ESP)
Norman, Magnus (SWE)
Novak, Jiri (CZE)
O'Brien, Alex (USA)
Pavel, Andrei (ROM)
Pescosolido, Stefano (ITA)
Philippoussis, Mark (AUS)
Pioline, Cedric (FRA)
Pozzi, Gianluca (ITA)
Puerta, Mariano
Rafter, Patrick (AUS)
Rios, Marcelo (CHI)
Rosset, Marc (SUI)
Rusedski, Greg (GBR)
Safin, Marat
Sampras, Pete (UAU)
Santoro, Fabrice (FRA)
Schalken, Sjeng (NED)
Siemerink, Jan (NED)
Tarango, Jeff (USA)
Woodforde, Mark (AUS)

Allison, Bobby	Bobby Allison Racing	140 Church Street	Hueytown, AL 35020
Andretti, John	Petty Enterprises	311 Branson Mill Rd.	Randleman, NC 27317
Andretti, Michael	Team Green	7615 Zionsville Rd.	Indianapolis, IN 46268
Atwood, Casey	Ultra Motorsports	6007 Victory Lane	Harrisburg, NC 28075
Barrichello, Rubens	Ferrari SpA	Via Ascari 55/57	41053 Maranello, Italy
Barron, Alex	Blair Racing	8227 Northwest Blvd., Suite 300	Indianapolis, IN 46278
Beechler, Donnie	A.J. Foyt Enterprises	19480 Stokes Rd.	Waller, TX 77484
Bell, Townsend	Visteon/Patrick Racing	8431 Georgetown Rd.	Indianapolis, IN 46268
Benson, Johnny	MBV Mototsports	3805 Downwind Blvd.	Concord, NC 28027
Bernoldi, Enrique	Arrows Grand Prix Intl.	Leafield Tech. Ctre Oakland Place	Oxon OX8 5PF England
Blaney, Dave	Jasper Motorsports	110 Knob Hill Rd.	Mooresville, NC 28117
Boat, Billy	Curb/Agajanian Racing	23045 North 15th Ave.	Phoenix, AZ 85027
Bodine, Brett	Scandia Bodine Racing	304 Performance Rd.	Mooresville, NC 28115
Bodine, Todd	Carter/Haas Racing	2670 Peachtree Rd.	Statesville, NC 28625
Brack, Kenny	Target/Chip Ganassi Racing	3821 Industrial Rd.	indianapolis, IN 46254
Buhl, Robbie	Dreyer & Reinbold Racing	4500 W. 99th St.	Indianapolis, IN 46268
Burton, Jeff	Roush Racing	122 Knob Hill Road	Mooresville, NC 28115
Burton, Ward	Bill Davis Racing	300 Old Thomasville Rd.	High Point, NC 27260
Busch, Kurt	Roush Racing	7050 Aviation Blvd.	Concord, NC 28078
Button, Jenson	Benetton Formula Ltd.	Whiteways Tech. Ctre Enstone Chipping	Norton Oxon OX7 4EE Eng.
Calkins, Buzz	Bradley Motorsports	4381 W. 96th St.	Indianapolis, IN 46268
Carpentier, Patrick	Player's/Forsythe Racing	7231 Georgetown Rd.	Indianapolis, IN 46268
Castroneves, Helio	Marlboro Team Penske	366 Penske Plaza	Reading, PA 19602
Cheever, Eddie Jr.	Cheever Indy Racing	8435 Georgetown Rd., Suite 600	Indianapolis, IN 46268
Compton, Stacey	A.J. Foyt Racing	128 Commercial Dr.	Mooresville, NC 28115
Coulthard, David	McLaren International	Unit 22, Woking Business Park Albert Drive	Woking Surrey GU21 5JY England
Craven, Ricky	Precision Preparation	3051 First Ave. Court SE	Hickory, NC 28602
da Matta, Cristiano	Newman/Haas Racing	500 Tower Parkway	Lincolnshire, IL 60069
de la Rosa, Pedro	Jaguar Racing	16 Tanners Dr. Blakelands Milton-Keynes	Bucks MK14 5BW England
Dixon, Scott	PacWest Racing	4001 Methanol Lane	Indianapolis, IN 46268
Dominguez, Mario	Herdez Competition	57A Gasoline Alley	Indianapolis, IN 46222
Earnhardt, Dale Jr.	Dale Earnhardt Inc.	1675 Coddle Creek Hwy.	Mooresville, NC 28115
Elliot, Bill	Everham Motorsports	7100 Weddington Road	Harrisburg, NC 28076
Fernandez, Adrian	Fernandez Racing	6950 Guion Rd., Suite 51	Indianapolis, IN 46268
Ferran, Gilde	Marlboro Team Penske	366 Penske Plaza	Reading, PA 19602
Fisher, Sarah	Walker Racing	4035 Championship Dr.	Indianapolis, IN 46268
Fisichella, Giancarlo	Jordan Grand Prix	Buckingham Rd., Silverstone	Norhants NN12 8TJ England
Fittipaldi, Christian	Newman/Haas Racing	500 Tower Parkway	Lincolnshire, IL 60069
Fittipaldi, Emerson	C/O Fittipaldi USA	950 So. Miami Ave.	Miami, FL 33130
Foyt, A.J.	6415 Toledo	Houston, TX 77008	
Franchitti, Dario	Team Green	7615 Zionsville Rd.	Indianapolis, IN 46268
Frentzen, Heinz-Harald	Arrows Grand Prix Intl.	Leafield Technical Centre Oakland Place	Oxon OX8 5PF England
Giaffone, Felipe	Hollywood Mo Nunn Racing	2920 Fortune Circle West, Suite E	Indianapolis, IN 46241
Gordon, Jeff	Hendrick Motorsports	4433 Papa Joe Hendrick Blvd.	Harrisburg, NC 28075
Gordon, Robby	Richard Childress Racing	236 Industrial Dr.	Welcome, Nc 27374

Green, Jeff	Richard Childress Racing	236 Industrial Dr.	Welcome, NC 27374
Hamilton, Bobby	Andy Petree Racing	1101 Upward Rd.	Flat Rock, NC 28731
Harvick, Kevin	RCR Team 3	236 Industrial Dr.	Welcome, NC 27374
Heidfeld, Nick	PP Sauber AG	Wildbachstrasse 9, 8340 Hinwil	Switzerland
Herb, Jon	Racing Professionals	1800 N. Meridian St.	Indianapolis, IN 46202
Hornish, Sam Jr.	Panther Racing	5101 Decatur Blvd., Suite P	Indianapolis, IN 26241
Irvan, Ernie	C/O Nasscar	1801 Nolusia	Daytona Beach, FL 32120
Irvine, Eddie	Jaguar Racing	16 Tanners Dr. Blakelands Milton-Keynes	Bucks MK14 5BW England
Jarrett, Dale	Robert Yates Racing	115 Dwelle St.	Charlotte, NC 28208
Johncock, Gordon	931 Bedtelyon Road	West Branch, MI 48661	
Johnson, Jimmy	Hendrick Motorsports	4443 Papa Joe Hendrick Blvd.	Harrisburg, NC 28075
Jones, Buckshot	Petty Enterprises	311 Branson Mill Rd.	Randleman, NC 27317
Jones, Parnelli	20550 Earl Street	Torrance, CA 90503	
Jourdain, Michel Jr.	Team Rahal	4601 Lyman Dr.	Hilliard, OH 43026
Junquiera, Bruno	Target/Chip Ganassi Racing	3821 Industrial Rd.	Indianapolis, IN 46254
Kanaan, Tony	Mo Nunn Racing	150 Gasoline Alley	Indianapolis, IN 46222
Kenseth, Matt	Roush Racing	7050 Aviation Blvd.	Concord, NC 28027
Kite, Jimmy	Team Scandia	701 S. Girls School Rd.	Indianapolis, IN 46231
Labonte, Bobby	Joe Gibbs Racing	13415 Reese Blvd.	Huntersville, NC 28078
Labonte, Terry	Hendrick Motorsports	4414 Papa Joe Hendrick Blvd.	Harrisburg, NC 28075
Lazier, Buddy	Hemelgarn Racing	130 Gasoline Alley	Indianapolis, IN 46222
Lazier, Jaques	701 Girls School Rd.	Indianapolis, IN 46231	
Lazzaro, Anthony	Sam Schmidt Motorsports	2202 Chatsworth Court	Henderson, NV 89014
Luyendyk, Arie	Treadway/Hubbard Racing	7991 W. 91st St., Building C	Indianapolis, IN 46214
Marcis, Dave	Marcis Auto Racing	71 Beale Rd.	Arden, NC 28704
Marlin, Sterling	Ganassi Racing	114 Meadow Hill Circle	Mooresville, NC 28115
Martin, Mark	Roush Racing	122 Knob Hill Road	Mooresville, NC 28115
Massa, Felipe	PP Sauber AG	Wildbachstrasse 9, 8340 Hinwil	Switzerland
Mast, Rick	Donlavey Racing	5011 Old Midlothian Pike	Richmond, VA 23224
Mayfield, Jeremy	Ray Evernham Motorsports	7100 Weddington Road	Harrisburg, NC 28076
McGehee, Robby	Cahill Racing	3330 Southgate Court, S.W.	Cedar Rapids, IA 52404
McNish, Allan	Toyota Motorsport GmbH	Toyota-Allee 7	50858 Koln, Germany
Mears, Rick	204 Spyglass Lane	Jupiter, Fl 33477	
Mears, Roger	PO Box 20729	Bakersfield, CA 93390	
Miller, Jack	Crest Racing Services	30F Gasoline Alley	Indianapolis, IN 46222
Montoya, Juan Pablo	BMW WilliamsF1	Grove, Wantage, Oxfordshire	OX12 0DQ England
Moran, Rocky Jr.	Cunningham Racing	7991 W. 21st St., Building B-1	Indianapolis, IN 46214
Muldowney, Shirley	79559 North Avenue	Armada, MI 48005	
Nadeau, Jerry	Hendrick Motorsports	4423 Papa Joe Hendrick Blvd.	Harrisburg, NC 28075
Nakano, Shinji	Fernandez Racing	6950 Guion Rd., Suite 51	Indianapolis, IN 46268
Nemechek, Joe	Travis Carter Enterprises	2668 Peachtree Rd.	Statesville, NC 28625
Newman, Ryan	Penske Racing South	156 Knob Hill Rd.	Mooresville, NC 28115
Panis, Olivier	British American Racing	Brackley, Northamptonshire	NN13 7BD England
Papis, Max	Sigma Autosport	7800 W. 71st St.	Bridgeview, IL 60455
Paul, John Jr.	PDM Racing	8135 Crawfordsville Rd	Indianapolis, IN 46214

Peck, Tom	PO Box 249	McConnersburg, PA 17233	
Petty, Kyle	Petty Enterprises	311 Branson Mill Rd.	Randleman, NC 27317
Petty, Richard	Route 3 Box 631	Randleman, NC 27317	
Prudhomme, Don	C/O NHRA	2035 Financial Way	Glendora, CA 91740
Rahal, Bobby	934A Cresent Blvd	Glenellyn, IL 60137	
Raikkonen, Kimi	McLaren International	Unit 22, Woking Business Park Albert Dr.	Woking Surrey GU21 5JY Eng.
Rathmann, Jim	14 Marina Iseles Blvd	Indian Harbor Beach, FL	32937
Ray, Greg	Kelly Racing	6803 Coffman Rd.	Indianapolis, IN 46268
Redon, Laurent	Mi-Jack/Conquest Racing	8010 Woodland Dr.	Indianapolis, IN 46278
Robertson, T. Wayne	C/O Nascar	1811 Volusia Avenue	Daytona Beach, FL 32015
Rudd, Ricky	Robert Yates Racing	292 Rolling Hills Rd.	Mooresville, NC 28117
Rutherford, Johnny	4919 Black Oak Lane	Fort Worth, TX 76114	
Sadler, Elliot	Wood Brothers Racing	21 Performance Dr.	Stuart, VA 24171
Salazar, Eliseo	A.J. Foyt Enterprises	19480 Stokes Rd.	Waller, TX 77484
Salo, Mika	Toyota Motorsport GmbH	Toyota-Allee 7	50858 Koln, Germany
Sato, Takuma	Jordan Grand Prix	Buckingham Rd., Silverstone	Norhants NN12 8TJ England
Schrader, Ken	MB2 Motorsports	185 McKenzie Rd.	Mooresville, NC 28115
Schroeder, Jeret	RDM Racing	8135 Crawfordsville Rd.	Indianapolis, IN 46214
Schumacher, Michael	Ferrari SpA	Via Ascari 55/57	41053 Maranello, Italy
Schumacher, Ralf	BMW WilliamsF1	Grove, Wantage, Oxfordshire	OX12 ODQ England
Sharp, Scott	Kelly Racing	6803 Coffman Rd.	Indianapolis, IN 46268
Shelby, Carroll	C/O Shelby Enterprises	19020 Anelo Avenue	Gardena, CA 90248
Skinner, Mike	Morgan-McClure Motorsports	26502 Newbanks Rd.	Abingdon, VA 24210
Sneva, Tom	3301 E. Valley Vista Lane	Paradise Valley, AZ 85253	
Spencer, Jimmy	Ganassi Racing	114 Meadow Hill Circle	Mooresville, NC 28115
Stewart, Tony	Joe Gibbs Racing	13415 Reese Blvd.	Huntersville, NC 28078
Stricklin, Hut	Bill Davis Racing	300 Old Thomasville Rd.	High Point, NC 27260
Sullivan, Danny	891 Washington Road	Grosse Pointe, Mi 48230	
Tagliani, Alex	Player's/Forsythe Racing	7231 Georgetown Rd.	Indianapolis, IN 46268
Takagi, Toranosuke	Walker Racing	4035 Championship Dr.	Indianapolis, IN 46268
Tracy, Paul	Team Green	7615 Zionsville Rd.	Indianapolis, IN 46268
Treadway, Rick	Treadway/Hubbard Racing	7991 W. 91st St., Building C	Indianapolis, IN 46214
Trulli, Jarno	Benetton Formula Ltd.	Whiteways Technical Ctre Enstone Chipping	Norton Oxon OX7 4EE England
Tyler, Brian	Chitwood Motorsports	4410 West Alva Street	Tampa, FL 33614
Unser, Al Jr.	Galles Racing	1300 Lomas Blvd.	Albuquerque, NM 87102
Unser, Al Sr.	7625 Central NW	Albuquerque, NM 87121	
Vasser, Jimmy	Team Rahal	4601 Lyman Dr.	Hilliard, OH 43026
Villeneuve, Jacques	British American Racing	Brackley, Northamptonshire	NN13 7BD England
Wallace, Kenny	Dale Earnhardt Inc.	1675 Coddle Creek Hwy.	Mooresville, NC 28115
Wallace, Mike	Andy Petree Racing	908 Upward Rd.	East Flat Rock, NC 28731
Wallace, Rusty	Penske Racing South	136 Knob Hill Road	Mooresville, NC 28115
Waltrip, Darrell	DARWAL	PO Box 293	Harrisburg, NC 28075
Waltrip, Michael	Dale Earnhardt Inc.	1675 Coddle Creek Hwy.	Mooresville, NC 28115
Wattles, Stan	Metro Racing Systems	7980 S.W. Jack James Dr.	Stuart, FL 34997
Webber, Mark	Minardi Team SpA	Via Spallanzani 21	48018 Faenza, Italy
Yarborough, Cal	1801 Volusian Ave	Daytona Beach, FL 32015	
Yoong, Alex	Minardi Team SpA	Via Spallanzani 21	48018 Faenza, Italy

Babilonia, Tai	13889 Valley Vista Blvd	Sherman Oaks, CA 91423	
Bannister, Roger	1 Church Row	Wandswoth Plain	London SW18, England
Baiul, Oksana	William Morris Agency	1325 Ave of Americas	New York, NY 10019
Blair, Bonnie	1907 W. Springfield	Champaign, IL 61820	
Bobeck, Nicole	US Figure Skating Assoc	20 First Street	Colorado Springs, CO 80906
Boitano, Brian	# 370	101 First Street	Los Altos, CA 94022
Browning, Curt	11160 River Valley Road	Edmonton, Alberta	I 5J 2G7 Canada
Bubka, Sergia	Ukrainian Athletic Fed.	Esplanadna Street	252023 Kiev, Ukraine
Comaneci, Nadia	4421 Hidden Hill Rd	Norman OK 73072	
Conner, Bart	2325 Westwood Drive	Norman, OK 73069	
Cousins, Robin	27307 Hiway 189	Blue Jay, CA 92317	
Devers, Gail	JJK & Associates	3466 Bridgeland Drive	Bridgeton, MI 63044
Evens, Janet	US Swimming	One Olympic Plaza	Colorado Springs, CO 80909
Gaylord, Mitch	Po Box 15001	Beverly Hills, CA 90209	
Hamill, Dorothy	World Figure Skating	20 First Street	Colorado Springs, CO 80906
Heiden, Eric	3505 Blackhawk Dr	Madison, WI 53705	
Jenner, Bruce	25254 Eldorado Meadow	Road	Hidden Hills, CA 91302
Johnson, Michael	C/O Gold Medal Mgmt.	1350 Pine Street	Boulder, CO 80302
Kulik, Ilia	Michael V. Carlisle	24 East 64th Street	New York, NY 10021
Kwan, Michelle	Proper Marketing	44450 Pinetree Drive#103	Plymouth, Mi 48071
Lewis, Carl	PO Box 571990	Houston, TX 77257	
Lipinski, Tara	C/O Detroit Skating Club	888 Denison Court	Bloomfield Hills, MI 48302
Louganis, Greg	PO Box 4130	Malibu, CA 90264	
Mathias, Bob	7469 East Pine Avenue	Fresno, CA 93727	
Miller, Shannon	2136 N. 13th Street	Reading, PA 19604-1200	
O'Brien, Dan	C/O Gold Medal Mgmt.	1350 Pine Street	Boulder, CO 80302
Retton, Mary Lou	114 White Avenue	Fairmont, WV 26554-2068	
Rigby, Cathy	# 200	110 East Wilshire	Fullerton, CA 92632
Samuelson, Joan	C/O Edwin Whitmore	114A Massachusetts Ave.	Arlington, MA 02174
Spitz, Mark	383 Dalehurst	Los Angeles, CA 90024	
Street, Picabo	C/O US Ski Team	PO Box 100	Park City, UT 84060
Strug, Kerri	USA Gymnastics	201 S. Capitol	Indianapolis, IN 46225
Toomey, Bill	1185 Linda Vista Drive	San Marcos, Ca 92069	
Torrence, Gwen	Gold Medal Mgmt.	1350 Pine Street	Boulder, CO 80302
Torvill & Dean	Box 16 Beeston	Nottingham, NG9	England
Torvill & Dean	MBE PO Box 32	Heathfield, East Sussex	TN21 OBW, England
Yamaguchi, Kristi	3650 Montecito Drive	Fremont, CA 94536	
Zmeleskal, Kim	C/O Karoly's Gymnastics	17203 Bamwood	Houston, TX 77090

Olympic Hall of Fame

Write to your Olympic Athletes at:
(Name of Athlete)
U.S. Olympic Committee
1750 East Boulder Street
Colorado Springs, CO 80909

1956 Basketball Team
Dick Boushka, Carl Cain, Chuck Darling,
Bill Evens, Gib Ford, Burdy Haldorson,
Bill Hougland, Bob Jeangerard, K.C. Jones,
Bill Russell, Ron Tomsic, Jim Walsh,
coach & Gerald Tucker

1960 Basketball Team
Jay Arnette, Walt Bellamy, Bob Boozer,
Terry Dischinger, Burdy Haldorson, Darrall
Imhoff, Allen Kelley, +Lester Lane, Jerry
Lucas, Oscar Robertson, Adrian Smith,
Jerry West and coach Pete Newell.

1964 Basketball Team
Jim Barnes, Bill Bradley, Larry Brown, Joe
Caldwell, Mel Counts, Richard Davies,
Walt Hazzard, Luke Jackson, John
McCaffrey, Jeff Mullins, Jerry Shipp,
George Wilson and coach +Hank Iba.

1960 Ice Hockey Team
Billy Christian, Roger Christian, Billy Cleary,
Bob Cleary, Gene Grazia, Paul Johnson,
Jack Kirrane, John Mayasich, Jack
McCartan, Bob McKay, Dick Meredith,
Weldon Olson, Ed Owen, Rod Paavola,
Larry Palmer, Dick Rodenheiser, +Tom
Williams and coach Jack Riley.

1980 Ice Hockey Team
Bill Baker, Neal Broten, Dave Christian,
Steve Christoff, Jim Craig, Mike Eruzione,
John Harrington, Steve Janaszak, Mark
Johnson, Ken Morrow, Rob McClanahan,
Jack O'Callahan, Mark Pavelich, Mike
Ramsey, Buzz Schneider, Dave Silk, Eric
Strobel, Bob Suter, Phil Verchota, Mark
Wells and coach Herb Brooks.

Weight Lifting
Davis, John (Deceased)
Kono, Tommy

Alpine Skiing
Mahre, Phil

Bobsled
Eagan, Eddie

Boxing
Clay, Cassius
Eagan, Eddie
Foreman, George
Frazier, Joe
Leonard, Sugar Ray
Patterson, Floyd

Cycling
Carpenter-Phinney, Connie

Diving
King, Miki
Lee, Sammy
Louganis, Greg
McCormick, Pat

Figure Skating
Albright, Tenley
Button, Dick
Fleming, Peggy
Hamill, Dorothy
Hamilton, Scott

Gymnastics
Conner, Bart
Retton, Mary Lou
Vidmar, Peter

Rowing
Kelly, Jack Sr.

Speed Skating
Heiden, Eric

Wrestling
Gable, Dan

Swimming
Babashoff, Shirley
Caulkins, Tracy
Daniels, Charles
de Varona, Donna
Kahanamoku, Duke
Madison, Helene
Meyer, Debbie
Naber, John
Schollander, Don
Spitz, Mark
Weissmuller, Johnny (Deceased)

Track & Field
Beamon, Bob
Boston, Ralph
Calhoun, Lee (Deceased)
Campbell, Milt
Davenport, Willie
Davis, Glenn
Didrikson, Babe (Deceased)
Dillard, Harrison
Evans, Lee
Ewry, Ray (Deceased)
Fosbury, Dick
Jenner, Bruce
Johnson, Rafer
Kraenzlein, Alvin (Deceased)
Lewis, Carl
Mathias, Bob
Mills, Billy
Morrow, Bobby
Moses, Edwin
O'Brien, Parry
Oerter, Al
Owens, Jesse (Deceased)
Paddock, Charley Deceased)
Richards, Bob
Rudolph, Wilma (Deceased)
Sheppard, Mel (Deceased)
Shorter, Frank
Thorpe, Jim (Deceased)
Toomey, Bill
Tyus, Wyomia
Whitfield, Mal
Wykoff, Frank (Deceased)

Armstrong, Lance	Lance Armstrong Fdt.	PO. Box 27483	Austin, TX 78755
Austin, Steve	World Wrestling Federation	1241 Main Street	Stamford, Ct 06902
Baiul, Oksana	PO Box 577	Simsbury, CT	
Bannister, Roger	16 Edwards Square	London W8, UK	
Borg, Bjorn	# 1300	1360 East 9th Street	Cleveland, OH 44114
Capriati, Jennifer	Saddlebrook Resort	5700 Saddlebrook Way	Wesley Chapel, FL 33543
Carter, Don	9895 South West 96th Street	Miami, FL 33176	
Costas, Bob	c/o NBC Sports	30 Rokefeller Plaza	New York, NY 10012
Craig, Jim	36 North Main Street	North Easton, MA 02156	
de Varona, Donna	Women's Sports Foundation	Eisenhower Park	East Meadow, NY 11554
Eldredge, Todd	888 Denison Court	Bloomfield Hills, MI 48302	
Fawcett, Joy	WUSA - 15th Floor	6205 Peachtree Dunwoody Rd	Atlanta, GA 30328
Finch, Jennifer	Octagon Worldwide	1270 Avenue of the Americas	New York, NY 10020
Hamill, Dorothy	William Morris Agency	One William Morris Place	Beverly Hills, CA 90212
Hawks, Tony	William Morris Agency	1325 Avenue of Americas	New York, NY 10019
Jackson, Keith	Turner Sports	One CNN Center- 13 So Tower	Atlanta, GA 30303
James, Bill	Boston Red Sox	4 Yawkey Way	Boston, MA 02215-3496
Kournikova, Anna	Octagon Mgmt.	1114 Avenue of the Americas	New York, NY 10036
Kwan, Michelle	Proper Marketing Associates	39555 Orchard Hill Place	Novi, MI 48375
Lee, Jeanette	Jeanette Lee Foundation	1427 West 86th Street	Indianapolis, IN 46260
LeMond, Greg	# 1800 Proserv	1101 Wilson Blvd.	Arlington, VA 22209
Lipinski, Tara	Progressive Artists	400 South Beverly Dr., Ste. 216	Beverly Hills, CA 90212
McKay, Jim	2805 Sheppard Rd.	Monton, MD 21111	
Navratilova, Martina	Rainbow Endowment	1501 Cherry Street	Philadelphia, PA 19402
Pele	Ministry Extraordinario	de dos tres Poderes	70150-900 Brasilia D.F. Brasilia, Brazil
Rampone, Christine	US Soccer Federation	1801 S. Prairie Avenue	Chicago, IL 60616
Santos, Jose	Saratoga Racetrack	267 Union Avenue	Saratoga Springs, NY 12866
Scully, Vinn	1555 Capri Drive	Pacific Palisades, CA	02/25/47
Shorter, Frank	558 Utica Court	Boulder, CO 80304-0773	
Stevens, Gary	Intl. Creative Mgmt.	8942 Wilshire Blvd	Beverly Hills, CA 90211
Storm, Hannah	645- 5th Avenue 10th Fl.	New York, NY 10022	
Wie, Michelle	511 Hahaione Street	Honolulu, HI 96825-1416	
Yagudin, Alexi	Intl. Skating Ctr. of Connecticut	PO Box 577	Simsbury, CT 06071

The Address Directory: Business & Technology

Business Leaders, CEO's & Entrepreneurs

The National Inventors Hall of Fame

Scientists and Nobel Prize Winners

W. James McNerney Jr.	3M	3M Center	St. Paul, MN 55144
Miles D. White	Abbott Labs	100 Abbott Park Rd.	Abbott Park, IL 60064
William Coors	Adolph Coors Co.	311 10th Street	Golden, CO 80401
John W. Rowe	Aetna	151 Farmington Avenue	Hartford, CT 06156
John Sweeney	AFL-CIO	815 16th Street, N.W.	Washington, DC 20006
Lawrence C. Johnston	Albertson's	250 Parkcenter Blvd	Boise, ID 83726
Alian J.P. Belda	Alcoa	201 Isabella St.	Pittsburgh, PA 15212
Cortesi Gaetano	Alfa Romeo	Via Gatternelata 45	Milan, 20149, Italy
Edward M. Liddy	Allstate Insurance	2775 Sanders Road	Northbrook, IL 60062
Scott T. Ford	Alltel	1 Allied Drive	Little Rock, AR 72202
Louis C. Camerilli	Altria Group	120 Parl Avenue	New York, NY 10017
Jeff Bezos	Amazon.com Bldg. 1200	1200 12th Ave. South	Seattle, WA 98144
Kenneth Chenault	American Express	200 Vessey Street	New York, NY 10285
Maurice R. Greenberg	American Intl. Group	70 Pine Street	New York, NY 10270
R. David Yost	Amerisourcebergen	1300 Morris Drive	Chesterbrook, PA 19087
Kevin W. Sharer	Amgen	1 Amgen Center Drive	Thousand Oaks, CA 91320
August A. Busch III	Anheuser-Busch	1 Busch Place	St Louis, MO 63118
Richard Parsons	AOL Time Warner	75 Rockefeller Plaza	New York, NY 10019
Stephen Wozniak	Apple Computer	1 Infinite Loop	Cupertino, CA 95014
Steven P. Jobs	Apple Computer	1 Infinite Loop	Cupertino, CA 95014
Robert K. Green	Aquila	20 Ninth Street	Kansas City, MO 64105
G. Allen Andreas	Archer Daniel Midland	4666 Faries Pkwy.	Decatur, IL 62526
Danny Goldberg	Artemis Records	130 Fifth Avenue	New York,NY 10011
David Dorman	AT&T	32 Sixth Avenue	New York, NY 10013
Michael J. Jackson	Autonation	110 SE 6th Street	Fort Lauderdale, FL 33301
Andrea Jung	Avon Products	1345 Sixth Avenue	New York, NY 10105
Kenneth Lewis	Bank of America Corp.	100 North Tryon Street	Charlotte, NC 28255
James Dimon	Bank One	1 Bank One Plaza	Chicago, IL 60607
Stephen Riggio	Barnes & Noble	122 5th avenue	New York, NY 10011
Steven Tamares	Bed Bath & Beyond	650 Liberty Avenue	Union, NJ 07083
F. Duane Ackermam	Bellsouth	1155 Peachtree St NE	Atlanta, GA 30309
Warren E. Buffett	Berkshire Hathaway	1440 Kiewit Plaza	Omaha, NE 68131
Bradbury H. Anderson	Best Buy	7601 Penn Avenue South	Richfield, MN 55423
Johnson, Robert	BET Television	1900 W Street	Washington, DC 20018
Nolan D. Archibald	Black & Decker	701 East Joppa Road	Towson, MD 21286
John Antioco	Blockbuster	1201 Elm Street	Dallas, TX 75270
Harry Stonecipher	Boeing Company	100 North Riverside	Chicago, IL 60606-1596
George J. Harad	Boise Cascade	1111 W. Jefferson Street	Boise, ID 83728
Peter R. Dolan	Bristol- Myers Squibb	345 Park Avenue	New York, NY 10154
Gertrude Elion	Burroughs Wellcome Co.	3030 Cornwallis Road	Research Triangle Park, NC 27709
Wallace R. Barr	Caesars Entertainment	3930 Howard Hughs Pkwy.	Las Vegas, NV 89109
Douglas C. Conant	Campbell Soup	Campbell Place	Camden, NJ 08103
Robert D. Walter	Cardinal Health	7000 Cardinal Place	Dublin, Ohio 43017
Glen A. Barton	Caterpillar	100 NE Adams Street	Peoria, IL 61629
Daniel Yergin	CERA Cambridge	55 Cambridge Parkway	Cambridge, MA 02142
Charles R. Schwab	Charles Schwab	101 Montgomery Street	San Francisco, CA 94101
David J. O'Reilly	Chevron Texaco	575 Market Street	San Francisco, CA 94105
W. Alan McCollough	Circuit City	9950 Mayland Drive	Richmond, VA 23233
John T. Chambers	Cisco Systems	170 W. Tasman Drive	San Jose, CA 95134
Charles O. Prince III	Citigroup	399 Park Avenue	New York, NY 10043
Robert Rubin	Citigroup	399 Park Avenue	New York, NY 10043
Sanford I. Weill	Citigroup	399 Park Avenue	New York, NY 10043
Maria Bartiroma	CNBC - US	2200 Fletcher Road	Fort Lee. NJ 07024
Douglas N. Daft	Coca-Cola	1 Coca-Cola Plaza	Atlanta, GA 30313
Reuben Mark	Colgate-Palmolive	300 Park Avenue	New York, NY 10022

Brian L. Roberts	Comcast	1500 Market Street	Philadelphia, PA 19102
Van B. Honeycutt	Computer Sciences	2100 E. Grand Avenue	El Segundo, CA 90245
Bruce C. Rohde	Conagra	1 Conagra Drive	Omaha, NE 68102
Archie Dunham	ConocoPhillips	600 N. Dairy Ashford Rd.	Houston, TX 77079
Thomas A. Dattilo	Cooper Tire & Rubber	701 Lima Avenue	Findlay, OH 45840
W. Leo Kiely III	Coors Brewing	311 Tenth Street	Golden, CO 80401
Rolf Eckrodt	Daimler Chrysler AG	Epplestrasse 225	Stuttgard, Germany 70546
Robert Lane	Deere	1 John Deere Place	Moline, IL 61265
Jeff Simmons	Def Jam Records	825 8th Avenue	New York NY 10019
Kamen, Dean	Deka Research	340 Commercial Street	Manchester, NH 03101
Michael Dell	Dell Computer	1 Dell Way	Round Rock, TX 78682
Leo F. Mullin	Delta Air Lines	1030 Delta Blvd	Atlanta, GA 30320
David H. Murdock	Dole Food	1 Dole Drive	Westlake Village, CA 91362
Tom Monaghan	Domino's Pizza	PO Box 997	Ann Arbor, MI 48106
William Stavropoulos	Dow Chemical	2030 Dow Center	Midland, MI 48674
Peter Kann	Dow Jones & Co.	105 Madison Avenue	New York, NY 10016
Charles O. Holliday	E. I. Du Pont Nemours	1007 Market Street	Wilmington, DE 19898
Daniel Carp	Eastman Kodak	343 State Street	Rochester, NY 14650
Meg Whitman	E-Bay	2125 Hamilton Avenue	San Jose, CA 95125
Esther Dyson	Edventure Holdings Inc.	104 5th Avenue	New York, NY 10011
Sidney Taurel	Eli Lilly	Lilly Corporate Center	Indianapolis, IN 46285
Kenneth L. Lay	Enron	1400 Smith Street	Houston, TX 77002
Stephen F. Cooper	Enron	1400 Smith Street	Houston, TX 77002
Fred Langhammer	Estee Lauder	767 Fifth Avenue	New York, NY 10153
Lee Iacocca	EV Global Motors Co.	16760 Schoenborn St.	North Hills, CA 91343
Lee Raymond	Exxon Mobile	5959 Las Colinas Blvd	Irving, TX 75039
Charles McClure	Federal-Mogul	26555 Northwestern Hwy.	Southfield, MI 48034
Frederick W. Smith	Fedex	924 S. Shady Grove Rd.	Memphis, TN 38132
Matthew D. Serra	Foot Locker	112 West34 th Street	New York, NY 10120
Steven Forbes	Forbes Magazine	60 Fifth Avenue	New York, NY 10011-8865
William C. Ford Jr.	Ford Motor Co.	1 American Road	Dearborn, MI 48126
Douglas McCorkindale	Gannett	7950 Jones Branch Dr.	McLean, VA 22107
Paul Pressler	Gap	1 Harrison St.	San Francisco, CA 94105
Melinda Gates	Gates Foundation	PO Box 23350	Seattle, WA 98102
Nicholas Chabraja	General Dynamics	3190 Fairview Park Drive	Falls Church, VA 22042
Jack Welch	General Electric	PO Box 861	Shelton, CT 06484
Jeffrey R. Immelt	General Electric	3135 Easton Turnpike	Faifield, CT 06431
Stephen W. Sanger	General Mills	1 General Mills Blvd.	Minneapolis, MN 55426
Richard Wagoner	General Motors	300 Renaissance Center	Detroit, MI 48265
A. D. Correll	Georgia-Pacific	133 Peachtree St. NE	Atlanta, GA 30303
James M. Kilts	Gillette	Prudential Tower Bldg.	Boston, MA 02199
Abby Joseph Cohen	Goldman & Sachs Co.	85 Broad Street	New York, NY 10004-2434
Henry Paulson	Goldman Sachs	85 Broad Street	New York, NY 10004
Robert Keegan	Goodyear Tire	1144 Market Street	Akron, OH 44316
Larry Page	Google	1600 Amphitheatre Pkwy	Mountain View, CA 94043
Sergey Brin	Google	1600 Amphitheatre Pkwy	Mountain View, CA 94043
William R. Johnson	H.J. Heinz	600 Grant Street	Pittsburgh, PA 15219
David J. Lesar	Halliburton	3600 Lincoln Plaza	Dallas, TX 75201
Jeffrey L. Bleustein	Harley-Davidson	3700 W. Juneau Ave.	Milwaukee, WI 53208
Gary W. Loveman	Harrah's Entertainment	1 Harrah's Court	Las Vegas, NV 89119
Alan Hassenfeld	Hasbro	1027 New Port Avenue	Providence, RI 02903
Richard H. Lenny	Hersey Foods	100 Crystal A Drive	Hersey, PA 17033
Carleton S. Fiorina	Hewlett-Packard	3000 Hanover St.	Palo Alto, CA 94304
Barron Hilton	Hilton Hotels	9336 Civic Center Dr.	Beverly Hills, CA 90210
Stephen Bollenbach	Hilton Hotels	9336 Civic Center Dr.	Beverly Hills, CA 90210

Robert I. Nardelli	Home Depot	2455 Paces Ferry Rd.NW	Atlanta, GA 30339
David M. Cote	Honeywell International	101 Columbia Road	Morristown, NJ 07962
Joel W. Johnson	Hormel Foods	1 Hormel Place	Austin, MN 55192
Samuel J. Palmisano	IBM	New Orchard Road	Armonk, NY 10504
Claire M. Fraser	Institute for Genomic Res.	9712 Medical Center Drive	Rockville, MD 20850
J. Craig Venter	Institute for Genomic Res.	9712 Medical Center Drive	Rockville, MD 20850
Andrew S. Grove	Intel Corporation	2200 College Mission Blvd	Santa Clara, CA 95052
Craig R. Barrett	Intel Corporation	2200 Mission College Blvd	Santa Clara, CA 95052
Gordon E. Moore	Intel Corporation	2200 Mission College Blvd	Santa Clara, CA 95052
Barry Diller	Interactive Corp.	152 West 57th Street	New York, NY 10019
Suze Orman	Intl. Creative Mgmt.	8942 Wilshire Blvd	Beverly Hills, CA 90211
Allen Questrom	J.C. Penny	6501 Legacy Dr.	Plano, TX 75024
William B. Harrison	J.P.Morgan Chase & Co.	270 Park Avenue	New York, NY 10017
David Neelman	Jet Blue Airways	118-29 Queens Blvd	Forest Hills, Ny 11375
William C. Weldon	Johnson & Johnson	1 Johnson & Johnson Plz.	New Brunswick, NJ 08933
Carlos M. Gutierrez	Kellogg	1 Kellogg Square	Battle Creek, MI 49016
Luke R. Corbett	Kerr-McGee	Ker McGee Center	Oklahoma City, OK 73125
Julian Day	K-Mart	3100 W. Big Beaver Rd.	Troy, MI 48084
David B. Dillon	Kroger	1014 Vine Street	Cincinnati, OH 45201
John E. Gherty	Land O' Lakes	4001 lexington Avenue	Arden Hills, MN 55126
Robert E. Rossiter	Lear	21557 Telegraph Rd.	Southfield, MI 48034
Philip Marineau	Levi Strauss	1155 Battery Street	San Francisco, CA 94111
Paul R. Charron	Liz Claiborne	1441 Broadway	New York, NY 10018
Vance D. Coffman	Lockheed Martin	6801 Rockledge Drive	Bethesda, MD 20817
Robert L. Tillman	Lowe's	1000 Lowe's Wat	Mooresville, NC 28117
Patricia F. Russo	Lucent Technologies	600 Mountain Avenue	Murray Hill, NJ 07974
Robert Eckert	Mattel Inc.	333 Continental Blvd	Segundo, CA 90245-5012
Felix Dennis	Maxim Magazine	1040 Avenue of America	New York, NY 10018
Ralph F. Hake	Maytag	403 W. Fourth St.	Newton, IA 50208
James Cantalupo	McDonald's	McDonald's Plaza	Oak Brook, IL 60523
Harold H. McGraw	McGraw - Hill	1221 Sixth Avenue	New York, NY 10020
Raymond V. Gilmartin	Merck	1 Merck Drive	Whitehouse Station, NJ 08889
David H. Komansky	Merrill Lynch	250 Vesey Street	New York, NY 10281
J. Terrence Lanni	MGM Mirage	3600 Las Vegas Blvd	Las Vegas, NV 89109
Jeno Paulucci	Michelina's Foods	P.O. Box 16630	Duluth, MN 55816
Steven R. Appleton	Micron Technology	8000 S. Federal Way	Boise, ID 83707
Bill Gates	Microsoft	One Microsoft Way	Redmond, WA 98052
Steven M. Ballmer	Microsoft	One Microsoft Way	Redmond, WA 98052
Hugh Grant	Monsato	800 Lindberg Blvd	St. Louis, MO 63179
Philip J. Purcell	Morgan Stanley	1585 Broadway	New York, NY 10036
Edward Zander	Motorola	1303 E. Algonquin Rd.	Schaumburg, IL 60196
John Thain	New York Stock Exchange	11 Wall Street	New York, NY 10005
Richard Grasso	New York Stock Exchange	11 Wall Street	New York, NY 10005
Russell T. Lewis	New York Times	229 West 43rd Street	New York, NY 10036
Rupert Murdoch	News Corporation	1211 Avenue of Americas	New York, NY 10036
Philip H. Knight	Nike	1 Bowerman Drive	Beaverton, OR 97005
Jorma Ollila	Nokia	Keilalahdentie 2-4	Finland
Ronald Sugar	Northrup Grumman	1840 Century Park	Los Angeles, CA 90067
M. Bruce Nelson	Office Depot	2200 Old Germantown Rd.	Delray Beach, FL 33445
Lawrence J. Ellison	Oracle	500 Oracle Pkwy.	Redwood Shores, CA 94065
David T. Brown	Owens Corning	1 Owens Corning Pkwy.	Toledo, OH 43659
Steven S. Reinemund	Pepsico	700 Anderson Hill Road	Purchase, NY 10577
Henry A. McKinnell	Pfizer	235 E. 42nd Street	New York, NY 10017
Hugh Hefner	Playboy Enterprises	10236 Charing Cross Rd	Los Angeles, CA 90024
Bob Metcalfe	Polaris Venture Partners	1000 Winter Street	Waltham, Ma 02451-1215

Alan G. Lafley	Procter & Gamble	1 P & G Plaza	Cincinnati, OH 45202
Arthur F. Ryan	Prudential of America	751 Broad Street	Newark, NJ 07102
Irwin Mark Jacobs	Qualcomm	5775 Morehouse Drive	San Diego, CA 92121
Joseph P. Nacchio	Qwest Communications	555 17th Street	Denver, CO 80202
Andrew R. Schindler	R.J. Reynolds Tobacco	401 North Main	Winston-Salem, NC 27201
Leonard H. Roberts	Radio Shack	100 Throckmorton St.	Fort Worth, TX 76102
William Swanson	Raytheon	870 Winter Street	Waltham, MA 02451
Paul Fireman	Reebock International	1895 J.W. Foster Blvd	Canton, MA 02021
Mary F. Sammons	Rite Aid	30 Hunter Lane	Camp Hill, PA 17011
C. Steven McMillan	Sara Lee	3 First National Plaza	Chicago, IL 60662
Edward Whitacre	SBC Communications	175 E. Houston	San Antonio, TX 78205
Alan Lacey	Sears Roebuck	3333 Beverly Road	Hoffman Estates, IL 60179
Christoper M. Connor	Sherwin Williams	101 Prospect Avenue	Cleveland, OH 44115
Muriel Siebert	Siebert Financial Corp.	885 Third Avenue	New York, NY 10022
Koichi Nishimura	Solectron	777 Gibraltar Drive	Milpitas, CA 95035
George Soros	Soros Foundation	888 7th Avenue	New York, NY 10106
William T. Esrey	Sprint	2330 Shawnee Mission Pwky	Westwood, KS 66205
Robert L. Sargent	Staples	500 Staples Drive	Framingham, MA 01702
Howard Schultz	Starbucks Coffee	PO Box 34067	Seattle, WA 98124
Orin C. Smith	Starbucks Coffee	2401 Utah Avenue South	Seattle, WA 98134
Scott G. McNealy	Sun Microsystems	901 San Antonio Rd.	Palo Alto, CA 94303
Jeffrey Noddle	Supervalu	11840 Valley View Road	Eden Prairie, MN 55344
Robert J. Ulrich	Target	777 Nicollet Mall	Minneapolis, MN 55402
Thomas J. Engibous	Texas Instruments	12500 Ti Blvd	Dallas, TX 75243
Richard D. Parsons	Time Warner	1271 Avenue of the Americas	New York NY 10020
John Eyler	Toys "R" Us	461 From Street	Paramus, NJ 07652
Kirk Kerkorian	Tracinda Corp. Suite 250	150 Rodeo Drive	Beverly Hills, CA 90212
Donald Trump	Trump Organization	725 Fifth Avenue	New York, NY 10022
John W. Creighton	UAL	1200 E. Algonquin Rd.	Elk Grove Tnshp, IL 60007
Lawrence A. Weinbach	Unisys	Unisys Way	Blue Bell, PA 19424
Michael L. Eskew	United Parcel Service	55 Glenlake Pkwy. NE	Atlanta, GA 30328
Thomas J. Usher	United States Steel	600 Grant Street	Pittsburgh, PA 15212
George David	United Technologies	1 Financial Plaza	Hartford, CT 06103
Barry Diller	USA Networks	152 W. 57th Street	New York, NY 10019
Ivan G. Seidenberg	Verizon Communications	1095 Sixth Ave.	New York, NY 10036
Sumner Redstone	Viacom	1515 Broadway	New York, NY 10036
Richard, Branson	Virgin Atlantic Airways	Sussex House	Crawley, Sussex RH10 1DQ, UK
Thomas Florio	Vogue Magazine	4 Times Square	New York, NY 10036-6563
Ferdinand Piech	Volkswagen	Brieffach 1880	Wolfsburg, Germany
David W. Bernauer	Walgreen	200 Wilmot Rd.	Deerfield, Il 60015
Alice Walton	Wal-Mart Stores	702 S.W. Eighth St.	Bentonville, AR 72716
H. Lee Scott Jr.	Wal-Mart Stores	702 S.W. Eighth St.	Bentonville, AR 72716
Helen Walton	Wal-Mart Stores	702 S.W. Eighth St.	Bentonville, AR 72716
Jim Walton	Wal-Mart Stores	702 S.W. Eighth St.	Bentonville, AR 72716
John Walton	Wal-Mart Stores	702 S.W. Eighth St.	Bentonville, AR 72716
Michael D. Eisner	Walt Disney	500 S. Buena Vista St.	Burbank, CA 91521
Roy Disney	Walt Disney	500 S. Buena Vista St.	Burbank, CA 91521
Donald Graham	Washington Post	1150 15th Street	Washington, DC 20009
Richard Kovacevich	Wells Fargo	420 Montgomery St.	San Francisco, CA 94163
David R. Whitwam	Whirlpool	2000 - 63 North	Benton Harbor, MI 49022
Bernard J. Ebbers	Worldcom	500 Clinton Center Blvd.	Clinton, MS 39056
William Wrigley Jr.	Wrigley Chewing Gum	410 N. Michigan Avenue	Chicago, IL 60611
Ann Mulcahy	Xerox	800 Long Ridge Rd.	Stamford, CT 06904
Carl Icahn	XO Communication	11111 Sunset Hills Road	Reston, VA 20190-5339
Richard Zamboni	Zamboni Machine	P.O. Box 1248	Paramount, CA 90723

The National Inventors Hall of Fame will forward mail to inductees. If you have a large item you want signed, please contact The Inventors Hall of Fame before sending item.

Please note on the envelope to forward the request to the member at:

Name of Inductee
Inventure Place
221 S. Broadway Street
Akron, OH 44308-1508

Inductee	Inducted	Accomplishment	Born
Bagley, Rodney	2002	Ceramic For Catalytic Convertors	1934
Binnig, Gerd K.	1994	STM Microscope	1947
Bird, Forrest	1995	Medical Respirator	1921
Blum, Samuel	2002	Excimer Eye Surgery	1920
Blumberg, Baruch S.	1993	Vaccine For Hepatitus	1925
Bohlin, Nils	2002	Three Point Safety Belt	1920
Bower, Robert W.	1997	Invented Mosfet	1936
Boyer, Herbert W.	2001	Recombinant DNA Technology	1936
Burckhalter, Joseph H.	1995	Antibody Labeling	1912
Cepollina, Frank	2003	Satellite Servicing Techniques	1936
Cohen, Stanley N.	2001	Recombinant DNA Technology	1935
Colton, Frank B.	1988	Organic Chemistry Resch.	1923
Conover, Lloyd H.	1992	Tetracycline	1923
Coover, Harry	2004	Superglue	1919
Damadian, Raymond W.	1989	Detecting Cancer In Tissue	1936
Dean, Mark	1997	Bus Plug-ins for Computer	1957
Dennard, Robert H.	1997	Invented Dram	1932
Djerssi, Carl	1978	Oral Contraceptives	1923
Dolby, Ray	2004	Dolby Noise Reduction	1933
Durant, Graham J.	1990	Developed Tagament Drug	1934
Emmett, John C.	1990	Developed Tagament Drug	1939
Engelbart, Douglas	1997	Computer Mouse	1925
Faget, Maxime	2003	Space Capsule Design	1921
Faggin, Federico	1996	Microprocessor	1941
Fergason, Jamess L.	1997	LSD Display Systems	1934
Flanigen, Edith	2004	Molecular Sieves	1929
Fogarty, Thomas J.	2001	Embolectomy Catheter	1934
Forrester, Jay W.	1979	Digital Storage Device	1918
Free, Helen	2000	Medical Dip and Read Tests	1923
Gallo, Robert	2004	HIV Isolation and Identification	1937
Ganellin, Charon R.	1990	Developed Tagament Drug	1934
George Carruthers	2003	Electrograph Ultraviolet Camera	1939
Gould, Gordon	1991	Laser	1920

Inductee-Continued	Inducted	Accomplishment	Born
Greatbatch, Wilson	1986	Cardiac Pacemaker	1919
Greene, Leonard M.	1991	Stall-warning for Airplane	1918
Hall, Robert N.	1994	Microwave Magnetron	1919
Heilman, M. Stephen	2002	Implantable Defibrillator	1933
Hillier, James	1980	Electronic Microscope	1915
Hoff, Ted	1996	Microprocessor	1937
Kaman, Charles	2003	Rotor Control Mechanism	1919
Keck, Donald B.	1993	Fiber-optic Wire	1941
Kelman, Charles D.	2004	Cataract Surgery	1930
Kilby, Jack S.	1982	Mini Electronic Curcuits	1923
Kolff, Willem J.	1985	Kidney Dialysis Machine	1911
Kurzweil, Raymond	2002	Reading Machine for the blind	1948
Kwolek, Stephanie	1995	Invented Kevlar	1923
Lachman, Irwin	2002	Ceramic For Catalytic Convertors	1930
Langer, Alois	2002	Implantable Defibrillator	1945
Ledley, Robert S.	1990	Invented CT X-ray Scanner	1926
Lewis, Ronald	2002	Ceramic For Catalytic Convertors	1936
Maiman, Theodore H.	1984	Ruby Laser System	1927
Maurer, Robert D.	1993	Fiber-optic Wire	1924
Mazor, Stanley	1996	Microprocessor	1941
Millman, Irving	1993	Vaccine for Hepatitus	1923
Moeller, Dennis	1997	Bus Plug-ins for Computer	1950
Molloy, Bryan	1999	Developed Prozac	1939
Montagnier, Luc	2004	HIV Isolation and Identification	1932
Mower, Morton	2002	Implantable Defibrillator	1933
Mullis, Kary B	1997	Amplifing Nucleic Acid	1944
Olsen, Kenneth H.	1990	Magnetic Core Memory	1926
Parkinson, Bradford	2004	Global Positioning System	1935
Parsons, John T.	1993	Numemical Control Machine	1913
Rines, Robert H.	1994	Sonar Scanning Devices	1922
Rohrer, Heinrich	1994	Stm Microscope	1933
Rosen, Harold	2003	Communications Satellite	1926
Rosinski, Edward J.	1979	Catalytic Cracking	1921
Rubin, Benjamin A.	1992	Vaccinating Needle	1917
Schawlow, Arthur	1996	Application Of Lasers	1921
Schmiegel, Klaus	1999	Developed Prozac	1939
Schultz, Peter C.	1993	Fiber-optic Wire	1942
Seiwald, Robert J.	1995	Antibody Labeling	1925
Sessler, Gerhard	1999	Foil Electret Microphone	1931
Sherman, Patsy O.	2001	Developed Scotchgard	1930
Smith, Samuel	2001	Developed Scotchgard	1927
Srinivasan, Rangaswamy	2002	Excimer Eye Surgery	1929
Townes, Charles H.	1976	Maser	1915
West, James	1999	Foil Electret Microphone	1931
Whitcomb, Richard	2003	Supercritical Wing	1921
Williams, Sam	2003	Small Fan-Jet Engine	1921
Wozniak, Steve	2000	Personal Computer	1950
Wynne, James	2002	Excimer Eye Surgery	1943

Date	Name	Born	Nationality	Acheivement
2004	Irwin Rose	1926	USA	ubiquitin-mediated protein degradation
2004	Avram Hershko	1937	Israel	ubiquitin-mediated protein degradation
2004	Aaron Ciechanover	1947	Israel	ubiquitin-mediated protein degradation
2003	Roderick Mackinnon	1956	USA	studies of ion channels
2003	Peter Agre	1949	USA	channels in cell membranes
2002	Kurt Wuthrich	1938	Switzerland	biological macromolecules
2002	Koichi Tanaka	1959	Japan	biological macromolecules
2002	John B. Fenn	1917	USA	biological macromolecules
2001	WIliam Knowles	1917	USA	Catalytic Asymmetric Synthesis
2001	Barry K. Sharpless	1941	USA	Catalytic Asymmetric Synthesis
2001	Ryoji Noyori	1938	Japan	Catalytic Asymmetric Synthesis
2000	Hidehi Shirakana	1936	Japan	Conductive Polymers
2000	Alan MacDiarmid	1927	USA	Conductive Polymers
2000	Alan Heeger	1936	USA	Conductive Polymers
1999	Ahmed Zwail	1946	Egyptian	Laser Pictures of Chemicals
1998	Walter Kohn	1923	USA	Quantum Chemistry
1998	John A. Pope	1925	USA	Quantum Chemistry
1997	Paul D. Boyer	1918	USA	Enzymatic Mechanics In Atp
1997	John E. Walker	1941	English	Enzymatic Mechanics In Atp
1997	Jens C. Skou	1918	Danish	Ion-transportinf Enzymes
1996	Robert Curl Jr.	1933	USA	Discovery of Fullerenes
1996	Richard E. Smalley	1943	USA	Discovery of Fullerenes
1996	Harold Kroto	1939	British	Discovery of Fullerenes
1995	Paul Crutzen	1933	Netherlands	Study of Decomposition of Ozone
1995	Mario Molina	1943	Mexico	Study of Decomposition of Ozone
1995	F. Sherwood Rowland	1927	USA	Study of Decomposition of Ozone
1994	George A. Olah	1937	USA	Disc. Ways To Use Hydrocarbons
1993	Michael Smith	1937	Canadian	Splicing of DNA Material
1993	Kary Mullis	1949	USA	Splicing of DNA Material
1992	Rudolph Marcus	1923	USA	Chemical Reaction Speeds
1991	Richard R. Ernst	1933	Swiss	Refinements in MRI Methodology
1990	Elias J. Corey	1928	USA	Synthesis Chemical Compounds
1989	Thomas R. Cech	1947	USA	Rna Acting as Enzyme
1989	Sidney Altman	1939	USA	Rna Acting As Enzyme
1988	Robert Huber	1937	German	Analysis of Atoms in Bacteria
1988	Johann Deisenhofer	1943	German	Analysis of Atoms in Bacteria
1988	Hartmut Michel	1948	German	Analysis of Atoms in Bacteria
1987	Jean-Marie Lehn	1939	French	Research in Molecular Binding

Nobel Prize Winners in Peace

Year	Winner (S)	Born	Nationality	Achievement
2004	Wangari Maathai	1940	Kenya	sustainable democracy and peace
2003	Shirin Ebadi	1947	Iran	for her efforts for democracy and human rights
2002	Jimmy Carter	1924	USA	to advance democracy and human rights
2001	Annan Kofi	1938	Ghana	More Organized & Peaceful World
2000	Kim Dae Jung	1924	Korea	Reconciliation with North Korea
1999	Médecins Sans Frontières	1971	International	Pioneering Humanity work
1997	Jody Williams	1950	USA	Banning Landmines
1997	Intl. Camp Ban Landmines	1992	USA	Banning Landmines
1996	Jose Ramos-Horta	1949	East Timor	Peace in East Timor
1996	Carlos F. X. Belo	1948	East Timor	Peace in East Timor
1995	Joseph Rotblat	1908	British	End to Nuclear Arms
1994	Yithak Rabin	Deceased	Israel	Mideast Peace Talks
1994	Yasser Arafat	Deceased	Gaza Strip	Mideast Peace Talks
1994	Shimon Peres	1923	Israel	Mideast Peace Talks
1993	Nelson Mandela	1918	So. Africa	End of Aparthied
1993	F.W. Deklerk	1936	So. Africa	End of Aparthied
1992	Rigoberta Menchu	1959	Guatemalan	Native American Rights
1991	Daw Aung San Suu Kyi	1945	Burmese	Democracy in Myanmar
1990	Mikhail Gorbachev	1931	Soviet	Help End Cold War
1989	Dalia Lama	1935	Tibetan	End China's Control Tibet
1988	UN Peacekeeping Force	1948	International	Role to Reduce Tension
1987	Oscar A. Sanchez	1941	Costa Rica	End Civil War in Central America
1986	Elie Wiesel	1928	USA	Peace & Dignity
1985	International Physicians	1980	USA	Against Nuclear War
1984	Desmond Tutu	1931	So. African	Against Apartheid
1983	Lech Walesa	1943	Polish	Rights to Unionize
1980	Adolfo P. Esquivel	1931	Argentine	Human Rights in Latin America
1976	Mairead Corrigan	1944	Irish	Movement to End Violence
1976	Betty Williams	1943	Irish	Movement to End Violence

Nobel Award Recipient	Year	Nobel Award Recipient	Year
Buck, LInda B.	2004	Sperry, Roger W.	1981
Axel, Richard	2004	Hubel, David H.	1981
Mansfield, Sir Peter	2003	Snell, George D.	1980
Lauterbur, Paul C.	2003	Dausset, Jean	1980
Sulston, John E.	2002	Benacerraf, Baruj	1980
Horvitz, Robert H.	2002	Hounsfield, Sir Godfrey N.	1979
Brenner, Sydney	2002	Cormack, Alan M.	1979
Nurse, Paul M.	2001	Smith, Hamilton O.	1978
Hunt, R. Timothy	2001	Nathans, Daniel	1978
Hartwell, Leland H.	2001	Arber, Werner	1978
Kandel, Eric	2000	Yalow, Rosalyn	1977
Greengard, Paul	2000	Schally, Andrew V.	1977
Carlsson, Arvid	2000	Guillemin, Roger	1977
Blobel, Guenter	1999	Gajdusek, D. Carleton	1976
Murad, Ferid	1998	Blumberg, Baruch S.	1976
Ignarro, Louis J.	1998	Temin, Howard Martin	1975
Furchgott, Robert F.	1998	Dulbecco, Renato	1975
Prusiner, Stanley B.	1997	Baltimore, David	1975
Zinkernagel, Rolf M.	1996	Palade, George E.	1974
Doherty, Peter C.	1996	De Duve, Christian	1974
Wieschaus, Eric F.	1995	Claude, Albert	1974
Nusslein-Volhard, Christiane	1995	Tinbergen, Nikolaas	1973
Lewis, Edward B.	1995	Lorenz, Konrad	1973
Rodbell, Martin	1994	Frisch, Karl Von	1973
Gilman, Alfred G.	1994	Porter, Rodney R.	1972
Sharp, Phillip A.	1993	Edelman, Gerald M.	1972
Roberts, Richard J.	1993	Sutherland, Earl W. Jr.	1971
Krebs, Edwin G.	1992	Katz, Sir Bernard	1970
Fischer, Edmond H.	1992	Euler, Ulf Von	1970
Sakmann, Bert	1991	Axelrod, Julius	1970
Neher, Erwin	1991	Luria, Salvador E.	1969
Thomas, E. Donnall	1990	Hershey, Alfred D.	1969
Murray, Joseph E.	1990	Delbruck, Max	1969
Varmus, Harold E.	1989	Nirenberg, Marshall W.	1968
Bishop, J. Michael	1989	Khorana, Har Gobind	1968
Hitchings, George H.	1988	Holley, Robert W.	1968
Elion, Gertrude B.	1988	Wald, George	1967
Black, Sir James W.	1988	Hartline, Haldan Keffer	1967
Tonegawa, Susumu	1987	Granit, Ragnar	1967
Levi-Montalcini, Rita	1986	Rous, Peyton	1966
Cohen, Stanley	1986	Huggins, Charles B.	1966
Goldstein, Joseph L.	1985	Monod, Jacoues	1965
Brown, Michael S.	1985	Lwoff, Andre	1965
Milstein, Cesar	1984	Jacob, Francois	1965
Koehler, Georges J.F.	1984	Lynen, Feodor	1964
Jerne, Niels K.	1984	Bloch, Konrad	1964
Clintock, Barbara Mc	1983	Huxley, Sir Andrew F.	1963
Vane, Sir John R.	1982	Hodgkin, Sir Alan L.	1963
Samuelsson, Bengt I.	1982	Eccles, Sir John Carew	1963
Bergstroem, Sune K.	1982	Wilkins, Maurice H.	1962
Wiesel, Torsten N.	1981	Watson, James Dewey	1962

Nobel Prize Winners in Physics

Name	Award Year	Name	Award Year
Wilczek, Frank	2004	Siegbahn, Kai M.	1981
Gross, David H.	2004	Schawlow, Arthur L.	1981
Leggett, Anthony J.	2003	Bloembergen, Nicolaas	1981
Ginzburg, Vitaly L.	2003	James, W. Cronin	1980
Abrikosov, Alexei A.	2003	Fitch, Val L.	1980
Koshiba, Masatoshi	2002	Weinberg, Steven	1979
Giacconi, Riccardo	2002	Salam, Abdus	1979
Davis, Raymond Jr.	2002	Glashow, Sheldon L.	1979
Wieman, Carl E.	2001	Wilson, Robert W.	1978
Ketterle, Wolfgang	2001	Penzias, Arno A.	1978
Cornell, Eric A.	2001	Kapitsa, Pyotr Leonidovich	1978
Kroemer, Herbert	2000	Vleck, John H. Van	1977
Kilby, Jack St. Clair	2000	Mott, Sir Nevill F.	1977
Alferov, Zhores I.	2000	Anderson, Philip W.	1977
Veltman, Martinus	1999	Ting, Samuel C. C.	1976
'T Hooft, Gerardus	1999	Richter, Burton	1976
Tsui, Daniel C.	1998	Rainwater, James	1975
Störmer, Horst	1998	Mottelson, Ben	1975
Laughlin, Robert B.	1998	Bohr, Aage	1975
Phillips, William D.	1997	Ryle, Sir Martin	1974
Cohen-Tannoudji, Claude	1997	Hewish, Antony	1974
Chu, Steven	1997	Josephson, Brian D.	1973
Richardson, Robert C.	1996	Giaever, Ivar	1973
Osheroff, Douglas D.	1996	Esaki, Leo	1973
Lee, David M.	1996	Schrieffer, J. Robert	1972
Reines, Frederick	1995	Cooper, Leon N.	1972
Perl, Martin L.	1995	Bardeen, John	1972
Shull, Clifford G.	1994	Gabor, Dennis	1971
Brockhouse, Bertram N.	1994	Neel, Louis	1970
Taylor, Joseph H. Jr.	1993	Alfven, Hannes	1970
Hulse, Russell A.	1993	Gell-Mann, Murray	1969
Charpak, Georges	1992	Alvarez, Luis W.	1968
De Gennes, Pierre-Gilles	1991	Bethe, Hans Albrecht	1967
Taylor, Richard E.	1990	Kastler, Alfred	1966
Kendall, Henry W.	1990	Tomonaga, Sin-Itiro	1965
Friedman, Jerome I.	1990	Schwinger, Julian	1965
Ramsey, Norman F.	1989	Feynman, Richard P.	1965
Paul, Wolfgang	1989	Townes, Charles H.	1964
Dehmelt, Hans G.	1989	Prokhorov, Aleksandr M.	1964
Steinberger, Jack	1988	Basov, Nicolay G.	1964
Schwartz, Melvin	1988	Wigner, Eugene P.	1963
Lederman, Leon M.	1988	Jensen, J. Hans D.	1963
Muller, K. Alexander	1987	Goeppert-Mayer, Maria	1963
Bednorz, J. Georg	1987	Landau, Lev Davidovich	1962
Ruska, Ernst	1986	Moessbauer, Rudolf L.	1961
Rohrer, Heinrich	1986	Hofstadter, Robert	1961
Binnig, Gerd	1986	Glaser, Donald A.	1960
Klitzing, Klaus Von	1985	Segre, Emilio Gino	1959
Rubbia, Carlo	1984	Chamberlain, Owen	1959
Meer, Simon Van Der	1984	Tamm, Igor Y.	1958
Fowler, William A.	1983	Frank, Il'ja Mikhailovich	1958
Chandrasekhar, Subra	1983	Cherenkov, Pavel A.	1958
Wilson, Kenneth G.	1982		

Nobel Prize for Economics	Year	Nobel Prize for Economics	Year
Kydland, Finn E.	2004	Miller, Merton M.	1990
Prescott, Edward C.	2004	Sharpe, William F.	1990
Engle, Robert F.	2003	Haavelmo, Trygve	1989
Granger, Clive W. J.	2003	Allais, Maurice	1988
Kahneman, Daniel	2002	Solow, Robert M.	1987
Smith, Vernon L.	2002	Buchanan, James M., Jr.	1986
Ackerlof, George A.	2001	Modigliani, Franco	1985
Spence, Michael A.	2001	Stone, Sir Richard	1984
Stiglitz, Joseph E.	2001	Debreu, Gerard	1983
Heckman, James	2000	Stigler, George J.	1982
McFadden, Daniel	2000	Tobin, James	1981
Mundell, Robert A.	1999	Klein, Lawrence R.	1980
Sen, Amartya	1998	Lewis, Sir Arthur	1979
Merton, Robert C.	1997	Schultz, Theodore W.	1979
Scholes, Myron S.	1997	Simon, Herbert A.	1978
Mirrlees, James A.	1996	Meade, James E.	1977
Vickrey, William	1996	Ohlin, Bertil	1977
Lucas, Robert	1995	Friedman, Milton	1976
Harsanyi, John C.	1994	Kantorovich, Leonid	1975
Nash, John F.	1994	Koopmans, Tjalling C.	1975
Selten, Reinhard	1994	Hayek, Friedrich August	1974
Fogel, Robert W.	1993	Myrdal, Gunnar	1974
North, Douglass C.	1993	Leontief, Wassily	1973
Becker, Gary S.	1992	Arrow, Kenneth J.	1972
Coase, Ronald H.	1991	Hicks, Sir John R.	1972
Markowitz, Harry M.	1990	Kuznets, Simon	1971

Nobel Prize for Literature	Year	Nobel Prize for Literature	Year
Elfriede Jelinek	2004	Camilo Jose Cela	1989
John Maxwell Coetzee	2003	Joseph Brodsky	1987
Imre Kertész	2002	Gao Xingjian	2000
V.S. Naipaul	2001	José Saramago	1998
Gunter Grass	1999	Wislawa Szymborska	1996
Dario Fo	1997	Kenzaburo Oe	1994
Seamus Heaney	1995	Derek Walcott	1992
Toni Morrison	1993	Octavio Paz	1990
Nadine Gordimer	1991	Naguib Mahfouz	1988

Addresses of Scientists & Nobel Prize Winners

'T Hooft, Gerardus	Spinoza Institute-Leuvenlaan 4	3508 TD Utrecht	the Netherlands
Abrikosov, Alexei A.	Bldg. 223 Room B-229	9700 South Cass Ave.	Argonne, IL 60439
Ackerlof, George A.	549 Evans Hall #3880	University of California, Berkeley	Berkeley, CA 94720-3880
Agre, Peter	420 Physiology Building	725 North Wolfe Street	Baltimore Maryland 21205
Alferov, Zhores I.	26 Polytekhnicheskaya	St. Petersburg 194021	Russian Federation
Arrow, Kenneth J.	Economics 342	Stanford University	Stanford, CA 94305
Axel, Richard	Howard Hughes Medical Inst.	701 West 168th Street	New York, NY 10032, USA
Bakker, Robert T.	1447 Sumac Avenue	Boulder, CO 80304	
Ballard, Dr. Robert	Oceanographic Institute	Woods Hole , MA 02543	
Baltimore, David	42 Church Street	Woods Hole, MA 02543	
Baulie, Ettienne-Emile	Lab. Des Hormones	Hopital De Bicetre	94270 Le Kremlin-Bicetre, France
Becker, Gary S.	Hoover Institution	Stanford University	Stanford, CA 94305
Beckman, Arnold O.	Beckman Institute	CalTech MC 139-74	Pasadena, CA 91125
Berg, Paul	Beckman Ctr. Room B062	Stanford University	Stanford, CA 94305
Berners-Lee, Tim	Room NE 43-356	545 Technology Square	Cambridge, MA 02139
Bethe, Hans	209 White Park Rd.	Ithaca, NY 14850	
Bishop, Michael J.	School of Medicine	Univ. of California	San Fracisco, CA 94143
Blaese, Michael R.	Kimeragen, Inc.	300 Pheasent Run	Newtown, PA 18940
Blobel, Gunter	Howard Hughes Medical Inst.	1230 York Avenue	New York, N.Y. 10021
Boyer, Paul D.	Dept. of Chemistry	Univ. of California	Los Angeles, CA 90024
Brenner, Sydney	The Molecular Sciences Inst.	2168 Shattuck Avenue	Berkeley, CA 94704
Brockhouse, Bertram	64 Lovers Lane	Ancaster, Ont. L9G 1G6	Canada
Brown, Michael S.	Univ. of Texas	Health Science Ctr.	Dallas, Texas 75235
Buck, Linda	Fred Hutchinson Cancer Res.	1100 Fairview Avenue North	Seattle, WA 98109-1024
Carlsson, Arvid	University of Göteborg	Medicinaregatan 7 Box 431	SE-405 30 Göteborg, Sweden
Carmona, Richard	Office of Surgeon General	5600 Fishers Lane Rm. 18-66	Rockville, MD 20857
Carter, Jimmy	The Carter Center	453 Freedom Parkway	Atlanta, GA 30307
Charpak, Georges	87 Rue De La Plaine	75020 Paris, France	
Chu, Steven	Varian Bldg. Room 230	Stanford University	Stanford, CA 94305
Ciechanover, Aaron	Technion	1 Efron Street	Haifa 31096, Israel
Coase, Ronald	1111 East 60th Street	Chicago, IL	60637
Cohen, Stanley	Vanderbilt Univ.	School Of Medicine	Nashville, Tn 37212
Collins, Francis	National Human Genome Inst.	9000 Rockville Pike Bldg 31/4B09	Bethesda, MD 20892
Cornell, Eric A.	Campus Box 440	University of Colorado	Boulder, Colorado 80309-0440
Corwin, Jeff	The Jeff Corwin Experience	2006 W. Olive Avenue	Burbank, CA 91506
Curl, Robert F.	1824 Bolsover Street	Houston, Tx 77005	
Dalai Lama	The Office of Tibet	241 East 32nd Street	New York, NY 19916
Damadian, Raymond V.	Fonar Corp.	110 Marcus Drive	Melville, NY 11747
Dausser, Jean	27, Rue Juliette Dodu	75010 Paris, France	
Davis, Raymond Jr.	Univ. of Penn. Physics Dept.	116 College Hall	Philadelphia, PA 19104-6377
De Gennes, Pierre	10 Rue Vauquelin	25005 Paris, France	
Debakey, Michael	Batlor College of Med.	One Baylor Plaza	Houston, TX 77030
Dees, Gerald M.	Scripps Research Inst.	10666 N. Torrey Pines Rd	La Jolla, CA 92037
Dehmelt, Hans	Univ. of Wash.- Physics	Box 351560	Seattle, WA 98195-1560
Doherty, Peter C.	St. Jude Hospital	Memphis, TN 37501	
Elion, Gertrude B.	Wellcome Research Lab	3030 Cornwallis Road	Triangle Park, NC 27709
Engle, Robert F.	New York University	44 West Fourth Street	New York, NY 10012-1126
Ernst, Richard	Kurlisr 24	8404 Winterthur	Switzerland
Fenn, John B.	Dept. of Chemistry	1001 W. Main St.	Richmond, VA 23284-2006
Folkman, Judah	Children's Hospital	300 Longwood Avenue	Boston, MA 02115
Friedman, Milton	Hoover Institute	Stanford University	Stanford, Ca 94305-6010
Furchgott, Robert	SUNY Health Science Center	450 Clarkson Avenue	Brooklyn, NY 11203
Gayle, Helene	Gates Foundation	PO Box 23350	Seattle, WA 98102
Geller, Margaret	Harvard-Smithsonian Ctr	60 Garden Street	Cambridge, MA 02138
Giacconi, Riccardo	Associated Universities, Inc.	1400 16 th St., NW	Washington, DC 20036

Gilbert, Walter	15 Gray Gardens Road	Cambridge, MA 02138	
Gilman, Alfred G.	Southwestern Medical Center	University of Texas	Dallas, TX 75390
Ginzburg, Vitaly L.	P.N. Lebedev Physical Institute	Leninskii Pr. 53	117924 Moscow
Goodall, Jane	Explorer in Residence	National Geographic	1145 17th Street NW
Gordimer, Nadine	C/O Russell- Volkening	50 West 29th Street	New York Ny 10001
Granger, Clive W. J.	U of California - Economics	9500 Gilman Drive	La Jolla, CA 92093-0508
Greengard, Paul	The Rockefeller University	1230 York Avenue	New York, NY 10021
Gross, David J.	Institute for Theoretical Physics	1219 University of California	Santa Barbara, CA 93106l
Hale, Alan	SW Inst. For Space Res.	15 East Spur Road	Cloudcroft, NM 88317
Hanna, Jack	PO Box 400	Powell, OH 43065	
Hartwell, Leland H.	1100 Fairview Ave N; D1-060	U. of Washington, Seattle	Seattle, WA 98109
Heckman, James	Univ. of Chicago - Economics	1126 East 59th Street	Chicago, IL 60637
Heeger, Alan J.	Department of Physics	UC at Santa Barbara	Santa Barbara, CA 93106-5090
Hershko, Avram	Technion	1 Efron Street	Haifa 31096, Israel
Ho, David	Aaron David Hospital	455 1st Ave.	New York, NY 10003
Horvitz, Robert H.	MIT Dept. of Biology Rm. 68-425	77 Massachusetts Avenue	Cambridge, MA 02139
Hunt, Timothy	Clare Hall Lab. PO Box 123	Lincoln's Inn Fields	London WC2 3PX, UK
Ignaro, Louis J.	UCLA Medical School	10833 Leconte Avenue	Los Angeles, CA 90095
Irwin, Steve	Autralia Zoo- Glass House	Mountain Tourist Route	Beerwah, Queensland 4519
Jackson, Shirley	Rensselaer Polytechnic	110 8th Street	Troy, Ny 12181
Kahneman, Daniel	Department of Psychology	Princeton University	Princeton, NJ 08544
Kandel, Eric	Center for Neurobiology	Columbia University	New York, NY 10032
Karle, Isabella	Naval Research Laboratory	4555 Overlook Avenue SW	Washington, DC 20375
Ketterle, Wolfgang	Room 26-243 at MIT	77 Massachusetts Avenue	Cambridge, MA 02139-4307
Kilby, Jack St. Clair	Texas Instruments Incorporated	12500 TI Boulevard	Dallas, TX 75243-4136
King, Mary-Claire	Molecular & Cell Biology	Univ. of Berkely-CA	Berkely, CA 94720
Kohn, Walter	Physics Department	U of C Santa Barbara	Santa Barbara, CA 93106
Koop, C. Everett	Childen's Natl. Med. Ctr	111 Michigan NW	Wasshington, DC 20010
Kornberg, Arthur	Beckman Ctr. Room 415	Stanford University	Stanford, CA 94305
Koshiba, Masatoshi	University of Tokyo	7-3-1 Hongo, Bunkyo-ku	Tokyo 113-0033
Kroemer, Herbert	Room 4107 Engineering I	University of California	Santa Barbara, CA 93106-9560
Kydland, Finn E.	GSIA	Carnegie Mellon University	Pittsburgh, PA 15213
Kyi, Daw Aung San Suu	Natl. League Democracy	54-56 University Ave.	Yangon, Mayanmar
Laughlin, Robert B.	Varian Bldg. Room 328	Stanford University	Stanford, CA 94305
Lauterbur, Paul C.	U of Illinois Magnetic Res. Lab.	2100 South Goodwin Avenue	Urbana, IL 61801
Leakey, Louise	Explorer in Residence	National Geographic	1145 17th Street NW
Leakey, Meave	Leakey Foundation	1002A O'Reilly Avenue	San Francisco, CA 94129-0346
Leakey, Richard	PO Box 24926	Nairobi, Kenya	
Lee, Henry C.	CT State Police Forensic	278 Colony Street	Merden, CT 06451
Leggett, Anthony J.	Univ. of Illinois-Physics Dept.	1110 West Green Street	Urbana, IL 61801-3080
Levy, David H.	C/O Plenum Publishing	233 Spring Street	New York, NY 10013
MacDiarmid, Alan G.	University of Pennsylvania	34th and Spruce Streets	Philadelphia, PA 19104
Mackinnon, Roderick	Howard Hughes Medical Institute	1230 York Avenue	New York, NY 10021
Mansfield, Sir Peter	Magnetic Resonance Centre	University of Nottingham	Nottingham, NG7 2RD, UK
Margulis, Lynn	Botany Department	U of Mass. at Amherst	Amherst, MA 01003
Marquez, Gabriel	Fuego 14Y	Pedregal De San Angel	Mexico DF, Mexico
Marshall, Barry J.	Heliobacter Foundation	PO Box 7965	Charlottesville,VA 22906
McFadden, Daniel	Department of Economics	University of California	Berkeley, CA 94720
Merton, Robert C.	Harvard Business School	Harvard University	Cambridge, MA
Molina, Mario	Department of Chemistry	MIT	Cambridge, MA 02138
Mundell, Robert A.	Department of Economics	Columbia University	New York, NY 10027
Murad, Ferid	U of Texas Med. School	PO Box 20708	Houston, TX 77225
Nash, John F.	Fine Hall - Washington Road	Princeton University	Princton, NJ 08544-1000
Neher, Erwin Dr.	Max Planck Inst. Bio/Che	Am Fass/ Post Fach 2841	D-3400 Gottingen, Germany
North, Douglass	Hoover Institution	Stanford Univ.	Stanford, CA 94305
Noyori, Ryoji	Nagoya University	Chikusa, Nagoya 464-8602	Japan

Addresses of Scientists & Nobel Prize Winners

Nurse, Paul M.	Cell Cycle Lab. PO Box 123	Lincoln's Inn Fields	London WC2 3PX, UK
Nye, Bill	C/O KCTS-TV	401 Mercer St.	Seattle, WA 98109
O'Keefe, Sean	NASA Administrator	300 E Street SW	Washington, DC 20546-0001
Osheroff, Douglas	Varian Bldg. Room 150	Stanford University	Stanford, CA 94305
Paul, Wolfgang	Physikalisches Institut der	Universitt Bonn Nussallee 12	D-5300 Bonn, Germany
Perl, Martin	Slac Mail Stop 61	Stanford University	Stanford, CA 94305
Phillips, William D.	Natl Inst Stnds & Tech.	Atomic Physics Div.	Gaithersburg, MD 20899
Plotkin, Mark	Ethnobiology	1655 North Fort Meyer	Arlington, Va 22209
Politzer, H. David	Mail Code 452-48 at CIT	1201 E. California Boulevard	Pasadena, CA 91106-3368
Pople, John	Chemistry-Northwestern Univ.	1801 Hinman Avenue	Evanston, IL 60204
Prescott, Edward C.	Research Dept. PO Box 291	Federal Reserve Bank of Mpls	Minneapolis, MN 55480-0291
Prusiner, Stanley B.	School Of Medicine	Univ. of California	San Francisco, CA 94143
Ramsey, Norman F.	Lyman Physics Laboratory	Harvard University	Cambridge, MA 02138
Richter, Burton	SLAC Mail Stop 80	Stanford University	Stanford, CA 94305
Roberts, Richard J.	New England Biolabs	32 Tozer Road	Beverly, MA 01915-5599
Rodbell, Martin	N.I. Environmental Health	Triangle Park, NC 27709	
Roosevelt, Anna	Field Museum	Roosevelt Rd & Lake Shore	Chicago, IL 60605
Rose, Irwin	College of Medicine	University of California, Irvine	Irvine, CA 92697
Sakmann, Bert Dr.	Max Planck Inst Med.Res.	Heidelberg, Germany	
Scholes, Myron S.	Hoover Institution	Standford University	Stanford, CA 94305-6010
Schwartz, Melvin	Digital Pathways, Inc.	PO Box 591171	San Francisco, CA 94159-1171
Sen, Amartya	6 Hilliard	Cambridge, MA 02138	
Sereno, Paul	University of Chicago	1027 East 57th Street	Chicago, IL 60637
Sharp, Phillip A.	Center for Cancer Research	MIT	Cambridge, MA 02138
Sharpe, William	Graduate Sch. Business	Stanford University	Stanford, CA 94305
Sharpless, Barry	10550 North Torrey Pines Blvd.	La Jolla, CA 92037	
Shirakawa, Hideki	Institute of Materials Sciences	University of Tsukuba	Sakura-mura, Ibaraki 305, Japan
Shirley, Donna	Mars Program	Jet Propulsion Lab	Pasadena, CA 91109
Skolnick, Mark	Myriad Genetics	390 Wakara Way	Salt Lake City, UT 84108
Skou, Jens C.	Dept. of Biophysics	Aarhus University	Denmark
Smalley, Richard E.	Rice University	6100 Main Street	Houston, TX 77005
Smith, Vernon L.	George Mason University	4400 University Drive	Fairfax, VA 22030-4444
Spelman, Lucy H.	Smithsonian National Zoo	3001 Connecticut Ave NW	
Spence, Michael A.	Stanford Business School	Stanford University	Stanford, CA 94305-5015
Stiglitz, Joseph E.	Columbia Univ. Economics Dept.	420 West 118th Street	New York, NY 10027
Stormer, Horst	Columbia University	538 West 120th Street	New York, NY 10025
Sulston, John E.	The Sanger Centre	Wellcome Trust Genome Campus,	Hinxton, Cambridge CB10 1SA, UK
Tanaka, Koichi	1. Nishinkokyo Kuwabaracho	Nakagyou-ku	Kyoto 604-8511, Japan
Taube, Henry	Chemistry Dept.	Stanford University	Stanford, CA 94305
Taylor, Richard E.	PO Box 4349	Stanford, CA 94309	(Nobel Prize 1990)
Tonegawa, Susumu	MIT	77 Massachusetts Avenue	Cambridge, MA 02138
Torvalds, Linus	Transmeta	3940 Freedom Circle	Santa Clara, Ca 95054
Tsui, Daniel C.	Dept. of Electrical Eng.	Princeton University	Princeton, NJ 08544
Tutu, Desmond	Claremount 7700	Johannesburgh	South Africa
Varmus, Harold	School of Medicine	Univ. of California	San Fracisco, CA 94143
Venter, J. Craig	The Institute for Genomic Res.	9712 Medical Center Drive	Rockville, MD 20850
Vogelstein, Bert	John Hopkins Oncology	424 North Bond Street	Baltimore, MD 21231
Watson, James D.	Cold Spring Harbor Lab.	One Bungton Road	Cold Spring Harbor, NY 11724
Wieman, Carl E.	Campus Box 440	University of Colorado	Boulder, Colorado 80309-0440
Wiesenthal, Simon	Salvatorgasse	1010 Vienna 1	Austria
Wilczek, Frank	Theoretical Physics at MIT 6-305	77 Massachusetts Ave.	Cambridge, MA 02139
Wilmut, Ian	Roslin Institute	Midlothian EH25 9PS	United Kingdom
Wuthrich, Kurt	Institute of Technology Zürich	ETH Hvnggerberg, HPK	CH-8093 Zürich, Schweiz
Zewail, Ahmed	Noyes Lab. Mail Code 127-72	California Institute of Technology	Pasadena, California 91125
Zinkernagel, Rolf M.	Immunology	University of Zurich	Zurich, Switzerland

The Address Directory: Government

The President and the Cabinet

The Supreme Court Judges

Members of the U.S. Senate

Members of the House of Representatives

State Governors

Mayors of Large U.S. Cities

Lawyers, Judges and Members of the Kennedy Family

World Leaders and Royalty

U. S. Astronauts

Advocates for Peace, Civil Rights and Human Rights

The President, Cabinet, Agencies & Supreme Court

Abraham, Spencer	Secretary of Energy	1000 Independence SW	Washington, DC 20585
Allbaugh, Joe	Director-FEMA	500 C Street SW	Washington, DC 20472
Arafat, Yassir	Arnesstonconseil	17 Belvedere	1002 Tunis, Tunisa
Ashcroft, John	Attorney General Justice Dept.	10th & Constitution Ave.	Washington, DC 20530
Bennett, Bill	# 890	1776 "I" Street	Washington, DC 20006
Bork, Robert	Am. Enterprise Inst.(AEI)	1150 17th Street, NW	Washington, D.C. 20036
Brzezinski, Zbigniew	Ctr.Strategic Studies (CSIS)	1800 K Street, NW	Washington, D.C. 20006
Bumpers, Dale	Ctr. for Defense Inform. (CDI)	1779 Mass. Ave.NW	Washington, D.C. 20036
Bush, George Herbert	10000 Memorial Drive	Houston, TX 77024	
Bush, George Walker	The White House	1600 Pennsylvania Ave	Washington, DC 20501
Bush, Laura	The White House	1600 Pennsylvania Ave	Washington, DC 20501
Carter, Jimmy	The Carter Center	453 Freedom Parkway	Atlanta, GA 30307
Carter, Rosalynn	The Carter Center	453 Freedom Parkway	Atlanta, GA 30307
Chao, Elaine	Secretary of Labor	200 Constitution Ave.NW	Washington, DC 20210
Chao, Linda L.	Hoover Institution	Stanford University	Stanford, CA 94305-6010
Cheney, Lynne	Am. Enterprise Inst.(AEI)	1150 17th Street, NW	Washington, D.C. 20036
Cheney, Richard	Office of The Vice President	Old Executive Bldg. NW	Washington, DC 20501
Clinton, Hillary Rodham	Senator of New York	US Senate	Washington, DC
Clinton, William Jefferson	Office of the President	55 West 125th Street	New York, NY 10027
D'Souza, Dinesh	Hoover Institution	Stanford University	Stanford, CA 94305-6010
Evans, Don	Secretary of Commerce	14th Street	Washington, DC 20301
Ford, Betty	40365 San Dune Road	Rancho Mirage, CA 92270	
Ford, Gerald	40365 San Dune Road	Rancho Mirage, CA 92270	
Fox, Vicente	President of Mexico	Los Pinas, Puerta 1, Col	Chapultepec 11850 Mexico
Frank, Tommy R.	U.S. Central Commander	Public Affairs Office	MacDill AFB, FL 33621
Friedman, Milton	Hoover Institution	Stanford University	Stanford, CA 94305-6010
Gilmore, James S.	Chairman-Republican Party	State Capital	Richmond, VA 23219
Gingrich, Newt	Hoover Institution	Stanford University	Stanford, CA 94305-6010
Giuliani, Rudolph	Guiliani Partners LLC	5 Times Square	New York, NY 10036
Greenspan, Alan	Chairman Federal Reserve	20th St. & Constitution	Washington, DC 20551
Haig, Alexander Jr.	Worldwide Asociates	4301 N. Fairfax Drive	Arlington, VA 22203
Healy, Bernadine Dr.	Director of the Red Cross	2025 E Street NW	Washington, DC 20006
Kirkpatrick, Jeane	Am. Enterprise Inst.(AEI)	1150 17th Street, NW	Washington, D.C. 20036
Kissinger, Henry A.	Ctr.Strategic Studies (CSIS)	1800 K Street, NW	Washington, D.C. 20006
Koplan, Jeffrey Dr.	Director of Ctr. Disease Ctl.	1600 Clifton Rd NE	Atlanta, GA 30333
La Rocque, Admiral Gene R.	Ctr. for Defense Inform. (CDI)	1779 Mass. Ave.NW	Washington, D.C. 20036
Martinez, Mel	Secretary of Housing	451 7th Street SW	Washington, DC 20410
McGovern, George	McGovern Family Fdt.	PO Box 33393	Washington, DC 20033
Meese, Edwin	Hoover Institution	Stanford University	Stanford, CA 94305-6010
Mineta, Norman Y.	Secretary of Transportation	400 7th Street SW	Washington, DC 20590
Mondale, Walter	2200 1st Bank Place East	Minneapolis, MN 55402	
Mueller, Robert	Director of the FBI	9th and Pennsylvania	Washington, DC 20535
Musharraf, Pervez	Leader of Pakistan	Chief Secretariat	Islamabad, Pakistan

The President, Cabinet, Agencies & Supreme Court

Myers, Richard General	Joint Chiefs of Staff	The Pentagon	Washington, DC 20318
Newbold, Gregory Lt. Gen.	Joint Chiefs of Staff	The Pentagon	Washington, DC 20318
Norton, Gale	Secretary of The Interior	18th & C Street	Washington, DC 20240
Nunn, Sam	Ctr.Strategic Studies (CSIS)	1800 K Street, NW	Washington, D.C. 20006
O'Connor, Sandra Day	The U.S. Supreme Court	First Street NE	Washington, DC 20543
Snow, John	Secretary of The Treasury	1500 Pennsylvania Ave.	Washington, DC 20220
Paige, Roderick R.	Secretary of Education	400 Maryland Ave. SW	Washington DC 20202
Panetta, Leon	Panetta Foundation	CSU, Monterey Bay	Seaside, California 93955
Perot, H. Ross	Perot Systems	2300 West Plano Parkway	Plano, TX 75075
Potter, John E.	Postmaster General	475 L'Enfant Plaza SW	Washington, DC 20260
Powell, Colin Luther	Secretary of State	2210 C Street NW	Washington, DC 20520
Powell, John	Chairman of the FCC	445 12th Street SW	Washington, DC 20554
Principi, Anthony	Secretary of Veterans Affair	810 Vermont Ave. NW	Washington, DC 20420
Putin, Vladimir	Office of the President	103073 The Kremlin	Moscow, Russia
Quayle, Dan	11711 N. Pennsylvania St.	Cornell, IN 46032	
Rehnquist, William H.	The U.S. Supreme Court	First Street NE	Washington, DC 20543
Reich, Robert B.	Center for Natl. Policy (CNP)	1779 Mass. Ave.NW	Washington, D.C. 20001
Rice, Condoleezza	Hoover Institution	Stanford University	Stanford, CA 94305-6010
Ridge, Tom	Director Homeland Security	The White House	Washington, DC 20502
Rumsfeld, Donald H.	Secretary of Defense	The Pentagon	Washington, DC 20301
Satcher, David	Center for Disease Control	1600 Clifton Rd NE	Atlanta, GA 30333
Scalia, Antonin	The U.S. Supreme Court	First Street NE	Washington, DC 20543
Schlesinger, James R.,	Ctr.Strategic Studies (CSIS)	1800 K Street, NW	Washington, D.C. 20006
Schwarzkopf, Norman	401 Staff Loop	Tampa, FL 33621	
Shalikashvili, John General	The Pentagon	Washington, DC 20318	
Sharon, Ariel	Prime Minister of Israel	Likud, 38 Rehov K George	Tel Aviv, Israel
Shelton, Henry General	The Pentagon	Washington, DC 20318	
Shultz, George P.	Hoover Institution	Stanford University	Stanford, CA 94305-6010
Solzhenitsyn, Alexander	Hoover Institution	Stanford University	Stanford, CA 94305-6010
Souter, David H.	The U.S. Supreme Court	First Street NE	Washington, DC 20543
Spitzer, Eliot	Attorney Generals Office	120 Broadway	New York, NY 10271
Starr, Kenneth	Kirkland & Ellis	655 Fifteenth Street, N.W.	Washington, D.C. 20005
Stevens, John Paul III	The U.S. Supreme Court	First Street NE	Washington, DC 20543
Tenet, George J.	Director of the CIA	Central Intelligence Agency	Washington, DC 20505
Thatcher, Margaret	Hoover Institution	Stanford University	Stanford, CA 94305-6010
Thomas, Clarence	The U.S. Supreme Court	First Street NE	Washington, DC 20543
Thompson, Tommy G.	Secretary of Health	200 Independence Ave.SW	Washington, DC 20201
Veneman, Ann	Secretary of Agriculture	The Mall, 12th & 14th St	Washington, DC 20250
Vessy, John W. Jr. General	Star Route Box 136A	Garrison, MN 56450	
Westmoreland, William General	107 1/2 Tradd Street	Charleston, SC29401	
Wilson, Pete	Hoover Institution	Stanford University	Stanford, CA 94305-6010
Zamperini, Louis (WWII POW)	1760 N. Gower Street	Hollywood, CA 90028	
Zinni, Anthony	College of William & Mary	P.O. Box 8795	Williamsburg, VA 23187

Due to the security issues that have arisen in the delivery of the U.S. mail to offices in Washington D.C. it is recommended that a person telephone the Congressperson at the listed phone numbers (Washington D.C. area code is 202) to request autographed material. If you have an item to send in for an autograph please be advised that a considerable wait may occur, however if you wish to mail an item the way to address a member of the U.S. Senate is given.

109th Congress Directory
Suite Codes:
SR-Russell Building - Zip Code 20510
SD-Dirksen Building - Zip Code 20510
SH-Hart Building - Zip Code 20510

Suggested Address And Salutation:
The Honorable Richard C. Shelby
U.S. Senate
110 Hart Building
Washington, D.C. 20510

Alabama	Suite	Phone	Alaska	Suite	Phone
Richard C. Shelby (R)	SH-110	224-5744	Ted Stevens (R)	SH-522	224-3004
Jeff Sessions (R)	SR-335	224-4124	Lisa H. Murkowski (R)	SR-C1	224-6665
Arizona			**Arkansas**		
John McCain (R)	SR-241	224-2235	Blanche L. Lincoln (D)	SD-355	224-4843
Jon Kyl (R)	SH-730	224-4521	Mark Pryor (D)	SR-217	224-2353
California			**Colorado**		
Dianne Feinstein (D)	SH-331	224-3841	Ken Salazar (D)	SD-B40A	224-5852
Barbara Boxer (D)	SH-112	224-3553	Wayne Allard (R)	SD-521	224-5941
Connecticut			**Delaware**		
Christopher J. Dodd (D)	SR-448	224-2823	Thomas R. Carper (D)	SH-513	224-2441
Joseph I. Leiberman (D)	SH-706	224-4041	Joseph R. Biden (D)	SR-201	224-5042
Florida			**Georgia**		
Mel Martinez (R)	SR-C2	224-3041	Johnny Isakson (R)	SR-C4	224-3643
Bill Nelson (D)	SH-716	224-5274	Saxby Chambliss (R)	SR-416	224-3521
Hawaii			**Idaho**		
Daniel K. Inouye (D)	SH-722	224-3934	Larry E. Craig (R)	SH-520	224-2752
Daniel K. Akaka (D)	SH-141	224-6361	Mike Crapo (R)	SD-239	224-6142
Illinois			**Indiana**		
Barack Obama (D)	SD-B40B	224-2854	Richard G. Lugar (R)	SH-306	224-4814
Richard J. Durbin (D)	SD-332	224-2152	Evan Bayh (D)	SR-463	224-5623
Iowa			**Kansas**		
Charles E. Grassley (R)	SH-135	224-3744	Sam Brownback (R)	SH-303	224-6521
Tom Harkin (D)	SH-731	224-3254	Pat Roberts (R)	SH-109	224-4774
Kentucky			**Louisiana**		
Jim Bunning (R)	SH-316	224-4646	David Vitter (R)	SH-825A	224-4623
Mitch McConnell (R)	SR-361A	224-2541	Mary Landrieu (D)	SH-724	224-5824
Maine			**Maryland**		
Olympia Snowe (R)	SR-154	224-5344	Paul S. Sarbanes (D)	SH-309	224-4524
Susan Collins (R)	SR-172	224-2523	Barbara A. Mikulski (D)	SH-709	224-4654

Massacheusetts	Suite	Phone	Michigan	Suite	Phone
Edward M. Kennedy (D)	SR-317	224-4543	Carl Levin (D)	SR-269	224-6221
John Kerry (D)	SR-304	224-2742	Debbie Stabenow (D)	SH-702	224-4822
Minnesota			**Mississippi**		
Norm Coleman (R)	SH-320	224-5641	Thad Cochran (R)	SD-113	224-5054
Mark Dayton (D)	SR-346	224-3244	Trent Lott (R)	SR-487	224-6253
Missouri			**Montana**		
Christopher S. Bond (R)	SR-274	224-5721	Max Baucus (D)	SH-511	224-2651
James Talent (R)	SR-493	224-6154	Conrad Burns (R)	SD-187	224-2644
Nebraska			**Nevada**		
Ben Nelson (D)	SH-720	224-6551	Harry Reid (D)	SH-528	224-3542
Chuck Hagel (R)	SR-248	224-4224	John Ensign (R)	SR-364	224-6244
New Hampshire			**New Jersey**		
John Sununu (R)	SR-111	224-2841	John Corzine (D)	SH-502	224-4744
Judd Gregg (R)	SR-393	224-3324	Frank Lautenerg (D)	SH-324	224-3224
New Mexico			**New York**		
Pete V. Domenici (R)	SH-328	224-6621	Hillary Rodham Clinton (D)	SR-476	224-4451
Jeff Bingaman (D)	SH-703	224-5521	Charles Schumer (D)	SH-313	224-6542
North Carolina			**North Dakota**		
Elizabeth Dole (R)	SR-120	224-6342	Kent Conrad (D)	SH-530	224-2043
Richard Burr (R)	SD-B40C	224-3154	Byron L. Dorgan (D)	SH-322	224-2551
Ohio			**Oklahoma**		
George Voinovich (R)	SH-317	224-3353	Tom Coburn (R)	SD-B40D	224-5754
Mike Dewine (R)	SR-140	224-2315	James M. Inhofe (R)	SR-453	224-4721
Oregon			**Pennsylvania**		
Ron Wyden (D)	SH-516	224-5244	Arlen Specter (R)	SH-711	224-4254
Gordon Smith (R)	SR-404	224-3753	Rick Santorum (R)	SD-511	224-6324
Rhode Island			**South Carolina**		
Lincoln Chafee (R)	SR-141A	224-2921	Lindsey Graham (R)	SR-290	224-5972
Jack Reed (D)	SH-728	224-4642	Jim DeMint (R)	SH-825	224-6121
South Dakota			**Tennessee**		
John Thune (R)	SD-B40E	224-2321	Alexander Lamar (R)	SH-302	224-4944
Tim Johnson (D)	SH-136	224-5842	Bill Frist (R)	SD-461	224-3344
Texas			**Utah**		
John Cornyn (R)	SH-517	224-2934	Orrin Hatch (R)	SH-104	224-5251
Kay Bailey Hutchinson (R)	SR-284	224-5922	Robert F. Bennett (R)	SD-431	224-5444
Vermont			**Virginia**		
Patrick J. Leahy (D)	SR-433	224-4242	John W. Warner (R)	SR-225	224-2023
James M. Jeffords (I)	SD-413	224-5141	George Allen (R)	SR-204	224-4024
Washington			**West Virginia**		
Maria Cantwell (D)	SH-717	224-3441	Robert C. Byrd (D)	SH-311	224-3954
Patty Murray (D)	SR-173	224-2621	John D. Rockefeller (D)	SH-531	224-6472
Wisconsin			**Wyoming**		
Herb Kohl (D)	SH-330	224-5653	Craig Thomas (R)	SD-307	224-6441
Russell Feingold (D)	SH-506	224-5323	Mike Enzi (R)	SR-379A	224-3424

Due to the security issues that have arisen in the delivery of the U.S. mail to offices in Washington D.C. it is recommended that a person telephone the Congressperson at the listed phone numbers (Washington D.C. area code is 202) to request autographed material. If you have an item to send in for an autograph please be advised that a considerable wait may occur, however if you wish to mail an item the way to address a member of the U.S. House of Representatives is given.

Suggested Address And Salutation:
The Honorable (John Doe)
United States House of Representatives
Washington, D.C. 20515

Representative	St.	Phone	Representative	St.	Phone	Representative	St.	Phone
Young, Don	AK	225-5765	Hunter, Duncan	CA	225-5672	Johnson, Nancy L.	CT	225-4476
Aderholt, Robert B.	AL	225-4876	Issa, Darrell E.	CA	225-3906	Larson, John B.	CT	225-2265
Bachus, Spencer	AL	225-4921	Lantos, Tom	CA	225-3531	Shays, Christopher	CT	225-5541
Bonner, Jo	AL	225-4931	Lee, Barbara	CA	225-2661	Simmons, Rob	CT	225-2076
Cramer, Robert Jr.	AL	225-4801	Lewis, Jerry	CA	225-5861	Norton, Eleanor H.	DC	225-8050
Davis, Artur	AL	225-2665	Lofgren, Zoe	CA	225-3072	Castle, Michael N.	DE	225-4165
Everett, Terry	AL	225-2901	Lungren, Daniel E.	CA	225-5716	Bilirakis, Michael	FL	225-5755
Rogers, Mike	AL	225-3261	McKeon, Howard P.	CA	225-1956	Boyd, Allen	FL	225-5235
Berry, Marion	AR	225-4076	Millender-McDonald, J	CA	225-7924	Brown, Corrine	FL	225-0123
Boozman, John	AR	225-4301	Miller, Gary G.	CA	225-3201	Brown-Waite, Ginny	FL	225-1002
Ross, Mike	AR	225-3772	Miller, George	CA	225-2095	Crenshaw, Ander	FL	225-2501
Snyder, Vic	AR	225-2506	Napolitano, Grace F.	CA	225-5256	Davis, Jim	FL	225-3376
Flake, Jeff	AZ	225-2635	Nunes, Devin	CA	225-2523	Diaz-Balart, Lincoln	FL	225-4211
Franks, Trent	AZ	225-4576	Pelosi, Nancy	CA	225-4965	Diaz-Balart, Mario	FL	225-2778
Grijalva, Raúl M.	AZ	225-2435	Pombo, Richard W.	CA	225-1947	Feeney, Tom	FL	225-2706
Hayworth, J. D.	AZ	225-2190	Radanovich, George	CA	225-4540	Foley, Mark	FL	225-5792
Kolbe, Jim	AZ	225-2542	Rohrabacher, Dana	CA	225-2415	Harris, Katherine	FL	225-5015
Pastor, Ed	AZ	225-4065	Roybal-Allard, Lucille	CA	225-1766	Hastings, Alcee L.	FL	225-1313
Renzi, Rick	AZ	225-2315	Royce, Edward R.	CA	225-4111	Keller, Ric	FL	225-2176
Shadegg, John B.	AZ	225-3361	Sánchez, Linda T.	CA	225-6676	Mack, Connie	FL	225-2536
Baca, Joe	CA	225-6161	Sanchez, Loretta	CA	225-2965	Meek, Kendrick B.	FL	225-4506
Becerra, Xavier	CA	225-6235	Schiff, Adam B.	CA	225-4176	Mica, John L.	FL	225-4035
Berman, Howard L.	CA	225-4695	Sherman, Brad	CA	225-5911	Miller, Jeff	FL	225-4136
Bono, Mary	CA	225-5330	Solis, Hilda L.	CA	225-5464	Putnam, Adam H.	FL	225-1252
Calvert, Ken	CA	225-1986	Stark, Fortney Pete	CA	225-5065	Ros-Lehtinen, Ileana	FL	225-3931
Capps, Lois	CA	225-3601	Tauscher, Ellen O.	CA	225-1880	Shaw, E. Clay Jr.	FL	225-3026
Cardoza, Dennis A.	CA	225-6131	Thomas, William M.	CA	225-2915	Stearns, Cliff	FL	225-5744
Costa, Jim	CA	225-3341	Thompson, Mike	CA	225-3311	Schultz, Debbie	FL	225-7931
Cox, Christopher	CA	225-5611	Waters, Maxine	CA	225-2201	Weldon, Dave	FL	225-3671
Cunningham, Randy	CA	225-5452	Watson, Diane E.	CA	225-7084	Wexler, Robert	FL	225-3001
Davis, Susan A.	CA	225-2040	Waxman, Henry A.	CA	225-3976	Young, C. W. Bill	FL	225-5961
Doolittle, John T.	CA	225-2511	Woolsey, Lynn C.	CA	225-5161	Barrow, John	GA	225-2823
Dreier, David	CA	225-2305	Beauprez, Bob	CO	225-2645	Bishop, Sanford Jr.	GA	225-3631
Eshoo, Anna G.	CA	225-8104	DeGette, Diana	CO	225-4431	Deal, Nathan	GA	225-5211
Farr, Sam	CA	225-2861	Hefley, Joel	CO	225-4422	Gingrey, Phil	GA	225-2931
Filner, Bob	CA	225-8045	Musgrave, Marilyn	CO	225-4676	Kingston, Jack	GA	225-5831
Gallegly, Elton	CA	225-5811	Salazar, John T.	CO	225-4761	Lewis, John	GA	225-3801
Harman, Jane	CA	225-8220	Tancredo, Thomas	CO	225-7882	Linder, John	GA	225-4272
Herger, Wally	CA	225-3076	Udall, Mark	CO	225-2161	Marshall, Jim	GA	225-6531
Honda, Michael M.	CA	225-2631	DeLauro, Rosa L.	CT	225-3661	McKinney, Cynthia	GA	225-1605

Representative	St.	Phone	Representative	St.	Phone	Representative	St.	Phone
Norwood, Charlie	GA	225-4101	Alexander, Rodney	LA	225-8490	Carnahan, Russ	MO	225-2671
Price, Tom	GA	225-4501	Baker, Richard H.	LA	225-3901	Clay, Wm. Lacy	MO	225-2406
Scott, David	GA	225-2939	Boustany, C.Jr.	LA	225-2031	Cleaver, Emanuel	MO	225-4535
Westmoreland, L.	GA	225-5901	Jefferson, William J.	LA	225-6636	Emerson, Jo Ann	MO	225-4404
Bordallo, Madeleine	GU	225-1188	Jindal, Bobby	LA	225-3015	Graves, Sam	MO	225-7041
Abercrombie, Neil	HI	225-2726	McCrery, Jim	LA	225-2777	Hulshof, Kenny C.	MO	225-2956
Case, Ed	HI	225-4906	Melancon, Charlie	LA	225-4031	Skelton, Ike	MO	225-2876
Boswell, Leonard L.	IA	225-3806	Capuano, Michael E.	MA	225-5111	Pickering, Charles	MS	225-5031
King, Steve	IA	225-4426	Delahunt, William D.	MA	225-3111	Taylor, Gene	MS	225-5772
Latham, Tom	IA	225-5476	Frank, Barney	MA	225-5931	Thompson, Bennie	MS	225-5876
Leach, James A.	IA	225-6576	Lynch, Stephen F.	MA	225-8273	Wicker, Roger F.	MS	225-4306
Nussle, Jim	IA	225-2911	Markey, Edward J.	MA	225-2836	Rehberg, Dennis R.	MT	225-3211
Otter, C. L. "Butch"	ID	225-6611	McGovern, James	MA	225-6101	Butterfield, G. K.	NC	225-3101
Simpson, Michael K.	ID	225-5531	Meehan, Martin T.	MA	225-3411	Coble, Howard	NC	225-3065
Bean, Melissa L.	IL	225-3711	Neal, Richard E.	MA	225-5601	Etheridge, Bob	NC	225-4531
Biggert, Judy	IL	225-3515	Olver, John W.	MA	225-5335	Foxx, Virginia	NC	225-2071
Costello, Jerry F.	IL	225-5661	Tierney, John F.	MA	225-8020	Hayes, Robin	NC	225-3715
Davis, Danny K.	IL	225-5006	Bartlett, Roscoe G.	MD	225-2721	Jones, Walter B.	NC	225-3415
Emanuel, Rahm	IL	225-4061	Cardin, Benjamin L.	MD	225-4016	McHenry, Patrick T.	NC	225-2576
Evans, Lane	IL	225-5905	Cummings, Elijah E.	MD	225-4741	McIntyre, Mike	NC	225-2731
Gutierrez, Luis V.	IL	225-8203	Gilchrest, Wayne T.	MD	225-5311	Miller, Brad	NC	225-3032
Hastert, J. Dennis	IL	225-2976	Hoyer, Steny H.	MD	225-4131	Myrick, Sue Wilkins	NC	225-1976
Hyde, Henry J.	IL	225-4561	Ruppersberger, C.	MD	225-3061	Price, David E.	NC	225-1784
Jackson, Jesse Jr.	IL	225-0773	Van Hollen, Chris	MD	225-5341	Taylor, Charles H.	NC	225-6401
Johnson, Timothy V.	IL	225-2371	Wynn, Albert R.	MD	225-8699	Watt, Melvin L.	NC	225-1510
Kirk, Mark Steven	IL	225-4835	Allen, Thomas H.	ME	225-6116	Pomeroy, Earl	ND	225-2611
LaHood, Ray	IL	225-6201	Michaud, Michael H.	ME	225-6306	Fortenberry, Jeff	NE	225-4806
Lipinski, Daniel	IL	225-5701	Camp, Dave	MI	225-3561	Osborne, Tom	NE	225-6435
Manzullo, Donald A.	IL	225-5676	Conyers, John Jr.	MI	225-5126	Terry, Lee	NE	225-4155
Rush, Bobby L.	IL	225-4372	Dingell, John D.	MI	225-4071	Bass, Charles F.	NH	225-5206
Schakowsky, Janice	IL	225-2111	Ehlers, Vernon J.	MI	225-3831	Bradley, Jeb	NH	225-5456
Shimkus, John	IL	225-5271	Hoekstra, Peter	MI	225-4401	Andrews, Robert E.	NJ	225-6501
Weller, Jerry	IL	225-3635	Kildee, Dale E.	MI	225-3611	Ferguson, Mike	NJ	225-5361
Burton, Dan	IN	225-2276	Kilpatrick, Carolyn	MI	225-2261	Frelinghuysen, R.	NJ	225-5034
Buyer, Steve	IN	225-5037	Knollenberg, Joe	MI	225-5802	Garrett, Scott	NJ	225-4465
Carson, Julia	IN	225-4011	Levin, Sander M.	MI	225-4961	Holt, Rush D.	NJ	225-5801
Chocola, Chris	IN	225-3915	McCotter, Thaddeus	MI	225-8171	LoBiondo, Frank A.	NJ	225-6572
Hostettler, John N.	IN	225-4636	Miller, Candice S.	MI	225-2106	Menendez, Robert	NJ	225-7919
Pence, Mike	IN	225-3021	Rogers, Mike	MI	225-4872	Pallone, Frank Jr.	NJ	225-4671
Sodrel, Michael E.	IN	225-5315	Schwarz, John	MI	225-6276	Pascrell, Bill Jr.	NJ	225-5751
Souder, Mark E.	IN	225-4436	Stupak, Bart	MI	225-4735	Payne, Donald M.	NJ	225-3436
Visclosky, Peter J.	IN	225-2461	Upton, Fred	MI	225-3761	Rothman, Steven R.	NJ	225-5061
Moore, Dennis	KS	225-2865	Gutknecht, Gil	MN	225-2472	Saxton, Jim	NJ	225-4765
Moran, Jerry	KS	225-2715	Kennedy, Mark R.	MN	225-2331	Smith, Christopher	NJ	225-3765
Ryun, Jim	KS	225-6601	Kline, John	MN	225-2271	Pearce, Stevan	NM	225-2365
Tiahrt, Todd	KS	225-6216	McCollum, Betty	MN	225-6631	Udall, Tom	NM	225-6190
Chandler, Ben	KY	225-4706	Oberstar, James L.	MN	225-6211	Wilson, Heather	NM	225-6316
Davis, Geoff	KY	225-3465	Peterson, Collin C.	MN	225-2165	Berkley, Shelley	NV	225-5965
Lewis, Ron	KY	225-3501	Ramstad, Jim	MN	225-2871	Gibbons, Jim	NV	225-6155
Northup, Anne M.	KY	225-5401	Sabo, Martin Olav	MN	225-4755	Porter, Jon C.	NV	225-3252
Rogers, Harold	KY	225-4601	Akin, W. Todd	MO	225-2561	Ackerman, Gary L.	NY	225-2601
Whitfield, Ed	KY	225-3115	Blunt, Roy	MO	225-6536	Bishop, Timothy H.	NY	225-3826

Representative	St.	Phone	Representative	St.	Phone	Representative	St.	Phone
Boehlert, Sherwood	NY	225-3665	Hooley, Darlene	OR	225-5711	Gonzalez, Charles	TX	225-3236
Crowley, Joseph	NY	225-3965	Walden, Greg	OR	225-6730	Granger, Kay	TX	225-5071
Engel, Eliot L.	NY	225-2464	Wu, David	OR	225-0855	Green, Al	TX	225-7508
Fossella, Vito	NY	225-3371	Brady, Robert A.	PA	225-4731	Green, Gene	TX	225-1688
Higgins, Brian	NY	225-3306	Dent, Charles W.	PA	225-6411	Hall, Ralph M.	TX	225-6673
Hinchey, Maurice D.	NY	225-6335	Doyle, Michael F.	PA	225-2135	Hensarling, Jeb	TX	225-3484
Israel, Steve	NY	225-3335	English, Phil	PA	225-5406	Hinojosa, Rubén	TX	225-2531
Kelly, Sue W.	NY	225-5441	Fattah, Chaka	PA	225-4001	Jackson-Lee, Sheila	TX	225-3816
King, Peter T.	NY	225-7896	Fitzpatrick, Michael	PA	225-4276	Johnson, Eddie	TX	225-8885
Kuhl, John R. Jr.	NY	225-3161	Gerlach, Jim	PA	225-4315	Johnson, Sam	TX	225-4201
Lowey, Nita M.	NY	225-6506	Hart, Melissa A.	PA	225-2565	Marchant, Kenny	TX	225-6605
Maloney, Carolyn B.	NY	225-7944	Holden, Tim	PA	225-5546	McCaul, Michael T.	TX	225-2401
McCarthy, Carolyn	NY	225-5516	Kanjorski, Paul E.	PA	225-6511	Neugebauer, Randy	TX	225-4005
McHugh, John M.	NY	225-4611	Murphy, Tim	PA	225-2301	Ortiz, Solomon P.	TX	225-7742
McNulty, Michael R.	NY	225-5076	Murtha, John P.	PA	225-2065	Paul, Ron	TX	225-2831
Meeks, Gregory W.	NY	225-3461	Peterson, John E.	PA	225-5121	Poe, Ted	TX	225-6565
Nadler, Jerrold	NY	225-5635	Pitts, Joseph R.	PA	225-2411	Reyes, Silvestre	TX	225-4831
Owens, Major R.	NY	225-6231	Platts, Todd Russell	PA	225-5836	Sessions, Pete	TX	225-2231
Rangel, Charles B.	NY	225-4365	Schwartz, Allyson	PA	225-6111	Smith, Lamar S.	TX	225-4236
Reynolds, Thomas	NY	225-5265	Sherwood, Don	PA	225-3731	Thornberry, Mac	TX	225-3706
Serrano, José E.	NY	225-4361	Shuster, Bill	PA	225-2431	Bishop, Rob	UT	225-0453
Slaughter, Louise M.	NY	225-3615	Weldon, Curt	PA	225-2011	Cannon, Chris	UT	225-7751
Sweeney, John E.	NY	225-5614	Kennedy, Patrick J.	RI	225-4911	Matheson, Jim	UT	225-3011
Towns, Edolphus	NY	225-5936	Langevin, James R.	RI	225-2735	Boucher, Rick	VA	225-3861
Velázquez, Nydia	NY	225-2361	Barrett, J. Gresham	SC	225-5301	Cantor, Eric	VA	225-2815
Walsh, James T.	NY	225-3701	Brown, Henry E. Jr.	SC	225-3176	Davis, Jo Ann	VA	225-4261
Weiner, Anthony D.	NY	225-6616	Clyburn, James E.	SC	225-3315	Davis, Tom	VA	225-1492
Boehner, John A.	OH	225-6205	Inglis, Bob	SC	225-6030	Drake, Thelma D.	VA	225-4215
Brown, Sherrod	OH	225-3401	Spratt, John M. Jr.	SC	225-5501	Forbes, J. Randy	VA	225-6365
Chabot, Steve	OH	225-2216	Wilson, Joe	SC	225-2452	Goode, Virgil H. Jr.	VA	225-4711
Gillmor, Paul E.	OH	225-6405	Herseth, Stephanie	SD	225-2801	Goodlatte, Bob	VA	225-5431
Hobson, David L.	OH	225-4324	Blackburn, Marsha	TN	225-2811	Moran, James P.	VA	225-4376
Jones, Stephanie	OH	225-7032	Cooper, Jim	TN	225-4311	Scott, Robert C.	VA	225-8351
Kaptur, Marcy	OH	225-4146	Davis, Lincoln	TN	225-6831	Wolf, Frank R.	VA	225-5136
Kucinich, Dennis J.	OH	225-5871	Duncan, John J. Jr.	TN	225-5435	Christensen, Donna	VI	225-1790
LaTourette, Steven	OH	225-5731	Ford, Harold E. Jr.	TN	225-3265	Sanders, Bernard	VT	225-4115
Ney, Robert W.	OH	225-6265	Gordon, Bart	TN	225-4231	Baird, Brian	WA	225-3536
Oxley, Michael G.	OH	225-2676	Jenkins, William L.	TN	225-6356	Dicks, Norman D.	WA	225-5916
Portman, Rob	OH	225-3164	Tanner, John S.	TN	225-4714	Hastings, Doc	WA	225-5816
Pryce, Deborah	OH	225-2015	Wamp, Zach	TN	225-3271	Inslee, Jay	WA	225-6311
Regula, Ralph	OH	225-3876	Barton, Joe	TX	225-2002	Larsen, Rick	WA	225-2605
Ryan, Tim	OH	225-5261	Bonilla, Henry	TX	225-4511	McDermott, Jim	WA	225-3106
Strickland, Ted	OH	225-5705	Brady, Kevin	TX	225-4901	McMorris, Cathy	WA	225-2006
Tiberi, Patrick J.	OH	225-5355	Burgess, Michael C.	TX	225-7772	Reichert, David G.	WA	225-7761
Turner, Michael R.	OH	225-6465	Carter, John R.	TX	225-3864	Smith, Adam	WA	225-8901
Boren, Dan	OK	225-2701	Conaway, K.	TX	225-3605	Baldwin, Tammy	WI	225-2906
Cole, Tom	OK	225-6165	Cuellar, Henry	TX	225-1640	Green, Mark	WI	225-5665
Istook, Ernest J. Jr.	OK	225-2132	Culberson, John	TX	225-2571	Kind, Ron	WI	225-5506
Lucas, Frank D.	OK	225-5565	DeLay, Tom	TX	225-5951	Moore, Gwen	WI	225-4572
Sullivan, John	OK	225-2211	Doggett, Lloyd	TX	225-4865	Obey, David R.	WI	225-3365
Blumenauer, Earl	OR	225-4811	Edwards, Chet	TX	225-6105	Petri, Thomas E.	WI	225-2476
DeFazio, Peter A.	OR	225-6416	Gohmert, Louie	TX	225-3035	Ryan, Paul	WI	225-3031
						Sensenbrenner, F.	WI	225-5101
						Capito, Shelley	WV	225-2711
						Mollohan, Alan B.	WV	225-4172
						Rahall, Nick J. II	WV	225-3452
						Cubin, Barbara	WY	225-2311

Alabama
Bob Riley
State Capitol
Montgomery, AL 36130

Alaska
Frank Murkowski
PO Box A
Juneau, AK 99811

Arizona
Janet Napolitano
State House
Phoenix, AZ 85007

Arkansas
Mike Huckabee
State Capitol
Little Rock, AZ 72201

California
Arnold Schwarzenegger
State Capitol
Sacramento, CA 95814

Colorado
Bill Owens
136 State Capitol
Denver, CO 80203

Connecticut
M. Jodi Rell
State Capitol
Hartford, CT 06106

Delaware
Ruth Ann Minner
Office of the Governor
Dover, DE 19901

Florida
Jeb Bush
State Capitol
Tallahassee, FL 32399-0001

Georgia
Sonny Perdue
203 State Capitol
Atlanta, GA 30334

Hawaii
Linda Lingle
State Capitol
Honolulu, HI 96813

Idaho
Dirk Kempthorne
State Capitol
Boise, ID 83720

Illinois
Rod Blagojevich
State Capitol
Springfield, IL 62706

Indiana
Joseph Kernan
Room 206 Statehouse
Indianapolis, IN 46204

Iowa
Tom Vilsack
State Capitol
Des Moines, IA 50319-0001

Kansas
Kathleen Sebelius
State House
Topeka, KS 66612-1590

Kentucky
Ernie Fletcher
State Capitol
Frankfort, KY 40601

Louisiana
Kathleen Blanco
State Capitol
Baton Rouge, LA 70804

Maine
John Baldacci
State House
Augusta, MA 04333

Maryland
Robert Ehrlich
Governor's State House
Annapolis, MD 21401

Massachusetts
Mitt Romney
State House
Boston, MA 02133

Michigan
Jennifer Granholm
State Capitol
Lansing, MI 48933

Minnesota
Tim Pawlenty
130 State Capitol
St.Paul, MN 55155

Mississippi
Haley Barbour
PO Box 139
Jackson, MS 39205

Missouri
Bob Holden
State Capitol
Jefferson City, MO 65102

Montana
Brian Schweitzer
State Capitol
Helena, MT 59620

Nebraska
Mike Johanns
State Capitol
Lincoln, NE 68509

Nevada
Kenny Guinn
State Capitol
Carson City, NV 89710

New Hampshire
John Lynch
State House Room 208
Concord, NH 03301

New Jersey
Richard Codey
State House, Governor
Trenton, NJ 08625

New Mexico
Bill Richardson
State Capitol
Santa Fe, NM 87503

New York
George Pataki
State Capitol
Albany, NY 12224

North Carolina
Mike Easley
State Capitol
Raleigh, NC 27603

North Dakota
John Hoeven
600 E. Blvd. State Capitol
Bismarck, ND 58505

Ohio
Bob Taft
Governor's House
Columbus, OH 43215

Oklahoma
Brad Henry
State Capitol Room 212
Oklahoma City, OK 73105

Oregon
Ted Kulongoski
State Capitol
Salem, OR 97310

Pennsylvania
Edward Rendell
State Capitol
Harrisburg, PA 17120

Rhode Island
Don Carcieri
State House
Providence, RI 02903

South Carolina
Mark Sanford
State House
Columbia, SC 29211

South Dakota
Mike Rounds
State Capitol
Pierre, SD 57501

Tennessee
Phil Bredesen
State Capitol
Nashville, TN 37243

Texas
Rick Perry
State Capitol
Austin, TX 78711

Utah
John Huntsman
210 State Capitol
Salt Lake City, UT 84114

Vermont
James H. Douglas
Pavilion Office Bldg
Montpelier, VT 05609

Virginia
Mark Warner
State Capitol
Richmond, VA 23219

Washington
Christine Gregoire
State Capitol
Olympia, WA 98504

West Virginia
Bob Wise
State Capitol
Charleston, WV. 25305

Wisconsin
Jim Doyle
State Capitol
Madison, WI 53707

Wyoming
Dave Freudenthal
State Capitol
Cheyenne, WY 82002

Mayor Michael Bloomberg [R]

City Hall Park, New York, NY 10007

website www.ci.nyc.ny.us

Mayor Howard Peak

1 Military Plaza, San Antonio, TX 78283

Website www.tristero.com/usa/tx/sa

Mayor Kurt Schmoke [D]

100 N. Holliday St, Baltimore, MD 21202

website www.ci.baltimore.md.us

Mayor Susan Golding [R]

202 C St, San Diego, CA 92101

website www.sannet.gov

Mayor Thomas M. Menino [D]

1 City Hall Square, Boston, MA 02201

website www.ci.boston.ma.us

Mayor Willie L. Brown, Jr. [D]

400 Van Ness Ave, San Francisco, CA 94102

website www.ci.sf.ca.us

Mayor Richard M. Daley [D]

121 N. LaSalle St, Chicago, IL 60602

website www.ci.chi.il.us

Mayor Lee P. Brown

901 Bagby St, Houston, TX 77251

website www.houston.org

Mayor Edward Rendell [D]

Broad & Market Sts, Philadelphia, PA 19107

website www.phila.gov

Mayor Stephen Goldsmith [R]

2501 City-County Building, Indianapolis, IN 46204

website www.indychamber.com

Mayor Skip Rimsza

251 W. Washington Ave, Phoenix, AZ 85003

website www.ci.phoenix.az.us

Mayor Anthony Williams [D]

441 4th St NW, Washington, DC 20004

website www.dchomepage.net

Mayor Ronald Kirk

1500 Marilla, Dallas, TX 75201

website www.gdc.org

Mayor Antonio Villaraigosa

200 N. Spring St, Los Angeles, CA 90012

website www.ci.la.ca.us

Joseph Patrick Kennedy* marries Rose Elizabeth Fitzgerald*
               Children   Deceased*
1. Joseph Patrick Kennedy Jr.*
2. Rosemary Kennedy
3. Kathleen Kennedy* marries William John Robert Cavendish
4. Eunice Mary Kennedy marries Robert Sargent Shriver Jr.
               Children
    4a. Robert Sargent Shriver III
    4b. Maria Owings Shriver marries Arnold Schwarzenegger
    4c. Timothy Perry Shriver
    4d. Mark Kennedy Shriver
    4e. Anthony Paul Shriver

5. Patricia Kennedy marries Peter Lawford* (divorced)
               Children
    5a. Christopher Kennedy Lawford
    5b. Sydney Maleia Lawford
    5c. Victoria Francis Lawford
    5d. Robin Elizabeth Lawford

6. Robert Francis Kennedy* marries Ethel Skakel
               Children
    6a. Kathleen Hartington Kennedy
    6b. Joseph Patrick Kennedy II
    6c. Robert Francis Kennedy Jr.
    6d. David Anthony Kennedy*
    6e. Mary Courtney Kennedy
    6f. Michael LeMoyne Kennedy*
    6g. Mary Kerry Kennedy
    6h. Christopher George Kennedy
    6i. Matthew Maxwell Taylor Kennedy
    6j. Douglas Harriman Kennedy
    6k. Rory Elizabeth Katherine Kennedy

7. Jean Ann Kennedy marries Stephen Edward Smith
               Children
    7a. Stephen Edward Smith Jr.
    7b. William Kennedy Smith
    7c. Amanda Mary Smith
    7d. Kym Marie Smith

8. Edward Moore Kennedy marries Virginia Joan Bennet marries Victoria Anne Reggie
               Children
    8a. Kara Ann Kennedy
    8b. Edward Moore Kennedy Jr.
    8c. Patrick Joseph Kennedy

9. John Fitzgerald Kennedy* marries Jaqueline Lee Bouvier*
               Children
    9a. unamed daughter(still born)
    9b. Caroline Bouvier Kennedy marries Edwin Arthur Schlossberg
    9c. John Fitzgerald Kennedy Jr.* marries Carolyn Bessette*
    9d. Patrick Bouvier Kennedy*

Bailey, F. Lee
66 Longwharf
Boston, MA 02110

Clark, Marcia
District Attorney Office
210 W Temple
Los Angeles, CA 90012

Darden, Christopher
William Morris Agency
151 El Camino
Beverly Hills, CA 90212

Dershowitz, Alan
Harvard Law School
Harvard University
Cambridge, MA 02138

Fujisaki, Hiroshi-Judge
Santa Monica Courthouse
Santa Monica, CA 90401

Hearst, Patty
The Gersh Agency
232 North Canon Drive
Beverly Hills, CA 90210

Ito, Lance- Judge
Dept 103
Superior Court
210 W Temple
Los Angeles, CA 90012

Kennedy, Edward
315 Russell Offfice Bldg
Washington, DC 20510

Kennedy, Patrick
U.S. House of Representatives
Washington, DC 20515

Kennedy, Joseph II
1210 Longworth House Building
Washington, DC 20510

Kennedy, Robert F.
78 North Broadway
White Plains, NY 10603

Moore, Michael
Attorney General
450 High Street
Jackson, MS 39201

Scheck, Barry
Cardozo School of Law
55 5th Avenue
New York, NY 10003

Schlosseberg, Carolin
888 Park Ave
New York, NY 10021

Shapiro, Robert L.
2121 Avenue of the Stars
Los Angeles, CA 90067

Shriver, Eunice Kennedy
Joseph P. Kennedy Jr. Foundation
1350 New York Ave NW
Washington DC 20005

Starr, Kenneth
Kirkland & Ellis
655 15th Street
Washington, DC 20005

Strossen, Nadine
New York Law School
57 Worth Street
New York, NY 10013

Shriver, Sargent
Director, Special Olympics
1325 G Street NW
Washington, DC 20005

Gary, Willie E.
Gary, Williams, Parenti
221 Osceola Street
Stuart, FL 34994

Abacha, Sani
Office of the President
Abuja, Nigeria

Ahern, Bertie
St. Luke's
161 Lower Drumcondra
Dublin 9, Ireland

Andrew, Duke Of York
Buckingham Palace
London W1 England

Annan, Kofi
Office of Secretary General
United Nations
New York, NY 10017

Anne, Princess Royal
Buckingham Palace
London England

Blair, Tony
11 Downing Street
London SW1A OAA, England

Cardoso, Fernando H.
President of Brazil
Palacio Do Planalto
Praca Dos Tres Poderes
70150 Brasilia.DF Brazil

Castro, Fidel
Office of the President
Palacia Del Gobierno
Havana, Cuba

Charles, Prince Of Wales
St. James Palace
London, England

Jospin, Lionel R.
Hotel De Matignon
57 Rue De Varenne
75700 Paris, France

Chretien, Jean
Office Of Prime Minister
Parliament Bldgs.
Ottawa, Ontario K1A OA2
Canada

Crown Princess Victoria
The Royal Palace
111 30 Stockholm, Sweden

D'alema, Massimo
Palazzo Del Quirinale
00187 Rome, Italy

De Lozada, Gonzalo
Palicio De Gobierno
Plaza Murillo
La Paz, Bolivia

Deby, Idriss
Office of President
N'djamena, Chad

Deklerk, F.W.
State President's Office
Union Bldg.(West Wing)
Private Bag X1000
0001 Pretoria, South Africa

Dos Santos, Jose
Gabinete De Presidente
Luanda, Angola

Ferguson, Sarah
Margaret
Buckingham Palace
London W1 England

Gandhi, Sonia
President India's Congress
10 Janpath Street
New Delhi, India

Gorbachev, Mikhail
Lenningradsky
Prospekt 49
Moscow, Russia

Havel, Vaclav, Prime Minister
Kancelar Prezidenta
Republiky
119 08 Prague Hrad
Czech Republic

Her Imperial Highness
Crown Princess Masako
Edo Castle
The Imperial Palace
Tokyo, Japan

Her Imperial Highness
Princess Nori
Edo Castle
The Imperial Palace
Tokyo, Japan

Her Imperial Highness
Princess Kako
Edo Castle
The Imperial Palace
Tokyo, Japan

Her Imperial Highness
Princess Mako
Edo Castle
The Imperial Palace
Tokyo, Japan

Her Imperial Highness
Princess Akishino
Edo Castle
The Imperial Palace
Tokyo, Japan

Her Imperial Majesty
Michiko Empress of Japan
Edo Castle
The Imperial Palace
Tokyo, Japan

Her Majesty
Queen Elizabeth II
Buckingham Palace
London W1 England

His Imperial Highness
Crown Prince Naruhito
Edo Castle
The Imperial Palace
Tokyo, Japan

His Imperial Highness
Prince Akishino of Japan
Edo Castle
The Imperial Palace
Tokyo, Japan

His Imperial Majesty
Akihito Emperor of Japan
Edo Castle
The Imperial Palace
Tokyo, Japan

His Majesty
King Fahd
Royal Palace
Riyadh, Saudi Arabia

Howard, John
Parliament House
Canberra, A.C.T.
Australia

Jiang, Zemin
Office of President
Beijing,
People's Republic Of
China

Khatami, Mohammad
Islamic Republic
Dr. Ali Shariati Avenue
Tehran, Iran

Kim Young Sam
Office of the President
Chong Wa Dae,
1 Sejong-No, Chongno-Ku
Seoul, South Korea

King Carl XVI Gustaf
The Royal Palace
111 30 Stockholm, Sweden

King Jaun Carlos I
Palacio De La Zarzuela
Madrid, Spain

Kiriyenko, Sergei
Prime Ministers Office
Krasnofriesnenskaya
Nab 2
Moscow 103274 Russia

Klestil, Thomas
Prasidentschaftskanzlie
Hofburg
1014 Vienna, Austria

Lee, Teng-Tui
Office of the President
Chiehshou Hall
122 Chung King South Rd
  Sec. 1 Tapei, Taiwan

Major, John
House of Commons
London Sw1 England

Mandela, Nelson
Private Bag X1000
Pretoria 0001
South Africa

Mankiller, Wilma P.
Principal Chief
Cherokee Nation
PO Box 948
Tahlequah, OK 74464

Putin, Vladimir
Office of the President
103073 The Kremlin
Moscow, Russia

Menem, Carlos
Casa De Gobierno
Balcarce 50
1064 Buenos Aires
Argentina

Mwinyi, Ali Hassan
C/O Office of President
Dar Es Salaam, Tanzania

Sharon, Ariel
Prime Minister of Israel
Likud, 38 Rehov K.george
Tel Aviv 61231, Israel

Obuchi, Keizo
Prime Minister Office
1-6 Nagato-cho
Chiyoda-Ku
Tokyo 100, Japan

Patterson, P.J.
Office of Prime Minister
1 Devon Road Po Box 272
Kingston 6, Jamaica

Prince Bernhard
C/O Soestdijk Palace
Baarn, Netherlands

Prince Carl Philip
The Royal Palace
111 30 Stockholm, Sweden

Prince Edward
Buckingham Palace
London W1 England

Prince Harry
St. James Palace
London England

Prince Philip
Duke of Edinburgh
Buckingham Palace
London W1 England

Prince Rainer III
Plais De Monaco
98015 Monte Carlo
Monaco

Prince William
St. James Palace
London England

Princess Madeleine
The Royal Palace
111 30 Stockholm, Sweden

Princess Margaret
Countess of Snowdon
Kensington Palace
London England

Queen Beatrix
Binnen Huf 19
The Hague 2513 AA
The Netherlands

Queen Silvia
The Royal Palace
111 30 Stockholm, Sweden

Rasmussen, Puol Nyrup
Prime Minister's Office
Christianborg
Prins Jorgens Gaardii
1218 Copenhaen, Denmark

Sabah, Jaber Al-Ahmad
Emir of Kuwait
Sief Palace
Amiry Diwan, Kuwait

Schroeder, Gerhard
Marbacher Strasse 11
6700 Ludwidshafen/Rhein
Federal Republic of Germany

Simitis, Costas
Office of the President
Odos Zalokosta 10
Athens, Greece

Thatcher, Margaret
Chester Square, Belgravia
London, England

Tutu, Desmond
Claremont 7700
Johannesburgh
South Africa

Walesa, Lech
Ul. Polanki 54
Gdansk-Oliwa, Poland

Yeltsin, Boris
The Kremlin
Moscow, Russia

Zedillo, Ponce De Leon
Ernesto-pres. of Mexico
Office of the President
Los Pinas, Puerta 1, Col
Chapultepec 11850, Mexico

Zeroual, Liamine
Presidence
De La Repulique
El Moradia, Algiers,
Algeria

Astronauts

Adamson, James C.	President	Honeywell Technology	7000 Columbia Gateway	Columbia, MD 21046
Akers, Thomas D.	Commander-ROTC	1870 Miner Circle	UMR-206 Harris Hall	Rolla, MT 65409
Aldrin, Buzz	10380 Wilshire Blvd	Los Angeles, CA 90024		
Allen, Andrew M.	Technical Operations	United Space Alliance	600 Gemini	Houston, TX 77058
Allen, Joseph P.	Chairman	Veridian	1200 South Hayes Street	Arlington, VA 22202
Altman, Scott D.	Astronaut Office	Code CB Bldg. 4S	2101 NASA Road One	Houston, TX 77058
Anders, William A.	Director	Heritage Flight Museum	PO Box 1630	Eastsound, WA 98245
Anderson, Clayton C.	Astronaut Office	Code CB Bldg. 4S	2101 NASA Road One	Houston, TX 77058
Antonelli, Dominic A.	Astronaut Office	Code CB Bldg. 4S	2101 NASA Road One	Houston, TX 77058
Apt, Jerome	The Carnegie Museum	Natural History	4400 Forbes Avenue	Pittsburgh, PA 15213
Archambault, Lee J.	Astronaut Office	Code CB Bldg. 4S	2101 NASA Road One	Houston, TX 77058
Armstrong, Neil A.	Chairman	AIL Systems	455 Commack Road	Deer Park, NY 11729
Ashby, Jeffrey S.	Astronaut Office	Code CB Bldg. 4S	2101 NASA Road One	Houston, TX 77058
Bagian, James P.	EPA	OMS-RSPD	2565 Plymouth Road	Ann Arbor, MI 48105
Baker, Ellen S.	Astronaut Office	Code CB Bldg. 4S	2101 NASA Road One	Houston, TX 77058
Baker, Michael A.	Asssitant Director	Code A6	Johnson Space Center	Houston, TX 77058
Barratt, Michael R.	Astronaut Office	Code CB Bldg. 4S	2101 NASA Road One	Houston, TX 77058
Barry, Daniel T.	Astronaut Office	Code CB Bldg. 4S	2101 NASA Road One	Houston, TX 77058
Bartone, John-David	Chief Scientist	Office of Space Station	Johnson Space Center	Houston, TX 77058
Bean, Alan L.	9173 Briar Forest	Houston, TX 77024-7222		
Behnken, Robert L.	Astronaut Office	Code CB Bldg. 4S	2101 NASA Road One	Houston, TX 77058
Blaha, John E.	VP Applied Research	USAA Corporation	9800 Fredericksburg Rd	San Antonio, TX 78288
Bloomfield, Michael J.	Astronaut Office	Code CB Bldg. 4S	2101 NASA Road One	Houston, TX 77058
Bluford, Guion S., Jr.	VP Aerospace Sector	Federal Data Corporation	3005 Aerospace Pkwy	Cleveland, OH 44124
Bobko, Karol J.	VP Product Development	Johnson Engineering	555 Forge River Road	Webster, TX 77598
Boe, Eric A.	Astronaut Office	Code CB Bldg. 4S	2101 NASA Road One	Houston, TX 77058
Bolden, Charles F., Jr.	Commanding General	PO Box 452038	MCAS Miramar	San Diego, CA 92145
Bondar, Roberta	Astronaut Office	Code CB Bldg. 4S	2101 NASA Road One	Houston, TX 77058
Borman, Frank	Chairman	Patlex Corporation	PO Box 1159	Fairacres, NM 88033
Bowen, Stephen G.	Astronaut Office	Code CB Bldg. 4S	2101 NASA Road One	Houston, TX 77058
Bowersox, Kenneth D.	SAIL	Johnson Space Center	Houston, TX 77058	
Brady, Charles E., Jr.	Astronaut Office	Code CB Bldg. 4S	2101 NASA Road One	Houston, TX 77058
Brand, Vance D.	Deputy Director	Aerospace Projects	NASA Dryden Flight Ctr.	Edwards, CA 93523
Brandenstein, Daniel	VP Customer Support	Lockheed Martin Space	595 Gemini Avenue	Houston, TX 77058
Bridges, Roy D., Jr.	Mail Code AA	Director	Kennedy Space Center	FL 32899
Brown, Curtis L., Jr.	19500 E Highway 6	Alvin, TX 77511-7458		
Brown, Mark N.	Director of Aerospace	General Research Corp.	2940 Presidential Drive	Fairborn, OH 45324
Buchli, James F.	Space Station Manager	United Space Alliance	1150 Gemini Road	Houston, TX 77058-2708
Buckey, Jay Clark	Dartmouth-Hitchcock	1 Medical Center Drive	Lebanon, NH 03756	
Bull, John S.	Aircraft Guidance & Nav	NASA Ames Research	Moffet Field, CA 94035	
Burbank, Daniel C.	Astronaut Office	Code CB Bldg. 4S	2101 NASA Road One	Houston, TX 77058
Bursch, Daniel W.	Astronaut Office	Code CB Bldg. 4S	2101 NASA Road One	Houston, TX 77058
Cabana, Robert D.	ISS Manager Intl. Op.	Bldg. 1 Room 522G	Johnson Space Center	Houston, TX 77058
Cagle, Yvonne D.	Astronaut Office	Code CB Bldg. 4S	2101 NASA Road One	Houston, TX 77058

Caldeiro, Fernando	Astronaut Office	Code CB Bldg. 4S	2101 NASA Road One	Houston, TX 77058
Caldwell, Tracy E.	Astronaut Office	Code CB Bldg. 4S	2101 NASA Road One	Houston, TX 77058
Camarda, Charles J.	Astronaut Office	Code CB Bldg. 4S	2101 NASA Road One	Houston, TX 77058
Cameron, Kenneth D.	Room 3-220	Saab Automobile	3044 West Grand Blvd	Detroit, MI 48202-3091
Carey, Duane G.	Astronaut Office	Code CB Bldg. 4S	2101 NASA Road One	Houston, TX 77058
Carpenter, M. Scott	PO Box 3161	4153 Spruce Way	Vail, CO 81657	
Carr, Gerald P.	President	CAMUS Inc.	PO Box 919	Huntsville, AR 72740
Casper, John H.	Director	Safety/Quality Assurance	Johnson Space Center	Houston, TX 77058
Cenker, Robert	Aerospace Consultant	GORCA, Inc.	155 Hickory Corner	East Windsor, NJ 08520
Cernan, Eugene A.	Chairman	Johnson Eng. Corp.	555 Forge River Road	Webster, TX 77598-4336
Chamitoff, Gregory E.	Astronaut Office	Code CB Bldg. 4S	2101 NASA Road One	Houston, TX 77058
Chang-Diaz, Franklin R.	Code CB-ASPL Bldg 4S	Advance Propulsion Lab.	Johnson Space Center	Houston, TX 77058
Chapman, Philip K.	Chief Scientist	Rotary Rocket Corp.	1250 Bayhill Drive	San Bruno, CA 94066
Cheli, Maurizio (ESA)	European Astronaut Ctr.	Linder Hohe,	Postfach 90 60 96	D-51127 Koln, Germany
Chiao, Leroy	Astronaut Office	Code CB Bldg. 4S	2101 NASA Road One	Houston, TX 77058
Chilton, Kevin P.	Deputy Director	Politico/Military AffairsJ-5	5104 Jnt. Staff Pentagon	Washington, DC 20318
Chrétien, Jean-Loup	CNES	Direction des Astronaute	2 Place Maurice Quentin	F-75039 Paris, France
Cleave, Mary L.	Code AS Room 7R86	Deputy Administrator	NASA Headquarters	Washington, DC 20546
Clervoy, Jean-Francois	European Astronaut Ctr.	Linder Hohe,	Postfach 90 60 96	D-51127 Koln, Germany
Clifford, Michael R.	Flight Op. Mgr. Intl.	Boeing Company	2100 Space Park Drive	Houston, TX 77058
Coats, Michael L.	VP Reusable Launch Sy.	Lockheed Martin	PO Box 179	Denver, CO 80201-0179
Cockrell, Kenneth D.	Astronaut Office	Code CB Bldg. 4S	2101 NASA Road One	Houston, TX 77058
Coleman, Catherine G.	Astronaut Office	Code CB Bldg. 4S	2101 NASA Road One	Houston, TX 77058
Collins, Eileen M.	Astronaut Office	Code CB Bldg. 4S	2101 NASA Road One	Houston, TX 77058
Collins, Michael	272 Polynesia Court	Marco Island, FL 34145		
Cooper, L. Gordon, Jr.	President	Galaxy Aerospace Inc.	16303 Waterman Drive	Van Nuys, CA 91406
Covey, Richard O.	VP Houston Operations	Boeing Company	2100 Space Park Drive	Houston, TX 77058
Creamer, Timothy J.	Astronaut Office	Code CB Bldg. 4S	2101 NASA Road One	Houston, TX 77058
Creighton, John O.	Production Test Pilot	Boeing Commercial	PO Box 3707	Seattle, WA 98124
Crippen, Robert L.	President	Cordant Technologies	PO Box 707	Brigham City, UT 84302
Crouch, Roger	ISS Chief Scientist	NASA Office of Life and	Microgravity Sciences	Washington, DC 20546
Culbertson, Frank L., Jr.	Deputy Program Mgr.	Code YA	Johnson Space Center	Houston, TX 77058
Cunningham, Walter	2425 West Loop South	Houston, TX 77027		
Curbeam, Robert L., Jr.	Astronaut Office	Code CB Bldg. 4S	2101 NASA Road One	Houston, TX 77058
Currie, Nancy J.	Astronaut Office	Code CB Bldg. 4S	2101 NASA Road One	Houston, TX 77058
Davis, N. Jan	Mail Code FDOI	Director, Flight Projects	George C. Marshall Ctr.	Huntsville, AL 35812
DeLucas, Lawrence	Ctr. Biophysical Science	University of Alabama	1530 3rd Avenue	Birmingham, AL 35294
Doi, Takao (NASDA)	Astronaut Office	NASDA	2-1-1 Segen, Tukuba-Shi	Ibaraki 305, Japan
Drew, B. Alvin	Astronaut Office	Code CB Bldg. 4S	2101 NASA Road One	Houston, TX 77058
Duffy, Brian	Code AC2 Bldg. 4S	Johnson Space Center	Houston, TX 77058	
Duke, Charles M., Jr.	Duke Ministry for Christ	PO Box 310345	New Braunfels,TX 78131	
Dunbar, Bonnie J.	Astronaut Office	Code CB Bldg. 4S	2101 NASA Road One	Houston, TX 77058
Dunlap, Alexander	Astronaut Office	Code CB Bldg. 4S	2101 NASA Road One	Houston, TX 77058
Duque, Pedro (ESA)	European Astronaut Ctr.	Linder Hohe,	Postfach 90 60 96	D-51127 Koln, Germany

Astronauts

Durrance, Samuel	Director of Technology	Final Analysis Inc.	9701-E Philadelphia Ct.	Lanham, MD 20708
Edwards, Joe F., Jr.	PO Box 1188	Enron Broadband Serv.	1400 Smith Street	Houston, TX 77251-1188
England, Anthony W.	Dept. of Electrical Eng.	University of Michigan	1301 Beal/3228 EECS	Ann Arbor, MI 48109
Engle, Joe H.	PO Box 58386	Houston, TX 77258-8386		
Eyharts, Léopold (ESA)	CNES	Direction des Astronaute	2 Place Maurice Quentin	F-75039 Paris, France
Fabian, John M.	100 Shine Road	Port Ludlow, WA 98365		
Favier, Jean-Jacques	CNES	Direction des Astronaute	2 Place Maurice Quentin	F-75039 Paris, France
Ferguson, Christopher J.	Astronaut Office	Code CB Bldg. 4S	2101 NASA Road One	Houston, TX 77058
Fettman, Martin	Department of Pathology	Colorado State Univ.	Fort Collins, CO 80523	
Feustel, Andrew J.	Astronaut Office	Code CB Bldg. 4S	2101 NASA Road One	Houston, TX 77058
Fincke, E. Michael	Astronaut Office	Code CB Bldg. 4S	2101 NASA Road One	Houston, TX 77058
Fisher, Anna L.	Astronaut Office	Code CB Bldg. 4S	2101 NASA Road One	Houston, TX 77058
Fisher, William F.	Emergency Specialist	Humana Hosp. Clear Lk.	500 Medical Center Blvd	Webster, TX 77598
Foale, C. Michael	Bldg. 1 Room 935A	Assistant Director	Johnson Space Center	Houston, Tx 77058
Ford, Kevin A.	Astronaut Office	Code CB Bldg. 4S	2101 NASA Road One	Houston, TX 77058
Foreman, Michael J.	Astronaut Office	Code CB Bldg. 4S	2101 NASA Road One	Houston, TX 77058
Forrester, Patrick G.	Astronaut Office	Code CB Bldg. 4S	2101 NASA Road One	Houston, TX 77058
Fossum, Michael E.	Astronaut Office	Code CB Bldg. 4S	2101 NASA Road One	Houston, TX 77058
Frick, Stephen N.	Astronaut Office	Code CB Bldg. 4S	2101 NASA Road One	Houston, TX 77058
Fuglesang, Christer	European Astronaut Ctr.	Linder Hohe,	Postfach 90 60 96	D-51147 Koln, Germany
Fulford, Millie	Dept. of Veteran Affairs	VA Medical Center	4150 Clement Street	San Francisco, CA 94121
Fullerton, Charles G.	Bldg. 4800-D/2066	Dryden Flight Rsrch. Ctr.	PO Box 273	Edwards AFB, CA 93523
Garan, Ronald J., Jr.	Astronaut Office	Code CB Bldg. 4S	2101 NASA Road One	Houston, TX 77058
Gardner, Dale A.	Site Manager	TRW	1555 N. Newport Road	Colorado Springs, CO 80916
Gardner, Guy S.	316 S. Taylor Street	Arlington, VA 22204		
Garneau, Marc (CSA)	Canadian Space Agency	6767 route de l'Aeroport	Saint-Hubert, Quebec	J3Y 8Y9, Canada
Garriott, Owen K.	111 Lost Tree Drive	Huntsville, Al 35824		
Gemar, Charles D.	Flight Test Operations	Bombardier Flight Test	1 Learjet Way	Witchita, KS 67209
Gernhardt, Michael L.	2765 Lighthouse Drive	Houston, TX 77058		
Gibson, Edward G.	VP Mgmt. Services	Aviation Mgmt. Syst.	3737 East Bonanza Way	Pheonix, AZ 85034
Gibson, Robert L.	First Officer	Southwest Airlines	7800 Airport Blvd	Houston, TX 77061
Glenn, John H., Jr.	School of Public Policy	Ohio State University	100 Bricker Hall	Columbus, OH 43210
Godwin, Linda M.	Astronaut Office	Code CB Bldg. 4S	2101 NASA Road One	Houston, TX 77058
Good, Michael T.	Astronaut Office	Code CB Bldg. 4S	2101 NASA Road One	Houston, TX 77058
Gordon, Richard F., Jr.	63 Antelope Drive	Sedona, AZ 86336-7150		
Gorie, Dominic L.	Astronaut Office	Code CB Bldg. 4S	2101 NASA Road One	Houston, TX 77058
Grabe, Ronald J.	General Manager	Orbital Sciences Corp.	21700 Atlantic Blvd.	Dulles, VA 20166
Graveline, Duane E.	PO Box 92	Underhill Ctr., VT 05490		
Gregory, Frederick D.	Safety/MissionAssurance	NASA Headquarters	Washington, DC 20546	
Gregory, William G.	Business Development	Honeywell Space Sys.	19019 North 59th Ave.	Glendale, AZ 85308
Grunsfeld, John M.	Astronaut Office	Code CB Bldg. 4S	2101 NASA Road One	Houston, TX 77058
Guidoni, Umberto (ESA)	European Astronaut Ctr.	Linder Hohe,	Postfach 90 60 96	51142 Koln, Germany
Gutierrez, Sidney M.	Mgr. Strategic Planning	Sandia National Labs	PO Box 5800 Dept. 5932	Albuquerque, NM 87185
Hadfield, Chris A. (CSA)	Canadian Space Agency	6767 route de l'Aeroport	Saint-Hubert, Quebec	J3Y 8Y9, Canada
Haise, Fred W., Jr.	CADATT	14316 FM 2354 Road	Baytown, TX 77520	
Halsell, James D., Jr.	Manager Room 3103	Code MK Bldg. M6-0399	Kennedy Space Center	FL 32899

Ham, Kenneth T.	Astronaut Office	Code CB Bldg. 4S	2101 NASA Road One	Houston, TX 77058
Hammond, L. Blaine, Jr.	Dept. 0926	Gulfstream Aircraft Corp.	4150 Donald Douglas Blvd	Long Beach, CA 90808
Harbaugh, Gregory J.	Astronaut Office	Code CB Bldg. 4S	2101 NASA Road One	Houston, TX 77058
Harris, Bernard A., Jr.	Chief Scientist	Spacehab Inc.	1331 Gemini Avenue	Houston, TX 77058
Hart, Terry J.	President	Loral Skynet	500 Hills Drive	Bedminster, NJ 07921
Hartsfield, Henry W., Jr.	NASA Training Operation	Raytheon Systems Co.	2224 Bay Area Blvd	Houston, TX 77058
Hauck, Frederick H.	President	AXA Space	4800 Montgomery Lane	Bethesda, MD 20814
Hawley, Steven A.	Code CA/SAH	Flight Crew Operations	Johnson Space Center	Houston, TX 77058
Helms, Susan J.	Astronaut Office	Code CB Bldg. 4S	2101 NASA Road One	Houston, TX 77058
Hennen, Thomas	Executive Director	The Atlantis Foundation	2800 NASA Road One	Seabrook, TX 77586
Henricks, Terence T.	PO Box 547	Timken Aerospace	Keene, NH 03431-0547	
Herrington, John B.	Astronaut Office	Code CB Bldg. 4S	2101 NASA Road One	Houston, TX 77058
Hieb, Richard J.	Orbital Sciences	21700 Atlantic Blvd	Dulles, VA 20166	
Higginbotham, Joan E.	Astronaut Office	Code CB Bldg. 4S	2101 NASA Road One	Houston, TX 77058
Hilliard Robertson, P.	Astronaut Office	Code CB Bldg. 4S	2101 NASA Road One	Houston, TX 77058
Hilmers, David C.	18502 Point Lookout Dr.	Houston, TX 77058		
Hire, Kathryn P.	Bldg. 2 Unit 3	2023 Enterprise	League City, TX 77573	
Hobaugh, Charles O.	Astronaut Office	Code CB Bldg. 4S	2101 NASA Road One	Houston, TX 77058
Hoffman, Jeffrey A.	NASA Office for Europe	2 Avenue Gabriel	F-75382 Paris Cedex 08	France
Holmquest, Donald L.	Homquist & Associates	109 Marrakech Court	Bellaire, TX 77401-5117	
Holt, R. Glynn	Dept. of Aerospace	Boston University	110 Cummington Street	Boston, MA 02215
Horowitz, Scott J.	Astronaut Office	Code CB Bldg. 4S	2101 NASA Road One	Houston, TX 77058
Hurley, Douglas G.	Astronaut Office	Code CB Bldg. 4S	2101 NASA Road One	Houston, TX 77058
Ivins, Marsha S.	Astronaut Office	Code CB Bldg. 4S	2101 NASA Road One	Houston, TX 77058
Jemison, Mae C.	Rm 306-6182 Steele Hall	The Jemison Institute	Dartmouth College	Hanover, NH 03755
Jernigan, Tamara E.	Astronaut Office	Code CB Bldg. 4S	2101 NASA Road One	Houston, TX 77058
Jett, Brent W.	NASA Office	Yuri Gagarin Centre	141 160 Zvezdny Gorodok	Mosk. Obl, Russia
Johnson, Gregory C.	Astronaut Office	Code CB Bldg. 4S	2101 NASA Road One	Houston, TX 77058
Johnson, Gregory H.	Astronaut Office	Code CB Bldg. 4S	2101 NASA Road One	Houston, TX 77058
Jones, Thomas D.	Astronaut Office	Code CB Bldg. 4S	2101 NASA Road One	Houston, TX 77058
Kadenyuk, Leonid	Ukrainian Space Agency	Academy of Sciences	252 127 Kiev 127	Ukraine
Kavandi, Janet L.	Astronaut Office	Code CB Bldg. 4S	2101 NASA Road One	Houston, TX 77058
Kelly, James M.	Astronaut Office	Code CB Bldg. 4S	2101 NASA Road One	Houston, TX 77058
Kelly, Mark E.	Astronaut Office	Code CB Bldg. 4S	2101 NASA Road One	Houston, TX 77058
Kelly, Scott J.	Astronaut Office	Code CB Bldg. 4S	2101 NASA Road One	Houston, TX 77058
Kerwin, Joseph P.	Life Sciences Systems	Wyle Laboratories	1290 Hercules Drive	Houston, TX 77058-2787
Kilrain, Susan L.	Room 5Y72 Code QS	Office of Space Flight	NASA Headquarters	Washington, DC 20546
Kopra, Timothy L.	Astronaut Office	Code CB Bldg. 4S	2101 NASA Road One	Houston, TX 77058
Kregel Kevin R.	Astronaut Office	Code CB Bldg. 4S	2101 NASA Road One	Houston, TX 77058
Lawrence, Wendy B.	Advanced Syst. & Tech.	Natl. Reconnaissance	14675 Lee Road	Chantilly, VA 20151
Lee, Mark C.	Astronaut Office	Code CB Bldg. 4S	2101 NASA Road One	Houston, TX 77058
Leestma, David C.	Flight Crew Operations	Bldg. 1 Room 920A	Johnson Space Center	Houston, TX 77058
Lenoir, William B.	Booz Allen & Hamilton	World Wide Technology	8283 Greensboro Drive	McLean, VA 22102
Leslie, Fred	Mail Stop 7795, SD 47	Bldg 4481 Room 315A	Marshall Space Flight Ctr.	Huntsville, AL 35812
Lind, Don L.	51 N. 376 E.	Smithfield, UT 84335		

Lindsey, Steven W.	Astronaut Office	Code CB Bldg. 4S	2101 NASA Road One	Houston, TX 77058
Linenger, Jerry M.	550 S. Stoney Point Rd.	Suttons Bay, MI 49682		
Linnehan, Richard M.	Astronaut Office	Code CB Bldg. 4S	2101 NASA Road One	Houston, TX 77058
Linteris, Gregory	Code B356 Bldg. 224	Fire Science Division	Natl. Inst. of Standards	Gaithersburg, MD 20899
Llewellyn, John A.	Bldg. ENB 345 LIB 618	University of So. Florida	4202 East Fowler Ave.	Tampa, FL 33620-5452
Lockhart, Paul S.	Astronaut Office	Code CB Bldg. 4S	2101 NASA Road One	Houston, TX 77058
Lopez-Alegria, Michael	Astronaut Office	Code CB Bldg. 4S	2101 NASA Road One	Houston, TX 77058
Loria, Christopher J.	Astronaut Office	Code CB Bldg. 4S	2101 NASA Road One	Houston, TX 77058
Lounge, John M.	Space Engineering	Spacehab Inc.	555 Forge River Road	Webster, TX 77589
Lousma, Jack R.	The Diamond General	Development Corp.	333 Parkland Plaza	Ann Arbor, MI 48108
Love, Stanley G.	Astronaut Office	Code CB Bldg. 4S	2101 NASA Road One	Houston, TX 77058
Lovell, James A., Jr.	PO Box 49	Lovell Communications	915 South Waukegan Rd	Lake Forest, IL 60045
Low, G. David	Global Data & Message	Orbcomm	2455 Horse Pen Road	Herdon, VA 20171
Lu, Edward T.	Astronaut Office	Code CB Bldg. 4S	2101 NASA Road One	Houston, TX 77058
Lucid, Shannon W.	1622 Gunwale Road	Houston, TX 77062-4538		
MacLean, Steven G.	Canadian Space Agency	6767 route de l'Aeroport	Saint-Hubert, Quebec	J3Y 8Y9, Canada
Magnus, Sandra H.	Astronaut Office	Code CB Bldg. 4S	2101 NASA Road One	Houston, TX 77058
Malerba, Franco	Alenia Spazio SpA	Corso Marche 41	I-10146 Torino, Italy	
Massimino, Michael J.	Astronaut Office	Code CB Bldg. 4S	2101 NASA Road One	Houston, TX 77058
Mastracchio, Richard A.	Astronaut Office	Code CB Bldg. 4S	2101 NASA Road One	Houston, TX 77058
Matthiesen, David	1564 Belle Avenue	Lakewood, OH 44107		
Mattingly, Thomas K., II	Chairman	Universal Space Network	10821 Bloomfield	Los Alamitos, CA 90720
Mayo, Itzhak	Astronaut Office	Code CB Bldg. 4S	2101 NASA Road One	Houston, TX 77058
McArthur, K. Megan	Astronaut Office	Code CB Bldg. 4S	2101 NASA Road One	Houston, TX 77058
McArthur, William S., Jr.	NASA Office	Yuri Gagarin Centre	141 160 Zvezdny Gorodok	Mosk. Obl, Russia
McBride, Jon A.	Suite 901	Image Development Grp.	1018 Kanawha Blvd	Charleston, WV 25301
McCandless, Bruce, II	M/S DC 3005	Lockheed Martin	PO Box 179	Denver, CO 80201-0179
McCulley, Michael J.	Chief Operating Officer	United Space Alliance	1150 Gemini Avenue	Houston, TX 77058-2708
McDivitt, James A.	9146 Cherry Avenue	Rapid City, MI 49676		
McMonagle, Donald R.	545 Apache Trail	Merritt Island, FL 32953		
Meade, Carl J.	X-33 Program Manager	Lockheed Martin	1011 Lockheed Way	Palmdale, CA 93599
Melnick, Bruce E.	Mail Stop FO 10	Boeing Company	Kennedy Space Center	FL 32815-0233
Melroy, Pamela A.	Astronaut Office	Code CB Bldg. 4S	2101 NASA Road One	Houston, TX 77058
Melvin, Leland D.	Astronaut Office	Code CB Bldg. 4S	2101 NASA Road One	Houston, TX 77058
Michel, F. Curtis	Dept. of Space Physics	Rice University	6100 Main Street	Houston, TX 77005-1892
Mitchell, Edgar D.	PO Box 540037	Lake Worth , FL	33454-0037	
Mohri, Mamoru (NASDA)	Astronaut Office	NASDA	2-1-1 Segen, Tukuba-Shi	Ibaraki 305, Japan
Morgan, Barbara R.	Astronaut Office	Code CB Bldg. 4S	2101 NASA Road One	Houston, TX 77058
Morin, Lee M.	Astronaut Office	Code CB Bldg. 4S	2101 NASA Road One	Houston, TX 77058
Mullane, Richard M.	1301 Las Lomas Rd. NE	Albequerque, NM 87106		
Musgrave, Story	8572 Sweetwater Trail	Kissimmee, FL 34747		
Nagel, Steven R.	Quality Assurance	Code CC4 Bldg 276	Johnson Space Center	Houston, TX 77058
Nelson, George D.	AAAS Project 2061	1333 H Street NW	PO Box 34446	Washington, DC 20005
Nespoli, Paolo (ESA)	Astronaut Office	Code CB Bldg. 4S	2101 NASA Road One	Houston, TX 77058
Newman, James H.	Astronaut Office	Code CB Bldg. 4S	2101 NASA Road One	Houston, TX 77058

Nicollier, Claude (ESA)	Astronaut Office	Code CB Bldg. 4S	2101 NASA Road One	Houston, TX 77058
Noguchi,Soichi (NASDA)	Astronaut Office	NASDA	2-1-1 Segen, Tukuba-Shi	Ibaraki 305, Japan
Noriega, Carlos I.	Astronaut Office	Code CB Bldg. 4S	2101 NASA Road One	Houston, TX 77058
Nowak, Lisa M.	Astronaut Office	Code CB Bldg. 4S	2101 NASA Road One	Houston, TX 77058
Nyberg, Karen L.	Astronaut Office	Code CB Bldg. 4S	2101 NASA Road One	Houston, TX 77058
Ochoa, Ellen	Astronaut Office	Code CB Bldg. 4S	2101 NASA Road One	Houston, TX 77058
Ockels, Wubbo J. (ESA)	Code ADM-RE ESTEC	Postbus 299	NL 2200 AG Noordwijk	Netherlands
O'Connor, Bryan D.	Engineering Department	Futron Corporation	400 Virginia Avenue	Washington, DC 20024
Oefelein, William A.	Astronaut Office	Code CB Bldg. 4S	2101 NASA Road One	Houston, TX 77058
O'Leary, Brian T.	Suite 21-200	1993 S. Kihei Road	Maui, HI 96753	
Olivas, John D.	Astronaut Office	Code CB Bldg. 4S	2101 NASA Road One	Houston, TX 77058
Oswald, Stephen S.	16806 Glenshannon Dr.	Houston, TX 77059		
Parazynski, Scott E.	Astronaut Office	Code CB Bldg. 4S	2101 NASA Road One	Houston, TX 77058
Parise, Ronald	System Science Division	Computer Science Corp.	10210 Greenbelt Road	Seabroke, MD 20706
Parker, Robert A. R.	Director	Jet Propulsion Lab.	4800 Oak Grove Drive	Pasadena, CA 91109
Patrick, Nicholas J. M.	Astronaut Office	Code CB Bldg. 4S	2101 NASA Road One	Houston, TX 77058
Pawelczyk, James	Applied Physiology	Penn State University	University Park Campus	University Park, PA 16802
Payette, Julie (CSA)	Canadian Space Agency	6767 route de l'Aeroport	Saint-Hubert, Quebec	J3Y 8Y9, Canada
Perrin, Philippe (CNES)	CNES	Direction des Astronaute	2 Place Maurice Quentin	F-75039 Paris, France
Peterson, Donald H.	President	Aerospace Operations	427 Pebblebrook	Seabrook, TX 77586
Pettit, Donald R.	Astronaut Office	Code CB Bldg. 4S	2101 NASA Road One	Houston, TX 77058
Phillips, John L.	Astronaut Office	Code CB Bldg. 4S	2101 NASA Road One	Houston, TX 77058
Pogue, William R.	4 Cromer Drive	Bella Vista, AR	72715-5318	
Poindexter, Alan G.	Astronaut Office	Code CB Bldg. 4S	2101 NASA Road One	Houston, TX 77058
Polansky, Mark L.	Astronaut Office	Code CB Bldg. 4S	2101 NASA Road One	Houston, TX 77058
Pontes, Marcos (Brazil)	Astronaut Office	Code CB Bldg. 4S	2101 NASA Road One	Houston, TX 77058
Precourt, Charles J., Jr.	Astronaut Office	Code CB Bldg. 4S	2101 NASA Road One	Houston, TX 77058
Pustovyi, Yaroslav	Ukrainian Space Agency	Academy of Sciences	252 127 Kiev 127	Ukraine
Readdy, William F.	Deputy Administrator	Code M-7 NASA Hdqtrs.	Washington, DC 20546	
Reightler, Kenneth S., Jr.	Eng. Analysis & Testing	Lockheed Martin Eng.	2400 NASA Road 1	Houston, TX 77058
Reilly, James F.	Astronaut Office	Code CB Bldg. 4S	2101 NASA Road One	Houston, TX 77058
Reisman, Garrett E.	Astronaut Office	Code CB Bldg. 4S	2101 NASA Road One	Houston, TX 77058
Richards, Paul W.	Astronaut Office	Code CB Bldg. 4S	2101 NASA Road One	Houston, TX 77058
Richards, Richard N.	Reusable Space Sys.	Boeing Company	5301 Bolsa Avenue	Huntington Beach, CA 92647
Ride, Sally K.	California Space Institute	University of California	9500 Gilman Drive	LA Jolla, CA 92093-0524
Robinson, Stephen K.	Astronaut Office	Code CB Bldg. 4S	2101 NASA Road One	Houston, TX 77058
Rominger, Kent V.	Astronaut Office	Code CB Bldg. 4S	2101 NASA Road One	Houston, TX 77058
Ronney, Paul	Mail Code OHE 430L	University So. California	3650 McClintock Avenue	Los Angeles, CA 90089
Ross, Jerry L.	Astronaut Office	Code CB Bldg. 4S	2101 NASA Road One	Houston, TX 77058
Runco, Mario, Jr.	Astronaut Office	Code CB Bldg. 4S	2101 NASA Road One	Houston, TX 77058
Sacco, Albert	Advanced Microgravity	Northeastern University	360 Huntingdon Avenue	Boston, MA 02115-5000
Schirra, Walter M., Jr.	PO Box 73	16834 Via de Santa Fe	Rancho Santa Fe, CA	92067
Schlegel, Hans (ESA)	European Astronaut Ctr.	PO Box 90 60 96	Linder Hohe D-51127	Koln, Germany
Schmitt, Harrison H.	437 Eng. Research Bldg	1500 Engineering Drive	University of Wisconsin	Madison, WI 53706
Schweickart, Russell L.	Low Earth Systems	CTA Commercial System	6116 Executive Blvd	Rockville, MD 20852

Scott, David R.	The Merces Group	Victoria Campbell-Johnson	30 Hackamore Lane	Bell Canyon, CA 91307
Scott, Winston E.	VP Student Affairs	Florida State University	313 Wescott	Tallahassee, FL 32306
Searfoss, Richard A.	24480 Silver Creek Way	Tehachapi, CA 93561		
Seddon, Margaret Rhea	Suite 3601	Vanderbilt Medical Group	Nashville, TN 37130	
Sega, Ronald M.	Eng. & Applied Science	University of Colorado	1420 Austin Bluff's Pkwy	Colorado Springs, CO80933
Sellers, Piers J.	Astronaut Office	Code CB Bldg. 4S	2101 NASA Road One	Houston, TX 77058
Shaw, Brewster H., Jr.	Intl. Space Station	Boeing Company	2100 Space Park Drive	Houston, TX 77058
Shepherd, William M.	Astronaut Office	Code CB Bldg. 4S	2101 NASA Road One	Houston, TX 77058
Shriver, Loren J.	Program Manager	United Space Alliance	1150 Gemini Avenue	Houston, TX 77058
Smith, Steven L.	Astronaut Office	Code CB Bldg. 4S	2101 NASA Road One	Houston, TX 77058
Spring, Sherwood C.	Suite 700	Pacific Sierra Corp.	1400 Key Blvd.	Arlington, VA 22209
Springer, Robert C.	Mail Stop ZA01	Boeing North America	555 Discovery Drive	Huntsville, AL 35806
Stafford, Thomas P.	Stafford, Burke & Hecker	1006 Cameron Street	Alexandria, VA 22314	
Stefanyshyn-Piper, H.	Astronaut Office	Code CB Bldg. 4S	2101 NASA Road One	Houston, TX 77058
Stewart, Robert L.	Canadian Space Agency	6767 route de l'Aeroport	Saint-Hubert, Quebec	J3Y 8Y9, Canada
Stott, Nicole P.	Astronaut Office	Code CB Bldg. 4S	2101 NASA Road One	Houston, TX 77058
Sturckow, Frederick W.	Astronaut Office	Code CB Bldg. 4S	2101 NASA Road One	Houston, TX 77058
Sullivan, Kathryn D.	President	Ctr. of Science / Industry	333 W Broad Street	Columbus, OH 43215
Swanson, Steven R.	Astronaut Office	Code CB Bldg. 4S	2101 NASA Road One	Houston, TX 77058
Tani, Daniel M.	Astronaut Office	Code CB Bldg. 4S	2101 NASA Road One	Houston, TX 77058
Tanner, Joseph R.	Astronaut Office	Code CB Bldg. 4S	2101 NASA Road One	Houston, TX 77058
Thagard, Norman E.	College Rel's FAMU-FSU	Florida State University	2525 Pottsdamer Street	Tallahassee, FL 32310
Thiele, Gerhard (ESA)	European Astronaut Ctr.	PO Box 90 60 96	Linder Hohe D-51127	Koln, Germany
Thirsk, Robert	Canadian Space Agency	6767 route de l'Aeroport	Saint-Hubert, Quebec	J3Y 8Y9, Canada
Thomas, Andrew S. W.	Astronaut Office	Code CB Bldg. 4S	2101 NASA Road One	Houston, TX 77058
Thomas, Donald A.	Astronaut Office	Code CB Bldg. 4S	2101 NASA Road One	Houston, TX 77058
Thornton, Kathryn C.	Dept. Eng. Applied Sci.	University of Virginia	A 237 Thornton Hall	Charlottesville, VA 22903
Thornton, William E.	701 Cowards Creek	Friendswood, TX 77546		
Thuot, Pierre J.	VP Administration	Orbital Sciences Corp.	21700 Atlantic Blvd.	Dulles, VA 20166
Tognini, Michel (ESA)	CNES	Direction des Astronaute	2 Place Maurice Quentin	F-75039 Paris, France
Trinh, Eugene	Microgravity Res. Rm. 8P11	300 E Street SW	Washington, DC 20546	
Truly, Richard H.	Director Code 1731	Natl. Renewable Lab.	1617 Cole Blvd	Golden, CO 80401-3393
Tryggvason, Bjarni V.	Canadian Space Agency	6767 route de l'Aeroport	Saint-Hubert, Quebec	J3Y 8Y9, Canada
Urbani, Luca	Agenzia Spaziale Italiana	Va di Patrizi 13	I-00161 Roma, Italy	
Van Hoften, James D. A.	333/14/C72 Senior VP	Bechtel Corporation	Box 193965	San Francisco, CA 94119
Vangen, Scott	Rm. 3002N Bldg. SSPF	NASA	Kennedy Space Center	FL 32815
Virts, Terry W., Jr.	Astronaut Office	Code CB Bldg. 4S	2101 NASA Road One	Houston, TX 77058
Vittori, Roberto (ESA)	Astronaut Office	Code CB Bldg. 4S	2101 NASA Road One	Houston, TX 77058
Voss, James S.	Associate Dean	107 Ramsay Hall	Auburn University	AL 36849-5338
Voss, Janice E.	Astronaut Office	Code CB Bldg. 4S	2101 NASA Road One	Houston, TX 77058
Wakata, Koichi	NASDA Houston Office	Johnson Space Center	2101 NASA Road One	Houston, TX 77058
Walheim, Rex J.	Astronaut Office	Code CB Bldg. 4S	2101 NASA Road One	Houston, TX 77058
Walker, Charles	Information Department	Boeing Company	1200 Wilson Blvd	Arlington, VA 22209
Walz, Carl E.	Astronaut Office	Code CB Bldg. 4S	2101 NASA Road One	Houston, TX 77058
Weber, Mary E.	Astronaut Office	Code CB Bldg. 4S	2101 NASA Road One	Houston, TX 77058
Weitz, Paul J.	3086 N. Tam O'Shatner Dr.	Flagstaff, AZ 86004		

Wetherbee, James D.	Astronaut Office	Code CB Bldg. 4S	2101 NASA Road One	Houston, TX 77058
Wheelock, Douglas H.	Astronaut Office	Code CB Bldg. 4S	2101 NASA Road One	Houston, TX 77058
Whitson, Peggy A.	Inst. of Biosciences	Rice University	Houston, TX 77005-1892	
Wilcutt, Terrence W.	Astronaut Office	Code CB Bldg. 4S	2101 NASA Road One	Houston, TX 77058
Williams, David R. (CSA)	Canadian Space Agency	6767 route de l'Aeroport	Saint-Hubert, Quebec	J3Y 8Y9, Canada
Williams, Donald E.	Senior Systems Engr.	SAIC	2200 Space Park Drive	Houston, TX 77058
Williams, Jeffrey N.	Astronaut Office	Code CB Bldg. 4S	2101 NASA Road One	Houston, TX 77058
Williams, Sunita L.	Astronaut Office	Code CB Bldg. 4S	2101 NASA Road One	Houston, TX 77058
Wilmore, Barry E.	Astronaut Office	Code CB Bldg. 4S	2101 NASA Road One	Houston, TX 77058
Wilson, Stephanie D.	Astronaut Office	Code CB Bldg. 4S	2101 NASA Road One	Houston, TX 77058
Wisoff, Peter J. K.	Astronaut Office	Code CB Bldg. 4S	2101 NASA Road One	Houston, TX 77058
Wolf, David A.	Astronaut Office	Code CB Bldg. 4S	2101 NASA Road One	Houston, TX 77058
Woodward III, Neil W.	Astronaut Office	Code CB	Johnson Space Center	Houston, TX 77058
Worden, Alfred M.	PO Box 8065	Vero Beach, FL	32963-8065	
Young, John W.	Associate Director	Mail Code AC5	Johnson Space Center	Houston, TX 77058
Zamka, George D.	Astronaut Office	Code CB Bldg. 4S	2101 NASA Road One	Houston, TX 77058

Additional Aviators & Space Figures

Binni, John	Scaled Composites	1624 Flight Line	Mojave, CA 93501-1663
Fossett, Steve	Steve Fossett Challenges	401 South La Salle	Chicago, Illinois 60605
Kittinger, Joe W. Jr	608 Mariner Way	Altamonte Springs, FL	32701
Kraft, Chris	14919 Village Elm Street	Houston, TX 77062	
Melvill, Mike	Scaled Composites	1624 Flight Line	Mojave, CA 93501-1663
Rutan, Burt	Scaled Composites	1624 Flight Line	Mojave, CA 93501-1663

Banks, Dennis
C/O Sacred Run
PO Box 315
Newport, KY 41071

Brady, James & Sarah
Handgun Control Inc.
1225 Bye St. NW
Washington, DC 20205

Brown, Denise
Nicole Brown Simpson
Charitible Foundation
Dana Point, CA 92629

Dobson, Dr. James C.
Focus on the Family
8605 Explorer Drive
Colorado Springs, CO 80920

Evers-Williams, Myrlie
NAACP
1072 W. Lynch Street
Jackson, MS 39203

Fuller, Millard
C/O Habitat for Humanity
121 Habitat Street
Americus, GA 31709-3498

Gorbachev, Mikhail
C/O Harper Collins
10 East 53rd St.
New York, NY. 10022

Graham, Billy
1300 Harmon Place
Minneapolis, MN 55403

Jackson, Jesse
National Rainbow Coalition
PO Box 27385
Washington, DC 20005

Jakobovits, Immanuel
Chief Rabbi of Britian
Office of Chief Rabbi
Adler House Tavistock
London WC1 England

King, Rodney
9100 Willshire Blvd
Beverly Hills, CA 90212

King, Coretta Scott
Martin Luther King Center
449 Auburn Avenue Ne
Atlanta, GA 30512

Meredith, James
929 Meadowbrook Drive
Jackson, MS 39206

Pope Benedict XVI
The Apostolic Palace
Vatican City

Roberts, Oral
7777 Lewis Street
Tulsa, OK 74130

Robertson, Pat
100 Centerville Turnpike
Virginia Beach, VA 23463

Smart, Ed
(Father of Elizabeth Smart)
1509 E. Kristianna Circle
Sal Lake City, UT 84103

Steinem, Gloria
118 East 73rd Street
New York, NY 10021

Walsh, John
America's Most Wanted
PO Box Crime-TV
Washington, DC 20016

Wiesel, Elie
40 Boston University
745 Commonwealth Ave.
Boston, MA 02115

Wu, Harry
168 Fontianblea Court
Milpatus, CA 95035

The Address Directory:
Appendix

Celebrity Birthdays

Celebrity Name Index

Satisfaction Guarantee

Celebrity Birthdays in 2008

Name	Birthday	Age	Born	Name	Birthday	Age	Born	Name	Birthday	Age	Born
Corzine, Jon	01-Jan	61	1947	Shelby, Carroll	11-Jan	85	1923	Seau, Junior	19-Jan	39	1969
Guzman, Luis	01-Jan	51	1957	Taylor, Rod	11-Jan	78	1930	Stapleton, Jean	19-Jan	85	1923
McCormack, Catherine	01-Jan	36	1972	Tinker, Grant	11-Jan	82	1926	Wayans, Shawn	19-Jan	37	1971
Ruiz, Olivia	01-Jan	28	1980	Amanpour, Christiane	12-Jan	50	1958	Aldrin, Edwin "Buzz"	20-Jan	78	1930
Salinger, J.D.	01-Jan	88	1920	Amerie "Marie Rogers"	12-Jan	28	1980	De Mayo, Neda	20-Jan	48	1960
Troyer, Verne	01-Jan	39	1969	Bezos, Jeff	12-Jan	44	1964	Eckstein, David	20-Jan	33	1975
Carrere, Tia	02-Jan	41	1967	Frazier, Joe	12-Jan	61	1947	Johnson, Arte	20-Jan	74	1934
Diggs, Taye	02-Jan	36	1972	Kirstie, Alley	12-Jan	53	1955	Maher, Bill	20-Jan	52	1956
Gooding, Cuba Jr.	02-Jan	40	1968	Limbaugh, Rush	12-Jan	57	1951	Neal, Patricia	20-Jan	82	1926
Hastert, Dennis	02-Jan	66	1942	Stern, Howard	12-Jan	54	1954	Perry, Rachel	20-Jan	32	1976
Shepard, Dax	02-Jan	33	1975	Yarborough, Glenn	12-Jan	78	1930	Provine, Dorothy	20-Jan	71	1937
Turlington, Christy	02-Jan	39	1969	Barry, Jennifer	13-Jan	25	1983	Wright, Will	20-Jan	48	1960
Coleman, Dabney	03-Jan	76	1932	Bingham, Traci	13-Jan	40	1968	Davis, Geena	21-Jan	51	1957
Gibson, Mel	03-Jan	52	1956	Bloom, Orlando	13-Jan	31	1977	Davis, Mac	21-Jan	66	1942
Loggia, Robert	03-Jan	78	1930	Dempsey, Patrick	13-Jan	42	1966	Domingo, Placido	21-Jan	67	1941
Manning, Eli	03-Jan	27	1981	Louis-Dreyfus, Julia	13-Jan	47	1961	Koons, Jeff	21-Jan	53	1955
Principal, Victoria	03-Jan	58	1950	Miller, Penelope Ann	13-Jan	44	1964	Nicklaus, Jack	21-Jan	68	1940
Cannon, Dyan	04-Jan	71	1937	Taylor, Rip	13-Jan	74	1934	Blair, Linda	22-Jan	49	1959
Loveless, Patty	04-Jan	51	1957	Bateman, Jason	14-Jan	40	1968	d' Abo, Olivia	22-Jan	41	1967
Ormand, Julia	04-Jan	43	1965	Bond, Julian	14-Jan	68	1940	Ford, Willa	22-Jan	27	1981
Patterson, Floyd	04-Jan	73	1935	Cavallari, Kristin	14-Jan	21	1987	Hurt, John	22-Jan	68	1940
Shula, Don	04-Jan	78	1930	Dunaway, Faye	14-Jan	67	1941	Lane, Diane	22-Jan	43	1965
Wyman, Jane	04-Jan	94	1914	Jones, Jack	14-Jan	70	1938	Wambaugh, Joseph	22-Jan	71	1937
Duvall, Robert	05-Jan	77	1931	Ladd, Jordan	14-Jan	33	1975	Anderson, Richard Dean	23-Jan	58	1950
Keaton, Diane	05-Jan	62	1946	LL Cool J	14-Jan	40	1968	Pele	23-Jan	68	1940
Manson, Marilyn	05-Jan	39	1969	Rooney, Andy	14-Jan	89	1919	Princess Caroline	23-Jan	51	1957
Mondale, Walter	05-Jan	80	1928	Smith, Shepard	14-Jan	44	1964	Rivera, Chita	23-Jan	75	1933
Rose, Charlie	05-Jan	66	1942	Soderberg, Steven	14-Jan	45	1963	Thiessen, Tiffani Amber	23-Jan	34	1974
Tenet, George	05-Jan	55	1953	Watson, Emily	14-Jan	41	1967	Villaraigosa, Antonio	23-Jan	55	1953
Atkinson, Rowan	06-Jan	53	1955	Charo "María Baeza"	15-Jan	57	1951	Ali, Tatyana	24-Jan	29	1979
Freeh, Louis	06-Jan	58	1950	Lowe, Chad	15-Jan	40	1968	Barton, Mischa	24-Jan	22	1986
Long, Howie	06-Jan	48	1960	Van Peebles, Mario	15-Jan	51	1957	Borgnine, Ernest	24-Jan	91	1917
Lopez-Melton, Nancy	06-Jan	51	1957	Adu, Sade	16-Jan	49	1959	Diamond, Neil	24-Jan	67	1941
Reece, Gabrielle	06-Jan	38	1970	Allen, Debbie	16-Jan	58	1950	Neville, Aaron	24-Jan	67	1941
Aiken, Liam	07-Jan	18	1990	Foyt, A.J.	16-Jan	73	1935	Retton, Mary Lou	24-Jan	40	1968
Cage, Nicolas	07-Jan	44	1964	Jones, Roy Jr.	16-Jan	39	1969	Smirnoff, Yakov	24-Jan	57	1951
Caruso, David	07-Jan	52	1956	Milsap, Ronnie	16-Jan	65	1943	Aquino, Corazon	25-Jan	75	1933
Couric, Katie	07-Jan	51	1957	Moss, Kate	16-Jan	34	1974	Harwell, Ernie	25-Jan	90	1918
Loggins, Kenny	07-Jan	60	1948	Pujols, Albert	16-Jan	28	1980	Jones, Dean	25-Jan	77	1931
Revere, Paul (singer)	07-Jan	70	1938	Schlessinger, Laura	16-Jan	61	1947	Keyes, Alicia	25-Jan	27	1981
Soriano, Alfonso	07-Jan	32	1976	Ali, Muhammad	17-Jan	66	1942	Kirshner, Mia	25-Jan	33	1975
Bassey, Shirley	08-Jan	71	1937	Carrey, Jim	17-Jan	46	1962	Davis, Angela	26-Jan	64	1944
Bowie, David	08-Jan	61	1947	Deschanel, Zooey	17-Jan	28	1980	DeGeneres, Ellen	26-Jan	50	1958
Eubanks, Bob	08-Jan	71	1937	Jones, James Earl	17-Jan	77	1931	Glenn, Scott	26-Jan	66	1942
Hawking, Stephen	08-Jan	66	1942	Kennedy, Robert F. Jr.	17-Jan	54	1954	Gretzky, Wayne	26-Jan	47	1961
Nichols, Rachel	08-Jan	28	1980	Kid Rock	17-Jan	37	1971	Newman, Paul	26-Jan	83	1925
Storch, Larry	08-Jan	85	1923	Povich, Maury	17-Jan	69	1939	Rue, Sara	26-Jan	29	1979
Baez, Joan	09-Jan	67	1941	Rodríguez, Freddy	17-Jan	33	1975	Uecker, Bob	26-Jan	73	1935
Enberg, Dick	09-Jan	73	1935	Sassoon, Vidal	17-Jan	80	1928	Van Halen, Eddie	26-Jan	53	1955
Gayle, Crysyal	09-Jan	57	1951	White, Betty	17-Jan	86	1922	Collinsworth, Chris	27-Jan	49	1959
Krantz, Judith	09-Jan	71	1937	Costner, Kevin	18-Jan	53	1955	Fonda, Bridget	27-Jan	44	1964
Martin, Mark	09-Jan	49	1959	Dolby, Ray	18-Jan	75	1933	O'Keefe, Sean	27-Jan	52	1956
Matthews, Dave	09-Jan	41	1967	Goldsboro, Bobby	18-Jan	67	1941	Roberts, John G. Jr.	27-Jan	53	1955
Benatar, Pat	10-Jan	55	1953	Arnez, Desi Jr.	19-Jan	55	1953	Rogers, Mimi	27-Jan	53	1955
Foreman, George	10-Jan	59	1949	Crawford, Michael	19-Jan	66	1942	Alda, Alan	28-Jan	72	1936
McCovey, Willie	10-Jan	70	1938	Everly, Phil	19-Jan	69	1939	Baryshnikov, Mikhail	28-Jan	60	1948
Shahi, Sarah	10-Jan	28	1980	Fabares, Shelly	19-Jan	64	1944	Clark, Roy	28-Jan	78	1930
Stewart, Rod	10-Jan	63	1945	Hedren, Tippi	19-Jan	77	1931	McLachlan, Sarah	28-Jan	40	1968
Blige, Mary J.	11-Jan	37	1971	Kinkade, Thomas	19-Jan	50	1958	Warren, Rick	28-Jan	54	1954
Crenshaw, Ben	11-Jan	56	1952	Parton, Dolly	19-Jan	62	1946	Wood, Elijah	28-Jan	27	1981
Judd, Naomi	11-Jan	62	1946	Reeves, Dan	19-Jan	64	1944	Burns, Edward	29-Jan	40	1968
				Rodriguez, Paul	19-Jan	53	1955	Gilbert, Sara	29-Jan	33	1975
								Graham, Heather	29-Jan	38	1970

Celebrity Birthdays in 2008

Name	Birthday	Age	Born	Name	Birthday	Age	Born	Name	Birthday	Age	Born
Jillian, Ann	29-Jan	58	1950	Cole, Natalie	06-Feb	58	1950	Asner, Jules	14-Feb	40	1968
Louganis, Greg	29-Jan	48	1960	Fabian "Fabiano Forte"	06-Feb	65	1943	Bernstein, Carl	14-Feb	64	1944
Ross, Katherine	29-Jan	65	1943	Farrell, Mike	06-Feb	69	1939	Bledsoe, Drew	14-Feb	36	1972
Selleck, Tom	29-Jan	63	1945	Gabor, Zsa Zsa	06-Feb	88	1920	Bloomberg, Michael	14-Feb	66	1942
Winfrey, Oprah	29-Jan	54	1954	Najimy, Kathy	06-Feb	51	1957	Downs, Hugh	14-Feb	87	1921
Bale, Christian	30-Jan	34	1974	Rose, Axl	06-Feb	46	1962	Fleming, Renee	14-Feb	49	1959
Butler, Brett	30-Jan	50	1958	Torn, Rip	06-Feb	77	1931	Henderson, Florence	14-Feb	74	1934
Cheney, Richard	30-Jan	67	1941	Brooks, Garth	07-Feb	46	1962	Highmore, Freddie	14-Feb	16	1992
Collins, Phil	30-Jan	57	1951	Ferrer, Miguel	07-Feb	54	1954	Kelly, Jim	14-Feb	48	1960
Hackman, Gene	30-Jan	78	1930	Izzard, Eddie	07-Feb	46	1962	Maxwell, Lois	14-Feb	81	1927
KIng Abdullah II Jordan	30-Jan	46	1962	Kutcher, Ashton	07-Feb	30	1978	Teller (Penn & Teller)	14-Feb	60	1948
Redgrave, Vanessa	30-Jan	71	1937	Majorino, Tina	07-Feb	23	1985	Tilly, Meg	14-Feb	48	1960
Spassky, Boris	30-Jan	71	1937	Nash, Steve	07-Feb	34	1974	Groening, Matt	15-Feb	54	1954
Banks, Ernie	31-Jan	77	1931	Rock, Chris	07-Feb	42	1966	Korman, Harvey	15-Feb	81	1927
Channing, Carol	31-Jan	87	1921	Spader, James	07-Feb	48	1960	Manchester, Melissa	15-Feb	57	1951
de Rossi, Portia	31-Jan	35	1973	Coleman, Gary	08-Feb	40	1968	Seymour, Jane	15-Feb	57	1951
Driver, Minnie	31-Jan	38	1970	Green, Seth	08-Feb	34	1974	Bettis, Jerome	16-Feb	36	1972
Gephardt, Richard	31-Jan	67	1941	Grisham, John	08-Feb	53	1955	Burton, LeVar	16-Feb	51	1957
Lapaglia, Anthony	31-Jan	49	1959	Klein, Robert	08-Feb	66	1942	Green, Ahman	16-Feb	31	1977
Mailer, Norman	31-Jan	85	1923	Koppel, Ted	08-Feb	68	1940	Icahn, Carl	16-Feb	72	1936
Pleshette, Susan	31-Jan	71	1937	Nolte, Nick	08-Feb	68	1940	Marrow, Tracy "Ice-T"	16-Feb	50	1958
Rylan, Nolan	31-Jan	61	1947	Steenburgen, Mary	08-Feb	55	1953	McEnroe, John	16-Feb	49	1959
Chapman, Duane "Dog"	01-Feb	55	1953	Williams, John	08-Feb	76	1932	Brown, Jim (football)	17-Feb	72	1936
Everly, Don	01-Feb	71	1937	Bennett, Jimmy	09-Feb	12	1996	Carlson, Kelly	17-Feb	32	1976
Ivey, Phil	01-Feb	32	1976	Farrow, Mia	09-Feb	63	1945	Holbrook, Hal	17-Feb	83	1925
Morris, Garrett	01-Feb	71	1937	King, Carole	09-Feb	66	1942	Jordan, Michael	17-Feb	45	1963
Presley, Lisa Marie	01-Feb	40	1968	Light, Judith	09-Feb	59	1949	Larry the Cable Guy	17-Feb	45	1963
Shore, Pauly	01-Feb	40	1968	Mudd, Roger	09-Feb	80	1928	Levitt, Joseph Gordon	17-Feb	27	1981
Yeltsin, Boris	01-Feb	77	1931	Pesci, Joe	09-Feb	65	1943	O'Connell, Jerry	17-Feb	34	1974
Brinkley, Chirstie	02-Feb	54	1954	Tritt, Travis	09-Feb	45	1963	Richards, Denise	17-Feb	37	1971
Diller, Barry	02-Feb	66	1942	Zhang, Ziyi	09-Feb	29	1979	Russo, Renee	17-Feb	54	1954
Erickson, Scott	02-Feb	40	1968	Apted, Michael	10-Feb	67	1941	Brown, Helen Gurley	18-Feb	86	1922
Fawcett, Farrah	02-Feb	61	1947	Dern, Laura	10-Feb	41	1967	Dillon, Matt	18-Feb	44	1964
Nash, Graham	02-Feb	64	1944	Flack, Roberta	10-Feb	69	1939	Dr. Dre "AndréYoung"	18-Feb	43	1965
Shakira "Isabel Ripoll"	02-Feb	31	1977	Norman, Greg	10-Feb	50	1958	Foreman, Milos	18-Feb	76	1932
Smothers, Tom	02-Feb	71	1937	Spitz, Mark	10-Feb	58	1950	Kennedy, George	18-Feb	83	1925
Stritch, Elaine	02-Feb	81	1927	Stephanopoulos, George	10-Feb	47	1961	Morrison, Toni	18-Feb	77	1931
Cimino, Michael	03-Feb	69	1939	Wagner, Robert	10-Feb	78	1930	Ono, Yoko	18-Feb	75	1933
Danner, Blythe	03-Feb	65	1943	Aniston, Jennifer	11-Feb	39	1969	Palance, Jack	18-Feb	88	1920
Fairchild, Morgan	03-Feb	58	1950	Bush, Jeb	11-Feb	55	1953	Ringwald, Molly	18-Feb	40	1968
Fisher, Isla	03-Feb	32	1976	Crow, Sheryl	11-Feb	46	1962	Shepherd, Sybill	18-Feb	58	1950
Hamilton, Laird	03-Feb	44	1964	Kilcher, Q'orianka	11-Feb	18	1990	Travolta, John	18-Feb	54	1954
Lane, Nathan	03-Feb	52	1956	Louise, Tina	11-Feb	70	1938	White, Vanna	18-Feb	51	1957
Tarkenton, Fran	03-Feb	68	1940	Nielsen, Leslie	11-Feb	82	1926	Bateman, Justine	19-Feb	42	1966
Tierney, Maura	03-Feb	43	1965	Norwood, Brandy	11-Feb	29	1979	Andrew, Duke of York	19-Feb	48	1960
Black, Clint	04-Feb	46	1962	Reynolds, Burt	11-Feb	72	1936	Daniels, Jeff	19-Feb	53	1955
Brenner, David	04-Feb	63	1945	Adams, Maud	12-Feb	63	1945	Del Toro, Benicio	19-Feb	41	1967
Cooper, Alice	04-Feb	60	1948	Blume, Judy	12-Feb	70	1938	Immelt, Jeffrey R.	19-Feb	52	1956
de La Hoya, Oscar	04-Feb	35	1973	Brolin, Josh	12-Feb	40	1968	Kebbel, Arielle	19-Feb	23	1985
Quayle, Dan	04-Feb	61	1947	Garagiola, Joe	12-Feb	82	1926	Robinson, Smokey	19-Feb	68	1940
Taylor, Lawrence	04-Feb	49	1959	Hall, Arsenio	12-Feb	53	1955	Seal "Henry Samuel"	19-Feb	45	1963
Aaron, Hank	05-Feb	74	1934	Kerns, Joanna	12-Feb	55	1953	Ambrose, Lauren	20-Feb	30	1978
Brown, Bobby	05-Feb	39	1969	Ricci, Christina	12-Feb	28	1980	Barkley, Charles	20-Feb	45	1963
Evans, Sarah	05-Feb	37	1971	Russell, Bill	12-Feb	74	1934	Crawford, Cindy	20-Feb	42	1966
Hersey, Barbara	05-Feb	60	1948	Channing, Stockard	13-Feb	64	1944	Duncan, Sandy	20-Feb	62	1946
Leigh, Jennifer Jason	05-Feb	46	1962	Gabriel, Peter	13-Feb	58	1950	Fenty, Robyn "Rihanna"	20-Feb	20	1988
Linney, Laura	05-Feb	44	1964	Kryzewski, Mike	13-Feb	61	1947	French, Stewart	20-Feb	44	1964
Mann, Michael	05-Feb	65	1943	Novak, Kim	13-Feb	75	1933	Griffiths, Rachel	20-Feb	40	1968
Meadows, Tim	05-Feb	47	1961	Segal, George	13-Feb	74	1934	Harris, Thomas	20-Feb	44	1964
Rampling, Charlotte	05-Feb	61	1947	Springer, Jerry	13-Feb	64	1944	Hearst, Patty	20-Feb	54	1954
Staubach, Roger	05-Feb	66	1942	Suvari, Mena	13-Feb	29	1979	O'Neill, Jennifer	20-Feb	60	1948
Waltrip, Darrell	05-Feb	61	1947	Tork, Peter	13-Feb	66	1942	Poitier, Sidney	20-Feb	81	1927
Brokaw, Tom	06-Feb	68	1940	Yeager, Chuck	13-Feb	85	1923	Trump, Ivana	20-Feb	59	1949

Celebrity Birthdays in 2008

Name	Birthday	Age	Born	Name	Birthday	Age	Born	Name	Birthday	Age	Born
Vanderbilt, Gloria	20-Feb	84	1924	Thicke, Allan	01-Mar	61	1947	Romney, Mitt	12-Mar	61	1947
Wilson, Nancy	20-Feb	71	1937	Webber, Chris	01-Mar	35	1973	Taylor, James	12-Mar	60	1948
Baldwin, William	21-Feb	45	1963	Bon Jovi, Jon	02-Mar	46	1962	Delany, Dana	13-Mar	52	1956
Church, Charlotte	21-Feb	22	1986	Bush, Reggie	02-Mar	23	1985	Hirsch, Emile	13-Mar	23	1985
Daly, Tyne	21-Feb	62	1946	Craig, Daniel	02-Mar	40	1968	Macy, William H.	13-Mar	58	1950
Grammer, Kelsey	21-Feb	53	1955	Gorbachev, Mikhail	02-Mar	77	1931	Rodrigue, George	13-Mar	64	1944
Hewitt, Jennifer Love	21-Feb	29	1979	Howard, Bryce Dallas	02-Mar	27	1981	Sedaka, Neil	13-Mar	69	1939
McClanahan, Rue	21-Feb	73	1935	Irving, John	02-Mar	66	1942	Bell, Jamie	14-Mar	22	1986
Page, Ellen	21-Feb	21	1987	Jovi, John Bon	02-Mar	46	1962	Borman, Frank	14-Mar	80	1928
Petersen, William	21-Feb	55	1953	Newman, Loraine	02-Mar	56	1952	Caine, Michael	14-Mar	75	1933
Anderson, Sparky	22-Feb	74	1934	Biel, Jessica	03-Mar	26	1982	Cernan, Gene	14-Mar	74	1934
Barrymore, Drew	22-Feb	33	1975	Joyner-Kersee, Jackie	03-Mar	46	1962	Crystal, Billy	14-Mar	61	1947
Erving, Julius	22-Feb	58	1950	Richardson, Miranda	03-Mar	50	1958	Jones, Quincy	14-Mar	75	1933
Frist, Bill	22-Feb	56	1952	Walker, Herschel	03-Mar	46	1962	Park, Grace	14-Mar	34	1974
Kennedy, Edward	22-Feb	76	1932	Bowen, Andrea	04-Mar	18	1990	Lee, H. Scott	14-Mar	59	1949
Bonilla, Bobby	23-Feb	45	1963	Heaton, Patricia	04-Mar	50	1958	Hirsch, Judd	15-Mar	73	1935
Dell, Michael	23-Feb	43	1965	Mancini, Ray	04-Mar	47	1961	Longoria, Eva	15-Mar	33	1975
Fanning, Dakota	23-Feb	14	1994	Prentiss, Paula	04-Mar	70	1938	Love, Mike	15-Mar	67	1941
Fonda, Peter	23-Feb	69	1939	Eggar, Samantha	05-Mar	69	1939	Burns, Brooke	16-Mar	30	1978
Richardson, Patricia	23-Feb	57	1951	Osteen, Joel	05-Mar	45	1963	Estrada, Erik	16-Mar	59	1949
Bostwick, Barry	24-Feb	62	1946	Stockwell, Dean	05-Mar	72	1936	Graham, Lauren	16-Mar	41	1967
Farentino, James	24-Feb	70	1938	Taylor, Niki	05-Mar	33	1975	Lewis, Jerry	16-Mar	82	1926
Folkman, Judah	24-Feb	75	1933	Arnold, Tom	06-Mar	49	1959	Woolery, Chuck	16-Mar	68	1940
Hewitt, Lleyton	24-Feb	27	1981	Barry, Marion	06-Mar	72	1936	Duffy, Patrick	17-Mar	59	1949
Jobs, Steve	24-Feb	53	1955	Greenspan, Alan	06-Mar	82	1926	Hamm, Mia	17-Mar	36	1972
Murray, Eddie	24-Feb	52	1956	Howard, Tom	06-Mar	29	1979	Lowe, Rob	17-Mar	44	1964
Olmos, Edward James	24-Feb	61	1947	Hughley, D.L.	06-Mar	45	1963	Russell, Kurt	17-Mar	57	1951
Vigoda, Abe	24-Feb	87	1921	McMahon, Ed	06-Mar	85	1923	Sinise, Gary	17-Mar	53	1955
Zahn, Paula	24-Feb	52	1956	O'Neal, Shaquille	06-Mar	36	1972	Blair, Bonnie	18-Mar	44	1964
Zane, Billy	24-Feb	42	1966	Park, Grace	06-Mar	29	1979	Cara, Irene	18-Mar	49	1959
Astin, Sean	25-Feb	37	1971	Reiner, Rob	06-Mar	63	1945	deKlerk, F.W.	18-Mar	72	1936
Irvin, Monte	25-Feb	89	1919	Stargell, Willie	06-Mar	67	1941	Graves, Peter	18-Mar	82	1926
Leoni, Tea	25-Feb	42	1966	Stevens, Gary	06-Mar	45	1963	Kander, John	18-Mar	81	1927
Monte, Irvin	25-Feb	89	1919	Eisner, Michael	07-Mar	66	1942	Pride, Charlie	18-Mar	70	1938
Raphael, Sally Jessy	25-Feb	73	1935	Fischer, Jenna	07-Mar	34	1974	Queen Latifah	18-Mar	38	1970
Santo, Ron	25-Feb	68	1940	Lendl, Ivan	07-Mar	50	1958	Updike, John	18-Mar	72	1936
Schieffer, Bob	25-Feb	71	1937	Scott, Willard	07-Mar	74	1934	Williams, Vanessa	18-Mar	45	1963
Carrot Top	25-Feb	41	1967	Skyes, Wanda	07-Mar	44	1964	Andress, Ursula	19-Mar	72	1936
Bolton, Michael	26-Feb	55	1953	Swann, Lynn	07-Mar	56	1952	Close, Glenn	19-Mar	61	1947
Domino, Fats	26-Feb	80	1928	Travanti, Daniel J.	07-Mar	68	1940	McGoohan, Patrick	19-Mar	80	1928
Faulk, Marshall	26-Feb	35	1973	Dolenz, Mickey	08-Mar	63	1945	Willis, Bruce	19-Mar	53	1955
Clinton, Chelsea	27-Feb	28	1980	Manheim, Camryn	08-Mar	47	1961	Hunter, Holly	20-Mar	50	1958
Groban, Josh	27-Feb	27	1981	Prinze, Freddie Jr.	08-Mar	32	1976	Hurt, William	20-Mar	58	1950
Hesseman, Howard	27-Feb	68	1940	Redgrave, Lynn	08-Mar	65	1943	Ireland, Kathy	20-Mar	45	1963
Nader, Ralph	27-Feb	74	1934	Van Der Beek, James	08-Mar	31	1977	Lee, Spike	20-Mar	51	1957
Taylor, Elizabeth	27-Feb	76	1932	Binoche, Juliette	09-Mar	44	1964	Linden, Hal	20-Mar	77	1931
Thomas, Rozonda "Chilli"	27-Feb	37	1971	Fischer, Bobby	09-Mar	65	1943	Reiner, Carl	20-Mar	86	1922
Woodward, Joanne	27-Feb	78	1930	Gibson, Charles	09-Mar	65	1943	Riley, Pat	20-Mar	63	1945
Andretti, Mario	28-Feb	68	1940	Snow, Brittany	09-Mar	22	1986	Broderick, Matthew	21-Mar	46	1962
Billick, Brian	28-Feb	44	1964	Burton, Lance	10-Mar	48	1960	Dalton, Timothy	21-Mar	64	1944
Durning, Charles	28-Feb	85	1923	Guy, Jasmine	10-Mar	44	1964	Lewis, Ananda	21-Mar	35	1973
Gehry, Frank	28-Feb	79	1929	Norris, Chuck	10-Mar	68	1940	O'Donnell, Rosie	21-Mar	46	1962
Gottfried, Gilbert	28-Feb	53	1955	Prince Edward	10-Mar	44	1964	Costas, Bob	22-Mar	56	1952
Larter, Ali	28-Feb	32	1976	Stone, Sharon	10-Mar	50	1958	Marceau, Marcel	22-Mar	85	1923
Peters, Bernadette	28-Feb	60	1948	Underwood, Carrie	10-Mar	25	1983	Modine, Matthew	22-Mar	49	1959
Smith, Dean	28-Feb	77	1931	Donaldson, Sam	11-Mar	74	1934	Robertson, Pat	22-Mar	78	1930
Belafonte, Harry	01-Mar	81	1927	McFerrin, Bobby	11-Mar	58	1950	Shatner, William	22-Mar	77	1931
Conrad, Robert	01-Mar	73	1935	Murdoch, Rupert	11-Mar	77	1931	Sonheim, Stephen	22-Mar	78	1930
Daltrey, Roger	01-Mar	63	1945	Scalia, Antonin	11-Mar	72	1936	Webber, Andrew Lloyd	22-Mar	60	1948
Davenport, Jack	01-Mar	35	1973	Albee, Edward	12-Mar	80	1928	Witherspoon, Reese	22-Mar	32	1976
Howard, Ron	01-Mar	54	1954	Eckhart, Aaron	12-Mar	40	1968	Bannister, Roger Sir	23-Mar	79	1929
Rozelle, Pete	01-Mar	82	1926	Feldon, Barbara	12-Mar	76	1932	Cole, Kenneth	23-Mar	54	1954
				Minnelli, Liza	12-Mar	62	1946	Corry, Rebecca	23-Mar	37	1971

Celebrity Birthdays in 2008

Name	Birthday	Age	Born	Name	Birthday	Age	Born	Name	Birthday	Age	Born
Davis, Hope	23-Mar	44	1964	Clapton, Eric	30-Mar	63	1945	Frost, David	07-Apr	69	1939
Kidd, Jason	23-Mar	35	1973	Coltrane, Robbie	30-Mar	58	1950	Garner, James	07-Apr	80	1928
Russell, Keri	23-Mar	32	1976	Dion, Celine	30-Mar	40	1968	Oates, John	07-Apr	59	1949
Strait, Steven	23-Mar	22	1986	Hammer, M.C.	30-Mar	46	1962	Annan, Kofi	08-Apr	70	1938
Yarboruogh, Cale	23-Mar	69	1939	Jones, Norah	30-Mar	29	1979	Arquette, Patricia	08-Apr	40	1968
Anderson, Louie	24-Mar	55	1953	Lucas, Jerry	30-Mar	68	1940	Brody, Adam	08-Apr	28	1980
Boyle, Lara Flynn	24-Mar	38	1970	Marshall, Peter	30-Mar	78	1930	Carter, Gary	08-Apr	54	1954
Hannigan, Alyson	24-Mar	34	1974	Reiser, Paul	30-Mar	51	1957	Guerrero, Lisa	08-Apr	44	1964
Jones, Star	24-Mar	46	1962	Alpert, Herb	31-Mar	73	1935	Lennon, Julian	08-Apr	45	1963
LeBrock, Kelly	24-Mar	48	1960	Chamberlain, Richard	31-Mar	73	1935	Penn, Robin Wright	08-Apr	42	1966
Mackie, Bob	24-Mar	68	1940	Gore, Albert	31-Mar	60	1948	Fanning, Elle	09-Apr	10	1998
Manning, Peyton	24-Mar	32	1976	Howe, Gordie	31-Mar	80	1928	Hefner, Hugh	09-Apr	82	1926
Allen, Marcus	25-Mar	48	1960	Jones, Shirley	31-Mar	74	1934	Jameson, Jena	09-Apr	34	1974
Bryant, Anita	25-Mar	68	1940	Kaplan, Gabe	31-Mar	63	1945	Learned, Michael	09-Apr	69	1939
Cross, Marcia	25-Mar	46	1962	McGregor, Ewan	31-Mar	37	1971	Nixon, Cynthia	09-Apr	42	1966
Franklin, Aretha	25-Mar	66	1942	Perlman, Rhea	31-Mar	60	1948	Quiad, Dennis	09-Apr	54	1954
Glaser, Paul Michael	25-Mar	65	1943	Walken, Christopher	31-Mar	65	1943	Babyface	10-Apr	49	1959
John, Elton	25-Mar	61	1947	Alito, Samuel A. Jr.	01-Apr	58	1950	Madden, John	10-Apr	72	1936
Lovell, Jim	25-Mar	80	1928	Maathai, Wangari	01-Apr	68	1940	Moore, Mandy	10-Apr	24	1984
Matchett, Kari	25-Mar	38	1970	McGraw, Ali	01-Apr	70	1938	Osment, Haley Joel	10-Apr	20	1988
McPhee, Katharine	25-Mar	24	1984	Niekro, Phil	01-Apr	69	1939	Seagal, Steven	10-Apr	56	1952
Michalka, Alyson	25-Mar	19	1989	Reagan, Michael	01-Apr	63	1945	Shariff, Omar	10-Apr	76	1932
Parker, Sarah Jessica	25-Mar	43	1965	Reynolds, Debbie	01-Apr	76	1932	von Sydow, Max	10-Apr	79	1929
Patrick, Danica	25-Mar	26	1982	Harris, Emmylou	02-Apr	60	1948	Brown, Tony	11-Apr	75	1933
Steinem, Gloria	25-Mar	74	1934	Smith, Reggie	02-Apr	63	1945	Esposito, Jennifer	11-Apr	35	1973
Wilkins, Roger	25-Mar	76	1932	Sutton, Don	02-Apr	63	1945	Garner, Kelli	11-Apr	24	1984
Allen, Marcus	26-Mar	48	1960	Baldwin, Alec	03-Apr	50	1958	Grey, Joel	11-Apr	76	1932
Arkin, Alan	26-Mar	74	1934	Bynes, Amanda	03-Apr	22	1986	Helfer, Tricia	11-Apr	34	1974
Caan, James	26-Mar	68	1940	Day, Doris	03-Apr	84	1924	Irwin, Bill	11-Apr	58	1950
Chesney, Kenny	26-Mar	40	1968	DeWitt, Joyce	03-Apr	59	1949	Stone, Joss	11-Apr	21	1987
Lawrence, Vicki	26-Mar	59	1949	Garth, Jennie	03-Apr	36	1972	Alexakis, Art	12-Apr	46	1962
Nimoy, Leonard	26-Mar	77	1931	Goodall, Jane	03-Apr	74	1934	Cassidy, David	12-Apr	58	1950
Huntsman, Jon Jr.	26-Mar	48	1960	Murphy, Eddie	03-Apr	47	1961	Clancy, Tom	12-Apr	61	1947
O'Conner, Sandra Day	26-Mar	78	1930	Newton, Wayne	03-Apr	66	1942	Danes, Claire	12-Apr	29	1979
Page, Larry	26-Mar	35	1973	Pierce, David Hyde	03-Apr	49	1959	Garcia, Andy	12-Apr	52	1956
Ross, Diana	26-Mar	64	1944	Spears, Aries	03-Apr	33	1975	Gill, Vince	12-Apr	51	1957
Short, Martin	26-Mar	58	1950	Angelou, Maya	04-Apr	80	1928	Letterman, David	12-Apr	61	1947
Smart, Amy	26-Mar	32	1976	Blaine, David	04-Apr	35	1973	O'Neill, Ed	12-Apr	62	1946
Woodward, Bob	26-Mar	65	1943	Davis, Clive	04-Apr	75	1933	Dow, Tony	13-Apr	63	1945
Carey, Mariah	27-Mar	38	1970	Downey, Robert Jr.	04-Apr	43	1965	Schroder, Rick	13-Apr	38	1970
Ferguson, Stacy "Fergie"	27-Mar	33	1975	Kelly, David E.	04-Apr	52	1956	Brody, Adrien	14-Apr	35	1973
Mitchell, Elizabeth	27-Mar	38	1970	Lahti, Christine	04-Apr	58	1950	Christie, Julie	14-Apr	68	1940
Song, Brenda	27-Mar	20	1988	Ledger, Heath	04-Apr	29	1979	Collins, Francis	14-Apr	58	1950
Tarantino, Quentin	27-Mar	45	1963	Weaving, Hugo	04-Apr	48	1960	Garrett, Brad	14-Apr	48	1960
Vaughan, Sarah	27-Mar	84	1924	Carver, Steve	05-Apr	63	1945	Gellar, Sarah Michelle	14-Apr	31	1977
York, Michael	27-Mar	66	1942	Kamen, Dean	05-Apr	57	1951	Justice, David	14-Apr	42	1966
Howard, Ken	28-Mar	64	1944	Powell, Colin	05-Apr	71	1937	Lynn, Loretta	14-Apr	73	1935
McEntire, Reba	28-Mar	53	1955	Braff, Zach	06-Apr	33	1975	Maddux, Greg	14-Apr	42	1966
Moakler, Shanna	28-Mar	33	1975	Haggard, Merle	06-Apr	71	1937	Rose, Pete	14-Apr	67	1941
Stiles, Julia	28-Mar	27	1981	Henner, Marilu	06-Apr	56	1952	Cardinale, Claudia	15-Apr	69	1939
Vaugh, Vince	28-Mar	38	1970	Levinson, Barry	06-Apr	66	1942	Clark, Roy	15-Apr	75	1933
Wiest, Diane	28-Mar	60	1948	Watson, James	06-Apr	80	1928	Thompson, Emma	15-Apr	49	1959
Capriati, Jennifer	29-Mar	32	1976	Williams, Billie Dee	06-Apr	71	1937	Griffin, Nikki	16-Apr	30	1978
Frazier, Walt	29-Mar	63	1945	Barber, Ronde	07-Apr	33	1975	Jabbar, Kareem Abdul	16-Apr	61	1947
Idle, Eric	29-Mar	65	1943	Barber, Tiki	07-Apr	33	1975	Lawrence, Martin	16-Apr	43	1965
Lawless, Lucy	29-Mar	40	1968	Black, Jack	07-Apr	39	1969	Pope Benedict XVI	16-Apr	81	1927
Logan, Lara	29-Mar	37	1971	Brown, Jerry	07-Apr	70	1938	Vinton, Bobby	16-Apr	73	1935
Macpherson, Elle	29-Mar	44	1964	Chan, Jackie	07-Apr	54	1954	Beckham, Victoria	17-Apr	34	1974
Major, John	29-Mar	65	1943	Coppola, Francis Ford	07-Apr	69	1939	Esiason, Boomer	17-Apr	47	1961
Sedaris, Amy	29-Mar	47	1961	Crowe, Russell	07-Apr	44	1964	Garner, Jennifer	17-Apr	36	1972
Sirtis, Marina	29-Mar	48	1960	Doerr, Bobby	07-Apr	90	1918	Bello, Maria	18-Apr	41	1967
Astin, John	30-Mar	78	1930	Dorsett, Tony	07-Apr	54	1954	Drury, James	18-Apr	74	1934
Beatty, Warren	30-Mar	71	1937	Ellsberg, Daniel	07-Apr	77	1931	Hart, Melissa Joan	18-Apr	32	1976

Celebrity Birthdays in 2008

Name	Birthday	Age	Born	Name	Birthday	Age	Born	Name	Birthday	Age	Born
McCormack, Eric	18-Apr	45	1963	Baker, James III	28-Apr	78	1930	Smith, Lovie	08-May	50	1958
Mills, Hayley	18-Apr	62	1946	Cruz, Penelope	28-Apr	34	1974	Ashcroft, John	09-May	66	1942
O'Brien, Conan	18-Apr	45	1963	Leno, Jay	28-Apr	58	1950	Bergen, Candice	09-May	62	1946
Roth, Eli	18-Apr	36	1972	Margret, Ann	28-Apr	67	1941	Dawson, Rosario	09-May	29	1979
Shawkat, Alia	18-Apr	19	1989	McDonnell, Mary	28-Apr	56	1952	Finney, Albert	09-May	72	1936
Woods, James	18-Apr	61	1947	Rohm, Elisabeth	28-Apr	35	1973	Jackson, Glenda	09-May	72	1936
Christensen, Hayden	19-Apr	27	1981	Hussein, Saddam	28-Apr	71	1937	Joel, Billy	09-May	59	1949
Donahue, Elinore	19-Apr	71	1937	Agassi, Andre	29-Apr	38	1970	Wallace, Mike	09-May	90	1918
Franco, James	19-Apr	30	1978	Aparicio, Luis	29-Apr	74	1934	Berman, Chris	10-May	53	1955
Hudson, Kate	19-Apr	29	1979	Pfeiffer, Michelle	29-Apr	50	1958	Bono "Paul Hewson"	10-May	48	1960
Judd, Ashley	19-Apr	40	1968	Seinfeld, Jerry	29-Apr	54	1954	Bradford, Barbara Taylor	10-May	75	1933
Electra, Carmen	20-Apr	36	1972	Thurman, Uma	29-Apr	38	1970	Domino, Fats	10-May	79	1929
Lange, Jessica	20-Apr	59	1949	Clayburgh, Jill	30-Apr	64	1944	Dyer, Wayne	10-May	68	1940
Lawrence, Joey	20-Apr	32	1976	Dunst, Kirsten	30-Apr	26	1982	Evangelista, Linda	10-May	43	1965
O'Neal, Ryan	20-Apr	67	1941	Garner, Phil	30-Apr	59	1949	Mahre, Phil	10-May	51	1957
Danza, Tony	21-Apr	57	1951	King Carl XVI Gustav	30-Apr	62	1946	Rowell, Victoria	10-May	48	1960
Grodin, Charles	21-Apr	73	1935	Leachman, Cloris	30-Apr	82	1926	Summerall, Pat	10-May	78	1930
MacDowell, Andie	21-Apr	50	1958	Nelson, Willie	30-Apr	75	1933	Burden, Eric	11-May	67	1941
Queen Elizabeth II	21-Apr	82	1926	Queen Beatrix	30-Apr	70	1938	d'Ambroise, Charlotte	11-May	44	1964
Romo, Tony	21-Apr	28	1980	Thomas, Isiah	30-Apr	47	1961	Farrakhan, Louis	11-May	75	1933
Sullivan, Nicole	21-Apr	38	1970	Vee, Bobby	30-Apr	65	1943	Ford, Harold (Politican)	11-May	38	1970
Campbell, Glen	22-Apr	72	1936	Waltrip, Michael	30-Apr	45	1963	Jarvik, Robert Dr.	11-May	62	1946
Nicholson, Jack	22-Apr	71	1937	Collins, Judy	01-May	69	1939	Leinart, Matt	11-May	25	1983
Spelling, Aaron	22-Apr	85	1923	Coolidge, Rita	01-May	64	1944	Richardson, Natasha	11-May	45	1963
Bertinelli, Valerie	23-Apr	48	1960	Mankoff, Robert	01-May	64	1944	Sahl, Mort	11-May	81	1927
Black, Shirley Temple	23-Apr	80	1928	McGraw, Tim	01-May	41	1967	Smalley, Stephen	11-May	78	1930
Cena, John	23-Apr	31	1977	Beckham, David	02-May	33	1975	Bacharach, Burt	12-May	79	1929
Davis, Judy	23-Apr	53	1955	Cannel, Steven J.	02-May	67	1941	Baldwin, Stephen	12-May	42	1966
De Witt, Joyce	23-Apr	59	1949	Gore, Lesley	02-May	62	1946	Berra, Yogi	12-May	83	1925
Krupa , Joanna	23-Apr	27	1981	Hughes, Sarah	02-May	23	1985	Biggs, Jason	12-May	30	1978
Lopez, George	23-Apr	47	1961	Humperdinck, Engelbert	02-May	72	1936	Byrne, Gabriel	12-May	58	1950
Spahn, Warren	23-Apr	87	1921	Jagger, Bianca	02-May	63	1945	Carlin, George	12-May	71	1937
Cedric the Entertainer	24-Apr	44	1964	Johnson, Dwayne	02-May	36	1972	Estevez, Emillio	12-May	46	1962
Clarkson, Kelly	24-Apr	26	1982	Gumbel, Greg	03-May	62	1946	Hawk, Tony	12-May	40	1968
Daly, Richard M.	24-Apr	66	1942	Henning, Doug	03-May	61	1947	Snyder, Tom	12-May	72	1936
Jones, Chipper	24-Apr	36	1972	Popeil, Ron	03-May	73	1935	Keitel, Harvey	13-May	69	1939
MacLaine, Shirley	24-Apr	74	1934	Valli, Frankie	03-May	71	1937	Rodman, Dennis	13-May	47	1961
Streisand, Barbra	24-Apr	66	1942	Bass, Lance	04-May	29	1979	Valentine, Bobby	13-May	58	1950
Ausbie, Geese	25-Apr	70	1938	Gasteyer, Ana	04-May	41	1967	Wonder, Stevie	13-May	58	1950
Azaria, Hank	25-Apr	44	1964	Gould, Alexander	04-May	14	1994	Zito, Barry	13-May	30	1978
Buck, Joe	25-Apr	39	1969	Travis, Randy	04-May	49	1959	Blanchett, Cate	14-May	39	1969
Clayson, Jane	25-Apr	41	1967	Wynette, Tammy	04-May	66	1942	Coppola, Sophie	14-May	37	1971
Lee, Jason	25-Apr	38	1970	Davis, Ann B.	05-May	82	1926	Lucas, George	14-May	64	1944
Lemon, Meadowlark	25-Apr	76	1932	Hogan, Brooke	05-May	20	1988	Perez, Tony	14-May	66	1942
Pacino, Al	25-Apr	68	1940	Palin, Michael	05-May	65	1943	Roth, Tim	14-May	47	1961
Shire, Talia	25-Apr	62	1946	Rhys-Davies, John	05-May	64	1944	Tamblyn, Amber	14-May	25	1983
Zellwegger, Renee	25-Apr	39	1969	Williams, Brian	05-May	49	1959	Zemeckis, Robert	14-May	57	1951
Brewster, Jordana	26-Apr	28	1980	Wynette, Tamy	05-May	66	1942	Ailes, Robert	15-May	68	1940
Burnett, Carol	26-Apr	75	1933	Yothers, Tina	05-May	35	1973	Alberghetti, Anna Marie	15-May	72	1936
Chen, Joan	26-Apr	47	1961	Bergeron, Tom	06-May	53	1955	Albright, Madeleine	15-May	71	1937
Clayson, Jane	26-Apr	41	1967	Blair, Tony	06-May	55	1953	Brett, George	15-May	55	1953
de Varona, Donna	26-Apr	61	1947	Clooney, George	06-May	47	1961	Johns, Jasper	15-May	78	1930
James, Kevin	26-Apr	43	1965	Downey, Roma	06-May	48	1960	Lopez, Trini	15-May	71	1937
Li, Jet	26-Apr	45	1963	Hope, Leslie	06-May	43	1965	Sigler, Jamie Lynn	15-May	27	1981
Milicevci, Ivana	26-Apr	34	1974	Mays, Willie	06-May	77	1931	Smith, Emmitt	15-May	39	1969
Pei, Ieoh M.	26-Apr	91	1917	Brewer, Teresa	07-May	77	1931	Brosnan, Pierce	16-May	55	1953
Santos, Jose	26-Apr	47	1961	Cherry, Eagle-Eye	07-May	39	1969	Carlson, Tucker	16-May	39	1969
Tatum, Channing	26-Apr	28	1980	Knievel, Robbie	07-May	46	1962	Gold, Traci	16-May	39	1969
Easton, Sheena	27-Apr	49	1959	Russert, Tim	07-May	58	1950	Jackson, Janet	16-May	42	1966
Kasem, Casey	27-Apr	76	1932	Benchley, Peter	08-May	68	1940	Korbut, Olga	16-May	53	1955
Klugman, Jack	27-Apr	86	1922	Cowher, Bill	08-May	51	1957	Spelling, Tori	16-May	35	1973
Stott, John	27-Apr	87	1921	Gilbert, Melissa	08-May	44	1964	Winger, Debra	16-May	53	1955
Alba, Jessica	28-Apr	27	1981	Iglesias, Enrique	08-May	33	1975	Enya	17-May	47	1961

The Address Directory

Name	Birthday	Age	Born	Name	Birthday	Age	Born	Name	Birthday	Age	Born
Hopper, Dennis	17-May	72	1936	Carter, Helen Bonham	26-May	42	1966	McKnight, Brian	05-Jun	39	1969
Leonard, Sugar Ray	17-May	52	1956	Gilsig, Jessalyn	26-May	35	1973	Moyers, Bill	05-Jun	74	1934
Nantz, Jim	17-May	49	1959	Goldthwait, Bobcat	26-May	46	1962	Orman, Suze	05-Jun	57	1951
O'Sullivan, Maureen	17-May	97	1911	Kravitz, Lenny	26-May	44	1964	Walberg, Mark	05-Jun	37	1971
Paxton, Bill	17-May	53	1955	Musberger, Brent	26-May	69	1939	Bernhard, Sandra	06-Jun	53	1955
Saget, Bob	17-May	52	1956	Nicks, Stevie	26-May	60	1948	Bond, Gary U.S.	06-Jun	69	1939
Fey, Tina	18-May	38	1970	Ride, Sally	26-May	57	1951	Borg, Bjorn	06-Jun	52	1956
Jackson, Reggie	18-May	62	1946	Williams, Hank Jr.	26-May	59	1949	Giamatti, Paul	06-Jun	41	1967
Roberts, Pernell	18-May	78	1930	Carolla, Adam	27-May	44	1964	Keanan, Staci	06-Jun	33	1975
Robinson, Brooks	18-May	71	1937	Fiennes, Joseph	27-May	38	1970	Kerkorian, Kirk	06-Jun	91	1917
Shriver, Lionel	18-May	51	1957	Gossett, Louis Jr.	27-May	72	1936	Iverson, Allen	07-Jun	33	1975
Strait, George	18-May	56	1952	Kissinger, Henry	27-May	85	1923	Jones, Jenny	07-Jun	62	1946
Yun-Fat, Chow	18-May	53	1955	Adams, Patch	28-May	63	1945	Jones, Tom	07-Jun	68	1940
Ephron, Nora	19-May	67	1941	Bradford, Jesse	28-May	29	1979	Kournikova, Anna	07-Jun	27	1981
Garnett, Kevin	19-May	32	1976	Cross, Joseph	28-May	22	1986	Neeson, Liam	07-Jun	56	1952
Jones, Grace	19-May	56	1952	Fogerty, John	28-May	63	1945	Osmond, Ken	07-Jun	65	1943
Lehrer, Jim	19-May	74	1934	Giuliani, Rudoph	28-May	64	1944	Prince "Roger Nelson"	07-Jun	50	1958
Manning, Archie	19-May	59	1949	Knight, Gladys	28-May	64	1944	Adderley, Herb	08-Jun	69	1939
Townshend, Pete	19-May	63	1945	Minogue, Kylie	28-May	40	1968	Bush, Barbara	08-Jun	83	1925
Cher "Cheryl LaPiere"	20-May	62	1946	West, Jerry	28-May	70	1938	Margulies, Julianna	08-Jun	42	1966
Cocker, Joe	20-May	64	1944	Benning, Annette	29-May	50	1958	Neiman, Leroy	08-Jun	81	1927
Olyphant, Timothy	20-May	40	1968	Etheridge, Melissa	29-May	47	1961	Rivers, Joan	08-Jun	75	1933
Pinchot, Bronson	20-May	49	1959	Jackson, LaToya	29-May	52	1956	Sinatra, Nancy	08-Jun	68	1940
Reagan, Ron	20-May	50	1958	Unser, Al	29-May	69	1939	Stiller, Jerry	08-Jun	81	1927
Stewart, Tony	20-May	37	1971	Judd, Wynonna	30-May	44	1964	Wayans, Keenan Ivory	08-Jun	50	1958
Wells, David	20-May	40	1968	Pollard, Michael J.	30-May	69	1939	West, Kanye	08-Jun	31	1977
Cox, Bobby	21-May	67	1941	Sayers, Gayle	30-May	65	1943	Cornwall, Patricia	09-Jun	52	1956
Edelstein, Lisa	21-May	41	1967	Walker, Clint	30-May	81	1927	Depp, Johnny	09-Jun	45	1963
Franken, Al	21-May	57	1951	Berenger, Tom	31-May	59	1949	Fox, Michael J.	09-Jun	47	1961
Mr. T	21-May	56	1952	Eastwood, Clint	31-May	78	1930	Mason, Jackie	09-Jun	77	1931
Williams, Ricky	21-May	31	1977	Farrell, Colin	31-May	32	1976	Portman, Natalie	09-Jun	27	1981
Campbell, Naomi	22-May	38	1970	Namath, Joe	31-May	65	1943	Vitale, Dick	09-Jun	69	1939
Eastwood, Alison	22-May	36	1972	Paycheck, Johnny	31-May	67	1941	Bailey, F. Lee	10-Jun	75	1933
John, Tommy	22-May	65	1943	Shields, Brook	31-May	43	1965	Bennett, Jonathan	10-Jun	27	1981
Ohno, Apolo	22-May	26	1982	Thompson, Lee	31-May	47	1961	Hurley, Elizabeth	10-Jun	43	1965
Pickens, T. Boone	22-May	80	1928	Boone, Pat	01-Jun	74	1934	Lipinski, Tara	10-Jun	26	1982
Quigley, Maggie	22-May	29	1979	Freeman, Morgan	01-Jun	71	1937	Sobieski, Leelee	10-Jun	26	1982
Shaw, Bernard	22-May	68	1940	Griffith, Andy	01-Jun	82	1926	Spitzer, Eliot	10-Jun	49	1959
Carey, Drew	23-May	50	1958	Klum, Heidi	01-Jun	35	1973	Barbeau, Adrienne	11-Jun	63	1945
Collins, Joan	23-May	75	1933	Morissette, Alanis	01-Jun	34	1974	Cisneros, Henry	11-Jun	61	1947
Hagler, Marvin	23-May	56	1952	Varekova, Veronica	01-Jun	31	1977	LaBeouf, Shia	11-Jun	22	1986
Jennings, Ken	23-May	34	1974	Brady, Wayne	02-Jun	36	1972	Laurie, Hugh	11-Jun	49	1959
Kilcher, Jewel	23-May	34	1974	Carvey, Dana	02-Jun	53	1955	Montana, Joe	11-Jun	52	1956
Monaco, Kelly	23-May	32	1976	Hamlisch, Marvin	02-Jun	64	1944	Reyes, Jose	11-Jun	25	1983
Burghoff, Gary	24-May	65	1943	Keach, Stacy	02-Jun	67	1941	Van Susteren, Greta	11-Jun	53	1955
Dylan, Bob	24-May	67	1941	Kellerman, Sally	02-Jun	70	1938	Wilder, Gene	11-Jun	73	1935
LaBelle, Patti	24-May	64	1944	Long, Justin	02-Jun	30	1978	Bush, George H. W.	12-Jun	84	1924
Presley, Priscilla	24-May	63	1945	Mathers, Jerry	02-Jun	60	1948	Nabors, Jim	12-Jun	76	1932
Redstone, Sumner	24-May	85	1923	Miller, Wentworth	02-Jun	36	1972	Rockefeller, David	12-Jun	93	1915
Reilly, John C.	24-May	43	1965	Petty, Kyle	02-Jun	48	1960	Allen, Tim	13-Jun	55	1953
Thomas, Kristin Scott	24-May	48	1960	Barris, Chuck	03-Jun	79	1929	Evans, Chris	13-Jun	27	1981
Carter, Dixie	25-May	69	1939	Castro, Raul	03-Jun	77	1931	Olsen, Mary-Kate	13-Jun	22	1986
Heche, Anne	25-May	39	1969	Cooper, Anderson	03-Jun	41	1967	Olsen, Ashley	13-Jun	22	1986
Hill, Lauren	25-May	33	1975	Curtis, Tony	03-Jun	83	1925	Sheedy, Ally	13-Jun	46	1962
McKellen, Sir Ian	25-May	70	1938	Ginsberg, Allen	03-Jun	82	1926	Thomas, Richard	13-Jun	57	1951
Myers, Mike	25-May	45	1963	McMurtry, Larry	03-Jun	72	1936	Tweeden, Leeann	13-Jun	35	1973
Selleca, Connie	25-May	53	1955	Shula, Mike	03-Jun	43	1965	Bleeth, Jasmine	14-Jun	40	1968
Shields, Mark	25-May	71	1937	Dern, Bruce	04-Jun	72	1936	Graf, Steffi	14-Jun	39	1969
Sims, Molly	25-May	35	1973	Jolie, Angelina	04-Jun	33	1975	Trump, Donald	14-Jun	62	1946
Sills, Beverly	25-May	79	1929	Phillips, Michelle	04-Jun	64	1944	Arquette, Courteney Cox	15-Jun	44	1964
Walker, Jimmie	25-May	61	1947	Wyle, Noah	04-Jun	37	1971	Baker, Dusty	15-Jun	59	1949
Altobelli, Joe	25-May	76	1932	Kenny G "Gorelick"	05-Jun	52	1956	Belushi, Jim	15-Jun	54	1954
Arness, James	26-May	85	1923	Follett, Ken	05-Jun	59	1949	Boggs, Wade	15-Jun	50	1958

Celebrity Birthdays in 2008

Name	Birthday	Age	Born	Name	Birthday	Age	Born	Name	Birthday	Age	Born
Holmgren, Mike	15-Jun	60	1948	Simon, Carly	25-Jun	63	1945	Griffin, Merv	06-Jul	83	1925
Hunt, Helen	15-Jun	45	1963	Reed, Willis	25-Jun	66	1942	"Dalai Lama"	06-Jul	73	1935
Ice-Cube	15-Jun	39	1969	Hayes, Sean	26-Jun	38	1970	Randolph, Willie	06-Jul	54	1954
Remini, Leah	15-Jun	38	1970	Jeter, Derek	26-Jun	34	1974	Reese, Della	06-Jul	76	1932
Rusesabagina, Paul	15-Jun	54	1954	LeMond, Greg	26-Jun	47	1961	Rush, Geoffrey	06-Jul	57	1951
Williams, Billy	15-Jun	70	1938	O'Donnell, Chris	26-Jun	38	1970	Stallone, Sylvester	06-Jul	62	1946
Mickelson, Phil	16-Jun	38	1970	Schwartzman, Jason	26-Jun	28	1980	Ward, Burt	06-Jul	63	1945
Van Ark, Joan	16-Jun	65	1943	Vick, Michael	26-Jun	28	1980	Collins, Mo	07-Jul	43	1965
Woods, Kerry	16-Jun	31	1977	Wilson, Gretchen	26-Jun	35	1973	Duvall, Shelly	07-Jul	59	1949
Gingrich, Newt	17-Jun	65	1943	Duffy, Julia	27-Jun	57	1951	Fox, Jorja	07-Jul	40	1968
Kinnear, Greg	17-Jun	45	1963	Maguire, Tobey	27-Jun	65	1943	Kwan, Michelle	07-Jul	28	1980
Manilow, Barry	17-Jun	62	1946	Morgan, Lorrie	27-Jun	49	1959	Starr, Ringo	07-Jul	68	1940
Rutan, Burt	17-Jun	65	1943	Perot, H. Ross	27-Jun	78	1930	Bacon, Kevin	08-Jul	50	1958
Williams, Venus	17-Jun	28	1980	Wang, Vera	27-Jun	59	1949	Beck	08-Jul	38	1970
Brock, Lou	18-Jun	69	1939	Bates, Kathy	28-Jun	60	1948	Bush, Sophia	08-Jul	26	1982
Ebert, Roger	18-Jun	66	1942	Brooks, Mel	28-Jun	82	1926	Huston, Anjelica	08-Jul	57	1951
McCartney, Paul	18-Jun	66	1942	Byner, John	28-Jun	70	1938	Keith, Toby	08-Jul	47	1961
Rossellini, Isabella	18-Jun	56	1952	Cusack, John	28-Jun	42	1966	Ventimiglia, Milo	08-Jul	31	1977
Abdul, Paula	19-Jun	46	1962	Elway, John	28-Jun	48	1960	Ames, Ed	09-Jul	81	1927
Maestro, Mia	19-Jun	30	1978	Yunus, Muhammad	28-Jun	68	1940	Cooper, Chris	09-Jul	57	1951
Nowitzki, Dirk Werner	19-Jun	30	1978	Basich, Tina	29-Jun	39	1969	Hanks, Tom	09-Jul	52	1956
Rashad, Phylicia	19-Jun	60	1948	Busey, Gary	29-Jun	64	1944	Koontz, Dean	09-Jul	63	1945
Rowlands, Gena	19-Jun	74	1934	Dierdorf, Dan	29-Jun	59	1949	Lee, Jeanette	09-Jul	37	1971
Salman, Rushdie	19-Jun	61	1947	Dogg, Snoop	29-Jun	37	1971	Love, Courtney	09-Jul	43	1965
Goodman, John	20-Jun	56	1952	Grandy, Fred	29-Jun	60	1948	McGillis, Kelly	09-Jul	51	1957
Kidman, Nicole	20-Jun	41	1967	Killebrew, Harmon	29-Jun	72	1936	Roundtree, Richard	09-Jul	66	1942
Landau, Martin	20-Jun	77	1931	Lewis, Richard	29-Jun	61	1947	Simpson, O.J.	09-Jul	61	1947
Lucas, Josh	20-Jun	37	1971	Ballard, Robert	30-Jun	66	1942	Smits, Jimmy	09-Jul	53	1955
Murray, Anne	20-Jun	63	1945	Caplan, Lizzy	30-Jun	26	1982	Guthrie, Arlo	10-Jul	68	1940
Richie, Lionel	20-Jun	59	1949	Horne, Lena	30-Jun	91	1917	Shriver, Eunice Kennedy	10-Jul	87	1921
Vila, Bob	20-Jun	62	1946	Tyson, Mike	30-Jun	42	1966	Simpson, Jessica	10-Jul	28	1980
Wilson, Brian	20-Jun	66	1942	Anderson, Pamela	01-Jul	41	1967	Vergara, Sofia	10-Jul	36	1972
Baxter, Meredith	21-Jun	61	1947	Aykroyd, Dan	01-Jul	56	1952	Armani, Giorgio	11-Jul	74	1934
Gross, Michael	21-Jun	61	1947	De Havilland, Olivia	01-Jul	92	1916	Corwin, Jeff	11-Jul	41	1967
Kopell, Bernie	21-Jun	75	1933	Farr, Jamie	01-Jul	74	1934	Lil 'Kim	11-Jul	33	1975
Mattea, Kathy	21-Jun	49	1959	Harry, Deborah	01-Jul	63	1945	Paolo, Connor	11-Jul	18	1990
Prince William	21-Jun	26	1982	Lewis, Carl	01-Jul	47	1961	Spinks, Leon	11-Jul	55	1953
Bradley, Ed	22-Jun	67	1941	Pollack, Sydney	01-Jul	74	1934	Ward, Sela	11-Jul	52	1956
Brockovich-Ellis, Erin	22-Jun	48	1960	Tyler, Liv	01-Jul	31	1977	Cliburn, Van	12-Jul	74	1934
Brown, Dan	22-Jun	44	1964	Branh, Michelle	02-Jul	25	1983	Cosby, Bill	12-Jul	71	1937
Brenneman, Amy	22-Jun	44	1964	Canseco, Jose	02-Jul	44	1964	Gary, Willie E.	12-Jul	61	1947
Daly, Carson	22-Jun	35	1973	David, Larry	02-Jul	61	1947	Ladd, Cheryl	12-Jul	57	1951
Drexler, Clyde	22-Jun	46	1962	Fox, Vincente	02-Jul	66	1942	Patty, Sandi	12-Jul	51	1957
Greene, Graham	22-Jun	56	1952	Lohan, Lindsay	02-Jul	22	1986	Yamaguchi, Kristi	12-Jul	37	1971
Hume, Brit	22-Jun	65	1943	Petty, Richard	02-Jul	71	1937	Crowe, Cameron	13-Jul	51	1957
Lauper, Cyndi	22-Jun	55	1953	Tisdale, Ashley	02-Jul	23	1985	Duke, David	13-Jul	58	1950
Streep, Meryl	22-Jun	59	1949	Cruise, Tom	03-Jul	46	1962	Ford, Harrison	13-Jul	66	1942
Wagner, Lindsay	22-Jun	59	1949	Smith, Shawnee	03-Jul	38	1970	Kemp, Jack	13-Jul	73	1935
Warner, Kurt	22-Jun	37	1971	Wilson, Patrick	03-Jul	35	1973	Mandrell, Louise	13-Jul	54	1954
McDormand, Frances	23-Jun	51	1957	Lollobrigida, Gina	04-Jul	81	1927	Marin, Cheech	13-Jul	62	1946
Parker, Robert M.	23-Jun	61	1947	Rivera, Geraldo	04-Jul	65	1943	Spinks, Michael	13-Jul	52	1956
Thomas, Clarence	23-Jun	60	1948	Saint, Eva Marie	04-Jul	84	1924	Stewart, Patrick	13-Jul	68	1940
Tomlinson, LaDainian	23-Jun	29	1979	Simon, Neil	04-Jul	81	1927	Bergen, Polly	14-Jul	78	1930
Vaugier, Emmanuelle	23-Jun	32	1976	Steinbrenner, George	04-Jul	78	1930	Bergman, Ingmar	14-Jul	90	1918
Fleetwood, Mick	24-Jun	66	1942	Falco, Edie	05-Jul	45	1963	Buell, Bebe	14-Jul	55	1953
Lee, Michelle	24-Jun	66	1942	Green, Eva	05-Jul	28	1980	Dyson, Esther	14-Jul	57	1951
Pataki, George	24-Jun	63	1945	Judge Joe Brown	05-Jul	61	1947	Gold, Missy	14-Jul	38	1970
Penny, Joe	24-Jun	52	1956	Lewis, Huey	05-Jul	57	1951	Grier, Roosevelt	14-Jul	76	1932
Cardellini, Linda	25-Jun	33	1975	Oates, Warren	05-Jul	80	1928	Kennedy, Patrick J.	14-Jul	41	1967
Lockhart, June	25-Jun	83	1925	Beatty, Ned	06-Jul	71	1937	Robertson, Dale	14-Jul	85	1923
Lumet, Sydney	25-Jun	84	1924	Bush, George W.	06-Jul	62	1946	Huffington, Arianna	15-Jul	58	1950
Michael, George	25-Jun	45	1963	Dryer, Fred	06-Jul	62	1946	Ronstadt, Linda	15-Jul	62	1946
Mutombo, Dikembe	25-Jun	42	1966	"50 Cent"	06-Jul	33	1975	Ventura, Jesse	15-Jul	57	1951

Celebrity Birthdays in 2008

Name	Birthday	Age	Born	Name	Birthday	Age	Born	Name	Birthday	Age	Born
Ferrell, Will	16-Jul	41	1967	Hays, Robert	24-Jul	61	1947	Whitman, Meg	04-Aug	52	1956
Flatley, Michael	16-Jul	50	1958	Krone, Julie	24-Jul	45	1963	Anderson, Loni	05-Aug	62	1946
Hellmuth, Phil	16-Jul	44	1964	Lopez, Jennifer	24-Jul	39	1969	Armstrong, Neil	05-Aug	78	1930
Johnson, Jimmy	16-Jul	65	1943	Malone, Carl	24-Jul	45	1963	Ewing, Patrick	05-Aug	46	1962
Myerson, Bess	16-Jul	84	1924	Paquin, Anna	24-Jul	26	1982	Kramer, Stepfanie	06-Aug	52	1956
Sanders, Barry	16-Jul	40	1968	Richards, Michael	24-Jul	59	1949	Shyamalan,M. Night	06-Aug	38	1970
Carroll, Diahann	17-Jul	73	1935	Sarandon, Chris	24-Jul	66	1942	Yeoh, Michelle	06-Aug	46	1962
Diller, Phyllis	17-Jul	91	1917	Tillis, Pam	24-Jul	51	1957	Cornish, Abbie	07-Aug	26	1982
Hasselhoff, David	17-Jul	56	1952	Brown, Louise	25-Jul	30	1978	Crosby, Sidney	07-Aug	21	1987
Linkletter, Art	17-Jul	96	1912	Getty, Estelle	25-Jul	84	1924	Duchovny, David	07-Aug	48	1960
Parker-Bowles,Camilla	17-Jul	61	1947	LeBlanc, Matt	25-Jul	41	1967	Keillor, Garrison	07-Aug	66	1942
Sutherland, Donald	17-Jul	73	1935	Renfro, Brad	25-Jul	26	1982	Larson, Don	07-Aug	79	1929
Bell, Kristen	18-Jul	28	1980	Beckinsale, Kate	26-Jul	35	1973	Theron, Charlize	07-Aug	33	1975
Branson, Richard	18-Jul	58	1950	Bullock, Sandra	26-Jul	44	1964	Thomas, B.J.	07-Aug	66	1942
Brolin, James	18-Jul	68	1940	Hamill, Dorothy	26-Jul	52	1956	Wales, Jimmy	07-Aug	42	1966
Diesel, Vin	18-Jul	41	1967	Jagger, Mick	26-Jul	65	1943	Chasez, J.C.	08-Aug	32	1976
Forbes, Steve	18-Jul	61	1947	Spacey, Kevin	26-Jul	49	1959	De Laurentiis, Dino	08-Aug	89	1919
Glenn, John H. Jr.	18-Jul	87	1921	Fleming, Peggy	27-Jul	60	1948	Hoffman, Dustin	08-Aug	71	1937
Mandela, Nelson	18-Jul	90	1918	Lear, Norman	27-Jul	86	1922	Leung, Katie	08-Aug	21	1987
Torre, Joe	18-Jul	68	1940	McGovern, Maureen	27-Jul	59	1949	Norville, Deborah	08-Aug	50	1958
Carr, Vicki	19-Jul	67	1941	Rodriguez, Alex	27-Jul	33	1975	Anderson, Gillian	09-Aug	40	1968
Edwards, Anthony	19-Jul	46	1962	Van Dyke, Jerry	27-Jul	77	1931	Bana, Eric	09-Aug	40	1968
McGovern, George	19-Jul	86	1922	Babbitt, Natalie	28-Jul	76	1932	Cousy, Bill	09-Aug	80	1928
Reeves, Martha	19-Jul	67	1941	Bradley, Bill	28-Jul	65	1943	Griffith, Melanie	09-Aug	51	1957
Schultz, Howard	19-Jul	55	1953	Davis, Jim	28-Jul	63	1945	Houston, Whitney	09-Aug	45	1963
Bundchen, Gisele	20-Jul	28	1980	Struthers, Sally	28-Jul	60	1948	Norton, Ken	09-Aug	63	1945
Carnes, Kim	20-Jul	63	1945	Young, Dey	28-Jul	53	1955	Sanders, Deion	09-Aug	41	1967
Epps, Omar	20-Jul	35	1973	Burns, Ken	29-Jul	55	1953	Tautou, Audrey	09-Aug	32	1976
Friedman, Thomas	20-Jul	55	1953	Dole, Elizabeth	29-Jul	72	1936	Banderas, Antonio	10-Aug	48	1960
Hillary, Sir Edmond	20-Jul	89	1919	McBride, Martina	29-Jul	42	1966	Bowe, Riddick	10-Aug	41	1967
Rigg, Diana	20-Jul	70	1938	Anka, Paul	30-Jul	67	1941	Brunson, Doyle	10-Aug	75	1933
Santana, Carlos	20-Jul	61	1947	Baker, Simon	30-Jul	39	1969	Dean, Jimmy	10-Aug	80	1928
Chastain, Brandi	21-Jul	40	1968	Bogdonovich, Peter	30-Jul	69	1939	Harmon, Angie	10-Aug	36	1972
Hartnett, Josh	21-Jul	30	1978	Fishburne, Lawrence	30-Jul	47	1961	Hogan, Hulk	11-Aug	55	1953
Landry, Ali	21-Jul	35	1973	Fox, Vivica	30-Jul	44	1964	Ward, Sela	11-Aug	52	1956
Lovitz, Jon	21-Jul	51	1957	Kudrow, Lisa	30-Jul	45	1963	Wozniak, Steve	11-Aug	58	1950
Stevens, Cat	21-Jul	60	1948	Pressly, Jaime	30-Jul	31	1977	vos Savant, Marilyn	11-Aug	62	1946
Trudeau, Gary	21-Jul	60	1948	Schwarzenegger, Arnold	30-Jul	61	1947	Hamilton, George	12-Aug	69	1939
Wallace, George	21-Jul	56	1952	Selig, Bud	30-Jul	74	1934	Lawson, Maggie	12-Aug	28	1980
Williams, Robin	21-Jul	56	1952	Swank, Hillary	30-Jul	34	1974	Sampras, Pete	12-Aug	37	1971
Brooks, Albert	22-Jul	61	1947	Rowling, J.K.	31-Jul	43	1965	Soros, George	12-Aug	78	1930
Dafoe, Willem	22-Jul	53	1955	Snipes, Wesley	31-Jul	46	1962	Bonaduce, Danny	13-Aug	49	1959
Dole, Bob	22-Jul	85	1923	Van Dyke, Barry	31-Jul	58	1950	Castro, Fidel	13-Aug	82	1926
Glover, Danny	22-Jul	61	1947	Coolio	01-Aug	45	1963	Ho, Don	13-Aug	78	1930
Henley, Don	22-Jul	61	1947	DeLuise, Dom	01-Aug	75	1933	Bell, Catherine	14-Aug	40	1968
Potente, Franka	22-Jul	34	1974	Mendes, Sam	01-Aug	43	1965	Berry, Halle	14-Aug	42	1966
Sherman, Bobby	22-Jul	65	1943	Barrett, Jacinda	02-Aug	36	1972	Brightman, Sarah	14-Aug	48	1960
Spade, David	22-Jul	44	1964	Craven, Wes	02-Aug	69	1939	Cheney, Lynne V.	14-Aug	67	1941
Trebek, Alex	22-Jul	68	1940	Foster, Sara	02-Aug	27	1981	Crosby, David	14-Aug	67	1941
Harrelson, Woody	23-Jul	47	1961	O'Toole, Peter	02-Aug	76	1932	Gorham, Christopher	14-Aug	34	1974
Hoffman, Philip	23-Jul	41	1967	Smith, Kevin	02-Aug	38	1970	Johnson, Magic	14-Aug	49	1959
Imus, Don	23-Jul	68	1940	Bennett, Tony	03-Aug	82	1926	Kunis, Mila	14-Aug	25	1983
Krauss, Alison	23-Jul	37	1971	Brady, Tom	03-Aug	31	1977	Martin, Steve	14-Aug	63	1945
LaSalle, Eriq	23-Jul	46	1962	Levy, Marv	03-Aug	83	1925	Steel, Danielle	14-Aug	61	1947
Radcliffe, Daniel	23-Jul	19	1989	Lilly, Evangeline	03-Aug	29	1979	Weaver, Earl	14-Aug	78	1930
Seymour, Stephanie	23-Jul	40	1968	McGinley, John C.	03-Aug	49	1959	Affleck, Ben	15-Aug	36	1972
Wayans, Marlon	23-Jul	36	1972	Sheen, Martin	03-Aug	68	1940	Breyer, Stephen	15-Aug	70	1938
Bonds, Barry	24-Jul	44	1964	Stewart, Martha	03-Aug	67	1941	Gates, Melinda	15-Aug	44	1964
Buzzi, Ruth	24-Jul	72	1936	Clemens, Roger	04-Aug	46	1962	Mazar, Debi	15-Aug	44	1964
Byrne, Rose	24-Jul	29	1979	Gordon, Jeff	04-Aug	37	1971	Messing, Debra	15-Aug	40	1968
Carter, Lynda	24-Jul	57	1951	Sprouse, Cole	04-Aug	16	1992	Quinn, Colin	15-Aug	49	1959
Chenoweth, Kristin	24-Jul	40	1968	Sprouse, Dylan	04-Aug	16	1992	Bassett, Angela	16-Aug	50	1958
Gallager,LeoAnthony	24-Jul	61	1947	Thornton, Billy Bob	04-Aug	53	1955	Bennett, Olivia	16-Aug	19	1989

Celebrity Birthdays in 2008

Name	Birthday	Age	Born	Name	Birthday	Age	Born	Name	Birthday	Age	Born
Braun, Carol	16-Aug	61	1947	Grossman, Rex	23-Aug	28	1980	Estefan, Gloria	01-Sep	51	1957
Cameron, James	16-Aug	54	1954	Kell, George	23-Aug	86	1922	Gibb, Barry	01-Sep	62	1946
Carell, Steve	16-Aug	45	1963	Long, Shelly	23-Aug	59	1949	Hardaway, Tim	01-Sep	42	1966
Culp, Robert	16-Aug	78	1930	Mohr, Jay	23-Aug	38	1970	McGraw, Phil Dr.	01-Sep	58	1950
Gifford, Frank	16-Aug	78	1930	Queen Norr	23-Aug	57	1951	Tomlin, Lily	01-Sep	69	1939
Gifford, Kathie Lee	16-Aug	55	1953	Russell, Mark	23-Aug	76	1932	Bradshaw, Terry	02-Sep	60	1948
Hutton, Timothy	16-Aug	48	1960	Springfield, Rick	23-Aug	59	1949	Connors, Jimmy	02-Sep	56	1952
Madonna	16-Aug	50	1958	Kilborn, Craig	24-Aug	46	1962	Grove, Andrew	02-Sep	72	1936
Newmar, Julie	16-Aug	75	1933	Matlin, Marlee	24-Aug	43	1965	Harmon, Mark	02-Sep	57	1951
Peres, Shimon	16-Aug	85	1923	Miller, Reggie	24-Aug	43	1965	Hayek, Salma	02-Sep	42	1966
Robison, Emily	16-Aug	36	1972	Ripken, Cal Jr.	24-Aug	48	1960	Lewis, Lennox	02-Sep	43	1965
DeNiro, Robert	17-Aug	65	1943	Bilson, Rachel	25-Aug	27	1981	Reeves, Keanu	02-Sep	44	1964
Felt, Mark W.	17-Aug	95	1913	Burton, Tim	25-Aug	50	1958	Ueberroth, Peter	02-Sep	71	1937
Hurd-Wood, Rachel	17-Aug	18	1990	Connery, Sean	25-Aug	78	1930	Perrine, Valerie	03-Sep	65	1943
Penn, Sean	17-Aug	48	1960	Costello, Elvis	25-Aug	54	1954	Sheen, Charlie	03-Sep	43	1965
Boosler, Elayne	18-Aug	56	1952	Cyrus, Billy Ray	25-Aug	47	1961	Walker, Mort	03-Sep	85	1923
Bugliosi, Vincent	18-Aug	74	1934	Fingers, Rollie	25-Aug	62	1946	Harvey, Paul	04-Sep	90	1918
Choudhury, Sarita	18-Aug	42	1966	Hall, Monty	25-Aug	84	1924	Knowles, Beyonce	04-Sep	27	1981
LaForce, Allie	18-Aug	19	1989	Philbin, Regis	25-Aug	75	1933	Piazza, Mike	04-Sep	40	1968
Leary, Denis	18-Aug	51	1957	Ray, Rachael	25-Aug	40	1968	Pinsky, Drew Dr.	04-Sep	50	1958
Norton, Edward	18-Aug	39	1969	Schiffer, Claudia	25-Aug	38	1970	Watson, Tom	04-Sep	59	1949
Polansky, Roman	18-Aug	75	1933	Simmons, Gene	25-Aug	59	1949	Wayons, Damon	04-Sep	48	1960
Redford, Robert	18-Aug	71	1937	Underwood, Blair	25-Aug	44	1964	Guisewite, Cathy	05-Sep	58	1950
Slater, Christian	18-Aug	39	1969	Bradlee, Ben	26-Aug	87	1921	Keaton, Michael	05-Sep	57	1951
Swayze, Patrick	18-Aug	56	1952	Culkin, Macaulay	26-Aug	28	1980	Lawrence, Carol	05-Sep	74	1934
Warner, Malcolm-Jamal	18-Aug	38	1970	Marsalis, Branford	26-Aug	48	1960	Mazeroski, Bill	05-Sep	72	1936
Clinton, William J.	19-Aug	62	1946	Pine, Chris	26-Aug	28	1980	Newhart, Bob	05-Sep	79	1929
Gallagher, Peter	19-Aug	53	1955	Ridge, Tom	26-Aug	63	1945	Welch, Raquel	05-Sep	68	1940
Gore, Tipper	19-Aug	60	1948	Bach, Barbara	27-Aug	61	1947	Curtain, Jane	06-Sep	61	1947
Lil' Romeo	19-Aug	19	1989	Chalke, Sarah	27-Aug	32	1976	Fiorina, Carle	06-Sep	54	1954
Matalin, Mary	19-Aug	55	1953	Ebbers, Bernard	27-Aug	67	1941	Foxworthy, Jeff	06-Sep	50	1958
McCourt, Frank	19-Aug	78	1930	Lear, Norman	27-Aug	86	1922	Harris, Naomi	06-Sep	32	1976
Morrison, Jennifer	19-Aug	29	1979	Least Heat-Moon, William	27-Aug	69	1939	Perez, Rosie	06-Sep	44	1964
Musgrave, Story	19-Aug	73	1935	Nechita, Alexandra	27-Aug	23	1985	Vargas, Elizabeth	06-Sep	46	1962
Perry, Matthew	19-Aug	39	1969	Reubens, Paul	27-Aug	56	1952	Worley, Jo Anne	06-Sep	71	1937
Sedgwick, Kyra	19-Aug	43	1965	Hammer, Armie	28-Aug	22	1986	Bernsen, Corbin	07-Sep	54	1954
St. John, Jill	19-Aug	68	1940	Piniella, Lou	28-Aug	65	1943	Everhart, Angie	07-Sep	39	1969
Stamos, John	19-Aug	45	1963	Priestley, Jason	28-Aug	39	1969	Inouye, Daniel	07-Sep	84	1924
Thoms, Tracie	19-Aug	33	1975	Rimes, LeAnn	28-Aug	26	1982	Mosley, Sugar Shane	07-Sep	37	1971
Womack, Lee Ann	19-Aug	42	1966	Roemer, Sarah	28-Aug	24	1984	Noonan, Peggy	07-Sep	58	1950
Adams, Amy	20-Aug	33	1975	Soul, David	28-Aug	65	1943	Wood, Evan Rachel	07-Sep	21	1987
Chung, Connie	20-Aug	62	1946	Twain, Shania	28-Aug	43	1965	Arquette, David	08-Sep	37	1971
Hayes, Isaac	20-Aug	66	1942	Gould, Elliott	29-Aug	70	1938	Burke, Brooke	08-Sep	37	1971
Roker, Al	20-Aug	54	1954	Gugino, Carla	29-Aug	37	1971	Caesar, Sid	08-Sep	86	1922
Brin, Sergey	21-Aug	35	1973	Jackson, Michael	29-Aug	50	1958	Pink "Alecia Moore"	08-Sep	29	1979
Case, Steve	21-Aug	50	1958	Leach, Robin	29-Aug	67	1941	Thomas, Jonathan Taylor	08-Sep	27	1981
Cattrall, Kim	21-Aug	52	1956	Lewis, Jamal	29-Aug	29	1979	Batali, Mario	09-Sep	48	1960
DeShannon, Jackie	21-Aug	64	1944	McCain, John	29-Aug	72	1936	Buble, Michael	09-Sep	33	1975
Hillenburg, Stephen	21-Aug	47	1961	Rubin, Robert	29-Aug	70	1938	Cartwright, Angela	09-Sep	56	1952
Moss, Carrie-Ann	21-Aug	41	1967	Alexander, Shaun	30-Aug	31	1977	Grant, Hugh	09-Sep	48	1960
Panettiere, Hayden	21-Aug	19	1989	Buffett, Warren	30-Aug	78	1930	Hooks, Bell	09-Sep	56	1952
Rogers, Kenny	21-Aug	73	1935	Diaz, Cameron	30-Aug	36	1972	Hunter, Rachel	09-Sep	39	1969
Amos, Tori	22-Aug	45	1963	Ling, Lisa	30-Aug	35	1973	Sandler, Adam	09-Sep	42	1966
Bradbury, Ray	22-Aug	88	1920	Lipton, Peggy	30-Aug	61	1947	Theismann, Joe	09-Sep	59	1949
Kroft, Steve	22-Aug	63	1945	Parish, Robert	30-Aug	55	1953	Columbus, Chris	10-Sep	50	1958
Molitor, Paul	22-Aug	52	1956	Gere, Richard	31-Aug	59	1949	Firth, Colin	10-Sep	48	1960
Parcells, Bill	22-Aug	67	1941	Morrison, Van	31-Aug	63	1945	Johnson, Randy	10-Sep	45	1963
Schwarzkopf, Norman	22-Aug	74	1934	Perlman, Itzhak	31-Aug	63	1945	O'Reilly, Bill	10-Sep	59	1949
Williams, Cindy	22-Aug	61	1947	Robinson, Frank	31-Aug	73	1935	Phillippe, Ryan	10-Sep	34	1974
Yastrzemski, Carl	22-Aug	69	1939	Tucker, Chris	31-Aug	36	1972	Simonyi, Charles	10-Sep	60	1948
Bryant, Kobe	23-Aug	30	1978	Bigelow, Scott	01-Sep	47	1961	Trudeau, Margaret	10-Sep	60	1948
Chapelle, Dave	23-Aug	34	1974	DeCarlo, Yvonne	01-Sep	86	1922	Bartiromo, Maria	11-Sep	41	1967
Eden, Barbara	23-Aug	74	1934	Dershowitz, Alan M.	01-Sep	70	1938	Connick, Harry Jr.	11-Sep	41	1967

Celebrity Birthdays in 2008

Name	Birthday	Age	Born
Falana, Lola	11-Sep	65	1943
Jackson, Phil	11-Sep	63	1945
Ludacris	11-Sep	31	1977
Holm, Ian	12-Sep	77	1931
Jones, George	12-Sep	77	1931
Ming, Yao	12-Sep	28	1980
Pantliano, Joe	12-Sep	57	1951
Rossum, Emmy	12-Sep	22	1986
Ward, Rachel	12-Sep	51	1957
Apple, Fiona	13-Sep	31	1977
Bisset, Jacqueline	13-Sep	64	1944
Duke, Annie	13-Sep	43	1965
Savage, Ben	13-Sep	28	1980
Smart, Jean	13-Sep	49	1959
Smiley, Tavis	13-Sep	44	1964
Ford, Faith	14-Sep	44	1964
Heatherton, Joey	14-Sep	64	1944
Neill, Sam	14-Sep	61	1947
Stafford, Michelle	14-Sep	40	1968
Crosby, Norm	15-Sep	81	1927
Jones, Tommy Lee	15-Sep	62	1946
Marino, Dan	15-Sep	47	1961
Murino, Caterina	15-Sep	34	1974
Olsen, Merlin	15-Sep	68	1940
Perry, Gaylord	15-Sep	70	1938
Prince Harry	15-Sep	24	1984
Stone, Oliver	15-Sep	62	1946
Anthony, Marc	16-Sep	39	1969
Bacall, Lauren	16-Sep	84	1924
Baylor, Elgin	16-Sep	74	1934
Bledel, Alexis	16-Sep	27	1981
Copperfield, David	16-Sep	52	1956
Hershiser, Orel	16-Sep	50	1958
King, B.B.	16-Sep	83	1925
Poehler, Amy	16-Sep	37	1971
Rourke, Mickey	16-Sep	52	1956
Schuller, Robert	16-Sep	82	1926
Shannon, Molly	16-Sep	44	1964
Yount, Robin	16-Sep	53	1955
Anastacia Lyn Newkirk	17-Sep	35	1973
Cepeda, Orlando	17-Sep	71	1937
Stafford, Thomas	17-Sep	78	1930
Armstrong, Lance	18-Sep	37	1971
Avalon, Frankie	18-Sep	69	1939
Hall, Tex G.	18-Sep	52	1956
Gandolfini, James	18-Sep	47	1961
Lohman, Alison	18-Sep	29	1979
Sandberg, Ryne	18-Sep	49	1959
Smith, Jada Pinkett	18-Sep	37	1971
Fallon, Jimmy	19-Sep	34	1974
Medley, Bill	19-Sep	68	1940
McCallum, David	19-Sep	75	1933
Morgan, Joe	19-Sep	65	1943
Scheck, Barry	19-Sep	59	1949
Snider, Duke	19-Sep	82	1926
Twiggy	19-Sep	62	1946
West, Adam	19-Sep	79	1929
Yearwood, Trisha	19-Sep	44	1964
Brothers, Joyce Dr.	20-Sep	80	1928
Chihuly, Dale	20-Sep	67	1941
Grant, Gogi	20-Sep	84	1924
Loren, Sophia	20-Sep	74	1934
Meara, Anne	20-Sep	79	1929
Bruckheimer, Jerry	21-Sep	63	1945
Elliott, David James	21-Sep	48	1960
Grace, Maggie	21-Sep	25	1983
Hagman, Larry	21-Sep	77	1931
Hill, Faith	21-Sep	41	1967
Hines, Cheryl	21-Sep	43	1965
King, Stephen	21-Sep	61	1947
Lake, Ricki	21-Sep	40	1968
Moynahan, Bridget	21-Sep	38	1970
Murray, Bill	21-Sep	58	1950
Richie, Nicole	21-Sep	27	1981
Resser, Autumn	21-Sep	28	1980
Wilson, Luke	21-Sep	37	1971
Alonso, Daniella	22-Sep	30	1978
Babilonia, Tai	22-Sep	49	1959
Baio, Scott	22-Sep	47	1961
Bocelli, Andrea	22-Sep	50	1958
Boone, Debbie	22-Sep	52	1956
Cavuto, Neil	22-Sep	50	1958
Hunt, Bonnie	22-Sep	44	1964
Jett, Joan	22-Sep	48	1960
Lasorda, Tommy	22-Sep	81	1927
Oxenberg, Catherine	22-Sep	47	1961
Alexander, Jason	23-Sep	49	1959
DeFer, Kaylee	23-Sep	22	1986
Iglesias, Julio	23-Sep	65	1943
Petersen, Paul	23-Sep	63	1945
Rooney, Mickey	23-Sep	88	1920
Springsteen, Bruce	23-Sep	59	1949
Kennedy, Joseph II	24-Sep	56	1952
McKay, Jim	24-Sep	87	1921
Palmeiro, Rafael	24-Sep	44	1964
Sorbo, Kevin	24-Sep	50	1958
Young, John	24-Sep	78	1930
Douglas, Michael	25-Sep	64	1944
Hasselbeck, Matt	25-Sep	33	1975
Locklear, Heather	25-Sep	47	1961
Pippen, Scottie	25-Sep	43	1965
Rizzuto, Phil	25-Sep	91	1917
Smith, Will	25-Sep	40	1968
Tiegs, Cheryl	25-Sep	61	1947
Walters, Barbara	25-Sep	77	1931
Zeta-Jones, Catherine	25-Sep	39	1969
Anderson, Lynn	26-Sep	61	1947
Barberie, Jullian	26-Sep	43	1965
Hamilton, Linda	26-Sep	52	1956
Kennedy, Ed Jr.	26-Sep	47	1961
LaLane, Jack	26-Sep	94	1914
McCord, Kent	26-Sep	66	1942
Milian, Christina	26-Sep	27	1981
Newton-John, Olivia	26-Sep	60	1948
Williams, Serena	26-Sep	27	1981
Cassidy, Shaun	27-Sep	50	1958
Lavigne, Arvil	27-Sep	24	1984
Schmidt, Mike	27-Sep	59	1949
Duff, Hilary	28-Sep	21	1987
Garofalo, Janeane	28-Sep	44	1964
Largent, Steve	28-Sep	54	1954
Paltrow, Gwyneth	28-Sep	36	1972
Sorvino, Mira	28-Sep	41	1967
Watts, Naomi	28-Sep	40	1968
Clay, Andrew Dice	29-Sep	50	1958
Gumbel, Bryant	29-Sep	60	1948
Ifill, Gwen	29-Sep	53	1955
Lewis, Jerry Lee	29-Sep	73	1935
Sizemore, Tom	29-Sep	47	1961
Walesa, Lech	29-Sep	65	1943
Chabert, Lacey	30-Sep	26	1982
Dickinson, Angie	30-Sep	77	1931
Drescher, Fran	30-Sep	51	1957
Elfman, Jenna	30-Sep	37	1971
Hingis, Martina	30-Sep	28	1980
Mathis, Johnny	30-Sep	73	1935
McCoo, Marilyn	30-Sep	65	1943
Roberts, Robin	30-Sep	82	1926
Stoltz, Eric	30-Sep	47	1961
Andrews, Julie	01-Oct	73	1935
Bosley, Tom	01-Oct	81	1927
Carew, Rod	01-Oct	63	1945
Carter, Jimmy	01-Oct	84	1924
McGwire, Mark	01-Oct	45	1963
Belle, Camilla	02-Oct	22	1986
Bracco, Lorraine	02-Oct	53	1955
Karan, Donna	02-Oct	60	1948
Leibovitz, Annie	02-Oct	59	1949
Ripa, Kelly	02-Oct	38	1970
Sting	02-Oct	57	1951
Campbell, Neve	03-Oct	35	1973
Checker, Chuby	03-Oct	67	1941
Couples, Fred	03-Oct	49	1959
Duke, Charles	03-Oct	73	1935
Eckersley, Dennis	03-Oct	54	1954
India.Arie "Simpson"	03-Oct	33	1975
Lee, Tommy	03-Oct	46	1962
Moloney, Janel	03-Oct	39	1969
Owen, Clive	03-Oct	44	1964
Sharpton, Al	03-Oct	54	1954
Simpson, Ashlee	03-Oct	24	1984
Sossamon, Shannyn	03-Oct	30	1978
Stefani, Gwen	03-Oct	39	1969
Winfield, Dave	03-Oct	57	1951
Collins, Jackie	04-Oct	67	1941
Cook, Rachael Leigh	04-Oct	29	1979
Heston, Charlton	04-Oct	84	1924
Rice, Ann	04-Oct	67	1941
Sarandon, Susan	04-Oct	62	1946
Silverstone, Alicia	04-Oct	32	1976
Simmons, Russell	04-Oct	51	1957
James, Bill	05-Oct	59	1949
Hill, Grant	05-Oct	36	1972
Hilton, Nicky	05-Oct	25	1983
Lin, Maya	05-Oct	49	1959
Mac, Bernie	05-Oct	50	1958
Pearce, Guy	05-Oct	41	1967
Winslet, Kate	05-Oct	33	1975
Dungy, Tony	06-Oct	53	1955
Eklund, Britt	06-Oct	66	1942
Lobo, Rebecca	06-Oct	35	1973
Shue, Elizabeth	06-Oct	45	1963
Behar, Joy	07-Oct	65	1943
Braxton, Toni	07-Oct	41	1967
Chen, Edison	07-Oct	28	1980
Cowell, Simon	07-Oct	49	1959
Ma, Yo Yo	07-Oct	53	1955
McAdams, Rachel	07-Oct	32	1976
Mellencamp, John	07-Oct	57	1951
Putin, Vladimir	07-Oct	56	1952
Tutu, Desmond	07-Oct	77	1931
Chase, Chevy	08-Oct	65	1943
Damon, Matt	08-Oct	38	1970

Celebrity Birthdays in 2008

Name	Birthday	Age	Born
Hammond, Daryl	08-Oct	48	1960
Hogan, Paul	08-Oct	69	1939
Jackson, Jesse	08-Oct	67	1941
Pastrana, Travis	08-Oct	25	1983
Procter, Emily	08-Oct	40	1968
Weaver, Sigourney	08-Oct	59	1949
Winans, CeCe	08-Oct	49	1959
Bakula, Scott	09-Oct	54	1954
Browne, Jackson	09-Oct	60	1948
Ferland, Jodelle	09-Oct	14	1994
Lamb, Brian	09-Oct	67	1941
Lott, Trent	09-Oct	67	1941
O'Hurley, John	09-Oct	54	1954
Osbourne, Sharon	09-Oct	56	1952
Routh, Brandon	09-Oct	29	1979
Shalhoub, Tony	09-Oct	55	1953
Singletary, Mike	09-Oct	50	1958
Sorenstam, Annika	09-Oct	38	1970
Williams, TylerJames	09-Oct	16	1992
Earnhardt, Dale Jr.	10-Oct	34	1974
Favre, Brett	10-Oct	39	1969
Lopez, Mario	10-Oct	35	1973
Roberts, Nora	10-Oct	58	1950
Roth, David Lee	10-Oct	53	1955
Tucker, Tanya	10-Oct	50	1958
Cusack, Joan	11-Oct	46	1962
Hall, Daryl	11-Oct	59	1949
Leonard, Elmore	11-Oct	83	1925
Morse, David	11-Oct	55	1953
Perry, Luke	11-Oct	42	1966
Wie, Michelle	11-Oct	19	1989
Young, Steve	11-Oct	47	1961
Jackman, Hugh	12-Oct	40	1968
Jones, Marion	12-Oct	33	1975
Maguire, Martie	12-Oct	39	1969
Pavarotti, Luciano	12-Oct	73	1935
Akins, Rhett	13-Oct	39	1969
Ashanti	13-Oct	28	1980
Campell-Martin, Tisha	13-Oct	40	1968
Cohen, Sacha Baron	13-Oct	37	1971
Jones, Jerry	13-Oct	66	1942
Osmond, Marie	13-Oct	49	1959
Preston, Kelly	13-Oct	46	1962
Rice, Jerry	13-Oct	46	1962
Simon, Paul	13-Oct	67	1941
Thatcher, Margaret	13-Oct	83	1925
Walsh, Kate	13-Oct	41	1967
Coogen, Steeve	14-Oct	43	1965
Dean, John	14-Oct	70	1938
Landis, Floyd	14-Oct	33	1975
Lauren, Ralph	14-Oct	69	1939
Maines, Natalie	14-Oct	34	1974
Moore, Roger	14-Oct	81	1927
Usher "Raymond IV"	14-Oct	30	1978
Venter, J. Craig	14-Oct	62	1946
Ferguson, Sarah	15-Oct	49	1959
Iaccoca, Lee	15-Oct	84	1924
Lagasse, Emeril	15-Oct	49	1959
Marcil, Venessa	15-Oct	39	1969
Marshall, Penny	15-Oct	65	1943
Palmer, Jim	15-Oct	63	1945
Roberts, Tanya	15-Oct	53	1955
Colson, Chuck	16-Oct	77	1931
Lansbury, Angela	16-Oct	83	1925

Name	Birthday	Age	Born
Martin, Kellie	16-Oct	33	1975
Mayer, John	16-Oct	31	1977
McCarver, Tim	16-Oct	67	1941
Robbins, Tim	16-Oct	50	1958
Somers, Suzanne	16-Oct	62	1946
Eminem	17-Oct	36	1972
Jackson, Alan	17-Oct	50	1958
Kidder, Margot	17-Oct	60	1948
Knievel, Evel	17-Oct	70	1938
Macdonald, Norm	17-Oct	45	1963
Puckett, Gary	17-Oct	66	1942
Wendt, George	17-Oct	60	1948
Berry, Chuck	18-Oct	82	1926
Ditka, Mike	18-Oct	69	1939
Hearns, Tommy	18-Oct	50	1958
Jackson, Keith	18-Oct	80	1928
Marsalis, Wynton	18-Oct	47	1961
Navratilova, Martina	18-Oct	52	1956
Wells, Dawn	18-Oct	70	1938
Holyfield, Evander	19-Oct	46	1962
Kattan, Chris	19-Oct	38	1970
LeCarre, John	19-Oct	77	1931
Lithgow, John	19-Oct	63	1945
Max, Peter	19-Oct	71	1937
Pennington, Ty	19-Oct	43	1965
Allen, Joan	20-Oct	52	1956
Hernandez, Keith	20-Oct	55	1953
Marichal, Juan	20-Oct	71	1937
Mortensen, Viggo	20-Oct	50	1958
Petty, Tom	20-Oct	58	1950
Snoop Dog	20-Oct	37	1971
Fisher, Carrie	21-Oct	52	1956
Ford, Whitey	21-Oct	80	1928
Sheindlin, JudgeJudy	21-Oct	66	1942
Boitono, Brian	22-Oct	45	1963
Devenue, Katherine	22-Oct	65	1943
Funicello, Annette	22-Oct	66	1942
Goldblum, Jeff	22-Oct	56	1952
Lloyd, Christopher	22-Oct	70	1938
Mencia, Carlos	22-Oct	41	1967
Roberts, Tony	22-Oct	69	1939
Bunning, Jim	23-Oct	77	1931
Crichton, Michael	23-Oct	66	1942
Flutie, Doug	23-Oct	46	1962
Yankovic, "Weird Al"	23-Oct	49	1959
Yoakam, Dwight	23-Oct	52	1956
Abraham, F. Murray	24-Oct	69	1939
Covey, Stephen	24-Oct	76	1932
Kline, Kevin	24-Oct	61	1947
Tittle, Y.A.	24-Oct	82	1926
Carville, James	25-Oct	64	1944
Ciara	25-Oct	23	1985
Knight, Bobby	25-Oct	68	1940
MacPhail, Lee	25-Oct	91	1917
Reddy, Hellen	25-Oct	67	1941
Ross, Marion	25-Oct	80	1928
Schweickart, Russell	25-Oct	73	1935
Cavanagh, Tom	26-Oct	40	1968
Cohen, Sasha	26-Oct	24	1984
Clinton, Hillary	26-Oct	61	1947
Farmer, Paul	26-Oct	49	1959
Heder, John	26-Oct	31	1977
McDermott, Dylan	26-Oct	47	1961

Name	Birthday	Age	Born
Merchant, Natalie	26-Oct	45	1963
Sajak, Pat	26-Oct	62	1946
Smith, Jaclyn	26-Oct	61	1947
Urban, Keith	26-Oct	41	1967
Benigni, Roberto	27-Oct	56	1952
Cleese, John	27-Oct	69	1939
Drudge, Matt	27-Oct	41	1967
Greenwood, Lee	27-Oct	66	1942
Kiner, Ralph	27-Oct	86	1922
Osbourne, Kelly	27-Oct	24	1984
Daniels, Charlie	28-Oct	72	1936
Franz, Dennis	28-Oct	64	1944
Gates, Bill	28-Oct	53	1955
Gertz, Jami	28-Oct	43	1965
Jenner, Bruce	28-Oct	59	1949
Nguyen, Scotty	28-Oct	48	1960
Paisley, Brad	28-Oct	36	1972
Phoenix, Joaquin	28-Oct	34	1974
Richter, Andy	28-Oct	42	1966
Roberts, Julia	28-Oct	41	1967
Ross, Tracee Ellis	28-Oct	36	1972
Dreyfuss, Richard	29-Oct	61	1947
Jackson, Kate	29-Oct	59	1949
Ryder, Winona	29-Oct	37	1971
Union, Gabrielle	29-Oct	36	1972
Hamlin, Harry	30-Oct	57	1951
Mitchell, Andrea	30-Oct	62	1946
Pollak, Kevin	30-Oct	51	1957
Slick, Grace	30-Oct	69	1939
Trump, Ivanka	30-Oct	27	1981
Winkler, Henry	30-Oct	63	1945
Vermeil, Dick	30-Oct	72	1936
Armstrong, Samaire	31-Oct	28	1980
Hall, Deidre	31-Oct	61	1947
Pauley, Jane	31-Oct	58	1950
Perabo, Piper	31-Oct	32	1976
Rather, Dan	31-Oct	77	1931
Anderson, Bill	01-Nov	71	1937
Collette, Toni	01-Nov	36	1972
Flynt, Larry	01-Nov	66	1942
Lovett, Lyle	01-Nov	51	1957
McCarthy, Jenny	01-Nov	36	1972
Player, Gary	01-Nov	73	1935
Rai, Aishwarya	01-Nov	35	1973
Buchanan, Pat	02-Nov	70	1938
Lange, K.D.	02-Nov	47	1961
Nelly	02-Nov	30	1978
Powers, Stephanie	02-Nov	66	1942
Schwimmer, David	02-Nov	41	1967
Arnold, Roseanne	03-Nov	56	1952
Capshaw, Kate	03-Nov	55	1953
Feller, Bob	03-Nov	90	1918
Ho, David	03-Nov	56	1952
Holmes, Larry	03-Nov	59	1949
Jackson, Hal	03-Nov	93	1915
Miller, Dennis	03-Nov	55	1953
Simms, Phil	03-Nov	53	1955
Bush, Laura	04-Nov	62	1946
Cronkite, Walter	04-Nov	92	1916
Mariucci, Steve	04-Nov	53	1955
McConaughey, Matthew	04-Nov	39	1969
Probst, Jeff	04-Nov	46	1962
Switt, Loretta	04-Nov	71	1937
Yanni "Chrysomallis"	04-Nov	54	1954

Celebrity Birthdays in 2008

Name	Birthday	Age	Born	Name	Birthday	Age	Born	Name	Birthday	Age	Born
Adams, Bryan	05-Nov	49	1959	Marsalis, Ellis	14-Nov	74	1934	Becker, Boris	22-Nov	41	1967
Garfunkel, Art	05-Nov	66	1942	Prince Charles	14-Nov	60	1948	Carmona, Richard	22-Nov	59	1949
Janssen, Famke	05-Nov	43	1965	Rice, Condoleezza	14-Nov	54	1954	Curtis, Jamie Lee	22-Nov	50	1958
O'Neal, Tatum	05-Nov	45	1963	Schilling, Curt	14-Nov	42	1966	Deutsch, Donny	22-Nov	51	1957
Pace, Peter	05-Nov	63	1945	Asner, Ed	15-Nov	79	1929	Hemingway, Mariel	22-Nov	47	1961
Shepard, Sam	05-Nov	65	1943	Clark, Petula	15-Nov	76	1932	Johansson, Scarlett	22-Nov	24	1984
Walton, Bill	05-Nov	56	1952	D'Angelo, Beverly	15-Nov	54	1954	King, Billie Jean	22-Nov	65	1943
Yashin, Alexei	05-Nov	35	1973	Eubanks, Kevin	15-Nov	51	1957	Mikkelsen, Mads	22-Nov	43	1965
Crier, Catherine	06-Nov	54	1954	Poitier, Sydney	15-Nov	35	1973	Van Zandt, Steve	22-Nov	58	1950
Field, Sally	06-Nov	62	1946	Wapner, Joseph A.	15-Nov	89	1919	Cyrus, Miley	23-Nov	16	1992
Hawke, Ethan	06-Nov	38	1970	Waterston, Sam	15-Nov	68	1940	Harvey, Steve	23-Nov	52	1956
Nichols, Mike	06-Nov	77	1931	Baiul, Oksana	16-Nov	31	1977	Hornsby, Bruce	23-Nov	54	1954
Romijn, Rebecca	06-Nov	36	1972	Gooden, Dwight	16-Nov	44	1964	Buckley, William F.	24-Nov	83	1925
Shriver, Marie	06-Nov	53	1955	Gyllenhaal, Maggie	16-Nov	31	1977	Heigl, Katherine	24-Nov	30	1978
Bundy, King Kong	07-Nov	51	1957	Helgenberger, Marg	16-Nov	50	1958	Henderson, Shirley	24-Nov	43	1965
Graham, Billy	07-Nov	90	1918	Saramago, Jose	16-Nov	86	1922	Applegate, Christina	25-Nov	37	1971
Kim, Yunjin	07-Nov	35	1973	Dean, Howard	17-Nov	60	1948	Bush, Barbara	25-Nov	27	1981
Mitchell, Joni	07-Nov	65	1943	DeVito, Danny	17-Nov	64	1944	Bush, Jenna	25-Nov	27	1981
Reid, Tara	07-Nov	33	1975	Fuentes, Daisy	17-Nov	42	1966	Gibbs, Joe	25-Nov	68	1940
Rivers, Johnny	07-Nov	66	1942	Hutton, Lauren	17-Nov	65	1943	Grant, Amy	25-Nov	48	1960
Mol, Gretchen	08-Nov	36	1972	Mathias, Bob	17-Nov	78	1930	Hennessy, Jill	25-Nov	39	1969
Posey, Parker	08-Nov	40	1968	Michaels, Lorne	17-Nov	64	1944	Larroquette, John	25-Nov	61	1947
Raitt, Bonnie	08-Nov	59	1949	Scorsese, Martin	17-Nov	66	1942	McNabb, Donovan	25-Nov	32	1976
Safer, Morley	08-Nov	77	1931	Seaver, Tom	17-Nov	64	1944	Stein, Ben	25-Nov	64	1944
Thome-Smith, Courtney	08-Nov	40	1968	Cosby, Rita	18-Nov	44	1964	Bedingfield ,Natasha	26-Nov	27	1981
Woodard, Alfre	08-Nov	55	1953	Evans, Linda	18-Nov	66	1942	Goulet, Robert	26-Nov	75	1933
Combs, Sean "Puffy"	09-Nov	39	1969	Moon, Warren	18-Nov	52	1956	Little, Rich	26-Nov	70	1938
Dane, Eric	09-Nov	36	1972	Nealon, Kevin	18-Nov	55	1953	Turner, Tina	26-Nov	69	1939
Duval, David	09-Nov	37	1971	Sevigny, Chloe	18-Nov	34	1974	Bond, Samantha	27-Nov	46	1962
Ferrigno, Lou "Hulk"	09-Nov	56	1952	Sullivan, Susan	18-Nov	66	1942	Kennedy, Caroline	27-Nov	51	1957
Gibson, Bob	09-Nov	73	1935	Wilson, Owen	18-Nov	40	1968	Nye, Bill	27-Nov	53	1955
Minnillo, Vanessa	09-Nov	28	1980	Wilson, Peta	18-Nov	38	1970	White, Jaleel	27-Nov	32	1976
Sisqo "Mark Andrews"	09-Nov	33	1975	Collins, Eileen	19-Nov	52	1956	Harris, Ed	28-Nov	58	1950
Cagle, Chris	10-Nov	40	1968	Curry, Ann	19-Nov	52	1956	Nelson, Judd	28-Nov	49	1959
Eve "Jihan Jeffers"	10-Nov	30	1978	Devers, Gail	19-Nov	42	1966	Kwanten, Ryan	28-Nov	32	1976
Fargo, Donna	10-Nov	59	1949	Farrell, Terry	19-Nov	45	1963	Newman, Randy	28-Nov	65	1943
Lambert, Miranda	10-Nov	25	1983	Foster, Jodie	19-Nov	46	1962	Shaffer, Paul	28-Nov	59	1949
Murphy, Brittany	10-Nov	31	1977	Glover, Savion	19-Nov	35	1973	Stewart, Jon	28-Nov	46	1962
Phillips, Mackenzie	10-Nov	49	1959	Howard, Ryan	19-Nov	29	1979	Winstead, Mary Elizabeth	28-Nov	24	1984
Rogers, Kenny	10-Nov	44	1964	Janney, Allison	19-Nov	48	1960	Cheadle, Don	29-Nov	44	1964
Scheider, Roy	10-Nov	73	1935	King, Larry	19-Nov	75	1933	Delaney, Kim	29-Nov	47	1961
Sinbad-David Adkins	10-Nov	52	1956	Klein, Calvin	19-Nov	66	1942	Emanuel, Rahm	29-Nov	49	1959
Boxer, Barbara	11-Nov	68	1940	Metzger, Mike	19-Nov	33	1975	Faris, Anna	29-Nov	32	1976
Christopher, Tyler	11-Nov	36	1972	Quinlan, Kathleen	19-Nov	54	1954	Gordy, Berry	29-Nov	79	1929
DiCaprio, Leonardo	11-Nov	34	1974	Ryan, Meg	19-Nov	47	1961	Ladd, Diane	29-Nov	66	1942
Flockhart, Calista	11-Nov	44	1964	Turner, Ted	19-Nov	70	1938	Mangione, Chuck	29-Nov	68	1940
Moore, Demi	11-Nov	46	1962	Bentley, Dierks	20-Nov	33	1975	Mandel, Howie	29-Nov	53	1955
Winters, Jonathan	11-Nov	83	1925	Biden, Joseph	20-Nov	66	1942	Nolin, Gena Lee	29-Nov	37	1971
Zoeller, Fuzzy	11-Nov	57	1951	Bolton, John R.	20-Nov	60	1948	Scully, Vin	29-Nov	81	1927
Comaneci, Nadi	12-Nov	47	1961	Dawson, Richard	20-Nov	76	1932	Shandling, Gary	29-Nov	59	1949
Gosling, Ryan	12-Nov	28	1980	Derek, Bo	20-Nov	52	1956	Clark, Dick	30-Nov	79	1929
Harding, Tonya	12-Nov	38	1970	Hamel, Veronica	20-Nov	65	1943	Guillaume, Robert	30-Nov	81	1927
Hathaway, Anne	12-Nov	26	1982	Smothers, Dick	20-Nov	69	1939	Jackson, "Bo"	30-Nov	46	1962
Michaels, Al	12-Nov	64	1944	Velazquesz, Nadine	20-Nov	30	1978	Liddy, G. Gordon	30-Nov	78	1930
Sosa, Sammy	12-Nov	40	1968	Woodruff, Judy	20-Nov	62	1946	Stiller, Ben	30-Nov	43	1965
Young, Neil	12-Nov	63	1945	Aikman, Troy	21-Nov	42	1966	Walsh, Bill	30-Nov	77	1931
Coleman, Monique	13-Nov	28	1980	Bjork	21-Nov	43	1965	Zimbalist, Efrem Jr.	30-Nov	85	1923
Conroy, Frances	13-Nov	55	1953	Brown, Tina	21-Nov	55	1953	Allen, Woody	01-Dec	73	1935
Goldberg, Whoopi	13-Nov	59	1949	Griffey, Ken Jr.	21-Nov	39	1969	Alt, Carol	01-Dec	48	1960
Kimmel, Jimmy	13-Nov	41	1967	Hawn, Goldie	21-Nov	63	1945	Midler, Bette	01-Dec	63	1945
Mantegna, Joe	13-Nov	61	1947	Musial, Stan	21-Nov	88	1920	Trevino, Lee	01-Dec	69	1939
McNealy, Scott	13-Nov	54	1954	Sheridan, Nicollette	21-Nov	45	1963	Furtado, Nelly	02-Dec	30	1978
Noth, Chris	13-Nov	54	1954	Tarver, Antonio	21-Nov	40	1968	Haig, Alexander Jr.	02-Dec	84	1924
Zahn, Steve	13-Nov	40	1968	Thomas, Marlo	21-Nov	71	1937	Karle, Isabella	02-Dec	87	1921

Celebrity Birthdays in 2008

Name	Birthday	Age	Born
Liu, Luci	02-Dec	40	1968
Phillips, Stone	02-Dec	54	1954
Silverman, Sarah	02-Dec	38	1970
Spears, Britney	02-Dec	27	1981
Allison, Bobby	03-Dec	71	1937
Dewan, Jenna	03-Dec	28	1980
Fraser, Brendan	03-Dec	40	1968
Hannah, Daryl	03-Dec	48	1960
Moore, Julianne	03-Dec	48	1960
Osbourne, Ozzy	03-Dec	60	1948
Seyfried, Amanda	03-Dec	23	1985
Williams, Andy	03-Dec	78	1930
Witt, Katerina	03-Dec	43	1965
Banks, Tyra	04-Dec	35	1973
Bridges, Jeff	04-Dec	59	1949
Jay-Z	04-Dec	39	1969
Martindale, Wink	04-Dec	74	1934
Tomei, Marisa	04-Dec	44	1964
Carreres, Jose	05-Dec	62	1946
Cho, Margaret	05-Dec	40	1968
Little Richard	05-Dec	73	1935
Muniz, Frankie	05-Dec	23	1985
Cuomo, Andrew	06-Dec	51	1957
King, Don	06-Dec	76	1932
Appleby, Shiri	07-Dec	30	1978
Bird, Larry	07-Dec	52	1956
Carter, Aaron	07-Dec	21	1987
Barnes, Pricsilla	07-Dec	53	1955
Bench, Johnny	07-Dec	61	1947
Burstyn, Ellen	07-Dec	76	1932
Owens, Terrell	07-Dec	35	1973
Wright, Jeffrey	07-Dec	43	1965
Basinger, Kim	08-Dec	55	1953
Carradine, David	08-Dec	68	1940
Coulter, Ann	08-Dec	47	1961
Hatcher, Teri	08-Dec	44	1964
Robb, AnnaSophia	08-Dec	15	1993
Bridges, Beau	09-Dec	67	1941
Butkus, Dick	09-Dec	66	1942
Daschle, Tom	09-Dec	61	1947
Dench, Judi	09-Dec	74	1934
Douglas, Kirk	09-Dec	90	1918
Huffman, Felicity	09-Dec	46	1962
Malkovich, John	09-Dec	55	1953
Metcalfe, Jesse	09-Dec	30	1978
Osmond, Donny	09-Dec	51	1957
Stossel, John	09-Dec	61	1947
Branagh, Kenneth	10-Dec	48	1960
Chriqui, Emmanuelle	10-Dec	31	1977
Dey, Susan	10-Dec	56	1952
Duncan, Michael Clark	10-Dec	51	1957
Nixon, Agnes	10-Dec	81	1927
Raven "Symone"	10-Dec	23	1985
Garr, Teri	11-Dec	59	1949
Kerry, John	11-Dec	65	1943
Mills, Donna	11-Dec	66	1942
Moreno, Rita	11-Dec	77	1931
Barker, Bob	12-Dec	85	1923
Connelly, Jennifer	12-Dec	38	1970
Fittipaldi, Emerson	12-Dec	62	1946
Koch, Ed	12-Dec	84	1924
Loring, Gloria	12-Dec	62	1946
Warwick, Dionne	12-Dec	68	1940
Bernanke, Ben	13-Dec	55	1953
Buscemi, Steve	13-Dec	51	1957
Foxx, Jamie	13-Dec	41	1967
Jenkins, Fergie	13-Dec	65	1943
Lee, Amy	13-Dec	27	1981
Nugent, Ted	13-Dec	59	1949
Van Dyke, Dick	13-Dec	83	1925
Zanuck, Richard	13-Dec	74	1934
Duke, Patty	14-Dec	62	1946
Hewitt, Don	14-Dec	86	1922
Ovitz, Michael	14-Dec	62	1946
Remick, Lee	14-Dec	73	1935
Conway, Tim	15-Dec	75	1933
Johnson, Don	15-Dec	59	1949
Leyland, Jim	15-Dec	64	1944
Warner, Mark Robert	15-Dec	54	1954
Bochco, Steven	16-Dec	65	1943
Bratt, Benjamin	16-Dec	45	1963
Perry, William	16-Dec	46	1962
Stahl, Lesley	16-Dec	67	1941
Guccione, Bob	17-Dec	78	1930
Hudson, Ernie	17-Dec	63	1945
Jovovich, Milla	17-Dec	33	1975
Levy, Eugene	17-Dec	62	1946
Thomas, SeanPatrick	17-Dec	38	1970
Aguilera, Christina	18-Dec	28	1980
Austin, Steve	18-Dec	44	1964
Holmes, Katie	18-Dec	30	1978
Liotta, Ray	18-Dec	53	1955
Pitt, Brad	18-Dec	45	1963
Richards, Keith	18-Dec	65	1943
Speilberg, Steven	18-Dec	62	1946
Angel, Criss	19-Dec	41	1967
Beals, Jennifer	19-Dec	45	1963
Gyllenhaal, Jake	19-Dec	28	1980
Kaline, Al	19-Dec	74	1934
Leakey, Richard	19-Dec	64	1944
Milano, Alyssa	19-Dec	36	1972
Baker, Anita	20-Dec	51	1957
Callas, Charlie	20-Dec	84	1924
JoJo "Levesque"	20-Dec	18	1990
Spencer, John	20-Dec	62	1946
Dick, Andy	21-Dec	43	1965
Donahue, Phil	21-Dec	73	1935
Evert, Chris	21-Dec	54	1954
Fonda, Jane	21-Dec	71	1937
Hu, Jintao	21-Dec	66	1942
Jackson, Samuel L.	21-Dec	60	1948
Kaczmarek, Jane	21-Dec	53	1955
Romano, Ray	21-Dec	51	1957
Sutherland, Kiefer	21-Dec	42	1966
Zappa, Frank	21-Dec	68	1940
Billingsley, Barbara	22-Dec	86	1922
Carlton, Steve	22-Dec	64	1944
Elizondo, Hector	22-Dec	71	1937
Fiennes, Ralph	22-Dec	46	1962
Garvey, Steve	22-Dec	59	1949
Gibb, Robin	22-Dec	59	1949
Johnson, Lady Bird	22-Dec	96	1912
Sawyer, Diane	22-Dec	63	1945
Clark, Wesley K.	23-Dec	64	1944
Bly, Robert	23-Dec	82	1926
Lucci, Susan	23-Dec	62	1946
QueenSilvia-Sweden	23-Dec	65	1943
Schmidt, Helmut	23-Dec	90	1918
Clark, Mary Higgins	24-Dec	81	1927
Martin, Ricky	24-Dec	37	1971
Seacrest, Ryan	24-Dec	34	1974
Buffett, Jimmy	25-Dec	62	1946
Henderson, Rickey	25-Dec	50	1958
Lennox, Annie	25-Dec	54	1954
Mandrell, Barbara	25-Dec	60	1948
Spacek, Sissy	25-Dec	59	1949
Davis, Gray	26-Dec	66	1942
Fisk, Carlton	26-Dec	61	1947
Leto, Jared	26-Dec	37	1971
Smith, Ozzie	26-Dec	54	1954
Walsh, John	26-Dec	63	1945
Amos, John	27-Dec	69	1939
de Ravin, Emilie	27-Dec	27	1981
Depardieu, Gerard	27-Dec	60	1948
Ford, Edsel II	27-Dec	60	1948
Oka, Masi	27-Dec	34	1974
Roberts, Cokie	27-Dec	65	1943
Ball, Taylor	28-Dec	21	1987
Ferlito, Vanessa	28-Dec	28	1980
Francisco, Don	28-Dec	68	1940
Lee, Stan	28-Dec	85	1923
Legend, John	28-Dec	30	1978
Miller, Sienna	28-Dec	27	1981
Milner, Martin	28-Dec	77	1931
Mullis, Gary	28-Dec	64	1944
Smith, Maggie	28-Dec	74	1934
Washington, Denzel	28-Dec	54	1954
Andrews, Jessica	29-Dec	25	1983
Banfield, Ashleigh	29-Dec	41	1967
Clarkson, Patricia	29-Dec	49	1959
Danson, Ted	29-Dec	61	1947
Faithfull, Marianne	29-Dec	62	1946
Law, Jude	29-Dec	36	1972
Moore, Mary Tyler	29-Dec	72	1936
Poundstone, Paula	29-Dec	49	1959
Voight, Jon	29-Dec	70	1938
Burrows, James	30-Dec	68	1940
Diddley, Bo	30-Dec	80	1928
James, Lebron	30-Dec	24	1984
Jones, Davy	30-Dec	63	1945
Koufax, Sandy	30-Dec	73	1935
Kreuk, Kristin	30-Dec	26	1982
Lauer, Matt	30-Dec	51	1957
Ullman, Tracey	30-Dec	49	1959
Vieira, Meredith	30-Dec	55	1953
Woods, Tiger	30-Dec	33	1975
Gong, Li	31-Dec	43	1965
Hopkins, Anthony	31-Dec	71	1937
Kilmer, Val	31-Dec	49	1959
Kingsley, Ben	31-Dec	65	1943
McCartney, Heather	31-Dec	46	1962
Neuwirth, Bebe	31-Dec	50	1958
Preston, "Amarillo Slim"	31-Dec	80	1928
Rigg, Rebecca	31-Dec	41	1967
Smith, Patti	31-Dec	62	1946
Summer, Donna	31-Dec	60	1948

The Address Directory

Celebrity Name Index

Name	Page	Name	Page	Name	Page	Name	Page
Bidwill, William V.	148	Bleustein, Jeffrey L.	178	Boros, Guy	159	Brennen, Eileen	44
Biedel, Alexis	43	Bliss, Caroline	75	Borstein, Alex	44	Brenner, David	80
Biel, Jessica	43	Blobel, Gunter	188	Boston, Ralph	173	Brenner, Sydney	188
Bikel, Theodore	43	Blood Sweat & Tears	94	Bostwick, Barry	44	Breslin, Spencer	44
Biletnikoff, Fred	137	Bloom, Orlando	44	Bosworth, Kate	44	Brett, George	117, 124
Billick, Brian	148	Bloomfield, Michael J.	208	Bouquet, Carole	75	Brewer, Teresa	97
Billingsley, Barbara	43	Blount, Mel	137	Bouton, Jim	124	Bridges, Angelica	44
Bingham, Tracy	43	Blue, Vida	124	Bova, Raoul	44	Bridges, Beau	44
Binni, John	215	Bluford, Guion S., Jr.	208	Bowa, Larry	124	Bridges, Jeff	44
Binnig, Gerd K.	181	Blum, Samuel	181	Bowden, Craig	159	Bridges, Roy D., Jr.	208
Binoche, Juliette	43	Blumberg, Baruch S.	181	Bowe, Riddick	136	Brin, Sergey	178
Bird, Forrest	181	Blume, Judy	85	Bowen, Julie	44	Brinkley, Christie	79
Bird, Larry	134	Bly, Robert	85	Bowen, Stephen G.	208	Briscoe, Brent	44
Birney, David	43	Boat, Billy	169	Bower, Robert W.	181	Brisky, Mike	159
Bisciotti, Stephen J.	148	Bobcats Dance Team	134	Bowersox, Kenneth D.	208	Brock, Lou	117,124
Bishop, Michael J.	188	Bobeck, Nicole	172	Bowlen, Pat	148	Brockhouse, Bertram	188
Bisset, Jacqueline	43	Bobko, Karol J.	208	Bowness, Rick	157	Broderick, Matthew	44
Bjork	97	Bocelli, Andrea	97	Bowrey, Lesley Turner	167	Brody, Adrien	44
Bjorkman, Jonas	168	Bochco, Steven	87	Bowser, Charles	148	Broeck, Lance Ten	159
Black, Byron	168	Bochner, Lloyd	44	Box Tops (The)	94	Brokaw, Tom	88
Black, Clint	97	Bochy, Bruce	124	Boxleitner, Bruce	44	Brolin, James	44
Black, Jack	44	Boddicker, Mike	124	Boyd, Billy	44	Brolin, Josh	44
Black, Ronnie	159	Bodine, Brett	169	Boyer, Herbert W.	181	Brookins, Gary	83
Black, Shirley Temple	44	Bodine, Todd	169	Boyer, Paul D.	188	Brooks & Dunn	94
Blackburn, Woody	159	Boe, Eric A.	208	Brack, Kenny	169	Brooks, Albert	80
Blackman, Honor	75	Bogdonovich, Peter	87	Bradbury, Brad	85	Brooks, Avery	44
Blackmar, Phil	159	Boggs, Wade	124	Bradbury, Ray	85	Brooks, David	85
Blades, Rubén	93	Bogues, Tyrone "Muggsy"	134	Bradlee, Ben	85	Brooks, Garth	97
Blaese, Michael R.	188	Bohlin, Nils	181	Bradley, Bill	173	Brooks, Mark	159
Blaha, John E.	208	Boitano, Brian	172	Bradley, Ed	88	Brooks, Mel	80
Blaine, David	91	Bolden, Charles F., Jr.	208	Bradley, Lonnie	136	Brosnan, Pierce	44, 75
Blair, Bonnie	172	Bollenbach, Stephen	178	Bradley, Michael	159	Broten, Neal	173
Blair, Tony	205	Bolt, Tommy	159	Bradshaw, John	85	Brothers, Dr. Joyce	88
Blake, Bud	83	Bolton, Michael	97	Bradshaw, Terry	137,148	Brown, Aaron	88
Blake, Robert	44	Boltz, Ray	97	Brady, Charles E., Jr.	208	Brown, Billy Ray	159
Blake, Teresa	75	Bon Jovi, Jon	97	Brady, James & Sarah	216	Brown, Bob (Boomer)	137
Blakely, Susan	44	Bond, Samantha	75	Brady, Tom	145	Brown, Campbell	88
Blakes, Anthony	129	Bondar, Roberta	208	Braff, Zach	44	Brown, Curtis L., Jr.	208
Blanchard, Rachel	44	Bonds, Barry	122	Braggs, Stephen	148	Brown, Dan	85
Blanchett, Cate	44, 78	Bone Thugs 'n' Harmony	94	Brame, Tom	159	Brown, David T.	179
Bland, John	159	Bonner, Frank	44	Branagh, Kenneth	44	Brown, Denise	216
Blanda, George	137,148	Booker, Eric	159	Branca, Ralph	124	Brown, James	97
Blaney, Dave	169	Boone, Debby	97	Brand, Vance D.	208	Brown, Jim	137
Blank, Arthur	148	Boone, Pat	97	Brandenstein, Daniel	208	Brown, Mark N.	208
Blankenship, Bob	159	Boosler, Elayne	80	Branigan, Laura	97	Brown, Michael S.	188
Blazer Dancers	134	Boreanaz, David	44	Bratt, Benjamin	44	Brown, Roosevelt	137
Bledsoe, Drew	142	Borg, Bjorn	167,174	Bratton, Alan	159	Brown, Sandra	85
Bleeth, Yasmine	44	Borgnine, Ernest	44	Braxton, Toni	97	Brown, Sawyer	96
Bleir, Rocky	148	Bork, Robert	193	Breed, Giff	159	Brown, Willie	137,148
Blethyn, Brenda	44	Borman, Frank	208	Brenneman, Amy	44		

Browne, Dik	83	Burstyn, Ellen	44
Browne, Jackson	93	Burton, Jeff	169
Browne, Olin	159	Burton, LeVar	45
Browning, Curt	172	Burton, Tim	87
Brue, Bob	159	Burton, Ward	169
Bruguera, Sergi	168	Buscemi, Steve	45
Bruton, Kris	129	Busch III, August A.	177
Bryant, Bart	159	Busch, Kurt	169
Bryant, Brad	159	Busey, Gary	45
Bryant, Kobe	132	Bush	95
Brzezinski, Zbigniew	193	Bush, George Herbert	193
Bubka, Sergia	172	Bush, George Walker	193
Buchanan, Pat	88	Bush, Laura	193
Buchli, James F.	208	Butkis, Dick	137
Buck, Joe	124	Butler, Brett	80
Buck, Linda	188	Button, Dick	173
Buckey, Jay Clark	208	Button, Jenson	169
Buckinghams (The)	94	Buttons, Red	45
Buckley, William F. Jr.	85	Buzzi, Ruth	80
Buckner, Bill	124	Byner, John	80
Bueno, Maria	167	Bynes, Amanda	45
Buffett, Jimmy	97	Byrds (The)	95
Buffett, Warren E.	177	Byrne, Gabriel	45
Buffoni, Brad	159	Byrnes, Edd	45
Buha, Jason	159	Byrum, Curt	160
Buhl, Robbie	169	Byrum, Tom	160
Bull, John S.	208	C & C Music Factory	95
Bullock, Sandra	44	Caan, James	45
Bumpers, Dale	193	Caan, Scott	45
Bundchen, Gisele	79	Cabana, Robert D.	208
Bunning, Jim	117	Cabrera, Orlando	119
Buoniconti, Nick	137	Caesar, Sid	80
Burbank, Daniel C.	208	Cage, Nicholas	45
Burbano, Mindy	88	Cagle, Yvonne D.	208
Burckhalter, Joseph H.	181	Caine, Michael	45
Burghoff, Gary	44	Calatrava, Santiago	91
Burke, Delta	44	Calcavecchia, Mark	160
Burke, Patrick	159	Caldeiro, Fernando	209
Burks, Ellis	119	Caldwell, Rex	160
Burnett, Carol	80	Caldwell, Tracy E.	209
Burnett, Mark	87	Calkins, Buzz	169
Burns, Bob	160	Call, Brandon	45
Burns, Brooke	44	Callazzo, Kim	160
Burns, Edward	44	Camacho, Hector	136
Burns, George	160	Camarda, Charles J.	209
Burns, Jere II	44	Cambell, Bebe Moore	85
Burns, Pat	157	Camerilli, Louis C.	177
Burrows, Saffron	44	Cameron, Julie	85
Bursch, Daniel W.	208	Cameron, Kenneth D.	209
Burstyn, Ellen	44	Cameron, Kirk	45
		Camp, Colleen	45

Campanella, Joseph	45	Carter, Deana	98
Campbell, Bruce	45	Carter, Dixie	45
Campbell, Glenn	98	Carter, Don	174
Campbell, Milt	173	Carter, Gene	117
Campbell, Naomi	79	Carter, Helena Bonham	45
Campbell, Neve	45	Carter, Jack	80
Campell, Earl	137	Carter, Jim	160
Canadeo, Tony	137	Carter, Jimmy	188,193
Canizares, Jose M.	160	Carter, Lynda	45
Cannel, Steven J.	87	Carter, Rosalynn	193
Cannon, Dyan	45	Carvey, Dana	45, 80
Cannon, Freddie	98	Casals, Rosemary 'Rosie'	167
Canseco, Joe	124	Cashman, Brian	124
Cantalupo, James	179	Casper, Billy	160
Cantone, Mario	45	Casper, Dave	137
Capers, Dom	148	Casper, John H.	209
Capital Steps	95	Cassel, Vincent	45
Capriati, Jennifer	174	Cassidy, David	98
Capshaw, Jessica	45	Cassidy, Joanna	45
Cara, Irene	98	Cassini, Oleg	91
Cardellini, Linda	45	Casta, Laetitia	79
Cardoso, Fernando H.	205	Castalda, Jean-Pierre	75
Carew, Rod	117,124	Castle-Hughes, Keisha	78
Carey, Chip	124	Castro, Fidel	205
Carey, Drew	80	Castroneves, Helio	169
Carey, Duane G.	209	Cattrall, Kim	45
Carey, Mariah	98	Cauffiel, Jessica	45
Carlin, George	80	Caulkins, Tracy	173
Carlsson, Arvid	188	Cavalier Girls	134
Carlton, Steve	117	Caviezel, James	45
Carmona, Richard	188	Cawley, Evonne Goolagong	167
Caron, Leslie	45	Cedric The Entertainer	45
Carp, Daniel	178	Cefalo, Jimmy	148
Carpenter, Charisma	45	Cenker, Robert	209
Carpenter, M. Scott	209	Cepeda, Orlando	117
Carpenter, Mary C.	98	Cepollina, Frank	181
Carpenter-Phinney, Connie	173	Cernan, Eugene A.	209
Carpentier, Patrick	169	Cey, Ron	124
Carr, Gerald P.	209	Chabert, Lacey	45
Carr, Vikki	98	Chabraja, Nicholas	178
Carradine, David	45	Chalke, Sarah	45
Carradine, Keith	45	Chalmers, Greg	160
Carrera, Barbara	75	Chamberlain, Richard	45
Carreras, Jose	98	Chambers, John T.	177
Carrere, Tia	45	Chambers, Justin	45
Carrey, Jim	45,80	Chambers, Nanci	45
Carroll, Val	160	Chambers, Tom	134
Carrot Top	80	Chamblee, Brandel	160
Carter, Benny	98	Chamitoff, Gregory E.	209
		Chan, Jackie	45

Chandler, Kyle	45	Christie, Lou	98	Coffman, Vance D.	179	Considine, John	46
Chang, Michael	168	Christoff, Steve	173	Cohen, Abby Joseph	178	Conti, Bill	93
Chang-Diaz, Franklin R.	209	Chu, Steven	188	Cohen, Sacha Baron	46	Conway, Tim	80
Channing, Stockard	46	Chung, Connie	88	Cohen, Scott	46	Coody, Charles	160
Chantels (The)	95	Church, Charlotte	98	Cohen, Stanley	188	Cook, John	160
Chao, Elaine	193	Ciechanover, Aaron	188	Cohen, Stanley N.	181	Cook, Rachael Leigh	46
Chao, Linda L.	193	Cimino, Michael	87	Cohn, Linda	88	Coolidge, Jennifer	46
Chapelle, Dave	80	Cink, Stewart	160	Colangelo, Jerry	134	Coolidge, Rita	98
Chapman, Philip K.	209	Claar, Brian	160	Colbert, Jim	160	Coolio	98
Chapman, Rex	134	Clancy, Sean	148	Cole, Bobby	160	Cooper, Alice	98
Chapman, Tracy	98	Clancy, Tom	85	Cole, Dennis	46	Cooper, Anderson	88
Chappelle, Dave	46	Clapp, Louise Brough	167	Cole, Gary	46	Cooper, Ashley	167
Charles, Bob	160	Clapton, Eric	93,98	Cole, Natalie	98	Cooper, Chris	46
Charles, Prince Of Wales	205	Clark, Dick	93	Cole, Paula	98	Cooper, Hank	160
Charlie Daniels Band(The)	95	Clark, Marcia	204	Coleman, Catherine G.	209	Cooper, Jackie	46
Charpak, Georges	188	Clark, Mary Higgins	85	Coleman, Dabney	46	Cooper, L. Gordon, Jr.	209
Charron, Paul R.	179	Clark, Roy	98	Coleman, Gary	46	Cooper, Stephen F.	178
Chase, Chevy	80	Clark, Susan	46	Collette, Toni	46,78	Coors, William	177
Chast, Roz	83	Clarke, Bob	157	Collins, Arthur W. "Bud"	167	Coover, Harry	181
Chavez, Jesus	136	Clarke, Darren	160	Collins, Clifton Jr.	46	Copperfield, David	91
Checker, Chubby	98	Clarkson, Kelly	46	Collins, Eileen M.	209	Coppola, Francis Ford	87
Cheever, Eddie Jr.	169	Clarkson, Patricia	46	Collins, Francis	188	Coppola, Sofia	46, 87
Chehak, Susan T.	85	Clary, Robert	46	Collins, Gary	46	Corbett, Luke R.	179
Cheli, Maurizio	209	Claxton, Paul	160	Collins, Jackie	85	Corduner, Allan	47
Chen, Joan	46	Clay, Andrew Dice	80	Collins, Judy	98	Cornell, Eric A.	188
Chen, T.C.	160	Clayburgh, Jill	46	Collins, Michael	209	Cornell, Lydia	47
Chenault, Kenneth	177	Clearwater, Keith	160	Collins, Mo	46	Cornwell, Patricia	85
Cheney, Lynne	193	Cleave, Mary L.	209	Collins, Phil	98	Correll, A. D.	178
Cheney, Richard	193	Cleese, John	46,75,80	Collins, Stephen	46	Corretja, Alex	168
Cher	46,98	Clemens, Roger	124	Colmes, Alan	88	Corwin, Jeff	188
Chesney, Kenny	98	Clervoy, Jean-Francois	209	Colson, Gary	134	Cosby, Bill	80
Chesnokov, Andrei	168	Cliburn, Van	93	Colton, Frank B.	181	Cosina, Dennis	160
Chiao, Leroy	209	Clifford, Michael R.	209	Coltrane, Robbie	46, 75	Costas, Bob	174
Chicago	95	Clinton, Hillary Rodham	193	Columbus, Chris	87	Costello, Elvis	98
Chicago Luvabulls	134	Clinton, William Jefferson	193	Comaneci, Nadia	172	Coster, Ritchie	47
Chieftains (The)	95	Clooney, George	46	Combs, Holly Marie	46	Costner, Kevin	47
Chihuly, Dale	91	Close, Glenn	46	Commodores (The)	95	Couch, Chris	160
Chiklis, Michael	46	Clowes, Daniel	83	Compton, Stacey	169	Coughlin, Tom	148
Chiles, Lois	46, 75	Coase, Ronald	188	Conant, Douglas C.	177	Coulthard, David	169
Chilton, Kevin P.	209	Coasters (The)	95	Connelly, Jenifer	46	Count Basie Orchestra	95
Chin, Tsai	75	Coates, Al	157	Conner, Bart	172,173	Couples, Fred	160
Cho, Margaret	46,80	Coats, Michael L.	209	Conner, Frank	160	Couric, Katie	88
Choi, K.J.	160	Cochran, Bobby	160	Connery, Sean	46,75	Courier, Jim	168
Chretien, Jean	205	Cochran, Russ	160	Connick, Harry Jr.	98	Court, Margaret Smith	167
Chrétien, Jean-Loup	209	Cochran, Tony	83	Connor, Christoper M.	180	Cousins, Robin	172
Chriqui, Emmanuelle	46	Cocker, Joe	98	Connor, George	137	Cousy, Bob	134
Christensen, Erika	46	Cockrell, Kenneth D.	209	Connors, Jimmy	167	Covey, Richard O.	209
Christensen, Hayden	46	Coen, Ethan	46	Conover, Lloyd H.	181	Covey, Stephen	85
Christian, Dave	173	Coen, Joel	46,87	Conrad, Robert	46	Cowell, Simon	88
Christie, Julie	46			Conroy, Frances	46	Cowher, Bill	148

Cox, Bobby	124	Culkin, Rory	47	Daniels, Charles (Athlete)	173	Deby, Idriss	205
Cox, Brian	47	Cullman, Joseph F.	167	Daniels, Charlie	99	DeCarlo, Dan	83
Cox, Courteney	47	Culp, Robert	47	Daniels, Jeff	47	DeCarlo, Yvonne	48
Cox, Nikki	47	Culp, Steven	47	Danson, Ted	47	Decker, Adam	160
Cox, Ronny	47	Culpepper, Daunte	145	Danza, Tony	47	Dees, Gerald M.	188
Coyote, Peter	47	Culver, Molly	47	Darden, Christopher	204	DeGeneres, Ellen	48, 80
Craig, Jim	173,174	Cumming, Alan	75	Dattilo, Thomas A.	178	Dehmelt, Hans	188
Craig, Roger	124,148	Cunningham, Walter	209	Dausser, Jean	188	Deklerk, F.W.	205
Craine, Jeanne	47	Cuoco, Kaley	47	Davenport, Willie	173	Del Rio, Jack	148
Crampton, Bruce	160	Cupit, Jacky	160	Davi, Robert	75	Del Toro, Benicio	48, 75
Craven, Ricky	169	Curbeam, Robert L., Jr.	209	David, George	180	DeLamielleure, Joe	137
Crawford, Cindy	47, 79	Curl, Robert F.	188	David, Larry	48,87	Delaney, Kim	48
Crawford, Johnny	47	Currie, Nancy J.	209	Davidson, Amy	48	Delany, Dana	48
Crawford, Marc	157	Curry, Ann	88	Davidson, Tommy	48	Dell, Michael	178
Crawford, Michael	98	Curry, Mark	47	Davies, Jeremy	48	Dellenbach, Jeff	148
Creamer, Timothy J.	209	Curtain, Jane	80	Davies, John Rhys	75	Delsing, Jay	160
Creed	95	Curtis, Jamie Lee	47	Davis, Al	137,148	DeLucas, Lawrence	209
Creekmur, Lou	137	Curtis, Tony	47,148	Davis, Ann B.	48	Deluise, Dom	80
Creighton, John O.	209	Cusack, John	47	Davis, Butch	148	DeMornay, Rebecca	48
Creighton, John W.	180	Cuthbert, Elisha	47	Davis, Geena	48	Dempsey, Patrick	48
Crenshaw, Ben	160	Cyrus, Billy Ray	98	Davis, Glenn	173	Dempsey, Rick	124
Crewson, Wendy	47	D'Abo, Maryam	75	Davis, Hope	48	Dench, Judi	48,75
Crichton, Michael	85	D'alema, Massimo	205	Davis, Jay	160	Deneuve, Catherine	48
Crickets (The)	95	D'Amato, Alfonse	88	Davis, Jim	83	DeNiro, Robert	48
Crier, Catherine	88	D'Angelo, Beverly	47	Davis, Kristin	48	Denisof, Alexis	48
Crippen, Robert L.	209	D'Arcy, James	47	Davis, N. Jan	209	Dennard, Mark	148
Criss, Peter	98	D'Lyn, Shea	49	Davis, Raymond Jr.	188	Dennard, Robert H.	181
Cristo	91	D'Onofrio, Vincent	49	Davis, Tommy	124	Dennehy, Brian	48
Cromwell, James	47	D'Souza, Dinesh	193	Davis, Willie	137	Dennis, Clark	160
Cronkite, Walter	88	da Matta, Cristiano	169	Davoli, Andrew	48	Dennis, Felix	179
Crosby, Mary	47	Dafoe, Willem	47	Dawber, Pam	48	Dent, Catherine	48
Crosby, Norm	80	Daft, Douglas N.	177	Dawson, Len	137	Dent, Jim	160
Cross, David	47	Dalai Lama	188	Dawson, Rosario	48	Denver, Bob	48
Crouch, Roger	209	Daley, Kevin	129	Day, Doris	48,99	Depardieu, Gerard	48
Crow, Sheryl	98	Dalton, Skip	160	Day, Glen	160	Depp, Johnny	48
Crowe, Russell	47,78	Dalton, Timothy	75	Day, Julian	179	Derek, Bo	48
Crown Prince Naruhito	206	Daltrey, Roger	98	De Gennes, Pierre	188	Dern, Bruce	48
Crown Princess Masako	205	Daly, Carson	88	De La Hoya, Oscar	136	Dern, Laura	48
Crown Princess Victoria	205	Daly, John	160	de la Rosa, Pedro	169	Dershowitz, Alan	204
Cruise, Tom	47	Daly, Timothy	47	de Lancie, John	48	Deschanel, Zooey	48
Crumb, R.	83	Daly, Tyne	47	De Lozada, Gonzalo	205	Destiny's Child	95
Crusan, Doug	148	Damadian, Raymond	181, 188	de Matteo, Drea	48	Detmer, Ty	142
Cruz, Penelope	47	Damon, Johnny	119	de Rossi, Portia	48, 78	Devers, Gail	172
Crystal, Billy	47, 80	Damon, Matt	47	De Souza, Edward	75	DeVito, Danny	48
Crystals (The)	95	Damone, Vic	98	de Varona, Donna	173,174	Devlin, Bruce	160
Csonka, Larry	137,148	Damron, Robert	160	Dean, Jeff	178	DeWitt, Joyce	48
Cuban, Mark	134	Dana, Bill	80	Dean, Jimmy	75	DeWitt, William O. Jr.	124
Culbertson, Frank L., Jr.	209	Dance, Charles	75	Dean, Mark	181	Dey, Susan	48
Culkin, Kieran	47	Danes, Claire	47	Debakey, Michael	188	Dhue, Laurie	88
Culkin, Macaulay	47	Daniel, Brittany	47				

Diamond, Neal	99	Donovan, Art	138	Dundee, Angelo	136	Ekland, Britt	76
Diana, Rich	148	Donovan, Carrie	88	Dungy, Tony	148	Eldard, Ron	50
Diaz, Cameron	48	Donovan, Kimberly	160	Dunham, Archie	178	Elder, Brad	160
Diaz, Yamila	79	Doobie Brothers (The)	95	Dunlap, Alexander	209	Elder, Lee	160
Dicaprio, Leonardo	48	Doody, Alison	76	Dunlap, Scott	160	Eldredge, Todd	174
Dick, Andy	48	Dooley, Adam	160	Dunne, Dominick	88	Electra, Carmen	50
Dickerson, Eric	138	Doors (The)	95	Duque, Pedro	209	Elfman, Jenna	50
Dickinson, Amy	85	Dorff, Stephen	49	Duran Duran	99	Elia, Lee	124
Dickinson, Angie	48	Dorfman, David	49, 177	Durant, Graham J.	181	Elion, Gertrude	177
Dierdorf, Dan	138	Dorsett, Tony	138,148	Durant, Joe	160	Elion, Gertrude B.	188
Diesel, Vin	49	Dorsey Bros. Orchestra	95	Durning, Charles	49	Elizondo, Hector	50
Difranco, Ani	99	Dos Santos, Jose	205	Durrance, Samuel	210	Eller, Carl	138,148
Dill, Terry	160	Dougherty, Ed	160	Dushku, Eliza	49	Ellerbee, Linda	88
Dillard, Harrison	173	Douglas, Donna	49	Duval, David	160	Elliot, Bill	169
Diller, Barry	179,180	Douglas, Illeana	49	Duval, James	49	Elliot, Chris	50
Diller, Phyllis	81	Douglas, Kirk	49	Duvall, Clea	49	Elliott, David James	50
Dillon, David B.	179	Douglas, Michael	49	Duvall, Robert	49	Elliott, Sam	50
Dillon, Matt	49	Down, Lesley-Anne	49	Duvall, Shelley	49	Ellis, Aunjanue	50
DiMarco, Chris	160	Downey, Robert Jr.	49	Dvoncova, Denisa	79	Ellis, Herb	93
Dimitriades, Alex	49	Downey, Roma	49	Dye, John	49	Ellison, Lawrence J.	179
Dimon, James	177	Downs, Hugh	88	Dyson, Esther	178	Ellman, Steve	157
DiNardo, Lenny	119	Doyle, Allen	160	Eagan, Eddie	173	Els, Ernie	160
Dion, Celine	99	Dr. John	93	Eagles (The)	95	Elson, Andrea	50
Discala, Jamie-Lynn	49	Drescher, Fran	49	Eaks, R.W.	160	Elway, John	138,149
Disney, Roy	180	Drew, B. Alvin	209	Earnhardt, Dale Jr.	169	Elwes, Cary	50
Ditka, Mike	138	Dreyfus, Julia Louise	49	Eastwood, Bob	160	Embree, Alan	119
Dixie Chicks (The)	95	Dreyfuss, Richard	49	Eastwood, Clint	49	Embry, Ethan	50
Dixon, Donna	49	Driegen, Dewi	79	Eaton, Shirley	76	Emerson, Roy	167
Dixon, Ivan	49	Drifters, (The)	95	Ebbers, Bernard J.	180	Eminem	50
Dixon, Scott	169	Driscoll, Paul	160	Eckersley, Dennis	117	Emmerich, Noah	50
Djerssi, Carl	181	Driver, Minnie	76	Eckert, Robert	179	Emmett, John C.	181
Djimon Hounsou	49	Drobny, Jaroslav	167	Eckhart, Aaron	49	Energee Dance Team	134
DMX	95, 99	Drucker, Mort	83	Eckrodt, Rolf	178	Engelbart, Douglas	181
Dobson, James C.	85, 216	Drudge, Matt	85	Eden, Barbara	49	Engibous, Thomas J.	180
Dodds, Trevor	160	Duchovney, David	49	Edgerson, Eugene	129	England, Anthony W.	210
Doden, Stanley	87	Dudley, Bill	138	Edie Falco	49	Engle, Joe H.	210
Doerr, Bobby	117	Duff, Hilary	49	Edwards, Anthony	50	Engle, Robert F.	188
Doherty, Denny	99	Duffy, Brian	209	Edwards, Herman	148	Englund, Robert	50
Doherty, Peter C.	188	Duffy, Julia	49	Edwards, Joe F., Jr.	210	Enqvist, Thomas	168
Doherty, Shannen	49	Duffy, Patrick	49	Edwards, Stacy	50	Enya	99
Doi, Takao	209	Duhamel, Josh	49	Egan, Susan	50	Epps, Omar	50
Dolan, Lawrence J.	124	Dukakis, Olympia	49	Eggar, Samantha	50	Epps, Mike	50
Dolan, Peter R.	177	Duke, Charles M., Jr.	209	Eggert, Nicole	50	Erbe, Kathryn	50
Dolby, Ray	181	Duke, Ken	160	Ehle, Jennifer	50	Erickson, Dennis	149
Dolenz, Micky	99	Duke, Patty	49	Ehlers, Beth	50	Ermy, R. Lee	50
Dominguez, Mario	169	Dunakey, Doug	160	Eikenberry, Jill	50	Ernst, Richard	188
Dominic Chianese	49	Dunaway, Faye	49	Eisner, Michael D.	180	Erskine, Carl	124
Donahoe, Tom	148	Dunbar, Bonnie J.	209	Eisner, Will	83	Eruzione, Mike	173
Donahue, Elinor	49	Dunbar, Lou "Sweet"	129	Ekberg, Anita	50	Erving, Julius	134
Donahue, Phil	88	Duncan, Michael Clarke	49	Ekington, Steve	160	Eskew, Michael L.	180

Esposito, Jennifer	50	Feherty, David	161	Flesch, Steve	161	Four Tops (The)	95
Esrey, William T.	180	Fehr, Brendan	51	Fletcher, Louise	51	Fouts, Dan	138
Estes, Bob	161	Fehr, Rick	161	Flockhart, Calista	51	Fox, John	149
Estes, Will	50	Feldon, Barbara	51	Florio, Thomas	180	Fox, Michael J.	51
Estevez, Emilio	50	Feller, Bob	117	Floyd, Raymond	161	Fox, Vicente	193
Estrich, Susan	88	Fenn, John B.	188	Flynt, Larry	85	Fox, Vivica A.	51
Ethan Coen	85	Fenn, Sherilyn	51	Foale, C. Michael	210	Foxx, Jamie	51
Eubanks, Kevin	93	Fergason, Jamess L.	181	Fogarty, Thomas J.	181	Foyt, A.J.	169
Evans, Don	193	Ferguson, Christopher J.	210	Fogerty, John	99	Franchitti, Dario	169
Evans, Lee	173	Ferguson, John	157	Foisman, Gerald A.	161	Franciosa, Anthony	51
Evans, Linda	50	Ferguson, Sarah	205	Foley, Scott	51	Francis, Connie	99
Eve	50	Fernandez, Adrian	169	Foley, Tom	124	Francisco, Don	88
Evens, Janet	172	Fernandez, Vincente	161	Folkman, Judah	188	Franco, Carlos	161
Everett, Chad	50	Ferran, Gilde	169	Foltz, Gerald	161	Francona, Terry	124
Everett, Jim	149	Ferraro, Geraldine	88	Fonda, Bridget	51	Frank, Tommy R.	193
Everly Brothers (The)	95	Ferreira, Wayne	168	Fonda, Jane	51	Franken, Al	51
Evers-Williams, Myrlie	216	Ferrell, Will	51	Fonda, Peter	51	Franken, Al	81
Evert, Chris	167	Ferrer, Miguel	51	Fontana, Isabeli	79	Frankes, Jonathan	51
Ewbank, Weeb	138	Ferrero, Juan Carlos	168	Foote, Horton	85	Franz, Dennis	51
Eyharts, Léopold	210	Fettman, Martin	210	Forbes, Steven	178	Fraser, Brenden	51
Eyler,	180	Feustel, Andrew J.	210	Ford Jr., William C.	178	Fraser, Claire M.	179
Fabian, John M.	210	Fey, Tina	51, 81	Ford, Betty	193	Fraser, Neale	167
Fabray, Nanette	50	Fidrych, Mark	124	Ford, Faith	51	Frazar, Harrison	161
Faget, Maxime	181	Fiducia, Donna	88	Ford, Gerald	193	Frazier, Joe	135, 173
Faggin, Federico	181	Field, Sally	51	Ford, Harrison	51	Free, Helen	181
Fair, Keith	161	Fiennes, Ralph	51	Ford, Kevin A.	210	Freeman, Morgan	51
Fairchild, Morgan	50	Finch, Jennifer	174	Ford, Scott T.	177	Freeman, Robin	161
Faithfull, Marianne	99	Fincke, E. Michael	210	Ford, Whitey	117	Frentzen, Heinz-Harald	169
Falco, Edie	50	Fingers, Rollie	117	Ford, William Clay	149	Frick, Stephen N.	210
Faldo, Nick	161	Finney, Albert	51	Foreigner	95	Fricker, Brenda	51
Falk, Peter	50	Fiori, Ed	161	Foreman, George	136, 173	Friedman, Milton	188,193
Falkenburg, Bob	167	Fiorina, Carleton S.	178	Foreman, Michael J.	210	Friedman, Thomas	85
Fanning, Dakota	50	Fireman, Paul	180	Forlani, Claire	51	Friend, Bob	161
Farentino, James	50	Fischbacher, Siegfried	91	Forrest, Vernon	136	Fromberg, Richard	168
Farina, Dennis	50	Fisher, Anna L.	210	Forrester, Jay W.	181	Frost, David	161
Faris, Anna	50	Fisher, Frances	51	Forrester, Patrick G.	210	Fryatt, Edward	161
Farr, Jamie	50	Fisher, Jeff	149	Forsbrand, Anders	161	Fry-Irvin, Shirley	167
Farrell, Colin	50	Fisher, Joely	51	Forsman, Dan	161	Fuentas, Daisy	88
Farrell, Mike	50	Fisher, Sarah	169	Forster, Robert	51	Fugit, Patrick	51
Farrell, Sharon	51	Fisher, William F.	210	Forsythe, John	51	Fuglesang, Christer	210
Farrell, Terry	51	Fisichella, Giancarlo	169	Forsythe, William	51	Fujisaki, Hiroshi-Judge	204
Farrow, Mia	51	Fisk, Carlton	117	Fortmann, Daniel	138	Fulford, Millie	210
Fauser, Mark	51	Fittipaldi, Christian	169	Fosbury, Dick	173	Fuller, Kurt	51
Favier, Jean-Jacques	210	Fittipaldi, Emerson	169	Fossett, Steve	215	Fuller, Millard	216
Favre, Brett	144	Flanery, Sean Patrick	51	Fossum, Michael E.	210	Fuller, Robert	52
Favreau, Jon	51	Flanigen, Edith	181	Foster, Ben	51	Fullerton, Charles G.	210
Fawcett, Farrah	51	Flatley, Michael	93	Foster, Bob	135	Fullerton, Fiona	76
Fawcett, Joy	174	Fleetwood Mac	95	Foster, Jodie	51	Fullmer, Gene	135
Faxon, Brad	161	Fleisher, Bruce	161	Foulke, Keith	119	Funicello, Annette	52
Fears, Tom	138	Fleming, Peggy	173	Four Freshmen	95	Funk, Fred	161

Furchgott, Robert	188	Gay, Brian	161	Gilchrist, Brad	83	Gooding, Cuba Jr.	52
Furlan, Renzo	168	Gayheart, Rebecca	52	Gilder, Bob	161	Gooding, Omar	52
Furlong, Edward	52	Gayle, Helene	188	Giles, Vinny	161	Goodman, John	52
Furness, Deborah-Lee	78	Gaylord, Mitch	172	Gilford, David	161	Goodwin, Doris	85
Furyk, Jim	161	Gayson, Eunice	76	Gillett, George N. Jr.	157	Gorbachev, Mikhail	205, 216
Gable, Dan	173	Gee, Prunella	76	Gilliam, Terry	52	Gordimer, Nadine	189
Gabriel, Peter	99	Gehry, Frank O.	91	Gillman, Sid	138	Gordon, Jeff	169
Gaetano, Cortesi	177	Geiberger, Al	161	Gilman, Alfred G.	189	Gordon, Lee (Porky)	52
Gaetti, Gary	124	Geiberger, Brent	161	Gilmartin, Raymond V.	179	Gordon, Richard F., Jr.	210
Gaffney, Paul	129	Geist, Bill	88	Gilmore, James S.	193	Gordon, Robby	169
Gallagher Jr., Jim	161	Gellar, Sarah Michelle	52	Gingrich, Newt	193	Gordon, Serena	76
Gallagher, David	52	Geller, Margaret	188	Ginzburg, Vitaly L.	189	Gordon-Levitt, Joseph	52
Gallagher, Jeff	161	Gemar, Charles D.	210	Girgrah, Isra	136	Gore, Jason	161
Gallagher, Leo	81	George Carruthers	181	Gish, Annabeth	52	Gorham, Christopher	52
Gallagher, Peter	52	George, Elizabeth	85	Giuliani, Rudolph	193	Gorie, Dominic L.	210
Gallant, Gerard	157	George, Melissa	52	Givens, Robin	52	Gorman, R.C.	91
Gallo, Robert	181	Gere, Richard	52	Glaser, Paul Michael	52	Gorshin, Frank	81
Galway, James	93	Gernhardt, Michael L.	210	Glass, David	124	Gossage, Goose	124
Gambill, Jan-Michael	168	Gershon, Gina	52	Glasson, Bill	161	Gosselin, Mario	157
Gamez, Rovert	161	Gertz, Jami	52	Glavine, Tom	122	Gossett, Louis Jr.	52
Gandhi, Sonia	205	Gervais, Ricky	52	Gleason, Joanna	52	Gotsche, Steve	161
Gandolfini, James	52	Gherty, John E.	179	Gleaton, Todd	161	Gottfried, Gilbert	81
Ganellin, Charon R.	181	Giacconi, Riccardo	188	Glen Miller Orchestra	95	Gould, Elliott	53
Garan, Ronald J., Jr.	210	Giaffone, Felipe	169	Glenn, John H., Jr.	210	Gould, Gordon	181
Garcia, Andy	52	Giamatti, Paul	52	Gless, Sharon	52	Goulet, Michael	157
Garcia, Sergio	161	Giannone, Alberto	161	Glover, Bruce	76	Gove, Jeff	161
Gardenhire, Ron	124	Giannulli, Mossimo	91	Glover, Danny	52	Goydos, Paul	161
Gardner, Dale A.	210	Giardello, Joey	135	Glover, Julian	76	Grabe, Ronald J.	210
Gardner, Guy S.	210	Gibbons, John	124	Glover, Savion	93	Grace, Bud	83
Garlin, Jeff	52	Gibbons, Leeza	88	Godfrey, Paul V.	124	Grace, Topher	53
Garneau, Marc	210	Gibbs, Alex	149	Godwin, Gail	85	Graf, Rick	149
Garner, James	52	Gibbs, Joe	138,149	Godwin, Linda M.	210	Graham, Alex	83
Garner, Jennifer	52	Gibson, Bob	117,124	Goetz, Dick	161	Graham, Billy	216
Garnett, Kevin	133	Gibson, Charles	88	Gogel, Matt	161	Graham, Dirk	157
Garofalo, Janeane	52, 81	Gibson, Deborah	99	Goggin, Matt	161	Graham, Donald	180
Garr, Terri	52	Gibson, Edward G.	210	Gold, Tracy	52	Graham, Heather	53
Garrett, Brad	81	Gibson, Fred	161	Goldberg, Danny	177	Graham, Lou	161
Garriott, Owen K.	210	Gibson, Henry	52	Goldberg, Stan	83	Graham, Paul	161
Garth, Jennie	52	Gibson, Kelly	161	Goldberg, Whoopi	52, 81	Grammer, Kelsey	53
Garvey, Steve	124	Gibson, Kirk	124	Goldblum, Jeff	52	Granato, Tony	157
Gary Trudeau	83	Gibson, Mel	52, 78	Goldman, William	85	Granger, Clive W. J.	189
Gary, Willie E.	204	Gibson, Robert L.	210	Goldthwait, Bobcat	81	Grant, Bud	138
Gary, Wise	83	Giffin, Doc	161	Golisano, B. Thomas	157	Grant, Hugh	53,179
Gasteyer, Ana	52	Gifford, Frank	138	Golmard, Jerome	168	Grant, Lee	53
Gates, Bill	179	Gifford, Kathie Lee	88	Golotta, Andrew	136	Grass Roots (The)	95
Gates, Melinda	178	Gilbert, Gibby Jr.	161	Gomez, Wilfred	135	Grassle, Karen	53
Gatlin Brothers (The)	95	Gilbert, Gibby Sr.	161	Goo Goo Dolls	95	Grasso, Richard	179
Gatski, Frank	138	Gilbert, Melissa	52	Good, Michael T.	210	Graveline, Duane E.	210
Gatti, Arturo	136	Gilbert, Sarah	52	Goodall, Jane	189	Graves, Peter	53
Gavilan, Kid	135	Gilbert, Walter	189	Goode, Matthew	52	Gray, Charles	76

Heldman, Gladys	167	Hilmers, David C.	211	Horne, Lena	99	Icahn, Carl	180
Helfgott, David	93	Hilton, Barron	178	Horning, Paul	138	Ice Cube	55
Helmond, Katherine	54	Hilton, Paris	54	Hornish, Sam Jr.	170	Ice-T	55
Helms, Susan J.	211	Hines, Cheryl	54	Horowitz, Scott J.	211	Idle, Eric	81
Henderson, Florence	54	Hinkle, Lon	162	Horsley, Lee	55	Ifans, Rhys	55
Henderson, Martin	54	Hinson, Larry	162	Horvitz, Robert H.	189	Iglesias, Enrique	99
Henderson, Ricky	124	Hirch, Judd	54	Hough, Charlie	124	Iglesias, Julio	99
Hendricks, Ted	138	Hire, Kathryn P.	211	Houston, Ken	138	Ignaro, Louis J.	189
Hendrickson, Dick	162	Hirsch, Elroy (Crazylegs)	138	Houston, Whitney	99	Iler, Robert	55
Hendry, Gloria	76	Hirsch, Emile	54	Howard, Bryce Dallas	55	Ilitch, Michael	124,157
Henke, Nolan	162	Hitchcock, Ken	157	Howard, Frank	124	Immature	95
Henman, Tim	168	Hjertstedt, Gabriel	162	Howard, John	206	Immelt, Jeffrey R.	178
Hennen, Thomas	211	Ho, David	189	Howard, Ron	55	Imperioli, Michael	55
Hennessy, Jill	54	Ho, Don	99	Howard, Traylor	55	Impressions (The)	95
Henning, Harold	162	Hobaugh, Charles O.	211	Howe, Art	124	Imus, Dick	89
Henninger, Brian	162	Hoch, Scott	162	Howe, Gordie	157	Imus, Don	89
Henricks, Terence T.	211	Hoff, Ted	182	Howe, Steve	124	India.Arie	99
Henry, J.J.	162	Hoffman, Dustin	54	Howell, Jamie	162	Indiana Pacemates	134
Herb, Jon	170	Hoffman, Glenn	124	Howison, Ryan	162	Indigo Girls	95
Herman's Hermits	95	Hoffman, Jeffrey A.	211	Hudson, Ernie	55	Ingram, James	99
Hernandez, Jay	54	Hoffman, Philip Seymour	54	Hudson, Kate	55	Ink Spots	95
Herrington, John B.	211	Hogan, Paul	55, 78	Huff, Sam	138	Innes, Laura	55
Herron, Alissa	162	Holbrook, Hal	55	Huffington, Arianna	89	Iovanna, Carol	89
Herron, Tim	162	Holden, Alexandra	55	Hughes, Bradley	162	Ireland, Kathy	55, 79
Hershey, Barbara	54	Holder, Geoffrey	76	Hughley, D.L.	81	Iron Butterfly	95
Hershiser, Orel	124	Holliday, Charles O.	178	Hulbert, Mike	162	Irons, Jeremy	55
Hershko, Avram	189	Holliman, Earl	55	Hume, Brit	89	Irsay, James	149
Herzigova, Eva	79	Hollis, John	76	Humperdinck, Engelbert	99	Irvan, Ernie	170
Hessmam, Howard	54	Holly, Lauren	55	Hunnam, Charlie	55	Irvin, Monte	117
Heston, Charlton	54	Hollyfield, Evander	136	Hunt, Bonnie	55	Irvine, Eddie	170
Hetfield, James	99	Holm, Celeste	55	Hunt, Helen	55	Irving, Amy	55
Hewitt, Bob	167	Holm, Ian	55	Hunt, Lamar	149,167	Irving, John	86
Hewitt, Don	89	Holmes, Katie	55	Hunt, Linda	55	Irwin, Hale	162
Hewitt, Jennifer Love	54	Holmes, Keith	136	Hunt, Timothy	189	Irwin, Steve	189
Hewitt, Lleyton	168	Holmes, Larry	136	Hunter, Holly	55	Isaacs, Jason	55
Hicks, Thomas O.	124	Holmgren, Mike	149	Hunter, Rachel	78,79	Ito, Lance- Judge	204
Hieb, Richard J.	211	Holmquest, Donald L.	211	Hunter, Torii	121	Ito, Robert	55
Hietala, Ryan	162	Holt, Lester	89	Hurdle, Clint	124	Ivanisevic, Goran	168
Higashi, Satoshi	162	Holt, R. Glynn	211	Hurley, Douglas G.	211	Ivins, Marsha S.	211
Higginbotham, Joan E.	211	Holtgrieve, Jim	162	Hurley, Elizabeth	55	Jacklin, Tony	162
Higgs, Mark	149	Holtz, Lou	149	Hurt, William	55	Jackman, Hugh	55,78
Hill, Faith	99	Honeycutt, Van B.	178	Huston, Anjelica	55	Jackson, Alan	99
Hill, Guy	162	Hooks, Bell	86	Huston, John	162	Jackson, Bo	149
Hill, Ike	149	Hooks, Robert	55	Hutson, Don	138	Jackson, Frank	149
Hill, Lauryn	99	Hooton, Burt	124	Hutton, Lauren	55	Jackson, Janet	99
Hill, Peter	162	Hope, Leslie	55	Hutton, Timothy	55	Jackson, Jesse	216
Hillenburg, Stephen	83	Hopkins, Anthony	55	Hutton, Tom	149	Jackson, Jonathan	55
Hillfiger, Tommy	91	Hopkins, Bo	55	Hyland, Scott	162	Jackson, Kate	55
Hilliard Robertson, P.	211	Hopper, Dennis	55	Hyzdu, Adam	119	Jackson, Keith	174
Hillier, James	182	Horn, Roy	91	Iacocca, Lee	178	Jackson, Latoya	99

Celebrity Name Index

Jackson, Matt	129	Johnson, Arte	56	Jones, Tommy Lee	56	Keach, Stacy	56
Jackson, Michael	99,177	Johnson, Curley	129	Jonze, Spike	87	Keaton, Diane	56
Jackson, Reggie	117,124	Johnson, Don	56	Joppy, William	136	Keaton, Michael	56,81
Jackson, Samuel L.	55	Johnson, Dwayne (The Rock)	56	Jordan, Michael	134	Kebebe, Liya	79
Jackson, Shirley	189	Johnson, Ervin "Magic"	134	Jordan, Oscar	100	Keck, Donald B.	182
Jacobs, Irwin Mark	180	Johnson, George	162	Jordan, Pete	162	Keegan, Andrew	56
Jacobs, Jeremy M.	157	Johnson, Gregory	211	Jospin, Lionel R.	205	Keegan, Robert	178
Jacobs, John	162	Johnson, Harold	135	Jourdain, Michel Jr.	170	Keel, Howard	56
Jacobsen, Peter	162	Johnson, Jimmy	138,170	Jourdan, Louis	76	Keen, Geoffrey	76
Jagger, Mick	99	Johnson, Joel W.	179	Judah, Zabdiel	136	Keenan, Mike	157
Jakobovits, Immanuel	216	Johnson, John	162	Judas Priest	96	Keener, Catherine	56
James, Bill	174	Johnson, John Henry	138	Judd, Ashley	56	Keillor, Garrison	86
James, Clifton	76	Johnson, Keyshawn	143	Judd, Naomi	100	Keitel, Harvey	56
James, Kevin	56	Johnson, Lynn-Holly	76	Judd, Wynonna	100	Kell, George	117
James, LeBron	132	Johnson, Michael	172	Julien, Claude	157	Kelleher, Robert	167
Jamison, Greg	157	Johnson, Rafer	173	Julio, Jorge	136	Kellerman, Faye	86
Jamison, Judith	93	Johnson, Randy	119	Jung, Andrea	177	Kellermen, Sally	56
Jan & Dean	95	Johnson, Robert	177	Junquiera, Bruno	170	Kelly, James M.	211
Janaszak, Steve	173	Johnson, Russell	56	Jurgensen, Sonny	138	Kelly, Jan	162
Janney, Allison	56	Johnson, William R.	178	Jurgensen, Steve	162	Kelly, Jerry	162
Jansen, Larry	124	Johnston, Jimmy	162	Kadenyuk, Leonid	211	Kelly, Jim	148,151
Janssen, Famke	76	Johnston, Lawrence C.	177	Kafelnikov, Yevgeny	168	Kelly, Leroy	138
Janzen, Lee	162	Johnston, Lynn	83	Kahanamoku, Duke	173	Kelly, Mark E.	211
Jarreau, Al	99	Johnston, Mark	162	Kahneman, Daniel	189	Kelly, Moira	56
Jarrett, Dale	170	Joiner, Charlie	138	Kaline, Al	117,125	Kelly, Scott J.	211
Jazz Dancers	134	Jolie, Angelina	56	Kaman, Charles	182	Kelly, Tim	86
Jeinsen, Elke	79	Jones, Ann Haydon	167	Kanaan, Tony	170	Kelman, Charles D.	182
Jemison, Mae C.	211	Jones, Buckshot	170	Kanada, Craig	162	Kemp, Will	56
Jenkins, Fergie	117	Jones, Cherry	56	Kanakaredes, Melina	56	Kendrick, Jill	162
Jenner, Bruce	172,173	Jones, Chipper	119	Kandel, Eric	189	Kennedy, Edward	204
Jensen, Jim	149	Jones, David "Deacon"	138	Kander, John	93	Kennedy, George	56
Jernigan, Tamara E.	211	Jones, Davy	100	Kane, Carol	56	Kennedy, Jamie	56
Jeter, Derek	122	Jones, Dean	56	Kann, Peter	178	Kennedy, Joseph II	204
Jett, Brent W.	211	Jones, George	100	Kaplan, Gabe	81,119	Kennedy, Patrick	204
Jett, Joan	99	Jones, Grace	76	Karan, Donna	91	Kennedy, Robert F.	204
Jewel	100	Jones, Jack	100	Karle, Isabella	189	Kenny G (Gorlick)	93
Jiang, Zemin	206	Jones, James Earl	56	Karon, Jan	86	Kenseth, Matt	170
Jillian, Ann	56	Jones, January	56	Karyo, Tcheky	76	Kerkorian, Kirk	180
Jimmy Dorsey Orshestra	96	Jones, Jenny	89	Kasem, Casey	89,93	Kerns, Joanna	56
Jobs, Steven P.	177	Jones, Jerry	149	Kass, Carmen	79	Kerr, Deborah	56
Joel, Billy	100	Jones, Kent	162	Katchor, Ben	83	Kerwin, Joseph P.	211
Jofre, Eder	135	Jones, Norah	100	Katt, Nicky	56	Ketchum, Hank	83
Johansson, Per-Ulrik	162	Jones, Parnelli	170	Kattan, Chris	56	Ketterle, Wolfgang	189
Johansson, Scarlet	56	Jones, Quincy	93	Katz, Richard	162	Key, Otis	129
Johansson, Thomas	168	Jones, Roy Jr.	136	Kaufman, Charlie	56	Khatami, Mohammad	206
John, Elton	100	Jones, Shirley	56,100	Kavandi, Janet L.	211	Kid Rock	100
John, Gottfried	76	Jones, Stan	138	Kaye, Johnathan	162	Kidder, Margot	56
John, Tommy	125	Jones, Steve	162	Kazami, Hiroshi	162	Kidman, Nicole	56
Johncock, Gordon	170	Jones, Thomas D.	211	Kazan, Lainie	100	Kiefer, Nicolas	168
Johns, Glynis	56	Jones, Tom	100	KC & The Sunshine Band	96	Kiel, Richard	76

Kiely III, W. Leo	178	Knight, Philip H.	179	Kroenke, E. Stanley	134	Lambert, Jack	138
Kilborn, Craig	89	Knight, Shirley	57	Kroslak, Jan	168	Lamoriello, Louis A.	157
Kilby, Jack S.	182	Knightley, Keira	57	Kruger, Diane	57	Lamotta, Jake	136
Kilby, Jack St. Clair	189	Knotts, Don	81	Krumholtz, David	57	Lancaster, Neal	163
Killebrew, Harmon	117,125	Knowles, Beyonce	57	Krzyzewski, Mike	134	Landers, Audrey	57
Kilmar, Val	56	Knox, Kenny	162	Kubek, Tony	125	Landers, Judy	57
Kilrain, Susan L.	211	Knoxville, Johnny	57	Kucera, Karol	168	Landry, Ali	57
Kilts, James M.	178	Koch, Gary	162	Kudrow, Lisa	57	Landry, Tom	138
Kim Young Sam	206	Kodes, Jan	167	Kuehne, Hank	162	Lane, Diane	57
Kimball, Ward	83	Kodjoe, Boris	57	Kuerten, Gustavo	168	Lane, Nathan	57
Kiner, Ralph	117	Koenig, Walter	57	Kulik, Ilia	172	Lane, Richard	138
King Carl XVI Gustaf	206	Kohl, Herb	134	Kulti, Nicklas	168	Lane, Robert	178
King Fahd	206	Kohn, Walter	189	Kunis, Mila	57	Lang, Herbert	129
King Jaun Carlos I	206	Kolff, Willem J.	182	Kurkova, Karolina	79	Lang, K.D.	100
King, BB	100	Komansky, David H.	179	Kurtz, Swoosie	57	Lange, Artie	57
King, Billie Jean	167	Kono, Tommy	173	Kurzweil, Raymond	182	Lange, Hope	57
King, Carole	100	Koolhaas, Rem	91	Kutcher, Ashton	57	Lange, Jessica	57
King, Coretta Scott	216	Koontz, Dean	86	Kwan, Michelle	172, 174	Langer, Alois	182
King, Don	136	Koop, C. Everett	189	Kwolek, Stephanie	182	Langer, Bernhard	163
King, Larry	89	Kopell, Bernie	57	Kwouk, Burt	76	Langer, Jim	138
King, Mary-Claire	189	Koplan, Jeffrey Dr.	193	Kydland, Finn E.	189	Langham, Franklin	163
King, Miki	173	Kopra, Timothy L.	211	Kyi, Daw Aung San Suu	189	Langhammer, Fred	178
King, Rodney	216	Korine, Harmony	57	La Beouf, Shia	57	Langton, Brooke	57
King, Stephen	86	Korman, Harvey	81	La Placa, Alison	57	Lanier, Willie	139
Kingsley, Ben	56	Kornberg, Arthur	189	La Rocque, Admiral Gene R.	193	Lanni, J. Terrence	179
Kingston Trio (The)	96	Kosar, Bernie	149	La Russa, Tony	125	Lansbury, Angela	57
Kingston, Alex	56	Koshiba, Masatoshi	189	La Voie, Fran	163	Laoretti, Larry	163
Kinkade, Thomas	91	Koskie, Corey	121	Labelle, Patti	100	Lapentti, Nicolas	168
Kinski, Nastassja	56	Kostis, Peter	162	Labine, Clem	125	Laracuente, Belinda	136
Kiriyenko, Sergei	206	Kotto, Yaphet	76	Labonte, Bobby	170	Largent, Steve	139
Kirkpatrick, Jeane	193	Koubek, Stefan	168	Labonte, Terry	170	Larroquette, John	57
Kirseborn, Vendela	79	Koufax, Sandy	117	Lacey, Alan	180	Larsen, Art	167
Kiss	96	Koufax, Sandy	125	Lachey, Nick	57	Larson, Jack	57
Kissinger, Henry A.	193	Kournikova, Anna	174	Lachman, Irwin	182	Larsson, Magnus	168
Kitchen, Mike	157	Kovacevich, Richard	180	Lacroix, Pierre	157	Lary, Yale	139
Kite, Jimmy	170	Krabbe, Jeroen	76	Lacy, Lee	125	Lasorda, Tommy	117,125
Kite, Tom	162	Kraft, Chris	215	Ladd, Cheryl	57	Lasswell, Fred	83
Kitt, Eartha	100	Kraft, Greg	162	Ladd, Diane	57	Lathan, Sanaa	57
Kittinger, Joe W. Jr	215	Krajicek, Richard	168	Ladd, Jordan	57	Latifah, Queen	57
Kiyabu, Sachiko	162	Kramer, Jack	167	Lafley, Alan G.	180	Laudau, Martin	57
Klein, Calvin	91	Kramer, Stanley	87	Lagasse, Emeril	91	Lauer, Matt	89
Klestil, Thomas	206	Kramer, Stepfanie	57	Lagrow, Lerrin	125	Laughlin, Robert B.	189
Kline, Kevin	56	Krantz, Judith	86	Lahoud, Joe	125	Lauper, Cyndi	100
Kline, Robert	81	Kratzert, Billy	162	Lahti, Christine	57	Laurie, Bill	157
Klugman, Jack	56	Krause, Paul	138	Laine, Frankie	100	Laurie, Hugh	57
Klum, Heidi	79	Krauss, Alison	100	Lake, Ricki	89	Lauterbur, Paul C.	189
Knicks City Dancers	134	Kravitz, Lenny	100	Laker Girls	134	Lavelli, Dante	139
Knight, Billy	134	Kregel Kevin R.	211	Lamas, Lorenzo	57	Laver, Rod	167
Knight, Bobby	134	Kreuk, Kristin	57	Lamb, Wally	86	Lavigne, Avril	100
Knight, Gladys	100	Kroemer, Herbert	189	Lambert, Christopher	57	Laviolette, Peter	158

Law, Jude	57	Lemaire, Jacques	158	Limbaugh, Tommy	163	Lopez, Al	117
Lawless, Lucy	57, 78	LeMond, Greg	174	Limeliters	96	Lopez, George	58,81
Lawrence, Martin	57, 81	Lennon Sisters	96	Limp Bizkit	100	Lopez, Jennifer	59, 101
Lawrence, Wendy B.	211	Lenny, Richard H.	178	Lin, Maya	91	Lopez, Jose Luis	136
Lawson, Maggie	58	Leno, Jay	81,89	Lin, T.Y	91	Lopez, Ricardo	136
Lay, Kenneth L.	178	Lenoir, William B.	211	Lincoln, Howard	125	Lopez-Alegria, Michael	212
Lazcano, Juan	136	Leon, Valerie	76	Lind, Don L.	211	Loren, Sophia	59
Lazenby, George	76	Leonard, Elmore	86	Linden, Hal	58	Loria, Christopher J.	212
Lazier, Buddy	170	Leonard, Justin	163	Lindner, Carl H.	125	Loria, Jeffrey H.	125
Lazier, Jaques	170	Leonard, Robert Sean	58	Lindner, Pernilla	79	Loring, Gloria	101
Lazzaro, Anthony	170	Leonard, Sugar Ray	136,173	Lindsay, Mark	100	Lott, Ronnie	139,149
Leach, Robin	89	Lerner, Randolf D.	149	Lindsey, George-Goober	58	Louganis, Greg	172,173
Leachman, Cloris	58	Lesar, David J.	178	Lindsey, Steven W.	212	Louis-Dreyfus, Julia	59
Leakey, Louise	189	Leskanic, Curtis	119	Lindvall, Angela	79	Louise, Tina	59
Leakey, Meave	189	Leslie, Fred	211	Linenger, Jerry M.	212	Lounge, John M.	212
Leakey, Richard	189	Leslie, Mann	58	Linklater, Art	89	Lousma, Jack R.	212
Learned, Michael	58	Leto, Jared	58	Linnehan, Richard M.	212	Loustaiot, Tim	163
Leary, Denis	58	Letterman (The)	96	Linney, Laura	58	Lovano, Joe	101
LeBlanc, Matt	58	Letterman, David	81,89	Linteris, Gregory	212	Love Hewitt, Jennifer	59
Lecarre, John	86	Levin, Harvey	89	Liotta, Ray	58	Love, Courtney	59,101
Led Zeppelin	100	Levinson, Barry	87	Lipinski, Tara	172,174	Love, Davis	163
Ledger, Heath	58, 78	Levy, Eugene	58	Lithgow, John	58	Love, Stanley G.	212
Ledley, Robert S.	182	Levy, David H.	189	Little Richard	101	Lovell, James A., Jr.	212
Lee, Brenda	100	Levy, Marv	139	Little, Larry	139	Loveman, Gary W.	178
Lee, Christopher	76	Lewis, Carl	172,173	Little, Rich	81	Lover, Ed	59
Lee, Henry C.	189	Lewis, Damian	58	Liu, Lucy	58	Lovett, Lyle	101
Lee, Jason Scott	58	Lewis, Daniel Day	58	Livingston, Ron	58	Lovio, Tresa	163
Lee, Jeanette	174	Lewis, Dave	158	LL Cool J	101	Lovitz, Jon	81
Lee, Mark C.	211	Lewis, Gary	100	Llewellyn, John A.	212	Low, G. David	212
Lee, Patrick	163	Lewis, Huey	100	Llewelyn, Doug	58	Lowe, Derek	119
Lee, Peggy	100	Lewis, Jason	58	Lloyd Webber, Andrew	93	Lowe, Rob	59
Lee, Sammy	173	Lewis, Jerry	81	Lloyd, Christopher	58	Lowell, Carey	59,76
Lee, Spike	87	Lewis, Jerry Lee	100	Locher, Dick	84	Lowery, Steve	163
Lee, Stan	83	Lewis, Juliette	58	Locke, Philip	76	Lu, Edward T.	212
Lee, Teng-Tui	206	Lewis, Kenneth	177	Lockhart, Anne	58	Lucas, George	87
Lee, Vic	84	Lewis, Lennox	136	Lockhart, Paul S.	212	Lucas, Jerry	134,173
Leen, Randy	163	Lewis, Ramsey	93,100	Locklear, Heather	58	Lucas, Josh	59
Leestma, David C.	211	Lewis, Ronald	182	Locklin, Loryn	58	Lucci, Susan	59
Leeves, Jane	58	Lewis, Russell T.	179	Lofton, James	139,149	Lucero, Emmanuel	136
Lefebvre, Jim	125	Leyritz, Jim	125	Lohan, Lindsay	58	Lucid, Shannon W.	212
Leggatt, Ian	163	Li, Jet	58	Lohman, Alison	58	Luckman, Sid	139
Leggett, Anthony J.	189	Libeskind, Daniel	91	Lohr, Bob	163	Ludacris	101
LeGros, James	58	Lickliter, Frank	163	Loken, Kristanna	58	Luft, Lorna	59
Leguizamo, John	58	Liddy, Edward M.	177	Lonborg, Jim	125	Lulu	101
Lehman, James M.	163	Light, Judith	58	London, Jeremy	58	Lumley, Joanna	77
Lehman, Tom	163	Lil' Kim	58	Long, Howie	139	Lundgren, Dolph	77
Lehrer, Jim	89	Lillard, Matthew	58	Long, Nia	58	Lunstrom, David	163
Leibovitz, Annie	91	Lillis, Bob	125	Long, Shelly	58	Luyendyk, Arie	170
Leigh, Jennifer Jason	58	Lilly, Bob	139	Lonsdale, Michael	76	Lye, Mark	163
Leipold, Craig	158	Limbaugh, Rush	89	Lopes, Davey	125	Lyman, Dorothy	59

Lynley, Carol	59	Malerba, Franco	212	Marsden, James	59	Maxwell, Lois	77
Lynskey, Melanie	59	Malick, Wendie	59	Marsh, Graham	163	May, Bob	163
Lyonne, Natasha	59	Malik, Art	77	Marshall, Barry J.	189	Mayfair, Billy	163
Mac, Bernie	59	Malkovich, John	59	Marshall, Penny	87	Mayfield, Jeremy	170
MacArthur, James	59	Malone, Darrell	149	Marshall, Peter	89	Maynard, Don	139
MacDiarmid, Alan G.	189	Malone, Gordon	129	Marshall, Susan	93	Mayo, Itzhak	212
Macdonald, Norm	59,81	Malone, Jena	59	Martin, Casey	163	Mayo, Virginia	60
MacDowell, Andie	59	Malone, Karl	132	Martin, Christy	136	Mays, Willie	117,125
MacGraw, Ali	59	Maltbie, Rodger	163	Martin, Doug	163	Mayweather, Floyd	136
Macha, Ken	125	Malzone, Frank	125	Martin, George	86, 93	Mazar, Debi	60
Macht, Gabriel	59	Mamas & Papas (The)	96	Martin, Jacques	158	Mazeroski, Bill	117
Macias, Jose	119	Mamet, David	86	Martin, Kellie	59	Mazor, Stanley	182
Mack, Tom	139	Manchester, Mellissa	101	Martin, Mark	170	Mazza, Valerie	79
Mackey, John	139	Mancini, Ray	136	Martin, Ricky	101	Mazzilli, Lee	125
Mackie, Bob	91	Mandela, Nelson	206	Martin, Steve	81	Mbenga, DJ	132
Mackinnon, Roderick	189	Mandlikova, Hana	167	Martin, Todd	168	McAdams, Rachel	60
MacLachlan, Kyle	59	Mandrell, Barbara	101	Martinez, Mel	193	McAfee, George	139
MacLaine, Shirley	59	Mandrell, Louise	101	Martinez, Pedro	119	McArthur, K. Megan	212
MacLean, Doug	158	Manheim, Camryn	59	Martino, Al	101	McArthur, William S., Jr.	212
MacLean, Steven G.	212	Manilow, Barry	101	Martz, Mike	149	McAuliffe, Dick	125
MacNee, Patrick	77	Mankiller, Wilma P.	206	Marvelettes (The)	96	McBride, Jon A.	212
MacPhail, Andrew B.	125	Mann, Herbie	94	Mascatello, John	163	McBride, Martina	101
MacPhail, Lee	117	Manning, Archie	149	Mason, Jackie	81	McCallum, David	60
MacPherson, Elle	79	Manning, Eli	146	Mason, Marsha	59	McCandless, Bruce, II	212
MacTavish, Craig	158	Manning, Payton	144	Massa, Felipe	170	McCann, Ronnie	163
Macy, Gary	101	Mansfield, Sir Peter	189	Massimino, Michael J.	212	McCarron, Scott	163
Macy, William H.	59	Mara, Wellington	139,149	Mast, Dick	163, 170	McCarthy, Andrew	60
Madden, John	149	Maraghy, Dave	163	Masterson, Christopher	60	McCarthy, Jenny	60
Maddux, Greg	119	Marceau, Sophie	77	Masterson, Danny	60	McCartney, Paul	101
Maddux, Mike	125	March, Stephanie	59	Masterson, Mary Stuart	60	McCarty, Dave	119
Madigan, Amy	59	Marchetti, Gino	139	Mastracchio, Richard A.	212	McClanahan, Rob	173
Madison, Helene	173	Marcil, Vanessa	59	Mastrantonia, Mary	60	McClatchy, Kevin S.	125
Madonna	59,101	Marcis, Dave	170	Matalin, Mary	89	McClenaghan, Eric	163
Madsen, Michael	59	Margret, Ann	59	Matera & Saunders	84	McClendon, Lloyd	125
Magadan, Dave	125	Margulies, Julianna	59	Mathers, Jerry	60	McClure, Charles	178
Magee, Andrew	163	Margulis, Lynn	189	Matheson, Hans	60	McCollough, W. Alan	177
Maggert, Jeff	163	Marichal, Juan	117	Mathias, Bob	172,173	McConaughey, Matthew	60
Magic Dancers	134	Marin, Cheech	59	Mathis, Johnny	101	McCord, Gary	163
Maginnes, John	163	Marineau, Philip	179	Matlin, Marlee	60	McCord, Kent	60
Magnus, Sandra H.	212	Marino, Dan	149	Matson, Ollie	139	McCorkindale, Douglas	178
Maguire, Tobey	59	Mariucci, Steve	149	Matsui, Hideki	122	McCormack, Catherine	60
Mahaffey, John	163	Mark, Reuben	177	Mattea, Kathy	101	McCormack, Eric	60
Maher, Bill	89	Markham, Monte	59	Matthiesen, David	212	McCormack, Mary	60
Mahre, Phil	173	Marlette, Doug	84	Mattinging, Don	125	McCormack, Mike	139
Mailer, Norman	86	Marlin, Sterling	170	Mattingly, Don	125	McCormack, Will	60
Maiman, Theodore H.	182	Marquez, Gabriel	189	Mattingly, Thomas K., II	212	McCormick, Maureen	60
Major, John	206	Marquina, Jose	163	Maurer, Robert D.	182	McCormick, Pat	173
Majors, Lee	59	Marsalis, Bradford	94	Mavs Dancers	134	McCourt, Frank	125
Mako, Gene	167	Marsalis, Ellis	94	Max, Peter	91	McCovey, Willie	117,125
Malave, Tina	59	Marsalis, Wynton	94	Maxim, Joey	135	McCoy, Glenn	84

Celebrity Name Index

McCracken, Craig	84	McNish, Allan	170	Millar, Kevin	119	Montagnier, Luc	182
McCready, Mindy	101	McPhee, George	158	Miller, Arthur	86	Montana, Ashley	79
McCulley, Michael J.	212	McRoy, Spike	163	Miller, Bebe	93	Montana, Joe	139,150
McCumber, Mark	163	Meade, Carl J.	212	Miller, Christa	61	Montgomerie, Colin	163
McCutcheon, Martine	60	Meadows, Jane	60	Miller, Dennis	81, 89	Montgomery, David	125
McDaniel, James	60	Meara, Ann	81	Miller, Jack	170	Montoya, Juan Pablo	170
McDaniel, Lindy	125	Mears, Rick	170	Miller, Johnny	163	Moody, Orville	163
McDermott, Dylan	60	Mears, Roger	170	Miller, Marcus	93	Moon, Wally	125
McDivitt, James A.	212	Meddick, Jim	84	Miller, Penelope Ann	61	Moore, Demi	61
McDonald, Tommy	139	Mediate, Rocco	163	Miller, Shannon	172	Moore, Gordon E.	179
McDonnell, Mary	60	Medvedev, Andrei	168	Miller, Wentworth	61	Moore, Julianne	61
McDonnell, Patrick	84	Meese, Edwin	193	Millman, Irving	182	Moore, Leonard	139
McDormand, Frances	60	Mellencamp, John	101	Mills, Alley	61	Moore, Mary Tyler	61
McDowell, Malcolm	60	Melnick, Bruce E.	212	Mills, Billy	173	Moore, Michael	204
McElhennny, Hugh	139	Melnyk, Steve	163	Mills, Sir John	61	Moore, Roger	61, 77
McEntire, Reba	101	Meloni, Christopher	60	Milner, Martin	61	Moorer, Michael	136
McFadden, Daniel	189	Melroy, Pamela A.	212	Milsap, Ronnie	101	Moores, John	125
McFadden, Gates	60	Melvill, Mike	215	Mineta, Norman Y.	193	Moorman, David	163
McFarlane, Seth	84	Melvin, Leland D.	212	Ming, Yao	132	Mora, Jim	150
McGehee, Robby	170	Mendes, Eva	60	Mirabelli, Doug	119	Moran, Erin	61
McGill, Bruce	60	Mendes, Sam	87	Mirren, Helen	61	Moran, Rocky Jr.	170
McGillis, Kelly	60	Menem, Carlos	206	Mitchell, Beverly	61	Moreau, Doug	150
McGinley, John C.	60	Menyes, Tom	163	Mitchell, Bobby	139	Moreno, Rita	61
McGinley, Ted	60	Meredith, James	216	Mitchell, Edgar D.	212	Moreno, Rita	101
McGoohan, Patrick	60	Meriwether, Lee	60	Mitchell, Shamba	136	Morgan, Barbara R.	212
McGovern, George	193	Merkerson, S. Epatha	60	Mitchell, Stiles	163	Morgan, Gil	163
McGovern, James	163	Merrill, Carrol	89	Mitra, Rhona	61	Morgan, Harry	61
McGowan, Rose	60	Merrill, Dina	60	Mix, Ron	139	Morgan, Joe	117
McGraw, Harold H.	179	Merton, Robert C.	189	Mize, Larry	163	Morgan, John	163
McGraw, Phillip	89	Meskimen, Jim	61	Mochrie, Colin	81	Morgan, Kelly	163
McGregor, Ewan	60	Messersmith, Andy	125	Modernaires	96	Morgan, Lorrie	101
McGregor, Ken	167	Messing, Debra	61	Modine, Matthew	61	Morgan, Walter	163
McGruder, Aaron	84	Metcalf, Laurie	61	Moeller, Dennis	182	Morgenstern, Maia	61
McKay, Jim	174	Metcalfe, Bob	179	Mohr, Jay	61	Morin, Lee M.	212
McKenzie, Benjamin	60	Meyer, Breckin	61	Mohri, Mamoru	212	Morissette, Alanis	101
McKeon, Jack	125	Meyer, Debbie	173	Mol, Gretchen	61	Morita, Pat	61
McKeon, Nancy	60	Michael, George	101	Molina, Alfred	61	Morris, Garrett	81
McLachlan, Sarah	101	Michaels, Lorne	89	Molina, Mario	189	Morris, Kathryn	61
McLanahan, Rue	60	Micheel, Shaun	163	Molinari, Susan	89	Morris, Robert	163
McMahon, Ed	89	Michel, F. Curtis	212	Molinaro, Al	61	Morrison, Toni	86
McMillan, C. Steven	180	Michener, James A.	86	Molitor, Paul	117,125	Morrow, Bobby	173
McMillan, Frew	167	Michiko Empress of Japan	206	Molloy, Bryan	182	Morrow, Ken	173
McMonagle, Donald R.	212	Mickelson, Phil	163	Moloney, Janel	61	Morse, David	61
McMurtry, Larry	86	Midler, Bette	61,101	Monaghan, Tom	178	Mortensen, Viggo	61
McNair, Barbara	101	Mientkiewicz, Doug	119	Moncrief, Michael	129	Mortimer, Emily	61
McNair, Robert C.	149	Mike & The Mechanics	96	Mondale, Walter	193	Morton, Samantha	61
McNeal, Don	149	Mikesell, Beverly	163	Monday, Rick	125	Moses, Edwin	173
McNealy, Scott G.	180	Milano, Alyssa	61	Monfort, Charles K.	125	Moss, Carrie-Ann	61
Mcnee, Patrick	60	Milbury, Mike	158	Monica	101	Moss, Kate	79
McNerney, W. James Jr.	177	Miley, Dave	125	Monkees (The)	96	Moss, Perry	163

Moss, Randy	145	Nacchio, Joseph P.	180	Newsome, Ozzie	139	Noth, Chris	62
Mota, Manny	125	Nadeau, Jerry	170	Newton, Thandie	62	Nottingham, Don	150
Motley, Marion	139	Nagel, Steven R.	212	Newton, Wayne	77, 102	Nouri, Michael	62
Mower, Morton	182	Naifeh, Steven	86	Newton-John, Olivia	102	Novak, Jiri	168
Moya, Carlos	168	Naimoli, Vincent J.	125	Nichols, Bobby	163	Nowak, Lisa M.	213
Moyers, Bill	89	Najimy, Kathy	62	Nichols, Paul	87	Noyori, Ryoji	189
Moynahan, Bridget	61	Nakano, Shinji	170	Nichols, Rick	164	Nugent, Ted	102
Muckler, John	158	Namath, Joe	139	Nicholson, Jack	62	Nuggets Dancers	134
Mueller, Bill	119	Napoles, Jose	135	Nicklaus, Gary	164	Nunn, Sam	194
Mueller, Robert	193	Nardelli, Robert I.	179	Nicklaus, Jack	164	Nurse, Paul M.	190
Mularkey, Mike	150	Nash, Graham	102	Nicollier, Claude	213	Nyberg, Karen L.	213
Mulcahy, Ann	180	Nash, John F.	189	Niedenfuer, Tom	125	Nye, Bill	190
Mulder, Karen	79	Nastase, Ilie	167	Niekro, Phil	117	O'Brian, Connan	89
Muldowney, Shirley	170	Nasty Boys (The)	96	Nielsen, Connie	62	O'Brien, Alex	168
Mullally, Megan	61	Navratilova, Martina	167, 174	Nielson, Brigitte	62	O'Brien, Dan	172
Mullane, Richard M.	212	Neal, Patricia	62	Nielson, Leslie	62	O'Brien, Parry	173
Mulligan, Richard	61	Necciai, Ron	125	Nimmer, Ann	164	O'Bryant, Eathan	129
Mullin, Leo F.	178	Nechita, Alexandra	91	Nimoy, Leonard	62	O'Callahan, Jack	173
Mullis, Kary B	182	Needham, Hal	87	Nine Inch Nails	96	O'Connell, Jerry	62
Mulloy, Gardnar	167	Neelman, David	179	Nishimura, Koichi	180	O'Connor Sinead	102
Mulroney, Dermot	61	Neeson, Liam	62	Nitschke, Ray	139	O'Connor, Bryan D.	213
Munchak, Mike	139	Neher, Erwin Dr.	189	Nitty Gritty Dirt Band	96	O'Connor, Christy Jr.	164
Mundell, Robert A.	189	Neill, Noel	62	Nixon, Cynthia	62	O'Connor, Frances	62
Muniz, Frankie	61	Neill, Sam	62	Nixon, Norman	91	O'Connor, Sandra Day	194
Munoz, Anthony	139	Neiman, Leroy	91	Nixon, Trot	119	O'Donnell, Chris	62
Munro, Caroline	77	Nelson, Craig T.	62	Nobilo, Frank	164	O'Donnell, Rosie	89
Murad, Ferid	189	Nelson, George D.	212	Noble, James	62	O'Hara, Maureen	62
Murdoch, Rupert	179	Nelson, Larry	163	Noddle, Jeffrey	180	O'Hare, Mark	84
Murdock, David H.	178	Nelson, M. Bruce	179	Noguchi,Soichi	213	O'Keefe, Sean	190
Murphy, Bob	163	Nelson, Tim Blake	62	Nolan, Christopher	62	O'Leary, Brian T.	213
Murphy, Brittany	62	Nelson, Willie	102	Nolan, Keith	164	O'Meara, Mark	164
Murphy, Eddie	62, 81	Nemcova, Petra	79	Nolin, Gena Lee	62	O'Neal, Ryan	62
Murphy, John C.	84	Nemechek, Joe	170	Noll, Chuck	139, 150	O'Neal, Shaquille	132
Murphy, Sean	163	Nemer, R.J.	163	Nolte, Nick	62	O'Neill, Ed	63
Murray, Andy	158	Neptune	93	Nomellini, Leo	139	O'Neill, Jennifer	63
Murray, Anne	102	Nesmith, Michael	102	Noone, Peter	102	O'Reilly, Bill	89
Murray, Bill	81	Nespoli, Paolo	212	Noriega, Carlos I.	213	O'Reilly, David J.	177
Murray, Bryan	158	Nettleson, Lois	62	Norman, Greg	164	O'Toole, Peter	63
Murray, Eddie	117	Neuwirth, Bebe	62, 93	Norman, Magnus	168	Oak Ridge Boys (The)	96
Musgrave, Story	212	Neville, Aaron	102	Norris, Chuck	62	Obuchi, Keizo	207
Musharraf, Pervez	193	New Jersey Nets	134	Norris, Tim	164	Ocean, Billy	102
Musial, Stan	117	Newbold, Gregory Lt. Gen.	194	North, Andy	164	Ochoa, Ellen	213
Mussina, Mike	122	Newcombe, Don	125	North, Douglass	189	Ockels, Wubbo J.	213
Musso, George	139	Newcombe, John	167	North, Oliver	89	Oefelein, William A.	213
Mwinyi, Ali Hassan	206	Newhart, Bob	62,81	North, Sheree	62	Oerter, Al	173
Myers, Mike	62,81,119	Newman, James H.	212	Norton, Edward	62	Offerdahl, John	150
Myers, Richard (General)	194	Newman, Paul	62	Norton, Gale	194	Ogilvie, Joe	164
N Sync	96	Newman, Randy	93	Norton, Ken	135	Ogrin, David	164
Naber, John	173	Newman, Ryan	170	Norville, Deborah	89	Olazabal, Jose Maria	164
Nabors, Jim	102	Newmar, Julie	62	Norwood, Brandy	62	Oldman, Gary	62

Olin, Ken	62	Palminteri, Chazz	63	Pavarotti, Luciano	102	Perry, Luke	64
Oliu, Ingrid	62	Palmisano, Samuel J.	179	Pavel, Andrei	168	Perry, Matthew	64
Oliva, Tony	125	Paltrow, Gwyneth	63	Pavelich, Mark	173	Pesci, Joe	64
Olivares, Ruben	135	Panetta, Leon	194	Pavin, Corey	164	Pescosolido, Stefano	168
Olivas, John D.	213	Panettiere, Hayden	63	Pawelczyk, James	213	Pestova, Daniela	79
Oliver, Louis	150	Panis, Olivier	170	Paxton, Bill	63	Peter, Paul & Mary	96
Ollila, Jorma	179	Pankow, John	63	Paycheck, Johnny	102	Peters, Bernadette	64
Olsen, Kenneth H.	182	Pantoliano, Joe	63	Payette, Julie	213	Petersen, William L.	64
Olsen, Mary Kate & Ashley	62	Papis, Max	170	Payne, Alexander	87	Petersen, Wolfgang	87
Olsen, Merlin	139, 150	Pappas, Deane	164	Payton, Nicholas	94	Peterson, Cristel Winther	79
Ontiveros, Lupe	63	Paquin, Anna	63	Payton, Walter	139	Peterson, Donald H.	213
Oosterhuis, Peter	164	Parazynski, Scott E.	213	Pearce, Guy	78	Peterson, Tony	164
Orlando, Tony	102	Parcells, Bill	150	Pearl Jam	96	Pett, Mark	84
Orman, Suze	179	Parise, Ronald	213	Pearson, Drew	150	Pettit, Donald R.	213
Ormond, Julia	63	Park, Ray	63	Peck, Dr. M. Scott	86	Petty, Kyle	171
Ortiz, Carlos	135	Parker & Hart	84	Peck, Tom	171	Petty, Richard	171
Ortiz, David	119	Parker, Clarence (Ace)	139	Pedrique, Al	125	Petty, Tom	102
Osborne, Ozzy	102	Parker, David K.	164	Peeples, Nia	63	Pfeiffer, Michelle	64
Osbourne, Jack	63	Parker, Fess	63	Peet, Amanda	63	Phifer, Mekhi	64
Osbourne, Kelly	63	Parker, Jim	139	Peete, Calvin	164	Phil Garner	125
Osbourne, Sharon	63	Parker, Mary-Louise	63	Peete, Holly Robinson	63	Philbin, Regis	89
Osheroff, Douglas	190	Parker, Robert A. R.	213	Pei, leoh Ming	91	Philippoussis, Mark	168
Osment, Haley Joel	63	Parker, Sarah Jessica	63	Pekar, Harvey	84	Phillippe, Ryan	64
Osmond, Donny	102	Parker, Thomas	164	Pele	174	Phillips, John L.	213
Osmond, Marie	102	Parker, Trey	84	Pelli, Cesar	91	Phillips, Lou Diamond	64
Osteen, Claude	125	Parkinson, Bradford	182	Peña, Tony	125	Phillips, Mackenzie	64
Oswald, Stephen S.	213	Parnevik, Jesper	164	Pendergast, Clancy	150	Phillips, Stone	89
Otto, Jim	139, 150	Parry, Craig	164	Penn & Teller	81, 91	Phillips, Ted	150
Otto, Miranda	63	Parsons, John T.	182	Penn, Robin Wright	63	Phillips, Wade	150
Owen, Clive	63	Parsons, Richard	177, 180	Penn, Sean	63	Phillips, William D.	190
Owen, Mickey	125	Parton, Dolly	102	Peoples, David	164	Phoenix, Joaquin	64
Owens, Buck	102	Pastore, Vincent	63	Pep, Willie	135	Phoenix, Rain	64
Ozaki, Joe	164	Pastorelli, Robert	63	Perabo, Piper	63	Phoenix, Summer	64
Ozaki, Joel	164	Pate, Jerry	164	Perez, Tony	117	Piano, Renzo	91
Pacino, Al	63	Pate, Steve	164	Perez, Vincent	63	Piazza, Mike	125
Padalecki, Jared	63	Patric, Jason	63	Perkins, Elizabeth	63	Pickles, Christina	64
Pafko, Andy	125	Patrick, Nicholas J. M.	213	Perks, Craig	164	Piech, Ferdinand	180
Page, Alan	139	Patrick, Robert	63	Perl, Martin	190	Pierce, David Hyde	64
Page, James	136	Patterson, Floyd	135	Perlman, Itzhak	94	Piers, Anthony	86
Page, Larry	178	Patterson, P.J.	207	Perlman, Rhea	63	Pietrangeli, Nicola	167
Page, Patti	102	Patty, Sandi	102	Perlman, Ron	64	Pietz, Amy	64
Paige, Elaine	63	Paul, Adrian	63	Pernice, Tom	164	Pihos, Pete	139
Paige, Roderick R.	194	Paul, John Jr.	170	Perot, H. Ross	194	Piniella, Lou	125
Palance, Jack	63	Paul, Wolfgang	190	Perranoski, Ron	125	Pinsky, Drew (Dr.)	89
Palin, Michael	81	Pauley, Jane	89	Perrin, Philippe	213	Pioline, Cedric	168
Palmeiro, Rafael	119	Paulsen, Pat	81	Perry, Chris	164	Piondexter, Buster	102
Palmer, Arnold	164	Paulson, Carl	164	Perry, Fletcher (Shorty)	139	Pippen, Scottie	134
Palmer, Geoffrey	77	Paulson, Dennis	164	Perry, Gaylord	117	Piraro, Dan	84
Palmer, Jim	117	Paulson, Henry	178	Perry, Jim	125	Pitino, Rick	134
		Paulucci, Jeno	179	Perry, Kenny	164	Pitney, Gene	102
						Pitt, Brad	64

Richardson, Patricia	65	Robertson, T. Wayne	171	Rosewall, Ken	167	Ryan, Meg	66
Richie, Lionel	103	Robinson, Brooks	117,126	Rosinski, Edward J.	182	Ryan, Nolan	117,126
Richter, Burton	190	Robinson, Frank	117,126	Ross, Diana	103	Rydell, Bobby	103
Richter, Gerhard	91	Robinson, Ivan	136	Ross, Gary	87	Ryder, Winona	66
Rickman, Alan	65	Robinson, Smokey	103	Ross, Jerry L.	213	Rymer, Charlie	165
Ricks, Charlie	164	Robinson, Stephen K.	213	Ross, Marion	66	Sabah, Jaber Al-Ahmad	207
Ride, Sally K.	213	Robinson, Zuleikha	66	Rossellini, Isabella	66	Sabato, Antonio Jr.	66
Riders In The Sky	96	Robustelli, Andy	140	Rosset, Marc	168	Sabbatini, Rory	165
Ridge, Tom	194	Rocca, Costantino	164	Rossiter, Robert E.	179	Sacco, Albert	213
Rigby, Cathy	172	Roche, Tony	167	Rossum, Emmy	66	Sade	103
Rigby, Terence	77	Rock, Chris	82	Roth, Tim	66	Sadler, Elliot	171
Rigg, Dame Dianna	77	Rockets Power Dancers	134	Roundtree, Richard	66	Sadler, Sandy	135
Rigg, Rebecca	78	Rockwell, Sam	66	Rourke, Mickey	66	Safer, Morley	90
Riggins, John	139	Rodbell, Martin	190	Rowe, John W.	177	Safin, Marat	168
Riggio, Stephen	177	Rodman, Dennis	134	Rowell, Victoria	66	Sagal, Katey	66
Riley, Chirs	164	Rodriguez, Alex	122	Rowlands, Gena	66	Saget, Bob	66, 82
Riley, Kevin	164	Rodriguez, Anthony	164	Rowling, J.K.	86	Sahl, Mort	82
Riley, Pat	134	Rodriguez, Chi Chi	164	Roxburgh, Richard	66, 78	Saint, Eve Maria	66
Rilly, Terry	164	Rodriguez, Luis	135	Royal, Billie Joe	103	Saint-Marie, Buffy	103
Rimes, LeAnn	103	Rodriguez, Paul	82	Royer, Hugh	165	Sajak, Pat	90
Rincon, Ricardo	122	Roe, Elwin 'Preacher'	126	Rozelle, Pete	140	Sakmann, Bert Dr.	190
Rines, Robert H.	182	Roebuck, Ed	126	Rubin, Benjamin A.	182	Salamone, Melissa	136
Ringo, Jim	139	Roenicke, Ron	126	Rubin, Robert	177	Salazar, Eliseo	171
Ringwald, Molly	65	Rogers, Kenny (Baseball)	123	Rudd, Ricky	171	Saliers, Emily	103
Rinker, Larry	164	Rogers, Kenny (Singer)	103	Rudner, Rita	82	Salinger, J.D.	86
Rinker, Lee	164	Rogers, Mimi	66	Ruehl, Mercedes	66	Salley, John	134
Rios, Marcelo	168	Rogers, Wayne	66	Ruff, Lindy	158	Salo, Mika	171
Ripa, Kelly	65	Rohde, Bruce C.	178	Ruffalo, Mark	66	Salt N' Pepa	96
Risebrough, Doug	158	Rohrer, Heinrich	182	Ruiz, John	136	Sammons, Mary F.	180
Ritchie, Nicole	65	Roker, Al	90	Rummells, David	165	Sampras, Pete	168
Ritter, Jason	66	Rollerson, Ron	129	Rumsfeld, Donald H.	194	Samuelson, Joan	172
Rivera, Geraldo	90	Rollins, John	164	Runco, Mario, Jr.	213	San Giacomo, Laura	66
Rivers, Joan	82	Romano, Ray	66, 82	Rusedski, Greg	168	Sanchez, Kiele	66
Rivers, Johnny	103	Romijn-Stamos, Rebecca	79	Rush, Geoffrey	66, 78	Sanchez, Roselyn	66
Rizzuto, Phil	117, 126	Rominger, Kent V.	213	Russel, Nipsey	82	Sanders, Barry	140, 150
Roach, O. Lynn Jr.	164	Ronney, Paul	213	Russell, Bill	134, 173	Sanders, Deion	150
Robbins, Tim	66	Ronstadt, Linda	103	Russell, Keri	66	Sanders, Doug	165
Roberts, Brian L.	178	Rooney, Andy	90	Russell, Kurt	66	Sanders, Jeff	165
Roberts, Cokie	90	Rooney, Dan	140	Russell, Mark	82	Sandler, Adam	66
Roberts, Dave	119	Rooney, Daniel M.	150	Russell, Raymond	165	Sandler, Adam	82
Roberts, Julia	66	Rooney, Mickey	66	Russert, Tim	90	Sanger, Stephen W.	178
Roberts, Leonard H.	180	Roosevelt, Anna	190	Russo, Patricia F.	179	Santana, Carlos	96, 103
Roberts, Loren	164	Rosa, Don	84	Russo, Rene	66	Santana, Johan	121
Roberts, Oral	216	Rosburg, Bob	165	Rustand, Eric	165	Santana, Manuel	167
Roberts, Richard J.	190	Rose, Calarence	165	Rutan, Burt	215	Santo, Ron	126
Roberts, Robin	117, 126	Rose, Charlie	90	Rutherford, Jim	158	Santoro, Fabrice	168
Roberts, Tanya	77	Rose, Irwin	190	Rutherford, Johnny	171	Santos, Jose	174
Robertson, Kathleen	66	Rose, Pete	126	Ryan, Blanchard	66	Sara, Mia	66
Robertson, Oscar	173	Roseanne	66, 82	Ryan, Chanel	79	Sarandon, Susan	66
Robertson, Pat	216	Rosen, Harold	182	Ryan, Jeri	66	Sargent, Robert L.	180

Sasso, Will	66	Schroeder, Jeret	171	Selig-Prieb, Wendy A.	126	Shelton, Marley	67
Sassoon, Vidal	91	Schroeder, John	165	Selleca, Connie	67	Shepard, Cybill	67
Satcher, David	194	Schroeder, Ted	167	Selleck, Tom	67	Shepard, Sam	67
Sather, Glen	158	Schultz, Howard	180	Sellers, Piers J.	214	Shepherd, Rita	165
Sato, Takuma	171	Schultz, Peter C.	182	Sellers, Victoria	67	Shepherd, William M.	214
Sauer, Hank	126	Schulz, Ted	165	Selmon, Lee Roy	140	Sheridan, Nicolette	67
Savage, Fred	67	Schumacher, Michael	171	Sen, Amartya	190	Sherman, Bobby	103
Savitt, Dick	167	Schumacher, Ralf	171	Sencion, Luis	136	Sherman, Cindy	91
Sawyer, Diane	90	Schwab, Charles R.	177	Senior, Peter	165	Sherman, Mike	150
Sax, Steve	126	Schwartz, Melvin	190	Sereno, Paul	190	Sherman, Patsy O.	182
Saxon, John	67	Schwartzman, Jason	67	Serkis, Andy	67	Sherry, Larry	126
Sayers, Gale	140	Schwarzenegger, Arnold	67	Serra, Matthew D.	178	Shields, Brook	67
Scacchi, Greta	67	Schwarzkopf, Norman	194	Sessler, Gerhard	182	Shine, Keiron	129
Scalia, Antonin	194	Schwarzrock, Brent	165	Severinsen, Doc	94	Shinn, George	134
Scalia, Jack	67	Schweickart, Russell L.	213	Sevigny, Chloe	67	Shirakawa, Hideki	190
Scarborough, Joe	90	Schwimmer, David	67	Sewell, Rufus	67	Shire, Talia	67
Schalken, Sjeng	168	Scioscia, Mike	126	Seymore, Stephanie	79	Shirelles	96
Schapiro, Miriam	86	Scoggins, Tracy	67	Seymour, Jane	67, 77	Shirley, Donna	190
Schawlow, Arthur	182	Score, Herb	126	Shadyac, Tom	67	Shore, Pauly	82
Scheck, Barry	204	Scorupco, Izabella	77	Shalhoub, Tony	67	Short, Bobby	94, 103
Schell, Catherine	77	Scott Jr., H. Lee	180	Shalikashvili, John (Gen.)	194	Short, Martin	67, 82
Schell, Maximilian	67	Scott, Antwan	129	Shanahan, Mike	150	Shorter, Frank	173, 174
Scherrer, George	165	Scott, Ashley	67	Sha-Na-Na	96	Shorter, Wayne	94
Scherrer, Tom	165	Scott, Darrion	145	Shandling, Garry	82	Showalter, Buck	126
Schiavelli, Vincent	77	Scott, David R.	214	Shannon, Molly	67	Shriver, Eunice Kennedy	204
Schiffer, Claudia	79	Scott, Jill	103	Shannon, Tim	165	Shriver, Loren J.	214
Schilling, Curt	119	Scott, Seann William	67	Shapiro, Robert L.	204	Shriver, Sargent	204
Schindler, Andrew R.	180	Scott, Willard	90	Sharer, Kevin W.	177	Shuba, George	126
Schirra, Walter M., Jr.	213	Scott, Winston E.	214	Sharif, Omar	67	Shue, Elisabeth	67
Schlegel, Hans	213	Scoular, Angela	77	Sharon, Ariel	194, 207	Shula, Dave & Don	150
Schlesinger, James R.,	194	Scully, Vin	126, 174	Sharp, Phillip A.	190	Shula, Don	140
Schlessinger, Laura	90	Seacrest, Ryan	90	Sharp, Scott	171	Shultz, George P.	194
Schlosseberg, Caroline	204	Seal	103	Sharpe, Sterling	151	Shyamalan, M. Night	86
Schmeling, Max	135	Seals, Dan	103	Sharpe, William	190	Siebert, Muriel	180
Schmidt, Joe	140	Searfoss, Richard A.	214	Sharpless, Barry	190	Siegel, Jeff	165
Schmidt, Mike	117,126	Seaver, Tom	117	Shashi Tharoor	86	Siegel, Scott	165
Schmiegel, Klaus	182	Seawell, David	165	Shatner, William	67	Siemerink, Jan	168
Schmitt, Harrison H.	213	Sebastian, John	103	Shaw, Bernard	90	Sifford, Charles	165
Schneider, Bonnie	67	Secada, John	103	Shaw, Billy	140	Silk, Dave	173
Schneider, Buzz	173	Sedaka, Neil	103	Shaw, Brewster H., Jr.	214	Silva, Henry	67
Schneider, Rob	67	Seddon, Margaret Rhea	214	Shaw, Fiona	67	Silver Dancers	134
Schoendienst, Red	117,126	Sedgman, Frank	167	Shear, Rhonda	67	Silverstone, Alicia	67
Scholes, Myron S.	190	Sedgwick, Kyra	67	Shearer, Bob	165	Simitis, Costas	207
Schollander, Don	173	Sega, Ronald M.	214	Sheedy, Ally	67	Simmons, Gene	103
Schott, Steve	126	Segura, Pancho	167	Sheen, Charlie	67	Simmons, Jean	68
Schottenheimer, Marty	150	Seidenberg, Ivan G.	180	Sheffield, Gary	126	Simmons, Jeff	178
Schrader, Ken	171	Seinfeld, Jerry	82	Shelby, Carroll	171	Simmons, Richard	90
Schramm, Tex	140	Seiwald, Robert J.	182	Shelby, John	126	Simon, Neal	86
Schreiber, Liev	67	Seixas, Vic	167	Shell, Art	140	Simon, Paul	103
Schroeder, Gerhard	207	Selig, Bud	126	Shelton, Henry General	194	Simpson, Ashlee	68

Turner, Clyde (Bulldog)	140	Van Dross, Luther	104
Turner, Ike	104	Van Dyke, Barry	71
Turner, Kathleen	70	Van Dyke, Dick	71
Turner, Morrie	84	Van Dyke, Jerry	71
Turner, Norv	150	Van Halen, Eddie	104
Turner, Robert	166	Van Hoften, James D. A.	214
Turner, Tina	104	Van Pelt, Bo	166
Turtles (The)	96	Van Susteren, Greta	90
Turturro, John	70	Van Zandt, Steve	71, 93
Tutu, Desmond	190, 207	Vangen, Scott	214
Twain, Shania	104	Vanner, Sue	77
Tway, Bob	166	Vardalos, Nia	71
Twiggs, Greg	166	Vargas, Fernado	136
Twiggy, Lawson	71	Varmus, Harold	190
T-wolves Dancers	134	Vartan, Michael	71
Tyler, Aisha	71	Vasser, Jimmy	171
Tyler, Brian	171	Vaughan, Bruce	166
Tyler, Liv	71	Vaughn, Vince	71
Tyson, Mike	136	Vee, Bobby	104
Tyus, Wyomia	173	Vel Johnson, Reginald	71
Ubach, Alanna	71	Velasquez, Patricia	71, 79
Ueberroth, Peter	126	Veneman, Ann	194
Uecker, Bob	126	Venora, Diane	71
Ullman, Tracey	82	Venter, J. Craig	179, 190
Ulrich, Robert J.	180	Ventures (The)	96
Underwood, Blair	71	Venturi, Ken	166
Union, Gabrielle	71	Verchota, Phil	173
Unser, Al Jr.	171	Vermeil, Dick	150
Unser, Al Sr.	171	Verplank, Scott	166
Updike, John	86	Versace, Dick	134
Upshaw, Gene	140	Versace, Donatella	91
Urban, Karl	71, 78	Versher, Wun	129
Urban, Keith	104	Veryzer, Tom	126
Urbani, Luca	214	Vessy, John W. Jr. (Gen)	194
Usher	104	Vidal, Christina	71
Usher, Thomas J.	180	Vidmar, Peter	173
Vaccara, Brenda	71	Vigorito, Tom	150
Valderrama, Wilmer	71	Vila, Bob	90
Vale, Jerry	104	Vilas, Guillermo	167
Valentine, Bobby	126	Villaraigosa, Antonio	202
Valentine, Darnell	134	Villeneuve, Jacques	171
Valentine, Karen	71	Vincent, Cerina	71
Valenzuela, Fernando	126	Vinton, Bobby	104
Vallie, Frankie	104	Virts, Terry W., Jr.	214
Van Ark, Joan	71	Visnjic, Goran	71
Van Arsdale, Dick	134	Vitale, Bob	134
Van Buren, Steve	140	Vittori, Roberto	214
Van Damme, Jean Claude	71	Vogelstein, Bert	190
Van Der Beek, James	71	von Detten, Erik	71
		Von Furstenberg, Diane	86
		von Sydow, Max	71, 77

Vonnegut, Kurt	86	Wannstedt, Dave	150
Voss, James S.	214	Wantanabe, Ken	71
Voss, Janice E.	214	Ward, Fred	71
Waddell, Don	158	Ward, Sela	71
Wade, Virginia	167	Warfield, Paul	140
Wadkins, Bobby	166	Wargo, Tom	166
Wadkins, Lanny	166	Warner, Kurt	146
Waggoner, Lyle	71	Warren, Charles	166
Wagner, Fred	84	Warren, Estella	72
Wagner, John	84	Warren, Lesley Ann	72
Wagner, Lindsay	71	Warrior Girls	134
Wagner, Robert	71	Warwick, Dionne	104
Wagoner, Porter	104	Washington, Denzel	72
Wagoner, Richard	178	Washington, Isaiah	72
Wahlberg, Mark	71	Waterston, Sam	72
Waite, Grant	166	Watson, Emma	72
Wakata, Koichi	214	Watson, James D.	190
Waldorf, Duffy	166	Watson, Tom	166
Walesa, Lech	207	Watterson, Bill	84
Walheim, Rex J.	214	Wattles, Stan	171
Walken, Christopher	71, 77	Watts, Brian	166
Walker, Alice	86	Watts, Naomi	72, 78
Walker, Charles	214	Wayans, Damon	82
Walker, Clint	71	Wayans, Keenan	82
Walker, Doak	140	Wayans, Marlon	72, 82
Waiker, Jimmy	82	Wayans, Shawn	82
Walker, Mort	84	Wayne, Patrick	72
Walker, Paul	71	Weatherly, Michael	72
Wallace, Chris	90	Weathers, Carl	72
Wallace, George	82	Weaver, Dennis	72
Wallace, Julie	77	Weaver, DeWitt	166
Wallace, Kenny	171	Weaver, Earl	117
Wallace, Mike	90, 171	Weaver, Sigourney	72
Wallace, Rusty	171	Weaver, Wayne	150
Wallach, Eli	71	Weaving, Hugo	72
Wallflowers (The)	96	Weaving, Hugo	78
Walsh, Bill	140	Webber, Mark	171
Walsh, John	216	Weber, Mary E.	214
Walter, Lisa Ann	71	Webster, Michael	140
Walter, Robert D.	177	Webster, Mitch	126
Walters, Julie	71	Wedge, Eric	126
Walton, Alice	180	Wedgeworth, Ann	72
Walton, Helen	180	Weilbring, D.A.	166
Walton, Jim	180	Weill, Sanford I.	177
Walton, John	180	Weinbach, Lawrence A.	180
Walton, Luke	132	Weinmeister, Arnie	140
Waltrip, Darrell	171	Weir, Mike	166
Waltrip, Michael	171	Weiskopf, Tom	166
Walz, Carl E.	214	Weisz, Rachel	72
Wang, Vera	91	Weitz, Paul J.	214

Letter Writing Service

Would you like to have a professionally written letter sent to your favorite celebrity? We offer a letter writing service that saves you time and offers a direct link to your celebrity. Here is how it works:

1. You write to your celebrity and send it to me via e-mail.
2. I take the letter and type it on an 8 x 11 page and send it by U.S. Postal Service to your celebrity.
3. I will place postage on the return envelope with your address.
4. Your celebrity will send the return request item back to you directly.
5. Your cost: 12.95 includes all postage and fees.

Great for collectors overseas wanting to contact celebrities in the United States

Satisfaction Guarantee

Every effort was made to locate and list the addresses of all well-known celebrities in "The Celebrity Address Directory & Autograph Collector's Guide." There are over 30,000 celebrities listed and celebrities change their addresses frequently. If you receive a "Return to Sender" request or do not find the name and address of the celebrity you are looking for, I will gladly research and provide you with the most current address of your celebrity.

E-mail your request to: american@pressenter.com
(E-mail is the fastest method of answering your requests)

Please use this format in your E-mail:

Name_____ Occupation_____